WYZAnt

Introduction to the Economics and Mathematics of Financial Markets

Introduction to the Economics and Mathematics of Financial Markets

Jakša Cvitanić and Fernando Zapatero

The MIT Press
Cambridge, Massachusetts
London, England

This book was set in 10/13 Times Roman by ICC and was printed and bound in the United States of America.

Library of Congress Cataloging-in-Publication Data

Cvitanić, Jakša
    Introduction to the economics and mathematics of financial markets / Jakša Cvitanić and Fernando Zapatero.
        p.   cm.
    Includes bibliographical references and index.
    ISBN 0-262-03320-8
    ISBN 0-262-53265-4 (International Student Edition)
    1. Finance—Mathematical models—Textbooks.   I. Zapatero, Fernando. II. Title.

HG106.C86   2004
332.632′01′515—dc22

                                            2003064872

To Vesela, Lucia, Toni
and
Maitica, Nicolás, Sebastián

Contents

Preface

Why We Wrote the Book

The subject of financial markets is fascinating to many people: to those who care about money and investments, to those who care about the well-being of modern society, to those who like gambling, to those who like applications of mathematics, and so on. We, the authors of this book, care about many of these things (no, not the gambling), but what we care about most is teaching. The main reason for writing this book has been our belief that we can successfully teach the fundamentals of the economic and mathematical aspects of financial markets to almost everyone (again, we are not sure about gamblers). Why are we in this teaching business instead of following the path of many of our former students, the path of making money by pursuing a career in the financial industry? Well, they don't have the pleasure of writing a book for the enthusiastic reader like yourself!

Prerequisites

This text is written in such a way that it can be used at different levels and for different groups of undergraduate and graduate students. After the first, introductory chapter, each chapter starts with sections on the single-period model, goes to multiperiod models, and finishes with continuous-time models. The single-period and multiperiod models require only basic calculus and an elementary introductory probability/statistics course. Those sections can be taught to third- and fourth-year undergraduate students in economics, business, and similar fields. They could be taught to mathematics and engineering students at an even earlier stage. In order to be able to read continuous-time sections, it is helpful to have been exposed to an advanced undergraduate course in probability. Some material needed from such a probability course is briefly reviewed in chapter 16.

Who Is It For?

The book can also serve as an introductory text for graduate students in finance, financial economics, financial engineering, and mathematical finance. Some material from continuous-time sections is, indeed, usually considered to be graduate material. We try to explain much of that material in an intuitive way, while providing some of the proofs in appendixes to the chapters. The book is not meant to compete with numerous excellent graduate-level books in financial mathematics and financial economics, which are typically written in a mathematically more formal way, using a theorem-proof type of structure. Some of those more advanced books are mentioned in the references, and they present a natural next step in getting to know the subject on a more theoretical and advanced level.

Structure of the Book

We have divided the book into three parts. Part I goes over the basic securities, organization of financial markets, the concept of interest rates, the main mathematical models, and ways to measure in a quantitative way the risk and the reward of trading in the market. Part II deals with option pricing and hedging, and similar material is present in virtually every recent book on financial markets. We choose to emphasize the so-called martingale, probabilistic approach consistently throughout the book, as opposed to the differential-equations approach or other existing approaches. For example, the one proof of the Black-Scholes formula that we provide is done calculating the corresponding expected value. Part III is devoted to one of the favorite subjects of financial economics, the equilibrium approach to asset pricing. This part is often omitted from books in the field of financial mathematics, having fewer direct applications to option pricing and hedging. However, it is this theory that gives a qualitative insight into the behavior of market participants and how the prices are formed in the market.

What Can a Course Cover?

We have used parts of the material from the book for teaching various courses at the University of Southern California: undergraduate courses in economics and business, a masters-level course in mathematical finance, and option and investment courses for MBA students. For example, an undergraduate course for economics/business students that emphasizes option pricing could cover the following (in this order):

• The first three chapters without continuous-time sections; chapter 10 on bond hedging could also be done immediately after chapter 2 on interest rates

• The first two chapters of part II on no-arbitrage pricing and option pricing, without most of the continuous-time sections, but including basic Black-Scholes theory

• Chapters on hedging in part II, with or without continuous-time sections

• The mean-variance section in chapter 5 on risk; chapter 13 on CAPM could also be done immediately after that section

If time remains, or if this is an undergraduate economics course that emphasizes equilibrium/asset pricing as opposed to option pricing, or if this is a two-semester course, one could also cover

• discrete-time sections in chapter 4 on utility.

• discrete-time sections in part III on equilibrium models.

Courses aimed at more mathematically oriented students could go very quickly through the discrete-time sections, and instead spend more time on continuous-time sections. A one-semester course would likely have to make a choice: to focus on no-arbitrage option pricing methods in part II or to focus on equilibrium models in part III.

Web Page for This Book, Excel Files

The web page **http://math.usc.edu/~cvitanic/book.html** will be regularly updated with material related to the book, such as corrections of typos. It also contains Microsoft Excel files, with names like ch1.xls. That particular file has all the figures from chapter 1, along with all the computations needed to produce them. We use Excel because we want the reader to be able to reproduce and modify all the figures in the book. A slight disadvantage of this choice is that our figures sometimes look less professional than if they had been done by a specialized drawing software. We use only basic features of Excel, except for Monte Carlo simulation for which we use the Visual Basic programming language, incorporated in Excel. The readers are expected to learn the basic features of Excel on their own, if they are not already familiar with them. At a few places in the book we give "Excel Tips" that point out the trickier commands that have been used for creating a figure. Other, more mathematically oriented software may be more efficient for longer computations such as Monte Carlo, and we leave the choice of the software to be used with some of the homework problems to the instructor or the reader. In particular, we do not use any optimization software or differential equations software, even though the instructor could think of projects using those.

Notation

Asterisk   Sections and problems designated by an asterisk are more sophisticated in mathematical terms, require extensive use of computer software, or are otherwise somewhat unusual and outside of the main thread of the book. These sections and problems could be skipped, although we suggest that students do most of the problems that require use of computers.

Dagger   End-of-chapter problems that are solved in the student's manual are preceded by a dagger.

Greek Letters   We use many letters from the Greek alphabet, sometimes both lowercase and uppercase, and we list them here with appropriate pronunciation: α (alpha), β (beta), γ, Γ (gamma), δ, Δ (delta), ε (epsilon), ζ (zeta), η (eta), θ (theta), λ (lambda), μ (mu), ξ (xi), π, Π (pi), ω, Ω (omega), ρ (rho), σ, Σ (sigma), τ (tau), φ, Φ (phi).

Acknowledgments

First and foremost, we are immensely grateful to our families for the support they provided us while working on the book. We have received great help and support from the staff of our publisher, MIT Press, and, in particular, we have enjoyed working with Elizabeth Murry, who helped us go through the writing and production process in a smooth and efficient manner. J. C.'s research and the writing of this book have been partially supported by National Science Foundation grant DMS-00-99549. Some of the continuous-time sections in parts I and II originated from the lecture notes prepared in summer 2000 while J. C. was visiting the University of the Witwatersrand in Johannesburg, and he is very thankful to his host, David Rod Taylor, the director of the Mathematical Finance Programme at Wits. Numerous colleagues have made useful comments and suggestions, including Krzysztof Burdzy, Paul Dufresne, Neil Gretzky, Assad Jalali, Dmitry Kramkov, Ali Lazrak, Lionel Martellini, Adam Ostaszewski, Kaushik Ronnie Sircar, Costis Skiadas, Halil Mete Soner, Adam Speight, David Rod Taylor, and Mihail Zervos. In particular, D. Kramkov provided us with proofs in the appendix of chapter 6. Some material on continuous-time utility maximization with incomplete information is taken from a joint work with A. Lazrak and L. Martellini, and on continuous-time mean-variance optimization from a joint work with A. Lazrak. Moreover, the following students provided their comments and pointed out errors in the working manuscript: Paula Guedes, Frank Denis Hiebsch, and Chulhee Lee. Of course, we are solely responsible for any remaining errors.

A Prevailing Theme: Pricing by Expected Values

Before we start with the book's material, we would like to give a quick illustration here in the preface of a connection between a price of a security and the optimal trading strategy of an investor investing in that security. We present it in a simple model, but this connection is present in most market models, and, in fact, the resulting pricing formula is of the form that will follow us through all three parts of this book. We will repeat this type of argument later in more detail, and we present it early here only to give the reader a general taste of what the book is about. The reader may want to skip the following derivation, and go directly to equation (0.3).

Consider a security S with today's price $S(0)$, and at a future time 1 its price $S(1)$ either has value s^u with probability p, or value s^d with probability $1 - p$. There is also a risk-free security that returns $1 + r$ dollars at time 1 for every dollar invested today. We assume that $s^d < (1 + r)S(0) < s^u$. Suppose an investor has initial capital x, and has to decide how many shares δ of security S to hold, while depositing the rest of his wealth in the bank account with interest rate r. In other words, his wealth $X(1)$ at time 1 is

$$X(1) = \delta S(1) + [x - \delta S(0)](1 + r)$$

The investor wants to maximize his expected utility

$$E[U(X(1))] = pU(X^u) + (1 - p)U(X^d)$$

where U is a so-called utility function, while X^u, X^d is his final wealth in the case $S(1) = s^u$, $S(1) = s^d$, respectively. Substituting for these values, taking the derivative with respect to δ and setting it equal to zero, we get

$$pU'(X^u)[s^u - S(0)(1 + r)] + (1 - p)U'(X^d)[s^d - S(0)(1 + r)] = 0$$

The left-hand side can be written as $E[U'(X(1))\{S(1) - S(0)(1 + r)\}]$, which, when made equal to zero, implies, with arbitrary wealth X replaced by optimal wealth $\hat{X}$,

$$S(0) = E\left[\frac{U'(\hat{X}(1))}{E(U'[\hat{X}(1)])} \frac{S(1)}{1 + r}\right] \tag{0.1}$$

If we denote

$$Z(1) := \frac{U'(\hat{X}(1))}{E\{U'(\hat{X}(1))\}} \tag{0.2}$$

we see that the today's price of our security S is given by

$$S(0) = E\left[Z(1)\frac{S(1)}{1 + r}\right] \tag{0.3}$$

We will see that prices of most securities (with some exceptions, like American options) in the models of this book are of this form: the today's price $S(0)$ is an expected value of the future price $S(1)$, multiplied ("discounted") by a certain random factor. Effectively, we get the today's price as a weighted average of the discounted future price, but with weights that depend on the outcomes of the random variable $Z(1)$. Moreover, in standard option-pricing models (having a so-called completeness property) we will not need to use utility functions, since $Z(1)$ will be independent of the investor's utility. The random variable $Z(1)$ is sometimes called **change of measure,** while the ratio $Z(1)/(1 + r)$ is called **state-price density, stochastic discount factor, pricing kernel,** or **marginal rate of substitution,** depending on the context and interpretation. There is another interpretation of this formula, using a new probability; hence the name "change of (probability) measure." For example, if, as in our preceding example, $Z(1)$ takes two possible values $Z^u(1)$ and $Z^d(1)$ with probabilities p, $1 - p$, respectively, we can define

$$p^* := pZ^u(1), \qquad 1 - p^* = (1 - p)Z^d(1)$$

The values of $Z(1)$ are such that p^* is a probability, and we interpret p^* and $1 - p^*$ as modified probabilities of the movements of asset S. Then, we can write equation (0.3) as

$$S(0) = E^* \left[\frac{S(1)}{1 + r} \right] \qquad (0.4)$$

where E^* denotes the expectation under the new probabilities, p^*, $1 - p^*$. Thus the price today is the expected value of the discounted future value, where the expected value is computed under a special, so-called **risk-neutral** probability, usually different from the **real-world probability.**

Final Word

We hope that we have aroused your interest about the subject of this book. If you turn out to be a very careful reader, we would be thankful if you could inform us of any remaining typos and errors that you find by sending an e-mail to our current e-mail addresses. Enjoy the book!

Jakša Cvitanić and Fernando Zapatero

E-mail addresses: cvitanic@math.usc.edu, zapatero@usc.edu

I THE SETTING: MARKETS, MODELS, INTEREST RATES, UTILITY MAXIMIZATION, RISK

1 Financial Markets

Imagine that our dear reader (that's you) was lucky enough to inherit one million dollars from a distant relative. This is more money than you want to spend at once (we assume), and you want to invest some of it. Your newly hired expert financial adviser tells you that an attractive possibility is to invest part of your money in the financial market (and pay him a hefty fee for the advice, of course). Being suspicious by nature, you don't completely trust your adviser, and you want to learn about financial markets yourself. You do a smart thing and buy this book (!) for a much smaller fee that pays for the services of the publisher and the authors (that's us). You made a good deal because the learning objectives of the first chapter are

- to describe the basic characteristics of and differences between the instruments traded in financial markets.
- to provide an overview of the organization of financial markets.

Our focus will be on the economic and financial use of financial instruments. There are many possible classifications of these instruments. The first division differentiates between securities and other financial contracts. A **security** is a document that confers upon its owner a financial claim. In contrast, a general **financial contract** links two parties nominally and not through the ownership of a document. However, this distinction is more relevant for legal than for economic reasons, and we will overlook it. We start with the broadest possible economic classification: bonds, stocks, and derivatives. We describe the basic characteristics of each type, its use from the point of view of an investor, and its organization in different markets.

Bonds belong to the family of **fixed-income securities,** because they pay fixed amounts of money to their owners. Other fixed-income instruments include regular savings accounts, money-market accounts, certificates of deposit, and others. Stocks are also referred to as **equities.** See figure 1.1 for a possible classification of financial instruments.

The financial instruments discussed in this chapter are **assets** a potential investor would consider as a part of his portfolio. This potential investor can be a person or an entity (a corporation, a pension fund, a country, . . .). In the economics and finance literature such a person or entity may be called a **trader,** an **agent,** a **financial investor,** and similar terms. We will name this investor **Taf.**

1.1 Bonds

In a very broad sense, a **bond** is a security (a document) that gives its owner the right to a fixed, predetermined payment, at a future, predetermined date, called **maturity.** The amount of money that a bond will pay in the future is called **nominal value, face value, par value,** or **principal.**

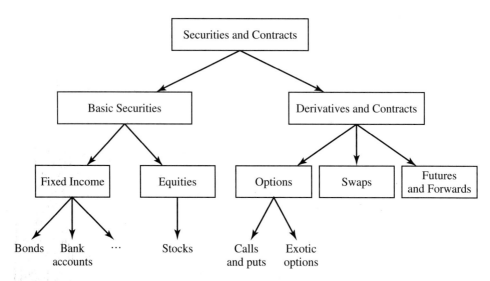

Figure 1.1
A classification of financial instruments: financial securities and contracts.

There are two sides to a bond contract: the party that promises to pay the nominal value, or the **debtor,** and the party that will get paid, or the **creditor.** We say that the debtor is a **counterparty** to the creditor in the bond contract, and vice versa. The debtor issues a bond in exchange for an agreed-upon amount called the **bond price** paid by the creditor. For example, the creditor may have to pay $95.00 today for a bond that pays $100.00 a year from today. The creditor can later sell the bond to another person who becomes the new creditor. The difference between the bond price the creditor pays to the debtor and the nominal value is called **interest.** The interest as a percentage of the total value is called **interest rate.** Typically, but not always, a bond with longer maturity pays a higher interest rate. A bond is characterized by its interest and its maturity. In principle, bonds represent the paradigm of **risk-free** securities, in the sense that there is a guaranteed payoff at maturity, known in advance. The lack of risk is the result of the certainty about that amount. In fact, in the models that we will examine in later chapters, we will always call bonds risk-free securities.

Money would fall into this broad definition of a bond. Money can be interpreted as a bond with zero interest rate and zero (immediate) maturity. The counterparty to the individual who has money is the government, guaranteeing the general acceptability of money as a payment instrument. A checking account is similar to money (although the counterparty is a bank). At the other extreme of the length of maturity, we have bonds issued by the government that expire in 30 years. Private corporations have issued bonds with longer maturities.

1.1.1 Types of Bonds

Depending on their maturity, bonds are classified into **short-term bonds,** or bonds of maturity no greater than one year, and **long-term bonds,** when their maturity exceeds one year. There are bonds that involve only an initial payment (the initial price) and a final payment (the nominal value). They are called **pure discount bonds,** since the initial price is equal to the discounted nominal value. Very often, however (especially with long-term bonds), the debtor will make periodic payments to the creditor during the life of the bond. These payments are usually a predetermined percentage of the nominal value of the bond and are called **coupons.** At maturity, the debtor will pay the last coupon and the nominal value. In this case, the nominal value part is called **principal.** The corresponding bonds are called **coupon bonds.** Actually, a coupon bond is equivalent to a collection, or a **basket,** of pure discount bonds with nominal values equal to the coupons. Pure discount bonds are also called **zero-coupon bonds,** because they pay no coupons. If the price at which the bond is sold is exactly the same as the nominal value, we say that the bond sells **at par.** If the price of the bond is different from the nominal value, we say that the bond sells **above par** if the price is higher than the nominal value, or **below par** if it is lower. Coupon bonds can sell at, above, or below par. Pure discount bonds always sell below par because the today's value of one dollar paid at a future maturity date is less than one dollar. For example, if Taf today lends $1,000 to his Reliable City Government for a ten-year period by buying a bond from the city, he should get more than $1,000 after ten years. In other words, a bond's interest rate is always positive.

1.1.2 Reasons for Trading Bonds

If a person has some purchasing power that she would prefer to delay, she could buy a bond. There are many reasons why someone might want to delay expending. As an example, our hard worker Taf may want to save for retirement. One way of doing so would be to buy bonds with a long maturity in order to save enough money to be able to retire in the future. In fact, if Taf knew the exact date of retirement and the exact amount of money necessary to live on retirement, he could choose a bond whose maturity matches the date of retirement and whose nominal value matches the required amount, and thereby save money without risk. He could also invest in bonds with shorter maturities and reinvest the proceeds when the bonds expire. But such a strategy will generally pay a lower interest rate, and therefore, the amount of money that will have to be invested for a given retirement target will be higher than if it were invested in the long-term bond.

Another example of the need to delay spending is the case of an insurance company, collecting premiums from its customers. In exchange, the insurance company will compensate the customer in case of fire or a car accident. If the insurance company could predict how much and when it will need capital for compensation, it could use the premiums to buy bonds with a given maturity and nominal value. In fact, based on their experience and information about their customers, insurance companies can make good estimates of the amounts that will be required for compensation. Bonds provide a risk-free way to invest the premiums.

There are also many reasons why someone might want to advance consumption. Individual consumers will generally do so by borrowing money from banks, through house and car loans or credit card purchases. Corporations borrow regularly as a way of financing their business: when a business opportunity comes up, they will issue bonds to finance it with the hope that the profits of the opportunity will be higher than the interest rate they will have to pay for the bonds. The bonds issued by a corporation for financing purposes are called **debt.** The owner of bonds, the creditor, is called the **bondholder.** The government also issues bonds to finance public expenses when collected tax payments are not enough to pay for them.

1.1.3   Risk of Trading Bonds

Even though we call bonds risk-free securities, there are several reasons why bonds might actually involve risk. First of all, it is possible that the debtor might fail to meet the payment obligation embedded in the bond. This risk is typical of bonds issued by corporations. There is a chance that the corporation that issues the bond will not be able to generate enough income to meet the interest rate. If the debtor does not meet the promise, we say that the debtor has defaulted. This type of risk is called **credit risk** or **default risk.** The bonds issued by the U.S. government are considered to be free of risk of default, since the government will always be able to print more money and, therefore, is extremely unlikely to default.

A second source of risk comes from the fact that, even if the amount to be paid in the future is fixed, it is in general impossible to predict the amount of goods which that sum will be able to buy. The future prices of goods are uncertain, and a given amount of money will be relatively more or less valuable depending on the level of the prices. This risk is called **inflation risk.** Inflation is the process by which prices tend to increase. When Taf saves for retirement by buying bonds, he can probably estimate the amount of goods and services that will be required during retirement. However, the price of those goods will be very difficult to estimate. In practice, there are bonds that guarantee a payment that depends on the inflation level. These bonds are called **real bonds** or **inflation-indexed** bonds. Because of the high risk for the debtor, these bonds are not common.

A final source of risk that we mention here arises when the creditor needs money before maturity and tries to sell the bond. Apart from the risk of default, the creditor knows with certainty that the nominal value will be paid at maturity. However, there is no price guarantee before maturity. The creditor can in general sell the bond, but the price that the bond will reach before maturity depends on factors that cannot be predicted. Consider, for example, the case of the insurance company. Suppose that the contingency the insurance company has to compensate takes place before the expected date. In that case, the insurance company will have to hurry to sell the bonds, and the price it receives for them might be lower than the amount needed for the compensation. The risk of having to sell at a given time at low prices is called **liquidity risk.** In fact, there are two reasons why someone who sells a bond might experience a loss. First, it might be that no one is interested in that bond at the time. A bond issued for a small corporation that is not well known might not be of interest to many people, and as a result, the seller might be forced to take a big price cut in the bond. This is an example of a liquidity problem. Additionally, the price of the bond will depend on market factors and, more explicitly, on the level of interest rates, the **term structure,** which we will discuss in later chapters. However, it is difficult in practice to distinguish between the liquidity risk and the risk of market factors, because they might be related.

1.2   Stocks

A **stock** is a security that gives its owner the right to a proportion of any profits that might be distributed (rather than reinvested) by the firm that issues the stock and to the corresponding part of the firm in case it decides to close down and liquidate. The owner of the stock is called the **stockholder.** The profits that the company distributes to the stockholders are called **dividends.** Dividends are in general random, not known in advance. They will depend on the firm's profits, as well as on the firm's policy. The randomness of dividend payments and the absence of a guaranteed nominal value represent the main differences with respect to the coupon bonds: the bond's coupons and nominal value are predetermined. Another difference with respect to bonds is that the stock, in principle, will not expire. We say "in principle," because the company might go out of business, in which case it would be liquidated and the stockholders will receive a certain part of the proceeds of the liquidation.

The stockholder can sell the stock to another person. As with bonds, the price at which the stock will sell will be determined by a number of factors including the dividend prospects and other factors. When there is no risk of default, we can predict exactly how much a bond will pay if held until maturity. With stocks there is no such possibility: future dividends are uncertain, and so is the price of the stock at any future date. Therefore, a stock is always a risky security.

As a result of this risk, buying a stock and selling it at a later date might produce a profit or a loss. We call this a **positive return** or a **negative return,** respectively. The return will have two components: the dividends received while in ownership of the stock, and the difference between the price at which the stock was purchased and the selling price. The difference between the selling price and the initial price is called **capital gain** or **loss.** The relation between the dividend and the price of the stock is called **dividend yield.**

1.2.1   How Are Stocks Different from Bonds?

Some of the cases in which people or entities delay consumption by buying bonds could also be solved by buying stock. However, with stocks the problem is more complicated because the future dividends and prices are uncertain. Overall, stocks will be more risky than bonds. All the risk factors that we described for bonds apply, in principle, to stocks, too. Default risk does not strictly apply, since there is no payment promise, but the fact that there is not even a promise only adds to the overall uncertainty. With respect to the inflation uncertainty, stocks can behave better than bonds. General price increases mean that corporations are charging more for their sales and might be able to increase their revenues, and profits will go up. This reasoning does not apply to bonds.

Historically, U.S. stocks have paid a higher return than the interest rate paid by bonds, on average. As a result, they are competitive with bonds as a way to save money. For example, if Taf still has a long time left until his retirement date, it might make sense for him to buy stocks, because they are likely to have an average return higher than bonds. As the retirement date approaches, it might be wise to shift some of that money to bonds, in order to avoid the risk associated with stocks.

So far we have discussed the main differences between bonds and stocks with respect to risk. From an economic point of view, another important difference results from the type of legal claim they represent. With a bond, we have two people or entities, a debtor and a creditor. There are no physical assets or business activities involved. A stockholder, however, has a claim to an economic activity or physical assets. There has to be a corporation conducting some type of business behind the stock. Stock is issued when there is some business opportunity that looks profitable. When stock is issued, wealth is added to the economy. This distinction will be crucial in some of the models we will discuss later. Stocks represent claims to the wealth in the economy. Bonds are financial instruments that allow people to allocate their purchasing decisions over time. A stock will go up in price when the business prospects of the company improve. That increase will mean that the economy is wealthier. An increase in the price of a bond does not have that implication.

In later chapters we will study factors that affect the price of a stock in more detail. For now, it suffices to say that when the business prospects of a corporation improve, profit prospects improve and the outlook for future dividends improves. As a result, the price of the stock will increase. However, if the business prospects are very good, the management of the company might decide to reinvest the profits, rather than pay a dividend. Such reinvestment is a way of financing business opportunities. Stockholders will not receive dividends for a while, but the outlook for the potential dividends later on improves. Typically, the stockholders have limited information about company prospects. For that reason, the dividend policy chosen by the management of the company is very important because it signals to the stockholders the information that management has.

1.2.2 Going Long or Short

Related to the question of how much information people have about company prospects is the effect of beliefs on prices and purchasing decisions: two investors might have different expectations about future dividends and prices. An "optimistic" investor might decide to buy the stock. A "pessimistic" investor might prefer to sell. Suppose that the pessimistic investor observes the price of a stock and thinks it is overvalued, but does not own the stock. That investor still can bet on her beliefs by **short-selling** the stock. Short-selling the stock consists in borrowing the stock from someone who owns it and selling it. The **short-seller** hopes that the price of the stock will drop. When that happens, she will buy the stock at that lower price and return it to the original owner. The investor that owes the stock has a **short position** in the stock. The act of buying back the stock and returning it to the original owner is called **covering the short position.**

Example 1.1 (Successful Short-Selling) Our reckless speculator Taf thinks that the stock of the company Downhill, Incorporated, is overvalued. It sells at $45 per share. Taf goes on-line, signs into his Internet brokerage account, and places an order to sell short one thousand shares of Downhill, Inc. By doing so he receives $45,000 and owes one thousand shares. After patiently waiting four months, Taf sees that the stock price has indeed plunged to $22 per share. He buys one thousand shares at a cost of $22,000 to cover his short position. He thereby makes a profit of $23,000. Here, we ignore transaction fees, required margin amounts, and inflation/interest rate issues, to be discussed later.

In practice, short-selling is not restricted to stocks. Investors can also short-sell bonds, for example. But short-selling a bond, for economic purposes, is equivalent to issuing the bond: the person who has a short position in a bond is a debtor, and the value of the debt is the price of the bond. In contrast to short-selling, when a person buys a security we say that she **goes long** in the security.

1.3 Derivatives

Derivatives are financial instruments whose payoff depends on the value of another financial variable (price of a stock, price of a bond, exchange rate, and so on), called **underlying.** As a simple example, consider a contract in which party A agrees to pay to party B $100 if the stock price of Downhill, Inc., is above $50 four months from today. In exchange party B will pay $10 today to party A.

As is the case with bonds, derivatives are not related to physical assets or business opportunities: two parties get together and set a rule by which one of the two parties will receive a payment from the other depending on the value of some financial variables. One party will have to make one or several payments to the other party (or the directions of payments might alternate). The profit of one party will be the loss of the other party. This is what is called a **zero-sum game.** There are several types of financial instruments that satisfy the previous characteristics. We review the main derivatives in the following sections.

1.3.1 Futures and Forwards

In order to get a quick grasp of what a forward contract is, we give a short example first:

Example 1.2 (A Forward Contract)   Our brilliant foreign currency speculator Taf is pretty sure that the value of the U.S. dollar will go down relative to the European currency, the euro. However, right now he does not have funds to buy euros. Instead, he agrees to buy one million euros six months from now at the exchange rate of \$0.95 for one euro.

Let us switch to more formal definitions: **futures** and **forwards** are contracts by which one party agrees to buy the underlying asset at a future, predetermined date at a predetermined price. The other party agrees to deliver the **underlying** at the predetermined date for the agreed price. The difference between the futures and forwards is the way the payments are made from one party to the other. In the case of a forward contract, the exchange of money and assets is made only at the final date. For futures the exchange is more complex, occurring in stages. However, we will see later that the trading of futures is more easily implemented in the market, because less bookkeeping is needed to track the futures contracts. It is for this reason that futures are traded on exchanges.

A futures or a forward contract is a purchase in which the transaction (the exchange of goods for money) is postponed to a future date. All the details of the terms of the exchange have to be agreed upon in advance. The date at which the exchange takes place is called **maturity.** At that date both sides will have to satisfy their part of the contract, regardless of the trading price of the underlying at maturity. In addition, the exchange price the parties agree upon is such that the today's value of the contract is zero: there is a price to be paid at maturity for the good to be delivered, but there is no exchange of money today for this right/obligation to buy at that price. This price to be paid at maturity (but agreed upon today!) is called the **futures price,** or the **forward price.**

The "regular," **market price** of the underlying, at which you can buy the underlying at the present time in the market, is also called the **spot price,** because buying is done "on the spot." The main difference with the futures/forward price is that the value the spot price will have at some future date is not known today, while the futures/forward price is agreed upon today.

We say that the side that accepts the obligation to buy takes a **long position,** while the side that accepts the obligation to sell takes a **short position.** Let us denote by $F(t)$ the forward price agreed upon at the present time t for delivery at maturity time T. By $S(t)$ we denote the spot price at t. At maturity time T, the investor with the short position will have to deliver the good currently priced in the market at the value $S(T)$ and will receive in exchange the forward price $F(t)$. The payoff for the short side of the forward contract can therefore be expressed as

$$F(t) - S(T)$$

The payoff for the long side will be the opposite:

$$S(T) - F(t)$$

Thus a forward contract is a zero-sum game.

1.3.2   Marking to Market

Futures are not securities in the strict sense and, therefore, cannot be sold to a third party before maturity. However, futures are **marked to market,** and that fact makes them equivalent, for economic purposes, to securities. Marking to market means that both sides of the contract must keep a cash account whose balance will be updated on a daily basis, depending on the changes of the futures price in the market. At any point in time there will be in the market a futures price for a given underlying with a given maturity. An investor can take a long or short position in that futures contract, at the price prevailing in the market. Suppose our investor Taf takes a long position at moment t, so that he will be bound by the price $F(t)$. If Taf keeps the contract until maturity, his total **profit/loss payoff** will be $F(t) - S(T)$. However, unlike the forward contract, this payoff will be spread over the life of the futures contract in the following way: every day there will be a new futures price for that contract, and the difference with the previous price will be credited or charged to Taf's cash account, opened for this purpose. For example, if today's futures price is $20.00 and tomorrow's price is $22.00, then Taf's account will be credited $2.00. If, however, tomorrow's price is $19.00, then his account will be charged $1.00. **Marking to market** is a way to guarantee that both sides of a futures contract will be able to cover their obligations.

More formally, Taf takes a long position at moment t, when the price in the market is $F(t)$. The next day, new price $F(t+1)$ prevails in the market. At the end of the second day Taf's account will be credited or charged the amount $F(t+1) - F(t)$, depending on whether this amount is positive or negative. Similarly, at the end of the third day, the credit or charge will be $F(t+2) - F(t+1)$. At maturity day T, Taf receives $F(T) - F(T-1)$. At maturity we have $F(T) = S(T)$, since the futures price of a good with immediate delivery is, by definition, the spot price. Taf's total profit/loss payoff, if he stays in the futures contract until maturity, will be

$$[S(T) - F(T-1)] + [F(T-1) - F(T-2)] + \cdots + [F(t+1) - F(t)] = S(T) - F(t)$$

This is the same as the payoff of the corresponding forward contract, except the payoff is paid throughout the life of the contract, rather than at maturity.

The investor, however, does not have to stay in the contract until maturity. She can get out of the contract by taking the opposite position in the futures contract with the same maturity: the investor with a long position will take a short position on the same futures contract. Suppose that the investor takes a long position at moment t and at moment $t + i$ wants out of the contract and takes a short position in the same contract with maturity T. The payoff of the long position is $S(T) - F(t)$, and the payoff of the short position is $F(t + i) - S(T)$, creating a total payoff of

$$S(T) - F(t) + F(t+i) - S(T) = F(t+i) - F(t)$$

Note that this is the same as the payoff of buying the contract at price $F(t)$ and selling it at price $F(t + i)$.

The system of marking to market makes it easy to keep track of the obligations of the parties in a futures contract. This process would be much more difficult for forward contracts, where for each individual contract it would be necessary to keep track of when the contract was entered into and at what price.

1.3.3 Reasons for Trading Futures

There are many possible underlyings for futures contracts: bonds, currencies, commodity goods, and so on. Whether the underlying is a good, a security, or a financial variable, the basic functioning of the contract is the same. Our investor Taf may want to use futures for **speculation,** taking a position in futures as a way to bet on the direction of the price of the underlying. If he thinks that the spot price of a given commodity will be larger at maturity than the futures price, he would take a long position in the futures contract. If he thinks the price will go down, he would take a short position. Even though a futures contract costs nothing to enter into, in order to trade in futures Taf has to keep a cash account, but this requires less initial investment than buying the commodity immediately at the spot price. Therefore, trading futures provides a way of borrowing assets, and we say that futures provide embedded **leverage.**

Alternatively, Taf may want to use futures for **hedging** risks of his other positions or his business moves. Consider, for example, the case of our farmer Taf who will harvest corn in four months and is afraid that an unexpected drop in the price of corn might run him out of business. Taf can take a short position in a futures contract on corn with maturity at the date of the harvest. In other words, he could enter a contract to deliver corn at the price of

$F(t)$ dollars per unit of corn four months from now. That guarantees that he will receive the futures price $F(t)$, and it eliminates any uncertainty about the price. The downside is that the price of corn might go up and be higher than $F(t)$ at maturity. In this case Taf still gets only the price $F(t)$ for his corn.

We will have many more discussions on hedging in a separate chapter later on in the text.

1.3.4 Options

In its simplest form, an **option** is a security that gives its owner the right to buy or sell another, underlying security, simply called **underlying,** at or before a future predetermined date for a predetermined price. The difference from the futures and forwards is that the owner of an option does not have to buy or sell if she chooses not to, which is why it is called an option. The option that provides its owner the right to buy is called a **call option.** For example, Taf can buy an option that gives him the right to buy one share of *Downhill, Inc.,* for $46.00 exactly six months from today. The option that provides its owner the right to sell is called a **put option.**

If the owner of the option can buy or sell *on a given date only,* the option is called a **European option.** If the option gives the right to buy or sell *up to (and including) a given date,* it is called an **American option.** In the present example, if it were an American option, Taf would be able to buy the stock for $46.00 at any time between today and six months from today.

If the owner decides to buy or sell, we say that the owner **exercises** the option. The date on which the option can be exercised (or the last date on which it can be exercised for American options) is called **maturity** or the **expiration date.** The predetermined price at which the option can be exercised is called the **strike price** or the **exercise price.** The decision to exercise an American option before maturity is called **early exercise.**

1.3.5 Calls and Puts

Consider a European call option with a maturity date T, providing the right to buy a security S at maturity T for the strike price K. Denote by $S(t)$ the value—that is, the spot price—of the underlying security at moment t. Each option contract has two parties involved. One is the person who will own the option, called a **buyer, holder,** or **owner** of the option. The other one is the person who sells the option, called a **seller** or **writer** of the option. On the one hand, if the market price $S(T)$ of the underlying asset at maturity is larger than the strike price K, then the holder will exercise the call option, because she will pay K dollars for something that is worth more than K in the market. On the other hand, if the spot price $S(T)$ is less than the strike price K, the holder will not exercise the call option, because the underlying can be purchased at a lower price in the market.

Example 1.3 (Exercising a Call Option)   Let us revisit the example of Taf buying a call option on the Downhill, Inc., stock with maturity $T = 6$ months and strike price $K = \$46.00$. He pays \$1.00 for the option.

a. Suppose that at maturity the stock's market price is \$50.00. Then Taf would exercise the option and buy the stock for \$46.00. He could immediately sell the stock in the market for \$50.00, thereby cashing in the difference of \$4.00. His total profit is \$3.00, when accounting for the initial cost of the option.

b. Suppose that at maturity the stock price is \$40.00. Taf would not exercise the option. He gains nothing from holding the option and his total loss is the initial option price of \$1.00.

Mathematically, the payoff of the European call option that the seller of the call pays to the buyer at maturity is

$$\max[0, S(T) - K] = [S(T) - K]^+ \tag{1.1}$$

Here, x^+ is read "x positive part" or "x plus," and it is equal to x if x is positive, and to zero if x is negative. The expression in equation (1.1) is the payoff the seller has to cover in the call option contract because the seller delivers the underlying security worth $S(T)$, and she gets K dollars in return if the option is exercised—that is, if $S(T) > K$. If the option is not exercised, $S(T) < K$, the payoff is zero. Figure 1.2 presents the payoff of the European call option at maturity.

For the European put—that is, the right to sell $S(T)$ for K dollars—the option will be exercised only if the price $S(T)$ at maturity is less than the strike price K, because otherwise

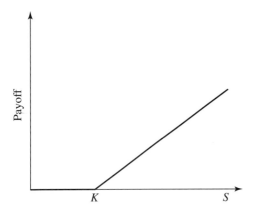

Figure 1.2
Call option payoff at exercise time.

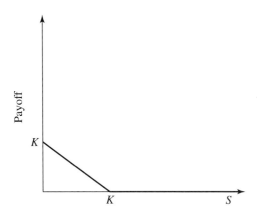

Figure 1.3
Put option payoff at exercise time.

the holder would sell the underlying in the market for the price $S(T) > K$. The payoff at maturity is then

$$\max[0, K - S(T)] = [K - S(T)]^+ \tag{1.2}$$

Figure 1.3 presents the payoff of the European put option at maturity.

An early exercise of an American option will not take place at time t if the strike price is larger than the stock price, $K > S(t)$, for a call, and if the strike price is smaller than the stock price, $K < S(t)$, for a put. However, it is not automatic that early exercise should take place if the opposite holds. For an American call, even when $S(t) > K$, the buyer may want to wait longer before exercising, in expectation that the stock price may go even higher. We will discuss in later chapters the optimal exercise strategies for American options.

In the case of a call (American or European), when the stock price is larger than the strike price, $S(t) > K$, we say that the option is **in the money.** If $S(t) < K$ we say that the option is **out of the money.** When the stock and the strike price are equal, $S(t) = K$, we say that the option is **at the money.** When the call option is in the money, we call the amount $S(t) - K$ the **intrinsic value** of the option. If the option is not in the money, the intrinsic value is zero. For a put (American or European), we say that it is in the money if the strike price is larger than the stock price, $K > S(t)$, out of the money if $K < S(t)$, and at the money when $S(t) = K$. When in the money, the put's intrinsic value is $K - S(t)$.

1.3.6 Option Prices

In an option contract, then, there are two parties: the holder has a right, and the writer has an obligation. In order to accept the obligation, the writer will request a payment. The payment is called the **premium,** although usually we will call it the **option price.** As indicated earlier, when a person accepts the option obligation in exchange for the premium, we say that the person is **writing an option.** When a person writes an option, we say that she has a short position in the option. The owner of the option, then, is said to be long in the option. This terminology is consistent with the terms used in the discussion of stocks.

We started this section by saying that the underlying of an option is a financial instrument. That was the case historically, but today options are written on many types of underlyings. For example, there are options on weather, on energy, on earthquakes and other catastrophic events, and so on. The payoffs of corresponding call and put options will be as in equations (1.1) and (1.2), where $S(T)$ represents the value of a certain variable (for example, a weather index) at maturity. Simple puts and calls written on basic assets such as stocks and bonds are common options, often called **plain vanilla options.** There are many other types of options payoffs, to be studied later, and they are usually referred to as **exotic options.**

When an option is issued, the buyer pays the premium to the writer of the option. Later on, the holder of the option might be able to exercise it and will receive from the writer the corresponding payoff. The gain of one party is the opposite of the other party's loss; hence an option is a zero-sum game. The buyer of the option does not have to hold the option until maturity: the option is a security, and the owner of the option can always sell it to someone else for a price. One of the topics we cover later is the pricing of options. The price of an option (like the price of a bond and the price of a stock) will depend on a number of factors. Some of these factors are the price of the underlying, the strike price, and the time left to maturity.

1.3.7 Reasons for Trading Options

Options offer an interesting investment possibility for several reasons. First, they are widely used for **hedging** risk. A portfolio with a stock and a put option is equivalent to a portfolio in the stock with a limit on a possible loss in the stock value: if the stock drops in price below the strike price, the put option is exercised and the stock/option holder keeps the strike price amount. For example, a put option on a market index may be a convenient way to ensure against a drop in the overall market value for someone who is heavily invested in the stocks. This is the basis for **portfolio insurance,** which we will discuss later. Similarly, risk exposure to exchange-rate risk can be hedged by using exchange-rate options.

Example 1.4 (Using a Put Option for Hedging) Our conservative investor Taf has purchased one hundred shares of the stock of Big Blue Chip company as a large part of his portfolio, for the price of $65.00 per share. He is concerned that the stock may go down during the next six months. As a hedge against that risk he buys one hundred at-the-money European put options with six months' maturity for the price of $2.33 each. After six months the Big Blue Chip stock has gone down to $60.00 per share. Taf has lost

$100 \cdot 5.00 = 500$ dollars in his stock position. However, by exercising the put options, he makes $100 \cdot 5.00 = 500$ dollars. His total loss is the cost of put options equal to $100 \cdot 2.33 = 233$ dollars.

In addition to hedging, options can be attractive from an investment point of view because of the implicit **leverage,** that is, as a tool for borrowing money. Buying options is similar to borrowing money for investing in the stocks. However, this might be risky, as shown in the following example.

Example 1.5   Suppose that the Big Blue Chip stock has today's price of $100. Imagine a weird stock market in which after one month there are only three possible prices of the stock: $105, $101, and $98. A European call option on that stock, with strike price $K = 100$ and maturity in one month, has a price of $2.50. Our optimistic investor Taf has $100 to invest, and believes that the most likely outcome is the highest price. He could invest all of his capital in the stock and, after one month, he would get a relative return of

$$(105 - 100)/100 = 0.05 = 5\%, \qquad (101 - 100)/100 = 1\%,$$
$$\text{or } (98 - 100)/100 = -2\%$$

depending on the final price. However, the call option is increasing in the price of the stock, so Taf might decide to invest all his capital in the call option. He would be able to buy $100/2.5 = 40$ calls. The payoff of each call will be $5.00 if the stock reaches the highest price, $1.00 in the middle state, and $0.00 in the lowest state (the option will not be exercised in that state). That payoff is all that will be left of the investment, since that is the end of the life of the option. The relative return for the investor in those states will then be

$$(5 \cdot 40 - 100)/100 = 1 = 100\%, \qquad (1 \cdot 40 - 100)/100 = -60\%,$$
$$\text{or } (0 - 100)/100 = -100\%$$

respectively.

We see that the investment in the call option really pays off if the stock increases to the highest value, but it means big losses otherwise. Investing in options is more risky than investing in stocks.

In the same way that buying a call is similar to buying the underlying, buying a put is similar to short-selling the underlying: the investor makes money when the price of the underlying goes down.

1.3.8   Swaps

Options and futures do not exhaust the list of financial instruments whose payoff depends on other financial variables. Another type of widely used derivative contract is a swap. We provide more details on swaps in a later chapter, and we only cover the basics here.

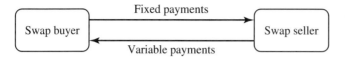

Figure 1.4
The buyer pays fixed interest and receives floating interest.

A **swap** is a contract by which two parties agree to exchange two cash flows with different features. For example, Taf has to pay a variable interest rate on his house mortgage loan, issued by bank A. However, he would rather be paying a fixed rate, because he does not like the fact that he cannot know what the variable rate will be each month. He could go to bank B, which trades swaps, and request a swap contract by which he would be paying bank B a fixed amount of interest each month, while in return bank B would be paying the variable interest to bank A. (This is an artificial example: in reality Taf would likely refinance his mortgage by having bank B pay the total debt to bank A at once, and not in monthly amounts.) A graphical illustration of a swap is given in figure 1.4.

A swap can be thought of as exchanging interest rates on two different types of bonds. Usually, only the interest-rate payments are exchanged, and not the principal. The principal amount is the same for both parties, and it is called the **notional principal.** It is only a reference amount, used to compute the coupon payments. In the most frequent type of swap, one party pays the other a **fixed interest rate** (on the notional principal) and receives in exchange a **floating interest rate.** Fixed interest means that the bond pays predetermined and constant coupons. Floating interest means that, each time a coupon is paid, the amount for the following payment is reset according to some rule. For example, the rate may be set equal to the current interest rate of the 30-year government bond plus 2%. The dates at which the exchanges take place and, therefore, the new coupons for the floating part are determined, are called **resetting dates.**

Very often the interest rates correspond to bonds denominated in different currencies. For example, one party pays the interest rate on a dollar-denominated bond, while the counter-party pays the interest rate on a yen-denominated bond. The two sides will exchange the interest rates as well as the currencies. The swaps where only the interest rate is exchanged are called **interest-rate swaps,** and they are called **currency swaps** if the currency is also exchanged. The side that will receive the floating rate **buys a swap,** while the side that will pay the floating rate **sells the swap.**

As in the case of options and futures, an investor might decide to buy or sell a swap for speculation purposes as a way to make money based on a change in interest rates, or swaps can be used as a hedging tool. In the former case, if Taf thinks that interest rates will go up, he would buy a swap, locking in the fixed rate he will have to pay in exchange for the variable interest payment that, if the prediction is correct, will go up. As a hedging instrument, swaps are usually used by investors who have to pay a floating rate and receive a fixed rate. For example, a bank might have many clients to whom it pays a floating rate on certain accounts. But suppose that the bank is also providing a lot of mortgage loans, the majority of which pay a fixed rate. This is a risky situation for the bank because, if the interest rates go up, it might face losses, since it will not be able to pass the higher costs to its mortgage customers. One possible way to avoid that risk is to buy a swap. The bank will be paying the fixed interest rate, the cost of which can be covered by the funds received through the mortgages, and it will be receiving a floating rate that will allow it to pay the floating interest on the floating-rate accounts.

At the resetting date, when the interest payments are exchanged, the net result will be computed, and a single payment in one direction will take place: if the floating rate is higher than the fixed rate, the party that sold the swap will pay the difference between the two interests on the principal to the party that bought the swap. As in the case of options and futures, swaps are zero-sum games. One side's profit is the other side's loss. Swaps are also contracts (and, like futures, not securities), and the parties cannot sell them, but they can get out of them by taking the opposite position.

1.3.9 Mortgage-Backed Securities; Callable Bonds

There are other securities with characteristics that make them similar to derivatives. We mention two: **mortgage-backed securities,** or **MBS,** and **callable bonds.** We first describe the MBS. Suppose that a bank is providing mortgages to its clients. If these mortgages are similar, the bank can pool them together and issue securities that represent a proportional part of the pool of mortgages. These securities will then be sold to investors. The security serves two purposes: On one hand, it makes the borrowing of money available to house buyers that are looking for a loan. On the other hand, it allows private investors to access a type of investment that may be attractive given its return rate and its safety. The bank serves as an intermediary and keeps a small fraction of the interest paid by the house buyers to the lenders (the investors who bought the MBS).

If the mortgage rate is fixed, this type of financial instrument behaves like a regular bond with predetermined coupons. However, there is one difference: at any time before the end of the mortgage term the house buyer can decide to pay off the mortgage. This action is called **prepayment.** It makes the investment in the MBS risky because the prepayments are more likely to happen when the interest rates are dropping and, therefore, when the coupon paid by the MBS is more attractive. In fact, one way to analyze the MBS is by considering it a standard bond minus a call option on the loan (see Problem 20). That is, the buyer of the MBS is simultaneously buying a bond with fixed coupon and writing an American call option on the bond with a strike price equal to the principal. If we can price both, we have a good approximation of the value of the MBS.

A similar interpretation is possible for callable bonds. **Callable bonds** are bonds with fixed interest rate and maturity, but such that the debtor has the possibility to repay the principal after some date prior to the scheduled maturity. As in the case of an MBS, a callable bond behaves like a standard bond minus a call on the bond with a strike price equal to the principal.

1.4 Organization of Financial Markets

Financial markets in the United States are the most developed financial markets, and we focus our attention on those. However, the organization of financial markets in most countries, in general, does not differ substantially from the structure that we will describe in the next few paragraphs.

Some securities and financial contracts can be purchased, or entered into, in markets with a physical location. Those markets are called **exchanges.** However, some securities and contracts are sold through sources without a physical location. We say that those financial instruments are traded **over the counter** or on an **OTC** market. Many contracts can be traded both on an exchange and on an OTC market. For example, many stocks, especially those of large companies, can be traded both on exchanges and OTC markets. However, treasury bonds, issued by the U.S. Treasury, the financial arm of the government, are traded on an OTC market, while corporate bonds are typically traded on exchanges. Another characteristic of exchanges as well as some organized OTC markets is the existence of a **market maker** that provides **liquidity** in a given security or contract. By this we mean that one of the obligations of the market maker is to guarantee that at every moment people can buy or sell a given security, or take a long or short position in a given contract, by offering these at appropriate prices.

1.4.1 Exchanges

In the United States there are two national stock exchanges, the **New York Stock Exchange,** or **NYSE,** which trades stocks of most of the largest companies, and the **American Exchange,** or **Amex,** which trades stocks of smaller companies. There are also several regional exchanges that list stocks of smaller companies. When an exchange lists a stock, the exchange guarantees that it can be bought or sold at the prevailing price in the market. At regional exchanges it is also possible to buy stocks of larger companies, like some of the companies listed on the NYSE. Stocks can also be bought OTC, without the need to go to any of those exchanges. There is also an organized OTC market that has become very important in recent years: **Nasdaq,** the **National Association of Security Dealers Automated Quotation.** This is basically a network of computers with some strict rules about the way to perform trades. Many of the high-tech companies that have become some of the largest companies in the world in the last two decades are listed here. Securities listed on the NYSE, or any regional exchange, can also be bought at Nasdaq.

Treasury bonds, as we said before, can be traded only in an organized OTC market that is also a network of a few authorized dealers. Any private investor who wants to buy or sell treasury bonds will have to do so through these dealers. Corporate bonds are listed in some of the exchanges we mentioned before.

Most of the options traded on the markets are standardized according to some specific rules about the maturity, the strike price, and the underlying. These options trade on exchanges. An investor does not need to find a counterparty in order to take a long or short position in such options. The market maker will take the role of the counterparty for a market price. The largest option exchange is the **Chicago Board of Options Exchange,** or **CBOE.** The second-largest options exchange is the Amex. The Amex started as a stock exchange but now generates a large part of its business through options trades. Other stock exchanges also trade options. There is also a very active OTC market for options. For example, exotic options do not trade on exchanges. Rather, they are actively bought and sold OTC by investment banks.

Futures contracts are listed on exchanges. The most important futures exchanges are the **Chicago Board of Trade,** or **CBOT,** and the **Chicago Mercantile Exchange,** or **CME.** As in the case of options, the market makers guarantee that an investor can take a long or a short position in a given futures contract, at any point in time, at the market price.

In the United States there are two federal agencies that oversee the proper functioning of financial markets: the **Securities and Exchange Commission,** or **SEC,** and the **Commodities and Futures Trading Commission,** or **CFTC.** The SEC oversees the securities markets, stocks, and options, and the CFTC is in charge of the futures markets.

1.4.2   Market Indexes

Thousands of securities and contracts are listed on different exchanges. In order to summarize the information contained in their prices, there are many market indexes. An **index** tries to express through a single number a summary of the level of the markets, or a subset of markets. We mention a few of them. First, the **Standard & Poor's 500,** or **S&P 500,** is an average of the prices of 500 of the largest stocks listed on the NYSE or Nasdaq. It is not strictly the largest 500 stocks because the index tries to cover all industries. The average is weighted by **market capitalization value,** or the number of outstanding shares times the stock price. This is the amount it would cost to buy all the stock of a given company at a given moment in time. Periodically, the components of the index are updated.

Another important index is the **Dow Jones Industrial Average,** or **DJIA,** which is a weighted average of 30 of the most important companies. This is the oldest index. Its correlation with the S&P 500 is very high.

We should also mention the Nasdaq index, which is a weighted average, using the market capitalization value, of all the securities listed on Nasdaq. Since most of the high-tech companies have been trading in that market, that index is considered an indicator of the performance of the technology sector (the "new economy"). The **Russell 3000** is a weighted average of the largest 3,000 stocks of the economy. Given the increase in the number of public companies, it attempts to fill the role that the S&P 500 was playing 20 years ago. The **Russell 2000** is structured like the Russell 3000, but excluding the largest 1,000 stocks. It is representative of the performance of the stocks of the midsized and small companies. Very often, the performance of these companies has differed from the performance of the rest of the market. Finally, the **Wilshire 6000** index includes more than 7,000 companies, almost every public company in the United States, and it intends to be the broadest possible market index. The index is constructed by aggregating the market capitalization value of those companies.

1.5   Margins

Taking a position in some of the securities or contracts we have reviewed involves a potential financial responsibility. For example, a short position in an option could end up in a financial liability, should the option end up in the money. The same is true for both a long and a short position in a futures contract. In order to guarantee that the investor will be solvent at maturity, **margin requirements** are imposed. We describe the general functioning of margin requirements.

As a part of a margin requirement, some assets have to be deposited as **collateral** for a given debt, meaning they can be used to pay off the debt, if necessary. The amount required as collateral at the beginning of the trade is known as the **initial margin.** The difference between the collateral and the debt may change in the future because the value of the assets and the debt are in general **stochastic,** meaning random. After the initial trade takes place the investor is required to keep a minimum **maintenance margin** between the value of his collateral assets and his debt, which is typically set to a value smaller than the initial margin. When the value of the debt goes up or the value of the collateral goes down in such a way that the maintenance margin is not satisfied, the intermediary sends the investor a **margin call** that involves a request for more collateral or a cancellation of the debt. Often, extra collateral will be requested so that the initial margin is currently satisfied. When the investor does not attend the margin call, the intermediary will liquidate the account by selling the assets and paying the debt. Margins are usually computed in such a way that there are enough assets to ensure the payment of the liability.

1.5.1   Trades That Involve Margin Requirements

Example 1.6 (Buying at Margin)   Our enthusiastic investor Taf really likes the stock of the company called Uphill, Incorporated. He would like to buy $100,000 worth of the stock, but he has only $40,000 to invest. He decides to **buy at margin.** He goes to an intermediary, asking it to buy $100,000 worth of Uphill, Inc. He pays $40,000 to the intermediary, effectively borrowing $60,000. The intermediary keeps all the stock as a collateral against the amount lent. It also requires a maintenance margin of $70,000, meaning that the total value of the collateral should be at least $70,000. Suppose that three months from now the value of the total stock purchased falls to $65,000. Then the intermediary would send Taf a margin call for $5,000.

Getting a loan from a financial intermediary in order to buy stock is common practice in financial markets. As in the preceding example, a specific way to do so is to ask the intermediary to buy a larger amount of stock than the investor is paying for and have the intermediary pay for the difference. The stock so purchased is kept by the intermediary as a guarantee. This procedure is called **buying at margin.** The initial margin and the maintenance margin will determine the value of the required collateral relative to the value of the loan (which is fixed, from the moment the purchase takes place). Initially, the collateral is the stock purchased, and its value exceeds that of the loan, since all the stock, including that which the investor paid for, is used as collateral. The stock price fluctuates later on, thereby making the value of the collateral uncertain.

Another type of trade that involves the potential of financial responsibility is short-selling. In a short sale, the investor borrows and sells the stock, with the hope that its price will go down. There is a risk, however, that the price will go up. In that case the investor may have to buy the stock at a high price in order to get out of the short position. In order to guarantee that the investor will be able to meet the potential financial liability, a margin is required. Typically, the proceeds of the sale of the borrowed stock, plus some additional assets (typically cash), are required to satisfy the initial margin. As the value of the stock, and therefore the value of the debt, changes, the collateral will change in value. Such changes are fine as long as the maintenance margin is kept.

When an investor buys an option, her only obligation is to pay the price of the option. However, when an investor writes an option, a potential financial liability arises. When the investor writes a call, one possible way to guarantee the payment of the financial liability that would result in case the option expires in the money is by holding the stock simultaneously.

Since the payoff of the option cannot be larger than the value of the stock [see equation (1.1)], the stock is an adequate guarantee. This is called a **covered call.** The opposite is called a **naked call.** Both naked calls and short positions in puts are guaranteed by setting some margin requirements that will depend on how much the option is in the money at a given point in time.

An infamous example of how important margins can be is the case of a hedge fund run successfully for many years by a famous Wall Street wizard. A **hedge fund** is a name for a mutual fund whose activity is actually often risky and speculative in nature. These funds seek very high returns, and this approach usually means that the risk involved is also high. At one point the wizard's fund had a lot of short positions, including short positions in puts on the market index. Then one day the index suddenly fell, making the intrinsic value of the puts very high and prompting substantial margin calls on the fund. The fund could not satisfy the calls and went bankrupt. Even though the market recovered in the ensuing days, it was too late for the hedge fund.

Finally, both long and short positions in futures contracts involve the possibility of a financial responsibility. Both sides of the contract are requested to have an account that is upgraded every day as the contract is marked to market. In addition to charging or crediting the difference of the futures prices between today and yesterday, the accounts may be required to keep additional collateral in order to satisfy margin requirements. Mounting losses might force the investor to exit the futures contract before maturity. It is then possible that the investor might lose money in a position in futures because she cannot keep up with the margin requirements, even though she would have made money had she been able to stay in the contract until maturity.

The combination of marking to market and margin requirements is very important in practice for the functioning of futures markets. However, in our theoretical discussions in later chapters on pricing futures contracts and derivatives in general, we will usually ignore margin considerations.

In the next section we discuss costs and fees an investor has to pay in order to purchase a security. Margins are also usually costly. The cost is, in general, the result of keeping some collateral in the margin account, without getting the prevailing interest return in exchange. For example, the cash that is kept as a guarantee for a short sale may not pay an interest rate, or it may pay an interest rate lower than what the investor could get elsewhere.

1.6   Transaction Costs

The main cost of buying a security is its price. However, there are other costs the investor has to pay in order to perform the transaction. We call them **transaction costs.** We now mention the main costs other than the price of the security that an investor will face.

Intermediaries often require a fee or a commission as a compensation for the services they provide. The smaller the trade, the larger the proportional costs will be. Very large investors will pay negligible proportional fees. On the exchanges there is typically a market maker whose obligation is to guarantee that the investors will be able to buy or sell a given security (take long or short positions in a contract). In order to do so, the market maker will quote the price at which it would be willing to buy the security, called the **bid price,** and the price at which it would be willing to sell the security, called the **ask price.** The bid will be lower than the ask. The difference between the bid and ask price is called the **bid-ask spread.** It achieves two purposes. First, it is a part of the compensation the market maker receives for its services. Second, it is a means of protection from the possibility that the price might move against the market maker by going down if the market maker is buying, or up if the market maker is selling. In fact, the size of the bid-ask spread is a good indicator of the market volatility or risk underlying a given security. The bid-ask spread tends to be larger for smaller stocks that are harder to trade and therefore more risky.

The main cost component in large trades is the **price impact.** For example, when a big investor wants to sell a large number of shares of a certain stock, this decision will increase its supply dramatically, and the demand may not be very high. We say that the selling puts pressure on the stock price in the market, and, as a consequence, the price is likely to drop significantly. The investor will probably have to accept a price considerably lower than the price at which the stock had been trading before the large transaction was announced. There are special channels for large trades, as well as different strategies investors can choose in the case of a large transaction, all of them aimed at minimizing the price impact of the trade.

Summary

We have introduced three main types of financial contracts: bonds, stocks, and derivatives. A zero-coupon or pure discount bond pays a guaranteed payment, called nominal, face, principal, or par value, at a given future date, called maturity. A coupon bond also pays intermediate payments. Since the payment amounts are known, bonds are called risk-free securities, even though they may be exposed to default/credit risk, inflation risk, and liquidity risk.

A stock is a risky security whose value is tied to the performance and prospects of the company issuing the stock. A stock can also pay dividends, whose values depend on the profit of the company. An investor can borrow stocks to sell. This process is called short-selling. If the investor buys stocks, that action is called taking a long position in the stock.

Derivatives are securities whose value is determined from the value of another security (or some other financial variable), called the underlying. Futures and forwards are contracts that allow buying the underlying at a predetermined price at maturity. Futures positions are marked to market. Options are frequently traded derivative securities. A call option gives the holder the right to buy one unit of the underlying for a predetermined strike price. A put option gives the holder the right to sell the underlying. If the buying/selling is done only at the final time (maturity), the option is European type. If the exchange can be done at any time before maturity, the option is American type. For this right, the investor who wants to hold the option has to pay a premium to the seller (writer) of the option. Options can be used for hedging risk or for speculation. Swaps enable two parties to exchange two different cash flows, such as a cash flow associated with a fixed interest rate and a cash flow associated with a floating interest rate. Mortgage-backed securities and callable bonds can also be considered as derivative instruments.

Securities are traded on exchanges or over the counter. Market movements are summarized in weighted averages of security prices, the best known ones being the S&P 500 index, Dow Jones index, and Nasdaq index. When engaged in financial contracts, investors might be asked to maintain a margin account, in order to be able to pay their liabilities if the market moves against them. When buying or selling securities, investors are exposed to transaction costs in the form of commissions, fees, and bid-ask spreads, or because of the price impact of a trade.

Problems

1. Why do bonds exist in financial markets?

†2. How "risk-free" are bonds as financial instruments?

3. What do you think the word "liquidity" refers to?

†4. Why are stocks usually more risky than bonds?

5. In the U.S. market in the last century stocks have paid higher returns than bonds on average. What are possible explanations for this difference?

†6. Being a sophisticated trader, you are not afraid to engage in selling shares short. You sell short 100 shares of Internet Bust Company at the market price of $20.00 per share. What is your profit or loss if you exit the short position five months from now and a share of the company is worth $15.00?

7. What is your profit or loss in the previous problem when you exit the short position at $24.00 per share?

†8. The company Nice Books International, owned by the authors of this book, promises to pay you back $50.00 for each copy of the book you buy this year if, five years from now, the book is out of print. For this promise, you have to pay an additional $10.00 when buying

a copy. If you agree to this proposal, are you buying the company's stock, the company's bond, or a derivative contract?

9. In the context of the previous problem, you need the book for the next semester, and there is a possibility that its today's price of $75.00 will change. Alternatively, the company offers to deliver the book to you at the beginning of the next semester, when you would have to pay the price of $80.00 for it. What kind of contract is this?

10. A share of ABCD stock can be purchased at $55.00 today or at $57.00 six months from now. Which of these prices is the spot price, and which is the forward price?

11. Explain the difference between entering into a long forward contract with the forward price $50.00 and buying a call option with a strike price of $50.00.

†12. Explain the difference between entering into a short forward contract with the forward price $50.00 and selling a call option with a strike price of $50.00.

13. You enter a short position in a corn futures contract with the futures price 70 cents per pound. The contract is for the delivery of 40,000 pounds. How much do you gain or lose if the corn price at the end of the contract is

a. 68 cents per pound?

b. 73 cents per pound?

†14. You buy a European put option on Up&Down, Inc., stock with maturity $T = 6$ months and strike price $K = \$54.00$. You pay $1.00 for the option.

a. Suppose that at maturity the stock's market price is $50.00. What is your total profit or loss?

b. What is the profit or loss when at maturity the stock price is $57.00?

15. A European put option with strike price $50.00 costs $3.00. Under what circumstances will the seller of the option make a profit? How about the buyer?

16. Do you think this statement is true: "An American option is always worth at least as much as the corresponding European option." Why?

17. At time zero you enter a long position in a forward contract on 10 shares of the stock XYZ at the forward price of $50.00. Moreover, you sell (write) 10 exotic options, each of which gives the holder one share of the stock (only) if the price of one share is above $55.00 and which pays the holder $40.00 (only) if the price is below $55.00. The today's selling price of one option of this kind is $45.00. The maturity of all of your positions is $T = 3$ months. What is your total profit or loss if

a. at maturity the price of one stock share is $60.00?

b. at maturity the price of one stock share is $48.00?

†18. At time zero you enter a short position in futures contracts on 20 shares of the stock XYZ at the futures price of $50.00. Moreover, you sell (write) 5 exotic options of the following type: they are put options, but using as the underlying asset the average of the today's stock price and the stock price at maturity, rather than using the stock price at maturity as the underlying asset. The option's strike price is $K = \$52.00$, the option selling price today is $5.00 per option, and the today's stock price is $S(0) = \$49.00$ per share. The maturity of all of your positions is $T = 2$ months. What is your total profit or loss two months from now if

a. at maturity the price of one stock share is $57.00?

b. at maturity the price of one stock share is $47.00?

19. One U.S. dollar is worth 1.2 euros today. Your company, based in the United States, will receive 2 million euros six months from now. You are concerned that the euro may lose its value relative to the dollar. You want to hedge this risk by buying put or call options on the exchange rate.

a. Describe in detail the kind of option you would want to buy.

b. Give a numerical example. More precisely, specify the strike price and the selling price of the option in part a, and assume that you buy n such options. If the value of one U.S. dollar is 1.3 euros six months from now, what is your total profit or loss?

*20. Construct a numerical example to show that an MBS behaves like a combination of a bond and an American call option.

21. You enter a futures contract on $\alpha\beta\gamma\delta$ stock at $34.00 today.

a. Tomorrow the futures price is $35.00. How much goes into or out of your margin account?

b. Same question as part a but with tomorrow's price equal to $32.00?

†22. You would like to buy $200,000 worth of the stock Good Potential, Inc., but you have only $60,000 to invest. You buy the $200,000 worth at margin. The intermediary requires a maintenance margin of $145,000. Four months from now the value of the total stock purchased falls to $125,000. What is the amount of the margin call the intermediary would send you?

23. Suppose that you are planning to buy 100 shares of company A and your broker charges you $15 per trade and $0.15 per share as his service fees. At the moment the trade takes place the price quoted for the stock A is

Bid	Ask
100.25	100.50

How much would you have to pay for 100 shares? What proportion of the value of the deal is transaction costs?

Further Readings

There are many excellent books that describe the organization and functioning of financial markets and institutions. Two popular MBA books on the general topic of investments, with good backgrounds on capital markets, are Bodie, Kane, and Marcus (2001) and Sharpe, Alexander, Bailey, and Sharpe (1998). A classic book on the organization of markets is Fabozzi, Modigliani, and Jones (2002). With respect to the organization (and much more) of futures and options markets, the standard reference is Hull (2002). Finally, a comprehensive book that explains in careful detail the trading process for all types of securities is Harris (2002).

2 Interest Rates

If you have ever taken a loan (from a bank, not your parents), you know that the method for calculating the amount that you have to pay back every month is a total mystery. If you have never taken a loan or will never take one, either you are too rich to be reading this book, or you have such poor credit eligibility that even this book cannot help you. The learning objectives of this chapter are to make the issue less mysterious and confusing (hopefully) by

- explaining how various interest rates are calculated.
- demonstrating how to find today's value of a cash flow of future payments.
- introducing the concepts of forward rates and term structure of interest rates.

The relative return of risk-free securities (bonds or bank account) is called the **interest rate.** In other words, the interest rate is the return that can be achieved in an investment without risk: anyone willing to invest money in the risk-free security will have the opportunity to lock in this return. Interest rate is a key component of economic models because it provides a benchmark against which to measure other possible investments. It also provides the simplest type of return, conceptually. In this chapter we review several aspects of this concept: different ways to compute the interest rate and the relation between interest rates and prices. Important notions of present value and of forward rates are directly related to interest rates. Finally, we explore a notion related to forward rates, the term structure of interest rates.

Unlike in other chapters, we here lump together the discrete-time analysis with the continuous-time analysis, because of the simplicity and usefulness of the concept of continuous-time interest rate.

2.1 Computation of Interest Rates

In pure discount bonds the interest rate is implicit in the difference between the purchase price and the amount that the holder of the bond will receive at maturity. For example, if a one-year zero-coupon bond pays $100.00 at maturity and its price today is $95.00, then the annual interest on this bond is

$$\frac{100 - 95}{95} = 0.0526 = 5.26\%$$

In general, consider a pure discount bond that sells today at a price $P(0)$ and matures with a nominal payment of $P(T)$. We will say that the **bond's interest rate** is the value r

that solves

$$P(0)(1+r) = P(T)$$

or

$$r = \frac{P(T) - P(0)}{P(0)}$$

This is the interest rate in a single-period model. In a multiperiod model this would be the way to compute the interest rate per period.

Coupon bonds make additional payments as part of the interest, in regular intervals until maturity. The interest has to be computed taking the coupon payments into account, as we shall explain. A bank account also behaves like a bond, at least if the interest rate is fixed, or known in advance.

2.1.1 Simple versus Compound Interest; Annualized Rates

Traditionally, interest rates have been classified as **simple** or **compound,** depending on whether interest is paid on the interest received or not. In practice, interest is always paid on accumulated interest, as long as the accumulated interest is not withdrawn from the investment. For example, if our investor Taf opens a bank account, the account will be periodically credited with interest on the existing balance, or, more typically, on the average balance over a period of time. If Taf keeps the interest in the account, it will become a part of the balance, and interest will be computed on it for the next period. If Taf holds a bond, coupons will be paid periodically. Coupons are detached from the rest of the investment, and therefore, unless Taf decides to use the interest received as coupon to buy more bonds, no interest will be paid on the coupon interest. In summary, the interest paid is always compounded, as long as it is reinvested.

An important issue with compound interest is the frequency of the interest payments: a bank can pay interest on the balance of the account every month, or every week, or some other time period. Both the rate and the periodicity of the payments will affect the final value of the investment. If r_Q is the quarterly simple rate, one dollar today is worth

$$1 + 4r_Q$$

dollars after a year. If r_Q is the quarterly rate and interest is compounded quarterly, one dollar today would increase to $1 + r_Q$ dollars three months from now, $(1+r_Q)(1+r_Q)$ dollars six months from now, and

$$(1+r_Q)^4$$

dollars after a year.

When two interest rates refer to payments of different frequencies, it is important to be able to compare them and see which one results in higher returns. For example, we want to compare a bank account that pays 1.5% interest over three-month intervals and a bank account with an interest of 2.9% paid over six-month periods. In order to make possible the comparison of interest rates paid at different frequencies, the common practice is to transform the rates into the corresponding rates for a common time interval, usually a year. That is, a rate paid over a three-month period will be "converted" into an **annual, or annualized, interest rate,** and in that way it can be compared with an interest rate paid over six months, also appropriately converted into an annual rate. A typical assumption when computing the annualized interest rate is that over the rest of the year the investment will pay the same interest rate. That is, if the bank account pays an interest r_Q over a three-month period, we assume that in the remaining three quarters of a year-long period it will also pay r_Q. The computation of the annualized rate depends on whether the bank pays simple or compound interest rate. Typically in practice a bank would quote a **nominal rate** of say 6% (not to be confused with the nominal rates introduced later in the inflation context). If the bank does the compounding on a quarterly basis, every three months, the nominal rate of 6% means that the quarterly rate r_Q is $6/4 = 1.5\%$. This is consistent with the usual convention of using the simple interest rule when quoting rates. The actual annual rate of interest, called **effective annual interest rate** and denoted r_{3m}, that corresponds to the quarterly compound rate r_Q, is determined from

$$1 + r_{3m} = (1 + r_Q)^4$$

With $r_Q = 1.5\%$ we get $r_{3m} = 6.1364\%$, showing that the effective rate is higher than the nominal rate. This can be compared, for example, with the annual rate r_{6m}, the result of annualizing the six-month, semiannual compound rate r_S:

$$1 + r_{6m} = (1 + r_S)^2$$

In our example $r_S = 3\%$ and $r_{6m} = 6.09\%$. Not surprisingly, more frequent compounding results in higher interest.

The same principle is applied in the case of interest rates for the periods longer than one year. For example, if the interest rate for a two-year period is r_2, the effective annual rate r_{2y} with annual compounding will be the result of

$$1 + r_{2y} = (1 + r_2)^{1/2}$$

The simple annual interest rate corresponding to r_2 is

$$r^{(2y)} = r_2/2$$

2.1.2   Continuous Interest

Let us recap the previous discussion: Suppose that a bank quotes its nominal annual rate as $r^{(2)}$ and the payments are every six months. The bank uses the simple rate convention; hence the interest rate paid every six months is $r^{(2)}/2$. The actual interest paid is compounded. Thus the effective annual rate r is given by

$$1 + r = \left(1 + \frac{r^{(2)}}{2}\right)^2$$

Similarly, if the bank makes daily payments and the quoted rate is $r^{(365)}$, the effective annual rate is computed from

$$1 + r = \left(1 + \frac{r^{(365)}}{365}\right)^{365}$$

The **continuously compounded interest rate** is the rate paid at infinite frequency. That is, we say that the bank pays a continuous rate r_C when the effective annual rate r is obtained from

$$1 + r = \lim_{n \to \infty} \left(1 + \frac{r_C}{n}\right)^n = e^{r_C}$$

(Here, $e = 2.7818\ldots$ is the base of the natural logarithm.) For example, if the quoted continuous rate is 6%, the effective annual rate is $r = e^{0.06} - 1 = 6.1837\%$.

If the continuous rate r_C is paid over a period t different from the year, the value of one dollar invested today will be

$$e^{r_C \cdot t}$$

at time t, where t represents the time period expressed in years. In order to see this result we represent (or approximate) t with k/n, where n represents a large number of short periods per year, and k is an integer. Then k is (approximately) equal to nt, and one dollar today results in the time t value (equivalently, the value after k periods) equal to

$$(1 + r_C/n)^k = (1 + r_C/n)^{nt} = [(1 + r_C/n)^n]^t \longrightarrow e^{r_C \cdot t}$$

The chosen time unit could be different from one year, but using time in years has become a standard that we follow. For example, when we write $t = 0.25$ we mean that t represents a three-month period.

In this deterministic (as opposed to random) framework the future value of investing in the bank is known in advance: if Taf invests amount $B(0)$ at time $t = 0$, at a continuous rate r_C, the value of the investment at time t will be

$$B(t) = B(0)e^{r_C \cdot t} \tag{2.1}$$

2.2   Present Value

A topic of great importance in the investment theory and practice is the derivation of criteria that would allow us to choose today between two different future payments, or **cash flows** of several payments. A typical approach is to assign to each cash flow its today's value, and compare those values. In later chapters this will be known as a **pricing theory,** and the payments will be random, in general. For the time being, we consider the simplest case, deterministic payments. An intuitive solution to this problem is to apply a similar technique to that presented in the previous section, but in the opposite direction: in the previous section we discussed how to transform an investment today into its future value, when the interest rate is known. Now, we are interested in transforming the future payments into a value today. This value, the today's worth of the future payments, is known as the **present value.**

DEFINITION 2.1   Present value of a future payment is that amount which, when invested today at a given interest rate, would result in the given value of the future payment.

For example, if we know that we will be paid $105 in a year, and the risk-free interest rate is $r = 5\%$, then the present value of this future payment is

$$105/(1 + 0.05) = 100$$

The explanation for this result is that we also would get $105 if we invested 100 today at 5% interest. Similarly, if we have to pay 105 in a year, the present value of that obligation is 100, at 5% interest. We see that the present value $V(0)$ is obtained as

$$V(0) = \frac{V}{1+r}$$

where V is the value of the future payment and r is the interest rate per period in question. We say that the future payoff amount V is **discounted,** since the present value is less than the future payment V. The factor

$$d = 1/(1+r)$$

by which we multiply the future payoff value is called the **discount factor.**
Consider now the case of a payment at a future date different from a year. The corresponding interest rate will be expressed in its equivalent annual rate. If the payment takes place in $1/n$ years and r is the corresponding equivalent annual rate using the simple interest rule, the discount factor is

$$d = \frac{1}{(1+r/n)}$$

When the compound rule is used to compute the equivalent annual rate, the discount factor is

$$d = \frac{1}{(1+r)^{1/n}}$$

In the case of continuous compounding with a continuous rate r_C and a period of t years, the discount factor is

$$d = e^{-r_c t}$$

2.2.1 Present and Future Values of Cash Flows

The previous discussion is easily extended to a stream of several payments, a **cash flow.** Consider a time interval $[0, T]$ consisting of m equally spaced periods, with interest rate r per period. Suppose that we receive a payment P_0 at time zero and invest it in the bank; in addition, we receive P_1 after the first period and invest it in the bank; we receive P_2 after the second period and invest it in the bank, and so on, until the final time T, at the end of the last time interval, at which moment we receive P_m. The values P_i can also be negative, which means a cost (instead of investing it, we have to borrow the amount P_i from the bank, at the same interest rate). The **future value of the cash flow** is (compounded every period)

$$P(T) = P_0(1+r)^m + P_1(1+r)^{m-1} + \cdots + P_m \tag{2.2}$$

In the case of continuous compounding, we replace $(1+r)^k$ with $e^{r(T-t_i)}$ where t_i is the time of payment P_i.

Similarly, we now extend the notion of the present value to cash flows of several payments. Given a cash flow of payments with values $V_0, \ldots, V_m$, where V_i is the payment at the end of the ith period, the **present value of the cash flow** is (compounded every period)

$$V(0) = V_0 + \frac{V_1}{(1+r)} + \cdots + \frac{V_m}{(1+r)^m} \tag{2.3}$$

We replace $(1+r)^k$ with e^{rt_i} for continuous compounding, where t_i is the time of payment V_i. It can be checked (see Problem 8) that the present value $V(0)$ and the future value $V(T)$ of a cash flow are related by

$$V(0) = \frac{V(T)}{(1+r)^m}$$

Example 2.1 (Project Value) The powerful CEO (chief executive officer) of the Enterprise Search Company, a gentleman with the familar name Taf, has to make a decision between two different business projects. His reliable research group tells him that project Amazing is certain to result in the cash flow $(-1.0, 1.5, 2.0)$ in millions of dollars. That is, the initial investment of one million dollars will result in the return of 1.5 million after one year and 2 million after two years. On the other hand, project Fabulous will have the cash flow $(-1.2, 1.2, 2.6)$. Taf recalls the investment class from his business school days, and decides to compare these two projects based on their present values. He estimates that the risk-free interest rate is likely to be around 6% for the next two years. The present value of project Amazing is then

$$-1 + \frac{1.5}{1.06} + \frac{2}{1.06^2} = 2.1951$$

and of project Fabulous

$$-1.2 + \frac{1.2}{1.06} + \frac{2.6}{1.06^2} = 2.2461$$

in millions. Taf concludes that project Fabulous might be a somewhat more profitable venture.

In order to compute the present values in various examples, it is convenient to recall the following **summation formula for a geometric sequence:**

$$\frac{1}{(1+r)} + \frac{1}{(1+r)^2} + \cdots + \frac{1}{(1+r)^m} = \frac{1}{r}\left(1 - \frac{1}{(1+r)^m}\right) \tag{2.4}$$

This expression means that the *cash flow of equal payments of P dollars after each of m periods has the present value*

$$V(0) = \frac{P}{r}\left(1 - \frac{1}{(1+r)^m}\right) \tag{2.5}$$

where r is the interest rate per period. The payments of P dollars are sometimes called **annuities.**

Equivalently, inverting equation (2.5), *in order to pay off a loan of $V(0)$ dollars in equal installments of P dollars at the end of each period, for m periods, the amount P is set equal to*

$$P = \frac{r(1+r)^m V(0)}{(1+r)^m - 1} \tag{2.6}$$

We say that the loan is **amortized** over m periods.

Example 2.2 (Mortgage Payments Calculation)   Our agent Taf has been doing well in the market and decides to buy a new house. Taf takes a 30-year loan on $400,000, at the fixed interest rate of 8%, compounded monthly. We want to compute the amount of Taf's monthly payments. There are 12 months in a year, so the number of periods is $m = 30 \cdot 12 = 360$.

The interest rate per period is $0.08/12 = 0.0067$. The value of the loan is $V(0) = 400,000$. Using formula (2.6) with $r = 0.0067$ and $m = 360$, we get approximately

$$P = 2,946$$

Taf will need to pay close to $3,000 in mortgage monthly payments. The way his balance is computed is as follows: After the first month the interest of $0.0067 \cdot 400,000 = 2,680$ is added to the initial balance of 400,000, resulting in the balance of 402,680. After he has paid the first installment of 2,946 his new balance will be $402,680 - 2,946 = 399,734$. After the second month before the payment the balance will be $399,734(1 + 0.0067)$, and so on.

The future value corresponding to these payments 30 years from now is

$$V(30) = 400,000(1 + 0.0067)^{360} = 4,426,747$$

In other words, if Taf invests $2,936 every month at 8% interest compounded monthly (that is, at a monthly rate of 0.67%) the final value of the investment after 30 years will be almost $4.5 million.

Example 2.3 (Loan Fees) When a bank advertises its mortgage products there are usually two rates listed. One is the mortgage interest rate and the other is called **APR** or **annual percentage rate.** The latter rate includes the fees for providing the loan. These fees are added to the loan amount and also paid through the monthly installments. As an example consider a bank that offers a 30-year mortgage loan of 400,000 at the rate of 7.8% compounded monthly, with the APR of 8.00%. As computed in the previous example the monthly payment at this APR is 2,936. Now, we use this monthly payment of 2,936 and the rate of $7.8/12 = 0.65\%$ in equation (2.5) to find that the total balance actually being paid is 407,851.10. This means that the total fees equal $407,851.10 - 400,000 = 7,851.10$.

Here is another example of evaluating a business venture by computing the so-called **annual worth,** using equation (2.6).

Example 2.4 (Annual Worth) A business venture is presented to Mr. Taf, a venture capitalist. It is projected that for the initial investment of $10 million the venture would return $2.2 million each year for the next 10 years. Mr. Taf thinks that he can find other risk-free investments returning 15% a year. He calculates that paying off $10 million in a course of 10 years at 15% annual compound rate would require paying $1.9925 million a year. Hence, he concludes that the annual worth of the venture is

$$2.2 - 1.9925 = 0.2075$$

million. This is a venture with a positive annual worth, and it should be explored further.

2.2.2 Bond Yield

Closely related to the interest-rate/present-value analysis is the analysis of a bond price and a bond yield, also called **yield to maturity,** or **YTM.** The yield of a bond is defined as that interest rate value for which the present value of the bond's payments (the coupons and the face value) equals the current bond price. For general investments, this concept is called the **internal rate of return** or **IRR.** The IRR of a bond is its yield.

Suppose that a bond pays a face value equal to V and n coupon payments per year, each of size C/n, at regular intervals (so that the annual coupon payment is C and the size of the intervals between payments, expressed in years, is $1/n$). Suppose also that there are T years left until maturity, for a total of $T \cdot n = m$ periods until maturity, and the current bond price is $P(t)$. Then the current yield $y(t)$ of the bond is determined from the equation

$$P(t) = \frac{V}{[1 + y(t)]^T} + \sum_{i=1}^{m} \frac{C/n}{[1 + y(t)]^{i/n}} \tag{2.7}$$

This equation gives the annualized yield using the compound interest rule. Very often, the yield is annualized using the simple interest rule. Expression (2.7) then becomes

$$P(t) = \frac{V}{[1 + y(t)/n]^m} + \sum_{i=1}^{m} \frac{C/n}{[1 + y(t)/n]^i} \tag{2.8}$$

We indeed see that the yield $y(t)$ is the interest rate implied by the bond. We also observe that the price of the bond and the yield move in opposite directions—higher yield implies lower price and vice versa—because paying less for a bond today means getting a higher return later.

2.2.3 Price-Yield Curves

A **price-yield curve** is a curve in which a bond price is plotted as a function of the bond's yield. We graph some price-yield curves in figure 2.1. Prices are shown as the percentages of the par value. The maturity is 30 years. A bond denoted as a 10% bond is a coupon bond paying 10% of the face value as coupons each year, meaning it pays a 5% coupon every six months.

As we have mentioned previously and as can be seen from the figure, the bond prices go down if the rates, hence also the yields, go up. Another obvious fact is that the bonds with a higher coupon rate cost more.

If the yield is equal to the coupon rate, then the price has to be equal to the face value; that is, the bond trades at par. For example the 10% bond with 10% yield and face value of 100 has price equal to 100. Because the coupons are exactly equal to the interest the bond pays, the present value is exactly equal to the face value.

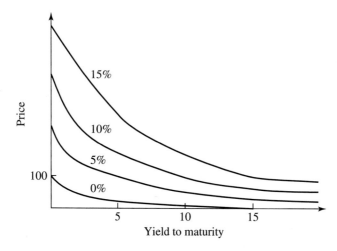

Figure 2.1
Price-yield curves for 30-year bonds with various coupon rates.

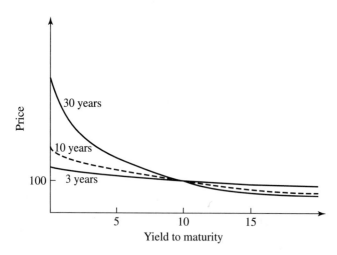

Figure 2.2
Price-yield curves for 10% coupon bonds with various maturities.

In figure 2.2 we sketch the price-yield curves for three 10% bonds of different maturities. They all have to pass through the point (10, 100) because they trade at par if the yield is 10%, as just explained. We see that a longer maturity corresponds to a steeper curve, meaning that the prices of long-term bonds are more sensitive to the changes in yield than are the prices of short-term bonds.

The specific relationship between the price and yield of a bond is the basis for the analysis of the risk of bond portfolios that we undertake in a later chapter.

2.3   Term Structure of Interest Rates and Forward Rates

A thorough study of the bond market requires looking at the rates for bonds of all maturities as they move over time. The corresponding structure of various rates is called the **term structure of interest rates.**

2.3.1   Yield Curve

The **yield curve** is the curve obtained by plotting the yields of bonds with different maturities against the maturity values. We focus here on the yield curve of government bonds. The shape of the yield curve varies over time and from country to country. The difference between longer maturity yields and shorter maturity yields determines the **slope of the term structure.** Typically, the yields for longer maturities are higher than the yields for shorter maturities, with the result that the yield curve is upward sloping. However, sometimes the short-term bonds yield more than the long-term bonds, and the curve is downward sloping, also called the **inverted yield curve.** That outcome occurs, for example, in situations of high inflation in which the government is applying strong inflationary measures and investors expect interest rates to drop in the future. In the United States the yield curve is usually upward sloping for most of the range and slightly downward sloping at the end. We say that it is "humped" shaped; see figure 2.3.

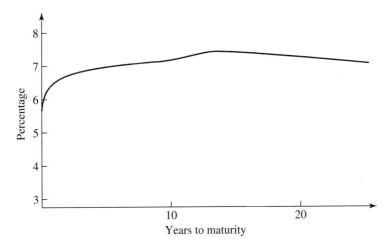

Figure 2.3
A possible shape of the yield curve.

The annualized nominal interest rate of a pure discount bond is called the **spot rate.** For pure discount bonds the spot rate is equal to the yield. As an example, consider a pure discount bond that matures in six months (a six-month pure discount bond), has a nominal value of $100, and is trading at $98. By equation (2.7) the annualized compound rate r_{6m} is determined from

$$98 = \frac{100}{(1 + r_{6m})^{1/2}}$$

with the solution $r_{6m} = 4.1233\%$. We say that the six-month spot rate is 4.1233%. This way of computing and quoting the six-month spot rate uses the six-month compounding convention. In practice the simple-rate convention is typically used. First, the implicit rate of return r is computed from

$$98 = \frac{100}{(1 + r)}$$

with the solution $r = 2.0408\%$. Then, the six-month annualized spot rate quoted is $2 \cdot 2.0408\% = 4.0816\%$. This computation is equivalent to the use of equation (2.8) for computing the yield of the bond. Using the compound method or the simple method is just a question of convention.

As an example of a second bond we consider a two-year pure discount bond with nominal value $100, which trades at $91. The two-year spot rate r_{2y} is obtained from

$$91 = \frac{100}{(1 + r_{2y})^2}$$

with the solution $r_{2y} = 4.8285\%$. Alternatively, we compute the rate of return from

$$91 = \frac{100}{(1 + r)}$$

giving $r = 9.8901\%$ and, according to the simple interest rule, this would give an annual rate of $0.5 \cdot 9.8901\% = 4.9451\%$.

The relationship between the yields of bonds with different maturities is of great interest to practitioners. The collection of the spot rates for all maturities is called the **term structure of interest rates.** If we do not mention otherwise, we refer to the term structure of default-free government bonds. In practice it is not possible to compute exactly the spot rates for all maturities simply because not all maturities are represented by the traded bonds. For example, there are no default-free bonds with maturity greater than 30 years.

2.3.2 Calculating Spot Rates; Rates Arbitrage

We need to introduce here the notion of arbitrage, which will be studied in much more detail in later chapters. By **arbitrage** we mean making potential profits with zero investment, and no risk of losing money. For example, suppose that we can sell a zero-coupon bond that pays $100 at maturity T for the price of $95 today, and that we can also construct a portfolio of other securities that pays $100 at the same maturity T for the initial investment of only $94. Then we can make risk-free, arbitrage profit of $1 by selling the bond for $95, and investing $94 in the portfolio. At maturity our positions cancel each other, while we have made $1 at the beginning. In fact, in a situation like this we would prefer to sell as many bond shares as possible, and buy the same number of the portfolio shares.

We will always assume in this book that the market is free of arbitrage (see those later sections for justifications of this assumption). Based on this assumption, oftentimes even when a default-free zero-coupon bond is not traded, the spot rates can be computed from default-free bonds that pay coupons by no-arbitrage arguments, as in the following examples.

Example 2.5 (Computing Spot Rates) Consider a default-free coupon bond that will pay a coupon of $3.00 in six months, and will make a final payment of $103.00 (the last coupon and the principal) in one year. This bond trades at $101.505. The coupon bond is equivalent to a portfolio of a six-month pure discount bond with a nominal value of $3.00, and another pure discount bond with a nominal value of $103.00. Assume also that a six-month zero-coupon bond is traded at 98.00, with the yield of 4.1233%, computed earlier. Using a combination of the six-month pure discount bond and the coupon bond maturing in a year, we can construct a portfolio that behaves like a one-year pure discount bond. We buy one unit of the coupon bond and we sell short 0.03 units of the six-month pure discount bond. (As usual in this book, we assume divisibility of the securities, meaning they can be traded in fractions.) The total cost of the basket of these bonds is

$$101.505 - 0.03 \cdot 98.00 = 98.565$$

In six months the short position in the discount bond requires paying $0.03 \cdot 100.00 = 3.00$. Simultaneously, the coupon for the same amount is paid, resulting in zero profit/loss. In one year the principal and the final coupon of the coupon bond are paid, generating a revenue of 103.00. No additional payments take place. The portfolio is thus equivalent to a pure discount bond with a cost of $98.565 with maturity of one year and a nominal value of $103.00. The corresponding one-year spot rate r_{1y} is derived from

$$98.565 = \frac{103}{1 + r_{1y}}$$

with the solution $r_{1y} = 4.4996\%$.

Alternatively, we first compute the six-month spot rate $r_{6m} = 4.1233\%$ and then, from the coupon bond, using the six-month spot rate, we compute the one-year spot rate using equation (2.7):

$$
\begin{aligned}
101.505 &= \frac{3}{(1 + r_{6m})^{1/2}} + \frac{103}{1 + r_{1y}} \\
&= \frac{3}{(1 + 0.041233)^{1/2}} + \frac{103}{1 + r_{1y}}
\end{aligned}
$$

The diligent reader can check that we get the same solution $r_{1y} = 4.4996\%$.

In addition to helping make financial decisions, the knowledge of the term structure of interest rates also allows us to spot potential arbitrage opportunities. We again illustrate it with an example.

Example 2.6 (Spot Rate Arbitrage) In the same setting as in Example 2.5, suppose that a one-year pure discount bond is also traded. Its price today (time zero) has to be

$$
P(0, 1) = \frac{100}{1 + r_{1y}} = \frac{100}{1.044996} = 95.6942 \tag{2.9}
$$

or else there are arbitrage opportunities. In order to show this fact, suppose first that the price of the one-year pure discount bond is $95.00, suggesting that the bond is **underpriced.** In order to take advantage of the arbitrage opportunity, we should buy the underpriced security and sell the equivalent portfolio. In this case we buy one unit of the one-year pure discount bond and pay $95.00 and take a short position in $100/103$ units of the portfolio described in Example 2.5, paying $103 after a year. That portfolio buys the coupon bond and sells 0.03 units of the six-month pure discount bond. Selling short $100/103$ units of this portfolio involves short-selling of $100/103$ units of the coupon bond and buying $0.03 \cdot 100/103$ units of the six-month pure discount bond. This strategy will initially generate $98.565 \cdot 100/103 = 95.6942$ dollars, in agreement with equation (2.9). After a year it pays $100/103 \cdot 103 = 100$, the same as the one-year pure discount bond. The combination of the long position in the one-year pure discount bond at the price of 95.00 and the short position in the portfolio behaving like a one-year discount bond at the price of 95.6942 generates a total profit/loss of $95.6942 - 95 = 0.6942$. This result means that there is an arbitrage opportunity—we make a positive initial profit, and the future profit/loss is zero.

To recap: in this example the same payoff of $100 can be generated by buying directly a one-year pure discount bond, or by a portfolio of a six-month pure discount bond and a one-year coupon bond. The costs of these two strategies have to be the same, or else there is arbitrage.

In the following example, we show how to derive different spot rates (points in the term structure) from existing bonds.

Example 2.7 (Deriving Points of the Term Structure)   Assume that today's date is 1/1/03. We want to determine as many points as possible in today's yield curve (or term structure of interest rates), given that we know that there are three risk-free bonds with the following characteristics: A pure discount bond that matures on 6/30/03 is selling today at $98. A 6% bond (that is, it pays annually 6% of its nominal value as coupons) that matures on 6/30/04 is selling today at $101. The coupon is paid out once a year on 6/30, so that the bond will pay coupons on 6/30/03 and 6/30/04. An 8% bond that matures on 6/30/04 is selling today at $105. The coupon is paid out once a year on 6/30. All the bonds have the face value of $100.

We first compute the six-month interest rate from

$$98 = \frac{100}{1+r}$$

with solution $r = 2.041\%$. We want to construct the term structure in annual terms. We can use the simple interest rate (the most common approach when reporting the term structure), so that the annual rate r_{6m} of the six-month bond is $r \times 2 = 4.082\%$. Alternatively, we could find the effective interest rate (using compounding), in which case $r_{6m} = (1+r)^2 - 1 = 4.12\%$. Similarly, we can compute the 18-month interest rate (since the second date for which there is a payment is 6/30/04). Using the already computed rate, we have

$$101 = \frac{6}{1.02041} + \frac{106}{1+r}$$

with solution $r = 11.438\%$. In annual terms, using the simple interest rate rule we have $r_{18m} = r \times 2/3 = 7.625\%$, or as the effective annual rate, $r_{18m} = (1+r)^{2/3} - 1 = 7.487\%$. We proceed in a similar way with the next maturity:

$$105 = \frac{8}{1.02041} + \frac{8}{1.11438} + \frac{108}{1+r}$$

and the solution is $r = 20.025\%$. We find the annual rate as $r_{30m} = r \times 2/5 = 8.010\%$ or $r_{30m} = (1+r)^{2/5} - 1 = 7.574\%$.

2.3.3   Forward Rates

An alternative way of analyzing the term structure of interest rates is by considering so-called forward rates. Forward rates are determined by the relationship between spot rates of different maturities. Consider, for example, the one-year and the two-year spot rates r_{1y}

and r_{2y}. The forward rate that connects these two rates, denoted by $f_{1y,2y}$, is given by

$$(1 + r_{1y})(1 + f_{1y,2y}) = (1 + r_{2y})^2$$

Effectively, *the* **forward rate** $f_{t,u}$ *for the period* $[t, u]$ *is the interest rate for the money invested between the dates t and u in the future, but agreed upon today.*

The preceding is a theoretical construction, and rates obtained in this way are sometimes called **implied forward rates**. In practice the actual **market forward rates** might be different because of various reasons including transaction costs and only an approximate knowledge of the term structure of interest rates.

Forward rates are similar to spot rates in their nature, and, therefore, the rules about the computation of annual equivalents apply. For example, using the six-month annualized spot rate r_{6m} and the one-year spot rate r_{1y} we get the annualized forward rate $f_{6m,1y}$ between the sixth month and the year as

$$(1 + r_{6m})^{1/2}(1 + f_{6m,1y})^{1/2} = 1 + r_{1y}$$

In general, the forward rate $f_{t,u}$ for the period $[t, u]$ with t and u expressed in years is determined from this **annualized forward rate formula with annual compounding:**

$$(1 + r_{ty})^t = (1 + r_{uy})^u (1 + f_{t,u})^{u-t} \tag{2.10}$$

For the compounding of m periods per year the formula for the **annualized forward rate** $f_{i,j}$ **between the ith and jth period** is

$$(1 + r_j/m)^j = (1 + r_i/m)^i (1 + f_{i,j}/m)^{j-i} \tag{2.11}$$

where r_k is the annualized spot rate for the interval between today and k periods from today.

The formula for the **annualized forward rate with continuous compounding** is

$$e^{r_{uy} \cdot u} = e^{r_{ty} \cdot t} \cdot e^{f_{t,u} \cdot (u-t)} \tag{2.12}$$

There is a one-to-one relationship between the collection of all spot rates and the collection of all forward rates. Hence it is sufficient to know either one of these collections in order to know the term structure of interest rates. As we will see later in the book there are models of the term structure of interest rates that focus on the specification of the dynamics of forward rates rather than on the dynamics of spot rates.

Forward rates are not only a theoretical tool. There are forward contracts in the market trading which one can lock in an interest rate today for a future period. Taf might find such a trade desirable if he thinks that the future interest rates will be different from the currently quoted forward rates.

Example 2.8 (Speculating on Forward Rates) The one-year pure discount bond with nominal $100 trades at $95, and the two-year pure discount bond with nominal $100 trades at \$89. The one-year spot rate r_{1y} is given by $95(1 + r_{1y}) = 100$ with the solution $r_{1y} = 5.2632\%$, and the two-year spot rate r_{2y} is given by $89(1 + r_{2y})^2 = 100$ with the solution $r_{2y} = 5.9998\%$. The forward rate $f_{1y,2y}$ is given by

$$1.052632(1 + f_{1y,2y}) = (1.059998)^2$$

with the solution $f_{1y,2y} = 6.7416\%$. If our fearless speculator Taf thinks that the rates will not change very much over the next year, he considers the forward rate to be relatively high. He wants to lock in the forward rate for his investment in the period between year one and year two. In order to do so (without using a forward contract), he buys the two-year pure discount bond at 89 and sells short 89/95 units of the one-year pure discount bond at 95. The cost of that portfolio today is zero. One year from now the one-year pure discount bond matures, and Taf has to pay

$$89/95 \cdot 100 = 93.6842$$

One year later, the two-year pure discount bond matures, and he receives \$100. The interest rate Taf gets in the second year with that trading strategy is

$$\frac{100 - 93.6842}{93.6842} = 0.067416$$

that is, the forward rate. If one year from now the one-year spot rate is less than 6.7416%, as Taf predicted, the price of the one-year bond at that time will be more than

$$\frac{100}{1 + 0.067416} = 93.6842$$

Consequently, after the first year Taf can sell the one-year bond short, get more than 93.6842, cover his short position in the 89/95 units of the previous one-year bond by paying 93.6842, and make a profit. At the end of the second year he gets 100 from the two-year bond, which is exactly enough to cover his short position in the one-year bond.

2.3.4 Term-Structure Theories

In addition to the knowledge of the term structure, it would be nice to have a model that could explain the shape of the term structure of interest rates, that is, the shape of the yield curve. As we will see in later chapters, a model that explains the dynamics of interest rates along with a pricing model for bonds will determine the possible shapes of the term structure. In this section we mention some broad theories that try to explain the general shape of the term structure, rather than to model the exact shape at a given moment. We thereby introduce some standard terminology and provide some basic benchmarks against which to measure more specific models of the term structure.

One standard theory is called the **expectation hypothesis** of the term structure. This theory suggests that the forward rates represent the values that investors expect the future spot rates to have. That is, the forward rate between years one and two is equal to the expected one-year spot rate one year from now. The problem with this theory is that it would be difficult to justify a constantly upward-sloping term structure: if the two-year spot rate is higher than the one-year spot rate, the forward rate between years one and two is higher than the one-year spot rate, which would indicate that people expect the one-year spot rate to be higher in the future. Thus an upward-sloping yield curve would seem to suggest that people expect interest rates to go up all the time, and this assumption is hard to justify. One way to avoid this difficulty with the theory is to assume that the investors add a **risk premium** to longer maturity rates, that is, to postulate that forward rates represent expected future spot rates plus a risk premium amount. The risk premium is added to compensate for the additional risk to which the long-term investor is exposed, for example, the inflation risk. (In an advanced later section on "change of numeraire" we will see that the forward rates can be interpreted as expected values of the spot rate, but not under the real-world probability.)

An alternative theory argues that different maturities are pretty much unrelated. The two-year spot rate is the result of a specific demand and supply for that maturity and is independent of the one-year and three-year spot rates. This is called the **segmentation hypothesis.** This approach provides flexibility for explaining peculiarities of the yield curve such as the hump typically observed in the term structure in the United States. For example, it might be the case that there is an extraordinary demand for pure discount bonds of very long maturities, and that demand makes them more expensive than long-term bonds of somewhat shorter maturities.

Yet another explanation is called **liquidity preference.** By this theory in general investors prefer short-term bonds to long-term bonds because the short-term bonds are less sensitive to the changes in market interest rates. To compensate for the higher risk, long-term bonds offer higher yields, according to the theory.

Summary

Money invested in a bank account or a bond earns interest at some interest rate. Interest is usually compounded at regular time periods. If the compounding is done on a continuous basis, the investment grows at an exponential rate. In order to be able to compare different risk-free investments, the associated interest rates are expressed in annualized terms.

The present value of a future payment is the value that would become equal to the future payment if invested at the given interest rate. It is obtained by discounting the future payment. Simple formulas are available for computing the present value of a cash flow of regular equal payments, as well as for the amount of the regular payments required to pay off a given loan value. The interest rate implicit in a bond return is called yield to maturity.

The spot rate is the annualized interest rate of a pure discount bond. The collection of spot rates associated to bonds with different maturities forms a term structure of interest rates. In order to avoid arbitrage, spot rates and bond prices have to be consistent across bonds with different maturities and different coupon payments. Forward rates are interest rates corresponding to future time periods. A forward rate can be locked in today for some period in the future by trading bonds with different maturities. There are different qualitative explanations for the relationship between forward rates and spot rates such as expectation hypothesis, segmentation hypothesis, and liquidity preference.

Problems

1. What is the annual interest rate for the one-year zero-coupon bond that pays $100.00 at maturity, trading today at $97.00?

†2. A bank quotes the nominal annual rate of 6%, and it compounds interest every two months. What is the value of one dollar deposited in this bank after a year?

3. A bank quotes the nominal annual rate of 5%, and it compounds interest every three months. What is the value of one dollar deposited in this bank after a year and a half?

†4. An investment opportunity guarantees total interest of 20% over a period of three years. What is the effective annual rate corresponding to annual compounding?

5. What is the effective annual rate for the quoted continuous rate of 7%?

†6. What is the value of $1.00 after 50 days if the continuous annual rate is 10%?

7. What is the present value of $100.00 paid nine months from now if

a. the annual nominal rate is 8%, and compounding is done quarterly?

b. the effective annual rate is 8%, and compounding is done quarterly?

c. the annual continuous rate is 8%?

8. Show that the present value $V(0)$ and the future value $V(T)$ of a cash flow $(P_0, \ldots, P_m)$ are related by

$$V(0) = \frac{V(T)}{(1+r)^m}$$

where r is the interest rate per period.

9. During your last year as a college student your parents give you two options:

a. They will pay you $5,000 at the beginning of the year, $4,500 after three months, and another $4,500 six months after the beginning of the year. They expect you to find a good job when you complete your degree and request that you pay them $7,000 two years from now, as a partial payback.

b. Alternatively, they will pay you $5,500, $5,000, and $5,000, and you have to pay back $9,000, at the same times as in part a.

What is the better deal for you, a or b? Assume that the nominal annual rate for the next two years is 8%, and compounding is done quarterly.

†10. You are facing two business opportunities with the following cash flows:

a. Investing $10,000 today, receiving $5,000 after three months, $4,500 after six months, and another $4,500 nine months from today.

b. Alternatively, you can invest $11,480 today, and receive $5,500, $5,000, and $5,000 after three, six, and nine months.

What is the better investment for you, a or b? Assume that the nominal annual rate is 5%, and compounding is done quarterly.

11. You are sick of living in a student dorm and decide to take a loan to buy a small apartment. You take a 15-year loan on $50,000, at the fixed interest rate of 9%, compounded monthly.

a. What is the amount of your monthly payments?

b. What is your balance after the second payment?

c. How much money would you have in 15 years if, instead, you deposited your monthly payments in a bank account at the same interest rate, with monthly compounding? In other words, what is the future value of the $50,000 in this context?

†12. Consider the framework of the previous problem. Before you take a loan you compare two banks: Bank A offers a 15-year mortgage loan of $50,000 at the nominal rate of 8.5%, with monthly compounding, with the APR of 9.00%. Bank B offers a 15-year mortgage loan of $50,000 at the nominal rate of 8.8%, with monthly compounding, with the APR of 9.2%. Which bank is charging you more in fees?

13. You take a loan on $200,000 for 30 years, at the annual nominal interest rate of 6%, compounded monthly. The loan installments also have to be paid monthly. The bank's APR is 6.8%. What is the amount of fees the bank is charging you?

†14. Suppose that if you invest in a money-market account you can get the annual return of 10% during the next five years. Your trustworthy friend Conman suggests that, instead, you should enter into a business with him, guaranteed to return $30,000 every year for the next five years, for the initial investment of $100,000. Assuming you believe him, what is your estimate of the annual worth of the business?

15. In order to buy a rental property you have to take a loan on $400,000 for 30 years, at the annual interest rate of 8%. The loan installments have to be paid monthly. The property

is expected to give revenue of $36,000 per year, for those 30 years, also paid in monthly installments (we assume that there is no increase in rent from one month to another). Will you be able to cover the loan payments from the rental income?

†16. Using the simple rate convention, find the yield of a two-year bond traded at par, with face value $100, paying coupons of $3.00 every six months.

17. The market trades a default-free coupon bond that pays a coupon of $4.00 every six months, and makes a final payment of $104.00 (the last coupon and the principal) in one year. This bond trades at $102.00. Moreover, a six-month zero-coupon bond is traded at $98.20. Find the one-year spot rate.

†18. In the previous problem what should the price P of the one-year pure discount bond be in order to prevent arbitrage opportunities? Explain how to construct arbitrage if the price is instead equal to $\tilde{P} = P + 0.5$.

19. The one-year pure discount bond with nominal $100 trades at $96, and the three-year pure discount bond with nominal $100 trades at $85. What is the forward rate for the period between one year and three years from today?

†20. In the context of the previous problem you want to lock in the forward rate for the period between year one and year three. How can you do that by trading in the one-year and the three-year bond?

*21. Go to your favorite source of the government bond prices and sketch an approximate shape of the today's yield curve.

Further Readings

The formalization of a general theory of interest rates is due to Fisher in 1930 (a modern edition of that work is Fisher 1965). Several papers in the 1950s and 1960s further articulated the theory of interest rates and its applications to valuation (see Hirshleifer 1970 for a survey). Additional early contributions are in Fama and Miller (1972) and Fama (1976). Modern treatments of interest rates and discounting can be found in any of the general texts on investments like Sharpe, Alexander, Bailey, and Sharpe (1998) or Bodie, Kane, and Marcus (2001), as well as in books dedicated to fixed-income securities, like Sundaresan (1997), Fabozzi (1999), Martellini and Priaulet (2001), and Martellini, Priaulet, and Priaulet (2003).

3 Models of Securities Prices in Financial Markets

When you play a lottery, with a little bit of effort and being an expert in basic probability, you can compute your chances of winning the jackpot if you invest $10.00. Even if you play every month, and the jackpot amount changes every month, you can still compute your chances of winning at least $10,000.00 during a period of one year, can't you? And if the number of lottery tickets you decide to buy changes from month to month, you could still do it, if you set yourself to it. But what if the lottery numbers do not all have the same chance of being picked, and worse, you are not told what these chances are, could you still do it? You would probably say "to heck with this lottery" and go bet your money on blackjack in a Las Vegas casino. Or, you could make some assumptions on the probabilities of the lottery numbers and use them to do your calculations. By doing so you make a **mathematical model** of the lottery. This is what researchers have been doing with prices of securities, and it leads us to the learning objectives of this chapter:

- To present the most popular mathematical models for basic securities
- To describe the wealth and portfolio processes of market investors given a model
- To develop mathematical tools to be able to use the models
- To outline basic differences between various models

The chapter presents the fundamental framework and tools for the rest of the book. Each section starts by considering simple single-period models, continues with more complex multiperiod models, and finishes with more sophisticated continuous-time models. In all of them the prices are modeled as random, stochastic processes whose values change with time. In the continuous-time sections we introduce the basics of the stochastic calculus, also called Itô calculus in honor of Kiyoshi Itô, the mathematician who invented it, and we also introduce the extremely important Brownian motion process. We briefly discuss stochastic models for interest rates and the distinction between real and nominal rates. Then we introduce two related concepts that will be instrumental throughout the rest of the book: arbitrage and complete markets.

In virtually all fields in which mathematical models are used, researchers face a trade-off between how realistic a model should be and how easy it is to perform computations and get solutions in the model. More complex models can be more realistic, but also harder to use. In economics and finance researchers sometimes use models that look ridiculously simplistic. The point is, they first try to understand the qualitative behavior of the objects being modeled (prices, investors, companies, ...), rather than getting reliable quantitative conclusions (such as exactly how much an investor should invest in a given stock). Once the initial understanding and interpretation are obtained, one can try to make the model more realistic and see whether the basic conclusions from the simple model change a lot or remain similar. It is surprising how many of the main insights in finance that we get by studying very simple models remain true, at least in spirit, in more complex models. Thus we hope that the readers will now have enough motivation to let us guide them through very simple models initially, even when those models look very distant from reality. The reader who needs more motivation may wish to jump ahead in the book and browse through section 9.3.1, where a very simple model is used to reduce the risk of selling a call option in an example from the real world.

3.1   Single-Period Models

All the theory of a financial market is based on a model of its basic securities. The simplest possible, but still interesting model, assumes that there are only two dates, initial and final. Therefore, the price of a security changes only once. More precisely, a security, let us call it S, starts with the value $S(0)$ at the initial time, $t = 0$, of the period, and ends with the value $S(1)$ at the end of the period, $T = 1$. Such a model is called the **single-period model.** If the security is risky (for example, a stock whose future value is unknown), then $S(1)$ is modeled as a random variable, whose value will be revealed at time 1. Despite its simplicity, the single-period model is useful not only as an educational vehicle: it may be used as a step in building multiperiod models; and it may be quite adequate in situations in which our brave investor Taf will hold the investment for a while and plans to be "passive" in the meantime.

3.1.1   Asset Dynamics

Depending on the purpose of a single-period model, the random variable $S(1)$ can be modeled as taking two possible values, three, four, and so on, including infinitely many values. In particular, $S(1)$ can be modeled as a discrete or a continuous random variable. A finite number of values is usually sufficient if the model is used as a building step in a multiperiod model. In particular, let us consider the **single-period finite-market model:**

We assume that $S(1)$ is a random variable that can take K possible values, $s_1, \ldots, s_K$, with probabilities $p_i = P[S(1) = s_i]$; see figure 3.1. More formally, consider a sample space $\Omega = \{\omega_1, \ldots, \omega_K\}$ of possible states of the world at time 1, each having a positive probability. If the state ω_i occurs, then $S(1) = s_i$.

We usually assume that there is a **risk-free asset** B in the market, a bond or a **bank account,** such that

$$B(0) = 1$$

and such that $B(1)$ is strictly positive for all states of the world. Typically, we also assume

$$B(1) \geq B(0)$$

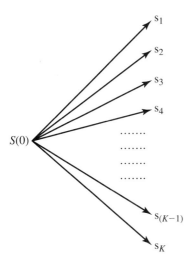

Figure 3.1
Single-period model: There are K possible values for the stock price at time 1.

The convention $B(0) = 1$ should be interpreted as meaning that *"one share" of the bank account, or one bond, is worth one dollar at time zero.* Therefore, $B(1)$ is the value at time 1 of one dollar invested in the bank at time 0. If we denote by r the bank **interest rate** in this period, we have

$$B(0) + rB(0) = B(1) \tag{3.1}$$

or, equivalently, $r = B(1) - 1$.

3.1.2   Portfolio and Wealth Processes

Consider now a market model in which there are N risky securities or stocks, $S_1, \ldots, S_N$ and bank account or bond B. Our investor Taf takes positions in market assets. We will denote by $X(t)$ the value of these positions at time t, called Taf's **wealth process.** We assume that Taf starts with some **initial wealth** amount at time zero

$$X(0) = x$$

and uses this amount to invest in the available securities. Since this is a single-period model, Taf trades only once, right at time zero. Denote by $\delta_i, i = 1, \ldots, N$ the number of security i shares that Taf holds between time zero and time one. We denote by δ_0 the amount invested in the bank account at time zero, "the number of shares" of the bank account. We assume that there are no transaction costs when transferring funds between securities. Then, Taf's wealth at the end of the period is given by

$$X(1) = \delta_0 B(1) + \delta_1 S_1(1) + \cdots + \delta_N S_N(1)$$

That is, the wealth is the sum of the amounts held in various assets. The vector of positions

$$\vec{\delta} = (\delta_0, \ldots, \delta_N)$$

is called a **portfolio strategy,** a **trading strategy,** or simply **portfolio.** Taf's portfolio has to satisfy some type of a **budget constraint.** The typical budget constraint is the so-called **self-financing condition:**

$$X(0) = \delta_0 B(0) + \delta_1 S_1(0) + \cdots + \delta_N S_N(0) \tag{3.2}$$

In other words, Taf cannot use funds other than the initial wealth to finance the positions in the market, and Taf is not allowed to spend money outside of the market (later we will allow such spending). Note that the condition implies that the amount δ_0 invested in the bank is automatically determined if we know how much is invested in the risky assets. There are no other restrictions on Taf's portfolio. In particular, a position δ_i in the ith security may be negative. This possibility is interpreted as taking a short position (as defined in a previous chapter) in security S_i. Short-selling the bank account is equivalent to borrowing from the bank. The **profit/loss, P&L,** of a portfolio strategy δ, denoted

$$G = X(1) - X(0)$$

will be called the **gains process.** If we denote

$$\Delta S_i = S_i(1) - S_i(0)$$

the gain of one share of security S_i, it follows from the above definitions and equation (3.1) that

$$G = \delta_0 r + \delta_1 \Delta S_1 + \cdots + \delta_N \Delta S_N$$

We have the following unsurprising relationship between the gains and wealth processes:

$$X(1) = X(0) + G$$

Since there are no goods in this model other than money, it is convenient to pick one of the securities as a reference and normalize the prices of all the others with respect to it. The usual choice for this so-called **numeraire** process is the bank account. More precisely, we introduce the **discounted prices:**

$$\bar{S}_i(t) := S_i(t)/B(t)$$

We use the same notation $\bar{Y}$ for any other discounted process Y. We define the discounted gains process as

$$\bar{G} := \delta_1 \Delta \bar{S}_1 + \cdots + \delta_N \Delta \bar{S}_N$$

where

$$\Delta \bar{S}_i = \bar{S}_i(1) - \bar{S}_i(0)$$

The reader is asked in Problem 2 to prove these intuitive relationships:

$$\bar{X}(1) = \delta_0 + \sum_{i=1}^{N} \delta_i \bar{S}_i(1) = X(0) + \bar{G} \tag{3.3}$$

In future chapters we will study portfolio strategies for different objectives Taf may have:

- Maximize the performance of a strategy
- Minimize risk
- Replicate (hedge) a position in the market

3.1.3 Arrow-Debreu Securities

Famous economists Kenneth Arrow (Nobel Prize in 1972) and Gerard Debreu (Nobel Prize in 1983) developed some of the basic framework of many of the economic ideas we will present throughout the book. We describe here the setting they use and some of their terminology. It is a very simple setting, but it makes it possible to explain some of the general concepts introduced later.

Consider the basic model described in section 3.1.1, where there are K possible states, or outcomes, at $t = 1$. A security S can be described as a K-dimensional vector $(s_1, \ldots, s_K)$ of payoffs in these states, where all the components of the vector are nonnegative. In this setting, consider risky securities that pay one unit of currency in a given state and zero in every other state. These securities are called **Arrow-Debreu securities;** see figure 3.2. There are K different Arrow-Debreu securities. A portfolio formed by holding one share of each of K Arrow-Debreu securities is a risk-free security that pays one unit of currency regardless of the state. It represents a pure discount bond that pays interest determined by the difference between the payoff of one unit at time $t = 1$ and the price at time $t = 0$. Arrow-Debreu securities are simple securities that can be used to describe any other security in a single-period model.

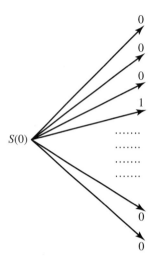

Figure 3.2
Arrow-Debreu security paying one at state 4 and paying zero at all other states.

3.2 Multiperiod Models

A **multiperiod model** is a direct extension of a single-period model—we simply divide the
time period we are considering into smaller time intervals, each modeled as single-period;
see figure 3.3.

3.2.1 General Model Specifications

We still denote by $t = 0$ the initial time, while we use $t = T$ as the notation for the end of
the period. More precisely, the time runs through the values $0, 1, \ldots, T$, and a security price
process S_i is represented as a sequence of random variables $S_i(0), \ldots, S_i(T)$. Similarly,
a portfolio strategy $\vec{\delta}$ changes (randomly) with time. We denote by $\vec{\delta}(t)$ the values of the
portfolio during the interval $[t - 1, t)$. In other words, the portfolio values $\delta_i(t)$ are chosen
at time $t - 1$, by convention. That is, we assume that the trades in the time period from $t - 1$
to t take place at the beginning of the period, namely at time $t - 1$, and thus *the portfolio*
values $\vec{\delta}(t)$ for the period $[t - 1, t)$ can only depend on the information known by time $t - 1$.
We say that $\vec{\delta}(t)$ is a **predictable** or a **previsible** process. Once the prices $S_i(t - 1)$ are
known, Taf chooses the portfolio $\vec{\delta}(t)$ that will determine the wealth at time t, after prices
$S_i(t)$ are known.

   Much of the single-period terminology and notation remains the same:

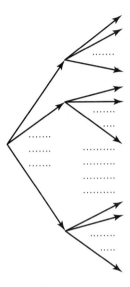

Figure 3.3
A two-period model with finitely many states.

Interest rate in the period $t - 1$ to t (assumed to be known already by time $t - 1$):

$$r(t) = \frac{B(t) - B(t - 1)}{B(t - 1)}$$

Wealth process:

$$X(t) = \delta_0(t)B(t) + \delta_1(t)S_1(t) + \cdots + \delta_N(t)S_N(t), \quad t = 1, \ldots, T$$

Self-financing condition:

$$X(t) = \delta_0(t + 1)B(t) + \delta_1(t + 1)S_1(t) + \cdots + \delta_N(t + 1)S_N(t), \quad t = 0, \ldots, T - 1$$

$$(3.4)$$

Together with the previous equation for $X(t)$, this condition means that the wealth just before a transaction takes place is equal to the wealth just after the transaction. In other words, there are no funds added to or withdrawn from the wealth process.

Gains process: We again denote by $G(t)$ the total profit or loss at time t, namely,

$$G(t) = \sum_{s=1}^{t} \delta_0(s)\Delta B(s) + \sum_{s=1}^{t} \delta_1(s)\Delta S_1(s) + \cdots + \sum_{s=1}^{t} \delta_N(s)\Delta S_N(s), \quad t = 1, \ldots, T$$

$$(3.5)$$

where $\Delta Y(t) = Y(t) - Y(t-1)$, for a given process Y. (The sums in this equation will become integrals in continuous-time models.) We still have

$$X(t) = X(0) + G(t) \tag{3.6}$$

and

$$\bar{X}(t) = \delta_0(t) + \sum_{i=1}^{N} \delta_i(t)\bar{S}_i(t) = X(0) + \bar{G}(t) \tag{3.7}$$

Here, as in the single-period model,

$$\bar{G}(t) = \sum_{s=1}^{t} \delta_1(s)\Delta\bar{S}_1(s) + \cdots + \sum_{s=1}^{t} \delta_N(s)\Delta\bar{S}_N(s)$$

where

$$\Delta\bar{S}_i(t) = \bar{S}_i(t) - \bar{S}_i(t-1)$$

We here show how to prove equation (3.6) in the case of two assets, B, S, and two periods, $t = 2$. The reader is asked in the Problems section to provide other proofs. In our case we have, for example,

$$\begin{aligned} G(2) = {} & \delta_0(1)[B(1) - B(0)] + \delta_0(2)[B(2) - B(1)] \\ & + \delta_1(1)[S(1) - S(0)] + \delta_1(2)[S(2) - S(1)] \end{aligned}$$

Using the self-financing condition

$$\delta_0(1)B(1) + \delta_1(1)S(1) = \delta_0(2)B(1) + \delta_1(2)S(1)$$

we see that

$$G(2) = \delta_0(2)B(2) + \delta_1(2)S(2) - [\delta_0(1)B(0) + \delta_1(1)S(0)]$$

By definition of $X(2)$ and the self-financing condition

$$\delta_0(1)B(0) + \delta_1(1)S(0) = \delta_0(0)B(0) + \delta_1(0)S(0)$$

we finally get

$$G(2) = X(2) - X(0)$$

3.2.2   Cox-Ross-Rubinstein Binomial Model

We want to model a market with only one risky asset S, the *stock*, and a *bank account*, with constant interest rate $r > 0$ for all the periods. A very simple but still stochastic multiperiod

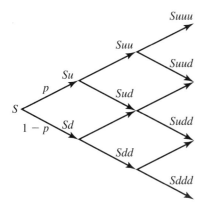

Figure 3.4
Binomial tree with three time periods.

model is a model in which the risky security S can jump to only two possible values at each point in time. To make it even simpler, consider the values $u > 1 + r$ and $d < 1 + r$, (u for *up* and d for *down*), and assume that the probabilities of the up and down moves are denoted by

$$p := P[S(t + 1) = uS(t)], \qquad q := 1 - p = P[S(t + 1) = dS(t)]$$

In other words, at each time point the stock price can go up by the factor u, or down by the factor d. We also assume that the price changes between different time periods are independent. This model is called the **binomial model** or **CRR (Cox-Ross-Rubinstein) model.** Its simplicity notwithstanding, the model is extremely useful as a good approximation to reality, while still very easy to implement in terms of computing and/or simulating prices of securities, as we will see in later chapters.

The model results in a so-called **binomial tree,** as in figure 3.4. We say that this tree is **recombining** because of the fact that an up-and-down move produces the same value for the stock as a down-and-up move. This property is convenient numerically because of the reduced number of possible values for the stock price. Nevertheless, as the length of each time period goes to zero (and, therefore, the number of the time periods increases), we get more and more possible values for the price of the stock. As we will discuss later, as the length of each time interval approaches zero, for specific parameter values, this model converges to a continuous-time model that will be extremely useful throughout the book.

3.3   Continuous-Time Models

(**Note on reading sequence:** The readers who are interested only in the basics of the Black-Scholes formula do not have to read the subsections following the first subsection on the simple facts about the Merton-Black-Scholes model. In chapter 7 we provide a brief exposition of the Black-Scholes formula that requires the first subsection here and the knowledge of normal distribution, but nothing else.)

Continuous-time finance deals with mathematical models of financial markets in which agents are allowed to trade continuously, rather than at discrete time periods only. Thus the market security prices have to be modeled as continuous-time processes, usually stochastic in nature. Since trading in modern financial markets can be executed in very short time intervals, the model is a reasonable approximation of the real markets (at least if we ignore changes in prices that happen overnight and over weekends and holidays). Why approximate discrete trading with continuous? Mainly for reasons of mathematical convenience and elegance. A problem with multiperiod discrete-time models is that they quickly become untractable for computational purposes and the notation tends to be cumbersome. Moreover, continuous-time models provide an opportunity to model complex price dynamics using a small number of model parameters that frequently have nice intuitive interpretation. For these reasons scholars have studied continuous-time models, which are often limits of discrete-time multiperiod models when the length of each time period $\Delta t = t_{k+1} - t_k$ goes to zero.

Continuous-time models require more advanced mathematical tools than discrete-time models. In return, they allow for explicit solutions of many standard pricing and investment problems, mainly thanks to the possibility of applying differential calculus. Nowadays, most derivative securities traders, not to mention analysts and researchers, have at least an intuitive understanding of continuous-time models.

3.3.1   Simple Facts about the Merton-Black-Scholes Model

We provide this section for readers who are interested only in the basics of the **Merton-Black-Scholes model** and do not want to have to learn about Brownian motion and stochastic calculus. Our exposition here requires only familiarity with the normal distribution. This section will enable the reader to get at least a superficial understanding of the Black-Scholes formula, and of the formula for the optimal strategies for maximizing utility of an investor in this model, as presented in chapters 7 and 4, respectively. The readers interested in more details on these topics can find them in section 3.3.6.

In the Merton-Black-Scholes model there is a **risk-free asset** B that we call a bond or a bank account, and which satisfies

$$B(t) = e^{rt} \tag{3.8}$$

with $r > 0$ as the constant, continuously compounded **interest rate.** There is also a **risky security,** that we call a **stock.** The stock price S satisfies

$$S(t) = S(0) \exp \left\{ (\mu - \tfrac{1}{2}\sigma^2)t + \sigma\sqrt{t}z(t) \right\} \tag{3.9}$$

Here, μ and $\sigma > 0$ are constants, and $z(t)$ is a standard normal random variable. If the constant σ was very close to zero, the stock would be almost risk-free, and would behave as a bank account with interest rate μ. The distribution of $S(t)$ is called **lognormal distribution,** because the logarithm of $S(t)$ is normally distributed.

The constant parameter μ represents the **expected return rate** of the stock, because it can be shown from the properties of the normal distribution that

$$E[S(t)] = S(0)e^{\mu t}$$

Therefore, we "expect" the stock price to grow exponentially at the constant rate μ. Written differently, we see that μ is equal to the **logarithm of expected relative return per unit time:**

$$\mu = \frac{1}{t} \log E \left[\frac{S(t)}{S(0)} \right]$$

This equation can be used to estimate μ from historical stock data. However, it should be mentioned that this procedure is quite difficult in practice. (Otherwise, it would be much easier to make money in the stock market!)

The constant σ measures the riskiness of the stock, which is why it is called the **volatility** of the stock. The squared volatility σ^2 is equal to the **variance of log-returns per unit time:**

$$\sigma^2 = \frac{\text{Var}[\log\{S(t)\} - \log\{S(0)\}]}{t} \tag{3.10}$$

This equation can be used as a basis for estimating σ^2 from historical data.

3.3.2 Brownian Motion Process

The basic continuous-time model is driven by a random process called **Brownian motion,** or the **Wiener process,** whose value at time t is denoted $W(t)$. We introduce it first in a heuristic way, as a limit of a discrete-time model:

$$W(t_{k+1}) = W(t_k) + z(t_k)\sqrt{\Delta t}, \qquad W(0) = 0 \tag{3.11}$$

Here, $z(t_k)$ are standard normal random variables (that is, with mean zero and variance one), independent of each other. It follows that the differences $W(t_{k+1}) - W(t_k)$ are normally distributed random variables with mean zero and variance Δt. More generally, for $k < l$,

$$W(t_l) - W(t_k) = \sum_{i=k}^{l-1} z(t_i)\sqrt{\Delta t}$$

It follows that $W(t_l) - W(t_k)$ is normally distributed with mean zero and variance $t_l - t_k$. The process W is called a **random walk** process (see chapter 16 for a somewhat different construction).

In the limit when Δt goes to zero, it can be shown that the random walk converges to a process called Brownian motion, also denoted W, with the following properties:

DEFINITION 3.1   (**Brownian Motion**)

a. $W(t) - W(s)$ is normally distributed with mean zero and variance $t - s$, for $s < t$.

b. The process W has independent increments: for any set of times $0 \le t_1 < t_2 < \cdots < t_n$, the random variables

$$W(t_2) - W(t_1), \; W(t_3) - W(t_2), \ldots, W(t_n) - W(t_{n-1})$$

are independent.

c. $W(0) = 0$.

d. The sample paths $\{W(t); t \ge 0\}$ are continuous functions of t.

Condition a says, in particular, that the "average size" (the expected value) of $[W(t + \Delta t) - W(t)]^2$ behaves like Δt, for small $\Delta t > 0$.

If we think of W as a price process, condition b says that the change in price tomorrow is independent of the change in price today.

Condition c is only a convention, convenient to keep the mean of the process equal to zero.

Despite their continuity, that is, condition d, Brownian motion paths are not differentiable anywhere. This is quite a property, if you think about it: it is not easy to imagine a function that is continuous but so irregular that it is not smooth anywhere. Intuitively, at every point in time over the next interval, however short, Brownian motion can go "anywhere" since the increment is a draw from a normal distribution. This "wild" behavior is also indicated by the fact that

$$E\left[\left(\frac{W(s) - W(t)}{t - s}\right)^2\right] = \frac{1}{t - s}$$

which tends to infinity as s goes to t. A simulated path of Brownian motion process is provided in figure 3.5.

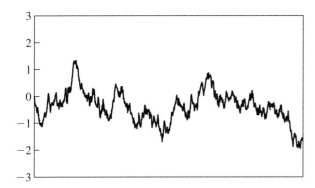

Figure 3.5
A simulated path of Brownian motion. Recalculating the Excel worksheet results in different sample paths.

It can be shown that Brownian motion is a **Markov process**—the distribution of its future values, conditional on the past and present values, depends only on the present value, and not on the past. Moreover, conditioning on the present information (which is then equivalent to conditioning on the past and present information), using properties of conditional expectations (see chapter 16) and the fact that $W(t) - W(s)$ is independent of $W(s)$, we get

$$
\begin{aligned}
E[W(t) \mid W(s)] &= E[W(t) - W(s) \mid W(s)] + E[W(s) \mid W(s)] \\
&= E[W(t) - W(s)] + W(s) \\
&= W(s)
\end{aligned}
$$

Therefore, the expected value of a future outcome of Brownian motion, conditional on the past and present information, is exactly equal to the present value. That is, the following so-called **martingale property** is satisfied:

$$
E[W(t) \mid W(s)] = W(s)
$$

One interpretation of this property is that **the best estimate of the future value** of Brownian motion is its present value. If the process W were a model for profits and losses of a gambling game, that would be a **fair game,** because we would not expect the future P&L to be different from today's P&L. We say that Brownian motion is a **martingale process.**

A Technical Remark   We also introduce the martingale property in chapter 4 in the less technical discrete-time framework, as well as in chapter 16.

A more precise definition of a martingale process in continuous time requires the notions of a σ-**algebra** or σ-**field** and conditional expectations with respect to a σ-algebra, discussed in chapter 16. Intuitively, a σ-algebra $\mathcal{F}(t)$ represents the information available up to time t. In this book we will always have $\mathcal{F}(s) \subset \mathcal{F}(t)$ for $s < t$, which is interpreted as having more information by time t than by time s. A collection of such σ-algebras $\mathbf{F} := \{\mathcal{F}(t)\}_{t \geq 0}$ is called a **filtration.** We say that a process $X(\cdot)$ is **adapted** to the filtration $\mathbf{F}$ if the random variable $X(t)$ is **measurable** with respect to σ-algebra $\mathcal{F}_t$, for every $t \geq 0$. (The definition of "measurable" is given in chapter 16.) Intuitively, $X(t)$ is known if the information given by $\mathcal{F}_t$ is known. Then we say that a process M is a martingale with respect to information filtration $\mathbf{F}$ if it is adapted to that filtration and if

$$E[X(t) \,|\, \mathcal{F}(t)] = X(s), \quad s \leq t \tag{3.12}$$

In words, *the conditional expectation of the future value given the current information is equal to the present value.* We also assume technical conditions that guarantee that the conditional expectation on the left-hand side exists.

3.3.3   Diffusion Processes, Stochastic Integrals

Brownian motion in itself is not sufficiently flexible for modeling various asset price processes. With this fact in mind, we generalize the approach of the previous section by considering processes of the form

$$X(t_{k+1}) = X(t_k) + \mu(t, X(t_k))\Delta t + \sigma(t, X(t_k))\sqrt{\Delta t} \cdot z(t_k), \qquad X(0) = x \tag{3.13}$$

Here, $z(t_k)$ are again independent standard normal random variables, while μ and σ are deterministic functions of the **time variable** t and the **state variable** x.

In the limit, when Δt goes to zero, we would expect to get

$$X(t) = x + \int_0^t \mu(u, X(u)) \, du + \int_0^t \sigma(u, X(u)) \, dW(u) \tag{3.14}$$

This relation is more often written as

$$dX(t) = \mu(t, X(t)) \, dt + \sigma(t, X(t)) \, dW(t), \qquad X(0) = x \tag{3.15}$$

This expression is called a **stochastic differential equation,** or **SDE,** for the process X, which is called a **diffusion process.** We call μ the **drift** and σ the **diffusion function** of process X. If the dW term were not present, it would be an ordinary differential equation. Later, as we model security prices as SDEs, we will see that they are very useful tools in modeling. Brownian motion will represent the uncertainty about the future price.

It is not clear in advance whether a process X satisfying a given SDE exists. In fact, a solution will exist only under certain technical conditions, routinely assumed to hold in finance literature. The integral

$$\int_0^t Y(u) \, dW(u)$$

for a given process Y is called a **stochastic integral** or **Itô integral.** We will argue that, under some conditions on Y, the Itô integral, as a process in time, is a martingale.

3.3.4   Technical Properties of Stochastic Integrals*

(**Note:** Sections with asterisks are needed mostly for technical arguments in the remainder of the book. They can be skipped or just browsed through at first reading.)

The Itô integral cannot be constructed in the same way as the usual Lebesgue/Riemann integral, because, as we discussed before, Brownian motion W is not differentiable. Nevertheless, a meaningful definition of the integral $\int_0^t Y(u)\,dW(u)$ is possible for a process Y which is such that $Y(t)$ is known if the past and present values $W(u), u \leq t$, of Brownian motion are known. We say that Y is a process **adapted** to the information generated by the Brownian motion process.

We now state the most important properties of the Itô integral:

THEOREM 3.1 (ITÔ INTEGRAL PROPERTIES)   Let Y be a process adapted to the information given by Brownian motion W. Let $T > 0$ be a given time horizon. Assume that

$$E\left[\int_0^T Y^2(u)\,du\right] < \infty \tag{3.16}$$

Then, for $t \leq T$, the integral process

$$M(t) := \int_0^t Y(u)\,dW(u)$$

is well defined. Moreover, it is a martingale with mean zero and variance process $E[\int_0^t Y^2(u)\,du]$. In other words, for all $s < t$,

$$E\left[\int_0^t Y(u)\,dW(u)\right] = 0$$

$$E\left[\int_0^t Y(u)\,dW(u) \,\bigg|\, W(u), 0 \leq u \leq s\right] = \int_0^s Y(u)\,dW(u)$$

$$E\left[\left(\int_0^t Y(u)\,dW(u)\right)^2\right] = E\left[\int_0^t Y^2(u)\,du\right]$$

In order to motivate the notion of stochastic integrals, the reader can think of Y as a portfolio process that is not allowed to look into the future; hence the requirement that $Y(t)$ is determined by information up to time t. And you can think of $M(t)$ as the corresponding gains process. The fact that $E[M(t)] = 0$ can be interpreted as saying that if we invest in process W with mean zero, then our gains will also have mean zero. In general, a wealth process of an investor in continuous time can be represented by an SDE. The Itô integral part of the SDE indicates that there is a risky, "noise" component of the wealth process because of which we do not know if the investment in the risky securities will go up or down in value, but the martingale property says that this noise component has zero mean.

We will only provide a discrete-time intuition for Theorem 3.1: Consider the discrete-time gains process

$$M(t_l) := \sum_{j=0}^{l-1} Y(t_j)[W(t_{j+1}) - W(t_j)], \qquad M(0) = 0$$

Note that by properties of conditional expectations we have, for all $k < l$,

$$E\left[\sum_{j=k}^{l} Y(t_j)\{W(t_{j+1}) - W(t_j)\}\right] = \sum_{j=k}^{l} E[E\{Y(t_j)[W(t_{j+1}) - W(t_j)] \mid W(0), \ldots, W(t_j)\}]$$

$$= \sum_{j=k}^{l} E[Y(t_j)E\{W(t_{j+1}) - W(t_j)\}] = 0 \qquad (3.17)$$

Therefore, $E[M(t_l)] = 0$, for all t_l. Next, using equation (3.17), we show the martingale property:

$$E[M(t_l) \mid W(0), \ldots, W(t_k)] = E\left[\sum_{j=0}^{k-1} Y(t_j)\{W(t_{j+1}) - W(t_j)\} \,\middle|\, W(0), \ldots, W(t_k)\right]$$

$$+ E\left[\sum_{j=k}^{l-1} Y(t_j)\{W(t_{j+1}) - W(t_j)\} \,\middle|\, W(0), \ldots, W(t_k)\right]$$

$$= \sum_{j=0}^{k-1} Y(t_j)[W(t_{j+1}) - W(t_j)]$$

$$+ E\left[\sum_{j=k}^{l-1} Y(t_j)\{W(t_{j+1}) - W(t_j)\}\right]$$

$$= M(t_k)$$

As for the variance, we only look at two periods:

$$E[\{Y(t_0)[W(t_1) - W(t_0)] + Y(t_1)[W(t_2) - W(t_1)]\}^2] = E[Y^2(t_0)\{W(t_1) - W(t_0)\}^2]$$
$$+ E[Y^2(t_1)\{W(t_2) - W(t_1)\}^2] + E[Y(t_0)Y(t_1)\{W(t_1) - W(t_0)\}\{W(t_2) - W(t_1)\}]$$

The second term on the right-hand side (and similarly the first term) can be computed as

$$E[Y^2(t_1)\{W(t_2) - W(t_1)\}^2] = E[E\{Y^2(t_1)[W(t_2) - W(t_1)]^2 \mid W(t_0), W(t_1)\}]$$
$$= E[Y^2(t_1)E\{[W(t_2) - W(t_1)]^2\}] = E[Y^2(t_1)\Delta t]$$

The last term is zero, as in equation (3.17):

$$E[Y(t_0)Y(t_1)\{W(t_1) - W(t_0)\}\{W(t_2) - W(t_1)\}]$$
$$= E[Y(t_0)Y(t_1)\{W(t_1) - W(t_0)\}E\{W(t_2) - W(t_1)\}] = 0$$

Combining these, and extending the process to more than two periods, we get

$$E[M^2(t_l)] = E\left[\sum_{j=0}^{l-1} Y^2(t_j)\Delta t\right]$$

This equation corresponds to the integral version in the continuous-time model, as in the statement of the theorem.

3.3.5 Itô's Rule

An indispensable tool for manipulating diffusion processes is the so-called **Itô's rule.** It is an extension of the differentiation rule in standard calculus

$$\frac{df(t, x(t))}{dt} = f_t(t, x(t)) + f_x(t, x(t))\frac{dx(t)}{dt}$$

where f_t and f_x denote partial derivatives with respect to t argument and x argument respectively. This rule can be written in an informal way, after multiplying by dt, as

$$df(x(t)) = f_t(t, x(t))\,dt + f_x(t, x(t))\,dx(t)$$

In Itô's calculus, there is an extra term appearing on the right-hand side. The intuition is the following: in standard calculus when we study how changes in an independent variable affect the value of another variable that depends on it, the first-order effect (the first derivative) is enough to analyze the "local" impact. That is not good enough when the independent variable itself depends on Brownian motion. The reason is that Brownian motion "can go anywhere" over the next time interval. As a result, we also have to take into account the second derivative, the second-order effect. Another intuitive mathematical reason is that, for small $\Delta t > 0$, the sum of the second-order terms $(W(t + \Delta t) - W(t))^2$ over a period $[0, T]$ behaves like T (not only on average, but path by path), hence cannot be neglected. More precisely, we have

THEOREM 3.2 (ITÔ'S RULE)   Let $f(t, x)$ be a function that has a continuous derivative with respect to t and two continuous derivatives with respect to x. Then, given the diffusion process

$$dX(t) = \mu(t, X(t))\,dt + \sigma(t, X(t))\,dW(t)$$

the process $f(t, X(t))$ satisfies

$$df(t, X(t)) = \left[f_t + \frac{1}{2}\sigma^2 f_{xx} \right] (t, X(t)) \, dt + f_x(t, X(t)) \, dX(t)$$

We see that the extra term involves the second derivative f_{xx}. If we substitute for $dX(t)$ and suppress in the notation the dependence on $(t, X(t))$, we get the following **useful form of Itô's rule:**

$$df = \left[f_t + \mu f_x + \frac{1}{2}\sigma^2 f_{xx} \right] dt + \sigma f_x \, dW \tag{3.18}$$

This is also valid when μ and σ are general random processes, as long as, for all t, their value at time t is completely determined by the history of W up to time t, that is, as long as they are adapted.

As a good way to remember it, we could write **Itô's rule in an informal way** as

$$df = f_t \, dt + f_x \, dX + \tfrac{1}{2} f_{xx} \, dX \cdot dX \tag{3.19}$$

using the following informal rules:

$$dt \cdot dt = 0, \qquad dt \cdot dW = 0, \qquad dW \cdot dW = dt \tag{3.20}$$

The last equality is due to the fact that a sum of small squared changes in W over a given interval $[0, t]$ is approximately t. The informal rules imply

$$dX \cdot dX = (\mu \, dt + \sigma \, dW) \cdot (\mu \, dt + \sigma \, dW) = \sigma^2 \, dt$$

In order to motivate a need for a rule like this, the reader can think of $X(t)$ as a stock-price process, and $f(t, X(t))$ as the price of an option written on the stock. Itô's rule gives us a connection between the two.

Example 3.1 (Brownian Motion Squared)   We want to find the dynamics of the process $Y(t) := W^2(t)$. We can think of process Y as a function $Y(t) = f(W(t))$ of Brownian motion, with $f(x) = x^2$, $f_x(x) = 2x$, and $f_{xx}(x) = 2$. Since

$$dW = 0 \cdot dt + 1 \cdot dW$$

Brownian motion is a diffusion process with the drift equal to zero and the diffusion term equal to one. Applying Itô's rule, we get

$$d(W^2(t)) = 2W(t) \, dW(t) + dt$$

This expression is the same as

$$2 \int_0^t W(u) \, dW(u) = W^2(t) - t$$

We see that the process $W^2(t) - t$ is a stochastic integral, hence a martingale. In general, if, for a given process Y there exists a process Q such that the process $Y^2 - Q$ is a martingale, we say that Q is a **quadratic variation** process of Y, often denoted $Q = \langle Y \rangle$. Thus the quadratic variation process of Brownian motion is the process $Q(t) = t$.

Example 3.2 (Exponential of Brownian Motion)   In this example we want to find the dynamics of the process

$$Y(t) = e^{aW(t) + bt}$$

We can think of process Y as a function $Y(t) = f(t, W(t))$ of Brownian motion and time, with

$$f(t, x) = e^{ax + bt}, \qquad f_t(t, x) = bf(t, x), \qquad f_x(t, x) = af(t, x),$$

$$f_{xx}(t, x) = a^2 f(t, x)$$

Applying Itô's rule we get

$$dY = \left[b + \frac{1}{2}a^2 \right] Y \, dt + aY \, dW$$

If we set

$$b = -\tfrac{1}{2}a^2$$

the drift term of Y will disappear, making it a stochastic integral $Y(t) = Y(0) + \int_0^t aY(u) \, dW(u)$, hence a martingale. In other words, the process

$$Y(t) = e^{aW(t) - \frac{1}{2}a^2 t}$$

is a martingale. In particular, this fact means that $E[Y(t)] = Y(0) = 1$, or

$$E\left[e^{aW(t)} \right] = e^{\frac{1}{2}a^2 t} \tag{3.21}$$

The reader familiar with the **moment-generating function** of a normal distribution will recognize this expression, because $W(t)$ is normally distributed with variance t.

Oftentimes in financial models we deal with more than one stock, or with other random factors in the market, with the result that we need a rule for functions of more than one process. We first present Itô's rule for the case of two processes. The general formula for n processes is provided in the appendix to this chapter.

Suppose we have a **two-dimensional Brownian motion** $(W_1(t), W_2(t))$, meaning that W_1 and W_2 are two *independent* one-dimensional Brownian motions. Consider two processes given by

$$dX = \mu_X \, dt + \sigma_{X,1} \, dW_1 + \sigma_{X,2} \, dW_2$$
$$dY = \mu_Y \, dt + \sigma_{Y,1} \, dW_1 + \sigma_{Y,2} \, dW_2$$

Then, for a sufficiently smooth function $f(x, y)$ (that is, a function that has at least two continuous derivatives with respect to x and y, plus continuous mixed partial derivatives between x and y), the process $f(X(t), Y(t))$ satisfies the **two-dimensional Itô's rule:**

$$
\begin{aligned}
df(X, Y) = f_x \, dX + f_y \, dY &+ \left[\tfrac{1}{2}\left(\sigma_{X,1}^2 + \sigma_{X,2}^2 \right) f_{xx} + \tfrac{1}{2}\left(\sigma_{Y,1}^2 + \sigma_{Y,2}^2 \right) f_{yy} \right. \\
&\left. + f_{xy}(\sigma_{X,1}\sigma_{Y,1} + \sigma_{X,2}\sigma_{Y,2}) \right] dt
\end{aligned}
\tag{3.22}
$$

Again, as a way to remember it, we could write the **two-dimensional Itô's rule in an informal way** as

$$df(X, Y) = f_x \, dX + f_y \, dY + \tfrac{1}{2}[f_{xx} \, dX \cdot dX + f_{yy} \, dY \cdot dY] + f_{xy} \, dX \cdot dY \tag{3.23}$$

where, in addition to the informal rules of equations (3.20), we also use

$$dW_1 \cdot dW_2 = 0$$

which is a consequence of W_1 and W_2 being independent of each other.

In some applications it is more convenient that W_1 and W_2 are not independent, but correlated, with **instantaneous correlation** equal to ρ, in the sense that

$$E[W_1(t)W_2(t)] = \rho t$$

for every t. Then the informal rule is

$$dW_1 \cdot dW_2 = \rho \, dt$$

and Itô's rule is

$$
\begin{aligned}
df(X, Y) = f_x \, dX + f_y \, dY &+ \left[\tfrac{1}{2}\left(\sigma_{X,1}^2 + \sigma_{X,2}^2 \right) f_{xx} + \tfrac{1}{2}\left(\sigma_{Y,1}^2 + \sigma_{Y,2}^2 \right) f_{yy} \right. \\
&\left. + f_{xy}(\sigma_{X,1}\sigma_{Y,1} + \sigma_{X,2}\sigma_{Y,2} + \rho\sigma_{X,1}\sigma_{Y,2} + \rho\sigma_{X,2}\sigma_{Y,1}) \right] dt
\end{aligned}
\tag{3.24}
$$

As a particular case of equation (3.24), we have the following **Itô's rule for the product** of two processes:

$$d(XY) = X\,dY + Y\,dX + [\sigma_{X,1}\sigma_{Y,1} + \sigma_{X,2}\sigma_{Y,2} + \rho\sigma_{X,1}\sigma_{Y,2} + \rho\sigma_{X,2}\sigma_{Y,1}]\,dt \qquad (3.25)$$

Example 3.3 (Product Rule) We want to find the dynamics of the process

$$Y(t) = W^2(t) \cdot e^{aW(t)}$$

We could do so using Itô's rule directly, or we can consider this process as a product of the processes from Examples 3.1 and 3.2. We choose to do the latter, and use the product rule:

$$dY = e^{aW} \cdot d(W^2) + W^2 \cdot d(e^{aW}) + d(W^2) \cdot d(e^{aW})$$

Using Examples 3.1 and 3.2, this gives us

$$dY = e^{aW}\left[t + \tfrac{1}{2}a^2W^2 + 2Wa\right]dt + ae^{aW}W^2\,dW$$

Here we give only a rough sketch of how to prove the one-dimensional Itô's rule, while a more detailed proof is provided in the appendix to this chapter (section 3.7):

"Proof" of Itô's Rule: For a process X define

$$\Delta X(t) = X(t + \Delta t) - X(t)$$

Expanding the function f in Taylor series we obtain

$$f(t + \Delta t, X(t + \Delta t)) = f(t, X(t)) + f_t \Delta t + f_x \Delta X + \tfrac{1}{2}f_{xx}(\Delta X)^2$$
$$+ \text{higher-order terms}$$

It can be shown that the higher-order terms converge to zero as $\Delta t \to 0$. Moreover, consider

$$\frac{(\Delta X)^2}{\Delta t} = \frac{1}{\Delta t}(\mu \Delta t + \sigma \Delta W)^2 = \mu^2 \Delta t + 2\mu\sigma \Delta W + \sigma^2 \frac{(\Delta W)^2}{\Delta t}$$

In the limit when $\Delta t \to 0$, the first two terms go to zero, and, because the sum of the terms $(\Delta W)^2$ over the interval $[0, t]$ behaves like t, we can approximate the third term by σ^2. In other words, we get, in the limit, and having in mind the integral interpretation, that

$$(dX)^2 = \sigma^2\,dt$$

Using this equation in the Taylor expansion indeed results in Itô's rule:

$$df = f_t\,dt + f_x\,dX + \tfrac{1}{2}f_{xx}\sigma^2\,dt \qquad\qquad \blacksquare$$

3.3.6 Merton-Black-Scholes Model

The idea to use Brownian motion in models for the stock market goes back to the thesis of the French mathematician Louis Bachelier in 1900. His work was way ahead of his time, and it was not noticed by economists and was mostly ignored by mathematicians. Nowadays he is given the credit for being the first person to study both the mathematical and finance applications aspects of Brownian motion. In the economics literature Brownian motion was introduced by Paul Samuelson (a Nobel Prize winner in economics in 1970) in the 1950s and 1960s. The finance theory of these models was further developed by Robert C. Merton, Samuelson's student, in the late 1960s and early 1970s. The model we introduce here was also used by Fischer Black and Myron Scholes in their landmark paper published in 1973. (Merton and Scholes jointly received a Nobel Prize in economics in 1997 for this work; sadly, Black had died of illness before that.) Although the model is a simplification of the actual price dynamics, it is intuitive enough for practitioners to be able to use it by adapting it to the situation at hand. Its beauty, and, at the same time its disadvantage, is that it requires only a small number of parameters to describe the basic asset prices and the prices of derivative securities based on those assets. Introducing models with more parameters means that we can better fit the model to the real-world data. However, having more parameters means less precision when estimating them and more complexity in analytical and numerical studies of the model and the price processes. Even worse, it means less confidence that the model will closely describe the real world in the future due to "overfitting"—using sufficiently many parameters the model can fit any given historical data set, without really working well for the future outcomes of the actual underlying processes.

The main economic justification for using Brownian motion in our models is the **random walk hypothesis,** which postulates that prices move completely randomly, at least after adjusting for the long-run average return. In this regard, it can be shown that a specific discrete-time Cox-Ross-Rubinstein model of the type we described in section 3.2.2 corresponds, in the limit as $\Delta t \to 0$, to the Merton-Black-Scholes model that we now introduce. (Cox, Ross, and Rubinstein were partially motivated by a desire to simplify the Merton-Black-Scholes model.)

First, there is a **risk-free asset** B that we call a bond or a bank account. We assume the following dynamics for the bank-account process:

$$dB(t) = rB(t)\,dt, \qquad B(0) = 1 \tag{3.26}$$

with $r > 0$ as the constant, continuously compounded **interest rate.** [The reader can find a detailed discussion of interest rates in the previous chapter, including the fact that the risk-free security of the Cox-Ross-Rubinstein model converges to the dynamics (3.26) when the length of each time interval converges to zero.] Equation (3.26) means that one dollar in the bank at time 0 results in

$$B(t) = e^{rt}$$

dollars at time t. We say that this security is "risk-free" because its dynamics do not have a stochastic component; that is, in equation (3.26) there is no Brownian motion. The future value of the security is known, as happens in reality with the payoff of a default-free bond.

There is also a **risky security,** which we call a **stock.** The stock price S satisfies the following **Merton-Black-Scholes model:**

$$dS(t) = \mu S(t)\, dt + \sigma S(t)\, dW(t), \qquad S(0) = s \tag{3.27}$$

If the constant $\sigma > 0$ was very close to zero, the stock would be almost risk-free and would behave like a bank account with interest rate μ.

In fact, there is an **explicit formula for the stock price** $S(t)$ in this model:

$$S(t) = S(0) \exp \left\{ \sigma W(t) + \left(\mu - \tfrac{1}{2}\sigma^2 \right) t \right\} \tag{3.28}$$

The distribution of $S(t)$ is called **lognormal distribution,** because the logarithm of $S(t)$ is normally distributed. We say that the stock price follows a **geometric Brownian motion** process. The modification $\tfrac{1}{2}\sigma^2 t$ in equation (3.28) comes from Itô's rule. Indeed, consider the function

$$f(t, w) = \exp \left\{ \sigma w + \left(\mu - \tfrac{1}{2}\sigma^2 \right) t \right\}$$

Noting that

$$f_t = \left(\mu - \tfrac{1}{2}\sigma^2 \right) f, \qquad f_w = \sigma f, \qquad f_{ww} = \sigma^2 f$$

and using Itô's rule on the process $S(t) = f(t, W(t))$ of equation (3.28), we easily check that this process satisfies the Merton-Black-Scholes model (3.27).

The constant parameter μ represents the **expected return rate** of the stock. In order to see what we mean by that statement, consider the process

$$M(t) = \exp \left\{ \sigma W(t) - \tfrac{1}{2}\sigma^2 t \right\} \tag{3.29}$$

This is exactly the process we would get for the stock price S for $\mu = 0$. Hence, it satisfies

$$dM = \sigma M\, dW, \qquad M(0) = 1$$

These equations mean that M is a stochastic integral process, namely,

$$M(t) = 1 + \int_0^t \sigma M(u) \, dW(u)$$

It is therefore a martingale, so that

$$E[M(t)] = 1, \qquad t \geq 0$$

This equation implies

$$E[S(t)] = E[s M(t) e^{\mu t}] = S(0) e^{\mu t}$$

Therefore, we "expect" the stock price to grow exponentially at the constant rate μ. The actual return, however, suffers a modification due to the market uncertainty, modeled by Brownian motion. Written differently, we see that μ is equal to the **logarithm of expected relative return per unit time:**

$$\mu = \frac{1}{t} \log E \left[\frac{S(t)}{S(0)} \right]$$

This can be used to estimate μ from historical stock data. However, it should be mentioned that this type of estimating is quite difficult in practice. (That's too bad: if we could easily conclude what the mean returns of publicly traded stocks are equal to, we would likely be able to make a very good living by investing in the market!) In the chapters on equilibrium in part III, we present some ways of estimating mean returns of individual assets from economic factors that are either observable or easier to estimate (such as the mean return of the whole market).

Another interpretation of μ can be obtained using technical properties of the Itô integral from which it follows that

$$E \left[\int_0^t \frac{dS(u)}{S(u)} \right] = \mu t$$

Thinking of dS/S as the relative return in a small time period, we could say that μ is the expected cumulative relative return per unit time. This is sometimes written formally as $\mu \, dt = E[dS/S]$.

As for the diffusion term σ, note that from equation (3.27) and the technical properties of stochastic integrals we have

$$\text{Var} \left[\int_0^t \frac{dS(u)}{S(u)} \right] = \sigma^2 t$$

This equation is sometimes written formally as $\sigma^2 \, dt = \text{Var}[dS/S]$. The constant σ measures the riskiness of the stock, which is why it is called the **volatility** of the stock. In order to find another economic interpretation for σ, consider the more general version of equation (3.28), with $t < u$:

$$S(u) = S(t) \exp \left\{ \sigma[W(u) - W(t)] + \left(\mu - \tfrac{1}{2}\sigma^2 \right)(u - t) \right\} \tag{3.30}$$

It follows that

$$\log[S(u)] - \log[S(t)] = \sigma[W(u) - W(t)] + \left(\mu - \tfrac{1}{2}\sigma^2 \right)(u - t)$$

The only random term on the right-hand side is $\sigma[W(u) - W(t)]$, which has standard deviation $\sigma\sqrt{u - t}$. As a result, the squared volatility σ^2 is equal to the **variance of log-returns per unit time:**

$$\sigma^2 = \frac{\mathrm{Var}[\log\{S(u)\} - \log\{S(t)\}]}{u - t} \tag{3.31}$$

This equation can be used as a basis for estimating σ^2 from historical data. For example, denote by X_i, $i = 1, \ldots, n$, the observed daily log returns, and by

$$\bar{X} = \frac{1}{n} \sum_{i=1}^{n} X_i$$

their **sample mean.** An estimate for the variance of daily returns is given by the **sample variance**

$$\hat{\sigma}^2_{day} = \frac{1}{n - 1} \sum_{i=1}^{n} (X_i - \bar{X})^2$$

If the time is measured in years we have $u - t = 1/365$, and by equation (3.31) the estimate of annual volatility $\hat{\sigma}$ is given by

$$\hat{\sigma}^2 = 365 \cdot \hat{\sigma}^2_{day} \tag{3.32}$$

In the **multidimensional version of the Merton-Black-Scholes model** there are N stocks and d Brownian motions (as we will explain, it turns out that $d = N$ is the easiest model to work with). In other words, the stocks would be modeled as

$$dS_i(t) = \mu_i S(t)\, dt + \sum_{j=1}^{d} \sigma_{ij} S_i(t)\, dW_j(t), \qquad i = 1, \ldots, N \tag{3.33}$$

The matrix with entries σ_{ij} is called the **volatility matrix.**

3.3.7 Wealth Process and Portfolio Process

Let us suppose now that our investor Taf faces markets with securities that satisfy the dynamics of the Merton-Black-Scholes model we have described. We denote by $\pi(t)$ the amount of money (not the number of shares!) held in the stock at time t. As usual, a negative value means that Taf is short-selling the stock. We call π a **portfolio process.** It is assumed that the agent cannot see the future, so $\pi(t)$ has to be determined from the information up to time t. In other words π is an adapted process, as defined earlier. We also require the technical condition

$$E\left[\int_0^T \pi^2(u)\,du\right] < \infty$$

which implies that $\int_0^t \pi(u)\,dW(u)$ is a well-defined martingale process. Such a portfolio is called **admissible.** (See section 3.6.3, on arbitrage in continuous time, for a reason for imposing this condition.)

We denote by $X = X^{x,\pi}$ the **wealth process** corresponding to the initial investment $x > 0$ and the portfolio strategy π. Typically, we require the portfolio strategy π to be **self-financing,** by which we mean that the amount held in the bank at time t is equal to $X(t) - \pi(t)$ and that X satisfies

$$dX = \frac{\pi}{S}\,dS + \frac{X - \pi}{B}\,dB \tag{3.34}$$

This is the analogue of equation (3.6) in discrete time. It says that the change in wealth X is equal to the change in S times the number of shares held in S, plus change in B times the "number of shares" held in B. The integral form of this equation is

$$X(t) = X(0) + \int_0^t \frac{\pi(u)}{S(u)}\,dS(u) + \int_0^t \frac{X(u) - \pi(u)}{B(u)}\,dB(u)$$

where the integral terms are interpreted as gains (profit/loss) from trade in S and gains from trade in B. Substituting for dS and dB we obtain the **wealth equation**

$$dX = [rX + \pi(\mu - r)]\,dt + \pi\sigma\,dW \tag{3.35}$$

For the **discounted wealth process**

$$\bar{X}(t) := e^{-rt}X(t)$$

we get, by Itô's rule for products,

$$d\bar{X} = [\bar{\pi}(\mu - r)]\,dt + \bar{\pi}\sigma\,dW \tag{3.36}$$

The same equation holds in the general version of the Merton-Black-Scholes model in which μ, r, and σ are random processes, and not constant. Similarly, we would still have the same expressions in a model with N stocks and d Brownian motions. The only differences would be that $\vec{\pi} = (\pi_1, \ldots, \pi_N)$ would be a vector of holdings in N stocks, $\vec{\mu} = (\mu_1, \ldots, \mu_N)$ would be a vector of stocks' return rates, $\vec{W} = (W_1, \ldots, W_d)$ would be a d-dimensional Brownian motion, and σ would be a volatility matrix of dimension $N \times d$.

3.4   Modeling Interest Rates

It is an essential property of interest rates that the rate is known ahead of time for the period committed. However, the interest rate might change in the next period, and not be known ahead of time. For example, a bank can credit to Taf's account an agreed monthly rate. Next month, though, the interest the bank will credit might be different. With a pure discount bond held until maturity, the value to be received is known, and, therefore, the interest to be received from the investment is known. However, if Taf decides upon maturity to reinvest the proceeds in another pure discount bond, the interest rate to be received will not be known until the new investment takes place. Similarly, if Taf decides to sell a bond before it matures, he cannot predict the price at which the bond will sell, and, therefore, the return is uncertain. This uncertainty occurs because, even though the payoff at maturity is known, the bond price fluctuates in the meantime. In practice, then, interest rates are stochastic.

3.4.1   Discrete-Time Models

In single-period discrete-time models the risk-free rate is fixed by construction: even if there are several possible states of the world at moment $t = 1$, the interest rate, by definition, will be the same in all states. In multiperiod models, however, it is possible to model the interest rate as a stochastic process, always known one period ahead of time. That is, at time $t - 1$ we know the payment of a bond at moment t (whether it is a coupon or a pure discount bond), but we do not know the payment at moment $t + 1$. In the case of a pure discount bond we know the payment to be received at maturity T, but we do not know the price of the bond at moment $T - 1$ and, therefore, the interest to be received between $T - 1$ and T.

There are multiple ways to model the randomness of the interest rate. In a model with finitely many states, we can assume that the interest rate to be received during the period $[t, t + 1]$ for an investment in the risk-free security will take at moment t a value $r(t, \omega)$ if the state ω occurs. If the model has an infinite state space, we can assume some specific dynamics for the interest rate. For example, we can assume that at moment t the interest rate is proportional to the interest rate at the previous time, plus some noise:

$$r(t) = \alpha r(t-1) + \epsilon(t)$$

where α is a given positive number, and $\epsilon(t)$ is a random variable with a normal distribution having zero mean. This is an example of an **autoregressive process.**

One problem with discrete-time models with an infinite state space is that they get untractable. As a result, it is often preferable to work in a continuous-time setting.

3.4.2 Continuous-Time Models

Consider the value of a bank account that pays a continuous interest rate $r = r_C$, as described by equation (2.1). Differentiating equation (2.1), we see that the dynamics of this value are given by

$$dB(t) = B(t)r\,dt \tag{3.37}$$

The interest rate can be time dependent and stochastic, in which case we modify the previous equation to

$$dB(t) = B(t)r(t)\,dt \tag{3.38}$$

and the value in the bank account at time t becomes

$$B(t) = B(0)e^{\int_0^t r(s)ds}$$

There are many possible continuous-time models for the dynamics of the interest rate. We mention the two models most widely known, postponing more detailed discussions for a later section on pricing interest-rate derivatives. Let W be a standard Brownian motion process. Oldrich Vasicek (1977) introduced the following model for the stochastic continuous interest rate r:

$$dr(t) = a[b - r(t)]\,dt + \sigma\,dW(t) \tag{3.39}$$

where a, b, and σ are positive constant parameters. This model satisfies a property called **mean reversion.** The parameter b is called the **long-term mean:** when the interest rate $r(t)$ is larger than b, the drift becomes negative and the tendency of the interest rate is to go down, until the level b is reached. The opposite trend takes place when the interest rate is lower than b. In other words, the interest rate has a tendency to move toward the long-term mean b. The parameter a is called the **speed of mean reversion,** since the intensity of the tendency to approach b depends on it. Mean reversion is a property that interest rates display in the real world.

Another very popular model was introduced by John Cox, Jonathan Ingersoll, and Stephen Ross (1985b). In their model, the dynamics of the interest rate is given by

$$dr(t) = a[b - r(t)]\, dt + \sigma \sqrt{r(t)}\, dW(t) \tag{3.40}$$

The difference between the model of Vasicek and the Cox-Ingersoll-Ross (CIR) model is the fact that the term $\sqrt{r}$ appears in the diffusion term. This has two consequences. First, the diffusion term itself, the **interest-rate volatility,** becomes stochastic. Second, the interest rate is always nonnegative: if the interest rate were to hit zero, the diffusion term would also hit zero, and the positive drift would move the interest rate back into positive values. A drawback of the Vasicek model (3.39) is that the interest rate can become negative.

In later chapters, we will analyze the effects on bond prices of using various ways to model interest-rate dynamics.

3.5   Nominal Rates and Real Rates

So far, we have frequently used the term "risk-free" for bonds or a bank account. However, there is one type of risk that the common bonds cannot eliminate: **inflation risk.** Bonds do not protect their holders against an unexpected increase of prices in the economy. When Taf buys a 10-year pure discount bond with no risk of default (issued by the government, for example), Taf knows with certainty the amount of money that the bond will pay in 10 years, at maturity. However, Taf cannot predict the purchasing power of that amount of money 10 years from now. If prices in the economy experience a high unexpected growth, Taf will find out in 10 years that the amount of money the bond pays does not allow him to buy as many things as expected and, therefore, Taf will be "less wealthy" than anticipated. The reason why bonds involve inflation risk is the fact that bonds guarantee a given amount of money, not of goods. The interest rate, computed as in section 2.1, that does not consider possible changes of the price levels in the economy is called the **nominal interest rate.** Sometimes it is useful to compute the interest rate net of changes in the price levels. We call it the **real interest rate,** and discuss it in the following sections.

3.5.1   Discrete-Time Models

The notion of inflation is the same in single-period and in multiperiod discrete-time models. Denote by $p(t)$ the general price level in the economy, that is, the average price of goods in the economy at moment t. We interpret this to mean that, at moment t, with an amount of money $X(t)$ Taf can buy $X(t)/p(t)$ units of goods. We focus on the single-period case. The amount of money $X(1)$ at moment $t = 1$ is equivalent to the amount $X(0)$ at moment

$t = 0$ for which $X(1)/p(1) = X(0)/p(0)$, that is, to the amount

$$X(0) = \frac{X(1)}{p(1)} p(0) = \frac{X(1)}{p(1)/p(0)}$$

In the discrete-time setting we define the **inflation rate** (or the growth rate in prices) i as

$$i = \frac{p(t) - p(t-1)}{p(t-1)}$$

Then, $p(1)/p(0) = 1 + i$ and the value of $X(1)$ at the $t = 0$ level becomes $\frac{X(1)}{1+i}$. The real interest rate is the return implicit in the bond net of the inflation effect. More precisely, a pure discount bond with a price $P(0)$ at $t = 0$ that will pay an amount $P(1)$ at $t = 1$ has a **real rate** r_R given by

$$r_R = \frac{\frac{P(1)}{1+i} - P(0)}{P(0)}$$

Since, by definition, the nominal rate r_N is given by $r_N = \frac{P(1) - P(0)}{P(0)}$, it is clear that

$$1 + r_N = (1 + r_R)(1 + i) \tag{3.41}$$

or

$$r_R = \frac{1 + r_N}{1 + i} - 1 = \frac{r_N - i}{1 + i}$$

When the inflation is small, then r_R is approximately equal to $r_N - i$.

We should remark that the prices in the economy are typically stochastic and unpredictable: the price level at moment t will depend on the state resulting at moment t and that is not known at moment $t - 1$. However, the nominal rate that links the payoff of the bond at t and its price at $t - 1$ is known at $t - 1$. In other words, while the nominal rate is predictable (one period ahead), the real rate is not.

Another peculiarity of real rates is that they can be negative, although this is a very rare occurrence. Nominal rates are almost always positive and usually incorporate expected inflation: the higher the expected growth in prices, the higher the nominal interest rates. In fact, the changes in inflation expectations are one of the main factors affecting nominal interest rates. However, sometimes inflation turns out to be higher than expected, in which case real rates might become negative.

The previous discussions also apply to multiperiod models.

3.5.2   Continuous-Time Models

In continuous time we assume that the risk-free investment follows the dynamics

$$dB(t) = B(t)r(t)\,dt$$

with a (possibly stochastic) interest rate r. The process B is **locally predictable,** in the sense that there is no Brownian motion component, so that knowing $r(t)$ at time t, we can find an approximate value for the increase $\Delta B(t)$ in a short time period Δt. The interest rate r is the nominal interest rate. In order to introduce real rates in this setting, we first have to model the price dynamics. Suppose that the process p, representing the general price level in the economy, satisfies the following dynamics:

$$dp(t) = p(t)[\mu(t)\,dt + \sigma(t)\,dW(t)]$$

If μ and σ are constant, this process is a geometric Brownian motion. In general, under mild conditions on the processes μ and σ, the process p is given by

$$p(t) = p(0)e^{\int_0^t [\mu(s) - \frac{1}{2}\sigma^2(s)]\,ds + \int_0^t \sigma(s)\,dW(s)}$$

as can be checked by Itô's rule. The general level of prices is not locally predictable, due to the presence of Brownian motion process.

As in the discrete-time case, the real rate is the interest rate net of price changes. The nominal rate per time unit is dB/B. The relative return corresponding to the real rate, $d(B/p)/(B/p)$, is the result of the change in the value of the risk-free asset normalized by the price level, which, by Itô's rule, is

$$\frac{d\left(\frac{B(t)}{p(t)}\right)}{\frac{B(t)}{p(t)}} = [r(t) - \mu(t) + \sigma^2(t)]\,dt - \sigma(t)\,dW(t)$$

It has a predictable dt component, but it also has an unpredictable component that is the result of the unpredictable component of inflation.

3.6   Arbitrage and Market Completeness

The theory of option pricing that we will develop later has been extremely successful, having had widespread use among practitioners. The theory relies on two fundamental notions that we explain in this section: complete markets and arbitrage, or absence of arbitrage. In addition, there are other properties required from a financial market model for the traditional theory of option pricing to work: there are no transaction costs, no restrictions or penalties on borrowing or short-selling, and no limitations of any other type on the portfolio choice.

A market satisfying those requirements is called a **perfect market.** We will assume perfect markets in our analysis of this section, as well as in most other sections in the book.

3.6.1   Notion of Arbitrage

We say that there is an **arbitrage opportunity** when someone has a positive probability of achieving a positive return with no risk of loss. An obvious example of an arbitrage opportunity is a situation in which it is possible to buy and sell an item simultaneously at different prices. An example of a market where arbitrage opportunities may arise is the foreign exchange market.

Example 3.4 (Arbitrage)   Suppose that our foreign exchange expert Taf observes two quotes from two different traders for the yen/U.S. dollar exchange rate of 115 yen/dollar and 115.5 yen/dollar, respectively: he should simultaneously buy yen at the 115.5 exchange rate and sell them at the 115 exchange rate. He pays $1/115.5$ dollars for a yen and gets in return $1/115$. If he can buy and sell large amounts to the two traders at these prices, he can make a lot of money.

Although arbitrage opportunities sometimes arise, they tend to disappear quickly. The investors who observe a mismatch in the quoted prices or rates will follow an arbitrage strategy as in example 3.4. As a result, in the context of that example, the yen demand will increase and the trader who is quoting an exchange rate of 115.5 will make yen more expensive. Similarly, given the increase in yen supply, the trader that is quoting an exchange rate of 115 will make yen cheaper. Soon the prices will match, and the arbitrage opportunity will disappear.

Mathematically, we say that there is **arbitrage,** or **free lunch,** in the market if there exists a trading strategy δ such that

$$X^\delta(0) = 0, \qquad X^\delta(T) \geq 0, \qquad P[X^\delta(T) > 0] > 0 \quad \text{for some } T > 0 \tag{3.42}$$

where $X^\delta(t)$ is the wealth at time t corresponding to portfolio strategy δ, and P denotes probability.

Since arbitrage opportunities cannot prevail in financial markets for long periods of time, standard models assume that there are no arbitrage opportunities. In fact, most of the financial literature is based on the nonexistence of arbitrage in order to study ways to price securities and hedge financial positions. In the following sections we briefly discuss arbitrage in various financial models; in later chapters we will discuss the consequences of the assumption of absence of arbitrage.

We should mention that the arbitrage in the yen example is model independent—no matter what the probability distribution of the exchange rate is, there is money to be made, if the trade can be performed instantaneously at the given prices. However, our definition of arbitrage is broader and considers as "free money" also those trades for which there is arbitrage under our fixed probability model and given the portfolio strategies that we admit in the model, even though there might not be arbitrage under another model with possibly a different set of admissible strategies. For example, our definition of arbitrage strategies may in principle include a complex portfolio strategy that requires continuous trading and depends on model parameters, and that would result in free money only if the model is correct. And this is not unreasonable: if our model is correct, we want it to be free of arbitrage.

It should also be emphasized that the assumption of no arbitrage is not a very strong one. What traders in practice call "arbitrage opportunities" are often not really arbitrage trades in the sense of the preceding definition. More precisely, most of those opportunities have low probability of losses (at least in the mind of the arbitrage trader) but not zero probability of losses. Thus most of the so-called "arbitrage trades" are not risk-free even if the trader uses a good model, and they are not considered arbitrage by our definition. For example, if in Example 3.4 we consider a more realistic situation in which when Taf issues an order for buying or selling yen he is not completely sure whether the price will remain the same by the time his order is exercised, then he faces a possibility of losing money.

3.6.2 Arbitrage in Discrete-Time Models

We first consider the single-period models. We denote by $S_i^k(1)$ the payoff of security i if outcome (state) k occurs at time 1, $k = 1, \ldots, K$. An arbitrage opportunity exists when there is a portfolio $\vec{\delta}$ such that

$$\delta_0 B(0) + \delta_1 S_1(0) + \cdots + \delta_N S_N(0) = 0$$

and

$$\delta_0 B(1) + \delta_1 S_1^k(1) + \cdots + \delta_N S_N^k(1) \geq 0, \qquad k = 1, \ldots, K$$

with at least one state k such that

$$\delta_0 B(1) + \delta_1 S_1^k(1) + \cdots + \delta_N S_N^k(1) > 0$$

It is left as an exercise (see Problem 21) that the previous condition is implied by the following: There is a portfolio such that

$$\delta_0 B(0) + \delta_1 S_1(0) + \cdots + \delta_N S_N(0) < 0$$

and

$$\delta_0 B(1) + \delta_1 S_1^k(1) + \cdots + \delta_N S_N^k(1) = 0, \qquad k = 1, \ldots, K$$

We illustrate the notion of arbitrage in the single-period model with a somewhat academic example:

Example 3.5 (Arbitrage with Arrow-Debreu Securities)   Consider a single-period model with two states. There are two Arrow-Debreu securities of the type described in section 3.1.3, with prices 0.45 and 0.45. There is a risk-free security that pays 1 in each of the two states and sells at moment $t = 0$ for 0.95. Here is an arbitrage strategy: buy each of the Arrow-Debreu securities and borrow (sell short) the risk-free security. Such a portfolio generates a revenue of $-0.45 - 0.45 + 0.95 = 0.05$ at moment $t = 0$. At moment $t = 1$ the portfolio has zero payoff in both states: a negative payment of 1.00 because of the short position in the risk-free security, and a positive payoff of 1.00 because of the long position in the two Arrow-Debreu securities.

The notion of arbitrage in finite-state multiperiod models is similar to the single-period model, and we let the enthusiastic reader work out the extension to the multiperiod case.

3.6.3   Arbitrage in Continuous-Time Models

In continuous-time models the notion of arbitrage can be much more delicate than in discrete-time models, because continuous trading allows for some weird trading strategies that might result in arbitrage even in normal market conditions. Such strategies may also be impossible to implement in practice and should, in principle, be excluded from consideration. This is one reason why we require our portfolios to be admissible, as defined earlier.

Once we restrict ourselves to "reasonable" portfolios, we can use condition (3.42) to characterize arbitrage in continuous-time models, too. Here we present an example when arbitrage can arise in continuous-time models. Consider the Merton-Black-Scholes model with two stocks that have the same volatility σ and are driven by the same Brownian motion W. Then there is arbitrage opportunity if

$$\mu_1 \neq \mu_2$$

For example, suppose that $\mu_1 > \mu_2$. Then we can sell short $S_1(0)/S_2(0)$ shares of stock 2 and buy one share of stock 1. The initial cost of this strategy is zero. However, by equation (3.28), we make the positive profit at time T equal to

$$S_1(T) - \frac{S_1(0)}{S_2(0)} S_2(T) = S_1(0)e^{\sigma W(T) - T\sigma^2/2}(e^{\mu_1 T} - e^{\mu_2 T})$$

This is arbitrage.

More generally, consider the economy described by d independent Brownian motion processes and with N risky securities S_i. Let C denote a linear combination of these securities,

$C(t) = \sum_{i=1}^{N} \lambda_i S_i(t)$, for some constant numbers λ_i. Suppose that C satisfies the dynamics

$$dC(t) = \mu_1(t)C(t)\,dt + \sum_{j=1}^{d} \sigma_j(t)C(t)\,dW_j(t)$$

with μ_1 and σ_j possibly random processes. Assume also that there is a security S with price dynamics having the same volatility structure, and driven by the same Brownian motion process:

$$dS(t) = \mu_2(t)S(t)\,dt + \sum_{j=1}^{d} \sigma_j(t)S(t)\,dW_j(t) \tag{3.43}$$

If there is a time interval on which $\mu_1(t) > \mu_2(t)$, we can construct arbitrage strategies as before by taking long or short positions in C and S. We can also do so if there is an interval on which $\mu_1(t) < \mu_2(t)$.

3.6.4   Notion of Complete Markets

The reason why the completeness property (definition to follow) is important is that, as we will see later, in complete markets every financial contract has a unique fair price (assuming absence of arbitrage). This crucial insight enables financial markets practitioners to price all kinds of complicated contracts in a consistent manner, that is, taking into account the worth of securities relative to each other.

Consider now any of the models we have introduced before, either in discrete time or in continuous time, and assume the model is arbitrage free. In order to describe market completeness we introduce a notion of a **contingent claim.** A contingent claim is a financial contract with a random payoff that can be positive or negative. The term "contingent" comes from the fact that the payoff is random, hence contingent (dependent) on which random outcome has occurred, that is, which state of nature is realized at the time of the payoff. All the securities that we have described are contingent claims.

We say that a portfolio **replicates** a contingent claim when the payoff of the portfolio matches the payoff of the contingent claim in all possible states (with probability one, in the language of probability theory). We require the **replicating portfolio** strategy to be self-financing.

Example 3.6 (Replication of a Risk-Free Security)   We again place ourselves in the single-period economy with two states, in which the two Arrow-Debreu securities are traded, paying 1 in one of the states and 0 in the other. Moreover, there is a risk-free security paying 1 in both states. A portfolio that holds one unit of each Arrow-Debreu security replicates the risk-free security.

We say that a **market is complete** when we can replicate any contingent claim with the existing securities. We now study the requirements for a market to be complete in various models.

3.6.5 Complete Markets in Discrete-Time Models

We first consider the single-period model. For simplicity, suppose that this is a finite single-period market model with one stock that has a random payoff $S(1)$ at $t = 1$, and with one bank account with interest rate r. Suppose further that Taf has a short position in a contingent claim (for example, an option) with a payoff $g(S(1))$, for some function g. In other words, at $t = 1$, Taf will have to pay $g(s_k)$ to the holder of the contingent claim if the stock price $S(1)$ at the end of the period takes the value s_k. As in section 3.1.1, we assume that there are K possible values for the stock, $s_1, \ldots, s_K$.

Suppose that Taf wants to find a strategy that would replicate the payoff of this option no matter what happens at time $t = 1$. Taf wants this because his objective is to construct a portfolio that guarantees that he will be able to meet the option payoff, regardless of which value the stock has at time 1. Therefore, the terminal value $X(1)$ of Taf's strategy $\vec{\delta}$ has to satisfy

$$X(1) = \delta_0 B(1) + \delta_1 s_k = g(s_k), \qquad k = 1, \ldots, K \tag{3.44}$$

This is a system of K equations with two unknowns, δ_0 and δ_1. Typically, we can find a solution only if $K \leq 2$. The case $K = 1$ is not very interesting because it corresponds to knowing the stock value in advance. So, the situation here is "ideal" if $K = 2$ and the system of equations (3.44) is nondegenerate: in that case the system has a unique solution, we can replicate any contingent claim, and the market is complete.

Example 3.7 (Replication in a Single-Period Model) Consider a single-period model with $r = 0.005$, $S(0) = 100$, $s_1 = 101$, and $s_2 = 99$. The payoff Taf is trying to replicate is the European call option

$$g[S(1)] = [S(1) - \tilde{K}]^+ = \max[S(1) - \tilde{K}, 0]$$

with $\tilde{K} = 100$. According to equation (3.44), Taf has to solve the system

$$\delta_0(1 + 0.005) + \delta_1 101 = 1$$
$$\delta_0(1 + 0.005) + \delta_1 99 = 0$$

The solution is $\delta_0 = -49.2537$, $\delta_1 = 0.5$. So, Taf has to borrow 49.2537 from the bank (short-sell the bond or bank account) and buy half a share of the stock. We note that the cost of the replicating strategy (the amount of necessary initial investment) is

$$\delta_0 B(0) + \delta_1 S(0) = 0.746$$

As will be argued later, this is the fair price of the option in this model.

   We present another example in which we have a **trinomial model** (three possible outcomes for the price of the stock in the next period). In order to have a complete market we need now three securities (instead of two as in a binomial setting).

Example 3.8 (Replication in a Trinomial Model)   Consider the single-period model in which the price of the stock today is $S(0) = \$100$. In the next period it can go up to \$120, stay at \$100, or go down to \$90. The price of the European call on this stock with strike price \$105 is \$5, and the price of the European call with strike price \$95 is \$10, with both options expiring in the next period. We want to replicate the payoff of the risk-free security that pays \$1 after one period regardless of what happens. We denote by δ_1 the number of shares of the stock, by δ_2 the number of calls with strike price 105, and by δ_3 the number of calls with strike price 95. By computing the payoffs of the three securities in each of the possible three states in the next period, we see that in order to replicate the risk-free security we need to have

$$120\delta_1 + 15\delta_2 + 25\delta_3 = 1$$
$$100\delta_1 + 5\delta_3 = 1$$
$$90\delta_1 = 1$$

The solution to this system is $\delta_1 = 1/90$, $\delta_2 = 2/135$, and $\delta_3 = -1/45$. We note that the cost of this portfolio is

$$\frac{1}{90}100 + \frac{2}{135}5 - \frac{1}{45}10 = 0.963$$

We will argue later that this should then be the price of the risk-free security. Since its relative return is $1/0.963 - 1 = 3.85\%$, this is the risk-free rate in this model.

   We argue next that the multiperiod Cox-Ross-Rubinstein binomial model of section 3.2.2 is complete. We will see that we have to solve a series of 2-by-2 equations of the type shown in Example 3.7. See also Problems 29 and 30 for more examples. We will discuss the replication of claims in this model again, in the chapters on hedging and on numerical methods (chapters 9–11).

   For concreteness, we consider a two-period binomial model. In such a model there are three possible payoff values of a given contingent claim C maturing at the end of the second period. Let us call these values C^{uu}, C^{ud}, and C^{dd}, corresponding to the stock price movements up-up, up-down, and down-down. Similarly for S^{uu}, S^{ud}, and S^{dd}. Likewise, we denote by $C^u(1)$, $C^d(1)$ the time-1 values of the wealth process that replicates the payoff C (and which we are trying to find). Also, denote by $\delta_1^u(1)$ the number of units of the risky asset the replicating portfolio holds at time 1 in the upper node, and by $\delta_0^u(1)$ the amount held in the risk-free asset in that node. Similarly for the lower node at time 1. In order to have replication at maturity, we start replicating backward, from the end of the tree. We need to have the sum of money in the bank and money in the stock equal to the payoff, that is,

$$\delta_0^u(1)(1+r) + \delta_1^u(1)S^{uu} = C^{uu}$$
$$\delta_0^u(1)(1+r) + \delta_1^u(1)S^{ud} = C^{ud} \tag{3.45}$$

This system can be solved as

$$\delta_0^u(1) = \frac{1}{1+r}\left[C^{uu} - \delta_1^u(1)S^{uu}\right]$$
$$\delta_1^u(1) = \frac{C^{uu} - C^{ud}}{S^{uu} - S^{ud}} \tag{3.46}$$

Then the replicating portfolio's value at time 1 in the upper node has to be

$$C^u(1) = \delta_1^u(1)S^u + \delta_0^u(1)$$

We can similarly find the value for $C^d(1)$. Then we need to replicate these two values in the first period; that is, we need to have

$$\delta_0(0)(1+r) + \delta_1(0)S^u = C^u(1)$$
$$\delta_0(0)(1+r) + \delta_1(0)S^d = C^d(1) \tag{3.47}$$

We can now solve this system as before. This result shows that the model is complete.

We mention that in this model the number of shares the replicating portfolio holds in the underlying asset is always of the same type as in equation (3.46); that is, it is equal to the change in the future values of the claim divided by the change in the future values of the underlying asset, denoted

$$\delta_1 = \frac{\Delta C}{\Delta S} \tag{3.48}$$

This number is known as the **delta** of the claim, and it is different at different nodes of the tree.

(**Note:** The rest of this section is somewhat technical and can be skipped at first reading.)

As a general case of a single-period model consider the Arrow-Debreu model described in section 3.1.3. A contingent claim in that setting is represented by a K-dimensional vector $\vec{y} = (y^1, \ldots, y^K)$, whose entries y^k correspond to the payoff of the claim in state k. We denote by x_j^k the payoff of the security j at state k, and by $\vec{x}_j$ the vector of all possible payoffs for the basic security j in this market, $j = 1, \ldots, N$. We also denote by A the matrix formed by stacking together the payoff vectors $\vec{x}_j$ for all the basic securities in the market. The following theorem states the requirement for market completeness in the Arrow-Debreu setting.

THEOREM 3.3   Consider the Arrow-Debreu setting described previously. A necessary and sufficient condition for the Arrow-Debreu market to be complete is that the matrix A be of rank K.

Proof   In order to find a replicating portfolio $\vec{\delta}$ for a given claim $\vec{y}$, we have to solve the system of equations

$$\delta_1 x_1^i + \delta_2 x_2^i + \cdots + \delta_N x_N^i = y^i, \qquad i = 1, \ldots, K$$

This system can be solved for any given vector $\vec{y}$ if and only if the rank of the matrix A is K.   ∎

It follows that for the single-period market with K states to be complete we need at least K securities. In fact, K **nonredundant securities** are enough. We say that a **security is redundant** when its payoff can be replicated by a portfolio of other existing securities. One case when this market is complete occurs when all the Arrow-Debreu securities are traded; see the Problems section.

In multiperiod discrete-time models the notions of a contingent claim and replication are similar to the single-period case, as we have already seen for the CRR model. We require that the replicating portfolio be self-financing, as defined in section 3.1.2. In order to find the replicating portfolio we simply have to solve a system of equations as in equation (3.44) at each time period, starting from the last and going backward. For example, suppose that we have N securities and K states at each moment t. A contingent claim pays $g(S(T))$ at the end of the considered horizon, with $S(T)$ random. We start with the system of equations corresponding to each of the states k:

$$X^k(T) = \delta_0^k(T) B^k(T) + \sum_{i=1}^{N} \delta_i^k(T) S_i^k(T) = g(S^k(T)), \qquad k = 1, \ldots, K \qquad (3.49)$$

We solve this system (if possible) for values $\delta_i^k(T)$ keeping in mind that *the solution can only depend on information available up to time $T - 1$* (the predictability property). We find the value of the replicating wealth process at time $T - 1$ from the self-financing condition:

$$X^k(T-1) = \delta_0^k(T) B^k(T-1) + \sum_{i=1}^{N} \delta_i^k(T) S_i^k(T-1), \quad k=1,\ldots,K$$

We then go one step backward, solving (if possible) the system

$$X^k(T-1) = \delta_0^k(T-1) B^k(T-1) + \sum_{k=1}^{N} \delta_i^k(T-1) S_i^k(T-1), \quad k=1,\ldots,K$$

again keeping in mind that the values $\delta_i^k(T-1)$ can only depend on the values known by time $T-2$. We proceed like this until we reach time zero. This problem will typically have a unique solution when $N = K$ and the securities are not redundant.

3.6.6 Complete Markets in Continuous-Time Models*

The study of completeness of continuous-time models is harder than that of discrete-time models, because they have an infinite state space. Nevertheless, the definition remains the same, as follows. In continuous-time Brownian motion models a contingent claim is any financial contract with a final payoff $C(T)$ that depends on the values of Brownian motion up to time T. This is usually equivalent to requiring that $C(T)$ be known from the history of the underlying asset prices up to time T. A typical example would be a **path-independent European option** with payoff $g(S(T))$ for some function g, where the random value $S(T)$ corresponds to a security or vector of securities whose price is modeled by a diffusion process driven by Brownian motion. In order for a market model to be complete, we require, as in discrete time, that the payoff of any contingent claim (satisfying certain mild technical conditions) can be replicated with a self-financing admissible portfolio of existing securities. The difference compared to discrete time is that the definition of admissibility may be different.

We now present a nonrigorous discussion on how to check whether a continuous-time market model is complete. (A more rigorous analysis will be provided in a later chapter, using the so-called martingale representation theorem.) We assume that there are no arbitrage opportunities in the model.

Consider the following argument: Denote by $C(t)$ the time-t price of a contingent claim with payoff $C(T)$ at time T. Since the uncertainty in the economy is explained by the evolution of a d-dimensional Brownian motion process, it is not unreasonable to assume that all the financial assets in the economy, including the contingent claim, will satisfy the price dynamics of the type

$$dC(t) = a(t)\,dt + \sum_{j=1}^{d} b_j(t)\,dW_j(t) \tag{3.50}$$

where a and b_j are some processes, possibly stochastic. Suppose that, in addition to the usual bank account, there are N securities in the economy that themselves satisfy the dynamics

$$dS_i(t) = \mu_i(t)S(t)\,dt + \sum_{j=1}^{d} \sigma_{ij}(t)S_i(t)\,dW_j(t), \quad i = 1, \ldots, N \tag{3.51}$$

The objective is, then, to start with initial wealth $X(0) = C(0)$ and compute at every time t the amount $\pi_0(t)$ to be invested in the bank and $\pi_i(t)$ to be invested in security S_i, such that the corresponding wealth process X matches the claim's price process. That is, we want to find a vector of portfolio holdings π such that $dX(t) = dC(t)$, or

$$\pi_0(t)\frac{dB(t)}{B(t)} + \sum_{i=1}^{N} \pi_i(t)\frac{dS_i(t)}{S_i(t)} = a(t)\,dt + \sum_{j=1}^{d} b_j(t)\,dW_j(t)$$

In particular, this approach guarantees that at maturity T we have $X(T) = C(T)$. If we substitute for dS/S, we get

$$\pi_0(t)\frac{dB(t)}{B(t)} + \sum_{i=1}^{N} \pi_i(t)\mu_i(t)\,dt + \sum_{i=1}^{N} \left[\pi_i(t) \sum_{j=1}^{d} \sigma_{ij}(t)\,dW_j(t) \right]$$

$$= a(t)\,dt + \sum_{j=1}^{d} b_j(t)\,dW_j(t)$$

It will be shown later that in order to determine $a(t)$ and $b_j(t)$ it is sufficient to match the dW terms in order to match the two sides of this equation. In other words, we need to have, at every time t

$$\sum_{i=1}^{N} \pi_i(t)\sigma_{ij}(t) = b_j(t), \quad j = 1, \ldots, d$$

This is a system of d equations for N unknowns $\pi_i(t)$, $i = 1, \ldots, N$, and it leads to the following necessary and sufficient condition for completeness in this model:

THEOREM 3.4   Consider the model (3.51) with d independent Brownian motion processes and N risky securities, in addition to the bank account. We denote by $\sigma(t)$ the matrix with entries $\sigma_{ij}(t)$, that is, the volatility matrix formed by stacking together the d-dimensional vectors $(\sigma_{i1}, \ldots, \sigma_{iN})$ of the diffusion coefficients of the N securities returns. This makes $\sigma(t)$ an $N \times d$ dimensional matrix. A necessary and sufficient condition for markets to be complete is that $\sigma(t)$ be of rank d for all $t \in [0, T]$ (with probability one).

In particular, we need to have $N \geq d$, that is, at least as many securities as Brownian motions. In fact, it is sufficient to have $N = d$ and the matrix $\sigma(t)$ be nonsingular, that is, that it has an inverse. That guarantees that, for $dX = dC$ to hold, we only need to solve a system of N independent equations with N unknowns. When $N = d$, the matrix process σ is singular when the vector of diffusion coefficients of one of the securities is a linear combination of the diffusion coefficients of other securities. If that is the case, we say that the security is redundant.

The simplest example of complete markets in continuous time is the Merton-Black-Scholes model of section 3.3.6. There is one Brownian motion, one stock with constant coefficients, and a bond or bank account with constant interest rate.

Example 3.9 (Replication in the Merton-Black-Scholes Model) Consider the Merton-Black-Scholes model of section 3.3.6 with a stock with constant coefficients μ and σ, and a bond or bank account with constant interest rate r. Suppose that the contingent claim follows the dynamics

$$dC(t) = a(t)\,dt + b(t)\,dW(t)$$

We want

$$\pi_0(t)r\,dt + \pi_1(t)\left[\mu\,dt + \sigma\,dW(t)\right] = a(t)\,dt + b(t)\,dW(t)$$

This means that the amount $\pi_1(t)$ invested in the stock has to be equal to $\frac{b(t)}{\sigma}$ and, by the self-financing condition, the amount in the bank is $\pi_0(t) = C(t) - \pi_1(t)$.

As mentioned earlier, market completeness is a desirable property in option-pricing applications, since it leads to unique prices. We will come back to the notion of complete markets and some of its important consequences in the option-pricing sections of the book.

Continuous-time models can be much more complex than those described by the Merton-Black-Scholes model. In particular, we can have continuous-time models that allow for **jumps** in the price processes, convenient for modeling sudden and sizable market moves; or we can have a diffusion model in which the volatility itself is a random process. These are called **stochastic volatility models.** Most continuous-time models with jumps or with stochastic volatility are incomplete. In this book we will focus mostly on complete models. This emphasis does not mean that they are more realistic—they are simply easier to work with.

3.7 Appendix

3.7.1 More Details for the Proof of Itô's Rule

We follow here a proof given in Steele (2000). We consider only the simplest case of Itô's rule:

$$f(W(t)) - f(0) = \int_0^t f'(W(s))\,dW(s) + \tfrac{1}{2}\int_0^t f''(W(s))ds \tag{3.52}$$

In addition to assuming that f'' exists and is continuous, we also assume, for simplicity, that f has compact support. This assumption means that f, f', and f'' are all bounded. We denote the bound for a given function g by $|g|_{max}$.

We first divide the time interval $[0, t]$ into n equal pieces, with endpoints $t_i = it/n$, $0 \le i \le n$. We represent the left side of equation (3.52) as

$$f(W(t)) - f(W(0)) = \sum_{i=1}^{n} [f(W(t_i)) - f(W(t_{i-1}))] \tag{3.53}$$

We want to use Taylor's formula on the differences in the sum, in the following form:

$$f(y) - f(x) = (y - x)f'(x) + \frac{1}{2}(y - x)^2 f''(x) + R(x, y) \tag{3.54}$$

where the remainder $R(x, y)$ is given by

$$R(x, y) = \int_x^y (y - u)(f''(u) - f''(x))\, du$$

By continuity of f'' it can be shown that

$$|R(x, y)| \le (y - x)^2 h(x, y) \tag{3.55}$$

where h is a uniformly continuous bounded function, with $h(x, x) = 0$, for all x. In order to reduce notation, we denote

$$W_i = W(t_i)$$

We use Taylor's formula in the sum in expression (3.53) to obtain

$$f(W(t)) - f(W(0)) = A_n + B_n + C_n = \sum_{i=1}^{n} f'(W_{i-1})(W_i - W_{i-1})$$

$$+ \frac{1}{2} \sum_{i=1}^{n} f''(W_{i-1})(W_i - W_{i-1})^2 + C_n \tag{3.56}$$

where

$$|C_n| \le \sum_{i=1}^{n} (W_i - W_{i-1})^2 h(W_{i-1}, W_i) \tag{3.57}$$

As n goes to infinity, the term A_n converges (in probability) to $\int_0^t f'(W(s))\, dW(s)$, the first term in equation (3.52).

Next, we represent the term B_n as

$$B_n = \sum_{i=1}^{n} f''(W_{i-1})(t_i - t_{i-1}) + \frac{1}{2} \sum_{i=1}^{n} f''(W_{i-1})[(W_i - W_{i-1})^2 - (t_i - t_{i-1})]$$

The first term on the right-hand side converges to the ordinary integral $\int_0^t f''(W(s))\, ds$. Together with the established convergence of A_n, we see that it only remains to show that the second sum of B_n and the term C_n converge to zero. Note that the expected values of the product of the summands in the second sum of B_n satisfy, as in equation (3.17),

$$E\{f''(W_{i-1})[(W_i - W_{i-1})^2 - (t_i - t_{i-1})] \cdot f''(W_{j-1})[(W_j - W_{j-1})^2 - (t_j - t_{j-1})]\} = 0$$

because

$$E[(W_j - W_{j-1})^2] = t_j - t_{j-1}$$

Using this, and denoting by $B_{2,n}$ the second sum of B_n, we see that

$$E\left[B_{2,n}^2\right] = \sum_{i=1}^{n} E\{f''(W_{i-1})^2[(W_i - W_{i-1})^2 - (t_i - t_{i-1})]^2\} \tag{3.58}$$

$$\leq |f''|_{max}^2 \sum_{i=1}^{n} E\{[(W_i - W_{i-1})^2 - (t_i - t_{i-1})]^2\} \tag{3.59}$$

$$= \frac{2t^2}{n}|f''|_{max}^2 \tag{3.60}$$

where we use the fact that for the normal random variable $X = W_i - W_{i-1}$ with mean zero and variance t/n, we have $\text{Var}[X^2] = 2t^2/n^2$. Moreover, Markov inequality says

$$P\left[B_{2,n}^2 > \lambda\right] \leq \frac{E\left[B_{2,n}^2\right]}{\lambda}$$

which implies that $B_{2,n}$ converges to zero in probability.

Finally, we show that the term C_n converges to zero in probability. Using Cauchy inequality in expression (3.57) we get

$$E[|C_n|] \leq \sum_{i=1}^{n} \sqrt{E[(W_i - W_{i-1})^4]} \sqrt{E[h^2(W_{i-1}, W_i)]} \tag{3.61}$$

Using known properties of the normal distribution, we get

$$E[(W_i - W_{i-1})^4] = 3t^2/n^2$$

Moreover, by uniform continuity of h and $h(x, x) = 0$, for each $\varepsilon > 0$ there exists a $\delta > 0$ such that $|h(x, y)| \leq \varepsilon$ if $|x - y| \leq \delta$; hence,

$$E[h^2(W_{i-1}, W_i)] \leq \varepsilon^2 + |h|_{max}^2 P[|W_{i-1} - W_i| \geq \delta]$$

$$\leq \varepsilon^2 + \frac{|h|_{max}^2}{\delta^2} E[|W_{i-1} - W_i|^2]$$

$$= \varepsilon^2 + \frac{|h|_{max}^2}{\delta^2} t/n$$

The last two equations applied to equation (3.61) give us

$$E[|C_n|] \leq n\sqrt{3t^2/n^2}\sqrt{\varepsilon^2 + \frac{|h|^2_{max}}{\delta^2} t/n}$$

Since ε is arbitrary, we see that $E[|C_n|]$ converges to zero, and by Markov's inequality we conclude that C_n converges to zero in probability, too.

To be completely rigorous, we also have to argue as follows: We can find a subsequence n_j so that all three terms A_{n_j}, B_{n_j}, and C_{n_j} converge to zero in probability, for fixed t. This fact means that for fixed t, Itô's rule holds with probability one. Since the intersection of a countable collection of sets of probability one is also of probability one, Itô's rule holds for all rational t's with probability one. Finally, by continuity of the terms in Itô's rule, it also holds for all $t > 0$.

3.7.2 Multidimensional Itô's Rule

Let $(W_1, W_2, \ldots, W_n)$ be an n-dimensional Brownian motion, meaning that the W_k's are independent one-dimensional Brownian motions. Consider d processes given by

$$dX_i = \mu_i \, dt + \sigma_{i,1} \, dW_1 + \cdots + \sigma_{i,n} \, dW_n, \quad i = 1, \ldots, d$$

Denote $\vec{X}(t) = (X_1(t), \ldots, X_d(t))$. Then, for a sufficiently smooth function $f(\vec{x})$ of $\vec{x} = (x_1, \ldots, x_d)$, the process $f(\vec{X}(t))$ satisfies the **multidimensional Itô's rule:**

$$df(\vec{X}) = \sum_{i=1}^{d} f_{x_i} \, dX_i + \left[\frac{1}{2} \sum_{i,j=1}^{d} \left(f_{x_i x_j} \sum_{k=1}^{n} \sigma_{i,k} \sigma_{j,k} \right) \right] dt \tag{3.62}$$

Summary

We have introduced some basic models for asset prices: single-period, multiperiod, and continuous-time models. They model the prices as random, stochastic processes whose values vary with time. Typically, one asset is risk-free; that is, its growth is completely determined by the interest rate during the investment period. This asset, which we call the bank account, is used as a discounting asset for the prices of all other securities. It is also convenient to discount the wealth process of an investor by the risk-free asset. The wealth process is the value process of the investor's portfolio. It is required to be self-financing, meaning it corresponds to a trading strategy that does not require additional funds to be deposited into or taken out of the portfolio.

The most popular multiperiod model is the binomial Cox-Ross-Rubinstein model. In the continuous-time limit it results in the most famous continuous-time model, the Merton-Black-Scholes model. This model is based on the stochastic process called Brownian motion.

Brownian motion is a martingale process and a Markov process. In order to be able to work in continuous-time models, one has to be familiar with Itô's rule for diffusion processes.

Interest rates can be modeled as discrete-time or continuous-time stochastic processes. Real interest rates correspond to risk-free returns adjusted for inflation.

Most market models allow no arbitrage opportunities in the market. Many also imply that the market is complete, so that every random payoff can be replicated in the market. Both the Cox-Ross-Rubinstein model and the Merton-Black-Scholes model are free of arbitrage and complete.

Problems

1. Suppose you want to model a stock index S (a weighted average of a great number of stocks) using a single-period model. The return $\Delta S = S(1) - S(0)$ in the period will be a weighted average of the returns of all the stocks comprising the index. What distribution(s) might be appropriate for modeling ΔS? Why?

†2. In the single-period model show that equation (3.3) holds.

3. Show that equation (3.6) holds in the multiperiod model.

†4. Show that equation (3.7) holds in the multiperiod model, or at least for the case of two assets and two periods.

*5. Consider a two-period model, with one risky security S and one risk-free security B, in which there are **proportional transaction costs** when trading S: in order to buy one share of S we need to spend $(1 + \lambda)S$, paid from B, and when we sell one share of S we receive $(1 - \mu)S$ in B. Here $\lambda > 0$ and $0 < \mu < 1$. Can you write down the wealth process $X(t)$ and the self-financing condition for this case? How about the gains process?

†6. Give an example of a Cox-Ross-Rubinstein model with expected relative stock return equal to 0.1, $E[S(t)/S(t-1)] = 0.1$, and variance equal to 0.2, $\mathrm{Var}[S(t)/S(t-1)] = 0.2$. That is, choose the values of parameters p, u, and d so that these conditions are satisfied.

7. Consider a Cox-Ross-Rubinstein model with $p = 0.5$, $S(0) = 100$, $u = 1.01$, $d = 1/u$, and with two periods. Find all the possible stock prices after one period and after two periods. What is the probability that the stock price after two periods will be at least 102?

*8. In the model from the previous problem, using a statistical package, simulate 1,000 values of $S(5)$ and 1,000 values of $S(20)$. Plot the corresponding histograms.

9. Two diffusion processes X and Y satisfy

$$dX = (2 + 5t + X) dt + 3 dW_1$$
$$dY = 4Y dt + 8Y dW_1 + 6 dW_2$$

where W_1 and W_2 are correlated Brownian motions with $\rho = 0.1$. Use Itô's rule to find the dynamics of the processes

$$X^4, \qquad e^X, \qquad X \cdot Y$$

†10. Continue the previous problem by finding the dynamics of

$$\sin(X), \qquad X^4 \cdot Y, \qquad \sin(X) \cdot Y$$

11. Use Itô's rule to find the SDE for Brownian motion cubed, W^3. Do the same for S^3 where S is the stock price in the Merton-Black-Scholes model.

†12. Show that the process $M(t) := W^2(t) - t$ is a martingale, that is, that $E[M(t) \mid M(s)] = M(s)$ for $s \leq t$.

13. For which value of A is the process

$$M(t) = W^3(t) - A \int_0^t W(u)\, du$$

a martingale?

*14. Let $M(t) := \int_0^t Y(u)\, dW(u)$, where $E\left[\int_0^\infty Y^2(u)\, du\right] < \infty$. Use Itô's rule to find the differential dQ of the process $Q(t) = M^2(t) - \int_0^t Y^2(u)\, du$ and to conclude that the process Q is a martingale. In particular, argue that this implies $E[M^2(t)] = E[\int_0^t Y^2(u)\, du]$.

15. In the Merton-Black-Scholes model, show that $\mathrm{Var}[S(t)] = e^{2\mu t}(e^{\sigma^2 t} - 1)$.

†16. In the Merton-Black-Scholes model, find $\mathrm{Var}[S^2(t)]$.

17. Suppose that our agent Taf has observed the following values of stock S, as recorded at the end of the last 6 weeks:

$$S(0) = 100, \qquad S(1) = 98, \qquad S(2) = 100, \qquad S(3) = 101, \qquad S(4) = 105,$$
$$S(5) = 104$$

Taf wants to estimate the mean weekly return, so he computes the average $\hat{\mu}$ of the returns $\Delta S(i) = S(i) - S(i-1)$, $i = 1, \ldots, 5$. He then compares this to the return for the whole period lasting five weeks, normalized to give a weekly figure: $\tilde{\mu} = [S(5) - S(0)]/5$. How do these two estimates of the expected weekly return μ for this stock compare? What does this mean in terms of how easy or difficult it is to estimate μ?

*18. Go to the Internet and find the values of daily prices of a stock or a stock index for the last n days, where you can choose the stock and n yourself, but n should not be too small. Assume that the stock follows the Black-Scholes model, and estimate its drift and its volatility, in annual terms.

19. Derive equation (3.36).

20. Consider the following interest-rate model: the continuous interest rate of a bank account in the time period $[0, 1]$ is a time-dependent process given by

$$r(t) = 0.08 \cdot e^{-t} + 1 - e^{-t}$$

a. How much is one dollar invested at time $t = 0$ worth at time $t = 1$?

b. What is the dynamics satisfied by the process r; that is, what is the function $f(t, r(t))$ such that

$$dr(t) = f(t, r(t)) \, dt$$

21. Show that our first definition of arbitrage in the single-period model is implied by the second definition.

†22. Suppose that in a single-period model the stock value at time 1 is not random, but known already at the beginning of the period. Suppose also that the interest rate r is fixed. Find the conditions on $S(0)$, r, and $S(1)$ under which there are no arbitrage opportunities in this market.

23. Consider a simple economy described by a single-period model with three states. There are three Arrow-Debreu securities of the type described in section 3.1.3, with prices 0.30, 0.30, and 0.35. There is also a risk-free security that pays 1 in each of the three states and sells at moment $t = 0$ for 0.90. Construct an arbitrage strategy in this economy.

†24. Argue that the single-period Arrow-Debreu market is complete if all Arrow-Debreu securities are traded.

25. Provide an example of a single-period model that is incomplete.

†26. Consider a single-period CRR model with interest rate 0.05, $S(0) = 10$, $u = 1.2$, and $d = 0.98$. Suppose you have written an option that pays the value of the square root of the absolute value of the difference between the stock price at maturity and $10.00; that is, it pays $\sqrt{|S(1) - 10|}$. How many shares of the stock should you buy to replicate this payoff? What is the cost of the replicating portfolio?

27. In the context of Example 3.7, find a replicating portfolio for the put option with the payoff function $g(s) = (100 - s)^+ = \max(100 - s, 0)$.

28. Consider the single-period model in which the price of the stock today is $S(0) = \$100$. In the next period it can go up to $110, stay at $100, or go down to $80. The price of the European put on this stock with strike price $105 is $8, and the price of the European put with strike price $95 is $5, with both options expiring in the next period. Find the portfolio that replicates the payoff of the risk-free security that pays $1 after one period regardless of what happens.

29. Consider a two-period Cox-Ross-Rubinstein model with $S(0) = 100$, $u = 1.01$, $d = 1/u$, and $r = 0.005$. Find a replicating portfolio in this model for the put option $g(s) = (100 - s)^+$.

*30. Write a computer code for a program that would compute the replicating portfolio values $\delta_0(0)$, $\delta_1(1)$ at time 0 in a Cox-Ross-Rubinstein model in which

$$1 + r = e^{\bar{r}\Delta t}, \qquad u = e^{\sigma\sqrt{\Delta t}}, \qquad d = \frac{1}{u}, \qquad \Delta t = T/n$$

The payoff to be replicated is the call option, $g(s) = (s - K)^+$. The input of the program should consist of $\bar{r}$, σ, K, $S(0)$, T, and n. The output should give $\delta_0(0)$, $\delta_1(0)$. Run the program for different values of n. You can check the correctness of your program by setting $K = 0$, which should produce $\delta(0) = 0$, $\delta(1) = 1$. (Why?) Note that the program has to compute the values backward from time T to $T - \Delta t$, $T - 2\Delta t$, and so on, until time 0.

Further Readings

The standard discrete-time representation of securities with uncertainty was developed in the 1950s by K. Arrow and G. Debreu. Arrow (1971) and Debreu (1959) are good summaries of their contributions. The binomial setting that has become standard for option pricing was introduced in Cox, Ross, and Rubinstein (1979). The modeling of security prices in continuous time was initiated by Samuelson (1969) and Merton (1969). An advanced textbook treatment of discrete-time models is Pliska (1997), and of continuous-time models Karatzas and Shreve (1998). Some of the books on stochastic calculus are Karatzas and Shreve (1997), Oksendal (1998), and Steele (2000).

4 Optimal Consumption/Portfolio Strategies

(**Note on the reading sequence:** The reader interested primarily in option pricing can skip chapters 4 and 5 in the first reading.)

You may decide to invest your money according to the approach "let me invest in the mutual fund that has the largest advertisement in the business section of my Internet portal." Alternatively, if you believe you have good ways of estimating the parameters of your model for market prices, you can use the methods developed in this chapter, whose learning objectives are

- to describe a classical way of measuring expected reward from investment strategies.
- to present different ways of computing optimal consumption/portfolio choices.
- to discuss qualitative features of optimal strategies.

One of the objectives of economics is to try to predict people's decisions and their impact on market variables such as prices. In order to do so, mathematical models are used. The point of departure of most of the models is the assumption that people are rational and try to achieve a certain financial objective. In mathematical terms, they try to optimize some criterion. One general approach is to apply a mathematical function to the consumption and wealth of an economic agent and assume that the decisions of the agent pursue the maximization of that function. The function is called the utility function, and it measures the level of satisfaction the agent derives from consumption and wealth. The agent decides how much to consume, how much to save, and how to allocate his capital between different assets in order to maximize his expected utility.

It should be remarked that this approach is more general and theoretical and, as a result, more difficult to use in practice than the option-pricing problem, studied later in the book. One reason for that limitation is the fact that the optimal solution depends on the mean return rates of the risky assets, which are difficult to estimate. It also depends heavily on the kind of utility function we choose. Nevertheless, this formulation has proved very useful in describing general qualitative features of investors' behavior in financial markets. Moreover, it may be used as a tool for pricing and hedging in incomplete market models, in which there is no unique way to price securities.

4.1 Preference Relations and Utility Functions

We study here ways to model preferences of an individual in a given economy. But first we have to introduce the notion of consumption, traditionally used by economists in studying economic behavior of individuals.

4.1.1 Consumption

Recall the concepts of wealth and portfolio that we introduced in chapter 3. We introduce here an additional basic notion that lies beneath the concept of individual preferences: **consumption.** We will assume that there is a single good in the economy (or maybe several goods, but we can express the aggregate consumption in terms of one good) that becomes the **numeraire.** This assumption means that the prices of all assets are expressed in the units of the numeraire good, which we always choose to be money. Our investor Taf has to decide what proportion of his wealth to invest, what proportion of wealth to save, and how much to consume.

Discrete-Time Models   We revisit the wealth equations of chapter 2 by adding the possibility of consuming money, that is, spending it outside of the financial market. We denote by $c(0)$ the amount consumed at time 0, and by $X(1)$ the wealth amount *before* consumption at time 1. The wealth at time 1, then, is given by

$$X(1) = \delta_0 B(1) + \sum_{i=1}^{N} \delta_i S_i(1) \tag{4.1}$$

and the **self-financing condition** is

$$X(0) - c(0) = \delta_0 B(0) + \delta_1 S_1(0) + \cdots + \delta_N S_N(0) \tag{4.2}$$

The extension to multiperiod models is straightforward. Consumption is described by a stochastic process $c(t)$, representing the amount of money consumed at time t. If we denote by $X(t)$ the wealth *before* consumption at time t, we have

$$X(t) = \delta_0(t) B(t) + \sum_{i=1}^{N} \delta_i(t) S_i(t) \tag{4.3}$$

We have to impose some conditions on the portfolio and consumption processes among which Taf can choose. These conditions are needed for both technical and economic reasons. A strategy—that is, a combination of a consumption and a portfolio process—that satisfies those conditions is called **admissible.** The strategy (c, δ) is admissible if

1. c is a nonnegative (for obvious economic reasons) adapted process; that is, $c(t)$ has to be determined from the information available at time t.

2. the corresponding terminal wealth satisfies $X(T) \geq c(T)$; that is, bankruptcy is not allowed.

3. the following **self-financing condition** is satisfied:

$$X(t) - c(t) = \delta_0(t+1) B(t) + \delta_1(t+1) S_1(t) + \cdots + \delta_N(t+1) S_N(t) \tag{4.4}$$

This means that the amount of money that Taf has in the assets after trading at time t is equal to the wealth $X(t)$ before trading, minus the consumed amount.

Continuous-Time Models   Consumption is described by a continuous-time nonnegative adapted stochastic process $c(t)$ that represents the rate of consumption. In other words, the cumulative consumption up to time t is $C(t) = \int_0^t c(u)du$. Using the notation of chapter 2, the wealth-process dynamics is given by

$$dX(t) = \{r(t)X(t) + \pi(t)[\mu(t) - r(t)] - c(t)\}\,dt + \pi(t)\sigma(t)\,dW(t) \qquad (4.5)$$

Taf chooses the rate of consumption that is subtracted in the dynamics of the wealth process. The remainder is allocated between the bank and the stocks.

4.1.2   Preferences

Utility functions are built upon a more basic idea, **preferences.** Investors do not think in terms of mathematical functions. However, investors are typically able to compare between different situations and to decide which one is better.

We usually assume that the investor whose behavior we are trying to model faces a finite horizon. The finite horizon can be interpreted as death, for example, if our investor Taf is a person, or the moment at which his performance will be evaluated, if Taf is the manager of an investment fund. However, it is sometimes convenient, for technical reasons, to assume that Taf faces an infinite horizon. The simplest case considered in economics is that our investor Taf only cares about consumption over a given time interval and/or about his final wealth. It is sometimes useful to think of the final wealth amount as being consumed, hence also considered a part of the consumption. While an average individual would be interested in consumption over time, and potentially in the final wealth for a bequest motive, a money manager would be interested only in the final wealth. In the case of an infinite horizon, there is no such a thing as the final wealth, and the assumption is then that Taf only cares about intertemporal consumption. In an uncertain world, Taf will be concerned about his consumption and/or wealth as related to the possible future states of the world.

Let us denote by x the values of consumption and/or the final wealth across different states. For example, a possible x in a two-state single-period model is consumption of 1 in state 1 and 0 in state 2. This can be denoted as

$x = (1, 0)$

In multiperiod models or continuous-time models, consumption over time will be a stochastic process, but the idea is the same. We will call a given x a **consumption choice.**

If consumption choice x_1 results in more money than consumption choice x_2 in all states, denoted $x_1 \geq x_2$, then we say that x_1 **dominates** x_2 and x_1 should be preferred. However, most of the time the outcomes of consumption choices are random, and one choice will produce more money in some states and less money in other states than the other choice. Consequently, Taf has to develop a way of comparing different consumption choices.

Example 4.1 (Comparing Consumption Choices)

a. Taf has a pleasant duty to choose between two winning but uncertain projects: Project A pays either $10 or $100. Project B pays either $15 at the same time project A pays $10, or $110 when project B pays $100. This is a no-brainer: Taf should go with project B.

b. In another case, project A pays as in part a, while project B pays $110 when project A pays $10, and it pays $15 when project A pays $100. It is not clear, without further information, which consumption choice Taf should choose.

Suppose that Taf has come up with preference relations for consumption choices. If Taf likes the consumption choice x_1 at least as much as the consumption choice x_2, we denote that by $x_1 \succeq x_2$. If Taf definitely prefers x_1 to x_2, we denote that by $x_1 \succ x_2$. When $x_1 \succeq x_2$ and $x_2 \succeq x_1$, we say that Taf is indifferent between x_1 and x_2, and we denote it by $x_1 \sim x_2$. The following two properties are usually assumed for a preference relation:

1. **Completeness:** For any two strategies x_1, x_2 we have either $x_1 \succeq x_2$ or $x_2 \succeq x_1$ (or both).

2. **Transitivity:** If $x_1 \succeq x_2$ and $x_2 \succeq x_3$, then $x_1 \succeq x_3$.

The completeness property means that Taf can compare any two given choices and rank them in terms of preferences. The transitivity property means that if Taf likes choice 1 at least as much as choice 2, and likes choice 2 at least as much as choice 3, then Taf must like choice 1 at least as much as choice 3. The transitivity property can be interpreted as consistency in economic choices. There are two other properties that, as we will try to justify, are relevant from the economics point of view.

3. **Monotonicity:** If $x_1 \geq x_2$, then $x_1 \succeq x_2$.

4. **Convexity:** Consider the consumption choice $x_3 = \alpha x_1 + (1 - \alpha)x_2, \alpha \in (0, 1)$. Then, $x_3 \succeq x$ whenever $x_1 \succeq x$ and $x_2 \succeq x$.

Monotonicity simply means that more is better, and that definition is typically consistent with human preferences. Convexity means that a weighted average of two choices is no worse than the less preferred individual choice. An investor with convex preferences tries to avoid risk. This investor is called **risk-averse,** as opposed to the **risk-seeking** investor, who prefers to takes chances, or the **risk-neutral** investor, who is indifferent between the weighted averages and the individual choices. We provide more details on these notions in what follows.

4.1.3 Concept of Utility Functions

A **utility function** is a mapping from the set of consumption choices into the real numbers. In other words, a utility function assigns a real number to every consumption choice and therefore determines preference relations between various choices as follows:

$$U(x_1) \geq U(x_2) \Rightarrow x_1 \succeq x_2$$
$$U(x_1) > U(x_2) \Rightarrow x_1 \succ x_2$$
$$U(x_1) = U(x_2) \Rightarrow x_1 \sim x_2$$

Suppose, for simplicity, that our agent Taf only cares about final wealth X, in a setting of uncertainty. Since wealth is random, a standard approach is to assume that Taf cares about average utility or **expected utility,** $E[U(X)]$.

Example 4.2 (Square-Root Utility) Our dear friend Taf has a choice between two investment opportunities. One pays $10,000 with certainty, while the other pays $22,500 with probability 0.3, $4,900 with probability 0.3, and $900 with probability 0.4. Taf decides that he likes the utility approach to establish his preferences, and he also thinks that the so-called power utility of the form $U(x) = x^\gamma$ suits his purpose. Here, γ is a positive number less than one. Consequently, his utilities from the two investment opportunities are

$$U(1) = (10,000)^\gamma, \qquad U(2) = 0.3 \cdot (22,500)^\gamma + 0.3 \cdot (4,900)^\gamma + 0.4 \cdot (900)^\gamma \qquad (4.6)$$

In order to decide what value of γ to use, he decides he is pretty much indifferent between the choice of receiving $100 for sure, or $144 and $64 with fifty-fifty chance. He uses this equality in preferences to find his γ from

$$(100)^\gamma = 0.5 \cdot (144)^\gamma + 0.5 \cdot (64)^\gamma$$

He sees that the value of $\gamma = 1/2$ will do the job. In other words, he decides he has the square-root utility, $U(x) = \sqrt{x}$. He can now evaluate the utility values of the two investments using equations (4.6), and he gets

$$U(1) = 100, \qquad U(2) = 0.3 \cdot \sqrt{22,500} + 0.3 \cdot \sqrt{4,900} + 0.4 \cdot \sqrt{900} = 78$$

Since $U(1) > U(2)$ he decides he prefers the first investment.

Note: It is often appropriate to use utility functions that change with time, of the form $U(t, x)$, or even more complex ways of measuring utility. For simplicity, we stick to the case $U(x)$.

It is easily shown that a preference relation defined by a utility function satisfies completeness and transitivity (see Problem 1). However, the converse is not always true; that is, not all complete and transitive preference relations can be represented by a utility function, unless some additional conditions are assumed on the preference relation.

Typically, preferences are assumed to be monotonic. This assumption corresponds to an increasing utility function. Similarly, utility functions that are concave (this notion is discussed in the following paragraphs) result in convex preferences, although the converse is not necessarily true. As we will see, concavity, besides this economic interpretation, is also convenient for technical reasons when solving Taf's optimization problems.

In order to motivate the choice of a concave function $U(\cdot)$ we compare the following two possibilities:

1. The future wealth is equal to $\frac{1}{2}x + \frac{1}{2}y$ with certainty.
2. The future wealth is x with probability $\frac{1}{2}$ and y with probability $\frac{1}{2}$.

For the first possibility, the expected utility is $U(0.5x + 0.5y)$. For the second, it is $0.5U(x) + 0.5U(y)$. If we think it is reasonable to prefer the certain amount $0.5x + 0.5y$ to the random amount equal to either x or y with the same probability 0.5 (that is, if we assume convex preferences) we need to have

$$U(0.5x + 0.5y) \geq 0.5U(x) + 0.5U(y)$$

More generally, we can require that the function U be **concave:**

$$U(\alpha x + (1 - \alpha)y) \geq \alpha U(x) + (1 - \alpha)U(y), \quad 0 \leq \alpha \leq 1$$

It can be shown that the concavity implies the so-called **Jensen's inequality:**

$$U(E[X]) \geq E[U(X)] \tag{4.7}$$

for any given random variable X. In other words, the investor prefers the certain average amount $E[X]$ to the random amount X. As we said before, this investor is called **risk-averse,** as opposed to the **risk-neutral** investor, who is indifferent between 1 and 2. We have equality in equation (4.7) only if the utility is a linear function, $U(x) = ax + b$. A convex function $U(\cdot)$, that is, such that function $-U(x)$ is concave, would imply that Taf likes risk (prefers 2 to 1) and is called **risk-seeking.**

A typical graph of a concave increasing function looks like the one in figure 4.1.

4.1.4   Marginal Utility, Risk Aversion, and Certainty Equivalent

We now introduce the notion of **marginal utility** as a measure of the change in utility when there is a change in wealth (or consumption). More precisely, if the utility function is differentiable, the marginal utility is the slope, the derivative, of the utility function. As can be seen from figure 4.1, the marginal utility of an increasing concave utility function is

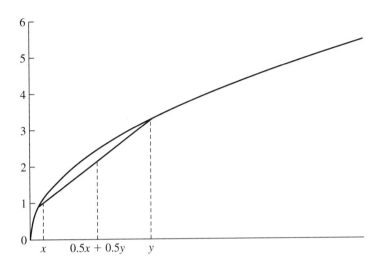

Figure 4.1
A graph of an increasing concave function.

decreasing. In other words, when Taf has a low level of wealth, the satisfaction provided by an extra unit of wealth is higher than when Taf has a high level of wealth. This is another appealing property from the economics point of view.

In accordance with previous considerations we will use utility functions $U(x)$ such that

1. U is strictly increasing.
2. U is twice differentiable.
3. U is concave; in particular, $U'' \leq 0$.

Differentiability is not required for economic reasons, but for technical reasons, in order to solve optimization problems of the investor. Typical examples of utility functions frequently used in financial models are

- **logarithmic utility:** $U(x) = \log(x)$.
- **power utility:** $U(x) = \frac{x^\gamma}{\gamma}, \quad \gamma \leq 1$.
- **exponential utility:** $U(x) = 1 - e^{-\alpha x}$.
- **quadratic utility:** $U(x) = x - \beta x^2$.

(We denote here by "log" the natural logarithm, sometimes denoted "ln.") Note that the logarithmic utility when applied to wealth requires that the wealth be positive, while the exponential utility, for example, allows for the possibility of negative wealth. The logarithmic utility can be considered as a limit of the utility $\frac{x^\gamma - 1}{\gamma}$ as γ tends to zero. (The utility $\frac{x^\gamma - 1}{\gamma}$ is equivalent to the power utility, in the sense that they result in the same preferences.) The quadratic utility corresponds to the so-called **mean-variance** objective of maximizing the mean of the return while keeping its variance low. Note that the quadratic utility is increasing only in a certain range of x values.

Since we will use concave utility functions, implying that we assume the investors to be risk-averse, it is convenient to have a measure of the degree of risk aversion. In that regard, we define **absolute risk aversion,** introduced by Arrow and Pratt, as

$$A(x) := -\frac{U''(x)}{U'(x)}$$

and **relative risk aversion** as

$$R(x) := x A(x)$$

Example 4.3 (Exponential Utility)   For exponential utility $U(x) = 1 - e^{-\alpha x}$, we have

$$U'(x) = \alpha e^{-\alpha x}, \qquad U''(x) = -\alpha^2 e^{-\alpha x}, \qquad A(x) = \alpha$$

In other words, the absolute risk aversion is constant, equal to α. For this reason exponential utility is said to belong to the family of utility functions with constant relative risk aversion, or the CRRA family.

In the case of the power utility, the parameter γ is called the **risk-aversion parameter.** Strictly speaking $1 - \gamma$ is the relative risk aversion. Sometimes power utility is parameterized as $x^{1-\gamma}/(1 - \gamma)$, for $\gamma > 0$, so that γ is the true relative risk aversion. For the parametrization we used previously, larger γ corresponds to the investors who are more risk-tolerant, while smaller γ corresponds to the investors who are more risk-averse.

In order to give some intuition to the definition of risk aversion, recall that the linear utility function corresponds to a risk-neutral investor. In this case, U'' is zero. Larger curvature of the utility function results in more risk-averse behavior. The curvature is measured by the second derivative, but it has to be normalized by the first derivative to make it invariant to linear transformations. We will see later that larger risk aversion implies investing more in the risk-free security, while smaller risk aversion means investing more in the risky securities, as it should. Later we will provide another interpretation for absolute risk aversion.

Another useful concept for applications is that of **certainty equivalent.** Given a random variable Y, the certainty equivalent is the constant amount of cash $\mathrm{CE}(Y)$ the utility of which is the same as the expected utility of Y:

$$U(\mathrm{CE}(Y)) = E[U(Y)] \tag{4.8}$$

In other words, in the eyes of the investor with utility U, the certain amount CE(Y) is equivalent to the random payoff Y. It follows from the risk-aversion property (4.7) that, for a risk-averse investor, the certainty equivalent is never larger than the expected value of Y:

$$\text{CE}(Y) \leq E[Y]$$

The certainty equivalent is often used for comparing and pricing random payoffs.

Example 4.4 (Buying Price) One way to use the certainty equivalent for pricing a given claim is to require that the certainty equivalent of the profit or loss without buying the claim is the same as the certainty equivalent of profit or loss when buying the claim for a given amount. Such amount is then called the **buying price** of the claim.

As an example, consider a single period with a simple claim that pays the random value Y at time 1, equal to Y_1 with probability p_1, or Y_2 with probability $p_2 = 1 - p_1$. These amounts can also be negative, meaning that they represent a payment rather than a payoff. Suppose also that our potential buyer Taf has at his disposal the amount of $X(0)$ dollars. If he does not buy the claim, we assume that he will invest the money in the risk-free asset, in which case he would have $(1 + r)X(0)$ at time 1, where r is the risk-free interest rate for the period. The buying price $b(0)$ is then obtained by setting

$$\text{CE}((1 + r)X(0)) = \text{CE}\{(1 + r)(X(0) - b(0)) + Y\} \tag{4.9}$$

In general, the buying price $b(0)$ will have a somewhat peculiar feature: it will depend on how rich the buyer is at the moment, meaning it will depend on $X(0)$. However, for exponential utility this price will not depend on $X(0)$. So, let us assume that Taf has exponential utility $U(x) = 1 - e^{-\alpha x}$. Then, in order to satisfy equation (4.9), the expected utilities of the two investment alternatives have to be the same, that is, the price $b(0)$ has to satisfy

$$e^{-\alpha(1+r)X(0)} = p_1 \cdot e^{-\alpha\{(1+r)[X(0)-b(0)]+Y_1\}} + p_2 \cdot e^{-\alpha\{(1+r)[X(0)-b(0)]+Y_2\}}$$

This reduces to

$$e^{-\alpha(1+r)b(0)} = p_1 \cdot e^{-\alpha Y_1} + p_2 \cdot e^{-\alpha Y_2}$$

The buying price $b(0)$ can be computed from this equation. We can write the equation in terms of the certainty equivalent as

$$b(0) = \frac{1}{1 + r}\text{CE}(Y) \tag{4.10}$$

where CE(Y) is the certainty equivalent of the random payoff Y. This representation shows the similarity of the present-value formula for deterministic payoffs to the buying price for random payoffs.

The quantity $E[Y] - CE[Y]$ is sometimes called the **risk premium.** We now derive an approximate relationship between the risk premium and the absolute risk aversion. Denote $\mu_Y = E[Y]$. Using Taylor's expansion, we have the approximation

$$U(Y) \approx U(\mu_Y) + (Y - \mu_Y)U'(\mu_Y) + \tfrac{1}{2}(Y - \mu_Y)^2 U''(\mu_Y) \qquad (4.11)$$

and taking expectations

$$E[U(Y)] \approx U(\mu_Y) + \tfrac{1}{2}\text{Var}[Y]U''(\mu_Y) \qquad (4.12)$$

However, again by Taylor's expansion and by definition of the certainty equivalent,

$$E[U(Y)] = U(CE[Y]) \approx U(\mu_Y) + [CE(Y) - \mu_Y]U'(\mu_Y) \qquad (4.13)$$

Comparing the last two equalities, we get the following expression for the risk premium in terms of the absolute risk aversion:

$$\mu_Y - CE[Y] \approx -\frac{1}{2}\frac{U''(\mu_Y)}{U'(\mu_Y)}\text{Var}[Y] \qquad (4.14)$$

Note from this equation that maximizing the certainty equivalent $CE[Y]$ is approximately equivalent to the mean-variance quadratic utility optimization.

4.1.5 Utility Functions in Multiperiod Discrete-Time Models

Suppose that Taf cares about both his consumption and the final wealth. We denote by $c(t)$ the amount consumed at time t, and by $X(t)$ the level of wealth at moment t. Suppose also that Taf faces a finite horizon $[0, T]$. Similarly to the single-period case considered before, Taf's objective will be the maximization of

$$E\left[\sum_{t=0}^{T} \beta^t U_1(c(t)) + U_2(X(T))\right]$$

where $U_1(\cdot)$ and $U_2(\cdot)$ are two utility functions and $0 < \beta < 1$ is a discount factor.

In the infinite-horizon case, the objective is similar, with $T = \infty$, but without utility from the final wealth.

4.1.6 Utility Functions in Continuous-Time Models

We use the notation introduced before. In the finite-horizon case, Taf's objective will be to maximize

$$E\left[\int_0^T e^{-\beta t}U_1(c(t))\, dt + U_2(X(T))\right]$$

where $\beta > 0$ is a discount rate. The infinite-horizon case, without final wealth, is treated similarly.

4.2 Discrete-Time Utility Maximization

Before we describe how to find optimal strategies in various models, let us illustrate by an example how frequent rebalancing of portfolio positions can be superior to simple buy-and-hold strategies. For example, consider the following two investment (or "gambling") opportunities:

1. Keep the money "under the mattress"; this opportunity has zero return.

2. Invest in an opportunity ("bet on a gambling game") that doubles your money or cuts your money in half at each time period, with a fifty-fifty chance.

The long-term (continuous) rate of return for these strategies is measured by $\log[X(t)]$, where $X(t)$ is the total wealth at time t. If we invest in opportunity 1, the average rate of return of the investment of one dollar is $E[\log(1)] = 0$. Similarly, if we invest one dollar in the second opportunity, the expected rate of return is also zero:

$$0.5 \log(2) + 0.5 \log \left(\tfrac{1}{2}\right) = 0$$

However, if we rebalance our portfolio at each period to keep, say, 60% of money we have in the first opportunity, and 40% in the second opportunity, the expected rate of return on one dollar is

$$0.5 \log(0.6 + 0.4 \cdot 2) + 0.5 \log \left(0.6 + 0.4 \cdot \tfrac{1}{2}\right) = 0.057$$

This means that on average one dollar results in $e^{0.057} = 1.058$ dollars in each period, a return of 5.8% per period. In other words, *by rebalancing the portfolio on a regular basis we can combine two opportunities with zero expected return into an investment with positive expected return.*

In effect, we use the strategy "buy low, sell high": when we have more than 40% of our money in the risky opportunity we transfer some money under the mattress, and when we have more than 60% under the mattress, we move some money into the risky opportunity.

The aim of the following sections is to find the optimal proportion of wealth to be held in the available assets at each trading period. We would also like to justify within our models the common recommendation of financial advisers to keep a certain constant percentage of your wealth in the risky assets (stocks) and the remaining percentage in the risk-free assets, independently of how much money you have. Such a strategy is of the type "buy low, sell high," and the optimal strategies we will find in most of our models will be of this type.

4.2.1 Single Period

Consider a single-period market model with N risky securities, whose prices we denote by $S_1, \ldots, S_N$, and a risk-free bank account (or bond) whose balance (or price) we denote by B. There might be a finite number of states or an infinite number of states (for example, the return of each risky security at time 1 is normally distributed). We assume that our agent Taf starts with x dollars and chooses the portfolio $\vec{\delta}$ to maximize the expected utility from wealth at time 1:

$$\sup_{\vec{\delta}} E[U(X(1))]$$

The maximization is performed over the set of portfolio strategies $\vec{\delta} = (\delta_0, \ldots, \delta_N)$, subject to the self-financing condition, or the budget constraint condition,

$$x = \delta_0 B(0) + \delta_1 S_1(0) + \cdots + \delta_N S_N(0)$$

Recall that

$$X(1) = \delta_0 B(1) + \delta_1 S_1(1) + \cdots + \delta_N S_N(1) = \sum_{i=0}^{N} \delta_i S_i(1)$$

where we denoted

$$S_0 := B$$

for notational simplicity. This is a standard optimization problem with the constraint given by the budget constraint condition. Such problems are solved by first forming the so-called **Lagrangian**

$$L := E\left[U\left(\sum_{i=0}^{N} \delta_i S_i(1) \right) \right] - \lambda \left[\sum_{i=0}^{N} \delta_i S_i(0) - x \right]$$

Then we differentiate it with respect to each δ_i inside the expected value, and set the derivatives equal to zero to get, denoting by $\hat{X}(1)$ the optimal terminal wealth,

$$E[U'(\hat{X}(1))S_i(1)] = \lambda S_i(0), \quad i = 0, \ldots, N \tag{4.15}$$

for a total of $N+1$ equations. Together with the budget constraint, we have $N+2$ equations for $N+2$ unknowns, $\delta_0, \ldots, \delta_N$ and λ. In particular, for $i = 0$, $S_0(0) = B(0) = 1$ and $S_0(1) = B(1) = 1 + r$, where r is the interest rate paid by the bank account, and we get

$$\lambda = E[U'(\hat{X}(1))(1 + r)]$$

Substituting this result in equation (4.15), we see that

$$S_i(0) = \frac{E[U'(\hat{X}(1))S_i(1)]}{E[U'(\hat{X}(1))(1+r)]} = \frac{1}{1+r} \frac{E[U'(\hat{X}(1))S_i(1)]}{E[U'(\hat{X}(1))]} \tag{4.16}$$

This provides us with an expression for the price of a risky asset S_i. It is the present value of the normalized expectation of a functional of the future payoff. This is a "preview" of a crucial pricing formula in economics that we will discuss later in the book, in sections on equilibrium; in particular, see section 12.3.1.

A variation of this single-period model is the case in which we allow consumption $c(0)$ at time 0. Our agent will try to solve the problem

$$\sup_{\vec{\delta}} \{U_1(c(0)) + E[U_2(X(1))]\}$$

The only difference is that the budget constraint is now

$$x - c(0) = \delta_0 B(0) + \delta_1 S_1(0) + \cdots + \delta_N S_N(0)$$

Example 4.5 (Log Utility)   Consider the single-period Cox-Ross-Rubinstein model, with stock $S(0)$ moving up to $S(0)u$ with probability p, and down to $S(0)d$ with probability q, $d < 1 + r < u$. Assume the log utility, $U(X(T)) = \log(X(T))$. Denoting by δ the number of shares Taf holds in the stock, the objective is to maximize

$$E[\log(\delta S(1) + (x - \delta S(0))(1+r))] = p \log(\delta S(0)(u - (1+r)) + x(1+r))$$
$$+ q \log(\delta S(0)(d - (1+r)) + x(1+r))$$

Note that we have already accounted for the budget constraint in this expression, and, therefore, we do not have to form a Lagrangian. Differentiating with respect to δ and setting the derivative equal to zero, we find the optimal number of shares $\hat{\delta}$:

$$\frac{\hat{\delta}S(0)}{x} = \frac{(1+r)[up + dq - (1+r)]}{((1+r) - d)(u - (1+r))} \tag{4.17}$$

We introduce the notation

$$\hat{\Pi} := \frac{\hat{\delta}S(0)}{x}$$

for the optimal **proportion of wealth** invested in the stock, also called **portfolio weight**. We can rewrite it as

$$\hat{\Pi} = \frac{(1+r)(E[S(1)/S(0)] - (1+r))}{((1+r) - d)(u - (1+r))} \tag{4.18}$$

We note that *for the logarithmic utility the optimal proportion of wealth held in the stock does not depend on the level of wealth x.*

This weight is proportional to the difference between the expected relative returns of stock and bank, $E[S(1)/S(0)] - (1 + r)$. We will see subsequently that the optimal solution in this logarithmic case remains the same even in the multiperiod Cox-Ross-Rubinstein model; see equation (4.26).

4.2.2 Multiperiod Utility Maximization: Dynamic Programming

We consider here multiperiod models with a finite number of states per period. The interest rate is also possibly stochastic. In principle, we could solve the multiperiod utility maximization problem following the same approach as in the single-period model: we can formulate it as an optimization problem under the self-financing budget constraints, and then take derivatives, set them equal to zero, and solve for the optimal strategy. When the number of periods is high, however, this approach becomes computationally very demanding. An alternative is to use the **principle of dynamic programming,** or the **Bellman equation.** We now describe that approach. Consider the problem of utility maximization from terminal wealth on a finite horizon $[0, 1, \ldots, T]$. At time 0, our agent Taf tries to solve

$$\sup_{\vec{\delta}^{[1]}} E[U(X^{\vec{\delta}^{[1]}}(T))]$$

Here,

$$\vec{\delta}^{[j]} := \{\vec{\delta}(j), \vec{\delta}(j + 1), \ldots, \vec{\delta}(T)\}$$

where $\vec{\delta}(i)$ is a vector of portfolio holdings in the period $[i - 1, i)$. In other words, $\vec{\delta}^{[j]}$ is the portfolio strategy for the period $[j - 1, T)$.

We introduce the concept of **value function** or **indirect utility,** which indicates, at a given time t and with a given level of wealth x, the maximum value an agent who pursues the preceding objective can achieve, starting with wealth x at time t. We denote it by $V(t, x)$:

$$V(t, x) := \sup_{\vec{\delta}^{[t+1]}} E_{t,x}[U(X^{\vec{\delta}^{[t+1]}}(T))] \tag{4.19}$$

The expectation $E_{t,x}$ is the conditional expectation corresponding to the "initial condition" $X(t) = x$, and conditioned on all the available information up to time t. The supremum is taken over all admissible portfolio strategies $\vec{\delta}^{(t+1)}$ over the period $[t, T]$.

Let $\hat{\delta}^{[1]} = \{\hat{\delta}(1), \hat{\delta}(2), \ldots, \hat{\delta}(T)\}$ be the optimal strategy in the interval $[0, T]$. The optimal portfolio holdings $\hat{\delta}(i)$ in the interval $[i - 1, i)$ provide the rules on how to distribute the wealth among different assets depending on the current values of the wealth and the asset prices. Intuitively, we would expect that the optimal rules for the subinterval $[j, T]$

are given by the subset

$$\hat{\delta}^{[j+1]} = \{\hat{\delta}(j+1), \hat{\delta}(j+2), \ldots, \hat{\delta}(T)\}$$

of the optimal holdings for the interval $[0, T]$. Formally, this relationship is expressed through the **principle of dynamic programming, DPP,** which says that

$$V(t, x) = \sup_{\vec{\delta}} E_{t,x}[V(t+1, X^{\vec{\delta}}(t+1))] \qquad (4.20)$$

where $\vec{\delta} = \vec{\delta}(t)$ is a portfolio strategy for the period $[t, t+1)$.

In other words, suppose that Taf knows how to trade optimally from time $t+1$ on, hence also knows the function $V(t+1, x)$. At moment t, Taf only has to find the optimal strategy $\hat{\delta}$ for the period $[t, t+1)$, the strategy that produces the "best" wealth $X^{\vec{\delta}}(t+1)$ at time $t+1$ (that is, the wealth level corresponding to the optimal allocation among existing securities) for the problem (4.20). Of course, the strategy is random and depends on the values of the market factors at time t, included in the information available up to time t.

This represents a great simplification over the problem initially considered: the supremum is taken only over all admissible portfolio strategies over the period $[t, t+1)$. We do not have to worry about the whole horizon, but just one period. A proof for equation (4.20) is outlined in an appendix to this chapter (section 4.7), and it requires certain assumptions.

The DPP enables us to reduce a multiperiod problem to a sequence of single-period problems, working backward in time, using a so-called **backward algorithm.** Indeed, we know the solution of the value function at the terminal time T:

$$V(T, x) = U(T, x)$$

We know it because at time T there is no optimization to be performed. Then we can use equation (4.20) to compute $V(T-1, x)$, and continue backward until we compute $V(0, x)$, which really is the value we are interested in. The optimal portfolio strategy obtained in this last step will be the optimal strategy to choose at time $t = 0$.

We illustrate the principle of dynamic programming with a couple of examples.

Example 4.6 (Square-Root Utility)   Consider the multiperiod Cox-Ross-Rubinstein model, where the stock price $S(t)$ can move up to $S(t)u$ with probability p, and down to $S(t)d$ with probability q, at each moment t. The bank account pays interest r each period. As before, we assume that $d < 1+r < u$. Our agent Taf has the square-root utility, $U(X(T)) = \sqrt{X(T)}$. We start the backward algorithm by setting

$$V(T, x) = \sqrt{x}$$

We want to find $V(T-1, x)$. Introduce the notation

$$\tilde{u} = u - (1+r), \qquad \tilde{d} = d - (1+r) \qquad (4.21)$$

Suppose that the current wealth at time $T-1$ is $X(T-1) = x$ and the current stock price is $S(T-1) = s$. By the principle of dynamic programming, we have

$$
\begin{aligned}
V(T-1, x) &= \max_{\delta} E_{T-1,x}[\sqrt{X(T)}] \\
&= \max_{\delta} E_{T-1,x}[\sqrt{\delta S(T) + (x - \delta s)(1+r)}] \qquad (4.22) \\
&= \max_{\delta}[p\sqrt{\delta s[u - (1+r)] + x(1+r)}} \\
&\quad + q\sqrt{\delta s[d - (1+r)] + x(1+r)}]
\end{aligned}
$$

As in the single-period case, we do not have to worry about the budget constraint, already accounted for in equation (4.22). Differentiating with respect to δ and setting the derivative equal to zero, we get

$$p\frac{s\tilde{u}}{\sqrt{\delta s\tilde{u} + x(1+r)}} = -q\frac{s\tilde{d}}{\sqrt{\delta s\tilde{d} + x(1+r)}}$$

We can then square both sides and solve for the optimal number of shares $\hat{\delta}$ at time $T-1$ and the optimal proportion $\hat{\Pi}$ to be held in the stock at time $T-1$:

$$\hat{\Pi} := \frac{\hat{\delta}s}{x} = -(1+r)\frac{p^2\tilde{u}^2 - q^2\tilde{d}^2}{p^2\tilde{u}^2\tilde{d} - q^2\tilde{d}^2\tilde{u}} \qquad (4.23)$$

We note that optimal proportion $\hat{\Pi}$ at time $T-1$ does not depend on wealth $X(T-1) = x$ nor on the stock price value $S(T-1) = s$ at time $T-1$, but only on model parameters. Substituting the optimal $\hat{\delta} \cdot s = x\hat{\Pi}$ back into equation (4.22), we see that we get

$$
\begin{aligned}
V(T-1, x) &= p\sqrt{x[\hat{\Pi}\tilde{u} + (1+r)]} + q\sqrt{x[\hat{\Pi}\tilde{d} + (1+r)]} \\
&= c\sqrt{x} \qquad (4.24)
\end{aligned}
$$

for some constant c that depends on model parameters only. The next step would be to find $V(T-2, x)$ as [with $S(T-2) = s$]

$$V(T-2, x) = \max_{\delta} E_{T-2,x}[c\sqrt{\delta S(T-1) + (x - \delta s)(1+r)}]$$

We see that this is of the same form as in equation (4.22), and thus the optimization will give the same result for the optimal proportion $\hat{\Pi}$ as before. Therefore, we can show by induction that the optimal proportion $\hat{\Pi}$ does not change with time, and it is always equal to the expression given by equation (4.23).

Example 4.7 (Log Utility) Consider the same model as in the previous example, but our agent Taf now has the log utility $U(X(T)) = \log(X(T))$. We start the backward algorithm by setting

$$V(T, x) = \log(x)$$

and we want to find $V(T-1, x)$. By the principle of dynamic programming, with $S(T-1) = s$, we have

$$
\begin{aligned}
V(T-1, x) &= \max_{\delta} E_{T-1,x}[\log\{\delta S(T) + (x - \delta s)(1 + r)\}] \\
&= \max_{\delta}[p \log\{\delta s \tilde{u} + x(1 + r)\} + q \log\{\delta s \tilde{d} + x(1 + r)\}]
\end{aligned}
\tag{4.25}
$$

Differentiating with respect to δ and setting the derivative equal to zero, we find the optimal number of shares $\hat{\delta}$ at time $T - 1$ and the optimal proportion to be held in the stock at time $T - 1$:

$$\hat{\Pi} := \frac{\hat{\delta}s}{x} = (1 + r)\frac{[1 + r - (up + dq)]}{\tilde{u}\tilde{d}} \tag{4.26}$$

This expression is of the same type as equation (4.17). We note again that the optimal proportion $\hat{\Pi}$ at time $T - 1$ does not depend on wealth $X(T - 1) = x$ nor on the stock price value $S(T - 1) = s$ at time $T - 1$. Substituting the optimal $\hat{\delta} = x\hat{\Pi}/s$ back into equation (4.25), we get

$$
\begin{aligned}
V(T-1, x) &= E_{T-1,x}[\log\{\hat{\delta} S(T) + (x - \hat{\delta}s)(1 + r)\} \\
&= E_{T-1,x}[\log\{x[\hat{\delta} S(T)/x + (1 - \hat{\delta}s/x)(1 + r)]\}] \\
&= \log(x) + p \log\{1 + r + \hat{\Pi}\tilde{u}\} + q \log\{1 + r + \hat{\Pi}\tilde{d}\} \\
&= \log(x) + A
\end{aligned}
\tag{4.27}
$$

where $A = p \log\{(1+r)(1 + \frac{1+r-(up+dq)}{d})\} + q \log\{(1+r)(1 + \frac{1+r-(up+dq)}{u})\}$ is a function that depends on model parameters only. The next step would be to find $V(T - 2, x)$ as [with $S(T - 2) = s$]

$$V(T-2, x) = \max_{\delta} E_{T-2,x}[\log\{\delta S(T - 1) + (x - \delta s)(1 + r)\}] + A$$

We see that the optimization will give the same result for the optimal proportion $\hat{\Pi}$ as before. Therefore, we can show by induction that the optimal proportion $\hat{\Pi}$ does not change with time, and it is always equal to the expression given by equation (4.26).

For the logarithmic utility, it is straightforward to check that the result is even more general: the optimal proportion of wealth to be held in the stock is of the same form, for all time periods, even if market parameters change randomly from one time period to another. This result is, however, specific to the log utility. In general, for other utility functions the optimal portfolio strategy would take into account future investment opportunities: for example, if the model is such that the today's interest rate of the bond is likely to be higher than the future interest rate (i.e., the dynamics of the interest rate are such that the expected future interest rate is lower than the current interest rate), Taf might invest more in the bond, to take advantage of the potential increase in its price resulting from a drop in interest rates. Because the optimal portfolio for logarithmic utility does not take into account the comparison between the today's and the future values of economic factors, we say that logarithmic utility induces short-sighted, **myopic behavior.**

We also point out that, in the setting of the preceding examples in which the values of the model parameters and the utility function do not change with time, the optimal proportion held in the stock is also time independent for the considered utility functions.

Another interesting property of logarithmic utility is that solving the problem of an agent that maximizes logarithmic utility is equivalent to solving the **optimal growth problem.** We denote by $R(t)$ the rate of return of wealth at moment t:

$$R(t) := \frac{X(t) - X(t-1)}{X(t-1)}$$

Denoting by $\Pi(t)$ the proportion of wealth invested in the risky security at moment t, and using computations similar to those in equation (4.27), we see that

$$1 + R(t) = \frac{X(t)}{X(t-1)} = \left[1 + r + \Pi(t) \left(\frac{S(t)}{S(t-1)} - (1+r) \right) \right] \tag{4.28}$$

We have

$$X(T) = [1 + R(T)][1 + R(T-1)] \cdot \ldots \cdot [1 + R(1)]X(0)$$

and taking logarithms we get

$$\log[X(t)] = \log[1 + R(T)] + \log[1 + R(T-1)] + \cdots + \log[1 + R(1)] + \log[X(0)]$$

Thus, maximizing $E[\log\{X(T)\}]$ is equivalent to maximizing expected growth rate $E[\log\{1 + R(t)\}]$ for every t independently. The maximization is easy, using equation (4.28), and gives the same result for the optimal $\hat{\Pi}$ as before.

In figure 4.2 we graph the log-optimal proportion $\hat{\Pi}$ held in the stock against the probability p of the upward move p. For example, if $p = 0.6$, Taf should have $\hat{\Pi} = 0.84$, or keep 84% of his wealth in the stock, while if $p = 0.4$, then $\hat{\Pi} = -0.84$, and the amount equal to 84% of his wealth should be sold short in the stock. We see that the proportion $\hat{\Pi}$ held

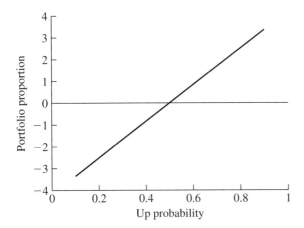

Figure 4.2
Logarithmic utility. The proportion of wealth in stock increases with the probability of an upward move. Here,
$r = 0.05, u = 1.3, d = 0.8$.

in the stock is very sensitive to the choice of the probability of the upward and downward
moves.

4.2.3   Optimal Portfolios in the Merton-Black-Scholes Model

For the reader who does not want to go through the continuous-time section that follows, we want to state here simple and elegant formulas for the optimal portfolios in the
Merton-Black-Scholes model introduced in section 3.3.1. For the logarithmic utility the portfolio weight $\hat{\Pi}$ in the risky asset S that maximizes expected utility from terminal wealth
$E[U(X(T))]$ is given by

$$\hat{\Pi}(t) = \frac{\mu - r}{\sigma^2}$$

at all times t. The rest is held in the risk-free asset. For example, if the risk-free rate is
$r = 5\%$, the mean log-return of asset S is $\mu = 8\%$, and the volatility is $\sigma = 20\%$, then the
investor with log utility should hold $(0.08 - 0.05)/0.04 = 0.75$ or 75% of his money in S
and 25% in the risk-free asset, at all times. For the power utility $U(x) = x^\gamma$, the optimal
portfolio weight is

$$\hat{\Pi}(t) = \frac{\mu - r}{(1 - \gamma)\sigma^2}$$

at all times t.

4.2.4 Utility from Consumption

In case Taf also cares about consumption, he would face the following optimization problem:

$$V(t, x) := \sup_{c, \vec{\delta}} E_{t,x} \left[\sum_{t=0}^{T-1} U_1(c(t)) + U_2(X^{c, \vec{\delta}}(T)) \right] \tag{4.29}$$

In addition to the maximization over portfolio processes $\vec{\delta}$, Taf also has to choose an optimal consumption process c. We state **the dynamic programming principle for optimal consumption choice,** similar to the one considered in the previous section:

$$V(t, x) = \sup_{c, \vec{\delta}} \{ U_1(c(t)) + E_{t+1,x}[V(t + 1, X^{c, \vec{\delta}}(t + 1))] \}, \qquad V(T, x) = U_2(x)$$

This equation can be used to compute the optimal strategy following the procedure we described previously.

4.3 Utility Maximization in Continuous Time

The principle of dynamic programming that we described in the multiperiod discrete-time setting can be extended to continuous-time models. The resulting optimality condition is known as the **Hamilton-Jacobi-Bellman partial differential equation (HJB PDE),** in recognition of the contributors to this very useful technical tool. This methodology was incorporated into financial economics by Merton. Almost 20 years later a completely different approach to solving the same type of problems was introduced. That approach is called **the martingale approach** or **convex duality.** Although the approach was introduced in continuous time, it is straightforward to extend it to multiperiod discrete-time models. However, the approach is simple to use only in complete-market models. Later in the book we will use the martingale approach to study the no-arbitrage pricing theory, both in discrete and in continuous time.

4.3.1 Hamilton-Jacobi-Bellman PDE

Consider now the continuous-time version of the portfolio optimization problem for our investor Taf, who only cares about final wealth and has to decide the allocation of wealth between stocks and the risk-free asset. We assume the simplest Merton-Black-Scholes setting, with one stock and the bank account. The problem of the individual is to find the **value function** V that satisfies

$$V(t, x) = \sup_{\pi} E_{t,x}[U(X^{\pi}(T))] \tag{4.30}$$

where we assume that the initial condition is $X(t) = x$; that is, Taf starts with x dollars at time t. The supremum is taken over all admissible portfolios. The theory for solving such problems is very technical, but some of its most useful results will not be too difficult to state, in the language of previous sections.

Recall the wealth equation

$$dX^\pi = [rX^\pi + \pi(\mu - r)]\,dt + \pi\sigma\,dW \tag{4.31}$$

For a given portfolio strategy π (not necessarily optimal) we introduce the associated expected utility

$$J(t, x; \pi) = E_{t,x}[U(X^\pi(T))] \tag{4.32}$$

Suppose that the portfolio strategy π is of the **feedback form**

$$\pi(t) = \pi(t, X^\pi(t))$$

for some deterministic function $\pi(t, x)$. In fact, it can be shown that the optimal strategy has to be of the feedback form in this model. Then the function $J = J(t, x)$ is an expected value of a function of a diffusion process X^π, and, as such, it is a function of (t, x) only. Such functions can be connected to partial differential equations. We now introduce a very important result in that regard, which will help solve the problem Taf faces. We denote by J_t the partial derivative of J with respect to the first argument and by J_x the partial derivative with respect to the second argument.

PROPOSITION 4.1   Consider the expected utility J of equation (4.32), with π being of the feedback form. Under technical conditions, it satisfies the PDE

$$J_t + \tfrac{1}{2}\pi^2\sigma^2 J_{xx} + \pi(\mu - r)J_x + rxJ_x = 0, \qquad J(T, x) = U(x)$$

"Proof" of the Proposition   Since $J(t, X^\pi)$ is a function of the diffusion process X^π, we can derive its dynamics using Itô's rule (assuming J is smooth enough) as

$$dJ = \left(J_t + J_x(\pi(\mu - r) + rX^\pi) + \tfrac{1}{2}J_{xx}\pi^2\sigma^2\right)dt + J_x\pi\sigma\,dW$$

or, integrating the previous expression from a starting point $J(t, x)$,

$$J(T, X^\pi(T)) = U(X^\pi(T))$$
$$= J(t, x) + \int_t^T \left[J_u + J_x(\pi(\mu - r) + rX^\pi) + \tfrac{1}{2}J_{xx}\pi^2\sigma^2\right]du$$
$$+ \int_t^T J_x\pi\sigma\,dW$$

Taking expectations on both sides of the previous equation and rearranging, we obtain

$$J(t, x) = E_{t,x}[U(X^\pi(T))] - E_{t,x}\left[\int_t^T [J_u + J_x(\pi(\mu - r) + rX^\pi) + \tfrac{1}{2}J_{xx}\pi^2\sigma^2]\,du\right]$$

because the expectation of the dW integral is zero (under some technical conditions). However, by definition, $J(t, x) = E_{t,x}[U(X^\pi(T))]$, and, therefore, the expectation of the integral on the right-hand side has to be equal to zero. Taking a derivative with respect to the time argument at the point t, we see that J has to satisfy the PDE from the statement of the proposition (again, assuming some technical conditions).   ∎

This is a special case of a more general result called the **Feynman-Kac theorem,** which we will state later in the book.

The following theorem presents the solution to our problem. We do not present the proof, which is very technical and is a consequence of the principle of dynamic programming in continuous time.

THEOREM 4.1   Consider the value function

$$V(t, x) = \sup_\pi J(t, x; \pi)$$

where J is as in equation (4.32). Under technical conditions, the value function V satisfies the **Hamilton-Jacobi-Bellman PDE (HJB PDE):**

$$V_t + \sup_\pi \left[\tfrac{1}{2}\pi^2\sigma^2 V_{xx} + \pi(\mu - r)V_x\right] + rxV_x = 0, \qquad V(T, x) = U(x) \qquad (4.33)$$

Moreover, if the supremum in this equation is attained at some function $\hat{\pi}(t, x)$ then the optimal portfolio process $\hat{\pi}(t)$ is given in the feedback form as

$$\hat{\pi}(t) = \hat{\pi}(t, X^{\hat{\pi}}(t)) \qquad (4.34)$$

In other words, we have the following remarkable result of the **stochastic control theory:** the value function $V(\cdot, \cdot)$, supremum of the functions $J(\cdot, \cdot; \pi)$, satisfies the PDE obtained from the PDE satisfied by the functions $J(\cdot, \cdot; \pi)$ simply by taking the supremum over π.

Expression (4.34) means that the optimal portfolio value at time t is obtained by evaluating the deterministic function $\hat{\pi}(t, \cdot)$ at the current value of the wealth process $X^{\hat{\pi}}(t)$. In our portfolio optimization problem it is easy to find the maximizing function $\hat{\pi}(t, x)$ in the HJB PDE: we differentiate $(1/2)\pi^2\sigma^2 V_{xx} + \pi(\mu - r)V_x$ with respect to π and set the derivative equal to zero to get

$$\pi\sigma^2 V_{xx} + (\mu - r)V_x = 0$$

This step yields an expression for the optimal portfolio function in terms of the value function:

$$\hat{\pi}(t, x) = -\sigma^{-1}\theta \frac{V_x(t, x)}{V_{xx}(t, x)} \qquad (4.35)$$

where

$$\theta = \sigma^{-1}(\mu - r)$$

This quantity is called **market price of risk, risk premium,** or **relative risk.** It compares the return rates of the risky asset and the risk-free asset, normalized by the volatility of the risky asset. We will meet this quantity again in later chapters.

Substituting the optimal $\hat{\pi}$ into the HJB equation (we can omit the supremum now), we obtain the equivalent version of the HJB PDE for our problem

$$V_t - \frac{\theta^2}{2}\frac{(V_x)^2}{V_{xx}} + rxV_x = 0, \qquad V(T, x) = U(x) \qquad (4.36)$$

Example 4.8 (Logarithmic Utility) The case of the logarithmic utility function

$$U(x) = \log(x)$$

is typically the easiest. We conjecture that the solution to the HJB PDE might be of the form

$$V(t, x) = \log(x) + K(T - t)$$

for some constant K. Indeed, using

$$V_t = -K, \qquad V_x = \frac{1}{x}, \qquad V_{xx} = -\frac{1}{x^2}$$

we see that this function satisfies the HJB PDE (4.36) if we take

$$K = r + \theta^2/2$$

From equation (4.35) we see that the optimal portfolio is given by

$$\hat{\pi}(t) = \sigma^{-1}\theta X^{\hat{\pi}}(t) \qquad (4.37)$$

Or, equivalently, the optimal proportion of wealth to be invested in the stock is constant and given by

$$\hat{\Pi}(t) := \frac{\hat{\pi}(t)}{X^{\hat{\pi}}(t)} = \sigma^{-2}(\mu - r)$$

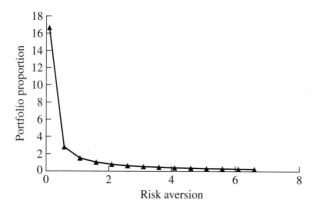

Figure 4.3
Power utility: proportion held in stock decreases as risk aversion gets higher. Here, $\mu = 0.2, \sigma = 0.3, r = 0.05$.

In other words, it is optimal to keep in the risky asset a percentage of wealth proportional to the difference between the return rates of the risky asset and the risk-free asset, and inversely proportional to the variance of log-returns.

In Problem 15 you are asked to show that for the power utility function

$$U(x) = \frac{x^{\gamma}}{\gamma}, \quad \gamma < 1$$

the optimal portfolio is

$$\hat{\Pi}(t) = \frac{\hat{\pi}(t)}{X^{\hat{\pi}}(t)} = \sigma^{-2}\frac{\mu - r}{1 - \gamma} \tag{4.38}$$

We see that the optimal portfolio depends heavily on the stock's drift μ and the investor's risk aversion γ. We also see that the larger the risk aversion of the investor (the smaller γ), the lower the optimal investment in the risky asset. Moreover, in this situation in which the model parameters and the utility function do not depend on time, the optimal proportion of wealth to be held in the stock is also time independent. We illustrate the dependence of the optimal proportion $\hat{\Pi}$ on the risk aversion $1 - \gamma$ in figure 4.3.

It should be pointed out that the log-utility case can be solved directly in the Merton-Black-Scholes setting, without resorting to the HJB PDE. We first replace the amount in the stock π by the proportion of wealth held in the stock $\Pi = \pi/X^{\pi}$ in the wealth equation (4.31) to get

$$dX^{\pi} = X^{\pi}[r + \Pi(\mu - r)]\,dt + \Pi\sigma\,dW] \tag{4.39}$$

An application of Itô's rule verifies that the solution to this equation is

$$X^\pi(t) = x \exp\left\{ \int_0^t \left[r + \Pi(u)(\mu - r) - \tfrac{1}{2}\sigma^2\Pi^2(u) \right] du + \int_0^t \Pi(u)\sigma \, dW(u) \right\}$$

Using this, we obtain

$$E[\log(X^\pi(T))]$$
$$= \log(x) + E\left[\int_0^T \left(r + \Pi(u)(\mu - r) - \tfrac{1}{2}\sigma^2\Pi^2(u) \right) du + \int_0^T \Pi(u)\sigma \, dW(u) \right]$$

Since the expectation of the stochastic integral is zero, we see that it is sufficient to maximize

$$\Pi(u)(\mu - r) - \tfrac{1}{2}\sigma^2\Pi^2(u) \tag{4.40}$$

Differentiating with respect to $\Pi(u)$ and setting the derivative equal to zero, we get the same expression for the optimal proportion $\hat{\Pi}$ as before.

We now consider the case of the agent who also derives utility from consumption. Recall that in continuous time we measure utility of the consumption rate, nonnegative adapted process c, such that the total (cumulative) amount of money $C(t)$ spent on consumption by time t is given by $C(t) = \int_0^t c(u) \, du$. The mixed, terminal wealth/consumption utility maximization problem is

$$V(t, x) = \sup_{\pi, c} E_{t,x}\left[U_1(X^{\pi,c}(T)) + \int_0^T U_2(c(u)) \, du \right] \tag{4.41}$$

The wealth equation becomes

$$dX^{\pi,c} = [rX^{\pi,c} + \pi(\mu - r)] \, dt + \pi\sigma \, dW - c \, dt \tag{4.42}$$

We leave as an exercise in Problem 26 the argument that the HJB PDE should be

$$V_t + \sup_{\pi, c}\left\{ \tfrac{1}{2}\pi^2\sigma^2 V_{xx} + [\pi(\mu - r) - c]V_x + U_2(c) \right\} + rxV_x = 0, \qquad V(T, x) = U_1(x) \tag{4.43}$$

Taking the derivative with respect to c we see that the optimal consumption is given by

$$\hat{c}(t) = (U_2')^{-1}(V_x(t, X^{\hat{\pi},\hat{c}}(t))) \tag{4.44}$$

The notation here is that f^{-1} denotes the inverse of function f; that is,

$$f^{-1}(f(x)) = x$$

In Problems 24 and 25 we ask for the solution to the log and power utility functions.

4.4   Duality/Martingale Approach to Utility Maximization

Dynamic programming is a standard approach for solving utility maximization problems. More recently, another approach has been developed within the finance and financial mathematics literature to solve such problems. It is based on a connection between the pricing/hedging of securities and the optimal solution to the utility maximization problem. We present it first in the simple single-period binomial model.

4.4.1   Martingale Approach in Single-Period Binomial Model

Consider a security with today's price $S(0)$, and at time one its price $S(1)$ has either value s^u with probability p or value s^d with probability $1 - p$. We assume that $s^d < (1+r)S(0) < s^u$, to avoid arbitrage. Suppose our investor Taf has initial capital x and wants to find the optimal number of shares δ of security to hold, while depositing the rest of his wealth in the bank account with single-period interest rate r. In other words, his wealth at time one is

$$X(1) = \delta S(1) + (x - \delta S(0))(1 + r)$$

Taf wants to maximize his expected utility

$$E[U(X(1))] = pU(X^u) + (1 - p)U(X^d)$$

where X^u, X^d is his terminal wealth $X(1)$ in the case $S(1) = s^u$, $S(1) = s^d$, respectively. Substituting for these values, taking the derivative with respect to δ, and setting it equal to zero, we get

$$pU'(X^u)(s^u - S(0)(1 + r)) + (1 - p)U'(X^d)(s^d - S(0)(1 + r)) = 0$$

The left-hand side can be written as $E[U'(X(1))(S(1) - S(0)(1 + r))]$, which, when made equal to zero, implies, with X replaced by $\hat{X}$,

$$S(0) = E\left[\frac{U'(\hat{X}(1))}{E[U'(\hat{X}(1))]}\frac{S(1)}{1 + r}\right] \tag{4.45}$$

This is a necessary condition for a random variable $\hat{X}(1)$ to be the optimal terminal wealth for our investor. Denote now

$$Z(1) := \frac{U'(\hat{X}(1))}{E[U'(\hat{X}(1))]} \tag{4.46}$$

Note that

$$E[Z(1)] = 1$$

Then, we see that the price of our security S is given by

$$S(0) = E\left[\frac{Z(1)}{1+r}S(1)\right]$$
(4.47)

The random variable $Z(1)$ is sometimes called **change of measure,** while the ratio $Z(1)/(1+r)$ is called **state-price density, stochastic discount factor, pricing kernel,** or **marginal rate of substitution,** depending on the context and interpretation. We will see that prices of most securities (with some exceptions, like American options) in the models of this book are of this form: the today's price $S(0)$ is an expected value of the future price $S(1)$, multiplied ("discounted") by a certain random factor.

There is another interpretation of this formula, using a new probability; hence the name "change of (probability) measure." More precisely, define

$$p^* := p\frac{U'(\hat{X}^u)}{E[U'(\hat{X}(1))]}, \qquad 1 - p^* = (1-p)\frac{U'(\hat{X}^d)}{E[U'(\hat{X}(1))]}$$

We can see that p^* is a probability, and we interpret p^* and $1 - p^*$ as modified probabilities of s^u and s^d. Then, we can write equation (4.45) as

$$S(0) = E^*\left[\frac{S(1)}{1+r}\right]$$
(4.48)

where E^* denotes the expectation under the new probabilities, p^*, $1 - p^*$. In multiperiod models, if r is the interest per period, this becomes

$$\frac{S(t)}{(1+r)^t} = E_t^*\left[\frac{S(T)}{(1+r)^T}\right]$$
(4.49)

where E_t^* is the expectation conditional on the information available by time t. In the terminology of probability theory, we say that the process

$$M(t) := \frac{S(t)}{(1+r)^t}$$

is a **martingale** under the new probabilities, since it satisfies the so-called **martingale property**

$$M(t) = E_t^*[M(T)]$$
(4.50)

To recap, we have seen that for a random variable $\hat{X}(1)$ to be optimal terminal wealth in our single-period model, a martingale-like property (4.45) has to be satisfied. We now want to ask a reverse question: among all random variables $Z(1)$ that satisfy equation (4.47) and have expectation equal to one, can we find the one that corresponds to the optimal terminal wealth through equation (4.46)? If we can, then we would also solve the utility maximization problem. This solution is not easy in general models, but it is not very hard in markets that are complete, that is, markets in which every contingent claim can be replicated. As we will see later, the reason is that in such markets there is only one random variable that satisfies equation (4.47), and it is usually not difficult to find. Let us see how this process works in our single-period binomial model.

In such a model, any random variable $Z(1)$ can take only two values, say z^u with probability p and z^d with probability $1 - p$. Since we require that $E[Z(1)] = 1$, we get

$$pz^u + (1 - p)z^d = 1$$

In addition, condition (4.47) becomes

$$(1 + r)S(0) = pz^u s^u + (1 - p)z^d s^d$$

Solving these two equations, we get

$$z^u = \frac{1}{p} \frac{(1 + r)S(0) - s^d}{s^u - s^d}, \qquad z^d = \frac{1}{1 - p} \frac{s^u - (1 + r)S(0)}{s^u - s^d} \tag{4.51}$$

From equation (4.46) we know that $Z(1) := U'(\hat{X}(1))/\lambda$, for some constant λ. Introduce now the inverse function of U',

$$I(z) = (U')^{-1}(z) \tag{4.52}$$

We see that

$$\hat{X}(1) = I(\lambda Z(1)) \tag{4.53}$$

We have almost solved our optimization problem: if we can find λ, then we know the optimal terminal wealth, and we can compute the optimal portfolio that attains it. We can now find the optimal $\hat{\delta}$ and λ from

$$\hat{X}(1) = \hat{\delta}S(1) + (x - \hat{\delta}S(0))(1 + r) = I(\lambda Z(1))$$

Note that this is a system of two equations (for the up state and the down state) with two unknowns, δ and λ, and it can be solved under mild conditions on the utility function U. See the next section and the Problems for examples.

4.4.2 Martingale Approach in Multiperiod Binomial Model

We now present a similar approach for maximizing expected utility $E[U(X(T))]$ from terminal wealth in the general binomial model. Motivated by the single-period model, we hope to identify a random variable $Z(T)$ such that

$$E[Z(T)\bar{S}(T)] = S(0)$$

where $\bar{S}(t) = S(t)/(1+r)^t$ is the discounted stock price. In fact, we hope for even more, to find a process $Z(t)$ such that

$$E_t[Z(T)] = Z(t), \qquad Z(0) = 1 \tag{4.54}$$

and

$$E_t[Z(T)\bar{S}(T)] = Z(t)\bar{S}(t) \tag{4.55}$$

for all T and $t < T$. Therefore, we want $Z(t)$ to be a martingale, as well as process $Z(t)S(t)$ to be a martingale. We want to argue that this property would imply that $Z(t)\bar{X}(t)$ is also a martingale, and in particular, that it satisfies

$$E[Z(T)\bar{X}(T)] = E[\bar{Z}(T)X(T)] = x \tag{4.56}$$

where $x = X(0)$ is the initial capital of the investor. In order to see this point, note that

$$E[Z(T)\bar{X}(T)] = E[E_{T-1}[Z(T)(\delta(T-1)\bar{S}(T) + \bar{X}(T-1) - \delta(T-1)\bar{S}(T-1))]]$$

where $\delta(T-1)$ is the number of shares of stock held at time $T-1$. Since

$$E[E_{T-1}[Z(T)\delta(T-1)\bar{S}(T-1)]] = E[Z(T-1)\delta(T-1)\bar{S}(T-1)]$$

by equation (4.54), then if equation (4.55) holds, we get

$$E[Z(T)\bar{X}(T)] = Z(T-1)\bar{X}(T-1)$$

Continuing in the same manner for $t = T-2, T-3, \ldots$, we get equation (4.56).

We can consider equation (4.56) to be a constraint in our maximization problem. In other words, we can consider the Lagrangian

$$E[U(X(T))] - \lambda(E[\bar{Z}(T)X(T)] - x)$$

where λ is a Lagrange multiplier. Then we take the derivative with respect to $X(T)$ and set it equal to zero. We do this step state by state, since $X(T)$ is a random variable. We get the following condition for the optimal $\hat{X}(T)$:

$$E[U'(\hat{X}(T)) - \lambda\bar{Z}(T)] = 0$$

In particular, this condition will be satisfied if we can find a portfolio strategy such that

$$\hat{X}(T) = I(\lambda\bar{Z}(T))$$

where I is again the **inverse function of marginal utility** U'. Since condition (4.56) has to hold, λ has to satisfy

$$E[\bar{Z}(T)I(\lambda\bar{Z}(T))] = x \tag{4.57}$$

and it will typically be uniquely determined by this equation. Moreover, if we are in a complete-market model such as our binomial model, we can find a portfolio for which $\hat{X}(T) = I[\lambda\bar{Z}(T)]$, and by conditions (4.56) and (4.57), this portfolio requires exactly x as initial capital. The portfolio can be found by a replication algorithm, such as the backward induction algorithm; see the log-utility example that follows and Problems 16, 17, 19, and 20 for other examples.

The only remaining question is whether we can find a process $Z(t)$ with the preceding properties. Problem 18 asks you to check that the process $Z(t)$, defined as the product of t independent copies of the random variable $Z(1)$ determined by equations (4.51), does indeed satisfy conditions (4.54) and (4.55) in the binomial model. Here, in equations (4.51) we have $s^u = S(0)u$, $s^d = S(0)d$, for some factors $d < 1 + r < u$.

To recap: *In the binomial model the optimal strategy is the strategy that replicates the claim $I(\lambda\bar{Z}(T))$, with λ and $Z(T)$ determined as in the preceding discussion.*

Example 4.9 (Log Utility)   Let $U(x) = \log(x)$. Then $I(z) = 1/z$ and $\lambda = 1/x$. Therefore, we need to have $\hat{X}(T) = x/\bar{Z}(T)$. Moreover, since $\bar{Z}(t)\hat{X}(t)$ is a martingale process,

$$\bar{Z}(t)\hat{X}(t) = E_t[\bar{Z}(T)\hat{X}(T)] = x$$

In particular, at time $t = 1$

$$\hat{X}(1) = x/\bar{Z}(1)$$

Evaluating this at the upper node at time $t = 1$, we see that

$$\delta(0)S(0)u + (x - \delta(0)S(0))(1 + r) = x(1 + r)/z^u$$

where z^u is given in equations (4.51). If we solve this equation, we will get that the optimal proportion at time $t = 0$ to be held in the stock is

$$\frac{\hat{\delta}(0)S(0)}{x} = \frac{(1 + r)[up + d(1 - p) - (1 + r)]}{[(1 + r) - d][u - (1 + r)]} \tag{4.58}$$

This is the same result as in equation (4.26), obtained by dynamic programming. Continuing the replication at times $t = 2, 3, \ldots$, we can see that the optimal proportion for logarithmic utility does not change with time.

4.4.3   Duality/Martingale Approach in Continuous Time*

Deriving the HJB PDE is a standard continuous-time approach for solving stochastic control problems such as the utility maximization problem. The alternative approach, described earlier in discrete time, when done in general models, is based on convex duality and the fact that in complete markets we can replicate any contingent claim. Intuitively, we can think of wealth at moment T as a random contingent claim, and the agent has to decide what contingent claim it is optimal to replicate (subject to the budget constraint, of course). The duality approach allows us to characterize the optimal contingent claim, that is, the optimal terminal wealth $\hat{X}(T)$. Then the optimal portfolio $\hat{\pi}$ is the one that replicates $\hat{X}(T)$.

Consider the simplest Merton-Black-Scholes setting, with one stock. Recall the market price of risk θ, the quantity given by

$$\theta := \sigma^{-1}(\mu - r)$$

We introduce the following auxiliary stochastic process:

$$Z(t) = e^{-\theta W(t) - \frac{1}{2}\theta^2 t} \tag{4.59}$$

For reasons that will be obvious when we discuss no-arbitrage pricing, this process is called the **risk-neutral density** or the **continuous-time Arrow-Debreu price**. A straightforward application of Itô's rule gives

$$dZ = -\theta Z \, dW, \qquad Z(0) = 1$$

Therefore, Z is a martingale, with expectation equal to 1. The purpose of introducing this process is to "modify" the dynamics of the discounted wealth process and transform it into a process without drift (that is, a process that only has the stochastic dW component and, therefore, under some technical conditions, is a martingale). Using Itô's rule for products, the dynamics (4.31), and recalling the notation $\bar{X}(t) = \exp\{-rt\}X(t)$, we obtain

$$d(Z\bar{X}) = \bar{Z}(\pi\sigma - \theta X)\, dW \tag{4.60}$$

or

$$Z(t)\bar{X}(t) = x + \int_0^t \bar{Z}(u)[\pi(u)\sigma - \theta X(u)]\, dW(u)$$

This expression means that (as we wanted) $Z\bar{X}$ *is a martingale,* if the integrand in the stochastic integral satisfies some technical conditions. Hereafter we assume that, indeed, those conditions are satisfied. As a consequence of the martingale property, we get

$$E_t[Z(T)\bar{X}(T)] = Z(t)\bar{X}(t) \tag{4.61}$$

where E_t denotes expectation conditional on the information available up to time t. In other words, *the expected value of the discounted wealth multiplied by the risk-neutral density is equal to the current wealth.* The dynamic self-financing property implicit in equation (4.31) now implies, by equation (4.61) with $t = 0$, the following ("static") **budget constraint:**

$$E[Z(T)\bar{X}(T)] = x \tag{4.62}$$

The dynamic problem has become a static problem, in the sense that we have to make a choice of what wealth is optimal at time T, as opposed to what process $\pi(t)$ is optimal on the interval $[0, T]$. We have to solve

$$\sup_{X(T)} E[U(X(T))]$$

subject to the constraint

$$E[Z(T)\bar{X}(T)] = x$$

This is equivalent to solving the optimization problem

$$\sup_{X(T),\lambda} E[U(X(T))] - \lambda(x - E[\bar{Z}(T)X(T)]) \tag{4.63}$$

We first present an informal way of finding the optimal solution. Ignoring expected values, differentiating in expression (4.63) with respect to $X(T)$ and setting the derivative equal to zero, we get

$$U'(\hat{X}(T)) = \lambda\bar{Z}(T)$$

for a candidate $\hat{X}(T)$ for optimal terminal wealth. Denoting

$$I(y) := (U')^{-1}(y)$$

the inverse function of marginal utility U', the last equation becomes

$$\hat{X}(T) = I(\lambda\bar{Z}(T)) \tag{4.64}$$

In words, we conjecture that *the optimal terminal wealth is equal to the inverse of marginal utility evaluated at the discounted risk-neutral density,* multiplied by a constant λ. In order to be able to have $\hat{X}(T)$ as the terminal wealth while starting with initial wealth x, we have to choose λ so that the budget constraint is satisfied:

$$E[\bar{Z}(T)I(\lambda\bar{Z}(T))] = x \tag{4.65}$$

We now present a rigorous argument based on convex duality. Introduce a **dual function** $\tilde{U}$ (or **Legendre-Fenchel conjugate function**) to the function U:

$$\tilde{U}(z) = \max_{y>0}[U(y) - yz], \quad z > 0 \tag{4.66}$$

If we differentiate the function inside the maximum with respect to y and set the derivative equal to zero, we get

$$U'(y) = z$$

which means that the optimal y is given by

$$\hat{y} = I(z) \tag{4.67}$$

where $I(z) = (U')^{-1}(z)$ was introduced above. Substituting $\hat{y}$ back into equation (4.66) (and omitting the maximum operator), we see that the dual function is given by

$$\tilde{U}(z) = U(I(z)) - zI(z) \tag{4.68}$$

Note also from the definition of the dual function that

$$U(y) \le \tilde{U}(z) + yz, \quad y > 0, z > 0 \tag{4.69}$$

In particular, setting $y = X^{x,\pi}(T)$ and $z = \lambda\bar{Z}(T)$, for some initial wealth $x > 0$, some portfolio π, some positive number λ, and the discounted risk-neutral density $\bar{Z}(T)$, we get

$$U(X^{x,\pi}(T)) \le \tilde{U}(\lambda\bar{Z}(T)) + \lambda Z(T)\bar{X}^{x,\pi}(T)$$

Taking expectations, and recalling the static budget constraint (4.62), we get the following **duality relationship:**

$$E[U(X^{x,\pi}(T))] \le E[\tilde{U}(\lambda\bar{Z}(T))] + \lambda x \tag{4.70}$$

This means that for every portfolio, for any given $\lambda > 0$, the expected utility is less than the right-hand side. Therefore, we conclude the following:

If we can find a number $\hat{\lambda} > 0$ and a portfolio $\hat{\pi}$ such that its expected utility is equal to the upper bound, that is, such that

$$E[U(X^{x,\hat{\pi}}(T))] = E[\tilde{U}(\hat{\lambda}\bar{Z}(T))] + \hat{\lambda}x \tag{4.71}$$

then $\hat{\pi}$ is optimal.

This conclusion is true because every other portfolio has expected utility that is less than the right-hand side of equation (4.71).

In order to have equality in expression (4.70), two conditions are necessary and sufficient:

1. The maximum in equation (4.66) must be attained; by equation (4.67), this fact means that the *optimal terminal wealth $\hat{X}(T) = X^{x,\hat{\pi}}(T)$ has to satisfy*

$$\hat{X}(T) = I(\hat{\lambda}\bar{Z}(T)) \tag{4.72}$$

2. The budget constraint has to hold; this requirement means that $\hat{\lambda}$ has to be chosen so that

$$E[\bar{Z}(T)\hat{X}(T)] = E[\bar{Z}(T)I(\hat{\lambda}\bar{Z}(T))] = x \qquad (4.73)$$

The following important result guarantees the existence of a portfolio $\hat{\pi}$ that, in our complete-market setting, replicates $\hat{X}(T)$ starting with initial investment x. This result is called the **martingale representation theorem.**

THEOREM 4.2   If a process M is a martingale adapted to the information generated by Brownian motion process W, then it has a representation of the form

$$M(t) = E_t[M(T)] = E[M(T)] + \int_0^t \varphi(u)\,dW(u) \qquad (4.74)$$

for some adapted process φ. In particular,

$$M(T) = E[M(T)] + \int_0^T \varphi(u)\,dW(u)$$

We use this result on the martingale $E_t[\bar{Z}(T)X]$ where

$$X := I(\hat{\lambda}\bar{Z}(T))$$

(See Problem 28 about $E_t[\bar{Z}(T)X]$ being a martingale.) We get

$$\begin{aligned} E_t[\bar{Z}(T)X] &= E[\bar{Z}(T)X] + \int_0^t \varphi(u)\,dW(u) \\ &= x + \int_0^t \varphi(u)\,dW(u) \end{aligned} \qquad (4.75)$$

Let us define processes $\hat{X}(t)$ and $\hat{\pi}$ such that

$$\bar{Z}(t)\hat{X}(t) := E_t[\bar{Z}(T)X], \qquad \bar{Z}[\hat{\pi}\sigma - \theta\hat{X}] := \varphi \qquad (4.76)$$

From equation (4.60) we see that $\hat{X}$ is a wealth process associated with the portfolio $\hat{\pi}$. Moreover, we see from the first equality in equations (4.76) and properties of conditional expectations that $\hat{X}(T) = X$ and $X(0) = E[\bar{Z}(T)X] = x$. Therefore, indeed, the portfolio $\hat{\pi}$ replicates the payoff X starting with initial amount x.

Combining all of the preceding together, we get the main result of this section:

THEOREM 4.3 (OPTIMAL TERMINAL WEALTH)   Consider the problem of maximizing utility from terminal wealth $E[U(X^{x,\pi}(T))]$, starting with initial amount of capital $x > 0$. Suppose that we can find a number $\hat{\lambda} > 0$ such that equation (4.73) is satisfied. Then the optimal portfolio $\hat{\pi}$ is the portfolio that replicates the terminal wealth equal to $I(\hat{\lambda}\bar{Z}(T))$.

We have already proved this theorem—we have shown that such a portfolio attains the maximum possible expected utility, equal to $E[\tilde{U}(\hat{\lambda}\bar{Z}(T))] + \hat{\lambda}x$.

Example 4.10 (Logarithmic Utility)   Let us revisit the example with $U(x) = \log(x)$. We have

$$U'(x) = \frac{1}{x}, \qquad I(z) = (U')^{-1}(z) = \frac{1}{z}$$

From equation (4.72), the optimal wealth level is then

$$\hat{X}(T) = \frac{1}{\hat{\lambda}\bar{Z}(T)}$$

The budget constraint equation for finding $\hat{\lambda}$ is

$$x = E[\bar{Z}(T)\hat{X}(T)] = E\left[\bar{Z}(T)\frac{1}{\hat{\lambda}\bar{Z}(T)}\right]$$

It follows that

$$\hat{\lambda} = \frac{1}{x}$$

We also know that $Z\bar{X}^{x,\hat{\pi}}$ is a martingale (recall equation (4.60)). This implies, using equation (4.72),

$$Z(t)\bar{X}^{x,\hat{\pi}}(t) = E_t[\bar{Z}(T)I(\lambda\bar{Z}(T))] = E_t\left[\bar{Z}(T)\frac{1}{\lambda\bar{Z}(T)}\right] = x$$

In other words, in the case of logarithmic utility the product $Z\bar{X}^{x,\hat{\pi}}$ is constant. However, recall equation (4.60):

$$d(Z\bar{X}) = \bar{Z}[\pi\sigma - \theta X]\,dW \qquad (4.77)$$

Since the differential dx of the constant x is zero, we must have

$$\hat{\pi}\sigma - \theta X^{x,\hat{\pi}} - 0$$

or

$$\hat{\pi}(t) = \sigma^{-1}\theta X^{x,\hat{\pi}}(t) \qquad (4.78)$$

This is, of course, the same result as equation (4.37), obtained by the HJB PDE approach.

In the case of an agent that cares about both consumption and terminal wealth, as in equation (4.41), a similar argument shows that the optimal consumption rate is given by

$$\hat{c}(t) = I_2(\hat{\lambda}\hat{Z}(t)) \qquad (4.79)$$

where I_2 is the inverse function of U_2' and U_2 is, as before, the utility from the consumption rate. Here, $\hat{\lambda}$ has to be chosen so that the following budget constraint is satisfied (see Problem 27):

$$E\left[\bar{Z}(T)I_1(\hat{\lambda}\bar{Z}(T)) + \int_0^T \bar{Z}(u)I_2(\hat{\lambda}\bar{Z}(u))\,du\right] = x \qquad (4.80)$$

As an example, in the case of $U_1 = 0$ and $U_2(c) = \log(c)$, we have

$$\hat{c}(t) = \frac{x}{T\bar{Z}(t)}$$

An advantage of the duality approach is that it is applicable to much more general complete-market models than the Merton-Black-Scholes model. For example, we would get the same expression (4.78) for the optimal log-portfolio even if the constant parameters r, σ, and μ in the model were, instead, adapted stochastic processes $r(t)$, $\sigma(t)$, and $\mu(t)$. For general utilities, however, numerical methods have to be used in order to find the optimal portfolio. The duality approach can also be applied in incomplete markets, but this procedure is much more involved.

4.5 Transaction Costs

We have seen that in many cases it is optimal to keep a certain constant percentage of wealth in each asset. Let us consider the case of one risky asset, stock, and a bank account, in a continuous-time setting. Suppose, for example, that Taf has logarithmic utility, and that $(\mu - r)/\sigma^2 = 0.7$, so that it is optimal to hold 70% of wealth in the stock. In order to keep this proportion at all times, Taf has to move money around continuously. However, this optimal solution has been derived under the assumption that there are no transaction fees when transferring money between stock and bank. This is not the case in practice. It can be mathematically shown (although it is not easy) that in the presence of transaction costs Taf would not trade continuously, but only when the percentage of the money in the stock moves too far away from 70%. There are two main cases, differing in the type of trade Taf should do when this happens:

1. If the transaction costs are proportional to the amount transferred, when the portfolio proportion gets far away from 70% in the stock, say to above 78%, Taf should trade just a little so as to get a bit closer to 70%, say back to 78%;

2. If the transaction costs are fixed regardless of the size of the transaction, when the portfolio proportion gets far away from 70% in the stock Taf should trade so as to get all the way back to 70%.

4.6   Incomplete and Asymmetric Information

In our previous presentation we have assumed that the different prices and parameters of the model were known by the investor. In this section, we consider models in which agents might have various levels of information regarding the asset prices and parameters determining their dynamics. The reason is twofold. First, it is more realistic to assume that people (at least, some people) do not have all available information, or are unsure about some values of economic variables. Second, when there are several agents in the economy, frequently they will not agree about the values of the parameters or prices. For example, one person might think that stock prices are overvalued, while another person thinks prices are fair. Or one person might think the economy will grow, while another person might think it will shrink. We introduce models that allow some flexibility in the quantity and quality of the information of a given agent. Such models are called **models with incomplete, imperfect, partial,** or (in the case of several agents) **asymmetric information.**

4.6.1   Single Period

In single-period models a standard way to model incomplete information and allow for various degrees of information is to assume that the agent "observes" at time 0 the price of the risky security at time 1, $S(1)$, but with some noise. More precisely, Taf observes a "corrupted" value of $S(1)$ given by

$$Y := S(1) + \varepsilon \tag{4.81}$$

where ε is a random variable representing the noise, usually assumed to be normally distributed with mean zero, and possibly correlated with $S(1)$. Frequently it is convenient to assume that the agent tries to maximize the exponential utility

$$\max E\left[-e^{-\alpha X(1)} \,\middle|\, Y\right]$$

where α is the coefficient of risk aversion, $X(1)$ represents wealth, and the expectation is conditional on the information contained in Y.

When $X(1)$ is normally distributed given the knowledge of Y, with mean $E[X(1) | Y]$ and variance $\mathrm{Var}[X(1) | Y]$, the previous objective has the representation

$$\max E\left[-e^{-\alpha X(1)} \,\middle|\, Y\right] = \max \left\{-e^{-\alpha E[X(1)|Y] + \frac{1}{2}\alpha^2 \mathrm{Var}[X(1)|Y]}\right\}$$

This equation can be derived because the **moment-generating function** of a normal random variable X with mean m and variance σ^2 is given by

$$E[e^{tX}] = e^{mt + \frac{1}{2}t^2\sigma^2}$$

Suppose that there is also a risk-free security or bank account that pays interest rate r. From the budget constraint of an individual who starts with initial wealth x and buys δ shares of the risky security, we get

$$X(1) = \delta S(1) + [x - \delta S(0)](1 + r) = \delta[S(1) - (1 + r)S(0)] + (1 + r)x$$

so that

$$E[X(1) \mid Y] = \delta[E[S(1) \mid Y] - (1 + r)S(0)] + (1 + r)x$$

and

$$\text{Var}[X(1) \mid Y] = \delta^2 \, \text{Var}[S(1) \mid Y]$$

The objective, then, is dependent only on the conditional mean and variance of the risky security, and is equal to

$$\max_{\delta} E \left[e^{-\alpha\{\delta(E[S(1)|Y]-(1+r)S(0))+(1+r)x\}+\frac{1}{2}\alpha^2\delta^2 \, \text{Var}[S(1)|Y]} \right]$$

We maximize the exponent in this expression and set the derivative with respect to δ equal to zero, obtaining the optimal strategy

$$\hat{\delta} = \frac{E[S(1) \mid Y] - (1 + r)S(0)}{\alpha \, \text{Var}[S(1) \mid Y]} \tag{4.82}$$

This has a familiar form: the optimal holding of the stock is proportional to the (conditional) expected return of the stock and inversely proportional to its (conditional) variance, adjusted by the degree of risk aversion. In the simple case, when both $S(1)$ and Y are normally distributed, we can compute explicitly the conditional expectation and variance.

4.6.2 Incomplete Information in Continuous Time*

We now consider a continuous-time model

$$dS(t) = S(t)[\mu(t)\, dt + \sigma \, dW(t)]$$

in which the stock drift μ is a given random process. Taf does not observe its value at t but knows its probability distribution. Taf observes stock prices and, through them, learns more and more about the value of μ as time goes by. This is the so-called **Bayesian approach,** and the distribution of μ is called **prior distribution.** The observed prices affect Taf's beliefs on the prior distribution of μ, and he updates that distribution as more information arrives.

This dynamic framework has an interpretation somewhat different than the previous single-period example: in the single-period case, the agent observes future price values, albeit with noise. The quality of the information depends on the "size" (standard deviation) of the noise. In the continuous-time case we are considering here, the agent only observes the present price values, and the quality of the information depends on the "dispersion" of the distribution of the stock drift: the greater the variance of $\mu(t)$, the less the agent knows about it. One of the features of the continuous-time and multiperiod case is the fact that the agent learns over time.

It turns out that the problem of utility maximization in this model can be reduced to a problem of maximization in a model with full information. We now explain this result. Consider the estimate $\tilde{\mu}(t)$ of the drift $\mu(t)$ given by

$$\tilde{\mu}(t) := E[\mu(t) \mid S(u), u \le t]$$

In other words, $\tilde{\mu}(t)$ is the expected value of $\mu(t)$ conditional on the available information provided by the historical stock prices. Mathematically, $\tilde{\mu}$ is the expected value of the **posterior distribution** of μ for an agent who had a prior distribution for μ and has observed the prices over time. Let us see what happens to the model for S if we "force $\tilde{\mu}$ to become the drift":

$$dS(t) = S(t)[\tilde{\mu}(t)\, dt + \sigma\, d\tilde{W}(t)] \tag{4.83}$$

For this equation to be true, we have to have

$$\tilde{W}(t) := W(t) + \int_0^t [\mu(u) - \tilde{\mu}(u)]\, du$$

This is the famous **innovation process** of the **filtering theory.** An agent who sees the price S, who knows the parameter σ, and who "believes" that the expected return is $\tilde{\mu}$, will "see" $d\tilde{W}$ as the noise part of the price change. For an agent with perfect information, we have $\tilde{\mu} = \mu$ and $\tilde{W}$ is exactly W, the true noise part of the return. A fundamental result of the filtering theory is as follows:

The innovation process $\tilde{W}$ is a Brownian motion process adapted to the information given by the observed stock prices.

That is, the agent with incomplete information "lives in a world" in which $\tilde{\mu}$ is the expected return and the innovation process $\tilde{W}$ is a Brownian motion process.

Looking back to equation (4.83) we see why this point is so important: *we have replaced the model with unobserved drift μ with a model with observed drift $\tilde{\mu}$.* Therefore, we can use the methods developed for the model with full information. In particular, we can use the duality approach, which says that the optimal strategy consists in setting the terminal wealth to

$$\hat{X}(T) = I(\hat{\lambda}\bar{Z}(T))$$

Here we have

$$Z(T) = e^{-\int_0^T \tilde{\theta}(u)d\tilde{W}(u) - \frac{1}{2}\int_0^T \tilde{\theta}^2(u)du}$$

with

$$\tilde{\theta}(t) = (\tilde{\mu}(t) - r)/\sigma$$

As in the standard case, the constant $\hat{\lambda}$ is found from the budget constraint

$$E[\bar{Z}(T)I(\hat{\lambda}\bar{Z}(T))] = x$$

Example 4.11 (Logarithmic Utility)   Let us again look at the log utility $U(x) = \log(x)$. We can use the same arguments as in the full-information case, that is, as in Example 4.10. Following the same steps as in that example, we get

$$\hat{\pi}(t) = \sigma^{-1}\tilde{\theta}(t)X^{x,\hat{\pi}}(t) \tag{4.84}$$

We see that the optimal portfolio is of the same form. The only difference is that we replace the unobserved market price of risk θ (equivalently, the unobserved drift μ) by its estimate $\tilde{\theta}$ (equivalently, $\tilde{\mu}$). However, it can be shown that this is not necessarily the case for other utility functions (such as the power utility): *in general, we cannot simply replace θ by $\tilde{\theta}$ in the formula for the optimal portfolio.*

Computing the conditional expectation $\tilde{\mu}$, hence also $\tilde{\theta}$, can sometimes be done explicitly, but, in general, only numerical methods are possible. We consider an example with an explicit formula in the next section.

4.6.3   Power Utility and Normally Distributed Drift*

The following is a fairly difficult example of computing the optimal portfolio under partial information, which requires some results from filtering theory. The reader may want to read the beginning of the example, containing the formula for the optimal portfolio, and skip the rest, that is, the proof of the formula.

Example 4.12 (Power Utility)   We consider power utility $U(x) = x^\gamma/\gamma$, $\gamma < 0$, and the problem of maximizing expected terminal wealth $E[U(X(T)]$. We assume a particularly simple case in which $\theta = (\mu - r)/\sigma$ is assumed to be a time-independent random variable with normal distribution with mean m and variance v, and independent of Brownian motion W. Then, as we will show, the **optimal portfolio proportion for power utility from terminal wealth in the case of normally distributed unobserved stock drift** is given by

$$\hat{\Pi}(t) = \frac{\sigma^{-1}\tilde{\theta}(t)}{1 - \gamma - \gamma V(t)(T - t)} \tag{4.85}$$

where $V(t)$ is the conditional variance of θ, and $\tilde{\theta}(t)$ is the conditional expectation of θ, with both values given subsequently. In particular, we get the optimal portfolio at today's time $t = 0$ by substituting $\tilde{\theta}(0) = m$ and $V(0) = v$.

Recall that the optimal portfolio with full knowledge of θ is given by equation (4.85) with $V(t) \equiv 0$. We see, in the case $\gamma < 0$, that the absolute size of the optimal portfolio proportion in the case of incomplete information on θ gets smaller relative to the case of full information, as the time to maturity $T - t$ is longer and as the conditional variance $V(t)$ (the uncertainty) of θ is larger. It should be mentioned that similar formulas can be obtained in the case of incomplete information on risk premiums of several stocks.

The rest of this example contains a technical proof of the preceding statement. We introduce the risk-neutral Brownian motion W^*, where the relationship between $\tilde{W}$, W^*, and W is given by

$$\tilde{W}(t) = W(t) - \int_0^t \left(\tilde{\theta}(s) - \theta \right) ds = W^*(t) - \int_0^t \tilde{\theta}(s)\, ds$$

Since $\tilde{W}$ is adapted to the price filtration, we see that W^* is also a process adapted to the price filtration. The price process can be written as

$$dS = S(r\, dt + \sigma\, dW^*)$$

as the reader is asked to show in the Problems. First, we have to compute the estimate $\tilde{\theta}(t) = E_t[\theta]$. Since θ is normally distributed, we are in the setting of the famous **Kalman-Bucy filter,** and the filtering theory provides us with the solution

$$\tilde{\theta}(t) = V(t) \left(W^*(t) + \frac{1}{V(0)} m \right) \tag{4.86}$$

where the function $V(t)$ is the conditional variance of the risk premium θ and is given by

$$V(t) := \text{Var}_t(\theta) = \frac{v}{1 + vt}$$

We now recall the duality arguments, as in the full-information case. First, note that we have

$$U'(x) = x^{\gamma - 1}, \qquad I(z) := (U')^{-1}(z) = z^{\frac{1}{\gamma - 1}}$$

Thus, using Theorem 4.3, the optimal terminal wealth is

$$\hat{X}(T) = \frac{x}{E\left[\bar{Z}^{\frac{\gamma}{\gamma - 1}}(T) \right]} \bar{Z}^{\frac{1}{\gamma - 1}}(T)$$

Here, the constant factor

$$c := \frac{x}{E\left[\bar{Z}^{\frac{\gamma}{\gamma-1}}(T)\right]}$$

is chosen so that the budget constraint $E[\hat{X}(T)\bar{Z}(T)] = x$ is satisfied.

We also know that $\bar{Z}X^{x,\hat{\pi}}$ is a martingale. This fact gives the following expression for the optimal wealth process:

$$\bar{Z}(t)X^{x,\hat{\pi}}(t) = c \cdot E_t\left[\bar{Z}^{\frac{\gamma}{\gamma-1}}(T)\right]$$

The so-called **Bayes rule** for conditional expectations says that

$$E_t^*[X] = \frac{1}{Z(t)} E_t[XZ(T)]$$

From this we get

$$X^{x,\hat{\pi}}(t) = c \cdot E^*\left[e^{-r(T-t)}\bar{Z}^{\frac{1}{\gamma-1}}(T)\right] = ce^{rt}e^{-\frac{\gamma}{\gamma-1}rT}Z^{\frac{1}{\gamma-1}}(t) \cdot Y_{\frac{1}{\gamma-1}}(t) \tag{4.87}$$

where

$$Y_\alpha(t) := E_t^*\left[\left(\frac{Z(T)}{Z(t)}\right)^\alpha\right] \tag{4.88}$$

Thus, in order to find the optimal wealth, we need to compute $Y_\alpha(t)$. This computation is done in the following lemma

LEMMA 4.1   For all $\alpha > -1 - \frac{1}{vT}$ we have

$$Y_\alpha(t) = g_\alpha(T - t, \tilde{\theta}(t), V(t)), \quad 0 \le t \le T \tag{4.89}$$

where the function g_α is given by

$$g_\alpha(\tau, x, y) = \sqrt{\frac{(1 + y\tau)^{\alpha+1}}{1 + y\tau(1 + \alpha)}} \exp\left(\frac{\alpha(1 + \alpha)x^2\tau}{2(1 + (1 + \alpha)y\tau)}\right)$$

Proof   We first note that

$$Z(t) = e^{-\int_0^t \tilde{\theta}(u)dW^*(u) + \frac{1}{2}\int_0^t \tilde{\theta}^2(u)du} \tag{4.90}$$

Next, denote

$$A(t) := \frac{v}{2}(W^*)^2(t) + mW^*(t)$$

Then, using Itô's rule, we can check that

$$\int_0^T \tilde{\theta}(t)\,dW^*(t) = \frac{1}{v}V(T)A(T) - A(0) + \int_0^T \left(A(t)\frac{V^2(t)}{v} - \frac{1}{2}V(t) \right) dt$$

Substituting this last identity in expression (4.88) for $Y_\alpha(0)$ and using equation (4.90), you are asked in Problem 30 to show that

$$Y_\alpha(0) = \sqrt{(1+vT)^\alpha}\, \exp\left(\frac{m^2\alpha}{2v} \right) E^*\left[\exp\left(-\frac{\alpha V(T)}{2}(W^*(T) + m/v)^2 \right) \right] \tag{4.91}$$

Moreover, it is well known (or it can be computed directly by integration) that

$$E^*[\exp\{-\beta[W^*(T) + x]^2\}] = \frac{1}{\sqrt{1+2\beta T}}\, \exp\left(-\frac{\beta x^2}{1+2\beta T} \right)$$

for each $\beta > -1/(2T)$ and for each x. Using this in equation (4.91) we finish the proof of the lemma for the case $t = 0$; that is, we see that $Y_\alpha(0) = g(T, m, v)$. A similar proof works for a general value of t, to give $Y_\alpha(t) = g(T - t, \tilde{\theta}(t), V(t))$. ∎

Finally, we want to justify formula (4.85). The preceding computations and equation (4.87) give us an expression for the optimal wealth $X^{x,\hat{\Pi}}(t)$ as a function of $t, W^*(t)$ and $Z(t)$. Using Itô's rule on that function and comparing with the usual representation

$$d\bar{X} = \bar{X}\Pi\sigma\,dW^*$$

we can check that $\hat{\Pi}$ is indeed given by equation (4.85), a task delegated to Problem 30.

4.7 Appendix: Proof of Dynamic Programming Principle

We provide an outline of the proof for the dynamic programming principle. In the general case, a complete rigorous proof is very technical because of the questions of measurability of defined functions and existence of expected values. If we assume a finite set of possible values for the random variables in the model, these difficulties disappear.

Recall the definition of the value function

$$V(t, x) := \sup_{\vec{\delta}^{[t]}} E_{t,x}\left[U\left(X^{\vec{\delta}^{[t]}}(T) \right) \right] \tag{4.92}$$

and the principle of dynamic programming

$$V(t, x) = \sup_{\vec{\delta}} E_{t,x}\left[V\left(t+1, X^{\vec{\delta}}(t+1) \right) \right] \tag{4.93}$$

where $\vec{\delta} = \vec{\delta}(t)$ is a vector of portfolio holdings on the interval $[t, t+1)$.

Assumption   We impose an important Markovian-type assumption here: the conditional expectation

$$E_{t+i}\left[U(X^{\vec{\delta}^{[t]}}(T))\right]$$

given information up to time $t + i \leq T$, depends only on the values of the model random variables at time $t + i$ (including $\vec{\delta}(t+i)$), and not on the past values of the random variables at times before time $t + i$.

In particular, this assumption implies that

$$\sup_{\{\vec{\delta}(t),\vec{\delta}(t+1),...,\vec{\delta}(T-1)\}} E_{t,x}\left[E_{t+1}\left[U(X^{\vec{\delta}^{[t]}}(T))\right]\right]$$

$$= \sup_{\vec{\delta}(t)} E_{t,x}\left[\sup_{\{\vec{\delta}(t+1),\vec{\delta}(t+2),...,\vec{\delta}(T-1)\}} E_{t+1}\left[U(X^{\vec{\delta}^{[t]}}(T))\right]\right]$$

We note that the left-hand side is equal to $V(t, x)$ and the right-hand side is equal to the right-hand side of equation (4.93), and we are done.

Summary

In order to make decisions, financial agents have to establish preference relations between different trading strategies. This purpose can be achieved by using utility functions, which serve as a measure of satisfaction with an individual's wealth and consumption. Utility functions differ in the level of risk aversion, that is, the level of the individual's attitude toward risk. There are several ways of computing optimal policies when maximizing expected utility. The most popular one is based on the principle of dynamic programming. In discrete time, this principle leads to a backward algorithm that finds the optimal policy for a given time period from the optimal behavior in the future periods. In continuous time, it leads to a partial differential equation, called the Hamilton-Jacobi-Bellman PDE. There is also a powerful modern method, called the duality/martingale approach, that works particularly well in the case of complete markets. It provides a way to find the optimal terminal wealth for the utility maximization problem, after which the optimal portfolio is found as the one that replicates this terminal wealth.

In the case of Cox-Ross-Rubinstein and Merton-Black-Scholes models, it is possible to solve explicitly the case of the logarithmic utility. In this case the optimal proportion of wealth held in stock depends only on model parameters. In particular, it is proportional to the difference between the mean return rate of the stock and the risk-free rate, and inversely proportional to the variance of the stock's log-returns. The log utility has a myopic behavior, in the sense that the corresponding optimal portfolio depends only on the current values of the model parameters, disregarding the possible future values.

There is no essential difficulty in extending all the developed methods to the case of maximizing the expected utility of intermediate consumption. However, the models with incomplete or asymmetric information allow nice solutions only in special cases. In the continuous-time complete-market model, the utility maximization problem with incomplete information about the drift of the risky asset can be reduced to a problem with full information on the drift, after taking conditional expectations with respect to the available information.

Problems

1. Show that a preference relation represented by a utility function has to satisfy completeness and transitivity.

†2. You have a choice between two investment opportunities. One pays $20,000 with certainty, while the other pays $30,000 with probability 0.2, $6,000 with probability 0.4, and $1,000 with probability 0.4. Your utility is of the type $U(x) = x^\gamma$, $0 < \gamma < 1$. Moreover, you decide that you are indifferent between the choice of receiving $1,000 for sure, or $1,728 and $512 with a fifty-fifty chance. Find your γ, and decide which opportunity you like better.

3. Consider two projects that you can invest in: project A pays $100 with certainty, while project B pays $200 with probability 0.1, $80 with probability 0.6, and $50 with probability 0.3. Your utility is of the type $U(x) = \alpha x - x^2$. You know that you are indifferent between the choice of receiving $1,000 for sure, or $2,000 and $400 with a fifty-fifty chance. Find your α, and decide which project you like better.

†4. Let $A(x)$ denote the absolute risk aversion of utility function $U(x)$. What is the absolute risk aversion of utility function $V(x) = a + bU(x)$?

5. Show that the logarithmic and the power utility functions have constant relative risk aversion.

†6. Suppose your utility function is $U(x) = \log(x)$. You are considering leasing a machine that would produce an annual profit of $10,000 with probability $p = 0.4$ or a profit of $8,000 with probability $p = 0.6$. What is the certainty equivalent for this random return?

7. Suppose your utility function is $U(x) = -e^{-0.0002x}$. You are considering entering a project which would produce an annual profit of $10,000 with probability $p = 0.6$ or an annual profit of $8,000 with probability $p = 0.4$. What is the certainty equivalent for this random return? What is its buying price if the interest rate is $r = 5\%$ and there is no initial cost of entering the project?

†8. Consider a single-period binomial model: The price of the stock at time 0 is $S(0) = 100$. At time 1 it can move up to 110 with probability $1/3$, and down to 90 with probability $2/3$.

There is also a bank account that pays interest $r = 5\%$ per period. The agent has exponential utility $U(X(1)) = -e^{-0.03X(1)}$. If the agent has \$100 as initial capital, how much should she invest in the stock in order to maximize her expected utility?

9. In the context of Example 4.5, find the optimal proportion of wealth invested in the stock for the power utility.

10. In the context of Example 4.6, use dynamic programming to compute the optimal portfolio for the general power utility, $U(x) = x^\gamma/\gamma$.

11. In the context of Example 4.7, use dynamic programming to compute the optimal portfolio for the exponential utility, $U(x) = 1 - e^{-x}$. It may be helpful to show, by induction, that

$$V(t, x) = 1 - f(t)e^{-(1+r)^{T-t}x}$$

for some function f that depends only on model parameters.

12. Compute the optimal portfolio proportion $\hat{\Pi}$ for the logarithmic utility for various values of the drift μ in the Black-Scholes model while keeping other parameters fixed. Draw a graph similar to figure 4.3 with μ on the horizontal axis.

13. Find the optimal consumption and portfolio strategy for the problem (4.29) for the log utility.

*14. Find the optimal portfolio for the exponential utility from terminal wealth in continuous time by solving the HJB PDE.

15. Show that the optimal portfolio for the power utility from terminal wealth in continuous time is given by equation (4.38), by solving the HJB PDE. Hint: try to find a solution of the HJB PDE of the form $V(t, x) = f(t)x^\gamma$.

†16. Using the martingale approach in the single-period binomial model, find the optimal portfolio strategy for maximizing $E[\log\{X(1)\}]$ and $E[X^\gamma(1)/\gamma]$, for $\gamma < 1$.

17. Using the martingale approach in the single-period binomial model, find the optimal portfolio strategy for maximizing $E[1 - \exp\{-\alpha X(1)\}]$.

18. Show that the process $Z(t)$, defined as the product of t independent copies of the random variable $Z(1)$ determined by equations (4.51) with $s^u = S(0)u$, $s^d = S(0)d$, for some factors $d < 1 + r < u$, does indeed satisfy equations (4.54) and (4.55) in the binomial CRR model.

19. Using the martingale approach in the two-period binomial model, find the optimal portfolio strategy for maximizing $E[X^\gamma(1)/\gamma]$, for $\gamma < 1$.

†20. Using the martingale approach in the two-period binomial model, find the optimal portfolio strategy for maximizing $E[1 - \exp\{-\alpha X(1)\}]$.

*21. In the context of Example 4.10, find the optimal portfolio for the power utility using the duality approach.

*†22. In the context of Example 4.10, find the optimal portfolio for the exponential utility using the duality approach.

**23. Consider a Black-Scholes model in which the constant risk-premium value is denoted $\theta = (\mu - r)/\sigma$. For simplicity, assume $r = 0$. Introduce the process Z by

$$dZ(t) = -\theta Z(t)\, dW(t), \qquad Z(0) = 1$$

a. Show, using the duality method, that the optimal terminal wealth for the problem of maximizing

$$P[X(T) \geq C(T)] = E\left[\mathbf{1}_{\{X(T) \geq C(T)\}}\right]$$

for a given claim $C(T)$, under the constraint $X(T) \geq A(T)$ [where $A(T)$ is another claim], is given as an "option" written on $A(T), C(T), Z(T)$ of the type

$$\hat{X}(T) = C(T)\mathbf{1}_{\{\lambda Z(T)[C(T) - A(T)] \leq 1\}} + A(T)\mathbf{1}_{\{\lambda Z(T)[C(T) - A(T)] > 1\}}$$

Here, $\lambda > 0$ is a constant chosen so that $E[Z(T)\hat{X}(T)] = x$.

b. Suppose now that

$$A(T) = C(T) - k$$

for some constant $k > 0$, and that $X(0) < C(0)$, where $C(t) = E_t[Z(T)C/Z(t)]$ is the replicating process for claim C. Show that the optimal wealth at time t [the price of option $\hat{X}(T)$] satisfies

$$\hat{X}(t) = C(t) - kN\left(\frac{-\theta W(t) + \log(k\lambda) + \frac{1}{2}|\theta|^2 T}{|\theta|\sqrt{T - t}}\right)$$

c. Continuing part b, show also that the optimal portfolio (amount in stock) that replicates this payoff satisfies

$$\hat{\pi}(t) = \pi_C(t) + k\frac{\theta}{|\theta|\sigma\sqrt{T - t}} n\left(N^{-1}\left(\frac{C(t) - \hat{X}(t)}{k}\right)\right)$$

where π_C is the replicating portfolio for claim $C(T)$. Here, N and n are the normal cumulative distribution function and density function, respectively.

*†24. Find the optimal portfolio and consumption strategies for the log utility in continuous time, by solving the HJB PDE (4.43). Hint: try to find a solution of the HJB PDE of the form $V(t, x) = f(t) + g(t)\log x$.

*25. Find the optimal portfolio and consumption strategies for the power utility in continuous time, by solving the HJB PDE (4.43).

*26. Justify equation (4.43) by finding the PDE satisfied by the expected utility

$$J(t, x) = E_{t,x}[U_1(X^\pi(T))] + E_{t,x}\left[\int_t^T U_2(c(u))\, du\right] \qquad (4.94)$$

*27. Use Itô's rule to find the expression for $d(\bar{Z}X)$ in case there is consumption, that is, in case dX is given by equation (4.42). Argue that, at least under technical conditions, the process

$$M(t) := \bar{Z}(t)X(t) + \int_0^t \bar{Z}(u)c(u)\, du$$

is a martingale. In particular, argue that the budget constraint is given by

$$E\left[\bar{Z}(T)X(T) + \int_0^T \bar{Z}(u)c(u)\, du\right] = x$$

*†28. Given a random variable C whose value is known by time T, and such that $E[|C|]$ is finite, show that the process $M(t) := E_t[C]$ is a martingale on the time interval $[0, T]$.

*29. In the continuous-time incomplete-information model, verify that the dynamics of the stock price can be written as

$$dS(t) = S(t)[r\, dt + \sigma\, dW^*(t)]$$

where

$$W^*(t) = W(t) + \int_0^t \theta(u)\, du = \tilde{W}(t) + \int_0^t \tilde{\theta}(u)\, du$$

Those are the dynamics of S in the risk-neutral world; that is, the discounted stock price $\bar{S}$ is a martingale under the probability P^* under which W^* is Brownian motion.

**30. Fill in all the details in the computations of Example 4.12, leading to the optimal portfolio formula (4.85).

Further Readings

The basic consumption-portfolio problem in discrete time is presented in Arrow (1970) and Debreu (1959) [for the notion of risk aversion see Arrow (1971) and Pratt (1964)]. Mas-Collel, Whinston, and Green (1995) study single-period models in detail. Dothan (1990) and Pliska (1997) have a comprehensive treatment of discrete-time models. The problem in continuous time is introduced by Merton (1969). The original book on dynamic programming is Bellman (1957). Dynamic programming pricing of securities in discrete time is presented in Samuelson (1969). The dynamic programming approach in continuous time is applied by Merton (1971). Textbook treatments include Duffie (2001) and Karatzas and Shreve (1998). Mehra and Prescott (1985) present a very influential practical application of this problem that we discuss in the equilibrium section. Optimal investment with transaction costs in continuous time is treated in Constantinides (1986), Davis and Norman (1990), and Cadenillas and Pliska (1999). Duality methods in continuous time are introduced by Karatzas, Lehoczky, and Shreve (1987) and Cox and Huang (1989). Related framework can be found in Duffie and Huang (1985) and Duffie (1986). The effect of incomplete information on security prices has been studied in discrete-time models in different ways. An important early paper in the area is Grossman (1976). The treatment of optimal consumption-portfolio problems with incomplete information in continuous time is originally due to Detemple (1986), Dothan and Feldman (1986), and Gennotte (1986). The derivation of the formula for power utility and normally distributed drift is taken from Cvitanić, Lazrak, Martellini, and Zapatero (2002). The problem of utility maximization in incomplete markets is very difficult in general, and beyond the scope of this book. Some papers on this topic include He and Pagés (1991), Karatzas, Lehozcky, Shreve, and Xu (1991), Cvitanić and Karatzas (1992), Cuoco (1997), and Schroeder and Skiadas (2002).

5 Risk

Which lottery ticket would you pay more for: lottery ticket 1, which pays $1 or $9 with equal probability, or lottery ticket 2, which pays $4 or $5 with equal probability? Lottery 1 has a 50% chance of high gain, but it is also more risky. Your decision is a question of a trade-off between risk and potential reward, and it is the subject of this chapter, which has the following learning objective:

• To present various ways of measuring risk and reward such as the classical mean-variance theory, and the more recent value-at-risk approach

While utility maximization is a sound theoretical way for making comparisons between various investment strategies, more specialized and streamlined methods have been used by practitioners in financial markets. This chapter describes the classic **mean-variance** approach of Harry Markowitz for evaluating different portfolios, which is also the basis for many later developments in the book. The approach is based on comparing the means and the variances of portfolios. We also discuss a modern way of measuring the risk of a portfolio, called **value-at-risk,** or **VaR,** an approach based on computing probabilities of large losses. Both these approaches are given in the one-period, static framework, although there exist extensions to multiperiod models.

5.1 Risk versus Return: Mean-Variance Analysis

The mean-variance analysis was derived by Harry Markowitz in the 1950s as a systematic approach to measuring risks in financial markets. He later received a Nobel Prize in economics for this work. His objective was to establish a criterion for the comparison of different securities and portfolios as a trade-off between their return—as measured by expected return—and risk—as measured by the variance of the return. Although in the original work (Markowitz, 1952) no reference is made to the preferences or utilities of the investors, we will see that, in his approach, there are several implicit assumptions with respect to the preferences of the investors or the probability distribution of the returns of the securities.

The mean-variance approach was originally developed for single-period models. Accordingly, we assume that the trade is established at time 0 and some random return is received at time 1. The approach can be extended to multiperiod models, as we discuss later. Despite the very strong assumptions behind the Markowitz framework, its simplicity makes it a popular tool for gauging whether a portfolio strategy is "efficient." We present this framework next.

5.1.1   Mean and Variance of a Portfolio

If our agent Taf starts with initial capital $X(0)$ and has $X(1)$ at the terminal time 1, the **rate of return** is given by

$$R_X = \frac{X(1) - X(0)}{X(0)}$$

As usual, we assume that $X(1)$ is a random variable, a result of trading in a market with assets whose future values are (possibly) random. As we already pointed out, Markowitz's framework does not assume any specific distribution for these assets. However, it is assumed that only the mean and the variance of a portfolio are relevant for evaluating its performance. There are two possible settings in which that assumption would be fully justified:

• When the distribution of the returns is normal, because a normal distribution is fully characterized by the mean and the variance.

• When the utility of the investors is quadratic. In a single-period model, the quadratic utility of an individual who only cares about final wealth $X(1)$ is represented by

$$E[aX(1) - bX^2(1)] \tag{5.1}$$

where a and b are constant. It is clear from this expression that this investor only cares about the first and the second moment (or, equivalently, the mean and the variance) of the final wealth.

   We therefore assume that the mean and the variance of a given portfolio exist, and we denote them by

$$\mu = \mu_X = E[R_X], \qquad \sigma^2 = \sigma_X^2 = \text{Var}[R_X]$$

We identify a portfolio strategy with a pair (σ, μ).

   Although we take these numbers as given, in practice they have to be computed. There are two basic approaches. First, using information about past returns of a given security, its expected value and variance can be estimated using the mean and the variance of a sample of observations. Second, we can assign probabilities to the possible future returns in our model, and then compute the (theoretical) mean and the variance. In practice, the former method is used more frequently, because it makes the parameters of the model consistent with past returns.

   Next, we want to be able to find the mean and the variance of a portfolio with positions in several assets, if we know the means and the variances of individual assets in the portfolio.

Assume there are N assets in the market, $S_1, \ldots, S_N$, with returns

$$R_i = \frac{S_i(1) - S_i(0)}{S_i(0)}$$

their expected values denoted μ_i, and variances σ_i^2, $i = 1, \ldots, N$. Denote by Π_i the proportion (weight) of the initial capital $X(0)$ held in asset i. Accordingly,

$$\sum_{i=1}^{N} \Pi_i = 1$$

A proportion Π_i can be negative, meaning that Taf is short that asset. Note also that the number of shares δ_i of asset i in the portfolio is given by

$$\delta_i = \frac{\Pi_i X(0)}{S_i(0)}$$

The rate of return of the strategy determined by a portfolio $\Pi = (\Pi_1, \ldots, \Pi_N)$ is

$$R_\Pi = \frac{\sum_{i=1}^{N} \frac{\Pi_i X(0)}{S_i(0)} S_i(1) - X(0)}{X(0)}$$

By dividing all terms in the previous expression by $X(0)$ we get

$$R_\Pi = \sum_{i=1}^{N} \frac{\Pi_i [S_i(1) - S_i(0)]}{S_i(0)} = \sum_{i=1}^{N} \Pi_i R_i \tag{5.2}$$

which means that the return rate of the portfolio is simply the weighted average of the asset return rates. Therefore, this statement is also true for the means:

$$\mu_\Pi = \sum_{i=1}^{N} \Pi_i \mu_i$$

As for the variance, let us first denote

$$\sigma_{ij} := \mathrm{Cov}[R_i, R_j] := E[(R_i - \mu_i)(R_j - \mu_j)]$$

the covariance of R_i and R_j. We compute the variance for the portfolio in the case $N = 2$:

$$\begin{aligned}
\sigma_\Pi^2 &= E[(R_\Pi - \mu_\Pi)^2] \\
&= E[\{\Pi_1 R_1 + \Pi_2 R_2 - (\Pi_1 \mu_1 + \Pi_2 \mu_2)\}^2] \\
&= E\left[\Pi_1^2 (R_1 - \mu_1)^2 + 2\Pi_1 \Pi_2 (R_1 - \mu_1)(R_2 - \mu_2) + \Pi_2^2 (R_2 - \mu_2)^2\right]
\end{aligned}$$

This produces the following **formula for the variance of the return rate** for a portfolio consisting of two assets:

$$\sigma_\Pi^2 = \Pi_1^2 \sigma_1^2 + \Pi_2^2 \sigma_2^2 + 2\Pi_1 \Pi_2 \sigma_{12} \tag{5.3}$$

In the Problems section you are asked to show this extension to N assets:

$$\sigma_\Pi^2 = \sum_{i,j=1}^{N} \Pi_i \Pi_j \sigma_{ij} \tag{5.4}$$

Here, we denote $\sigma_{ii} = \sigma_i^2$.

From this formula we can see how diversifying your portfolio among different assets can reduce your risk. In particular, assume that there are N independent assets (and, therefore, with $\sigma_{ij} = 0$, $i \neq j$), all with the same variance σ^2 and the same mean μ. If we hold each asset with the same proportion $1/N$, the portfolio mean is still equal to μ, and its variance is

$$\frac{1}{N^2} \sum_{i=1}^{N} \sigma^2 = \sigma^2/N$$

In other words, the variance gets smaller with the number of independent assets in the portfolio. Recall now that the correlation ρ between two random variables R_1 and R_2, with variances σ_1^2, σ_2^2 and covariance σ_{12}, is defined as

$$\rho := \frac{\sigma_{12}}{\sigma_1 \sigma_2} \tag{5.5}$$

and we have $-1 \leq \rho \leq 1$. If the assets are not completely independent (that is, if their covariance is different from zero) but they are less than perfectly correlated (the correlation coefficient is smaller than one in absolute value), then diversification also reduces the portfolio variance, but less effectively.

When two securities are perfectly correlated and have different means, it is possible to construct a risk-free portfolio with positive return. We illustrate this point in the following example.

Example 5.1 (Deriving a Risk-Free Portfolio)   Suppose that the stock of company A has an expected return of 10% and a standard deviation of 8%. The stock of company B has an expected return of 14% and a standard deviation of 18%. The correlation between A and B is 1. We want to find the risk-free rate, consistent with no arbitrage. We do so by constructing a portfolio with zero volatility, hence risk-free, and its return rate has to equal the risk-free rate. From equations (5.3) and (5.5), we get

$$\sigma_\Pi^2 = \Pi_A^2 \sigma_A^2 + \Pi_B^2 \sigma_B^2 + 2\Pi_A \Pi_B \sigma_{AB} = (\Pi_A \sigma_A + \Pi_B \sigma_B)^2$$

where we have used the fact that $\rho_{AB} = 1$. We want the variance to be zero, so, since $\Pi_B = 1 - \Pi_A$, we need to have

$$0 = \Pi_A 0.08 + (1 - \Pi_A)0.18$$

with solution $\Pi_A = 1.8$ and, therefore, $\Pi_B = -0.8$. This condition means that for each $100 of investment, we sell short stock B for a total of $80 and we invest $180 in A. The return of this portfolio is

$$\mu_\Pi = \Pi_A \mu_A + \Pi_B \mu_B = 1.8 \cdot 0.1 + (-0.8) \cdot 0.14 = 0.068$$

The risk-free asset has to have the same return, that is, the risk-free rate has to be 6.8%.

5.1.2   Mean-Variance Efficient Frontier

Suppose now that given two portfolios with the same variance, an investor will prefer the one with the higher expected return. Different trading strategies will produce different points (σ, μ) in the plane. We want to get an idea of what kind of mean-variance points we can achieve by investing in two assets only. Let us represent these two assets by points (σ_1, μ_1) and (σ_2, μ_2). Denote the proportion invested in the first asset by Π, so that the proportion invested in the second asset is $1 - \Pi$. For now, we consider only the case when there is neither borrowing nor short-selling, so $0 \leq \Pi \leq 1$. The mean of the portfolio is

$$\mu = \Pi \mu_1 + (1 - \Pi)\mu_2$$

The variance will depend on the covariance between the two assets. Recall the correlation coefficient, defined in equation (5.5). Consider first the case when the two assets are perfectly correlated, with $\rho = 1$. In this case we have $\sigma_{12} = \sigma_1 \sigma_2$. Then the variance of the portfolio is, by equation (5.3),

$$\sigma^2 = \Pi^2 \sigma_1^2 + (1 - \Pi)^2 \sigma_2^2 + 2\Pi(1 - \Pi)\sigma_1 \sigma_2 = [\Pi \sigma_1 + (1 - \Pi)\sigma_2]^2$$

Therefore,

$$\sigma = \Pi \sigma_1 + (1 - \Pi)\sigma_2$$

This expression means that both the mean and the standard deviation of the portfolio are linear combinations of the individual assets' means and standard deviations, respectively. Therefore, by varying the proportion Π, we will trace a straight line in the (σ, μ) plane, between the two assets; see figure 5.1. Similarly, if $\rho = -1$, we can see that (see Problem 3)

$$\sigma = |\Pi \sigma_1 - (1 - \Pi)\sigma_2| \tag{5.6}$$

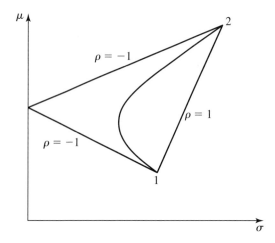

Figure 5.1
Mean-variance graph for portfolios of two assets.

This is represented by the two lines connecting at the μ-axis in figure 5.1. For the values of ρ between -1 and 1, the variance is given by equation (5.3), and varying Π corresponds to a curve between the two assets, such as the one in figure 5.1.

More generally, with N assets, one can obtain portfolios in the region to the right of a curve such as the one in figure 5.2. This region is called the **feasible region.** For a fixed mean return μ, the standard deviation σ for which the point (σ, μ) is on this curve is the smallest standard deviation that can be obtained by trading in these assets, because the point on the curve is the leftmost point in the feasible region with that value of μ. The very leftmost point on the curve is called the **minimum variance portfolio,** because it represents the portfolio that has the smallest possible variance. The part of the curve below this point is not interesting—for each point on the lower part of the curve there is a point on the upper part that has the same variance but a higher mean. The upper part of the curve is called the **efficient frontier,** since our investor Taf prefers smaller variance and higher mean for a portfolio:

The points on the efficient frontier are the points that correspond to the highest mean for a given level of variance, as well as the points that correspond to the lowest variance for a given mean level.

If one of the available assets is a risk-free asset (therefore, with zero variance) and has a (nonrandom) return R, then the feasible region looks like the one in figure 5.3. In order to see that fact, note that a combination of an asset (μ_1, σ_1) with the risk-free asset results in

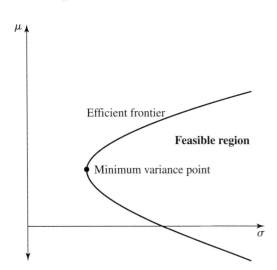

Figure 5.2
The efficient frontier is the upper part of the curve.

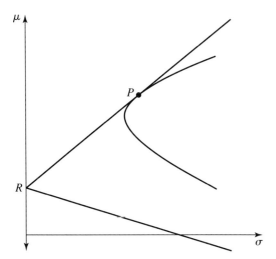

Figure 5.3
Efficient frontier with risk-free asset: The efficient frontier is the upper line. Point P is the mutual fund of risky assets that can be used for creating efficient portfolios of risky assets and the risk-free asset.

the mean and standard deviation

$$\mu = \Pi R + (1 - \Pi)\mu_1, \qquad \sigma = (1 - \Pi)\sigma_1$$

(Recall that any nonrandom quantity has zero variance and zero covariance with any other quantity.) So, when we invest in the risk-free security and any portfolio on the efficient frontier, we can attain any combination (σ, μ) on the straight line between the portfolio and the risk-free rate of return R on the y-axis by changing the proportion Π. The efficient frontier is now the upper line of the feasible region. The curve inside the feasible region in figure 5.3 is the boundary of the feasible region when there is no risk-free asset. The point P where this curve is tangent to the efficient frontier line corresponds to a special portfolio (or mutual fund):

Any portfolio on the efficient frontier line can be obtained by trading in the fund P and the risk-free asset.

This result is called the **one-fund theorem.** It holds because any point on a line can be obtained as a linear combination of the two points R and P on the line. It means that, for the mean-variance investors, in order to be optimal it is sufficient to invest in the single mutual fund P and the risk-free asset. Among all the points on the efficient frontier without the risk-free asset, P is the most important point, because it allows the investor to attain the portfolios on the line that is the efficient frontier in the presence of the risk-free asset. We also observe that the points on this line to the right of and above P can be attained by short-selling the risk-free security and investing the proceeds in the portfolio P.

5.1.3   Computing the Optimal Mean-Variance Portfolio

The mean-variance optimization problem postulates that we consider only portfolios with a given mean return rate equal to μ. Among those, we want to find the portfolio that results in the smallest variance. In other words, with N assets and portfolio weights denoted by $\Pi_i, i = 1, \ldots, N$, we need to solve the optimization problem that consists in minimizing the variance of the portfolio,

$$\frac{1}{2} \min \sum_{i,j=1}^{N} \Pi_i \Pi_j \sigma_{ij}$$

subject to the constraints

$$\sum_{i=1}^{N} \Pi_i \mu_i = \mu, \qquad \sum_{i=1}^{N} \Pi_i = 1 \tag{5.7}$$

The factor $\frac{1}{2}$ in the optimization problem is introduced for convenience only: it simplifies some of the resulting expressions, and, obviously, minimizing the value of half the variance is equivalent to minimizing the variance. Since this is an optimization problem with two constraints, we use two Lagrange multipliers λ_1 and λ_2, and form a **Lagrangian:**

$$L = \frac{1}{2} \sum_{i,j=1}^{N} \Pi_i \Pi_j \sigma_{ij} - \lambda_1 \left(\sum_{i=1}^{N} \Pi_i \mu_i - \mu \right) - \lambda_2 \left(\sum_{i=1}^{N} \Pi_i - 1 \right)$$

Then we differentiate the Lagrangian with respect to all Π_i and set derivatives equal to zero. This step would give us the following N **equations for the optimal mean-variance weights:**

$$\sum_{j=1}^{N} \sigma_{ij} \Pi_j - \lambda_1 \mu_i - \lambda_2 = 0, \qquad i = 1, \ldots, N \tag{5.8}$$

However, we have $N + 2$ unknowns, Π_i's, and λ_i's. The remaining two equations are the constraint equations (5.7).

We show equations (5.8) for the case $N = 2$:

$$L = \frac{1}{2} \left(\Pi_1^2 \sigma_1^2 + \Pi_2^2 \sigma_2^2 + 2\Pi_1 \Pi_2 \sigma_{12} \right) - \lambda_1 (\Pi_1 \mu_1 + \Pi_2 \mu_2 - \mu) - \lambda_2 (\Pi_1 + \Pi_2 - 1)$$

Setting the derivative of L with respect to Π_1 equal to zero, we get

$$\Pi_1 \sigma_1^2 + \Pi_2 \sigma_{12} - \lambda_1 \mu_1 - \lambda_2 = 0$$

Similarly for the derivative with respect to Π_2. This result is in agreement with equation (5.8) when $N = 2$.

Example 5.2 (Two Assets)   In the case of only two assets, the problem becomes degenerate, in the sense that the portfolio weights are determined directly from the constraints (5.7). Indeed, suppose that we want to achieve a mean μ with two assets. Then, denoting by Π the proportion in asset 1 [and, therefore, $(1 - \Pi)$ the proportion in asset 2], we need to have

$$\Pi \mu_1 + (1 - \Pi) \mu_2 = \mu$$

This gives

$$\Pi = \frac{\mu - \mu_2}{\mu_1 - \mu_2}$$

Suppose for example that $\mu_1 = 0.15$ and $\mu_2 = 0.10$. Then we have

$$\Pi_1 = 20(\mu - 0.1), \qquad \Pi_2 = 3 - 20\mu$$

The portfolio variance is given by

$$\sigma^2 = 400(\mu - 0.1)^2 \sigma_1^2 + (3 - 20\mu)^2 \sigma_2^2 + 40(\mu - 0.1)(3 - 20\mu)\sigma_{12}$$

This equation determines the mean-variance curve in the (σ, μ) plane. Suppose, for simplicity, that the assets are uncorrelated, $\sigma_{12} = 0$, and that $\sigma_1^2 = \sigma_2^2 = 0.01$. The variance is then

$$\sigma^2 = 4(\mu - 0.1)^2 + (0.3 - 2\mu)^2$$

Let us find the minimum-variance portfolio. We look for an expected return μ such that the portfolio with such a return has the lowest possible variance. Setting the derivative with respect to μ equal to zero, we obtain

$$\mu = 0.125$$

The variance corresponding to this mean is

$$\sigma^2 = 0.005$$

and it is the minimum variance for the portfolios consisting of these two assets. The proportions to be held in the two assets are

$$\Pi_1 = 20(0.125 - 0.1) = 0.5 = 50\%, \qquad \Pi_2 = 50\%$$

Example 5.3 (Three Assets) Consider now the case of three uncorrelated assets, all having the same variance equal to 0.01. Suppose also that

$$\mu_1 = 0.1, \qquad \mu_2 = 0.2, \qquad \mu_3 = 0.3$$

Then, equations (5.8) become

$$0.01\Pi_1 - 0.1\lambda_1 - \lambda_2 = 0$$
$$0.01\Pi_2 - 0.2\lambda_1 - \lambda_2 = 0$$
$$0.01\Pi_3 - 0.3\lambda_1 - \lambda_2 = 0$$

Together with the constraints

$$0.1\Pi_1 + 0.2\Pi_2 + 0.3\Pi_3 = \mu, \qquad \Pi_1 + \Pi_2 + \Pi_3 = 1$$

these equations can be solved for Π_i, $i = 1, 2, 3$, in terms of μ (see Problem 9).

To recap, equations (5.8) give us a way to find optimal weights for the assets in our portfolio (that is, the weights that yield the lowest possible variance for a given expected return) in a single-period model, assuming we know the variance-covariance structure, as well as the expected return of the assets. We will use mean-variance optimization later, in our discussion of equilibrium in chapter 13.

5.1.4 Computing the Optimal Mutual Fund

It may be useful for practical purposes to identify the mutual fund P from the one-fund theorem. We first point out that the first-order condition (5.8) is satisfied regardless of the pool of assets. That is, even if one of the assets is risk-free with zero variance and zero covariance with all other assets, equation (5.8) has to hold. Then the straight line that goes through R and P is also characterized by equation (5.8). Out of all the points on that line, we look for the point P that implies zero investment in the risk-free asset.

More precisely, suppose that there is a risk-free asset with mean return $\mu_1 = R$, and that Taf wants to find the proportions Π_i, $i = 2, \ldots, N$ of the risky assets held in the fund P. This fund is on the efficient frontier (which is the straight line that goes through R and P), and hence, the proportions Π_i can be found from equation (5.8), taking into account that the proportion Π_1 of the risk-free asset in the fund is zero. In other words, we have to solve the mean-variance optimization problem with

$$\Pi_1 = 0, \qquad \sum_{i=2}^{N} \Pi_i = 1$$

Since $\sigma_{1j} = 0$, $j = 1, \ldots, N$, from the equation with $i = 1$ in equation (5.8) we get

$$\lambda_2 = -\lambda_1 R$$

Substituting this in equations (5.8) with $i = 2, \ldots, N$, we get the system

$$\sum_{j=2}^{N} \sigma_{ij} \Pi_j = \lambda_1 (\mu_i - R), \qquad i = 2, \ldots, N \tag{5.9}$$

We can solve this system for Π_i's in terms of λ_1, and then find λ_1 from the condition $\sum_{i=2}^{N} \Pi_i = 1$.

Example 5.4 (Optimal Mutual Fund) Taf can invest in asset 1 with $\mu_1 = 0.2$, $\sigma_1 = 0.4$ and asset 2 with $\mu_2 = 0.3$, $\sigma_2 = 0.5$, with correlation $\rho = 0.2$, and in the risk-free asset with return $R = 0.05$. He wants to identify the weights of asset 1 and asset 2 in the mutual fund P. The system (5.9) becomes

$$\sigma_1^2 \Pi_1 + \sigma_{12} \Pi_2 = \lambda_1 (\mu_1 - R)$$
$$\sigma_2^2 \Pi_2 + \sigma_{21} \Pi_1 = \lambda_1 (\mu_2 - R)$$

Since $\sigma_{12} = \sigma_{21} = \rho \sigma_1 \sigma_2 = 0.04$, we get

$$0.16 \Pi_1 + 0.04 \Pi_2 = 0.15 \lambda_1$$
$$0.25 \Pi_2 + 0.04 \Pi_1 = 0.25 \lambda_1$$

Solving this system we get

$$\Pi_1 = 0.7162\lambda_1, \qquad \Pi_2 = 0.8854\lambda_1$$

From $\Pi_1 + \Pi_2 = 1$, we get $\lambda_1 = 0.6244$ and

$$\Pi_1 = 0.4472, \qquad \Pi_2 = 0.5528$$

This result means that first Taf should decide how much money to invest in the risk-free asset and how much in the risky assets, and the money in the risky assets should be split into about 45% in asset 1 and 56% in asset 2.

5.1.5 Mean-Variance Optimization in Continuous Time*

The mean-variance optimization problem is usually considered in the single-period framework. However, using the duality/martingale approach to portfolio optimization, we can analyze the problem in continuous time, too. For simplicity, we adopt the Black-Scholes model with one stock with price S and one risk-free security with price B, that is,

$$\frac{dS(t)}{S(t)} = \mu \, dt + \sigma \, dW(t)$$

$$\frac{dB(t)}{B(t)} = r \, dt$$

with μ, σ, and r constant. In this setting, our investor Taf tries to minimize the variance of the value of the discounted final wealth $\bar{X}(T)$:

$$\min E[\bar{X}^2(T)] - (E[\bar{X}(T)])^2 \tag{5.10}$$

under the constraint on the mean

$$E[\bar{X}(T)] = m \tag{5.11}$$

and the usual budget constraint

$$E[Z(T)\bar{X}(T)] = x \tag{5.12}$$

where x is Taf's initial wealth and Z is the risk-neutral density process discussed in chapter 4. We formulate the problem with the discounted wealth for convenience only, and without loss of generality. We have to assume that the market price of risk θ is different from zero, so that $Z(T)$ is different from one.

We could solve the problem using the rigorous duality approach as in utility maximization sections, but we choose to present the more intuitive Lagrange-multipliers approach. We write the Lagrangian as

$$E[\bar{X}^2(T)] - m^2 - 2\lambda_1\{E[\bar{X}(T)] - m\} - 2\lambda_2\{E[Z(T)\bar{X}(T)] - x\}$$

The factor 2 in front of the multipliers λ_i is introduced for convenience only. Proceeding in a heuristic fashion, we take a derivative with respect to $\bar{X}(T)$ and set it equal to zero to get the following expression for the discounted optimal terminal wealth:

$$\bar{X}(T) = \lambda_1 + \lambda_2 Z(T) \tag{5.13}$$

In particular, since Z is a martingale with expectation one, taking expectations we calculate the mean as

$$E[\bar{X}(T)] = \lambda_1 + \lambda_2$$

which, using equation (5.11), gives us

$$\lambda_2 = m - \lambda_1 \tag{5.14}$$

As for the budget constraint, we multiply all terms of equation (5.13) by $Z(T)$ and take expectations. Using again the fact that $Z(T)$ is a martingale with initial value 1, we get

$$E[Z(T)\bar{X}(T)] = \lambda_1 + \lambda_2 E[Z^2(T)]$$

From equation (5.12) this expression has to be equal to x, and, also using equation (5.14), we deduce

$$\lambda_1 = \frac{x - mE[Z^2(T)]}{1 - E[Z^2(T)]}, \qquad \lambda_2 = \frac{m - x}{1 - E[Z^2(T)]} \tag{5.15}$$

Since

$$Z^2(T) = e^{-2\theta W(T) - \frac{4}{2}\theta^2 T} e^{\theta^2 T} = M(T)e^{\theta^2 T}$$

where

$$M(t) := e^{-2\theta W(t) - \frac{4}{2}\theta^2 t}$$

is a martingale process, we get

$$E_t[Z(T)] = Z(t), \qquad E_t[Z^2(T)] = M(t)e^{\theta^2 T} \tag{5.16}$$

and, since $M(t)$ is a martingale with $M(0) = 1$,

$$E[Z^2(T)] = e^{\theta^2 T} \tag{5.17}$$

Substituting in equations (5.15), we get the values of the multipliers.

Next, we want to compute the optimal portfolio process. We recall that $Z\bar{X}$ is a martingale process, so that, using equation (5.13),

$$Z(t)\bar{X}(t) = E_t[Z(T)\bar{X}(T)] = E_t[\lambda_1 Z(T) + \lambda_2 Z^2(T)] \qquad (5.18)$$

Hence, using equations (5.16) in equation (5.18),

$$Z(t)\bar{X}(t) = \lambda_1 Z(t) + \lambda_2 e^{\theta^2 T} M(t) \qquad (5.19)$$

Using Itô's rule, we get

$$d[Z(t)\bar{X}(t)] = -\lambda_1\theta Z(t)\,dW(t) - 2\lambda_2 e^{\theta^2 T}\theta M(t)\,dW(t) \qquad (5.20)$$

However, we recall that

$$d[Z(t)\bar{X}(t)] = \bar{Z}(t)[\pi(t)\sigma - \theta X(t)]\,dW(t) \qquad (5.21)$$

where π is the amount held in the stock. We can now compute the optimal portfolio π matching the right-hand sides of equations (5.20) and (5.21):

$$\bar{Z}(t)[\pi(t)\sigma - \theta X(t)] = -\lambda_1\theta Z(t) - 2\lambda_2 e^{\theta^2 T}\theta M(t)$$

This, along with equation (5.19), implies

$$\bar{Z}(t)\pi(t)\sigma = -\lambda_2 e^{\theta^2 T}\theta M(t) \qquad (5.22)$$

where λ_2 is given by equations (5.15) and (5.17), which depend on m, so that the amount to be invested in the risky security is a function of the desired expected value of wealth. In particular, at initial time $t = 0$ when $\bar{Z}(0) = M(0) = 1$, we get

$$\pi(0)\sigma = -\lambda_2 e^{\theta^2 T}\theta \qquad (5.23)$$

Finally, let us compute the equation of the efficient frontier in this setup. The variance of the discounted terminal wealth can be calculated as

$$E[\bar{X}^2(T)] - m^2 = E[\bar{X}(T)\{\lambda_1 + \lambda_2 Z(T)\}] - m^2 = \lambda_1 m + \lambda_2 x - m^2$$

where the first equality follows from equation (5.13) and the second equality uses the constraint (5.12). Substituting for the values of λ_i, we can calculate this expression as

$$\mathrm{Var}[\bar{X}(T)] = \frac{(m-x)^2}{E[Z^2(T)] - 1}$$

This expression means that the mean-variance frontier is described by the linear relationship

$$\sigma_{\bar{X}(T)} = \frac{|m-x|}{\sqrt{E[Z^2(T)] - 1}}$$

We make the obvious observation that, in order to achieve the mean discounted wealth equal to the initial capital, that is, if $m = x$, the investor should put all the money in the risk-free security.

5.2   VaR: Value at Risk

A company doing business in world markets is exposed to all kinds of market risks: risks of fluctuating foreign exchange rates, of fluctuating stock prices and interest rates, of fluctuating commodity prices, of fluctuating correlations between various market variables, and so on. For the purposes of risk management by company executives or supervision by **regulatory agencies,** it is convenient to have simple measures of risk that can be easily understood and interpreted. In particular, it is convenient to be able to come up with only a single number as a measure of risk. It has become the industry standard to use, for this purpose, a number related to the probability of large losses. This is called the **value-at-risk** approach, or **VaR** approach (not to be confused with Var[·] as in "variance"). For example, a VaR of an investment company that is too high is an indication that the company's positions are too risky and have to be modified. Like most other successful approaches or models, this too is based on a simplification of reality and has a number of shortcomings. Nevertheless, it is a benchmark method and a standard for measuring risk, from which other, more complex and more sophisticated approaches can be developed and to which they may be compared.

5.2.1   Definition of VaR

Suppose we are interested in large losses of a given portfolio and, specifically, in those losses that are likely to happen not more often than once in hundred trading days. We say that we are interested in the 99% **confidence level** and in a **daily value at risk.** For example, a company might report its daily VaR at the 99% level to be $1 million. This statement means that the company estimates that there is less than a 1% chance that the company will lose $1 million during the next day. We have the following exact definition:

Daily value at risk at a 99% confidence level is the smallest number x *for which the probability that the next day's portfolio loss will exceed* x *is not more than 1%.*

In mathematical notation, if we denote by L the loss of the next day, we have

$$P[L \geq x] \leq 0.01 \tag{5.24}$$

and VaR is the smallest number x for which condition (5.24) holds. See figure 5.4 for a graphical illustration, when we assume a normal distribution (we discuss this assumption later).

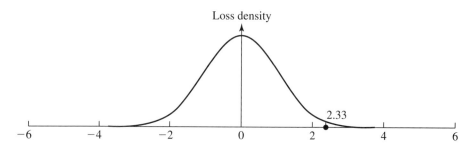

Figure 5.4
Value at risk: There is 1% probability (area) that the loss will be larger than the value 2.33 on the x-axis.

We can define VaR for other time periods. For regulatory purposes, a 10-day VaR is typically used. For example, if we say that a **10-day VaR** is $20 million, at a 95% level, we mean that there is less than 5% chance our portfolio will lose more than $20 million in the next 10 days.

For concreteness, from now on we consider only the daily VaR at the 99% level.

5.2.2 Computing VaR

How do we compute the VaR of a portfolio? The most difficult thing about this question is deciding what kind of distribution to assume for the portfolio returns. Are they normally distributed? Could there be jumps in the returns? Should we believe past experience? There are several approaches to this problem:

Historical, Nonparametric VaR   In the historical, nonparametric approach, we look at the sample of past returns, and we find the historical loss size for which there were only 1% of days with larger losses. This gives us the estimated VaR of the portfolio. Even if we believe that the past is a good estimate of the future in a particular situation, there are still difficulties in this approach: How large a sample (how many days in the past) should we choose? Should we discard unusual days with extremely high losses, say, during a market crash? Should we count only the trading days, or all days? How do we deal with a portfolio that is dynamic and has changed a lot with regard to the positions held in various assets? In short, this is a simple approach conceptually, but often tricky to successfully implement in practice.

Model-Based, Parametric VaR   The model-based, parametric approach is more frequently used. We assume that the portfolio returns have a particular distribution, and we compute the VaR using probabilistic methods. There are two main tasks: we have to choose which distribution the returns come from, and we have to estimate the parameters of that distribution, using historical data or otherwise.

One of the easiest solutions, though not always very realistic, is to assume that the rates of return (sometimes it is more realistic to use log-returns) have a normal distribution with mean μ and variance σ^2. The parameters μ and σ^2 have to be estimated. Denoting by R the rate of return and by $X(t)$ the portfolio value at time t, we have

$$R = \frac{X(1) - X(0)}{X(0)}$$

so that the actual loss {which is the negative of the profit, that is $-[X(1) - X(0)]$} is

$$L = -X(0)R$$

For example, if the portfolio returns -10% on the initial investment of \$100,000, the loss is \$10,000.

When R is normally distributed, the variable $Z = (R - \mu)/\sigma$ has the standard normal distribution, and we can compute the VaR from the following equation:

$$
\begin{aligned}
0.01 = P[L \geq x] = P[-X(0)R \geq x] = P[X(0)R \leq -x] &= P[R \leq -x/X(0)] \\
= P\left[\frac{R - \mu}{\sigma} \leq \frac{-x/X(0) - \mu}{\sigma}\right] &= P\left[Z \leq \frac{-x/X(0) - \mu}{\sigma}\right]
\end{aligned}
\tag{5.25}
$$

Using a standard normal distribution table (Z-table) or a software package such as Excel, we can find that

$$P[Z \leq -2.33] = 0.01$$

Therefore, we get the VaR from

$$\frac{-x/X(0) - \mu}{\sigma} = -2.33$$

resulting in the **formula for 99% VaR with normal distribution:**

$$\text{VaR} = X(0)[2.33\sigma - \mu] \tag{5.26}$$

For example, if a portfolio has a mean daily return of 0.03% and a standard deviation of 1%, and its current value is \$1 million, then $\text{VaR} = 0.023X(0) = \$23,000$.

Excel Tip: In order to find x for which $P[Z \leq x] = y$, use the command

NORMSINV(y)

5.2.3 VaR of a Portfolio of Assets

If a portfolio is changing its positions in different assets in a dynamic fashion, it may not be appropriate to model the returns of the portfolio directly as coming from a fixed distribution. Rather, it makes more sense to model the returns of the individual assets in the portfolio and then to derive conclusions for the whole portfolio. As an example, consider a portfolio of two stocks, with δ_1 shares of stock S_1 and δ_2 shares of stock S_2:

$$X = \delta_1 S_1 + \delta_2 S_2$$

Denote by Π_i the weight of stock i in the portfolio:

$$\Pi_i = \frac{\delta_i S_i}{X}$$

Recall that the rate of the return R of the portfolio is the weighted sum of the rates of return of the assets in the portfolio:

$$R = \Pi_1 R_1 + \Pi_2 R_2$$

If we assume that the stocks' return rates are normally distributed with means μ_i, variances σ_i^2, and correlation ρ, then the return rate R of the portfolio is also normally distributed with mean

$$\mu = \Pi_1 \mu_1 + \Pi_2 \mu_2$$

and variance

$$\sigma^2 = \Pi_1^2 \sigma_1^2 + \Pi_2^2 \sigma_2^2 + 2 \Pi_1 \Pi_2 \sigma_1 \sigma_2 \rho$$

With this knowledge, we can compute the VaR of the portfolio using equation (5.26). See Problems 18 and 19 for examples.

We mentioned that the normal distribution is easier to use than other distributions. This property is not so much true for one-dimensional distributions, but it becomes more relevant when dealing with a joint distribution of many random variables. One of the biggest difficulties in computing VaR is estimating the correlations between the different assets in a portfolio. Everything becomes simpler if we assume that the assets' return rates follow a multivariate normal distribution. Theoretically, the normal-distribution assumption is justified by the **central limit theorem** if the portfolio is well diversified, that is, if it consists of many assets that are close to being independent. The central limit theorem says that a sum of a large number of independent random variables behaves approximately as a normal random variable (see chapter 16).

5.2.4 Alternatives to VaR

The VaR approach is widely accepted and easy to understand. However, it has some disadvantages. One disadvantage of VaR is that, if a large loss happens, VaR tells us nothing about the actual size of the loss. Moreover, when calculating VaR, it is usually assumed that normal market conditions prevail, disregarding possible market crashes or extreme moves of market variables. And VaR, being a single number, does not indicate which of the portfolio components is responsible for the largest risk exposure. For these reasons, other methods for risk measurement have been developed, such as **stress testing** and **scenario analysis.** These methods typically involve many simulations of possible changes in variables affecting the portfolio, such as prices, interest rates, and correlations. For every simulation the profit or loss is calculated, giving us an idea of how the portfolio would behave in adverse market conditions. These simulations can be random, or they can be based on market moves from the past when they were of extreme size, such as during market crashes.

Another problem with VaR is that the VaR of a combination of two positions may be larger than the sum of the VaRs of the individual positions. This possibility goes against the usual diversification feature, that the risk of a diversified portfolio is no larger than the combined risk of the portfolio components.

In the next section we mention a real-world example that shows a need for risk management.

5.2.5 The Story of Long-Term Capital Management

Perhaps the best known recent example of how things can go wrong even when sophisticated modeling is used is the example of the hedge fund Long-Term Capital Management (LTCM) and its near demise in September 1998. The principals of the fund included Wall Street star traders, as well as two scholars whose names we encounter a lot in this book: Robert C. Merton and Myron Scholes. The fund lost more than 50% of its value (measured in hundreds of billions of dollars) during the crisis triggered by the devaluation of the Russian ruble and Russia's freeze on its debt payments. A part of the LTCM strategy was to anticipate that the spreads between different rates would become narrower. In particular, the spreads between the rates of treasury bonds and corporate bonds were at an unusually high historical level. Similarly, it was expected that the spreads between the interest rates of several Western European countries would become smaller, as a result of their becoming part of the European Union. However, the Russian crisis made investors "fly to safety" and become very conservative. This trend forced the spreads to go the other direction and become wider. Like most other hedge funds, LTCM was highly leveraged, meaning it had to use a lot of borrowed funds to sustain its positions. Once the crisis started, the fund started receiving margin calls, forcing it to try to sell some of its assets. Unfortunately, there was a sudden drop in liquidity, and it was difficult for LTCM to unwind positions (sell portfolio assets) at fair market prices. Even worse, many market participants were copying the trades of the previously successful LTCM, thus amplifying price movements. Eventually, the fund was bailed out by the concerted effort of a number of financial institutions that provided enough cash for its survival. The effort was initiated by the U.S. government, through mediation led by the Federal Reserve Bank of New York. The motivation for this effort was to help stabilize the markets, because a bankruptcy of such a big fund as LTCM would have had a major destabilizing effect.

The LTCM fund had its risk management system, including VaR and scenario testing. However, it seems that the testing was done in conditions that did not include market moves as extreme as the ones that actually occurred, partly because such moves had never before been experienced.

Summary

The mean-variance theory compares portfolio strategies on the basis of the mean and the variance of their return. The strategies can be represented as points in the mean-variance plane. The strategies with the lowest variance for a given level of the mean return form the efficient frontier in the plane. In order to have an efficient strategy composed of holdings in risky assets and a risk-free asset, it is sufficient to invest in one mutual fund of risky assets and in the risk-free asset. Optimal mean-variance strategies can be computed in various models.

A modern way of measuring the risk of a portfolio is using value at risk, or VaR. It is related to the probability of large losses. There are different models in which we can compute VaR. Even if a company calculates the VaR of its positions and other measures of risk on a regular basis, it can still run into big losses if the models are not adequate.

Problems

1. Consider two investors who care only about the means and variances of their investments. Investor A is indifferent between portfolio 1 with expected return of 10% and standard deviation of 15% and portfolio 2 with expected return of 18% and standard deviation of 20%. Investor B is indifferent between portfolio 3 with expected return of 12% and portfolio 4 with expected return of 15%, where the standard deviation of portfolios 3 and 4 are the same as of portfolios 1 and 2, that is, equal to 15% and 20%, respectively. Which of the two investors would you say is more risk-averse?

2. Prove equation (5.4).

3. Prove equation (5.6) for σ in terms of Π in the case of two assets with correlation $\rho = -1$, means μ_1 and μ_2, and standard deviations σ_1 and σ_2. What does this equation look like in terms of μ rather than in terms of Π?

†4. Consider a mutual fund F that invests 50% in the risk-free security and 50% in stock A, which has expected return and standard deviation of 10% and 12%, respectively. The risk-free rate is 5%. You borrow the risk-free asset and invest in F so as to get an expected return of 15%. What is the standard deviation of your investment?

5. Suppose that securities A and B are perfectly and positively correlated, meaning that $R_A = a + bR_B$ for some constants a and $b > 0$, with expected returns 8% and 12%, respectively, and standard deviations 15% and 25%, respectively. Compute the risk-free rate (or the rate of return of a risk-free portfolio).

6. You can invest in asset 1 with $\mu_1 = 0.1$, $\sigma_1 = 0.3$ and asset 2 with $\mu_2 = 0.2$, $\sigma_2 = 0.5$, with correlation $\rho = 0.2$. Find the minimum variance point and the portfolio strategy that attains it.

7. Repeat the previous problem if a risk-free asset with return $R = 0.05$ is also available.

8. Find the portfolio weights in the optimal mutual fund P for the two risky assets from the two previous problems.

9. Complete the solution to Example 5.3.

†10. You can invest in asset 1 with $\mu_1 = 0.1$, $\sigma_1 = 0.3$ and asset 2 with $\mu_2 = 0.2$, $\sigma_2 = 0.5$, with correlation $\rho = 0.2$. You can also invest in the risk-free asset with return $R = 0.05$. Find the optimal mean-variance portfolio for the given mean return $\mu = 0.2$.

11. Consider three securities A, B, and C with expected returns of 10%, 15%, and 12%, respectively, and standard deviations of 8%, 18%, and 20%. The correlation coefficients are 0.7 between A and B, 0.1 between A and C, and 0.4 between B and C. What is the portfolio on the efficient frontier that corresponds to an expected return of 12%? **Note:** You can provide either an exact answer to this question or an approximate answer. It is acceptable to find the variance for a number of portfolios (say 50) and choose the one with the smallest variance. (You can use a software program for this purpose.)

†12. Suppose that the risk-free rate is 5%. There are three risky portfolios A, B, and C with expected returns 15%, 20%, and 25%, respectively, and standard deviations 5%, 10%, and 14%. You can invest in the risk-free security and only one of the risky portfolios. Which one of them would you choose? What if the risk-free rate is 10%?

*13. Consider a Black-Scholes model with $\mu = 0.1$, $\sigma = 0.3$, $r = 0$, and a mean-variance investor starting with initial capital $x = 1$ who wants to attain the mean wealth level of m in $T = 1$ year. Draw a graph of the optimal portfolio amounts $\pi(0)$ to be held in the stock today for the values of $m = 1, 1.1, \ldots, 1.9, 2$.

†14. Compute the historical daily 90% VaR of a portfolio whose daily losses in the last 10 days were, in millions of dollars (minus sign indicates a profit):

$1, -0.5, -0.1, 0.7, 0.2, 0.1, -0.2, -0.8, -0.3, 0.5$

15. Compute the historical daily 80% VaR of a portfolio whose daily losses in the last five days were, in millions of dollars (minus sign indicates a profit):

$0.3, -0.4, 0.1, -0.2, 0.2$

†16. Compute the daily 99% and 95% VaR of a portfolio whose daily return is normally distributed with a mean of 1% and a standard deviation of 0.5%. The current value of the portfolio is $1 million.

17. Compute the daily 99% and 95% VaR of a portfolio whose daily profit or loss size is normally distributed with a mean of $10,000 and a standard deviation of $5,000. The current value of the portfolio is $2 million.

†18. Small investor Taf has 70% of his portfolio invested in a major market-index fund and 30% in a small-stocks fund. The mean monthly return rate of the market-index fund is 1.5%, with standard deviation 0.9%. The small-stocks fund has the mean monthly return rate of 2.2% with standard deviation of 1.2%. The correlation between the two funds is 0.13. Assume normal distribution for the return rates. What is the monthly VaR at 99% level for Taf's portfolio if the portfolio value today is $100,000?

19. Your portfolio is made up like this: you hold 60% in the U.S. stock market, with a mean monthly return rate of 1% and standard deviation 2%; you hold 10% in the global stock market, with a mean monthly return rate of 0.6% and standard deviation 1%; you hold 30% in risk-free assets with annual interest rate 5%. Assume normal distribution for the return rates of the stock markets. The correlation between the U.S. market and the global market is 0.25. What is the monthly VaR at a 99% level for your portfolio if the portfolio value today is $100,000?

*20. Choose a company listed on the NYSE and collect the daily stock prices for the last 100 days. (Alternatively, simulate 100 stock prices from some distribution.)

a. Compute the daily historical VaR.

b. Compute the daily parametric VaR, assuming the normal distribution for the relative returns.

Further Readings

The original mean-variance approach is due to Markowitz (1952). A general advanced exposition can be found in LeRoy and Werner (2001). The continuous-time treatment of the mean-variance frontier is taken from Cvitanić, Lazrak, and Wang (2003). Nice treatments of the value-at-risk approach are Duffie and Pan (1997) and Jorion (1997). An application of VaR to optimal portfolios is in Basak and Shapiro (2001). More general treatment for loss distributions can be found in Embrechts, Kluppelberg, and Mikosch (1997).

II PRICING AND HEDGING OF DERIVATIVE SECURITIES

6 Arbitrage and Risk-Neutral Pricing

By arbitrage we mean making money out of nothing without risk. For example, suppose that for a given exchange rate—say, U.S. dollars versus Japanese yen—we get two different quotes by two different traders, simultaneously, so that we can buy yen in the cheaper market and sell them in the more expensive. Even though there might be short time periods in a financial market when there is an arbitrage opportunity, such opportunities tend to disappear quickly. As other market participants observe the mismatch, the demand for the cheap yen will increase and the supply of the expensive yen will decrease, and that process will drive the quoted exchange rates to the no-arbitrage level at which they are identical. The assumption of absence of arbitrage in market models is crucial for getting any kind of sensible general results.

The formalization of this notion and its path-breaking application to finance were accomplished in the 1970s by Black and Scholes (1973), Merton (1973b, 1976, 1977), Cox and Ross (1976), Harrison and Kreps (1979), and Harrison and Pliska (1981). The revolutionary contribution of the theory of arbitrage was the realization that the absence of arbitrage implies a unique price for the claims (securities) that can be replicated in the market. Perhaps equally important for practical applications, the theory of arbitrage pricing (or pricing by no arbitrage) has developed methods for computing this unique price of a security, as well as for hedging risks of holding a position in a security. As we will see, the price of the claim that can be replicated is equal to the expected value of the payoff of the claim, discounted by the risk-free rate; however, the expected value is not taken under the "real world" probability, but under the "risk-neutral probability" or "equivalent martingale measure" (EMM).

In the following sections we show how the absence of arbitrage results in some simple bounds for the prices of standard derivative securities. We also explain the connection between arbitrage and the notion of risk-neutral probabilities. It should be remarked that the arbitrage relationships we obtain do not always hold in practice because of the idealized assumptions we make, such as the absence of transaction fees when trading.

6.1 Arbitrage Relationships for Call and Put Options; Put-Call Parity

In this chapter, as we do throughout the rest of the book, we assume that there are no arbitrage opportunities in the market. More precisely, we assume that any strategy that starts with zero investment cannot have a positive probability of producing a positive profit while at the same time having zero probability of resulting in a loss. We also assume that the bank interest rate r is positive and constant, and that there are no transaction costs in the market. (Instead of assuming a constant interest rate, we could assume that we can trade in the bond market, and by holding long or short positions in risk-free bonds, we could invest or borrow at the interest rate r.) For concreteness, we suppose continuous compounding, so that the value of K dollars at time T is worth $Ke^{-r(T-t)}$ at time t. Let us denote by $C(t)$, $c(t)$, $P(t)$, and $p(t)$ the time-t values of the American call option, the European call option, the American put option, and the European put option, respectively. Denote also by S the price of the stock that is the underlying security of all the options, by T the time of maturity, and by K the strike price for a given option. We now establish several comparisons among these values, which must hold, or arbitrage opportunities would exist.

We should emphasize that the results we get in this part of the chapter are model independent. More precisely, the arbitrage opportunities we will construct in the examples consist of taking a **static position** (one-time trade) in given securities and waiting until maturity. The positions are constructed in such a way that there is arbitrage regardless of what probability distributions those securities have.

The first of the relationships we get is that, for a European and an American call written on the same stock, and with the same maturity, we have

$$c(t) \le C(t) \le S(t) \tag{6.1}$$

The first inequality says that *the value of the European call is never larger than the value of the American call.*

This statement is true because the holder of the American call can always wait until maturity, in which case the payoff he gets is the same as that of the European call. That is, the American call gives the same right as the European call, plus an additional possibility of exercising before maturity. More formally, suppose $c(t) > C(t)$. Then we could sell the European call, buy the American call, and put the (positive) difference in the bank. We could then wait until maturity, when both calls have the same payoffs that would cancel each other in our portfolio, while we would have positive profit in the bank.

The second inequality says that *the value of a call option is never larger than the value of the stock.*

This statement is true because call options give holders the right to get one share of the stock, but they have to pay the strike price in order to get it.

For the put option we have

$$p(t) \le P(t) \le K \tag{6.2}$$

In other words, *the value of the European put is no larger than the value of the American put,* by the same argument as for the European and American calls, and *the value of a put option is never larger than the strike price.*

The latter statement is true because the holder of the put option gets K dollars if the option is exercised, but only upon the delivery of the stock.

In fact, since the European put payoff at maturity is at most K, *the value of the European put at time t is no larger than the value that results in K dollars in the bank at time T, when* *invested in the bank at time t:*

$$p(t) \leq Ke^{-r(T-t)} \tag{6.3}$$

Otherwise, we would write the put and deposit $p(t) > Ke^{-r(T-t)}$ in the bank. At maturity, we would have more than K in the bank. This amount is enough to pay the put holder if the put is exercised, and in exchange we would get the stock, with a value of at least zero. Therefore, we have a positive profit (arbitrage opportunity).

The next result says that *the value of the European call of a stock that pays no dividends is no smaller than the difference between the stock price and the discounted strike price:*

$$c(t) \geq S(t) - Ke^{-r(T-t)} \tag{6.4}$$

Suppose that this statement is not true, so that $c(t) + Ke^{-r(T-t)} < S(t)$. In other words, it looks like the call and the cash might be cheap while the stock might be expensive. We take advantage of this difference by constructing an arbitrage portfolio. More precisely, consider the strategy consisting of the following two positions at time t:

1. Sell the stock short.
2. Buy the call and deposit $Ke^{-r(T-t)}$ dollars in the bank.

Because we assumed $c(t) + Ke^{-r(T-t)} < S(t)$, when we take these positions, we have extra money to deposit in the bank at time t. However, at maturity time T, we have $-S(T)$ in position 1; as for position 2, if the option is in the money, that is, $S(T) > K$, our payoff will be $S(T) - K + K = S(T)$, and if the option is out of the money, we will have $K \geq S(T)$. Therefore, in any case we have no loss at time T [and maybe a profit, if $K > S(T)$], and we made a positive profit (money in the bank) at time t. We point out that this strategy might not work if the stock pays dividends before maturity. The reason is that, in this case, the short position in the stock will involve the obligation to pay the dividends. Then we cannot guarantee that there will be no loss.

For the put option we have the following: *The value of the European put on a stock that pays no dividends until maturity is never smaller than the discounted strike price minus the stock price:*

$$p(t) \geq Ke^{-r(T-t)} - S(t) \tag{6.5}$$

We argue as before. If the previous inequality does not hold, implement the strategy consisting of the following two positions at time t:

1. Borrow $Ke^{-r(T-t)}$ dollars.
2. Buy the put and the stock.

This strategy yields a profit at time t, and it can be verified that it yields a zero profit at maturity, at worst.

Thus far, we have only obtained bounds (inequalities) on option prices. The following classical result gives precise information (as an equality) on the relationship between the European and the American call prices:

The price of an American call on a stock that pays no dividends until maturity is equal to the price of the corresponding European call (that is, written on the same stock and with the same maturity).

Suppose that this is not the case. We only show that we cannot have $C(t) > c(t)$, because we already know that $C(t) \geq c(t)$ [we showed how to construct an arbitrage portfolio if $C(t) < c(t)$]. If $C(t) > c(t)$, we could sell the American call and buy the European call, while depositing the extra money in the bank. If at time $\tau \leq T$ the American option is exercised, we need to pay $S(\tau) - K$. We can cover that expense by selling the call option, because we know from expression (6.4) that $c(\tau) \geq S(\tau) - Ke^{-r(T-\tau)} \geq S(\tau) - K$. If the American option is never exercised, there is no obligation to cover. This is an arbitrage opportunity, so we cannot have $C(t) > c(t)$.

A corollary of previous arguments is the fact that *an American call written on a stock that does not pay dividends until maturity should not be exercised before maturity.*

Indeed, if the American option is exercised early at $\tau < T$, its payoff is $S(\tau) - K$, which is lower than the price of the option $C(\tau)$, because we know that we have $C(\tau) \geq c(\tau) \geq S(\tau) - Ke^{-r(T-\tau)} > S(\tau) - K$. Thus, if the option holder wants to get out of the option position, it is more profitable to sell it than to exercise it.

When the underlying stock pays dividends before maturity, the previous statement is not necessarily true, and it may be better to exercise the American option earlier, in order to be able to collect the dividends. Our argument might not hold anymore because, as we observed previously, inequality (6.4) might not be satisfied if the stock pays a dividend and we cannot conclude that $C(t) > S(t) - K$. For the American put option, even if the stock pays no dividends, it may be optimal to exercise early. As an extreme example, suppose that the stock is worth zero (or very close to zero) at some time $t < T$ (the company went bankrupt, or almost bankrupt). If the option is exercised at t, its payoff is K (or very close to K), and when we deposit it in the bank we will have more than K dollars at time T. This action is definitely better than waiting until time T to exercise, when the highest possible payoff is K dollars. Thus it is better to exercise at time t.

Let us also mention that for an American call option on a stock that pays dividends, if the option is exercised before maturity, it should be exercised only immediately before one of the times the dividend is paid. We have shown that in the absence of dividends it is optimal to wait until maturity. If there is a dividend to be paid, before the payment date the option behaves as an option on a non-dividend-paying stock, so it should not be exercised until that date.

Assuming that the stock pays no dividends, we finish this section by discussing another classical result that relates the prices of the European call and the European put, called **put-call parity:**

$$c(t) + Ke^{-r(T-t)} = p(t) + S(t) \tag{6.6}$$

In words, *the call price plus the present value of K dollars in the bank is equal to the put price plus the stock price.*

This result follows from looking at the payoffs of these two positions at maturity: holding a call plus discounted K dollars in the bank results in a payoff of one share $S(T)$ at maturity if $S(T) > K$, and it results in K dollars if $S(T) \leq K$. Holding a put and a share of the stock results in the same payoff at maturity. Consequently, since there is no possibility of early exercise, the prices of the two positions have to be the same. In the following example we show how to extract arbitrage profit when the put-call parity does not hold.

Example 6.1 (Deviation from the Put-Call Parity)   Suppose that the today's price of stock S is $S(0) = \$48$. The European call and put on S with strike price 45 and maturity T of three months are trading at \$4.95 and \$0.70, respectively. Three-month T-bills (nominal value \$100) are trading at \$98.50. We want to see whether there is arbitrage and take advantage if there is. We can find the discount factor, call it d, from the price of the T-bill:

$$98.5 = 100d$$

from which $d = 0.985$. We now compute the value of the left-hand side of the put-call parity,

$$c(t) + Kd = 49.275$$

and the value of the right-hand side,

$$p(t) + S(t) = 48.7$$

The left- and the right-hand sides are not equal; therefore, there is an arbitrage opportunity. We sell overvalued securities; that is, we write one call and sell short T-bills with a nominal value of \$45, from which we receive \$49.275. We buy the undervalued securities using this money; that is, we buy one put and one share of the stock at the cost of \$48.7. We still have left $49.275 - 48.7 = \$0.575$ at our disposal. We hold our positions until maturity. If $S(T) > 45$, then we have to deliver one share of the stock that we hold to cover the call position, and we use \$45 that we get for that share to cover our short position in the T-bill. If $S(T) \leq 45$, the call we wrote is out of the money, while we get \$45 for the share of the stock we have, by exercising the put. We use \$45 to cover our short position in the T-bill. In both cases the net cash flow of liquidating the portfolio is zero. This outcome is arbitrage, because the amount \$0.575 that we had at our disposal was not used to liquidate the portfolio.

Put-call parity does not apply to American options. The most we can say, if the stock pays no dividends, is

$$C(t) + Ke^{-r(T-t)} \leq P(t) + S(t) \tag{6.7}$$

This result follows from the put-call parity for the European options and from the fact that $P(t) > p(t)$ and $C(t) = c(t)$. In fact, we have

$$S(t) - K \leq C(t) - P(t) \leq S(t) - Ke^{-r(T-t)}$$

The right-hand-side inequality follows from expression (6.7). As for the left-hand side, suppose that it is not true, that is, $S(t) + P(t) > C(t) + K$. Then we could sell short one share of the stock, sell the put, buy the call, and deposit more than K dollars in the bank. If the put is exercised at time τ, we get one share of the stock to cover our short position, and we have to pay for it K dollars, which is less than what we already have in the bank. If the put is never exercised, we are short one share of the stock at maturity, which can be covered by exercising the call option we have, that is, by buying the share for K dollars from the bank. In any case, we make money out of nothing; therefore, there is an arbitrage opportunity.

6.2   Arbitrage Pricing of Forwards and Futures

6.2.1   Forward Prices

Let us first consider the problem of pricing a forward on an asset S that pays no dividends (or coupons). For concreteness, we call that asset a stock. We claim that, at least in theory, the **no-arbitrage forward price** $F(t)$, agreed upon at time t, has to satisfy

$$F(t) = S(t)e^{r(T-t)} \tag{6.8}$$

In other words, *the forward price is equal to the time-T value (that is, compounded at the appropriate interest rate) of one share's worth deposited in the bank at time t.*

In order to see this point, suppose it is not true. For example, suppose $F(t) > S(t)e^{r(T-t)}$. We can then, at time t, take a short position in the forward contract and buy the stock by borrowing $S(t)$ from the bank. At time T, we have to return $S(t)e^{r(T-t)}$ to the bank, and we can do so even while making a positive profit, because we deliver the stock and get in exchange $F(t)$ dollars, with $F(t) > S(t)e^{r(T-t)}$. This outcome is arbitrage. Conversely, we can construct an arbitrage portfolio if $F(t) < S(t)e^{r(T-t)}$ by selling the stock short, depositing the proceeds in the bank, and taking a long position in the forward contract.

Next, suppose the stock pays known dividends during the time interval $[t, T]$, whose present time-t value (the discounted future payments) is denoted $\bar{D}(t)$. We can then use a similar argument (see Problem 12) to show

$$F(t) = [S(t) - \bar{D}(t)]e^{r(T-t)} \tag{6.9}$$

The intuition for this result is that the dividend makes a long position in the stock cheaper, since the holder of the stock will later receive the dividends. Thus the present value of dividends is subtracted from the stock value on the right-hand side of equation (6.9). Similarly, if the stock pays the dividends continuously at the constant rate q, the present value of the stock net of dividends becomes $S(t)e^{-q(T-t)}$, and we have

$$F(t) = S(t)e^{(r-q)(T-t)} \tag{6.10}$$

Example 6.2 (Forward Pricing with Dividends)   A given stock trades at \$100, and in six months it will pay a dividend of \$5.65. The one-year continuous interest rate is 10%, and the six-month continuous interest rate is 7.41%. According to the analogue of expression (6.9) with different annualized interest rates for six months and for one year, we find the forward price as

$$F(t) = e^{0.1}[100 - 5.65e^{-0.0741 \times 0.5}] = 104.5$$

Suppose that the price is instead 104; that is, the forward contract is undervalued. We now construct an arbitrage strategy. We take a long position in the forward contract (at zero initial cost) and sell the stock short for \$100. We buy the six-month bond in the amount of $5.65e^{-0.0741 \times 0.5} = 5.4445$. We invest the remaining balance, $100 - 5.4445 = 94.5555$, in the one-year bond. In six months, we have to pay the dividend of \$5.65 and we can do it by using the proceeds of our investment in the six-month bond. In one year, we have bonds maturing for a nominal rate of $94.5555e^{0.1} = 104.5$. We pay \$104 for the stock (according to the conditions of the forward contract), deliver the stock to cover the short position, and keep $104.5 - 104 = 0.5$, which is an arbitrage profit.

Consider now a **forward contract on a foreign currency.** Here, $S(t)$ denotes the current price in dollars of one unit of the foreign currency. We denote by r_f the foreign risk-free interest rate (with continuous compounding). We observe that the foreign (continuously paid) interest rate is equivalent to a (continuously paid) dividend: the holder of the foreign currency will receive the interest rate very much as the holder of the stock will receive the dividend. We then have

$$F(t) = S(t)e^{(r-r_f)(T-t)} \tag{6.11}$$

If, for example, we had $F(t) < S(t)e^{(r-r_f)(T-t)}$, we could take a long position in the forward contract, borrow $e^{-r_f(T-t)}$ units of foreign currency, and deposit its value in dollars of

$S(t)e^{-r_f(T-t)}$ in the domestic bank. At time T we would have to pay $F(t)$ to get one unit of foreign currency; this unit would cover our debt to the foreign bank (remember that we had borrowed $e^{-r_f(T-t)}$, and this amount, compounded at the foreign rate r_f, becomes equal to one), and we would still have $S(t)e^{(r-r_f)(T-t)}$ in the domestic bank to more than cover the expense $F(t)$. We can similarly construct an arbitrage portfolio if $F(t) > S(t)e^{(r-r_f)(T-t)}$.

6.2.2 Futures Prices

We recall that the main difference between a futures contract and a forward contract is that the position in the futures contract is updated ("marked to market") periodically (typically, daily): the changes in the futures price for a given contract are credited or charged to the account of the investor with a position in the contract. The main result affecting the futures prices is the **futures-forward price equivalence:**

If the interest rate is deterministic, the futures price is equal to the forward price.

In order to show this point, assume for simplicity that the length of the period between two resettlement dates (when the contract is marked to market) for the futures contract is equal to one unit of time (say, one day) and that the continuously compounded interest rate for every period is equal to the constant r. Consider the following strategy:

1. At time 0 take a long position in $e^{-r(T-1)}$ futures contracts with price $F(0)$.

2. At time 1 increase the position to $e^{-r(T-2)}$ contracts, and so on, until time $T-1$, when the position is increased to one contract. During each period invest the profit or loss in the bank at rate r.

This strategy is not possible if the interest rate is stochastic because we need to know the value of the interest rate in the future.

The profit or loss in the period $(k, k+1)$ is

$$[F(k+1) - F(k)]e^{-r[T-(k+1)]}$$

which, being invested in the bank, increases to

$$F(k+1) - F(k)$$

at time T. The total profit or loss is therefore equal to

$$\sum_{i=0}^{T-1}[F(k+1) - F(k)] = F(T) - F(0) = S(T) - F(0)$$

However, the profit of the form $S(T) - G(0)$ is also the profit of the forward contract with price $G(0)$. Since these strategies both require zero investment, we need to have $F(0) = G(0)$, or, otherwise, there would be an arbitrage opportunity. Indeed, if, for example,

$G(0) > F(0)$, we could use the futures strategy we have described with zero initial invest-ment, while taking a short position in the forward contract, therefore having a profit equal to $S(T) - F(0) - [S(T) - G(0)] = G(0) - F(0) > 0$ at time T.

In general, if the interest rates are random, then the theoretical futures price is not equal to the theoretical forward price. We say "theoretical" because in practice there may be other factors influencing these prices in different ways, like taxes or liquidity considerations. One general rule of thumb for their relation is as follows: if the underlying asset S is strongly positively correlated with the interest rate, then the futures price will tend to be higher than the forward price, because increases in S tend to happen together with increases in the interest rate, so that the profit of holding a futures contract may typically be invested in the bank at a high rate of interest. Also, a decrease in S will tend to happen together with a decrease in the interest rate, so that the loss of holding a futures contract can typically be financed by borrowing from the bank at a low rate of interest. These two effects make the futures contract more valuable, while they do not affect the forward contract, for which there is no marking to market. However, if the underlying asset S is strongly negatively correlated with the interest rate, the futures price will tend to be lower than the forward price, by similar reasoning (see Problem 16).

We discuss the theoretical relationship between the forward price and the futures price more carefully in a later section.

6.2.3   Futures on Commodities

We assume in this section that the futures price is equal to the forward price. Thus far we have considered futures on financial assets. If a futures contract is written on a commodity (gold, silver, corn, oil, and so on), the preceding formulas may not be valid, even in theory. For example, it may be costly to hold a commodity because of **storage costs.** First, we suppose that there is no advantage in holding a commodity (we will explore this issue later). Storage costs can be interpreted as negative dividends (an additional payment the holder of the commodity has to make). So, by analogy with equation (6.9), if the total storage cost is known, denoting its present value by $\bar{U}(t)$, we have

$$F(t) = [S(t) + \bar{U}(t)]e^{r(T-t)} \tag{6.12}$$

Similarly, by analogy with equation (6.10), if the storage cost is proportional to the price of the commodity and is paid continuously in time at the constant rate u, we get

$$F(t) = S(t)e^{(r+u)(T-t)} \tag{6.13}$$

Recall that these relations are obtained with the assumption that there is no advantage in holding a commodity. However, for some commodities it may be the case that holding them is preferable to taking a position in the futures contract and getting them only in the future. For example, there may be benefits to owning the commodity in the case of shortages, or to keep a production process running, or because of their consumption value. In such situations, the value of the futures contract becomes smaller than in the case in which there are no benefits in holding the commodity, so we conclude

$$F(t) \leq [S(t) + \bar{U}(t)]e^{r(T-t)}$$

or

$$F(t) \leq S(t)e^{(r+u)(T-t)}$$

as the case may be. As a measure of how much smaller the futures price becomes, we define the **convenience yield** (which represents the value of owning the commodity) as the value y for which

$$F(t)e^{y(T-t)} = [S(t) + \bar{U}(t)]e^{r(T-t)}$$

or

$$F(t)e^{y(T-t)} = S(t)e^{(r+u)(T-t)}$$

In general, any type of cost or benefit associated with a futures contract (whether it is a storage cost, a dividend, or a convenience yield) is called **cost of carry.** We define it as the value c for which

$$F(t) = S(t)e^{(r+c)(T-t)}$$

6.3   Risk-Neutral Pricing

We have hinted before that the absence of arbitrage implies that the contingent claims that can be replicated by a trading strategy could be priced by using expectations under a special, risk-neutral probability measure. In the present section we explain why this is the case. The main results of this section are summarized in figure 6.1.

6.3.1   Martingale Measures; Cox-Ross-Rubinstein (CRR) Model

The modern approach to pricing financial contracts, as well as to solving portfolio-optimization problems, is intimately related to the notion of **martingale probability measures.** As we shall see, prices are expected values, but not under the "real-world" or "true" probability; rather, they are expected values under an "artificial" probability, called **risk-neutral probability** or **equivalent martingale measure (EMM).**

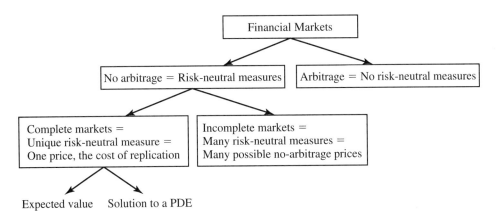

Figure 6.1
Risk-neutral pricing: no arbitrage, completeness, and pricing in financial markets.

We first recall the notion of a martingale: Consider a process X whose values on the interval $[0, s]$ provide information up to time s. Denote by E_s the conditional expectation given that information. We say that a process X is a martingale if

$$E_s[X(t)] = X(s), \qquad s \leq t \tag{6.14}$$

(We implicitly assume that the expected values are well defined.) This equation can be interpreted as saying that the best possible prediction for the future value $X(t)$ of the process X is the present value $X(s)$. Or, in profit/loss terminology, a martingale process, on average, makes neither profits nor losses. In particular, taking unconditional expected values in equation (6.14), we see that $E[X(t)] = E[X(s)]$. In other words, *expected values of a martingale process do not change with time.*

Recall our notation $\bar{A}$ that we use for any value A discounted at the risk-free rate. We say that a probability measure is a **martingale measure** for a financial-market model *if the discounted stock prices $\bar{S}_i$ are martingales.*

Let us see what happens in the Cox-Ross-Rubinstein model with one stock. Recall that in this model the price of the stock at period $t+1$ can take only one of the two values, $S(t)u$ or $S(t)d$, with u and d constants such that $u > 1 + r > d$, where r is the constant risk-free rate, and we usually assume $d < 1$. At every point in time t, the probability that the stock takes the value $S(t)u$ is p, and, therefore, $q := 1 - p$ is the probability that the stock will take the value $S(t)d$. Consider first a single-period setting. A martingale measure will be given by probabilities p^* and $q^* := 1 - p^*$ of up and down moves, such that the discounted stock price is a martingale:

$$S(0) = \bar{S}(0) = E^*[\bar{S}(1)] = p^* \frac{S(0)u}{1+r} + (1 - p^*) \frac{S(0)d}{1+r}$$

Here, $E^* = E_0^*$ denotes the (unconditional, time $t = 0$) expectation under the probabilities $p^*, 1 - p^*$. Solving for p^* we obtain

$$p^* = \frac{(1+r) - d}{u - d}, \qquad q^* = \frac{u - (1+r)}{u - d} \tag{6.15}$$

We see that the assumption $d < 1 + r < u$ guarantees that these numbers are indeed positive probabilities. Moreover, these equations define the only martingale measure with positive probabilities. Furthermore, p^* and q^* are strictly positive, so that events that have zero probability under the "real-world" probability measure also have zero probability under the martingale measure, and vice versa. We say that the two **probability measures are equivalent** and that the probabilities p^*, q^* form an **equivalent martingale measure** or **EMM**.

In order to make a comparison between the actual, real probabilities $p, 1 - p$ and the risk-neutral probabilities $p^*, 1 - p^*$, introduce the mean return rate μ of the stock as determined from

$$S(0)(1 + \mu) = E[S(1)]$$

Then a calculation similar to the preceding implies that we get expressions analogous to equations (6.15):

$$p = \frac{(1+\mu) - d}{u - d}, \qquad 1 - p = \frac{u - (1+\mu)}{u - d} \tag{6.16}$$

Thus we can say that

the risk-neutral world is the world in which there is no compensation for holding the risky assets, hence in which the expected return rate of the risky assets is equal to the risk-free rate r.

We want to make a connection between the price of a contingent claim and the possibility of replicating the claim by trading in other securities, as discussed in chapter 3. Denote now by δ the number of shares of stock held in the portfolio and by x the initial level of wealth, $X(0) = x$. The rest of the portfolio, $x - \delta S(0)$, is invested in the bank at the risk-free rate r. Therefore, from the budget constraint of the individual, the discounted wealth $\bar{X}(1)$ at time 1 is given by

$$\bar{X}(1) = \delta \bar{S}(1) + x - \delta S(0)$$

Since the discounted stock price is a martingale under probabilities p^*, $1 - p^*$, we have $E^*[\bar{S}(1)] = S(0)$, hence

$$E^*[\bar{X}(1)] = \delta S(0) + x - \delta S(0) = x \tag{6.17}$$

In other words, *the discounted wealth process is also a martingale under the equivalent martingale measure.*

We say that *the expected value of the discounted future wealth in the risk-neutral world is equal to the initial wealth.*

In fact, we have the following result on the possibility of replicating a contingent claim C (that is, a security with a payoff C at moment 1) starting with initial amount x. We denote by C^u the value of the contingent claim in the up state [if the stock goes up to $uS(0)$] and by C^d the value of the contingent claim in the down state.

THEOREM 6.1   A claim C can be replicated starting with initial wealth $C(0)$ if and only if $E^*[\bar{C}] = C(0)$.

Proof   We have already shown that if $X(1) = C$, then $E^*[\bar{X}(1)]$ is equal to the initial wealth $x = C(0)$. Conversely, suppose that $E^*[\bar{C}] = C(0)$; that is,

$$p^*\bar{C}^u + q^*\bar{C}^d = C(0) \tag{6.18}$$

However, a strategy δ^C with initial cost $D(0)$ replicates C if

$$C^u = \delta S(0)u + [D(0) - \delta S(0)](1 + r), \qquad C^d = \delta S(0)d + [D(0) - \delta S(0)](1 + r)$$

These last two equations determine the unique strategy δ and the cost $D(0)$ of replicating C. Using equations (6.15) we can easily verify that this amount $D(0)$ is equal to $C(0)$ given by equation (6.18). Therefore, $C(0)$ is indeed the initial amount needed to replicate C.   ∎

For the sake of completeness, we also mention another way of studying replication, without using risk-neutral probabilities. Introduce the following random variable, called **risk-neutral density:**

$$Z(1) := \begin{cases} p^*/p & \text{with probability } p \\ q^*/q & \text{with probability } q \end{cases} \tag{6.19}$$

We have

$$E[Z(1)\bar{X}(1)] = p\left[\frac{p^*}{p}\left(\delta\frac{S(0)u}{1+r} + x - \delta S(0)\right)\right] + q\left[\frac{q^*}{q}\left(\delta\frac{S(0)d}{1+r} + x - \delta S(0)\right)\right]$$
$$= E^*[\bar{X}(1)] = x$$

In other words, a different way to write equation (6.17), that is, the **budget constraint for the wealth process,** is

$$E^*[\bar{X}(1)] = E[Z(1)\bar{X}(1)] = x \tag{6.20}$$

Results similar to the preceding results for the single-period model are also valid in the multiperiod Cox-Ross-Rubinstein model. First, it can be verified that the martingale probabilities are still given by the same expressions as in equations (6.15). {Verification is accomplished by solving the equation $E_t^*[\bar{S}(t + 1)] = \bar{S}(t)$.} Next, we define the risk-neutral density $Z(T)$ as the product of T independent copies of the random variable $Z(1)$ in definition (6.19). We then have **the budget constraint**

$$E^*[\bar{X}(T)] = E[Z(T)\bar{X}(T)] = x \tag{6.21}$$

Moreover, Theorem 6.1 is still valid (see Problem 19).

6.3.2   State Prices in Single-Period Models

Consider now a more general single-period model with N stocks. For stock j, the value $S_j(1)$ at the end of the period is a random variable that can take K possible values, $s_j^1, \ldots, s_j^K$. We say that there are K possible states of the world at time 1. A vector $d = (d_1, \ldots, d_K)$ is called a **state-price vector** or a **vector of Arrow-Debreu prices,** if $d_i > 0$ for all $i = 1, \ldots, K$, and we have

$$S_j(0) = \sum_{i=1}^{K} d_i s_j^i \tag{6.22}$$

for all stocks $j = 1, \ldots, N$. This equation means that *the stock price today is obtained as a weighted average of its future values, with the weights being the state prices.*

We observe that the elements d_i of the vector d "measure" the value at moment 0 of one unit of currency at moment 1, in state i. That is, d_i is the price of a security with possible values $s_i = 1$, $s_k = 0$ for all $k \neq i$. If we assume, as usual, that there is a risk-free asset S_0 such that $S_0(0) = 1$, $S_0(1) = 1 + r$, where $r > 0$ is a constant, and that equation (6.22) is also valid for S_0, we get

$$\frac{1}{1 + r} = \sum_{i=1}^{K} d_i$$

Denote

$$p_i^* := \frac{d_i}{\sum_{j=1}^{K} d_j} = (1 + r)d_i$$

Note that $p_i^*, i = 1, \ldots, K$, are probabilities (although, most likely, different from the "true" probability): they are positive, and they add up to one. We can then write equation (6.22) as

$$S_j(0) = \sum_{i=1}^{K} p_i^* \frac{s_j^i}{1+r} = E^*[\bar{S}_j(1)] \tag{6.23}$$

where E^* is the expected value under the probabilities p_i^*, and $\bar{S}$ is the discounted price of stock S. The last equality implies that the discounted stock prices are martingales under the probabilities p_i^*. We recall that such probabilities are said to define a **risk-neutral probability measure** or an **equivalent martingale measure.** We have shown that *the existence of state prices is equivalent to the existence of a risk-neutral probability measure.*

6.3.3   No Arbitrage and Risk-Neutral Probabilities

We state now a classical result in finance, the so-called **fundamental theorem of asset pricing.** It shows why the concept of martingale measures is so important. The theorem says,

No arbitrage = Existence of at least one equivalent martingale measure

This is stated more precisely in the following theorem:

THEOREM 6.2   Consider a discrete-time financial-market model with finitely many possible random outcomes. If there exists a martingale measure with positive probabilities, then the market is arbitrage-free. Conversely, if the market is arbitrage-free, then there exists a martingale measure with positive probabilities.

Another classical result in the theory of arbitrage-free markets is the following:

Market completeness = Existence of a unique equivalent martingale measure

This theorem can be stated more precisely:

THEOREM 6.3   Consider a discrete-time financial-market model with finitely many possible random outcomes. If there exists a unique martingale measure with positive probabilities, then the market is complete and arbitrage-free. Conversely, if the market is arbitrage-free and complete, then there exists a unique martingale measure with positive probabilities.

Somewhat weaker versions of these two theorems are also true in more complex market models.

Let us restate Theorem 6.2 in our single-period model:

THEOREM 6.4   Consider a single-period financial-market model like the one described earlier. If there exist strictly positive risk-neutral probabilities p_i^*, then the market is arbitrage-free. Conversely, if the market is arbitrage-free, then there exist strictly positive risk-neutral probabilities p_i^*.

One direction is easy to prove, that the existence of risk-neutral probabilities assures absence of arbitrage. In order to show that fact, recall from equation (3.3) that the discounted wealth at time 1 is

$$\bar{X}(1) = \delta_0 + \sum_{i=1}^{N} \delta_i \bar{S}_i(1)$$

(where δ_0 is the number of units of the risk-free security), so that

$$E^*[\bar{X}(1)] = \delta_0 + \sum_{i=1}^{N} \delta_i S_i(0) = X(0)$$

by the self-financing condition (3.2). This expression means that (as observed previously with one risky asset) *the discounted wealth process is also a martingale under the risk-neutral probability measure.*

In particular, suppose that at time 1 we never lose, so that $\bar{X}(1)$ is always nonnegative. Assume also it is strictly positive in some states of the world. Then $E^*[\bar{X}(1)] = X(0)$ has to be strictly positive; that is, the initial investment $X(0)$ is strictly positive. But this conclusion means that there is no possibility of arbitrage—if we start with zero initial investment, we cannot end with nonnegative, and sometimes strictly positive, wealth.

The reverse statement—that is, that the absence of arbitrage implies the existence of a risk-neutral probability measure—is proved in the appendix to this chapter (section 6.4) in a simple model, as is Theorem 6.3. For the proofs of these theorems in more complex models, see the more advanced books mentioned in the references.

6.3.4 Pricing by No Arbitrage

An important practical question when trading contingent claims is, What is a fair price for the claim, and is there only one? This question is related to the possibility of replicating the claim. Recall that we say that a contingent claim C, with payoff at time T, can be replicated if there exists a strategy whose time-T wealth $X(T)$ is equal to C in all states of the world.

Denote by $C(0)$ the initial cost of that strategy. One of the most important principles in this book is this:

If a claim C can be replicated, then the price of the claim has to be equal to its replication cost C(0), or there is an arbitrage opportunity.

We call this amount $C(0)$ the **no-arbitrage price** of C or, simply, the price of C. Let us first support the preceding statement by an example.

Example 6.3 (Arbitrage by Replication)   Recall Example 3.7: a single-period model with $r = 0.005$, $S(0) = 100$, $s_1 = 101$, and $s_2 = 99$, where s_1 and s_2 are the two possible prices of the stock at moment 1, that is, $u = 1.01$, $d = 0.99$. The payoff is a European call option,

$$g[S(1)] = [S(1) - K]^+ = \max[S(1) - K, 0]$$

For the strike price $K = S(0) = 100$, the payoff will be 1 if the stock goes up and 0 if the stock goes down. Looking for the replicating portfolio, we solve

$$\delta_0(1 + 0.005) + \delta_1 101 = 1$$
$$\delta_0(1 + 0.005) + \delta_1 99 = 0$$

where δ_0 is the dollar amount invested in the bank account or bond, while δ_1 is the number of shares of the stock. The solution to these two equations is $\delta_0 = -49.2537$, $\delta_1 = 0.5$. That is, we borrow 49.2537 from the bank and buy half a share of the stock. The cost of the replicating strategy is

$$C(0) = \delta_0 + \delta_1 S(0) = \$0.746$$

   On the one hand, suppose, for example, that the price of the option is larger than the replication cost, say, equal to $c = \$1.00$. Taf can then sell the option for $1.00, deposit $0.254 of that amount in the bank, and use the remaining $0.746 to replicate the option's payoff. Suppose first that at time $T = 1$ the stock price is $S(1) = 101$. Then the payoff is $1.00, which is also the value of Taf's replicating portfolio, so Taf can deliver it to the holder of the option. Taf still has $0.254(1 + r)$ in the bank. The same reasoning applies if $S(1) = 99$. This result is arbitrage.
   On the other hand, suppose next that the price c is less than $C(0)$, say, equal to $0.50. Then Taf can borrow $0.746, buy the option for $0.50, and set aside $0.246 (or deposit it in the bank). Then, starting with $-$0.746$, Taf can use the strategy $-\delta$, that is, sell short 0.5 shares of the stock and deposit $\delta_0 = \$49.2537$ in the bank. Suppose first that the stock price is $S(1) = 101$ at time $T = 1$. Taf's option is then worth one dollar, which is exactly how much Taf owes in this replicating strategy. But, Taf still has $0.246 that was set aside at time $t = 0$. This is an arbitrage opportunity again. Similar steps may be followed if $S(1) = 99$.

   We now provide a more general argument for the statement that the price of C has to be equal to its replicating cost:

   Suppose, first, that the price c of the contingent claim that pays the random amount C at maturity is larger than the cost $C(0)$ of the strategy that replicates the payoff of that contingent claim. Then we can sell the contingent claim for the amount c larger than $C(0)$, invest $C(0)$ to replicate it, and deposit the extra money $c - C(0)$ in the bank. This result is arbitrage, because at time T we pay C (whatever it might be), and we still have the money in the bank. Conversely, suppose that the price c of the contingent claim that pays C is less than the cost $C(0)$ of its replicating portfolio. We first borrow an amount of cash $C(0) > c$, so that our initial wealth is equal to $-C(0)$. We buy the contingent claim and keep the difference $C(0) - c$ in the bank. We take exactly the opposite positions in the replicating portfolio (short when we needed to be long and the other way around). At maturity, having followed the opposite of the replicating strategy, we will have to pay C, but that is exactly the payoff of the contingent claim that we bought, so they exactly match, and we still have the money in the bank. This outcome is arbitrage.

How extraordinarily important this result is became clear in the 1970s, when researchers built mathematical models in which every claim can be replicated (the reader will recall that we say that such market models are **complete**). In addition, these models were sophisticated enough to make possible a sufficiently realistic description of the real financial markets. In other words, suddenly *we have usable models in which every claim can be priced in a unique way by the principle of no arbitrage, without knowing individual risk preferences!* In particular, researchers found ways of computing these prices in the Merton-Black-Scholes and Cox-Ross-Rubinstein models. We will see how these computations are done in the next chapter. But we first discuss a general, probabilistic representation for the no-arbitrage price of a claim.

6.3.5 Pricing by Risk-Neutral Expected Values

We have just argued that the price of a contingent claim with random payoff C at maturity that can be replicated by trading in the market has to be equal to the cost of its replicating strategy. Let us denote by X^C the replicating wealth process, so that $X^C(T) = C$ and $C(0) = X^C(0)$ is the price of C. Remember also that, at least in the single-period market model, a discounted wealth process is a martingale under the risk-neutral probability measure P^*. This fact implies that $X^C(0) = E^*[\bar{X}^C(T)]$, or, equivalently,

$$C(0) = E^*[\bar{C}] \tag{6.24}$$

In words, *the price of a claim C is equal to the risk-neutral expected value of its discounted payoff.*

While we have proved this result only for the single-period model, it can also be shown to be true in most other models, that is, in those in which the discounted wealth processes are martingales under the risk-neutral probability. This formulation can be used even if the contingent claim with payoff C cannot be replicated. This would be the case in an incomplete-markets setting, in which there are many risk-neutral probability measures. What is often assumed in such a situation is that there is one risk-neutral probability measure P^* among those many possible probability measures, which the market chooses to price the contingent claim via equality (6.24). However, in order to decide which probability P^* is chosen, typically we need to introduce the risk preferences of the investors into the picture (through utility functions), something that is not necessary in the complete-market models.

Equation (6.24) may look familiar because we have already obtained such a result in Theorem 6.1.

It may be surprising that the prices are computed as expected values under a risk-neutral probability. The reader familiar with insurance mathematics may recall that insurance contracts are priced under the true probability. However, in insurance the contracts are priced directly using the values of the expected losses and gains, while financial contracts should be priced taking into the account the prices of other securities that can be traded, because investors can and will trade in all the available securities if it is in their interest to do so. For example, a call option has to be priced relative to the price of the underlying.

Example 6.4 (Replication Cost as Expected Value)   Consider again the setting of Example 6.3, with $r = 0.005$, $S(0) = 100$, $s_1 = 101$, $s_2 = 99$, and the price of the call option equal to the replication cost $C(0) = 0.746$. Let us compute the risk-neutral probabilities in this example. For the discounted stock to be a martingale, we must have $E^*[\bar{S}(1)] = S(0)$, or

$$p^* \frac{101}{1.005} + (1 - p^*) \frac{99}{1.005} = 100$$

Solving for p^*, we obtain $p^* = 0.75$. Then, computing the risk-neutral expected value of the discounted payoff of the call option, we get

$$E^*[\bar{C}(1)] = p^* \frac{100 - 1}{1.005} = 0.746$$

which is the same amount we obtained for the replication cost $C(0)$ of the option.

6.3.6   Martingale Measure for the Merton-Black-Scholes Model

Consider the Merton-Black-Scholes model, with stock S that satisfies $dS = S[\mu \, dt + \sigma \, dW]$ and with a bank account with constant interest rate r. It will be convenient to "modify" the discounted wealth process $\bar{X}$ to get a martingale process. (We have already done so in chapter 4, but we repeat it here for the reader's convenience.) We recall the **market price of risk θ**, given by

$$\theta := \sigma^{-1}(\mu - r)$$

also called **risk premium** or **relative risk.** This quantity compares the return rates of the risky asset and the risk-free asset, normalized by the volatility of the risky asset. We also recall the **risk-neutral density** process or the **continuous-time Arrow-Debreu price process:**

$$Z(t) = \exp\left\{-\theta W(t) - \tfrac{1}{2}\theta^2 t\right\} \tag{6.25}$$

Itô's rule implies

$$dZ = -\theta Z\, dW, \qquad Z(0) = 1$$

In particular, as a stochastic integral, Z is a martingale, with expectation equal to one. Using Itô's rule for products and the dynamics (3.36), we get

$$d(Z\bar{X}) = \bar{Z}[\pi\sigma - \theta X]\, dW \tag{6.26}$$

or

$$Z(t)\bar{X}(t) = x + \int_0^t \bar{Z}(u)[\pi(u)\sigma - \theta X(u)]\, dW(u) \tag{6.27}$$

This equation means that

$Z\bar{X}$ is a martingale $\hfill$ (6.28)

if the integrand in the stochastic integral satisfies some technical conditions, which we assume to be the case. As a consequence of the martingale property, we get

$$E_t[Z(T)\bar{X}(T)] = Z(t)\bar{X}(t) \tag{6.29}$$

where E_t, as usual, denotes expectation conditional on the information available up to time t. In particular, we have the **budget constraint**

$$E[Z(T)\bar{X}(T)] = x \tag{6.30}$$

In other words, the initial wealth amount can be obtained as the expected value (under the "true" probability measure) of the discounted wealth multiplied by the risk-neutral density. As in the Cox-Ross-Rubinstein model, we have the following result on the possibility of replicating a contingent claim with random payoff C, starting with initial amount x:

THEOREM 6.5   A contingent claim with random payoff C at maturity T can be replicated, starting with initial wealth $C(0)$, if and only if

$$E[Z(T)\bar{C}] = C(0)$$

Proof   We have already shown that if $X(T) = C$ then $E[Z(T)\bar{X}(T)]$ is equal to the initial wealth $x = C(0)$. Let us discuss the converse: there exists a strategy that replicates C starting with initial amount $C(0) = E[Z(T)\bar{C}]$. In order to show this fact we need to recall a deep result from the theory of stochastic analysis called the **martingale representation theorem:**

THEOREM 6.6   If a process M is a martingale with respect to the information generated by Brownian motion W, then it has a representation of the form

$$M(t) = E_t[M(T)] = E[M(T)] + \int_0^t \varphi(u)\, dW(u) \tag{6.31}$$

for some (adapted) process φ. In particular,

$$M(T) = E[M(T)] + \int_0^T \varphi(u)\, dW(u)$$

We use this result on the martingale $E_t[Z(T)\bar{C}]$ (see Problem 22 for the martingale property of $E_t[Z(T)\bar{C}]$):

$$E_t[Z(T)\bar{C}] = E[Z(T)\bar{C}] + \int_0^t \varphi(u)\, dW(u) \tag{6.32}$$

If we define $X(t)$ and $\pi^C(t)$ such that

$$Z(t)\bar{X}(t) := E_t[Z(T)\bar{C}], \qquad \bar{Z}[\pi^C \sigma - \theta X] := \varphi \tag{6.33}$$

we see that equations (6.27) and (6.32) are the same. Hence, X is a wealth process associated with the portfolio π^C [since this choice for the portfolio guarantees that the wealth follows the process (6.27)]. Moreover, we see from the first expression in equations (6.33) and properties of conditional expectations that $X(T) = C$ and $X(0) = E[Z(T)\bar{C}] = C(0)$. Therefore, indeed, the portfolio π^C replicates the claim C starting with initial amount $C(0)$.   ∎

We now want to reexpress the preceding results using the notion of the risk-neutral, martingale measure. Consider a contingent claim paying a random amount C with maturity at time T. It follows from Theorem 6.5 that the initial capital $x = X^C(0)$ needed to finance the replicating strategy is then

$$X^C(0) = E[Z(T)\bar{C}] \tag{6.34}$$

More generally, from the martingale property of ZX, we have

$$Z(t)\bar{X}^C(t) = E_t[Z(T)\bar{C}] \tag{6.35}$$

In order to avoid the multiplication with the risk-neutral density $Z(T)$, we introduce the **risk-neutral probability** or **equivalent martingale measure** P^*, on events corresponding to the time interval $[0, T]$:

$$P^*[A] := E\left[Z(T)\mathbf{1}_A\right] \tag{6.36}$$

Here, the **indicator function** $\mathbf{1}_A$ is equal to one if the event A occurs, and it is equal to zero otherwise. In Problem 23 you are asked to show that P^* is indeed a well-defined probability. We denote by E^* expectation taken under the risk-neutral probability P^*. From the definition of P^* it is not too surprising that we have, for a given random variable X (measurable with respect to the information $\mathcal{F}_T$ available at time T),

$$E[Z(T)X] = E^*[X] \tag{6.37}$$

From this we show in the appendix to this chapter (section 6.4) that the following **Bayes' rule** for conditional expectations under the two probability measures holds:

$$E_t[Z(T)X] = Z(t)E_t^*[X] \tag{6.38}$$

We see then that equation (6.34) can be written as

$$X^C(0) = E^*[\bar{C}] \tag{6.39}$$

Similarly, from equations (6.35) and (6.38) with $X = \bar{C}$, it can also be concluded that *the discounted replicating process $\bar{X}^C$ of C is given as the risk-neutral conditional expected value of its discounted payoff:*

$$\bar{X}^C(t) = E_t^*[\bar{C}] \tag{6.40}$$

In particular, for the stock price itself, we have

$$\bar{S}(t) = E_t^*[\bar{S}(T)]$$

In other words, the *discounted stock-price process $\bar{S}$ is a martingale under probability* P^*. Hence the name "equivalent martingale measure." It may be shown from the martingale representation theorem that, as a P^*-martingale, the discounted stock price has to satisfy

$$d\bar{S} = \bar{S}\sigma \, dW^* \tag{6.41}$$

for some P^*–Brownian motion W^*. Using Itô's rule on the product $S(t) = e^{rt}\bar{S}(t)$, we see that the stock-price process S has the drift equal to the interest rate under the risk-neutral probability P^*:

$$dS = S[r \, dt + \sigma \, dW^*] \tag{6.42}$$

Comparing equation (6.42) to $dS = S[\mu\,dt + \sigma\,dW]$, we see that we need to have

$$W^*(t) = W(t) + \sigma^{-1}(\mu - r)t \tag{6.43}$$

Another famous theorem from stochastic analysis, the **Girsanov theorem,** says that W^* is, indeed, Brownian motion under P^*. Note that from equation (3.36) we have

$$d\bar{X} = \bar{\pi}\sigma\,dW^* \tag{6.44}$$

In particular, under technical conditions, which we assume,

The discounted wealth process $\bar{X}$ is a P^*-martingale $\tag{6.45}$

It can also be shown that *there is only one risk-neutral probability in the Merton-Black-Scholes model,* the one described earlier. As mentioned before, this is a characteristic of complete markets, in which all payoffs (up to technical conditions) can be replicated by a self-financing portfolio strategy. In the Merton-Black-Scholes model, we have one Brownian motion process and one stock, allowing us to replicate any payoff that depends on the Brownian motion. That would not be the case if we had two Brownian motion processes and one stock (in general, if we have more Brownian motion processes than stocks).

6.3.7   Computing Expectations by the Feynman-Kac PDE

We have seen in equations (6.34) and (6.39) that the cost of replicating a given random amount can be computed as an expected value. We will need this fact later in order to describe a way of calculating prices of derivative securities. In particular, we will use the following result:

Expected values of diffusion processes can be computed by solving the Feynman-Kac partial differential equation.

More precisely, we have the following important result from the theory of diffusion processes:

THEOREM 6.7 (FEYNMAN-KAC THEOREM)   Let X be a diffusion process satisfying

$$dX(t) = \mu(t, X(t))\,dt + \sigma(t, X(t))\,dW(t)$$

Denote by $E_{t,x}$ the expectation conditioned on the event $X(t) = x$. Consider the function

$$V(t, x) := E_{t,x}\left[e^{-\int_t^T r(u, X(u))du}\, g(X(T)) + \int_t^T e^{-\int_t^u r(z, X(z))dz} f(u, X(u))\,du \right]$$

for some given functions r, g, and f. Under technical conditions, function V is the solution to the **Feynman-Kac PDE,** or F-K PDE, and the boundary condition

$$V_t + \frac{1}{2}\sigma^2 V_{xx} + \mu V_x - rV + f = 0, \qquad V(T, x) = g(x) \tag{6.46}$$

(Subscripts denote partial derivatives. For example, V_{xx} is the second partial derivative with respect to the variable x.) If we think of X as an underlying financial process on which someone writes an option that pays a continuous dividend stream with the cumulative value $\int_0^t f(u, X(u))\, du$ and also pays $g(X(T))$ at maturity T, then V can be thought of as the initial cost of replicating this option (that is, if we assume that the dynamics of X are given under the risk-neutral probability). We point out that, although in the Merton-Black-Scholes model the interest rate is constant, we consider here the more general case in which it might be a function of the underlying security.

"Proof" of F-K Theorem   We use Itô's rule on the solution $V(t, X(t))$ of the F-K PDE to obtain

$$V(T, X(T)) = V(t, x) + \int_t^T \left[V_u + \frac{1}{2}\sigma^2 V_{xx} + \mu V_x \right] du + \int_t^T [\ldots]\, dW$$

Then, denoting $r(z) = r(z, X(z))$, and again using Itô's rule on the product $\exp\{-\int_t^u r(z)dz\} V(u)$, we deduce

$$e^{-\int_t^T r(u)du} V(T, X(T))$$
$$= V(t, x) + \int_t^T e^{-\int_t^u r(z)dz} \left[V_u + \frac{1}{2}\sigma^2 V_{xx} + \mu V_x - rV \right] du + \int_t^T [\ldots]\, dW$$

However, V satisfies the F-K PDE, that is, $V_t + \frac{1}{2}\sigma^2 V_{xx} + \mu V_x - rV = f$, and the boundary condition $V(t, x) = g(x)$. Substituting these in the previous expression, we get

$$e^{-\int_t^T r(u)du} g(X(T)) = V(t, x) - \int_t^T e^{-\int_t^u r(z)dz} f(u, X(u))\, du + \int_t^T [\ldots]\, dW$$

Under technical conditions, the conditional expectation $E_{t,x}$ of the last term (the stochastic integral) will be zero. In that case, taking expectations we get that $V(t, x)$ is, indeed, equal to the conditional expectation from the statement of the theorem. ∎

6.3.8   Risk-Neutral Pricing in Continuous Time

Let us recall now from equation (6.42) that in the Merton-Black-Scholes model the price process of the stock satisfies

$$dS = S[r\, dt + \sigma W^*] \tag{6.47}$$

for some Brownian motion W^* under the risk-neutral probability P^*, which is unique, meaning, we also recall, that in this model the market is complete. Thus, "every" contingent claim can be replicated. Hence, a price of the contingent claim with random payoff C is again given by

$$C(0) = E^*[\bar{C}]$$

(Strictly speaking, we at least have to assume that the claim is such that the expectation $E^*[\bar{C}]$ exists; it is for this reason that we write "every.") For example, consider a contingent claim with a payoff of the form $C = g(S(T))$, for some function g. Then the price of this option in the Merton-Black-Scholes model is $E^*[e^{-rT}g(S(T))]$, where the expectation is computed under the risk-neutral dynamics (6.47). Note that this dynamics does not depend on the actual drift of the stock μ, which has been replaced by the interest rate r. Therefore, also, *the price of an option in the Merton-Black-Scholes model does not depend on the stock's drift μ.*

This result is very nice from the practical point of view, since the expected return rate μ is difficult to estimate in practice. A partial intuition for it is that the option is priced relative to the stock: since we can go long or short in the stock in order to replicate the payoff of the option, it does not matter whether the stock tends to go up or down on average (which is what the drift μ measures).

6.3.9 Futures and Forwards Revisited*

Let us consider now the risk-neutral pricing of futures and forwards. We assume that the conditions under which we can price contingent claims under a risk-neutral measure P^* hold. We do not assume anything else about the dynamics of security prices. Recall our notation for the price of the risk-free asset,

$$B(t) = e^{\int_0^t r(u)du}, \qquad B(0) = 1$$

where r is the interest rate, possibly stochastic. Recall also that $B(t)/B(T) = e^{-\int_t^T r(u)du}$ is the discount factor to be applied in order to compute the present value at moment t of some financial variable valued at moment T. The forward contract with maturity T on a non-dividend-paying stock S is the contract with the payoff

$$S(T) - F(t)$$

where $F(t)$ is the forward price, agreed upon at time t. The value of this claim at time t is the risk-neutral expected value of the discounted payoff, that is,

$$E_t^* \left[\frac{\{S(T) - F(t)\}B(t)}{B(T)} \right]$$

We recall that the forward contract has a zero cost. In order for the previous expression to be zero at time t, and considering that the discounted value $S(t)/B(t)$ of the stock is a martingale under P^*, so that $E_t^*[S(T)/B(T)] = S(t)/B(t)$, we get

$$0 = S(t) - F(t)B(t)E_t^*[1/B(T)]$$

Therefore, the forward price is

$$F(t) = \frac{S(t)}{B(t)E_t^*[1/B(T)]} \qquad (6.48)$$

In the case of the constant interest rate r we get the familiar expression

$$F(t) = S(t)e^{r(T-t)}$$

already obtained before by no-arbitrage arguments.

As for a futures contract on the stock, the time–t discounted profit or loss of a long position in a futures contract in an interval $[t_i, t_{i+1}]$ is

$$\frac{B(t_i)[f(t_{i+1}) - f(t_i)]}{B(t_{i+1})}$$

where $f(t)$ is the futures price at time t. The total discounted profit or loss $G(t, T)$ on the interval $[t, T]$ is the sum of these terms over all intervals. Assuming that marking to market takes place at very short time intervals, the continuous-time approximation of the sum is

$$G(t, T) = B(t) \int_t^T \frac{1}{B(u)}\, df(u)$$

Since the futures contract costs nothing to enter into, we want the value of the total profit or loss—that is, the risk-neutral expectation of the discounted profit or loss—to be zero for all $t \leq T$. That is, we want to have

$$E_t^* \left[\int_t^T \frac{1}{B(u)} df(u) \right] = 0 \qquad (6.49)$$

for all $t \leq T$. We also need to have

$$f(T) = S(T) \qquad (6.50)$$

This condition states the obvious fact that the value of a futures contract with immediate maturity has to be equal to the value of the underlying. We now argue that these two conditions will be satisfied if

$$f(t) = E_t^*[S(T)] \qquad (6.51)$$

The reason is that the process $f(t)$ as defined here is a P^*-martingale, which also implies (by results of stochastic analysis) that the integral process $M(s) := \int_0^s \frac{1}{B(u)} df(u)$ is a P^*-martingale (if $1/B$ satisfies mild regularity conditions); this result, in turn, means that $E_t^*[M(T) - M(t)] = 0$, which is equivalent to equation (6.49).

In words, we have shown that, at least in theory, *the futures price is the risk-neutral expected value of the underlying spot price at maturity (without discounting).*

When the interest rate is constant, so that $B(t) = e^{rt}$, and given that $E_t^*[e^{-rT} S(T)] = e^{-rt} S(t)$ by the martingale property, we see that $f(t) = e^{r(T-t)} S(t)$, which is also the forward price. In general, the forward price and the futures price are not the same, and the difference is

$$F(t) - f(t) = \frac{S(t)}{B(t) E_t^*[1/B(T)]} - E_t^*[S(T)] \qquad (6.52)$$

Note that this equation implies that the risk-neutral covariance of $S(T)$ and $1/B(T)$ at time t is

$$\begin{aligned} \text{Cov}_t^*[S(T), 1/B(T)] &= E_t^*[S(T)/B(T)] - E_t^*[S(T)] E_t^*[1/B(T)] \\ &= S(t)/B(t) - E_t^*[S(T)] E_t^*[1/B(T)] \\ &= [F(t) - f(t)] E_t^*[1/B(T)] \end{aligned}$$

where we have again used the fact that $S(t)/B(t)$ is a P^*-martingale. This equation provides another expression for the **forward-futures spread:**

$$F(t) - f(t) = \frac{\text{Cov}_t^*[S(T), 1/B(T)]}{E_t^*[1/B(T)]} \qquad (6.53)$$

We see that the theoretical forward price and the futures price are equal if and only if $S(T)$ and $1/B(T)$ are uncorrelated under the risk-neutral probability P^*. Of course, that is the case if the interest rate is constant.

We have seen that the theoretical futures price $f(t)$ is the expected value $E_t^*[S(T)]$ of the spot price at maturity under the risk-neutral probability. Historically, economists have studied the relation between the futures price $f(t)$ and the expected spot price $E[S(T)]$ under the real-world probability. In fact, this topic has been of such a great interest that it was given really cute names: the situation in which $f(t) < E[S(T)]$ is called **normal backwardation.** The case in which $f(t) > E[S(T)]$ is called **contango.** It has been argued that when the hedgers mostly hold short positions in futures while speculators balance the market by holding long positions, the typical outcome is $f(t) < E[S(T)]$. This outcome occurs because the speculators require compensation for the risk of holding long positions and expect the futures price to increase over time, while the hedgers are willing to pay that compensation in order to avoid risk. Conversely, if the speculators tend to hold a short position, it is argued that we have $f(t) > E[S(T)]$, by similar reasoning.

6.4   Appendix

6.4.1   No Arbitrage Implies Existence of a Risk-Neutral Probability*

We provide here a proof of the second part of Theorem 6.4, that is, that the absence of arbitrage implies the existence of a risk-neutral probability. Consider the set A of all random variables $\bar{X}(1)$ such that $\bar{X}(1)$ is the time-1 discounted wealth of a strategy for which the initial investment $X(0)$ is zero. Denote by B the set of all random variables Y such that Y is always nonnegative, and $E[Y] \geq 1$. (We could require $E[Y] \geq a$ for any fixed positive number a; we set $a = 1$ for convenience only; we cannot set $a = 0$ because doing so might destroy the closedness property, needed later.) In particular, this condition implies that Y is positive in at least some states of the world. The absence of arbitrage implies that the sets A and B cannot have common elements. Note that the set A can be thought of as a vector space that is a subset of the vector space of dimension K, the number of possible values for $\bar{X}(1)$. Similarly, the set B can be thought of as a subset of the K-dimensional vector space, and this subset is closed and convex. [*Closed* means that a limit of a sequence of elements in B is an element of B; *convex* means that a line connecting two elements of B is inside B; equivalently, for any two elements b_1, b_2 of B, and $0 < \lambda < 1$, the point $\lambda b_1 + (1 - \lambda)b_2$ is also in B.] There is an important theorem of functional analysis, called the **separating hyperplane theorem** or **Hahn-Banach theorem,** that says that, under these conditions, there exists a plane that separates A and B. (Just imagine an oval-shaped subset B in the three-dimensional space that does not intersect with a two-dimensional plane A—it is obvious that we can draw a plane that separates those two sets A and B.) Mathematically, therefore, there exists a vector $d = (d_1, \dots, d_K)$ such that

$$\sum_{i=1}^{K} d_i a_i = 0, \qquad \sum_{i=1}^{K} d_i b_i > 0 \tag{6.54}$$

for every vector $a = (a_1, \dots, a_K)$ in A and every vector $b = (b_1, \dots, b_K)$ in B. For a given $j \leq K$, we can always choose a vector b in B such that all its coordinates are zero, except b_j, which is strictly larger than zero. The second relation in equations (6.54) implies then that $d_j > 0$, and this statement is true for all $j = 1, \dots, K$. We can then define positive probabilities

$$p_j^* = \frac{d_j}{\sum_{i=1}^{K} d_i}$$

It remains to show that these are risk-neutral probabilities. The first equality in equations (6.54) implies

$$\sum_{i=1}^{K} p_i^* a_i = 0 \tag{6.55}$$

for every vector a in A. For a given stock S consider now the strategy of borrowing $S(0)$ from the bank and buying one share of S. This strategy has zero initial investment, hence its time-1 discounted value, equal to $-S(0) + \bar{S}(1)$, belongs to the set A. By equation (6.55),

$$\sum_{i=1}^{K} p_i^* [\bar{s}_i - S(0)] = 0$$

or, written differently,

$$E^*[\bar{S}(1)] = S(0)$$

This result shows that, indeed, p_i^*, $i = 1, \ldots, K$, are risk-neutral probabilities.

6.4.2 Completeness and Unique EMM*

We now present a proof of Theorem 6.3 in the single-period model with finitely many outcomes. We are indebted to Dmitry Kramkov for this proof.

We first show that completeness implies existence of a unique equivalent martingale measure. Let us denote the possible outcomes (states of the world) by $\omega_1, \ldots, \omega_K$, corresponding to the possible stock values $s_1, \ldots, s_K$. In other words, the stock takes the value s_i if and only if the outcome ω_i occurs. For a contingent claim with payoff C at time 1, denote by $C(\omega_i)$ the amount of the payoff if the outcome ω_i occurs. Introduce the indicator functions $\mathbf{1}_i(\omega)$ equal to one if realized outcome ω is equal to ω_i, and to zero otherwise. Since the market is complete, we can replicate the payoffs $\mathbf{1}_i$. Denote by x_i the associated initial cost of replication. We have the following properties (see Problem 24):

1. All x_i's are positive, because otherwise there would be arbitrage.

2. We have

$$\sum_{i=1}^{K} x_i = 1/(1+r)$$

This relation holds because $\sum_{i=1}^{K} \mathbf{1}_i = 1$ and the initial cost of 1 dollar is $1/(1+r)$.

3. The initial cost for replicating a claim C is

$$c_0 = \sum_{i=1}^{K} C(\omega_i) x_i$$

This relation holds because for any outcome ω we have $C(\omega) = \sum_{i=1}^{K} C(\omega_i) \mathbf{1}_i(\omega)$.

We can now define a new probability

$$P^*[\omega_i] := \frac{x_i}{1+r}$$

It is now easily checked from properties 1–3 that this is an equivalent martingale measure. Suppose that $\tilde{P}$ is another EMM. Then, since the cost of replication has to satisfy $x_i = \tilde{E}[\mathbf{1}_i/(1+r)]$, we get

$$\tilde{P}[\omega_i] = \tilde{E}[\mathbf{1}_i] = x_i(1+r) = P^*[\omega_i]$$

Thus, $P^* = \tilde{P}$, and the EMM is unique.

We now show the reverse, that existence of a unique EMM P^* implies that the market is complete. First, we already know that if an EMM exists the market is arbitrage-free. Next, denote by A the set of all random variables $X(1)$ such that $X(1)$ is the time-1 wealth of a strategy for which the initial investment $X(0)$ is zero. Let us consider a claim C such that $E^*[C] = 0$, and denote by X^* an element of A that attains the minimum

$$\min_{X \in A} E^*[(X - C)^2]$$

For any given $X \in A$ and number y we have $yX + (1-y)X^* \in A$, and the function

$$f(y) := E^*[\{yX + (1-y)X^* - C\}^2]$$

attains its minimum at $y = 0$. Taking a derivative we get

$$0 = f'(0) = 2E^*[(X^* - C)(X - X^*)]$$

hence

$$E^*[X(X^* - C)] = E^*[X^*(X^* - C)]$$

and $E^*[X(X^* - C)]$ has the same value for all $X \in A$. In particular, since $0 \in A$ this value has to be zero:

$$E^*[X(X^* - C)] = 0, \quad X \in A$$

Now choose ε small enough to have

$$1 + \varepsilon[X^*(\omega) - C(\omega)] > 0$$

for all possible outcomes $\omega = \omega_1, \ldots, \omega_K$. Moreover, define

$$\tilde{P}(\omega) := P^*(\omega)[1 + \varepsilon\{X^*(\omega) - C(\omega)\}] \qquad (6.56)$$

We can see the following:

1. $\tilde{P}(\omega) > 0$.

2. Since $E^*[C] = 0$ and the cost $E^*[X^*/(1+r)]$ of replicating X^* is also zero (because $X^* \in A$), we get

$$\sum_{i=1}^{K} \tilde{P}(\omega_i) = \sum_{i=1}^{K}[1 + \varepsilon\{X^*(\omega_i) - C(\omega_i)\}]P^*[\omega_i] = E^*[1 + \varepsilon(X^* - C)] = 1$$

3. Let X be the final wealth of a strategy with initial cost x. Then the random variable

$$Y := X - x(1 + r)$$

is an element of A, and therefore

$$\tilde{E}[Y] = E^*[Y\{1 + \varepsilon(X^* - C)\}] = 0$$

Hence,

$$\tilde{E}[X] = x(1 + r) + \tilde{E}[Y] = x(1 + r)$$

Properties 1–3 imply that $\tilde{P}$ is an EMM. Since we assumed that the EMM is unique, we get $\tilde{P}[\omega] = P^*[\omega]$, which, from definition (6.56), implies

$$X^* = C$$

Therefore, any claim C for which $E^*[C] = 0$ can be replicated. In general, we denote

$$c_0 := E^*\left[\frac{C}{1+r}\right]$$

and define D by

$$C = D + c_0(1 + r)$$

Then D is an element of A, so we can replicate C by replicating D and investing c_0 in the bank. To recap, any claim C can be replicated, and the market is complete.

6.4.3 Another Proof of Theorem 6.4*

We now present an alternative proof, in the single-period model, for the fact that the absence of arbitrage implies existence of an EMM. This proof does not use the separating hyperplane theorem. The idea is the following: we first make the market complete, and then use Theorem 6.3, which we have just proved. We are again indebted to Dmitry Kramkov for providing us with this proof. We use the same notation as in the previous section. First we need the following lemma:

LEMMA 6.1   Consider an arbitrage-free single-period market with finitely many outcomes. Suppose that we add an arbitrary claim C to the market. There is a price c_0 for this claim such that the new, extended market is also arbitrage-free.

Proof   Consider all the strategies with final wealth X that dominates C, that is, such that

$$X(\omega) \geq C(\omega)$$

for all possible outcomes ω. Denote by x^u the smallest initial cost of all such strategies. Similarly, denote by x^d the largest initial cost of all the strategies that are dominated by C. It can be shown (but it is not very easy) that there exists a strategy with initial cost x^u (x^d) which dominates (is dominated by) C.

We note that we must have $x^d \leq x^u$, or else there is arbitrage (see Problem 25). Suppose first that $x^d < x^u$. Then we can set c_0 to be any number such that $x^d < c_0 < x^u$. The reader is asked in Problem 25 to show that the extended market is still arbitrage-free with this choice of c_0. If, however, $x^d = x^u$, consider the strategies with final wealths X and Y and initial wealths $x^d = x^u$ such that

$$X(\omega) \geq C(\omega) \geq Y(\omega)$$

for all outcomes ω. The absence of arbitrage in the original market implies that we must have

$$X(\omega) = C(\omega) = Y(\omega)$$

for all outcomes ω. This result means that C can be replicated and that its only no-arbitrage price is $c_0 = x^u = x^d$. This fact proves the lemma.   ∎

Using the lemma, we can add, one by one, the claims $\mathbf{1}_i$ introduced in the previous section as new securities into the market, while still preserving the no-arbitrage property. But this extended market is complete, since any claim C can be represented as

$$C(\omega) = \sum_{i=1}^{K} C(\omega_i)\mathbf{1}_i(\omega)$$

and can therefore be replicated by trading in $\mathbf{1}_i$ securities, holding $C(\omega_i)$ shares of the security $\mathbf{1}_i$. We can now use Theorem 6.3 to conclude that there exists an EMM P^* for the extended market. This is also an EMM for the original market, and we are done.

6.4.4 Proof of Bayes' Rule**

We provide the proof of Bayes' rule

$$E_t[Z(T)X] = Z(t)E_t^*[X] \tag{6.57}$$

using the fact that

$$E[Z(T)X] = E^*[X] \tag{6.58}$$

For this we need the definition of conditional expectations from the measure theory: Conditional expectation $Y = E_t[X]$ with respect to the information given by the σ-algebra $\mathcal{F}_t$ (see the chapter 16 definitions) is the random variable Y that is $\mathcal{F}_t$-measurable, and such that $E[\mathbf{1}_A Y] = E[\mathbf{1}_A X]$, for each event A in the σ-algebra $\mathcal{F}_t$ (which means that A is an event known at time t). Therefore, in order to prove equation (6.57), it is sufficient to show that for each event A in the σ-algebra $\mathcal{F}_t$ we have

$$E^* \left[\mathbf{1}_A \frac{E_t[Z(T)X]}{Z(t)} \right] = E^* [\mathbf{1}_A X] \tag{6.59}$$

From equation (6.58), the left-hand side is equal to

$$E \left[Z(T)\mathbf{1}_A \frac{E_t[Z(T)X]}{Z(t)} \right]$$

Next, by the martingale property and properties of conditional expectations (see chapter 16), this last expression is equal to

$$E \left[E_t \left\{ Z(T)\mathbf{1}_A \frac{E_t[Z(T)X]}{Z(t)} \right\} \right] = E[\mathbf{1}_A E_t\{Z(T)X\}] = E[\mathbf{1}_A Z(T)X]$$

Using equation (6.58) again, we see that the last expression is the same as $E^*[\mathbf{1}_A X]$, which is the right-hand side in equation (6.59), thereby completing the proof.

Summary

The principle of no arbitrage requires that no money can be made out of nothing without risk. This simple assumption enables us to obtain bounds on the prices of standard options, namely, American and European put and call options. It also implies that the price of an

American call option written on a stock that pays no dividends has to be equal to the price of the corresponding European call option. This statement is not true for put options. The price of the European put can be obtained from the price of the European call with the help of the so-called put-call parity relation.

Absence of arbitrage tells us that the theoretical price of a forward contract on a financial asset has to be equal to the value the current price of the asset would yield at maturity if invested in the bank. A similar expression is obtained if the asset pays dividends, as well as for the forward contract on foreign currency. If the interest rate is constant, the forward price has to be equal to the futures price, in theory. The price of futures on commodities has to be modified by including the cost of storage. Moreover, it may be advantageous to actually own a commodity rather than holding a futures contract. In this case we only know that its futures price has to be lower than it would otherwise be.

It is reasonable to expect, in discrete-time models, that the price of a contingent claim today is equal to a weighted average of its possible future price values. If that is the case, the weights are called state prices. They can be normalized to be probabilities, which constitute a risk-neutral probability measure or an equivalent martingale measure, that is, a probability system in which the discounted asset prices are martingales.

The fundamental theorem of asset pricing says that the absence of arbitrage holds if and only if there exists at least one risk-neutral probability measure. If there is only one such measure, the market is complete. These results hold in finite discrete-time models, and (possibly in a modified version) in other more complex models.

The importance of risk-neutral probabilities becomes clear when we deduce that the absence of arbitrage implies that if a claim can be replicated, then its price has to be equal to the cost of replication (i.e., to the amount needed to invest in the market in order to replicate the claim). This cost, and hence also the price of the claim, is equal to the risk-neutral expected value of the discounted payoff of the claim. In particular, in complete-market models, every contingent claim has a unique no-arbitrage price, equal to the expectation under the equivalent martingale measure. In the Merton-Black-Scholes model, this principle means that in order to compute the price of a contingent claim, we replace the drift of the stock with the interest rate. Therefore, the price of a contingent claim in the Merton-Black-Scholes model does not depend on the drift of the stock. Taking expectations under the risk-neutral probability is equivalent to taking expected values under the original probability, after multiplying by the risk-neutral density. In continuous-time models expectations of this type can also be computed as solutions to the Feynman-Kac PDE.

Using martingale methods, it is not difficult to find theoretical expressions for the forward price and the futures price of an asset. These are equal if the asset is independent of the risk-free asset under the risk-neutral probability.

Problems

1. Provide detailed no-arbitrage arguments for expression (6.3).

†2. Provide detailed no-arbitrage arguments for expression (6.5).

3. Consider a non-dividend-paying stock worth $9.00 today in a market with a continuously compounded interest rate of 10% per year. What are the bounds for the difference between an American call option and an American put option on this stock, with maturity five months and strike price $10.00? If we know that the price of the corresponding European call is $1.50, what are the bounds for the price of the American put?

†4. Assume that the future dividends on a given stock S are known, and denote their discounted value at the present time t by $\bar{D}(t)$. Argue the following:

$$c(t) \geq S(t) - \bar{D}(t) - Ke^{-r(T-t)}, \qquad p(t) \geq \bar{D}(t) + Ke^{-r(T-t)} - S(t) \qquad (6.60)$$

5. In the context of the previous problem show

$$c(t) + \bar{D}(t) + Ke^{-r(T-t)} = p(t) + S(t),$$
$$S(t) - \bar{D}(t) - K \leq C(t) - P(t) \leq S(t) - Ke^{-r(T-t)}$$

†6. Why is an American option always worth more than its intrinsic value? {As an example, recall that the intrinsic value at time t for the call option is $\max[S(t) - K, 0]$.}

7. Consider a European call and a European put, both with maturity in three months and strike price $100, written on a stock with a current price of $100. The stock will pay a dividend of $3 in one month. The prices of the options are $3.50 and $5 respectively. The price of a one-month pure-discount bond (nominal $100) is $99.65, and the interest rate is constant. Suppose that there are no arbitrage opportunities with these securities. There is also another European call and European put with maturities three months and strike prices $50, written on another, non-dividend-paying stock. The prices of these options are $4 and $1.5, respectively. What should be the no-arbitrage price of this stock? Suppose its price is $50. Describe the arbitrage strategy.

†8. A given stock trades at $95, and the European calls and puts on the stock with strike price 100 and maturity three months are trading at $1.97 and $6, respectively. In one month the stock will pay a dividend of $1. The prices of one-month and three-month T-bills are $99.60 and $98.60, respectively. Construct an arbitrage strategy, if possible.

9. Prove using a no-arbitrage argument that a European put option on a non-dividend-paying stock is a convex function of the strike price; that is, if we denote by $p(K)$ the put

price when the strike price is K, then

$$\alpha p(K_1) + (1 - \alpha)p(K_2) > p[\alpha K_1 + (1 - \alpha)K_2]$$

for $0 < \alpha < 1$.

†10. Consider two European call options on the same underlying and with the same maturity, but with different strike prices, K_1 and K_2, respectively. Suppose that $K_1 > K_2$. Prove that the option prices $c(K_i)$ satisfy

$$K_1 - K_2 > c(K_1) - c(K_2)$$

11. Find the forward price of a non-dividend-paying stock traded today at \$10.00, with the continuously compounded interest rate of 8% per year, for a contract expiring seven months from today.

†12. Provide no-arbitrage arguments for equation (6.9).

13. Provide no-arbitrage arguments for equation (6.10).

*14. Consider two forward contracts written on the same stock, with maturities one and four months and prices \$35 and \$34, respectively. The stock will pay a dividend of \$1 in two months. Prices of one-month, two-month, and four-month pure-discount bonds (nominal \$100) are \$99.60, \$99.15, and \$98.20, respectively. Construct an arbitrage strategy, if possible.

15. Complete the proof of equation (6.11).

16. Explain why the futures price will tend to be lower than the forward price, if the underlying asset S is strongly negatively correlated with the interest rate.

17. Argue equation (6.12) for forward contracts.

†18. Argue equation (6.13) for forward contracts.

*19. a. Show that the risk-neutral probabilities in the Cox-Ross-Rubinstein model are given by equations (6.15).

b. Moreover, if we define the risk-neutral density $Z(T)$ as the product of T independent copies of the random variable $Z(1)$ in definition (6.19), then equation (6.21) holds, and Theorem 6.1 is still valid.

†20. Consider a single-period binomial model of Example 6.3. Suppose you have written an option that pays the value of the squared difference between the stock price at maturity and \$100.00; that is, it pays $[S(1) - 100]^2$. What is the cost $C(0)$ of the replicating portfolio? Construct arbitrage strategies in the case that the option price is less than $C(0)$ and in the case that it is larger than $C(0)$. Compute the option price as a risk-neutral expected value.

21. In the context of Example 6.3, find the cost of replication $C(0)$ for the put option with the payoff function $g(s) = (100 - s)^+ = \max(100 - s, 0)$. Construct arbitrage strategies in the case that the option price is less than $C(0)$ and in the case that it is larger than $C(0)$. Compute the option price as a risk-neutral expected value.

*†22 Given a random variable C whose value is known by time T, and such that $E[|C|]$ is finite, show that the process $M(t) := E_t[C]$ is a martingale on the time interval $[0, T]$.

*23. Show that the risk-neutral probability P^* defined in expression (6.36) is indeed a well-defined probability; that is,

$$P^*[\emptyset] = 0, \qquad P^*[\Omega] = 1$$

where $\emptyset$ is the empty set and Ω is the set of all possible outcomes, and

$$P^*\left[\cup_{i=1}^\infty A_i \right] = \sum_{i=1}^\infty P^*[A_i]$$

for a partition $\{A_i\}$ of Ω. You can use the fact that the probability P itself satisfies these properties.

*24. Work out all the missing details for the proof of Theorem 6.3 given in section 6.4.2.

*25. Work out the missing details for the alternative proof of Theorem 6.4 given in section 6.4.3.

Further Readings

Arbitrage pricing of forward and futures contracts was analyzed in Cox, Ingersoll, and Ross (1981). Textbook treatments include Duffie (1989) and Hull (2002). An early version of Theorems 6.2 and 6.4 can be found in Ross (1976b). The idea of a risk-neutral pricing probability is used for options in Merton (1973b) and Cox and Ross (1976a and 1976b). It was extended to continuous-time settings by Ross (1978) and formalized by Harrison and Kreps (1979) and Harrison and Pliska (1981). More advanced treatments can be found in Dothan (1990) and Pliska (1997) in discrete time, and in Bjork (1999), Dana and Jeanblanc (2002), Duffie (2001), Elliott and Kopp (1999), Lamberton and Lapeyre (1997), Musiela and Rutkowski (1997), and Karatzas and Shreve (1998) in continuous time. Presentations of the martingale representation theorem and Girsanov theorem can be found in Karatzas and Shreve (1997) and Steele (2000). Pricing under risk-neutral probabilities has given rise to a large number of empirical studies, often called "tests of the stochastic discount factor." We mention here the influential work of Hansen and Jagannathan (1991). Reviews of that literature can be found in Campbell, Lo, and MacKinlay (1996) and Cochrane (2001).

7 Option Pricing

In the previous chapter we learned that the price of a contingent claim that can be replicated with the existing securities is equal to the risk-neutral expected value of its discounted payoff. Since in the binomial Cox-Ross-Rubinstein (CRR) model every contingent claim can be replicated, we can price all securities by computing this expected value. We will show how to do so in this chapter. Moreover, we will see how to compute option prices in the Merton-Black-Scholes (MBS) model. As an example, we will derive the famous Black-Scholes formula for the European call option. The formula can be obtained in several ways, including the following: as a limit of the CRR model price; directly computed as the risk-neutral expected value of the final payoff; and as a solution to a partial differential equation. We will also discuss pricing of options on stocks that pay dividends, pricing of American and exotic options, pricing of derivatives on an underlying with stochastic volatility, and other, possibly incomplete, market models.

7.1 Option Pricing in the Binomial Model

7.1.1 Backward Induction and Expectation Formula

We recall the binomial CRR model with one stock with price S and a bank account with constant interest rate r. For concreteness, let us assume that the interest rate is continuously compounded. Denote by Δt the length of the time period between two time steps. The model parameters $u > e^{r\Delta t}$ and $d < 1$ are given (actually, $d < e^{r\Delta t}$ is sufficient). During each time period, the stock $S(t)$ moves up to $uS(t)$ or down to $dS(t)$, with probabilities p and $1 - p$, respectively. In order to price options we do not have to know p. Instead, we need to know the risk-neutral probability p^*, which we computed in equations (6.15) in the case of the single-period interest rate r. (There is only one risk-neutral probability, and the CRR model is complete.) For the continuously compounded interest rate r, these formulas become

$$p^* = \frac{e^{r\Delta t} - d}{u - d}, \qquad q^* = 1 - p^* = \frac{u - e^{r\Delta t}}{u - d} \tag{7.1}$$

It is straightforward to check the martingale property, that $S(t) = e^{-r\Delta t}[p^* uS(t) + q^* dS(t)]$. In general (in a complete market), we have shown that the price of a stochastic payoff of C dollars at time T is equal to $C(0) = E^*[e^{-rT}C]$. In particular, suppose that the payoff is given by $C = g(S(T))$ for some nonnegative function g of the stock price value at maturity. Suppose first that there is only one time step between time 0 and time T. Under the risk-neutral probability, at T, the price of the stock is $S(0)u$ with probability p^* and $S(0)d$ with probability $1 - p^*$. Therefore, the option price is

$$C(0) = e^{-rT}[p^* g(S(0)u) + (1 - p^*)g(S(0)d)]$$

More generally, suppose that there are n time periods between time $t = 0$ and time $t = T$. Then, at maturity T, the stock price can have any value of the form $S(0)u^k d^{n-k}$, where k is the number of upward movements, while $n - k$ is the number of downward movements. The risk-neutral probability of having exactly k upward movements is given by the binomial probability

$$P^*(k \text{ upward movements}) = \binom{n}{k}(p^*)^k(1 - p^*)^{n-k}$$

where

$$\binom{n}{k} = \frac{n!}{k!(n-k)!}$$

(Here, $n! = n \cdot (n-1) \cdots 2 \cdot 1$ is n factorial, and $\binom{n}{k}$, to be read "n choose k," is the number of different ways in which it is possible to have exactly k upward steps out of n steps.) Therefore, the option price is

$$C(0) = \sum_{k=0}^{n} \left[e^{-rT} \binom{n}{k}(p^*)^k(1 - p^*)^{n-k} g(S(0)u^k d^{n-k}) \right] \tag{7.2}$$

There is an easy method to compute the previous expression, called the **backward induction** method in the binomial tree. That method can also be generalized to more complex settings in which we do not have a nice formula for the option price like the preceding, and it is particularly well suited for computer programs. Denote by $C^u(t + \Delta t)$ the value of the option at time $t + \Delta t$ if the stock went up between t and $t + \Delta t$, and by $C^d(t + \Delta t)$ the value of the option at time $t + \Delta t$ if the stock went down. Then the price of the option at time t can be derived from its value at time $t + \Delta t$ using the following **expectation formula:**

$$C(t) = E_t^*[e^{-r\Delta t}C(t + \Delta t)] = e^{-r\Delta t}[p^*C^u(t + \Delta t) + (1 - p^*)C^d(t + \Delta t)] \tag{7.3}$$

This is true because the value of the option at a given time is the discounted expected value, under the risk-neutral probability, of the future payoff (which, when we consider one period ahead, is the expression on the right-hand side). Mathematically, the option price $C(t)$ at time t is equal to the value of the replicating wealth process, and this discounted wealth process $C(t)$ is a martingale in the risk-neutral world. Therefore, by the martingale property,

$$e^{-rt}C(t) = E_t^*\left[e^{-r(t+\Delta t)}C(t + \Delta t)\right]$$

which implies expression (7.3).

Expression (7.3) gives us a very simple backward-induction algorithm to compute the option price at time 0, illustrated in figure 7.1:

• Start at the top of the tree (the right-hand side), at time T, and compute the value of the option's payoff $g(S(T))$ at all time-T nodes, that is, for all possible values of $S(T)$.

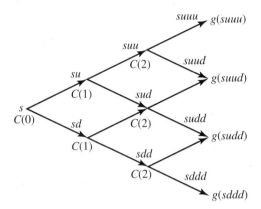

Figure 7.1
Backward induction: Algorithm for computing the option price. The values of C are computed using the expectation formula.

• At a given $T - \Delta t$ node, compute the option value $C(T - \Delta t)$ using the expectation formula (7.3), from the two option values at time T, corresponding to the two branches from the $T - \Delta t$ node.

• Continue the previous step at $T - 2\Delta t$ nodes, and so on, until you reach time 0, that is, the leftmost end node of the tree. This value is the option price today, in the binomial model.

Example 7.1 (Backward Induction)   Consider a two-period CRR model with continuously compounded interest rate $r = 0.05$, $S(0) = 100$, $u = 1.1$, and $d = 0.9$. The payoff is the European at-the-money call option with strike price $K = S(0) = 100$. We take $\Delta t = 1$. We compute first the possible values of the stock price at times 1 and 2, and payoff values $g(S(2)) = max(S(2) - 100, 0)$ at time 2. See figure 7.2: the values above the nodes are the stock-price values, and the values below the nodes are the corresponding option values. For example, the top two nodes at time 2 result in the stock prices 121 and 99, hence the option values of 21 and 0, respectively. We compute the risk-neutral probability

$$p^* = \frac{e^{r\Delta t} - d}{u - d} = 0.7564$$

We can then compute the option value at the previous node as

$$e^{-r\Delta t}[p^* \cdot 21 + (1 - p^*) \cdot 0] = 15.1088$$

Similarly, the bottom node at time 2 also has the option payoff equal to zero, so that the bottom node at time 1 corresponds to the option value equal to zero. Finally, from the option

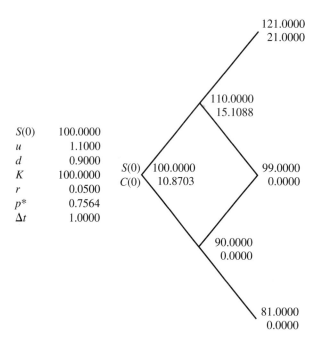

Figure 7.2
Computing a European option price in two periods.

values at time 1, we compute the time-0 option price as

$$e^{-r\Delta t}[p^* \cdot 15.1088 + (1 - p^*) \cdot 0] = 10.87$$

Alternatively, we could have computed the option price directly as a two-period risk-neutral expectation of the type (7.2). For our tree this is simply

$$e^{-2r\Delta t}(p^*)^2 \cdot 21 = 10.87$$

We will have more examples with option-price computations later, in chapter 11 on numerical methods.

7.1.2 Black-Scholes Formula as a Limit of the Binomial Model Formula

In the case of the European call, expression (7.2) can be developed further, in an alternative form. First, for a European call, expression (7.2) becomes

$$C(0) = \sum_{k=0}^{n} \left\{ e^{-rT} \binom{n}{k} (p^*)^k (1 - p^*)^{n-k} \max[S(0)u^k d^{n-k} - K, 0] \right\} \tag{7.4}$$

We note that a minimum number of upward movements of the stock are necessary for the call to end up in the money. For instance, in the example of figure 7.2, that number is 2. For a call option that expires after n periods let us denote by $a = a_n$ this minimum number k of upward movements of the stock such that $u^k d^{n-k} S(0) > K$. Then we can rewrite expression (7.4) by ignoring the terms in which the option payoff is zero, starting from $k = a$, as

$$C(0) = \sum_{k=a}^{n} \left\{ e^{-rT} \binom{n}{k} (p^*)^k (1 - p^*)^{n-k} [S(0) u^k d^{n-k} - K] \right\} \tag{7.5}$$

or as

$$C(0) = \sum_{k=a}^{n} \left[e^{-rT} \binom{n}{k} (p^*)^k (1 - p^*)^{n-k} S(0) u^k d^{n-k} \right]$$

$$- e^{-rT} K \sum_{k=a}^{n} \left[\binom{n}{k} (p^*)^k (1 - p^*)^{n-k} \right] \tag{7.6}$$

The two sums on the right-hand side look like binomial probabilities. More precisely, let X_p be a binomial random variable that counts the number of successes in n independent trials, with probability of success equal to p in each trial, and denote

$$N(n, p, a) := P[X_p \geq a] = \sum_{k=a}^{n} \left[\binom{n}{k} (p)^k (1 - p)^{n-k} \right]$$

Moreover, denote

$$\Delta t = T/n$$

introduce another probability

$$\tilde{p} = e^{-r\Delta t} u p^*$$

and note that by the definition of p^* in the binomial model we have

$$1 - \tilde{p} = e^{-r\Delta t} d(1 - p^*)$$

We can then reexpress the call price in equation (7.6) as

$$C(0) = S(0) N(n, \tilde{p}, a) - e^{-rT} K N(n, p^*, a) \tag{7.7}$$

This formula has the same structure as the famous Black-Scholes formula (7.13) for the European call price, which we discuss in the next section. The Black-Scholes formula can be obtained as a limit of the binomial formula (7.7), as $n \to \infty$, if we choose the following parametrization:

$$u = e^{\sigma \sqrt{\Delta t}}, \qquad d = \frac{1}{u}$$

for some given number $\sigma > 0$ (see Problem 7). This result is not too surprising, since, by the central limit theorem, the binomial probabilities $N(\cdot)$ in the preceding formula should converge to the corresponding probabilities for the normal distribution.

7.2 Option Pricing in the Merton-Black-Scholes Model

7.2.1 Black-Scholes Formula as Expected Value

For the reader who does not want to go through the details of the continuous-time sections of this chapter, we mention here how we compute the Black-Scholes formula directly from the model introduced in section 3.3.1. First, recall from equation (3.9) in that section that in the Merton-Black-Scholes model the stock price at time T is given by

$$S(T) = S(0) \exp\left\{ \left(\mu - \frac{1}{2}\sigma^2\right)T + \sigma\sqrt{T}Z \right\} \tag{7.8}$$

where Z has standard normal distribution. The Black-Scholes formula (7.13), for the European call price, in which we set the present time to be $t = 0$, is obtained by computing

$$E[e^{-rT}\{S(T) - K\}^+]$$

where, however, the value μ in equation (7.8) is replaced by r. This result arises because under the risk-neutral probability, the mean log-return of S becomes equal to the risk-free return rate r. The actual computation of this expected value leading to equation (7.13) is done in the appendix to this chapter (section 7.9).

7.2.2 Black-Scholes Equation

As we have shown, the price of a contingent claim with random payoff C and maturity T is $C(0) = E^*[\bar{C}]$. In particular, in the Merton-Black-Scholes (MBS) model described before, with one stock that follows a geometric Brownian motion process with constant drift μ and constant volatility σ and a bank account with constant interest rate r, E^* denotes the expectation with respect to P^*, the probability measure under which the drift μ is replaced by the interest rate r. Our problem now is the actual computation of the prices of contingent claims in the MBS model. One possibility is simulation (discussed later).

Another possibility is approximating the MBS model by a discrete-time binomial tree model, as discussed in the previous section. However, the original method, as presented in the pathbreaking work of Black and Scholes (1973), uses the partial differential equation (PDE) approach.

THEOREM 7.1 (BLACK-SCHOLES EQUATION)   Consider an option with a payoff $g(S(T))$. The price at time t of this option is given by $C(t, S(t))$, where function C is a solution to the **Black-Scholes PDE** and the boundary condition (subscripts denote partial derivatives)

$$C_t + \frac{1}{2}\sigma^2 s^2 C_{ss} + r(sC_s - C) = 0, \qquad C(T, s) = g(s) \tag{7.9}$$

(if a smooth unique solution exists).

Note that only the boundary condition depends on the payoff to be priced, not the PDE. Also, as expected, this PDE, hence also the option price, does not depend on the drift of the stock μ. The reason why it does not is that in the MBS model we can track (replicate) the value of the option by continuously trading between the stock and the bank account, no matter which direction the stock tends to move on average. In other words, the option is priced (and replicated) relative to the stock, and the expected return of the stock becomes irrelevant. As mentioned before, this result is very fortunate from the practical point of view, since the mean return rate μ is very hard to estimate in practice.

Proof of BS Equation   Let us use Itô's rule on the process $C(t, S(t))$:

$$dC(t, S(t)) = \left[C_t + \frac{1}{2}\sigma^2 S^2 C_{ss} + \mu S C_s\right] dt + \sigma S C_s \, dW$$

We want $C(t, S(t))$ to be the value of a portfolio that replicates the value of the option, which will, in particular, imply that $C(0, S(0))$ is the replication cost, hence the price of the option at the initial time. Consider, then, the problem of an investor (the option writer) who starts with wealth $C(0, S(0))$ and allocates the wealth between the stock and the bank account, so as to track the value of the option. As we know from equation (3.35), the value of the investor's wealth process evolves according to

$$dX = [rX + \pi(\mu - r)] \, dt + \pi\sigma \, dW \tag{7.10}$$

where π is the dollar amount invested in the stock. (The rest is invested in the bank account.) To make sure that the portfolio of this investor does indeed replicate the value of the option, we need to have

$$X(T) = g(S(T)) = C(T, S(T))$$

The investor wants to find the amount of money π^g to be invested in the stock at each point in time, such that, starting with initial wealth $X(0) = C(0, S(0))$,

$$C(t, S(t)) = X(t) \tag{7.11}$$

Comparing the dW terms of dC and dX, we see that we need to have

$$\pi^g(t) = S(t)C_s(S(t)) \tag{7.12}$$

This result gives us the formula for the replicating portfolio. Next, using equations (7.11) and (7.12) and comparing the dt terms, we see that we need to have

$$C_t + \tfrac{1}{2}\sigma^2 S^2 C_{ss} + \mu S C_s = (\mu - r)S C_s + rC$$

which, after a straightforward simplification, yields the Black-Scholes equation (7.9)! We conclude that if C solves the Black-Scholes equation, then $dC = dX$, and equality (7.11) does hold. Thus, C is a replicating wealth process, which, by no-arbitrage arguments, implies that it has to be equal to the price process of the option with payoff $g(S(T))$. ∎

There is another way of proving that the option price has to satisfy the Black-Scholes equation, based on the fact that the price is given by the risk-neutral expected value $E^*[\bar{g}(S(T))]$. We recall from the Feynman-Kac Theorem 6.7 that such an expectation can be computed as a solution to a PDE. Recalling that

$$dS = S[r\,dt + \sigma\,dW^*]$$

we see that the corresponding PDE from that theorem is exactly the Black-Scholes equation.

In equation (7.12) we found the amount π^g to be held in the stock, if we want to replicate (hedge) the option. We then see that the derivative of the option value with respect to the underlying satisfies

$$C_s = \frac{\pi^g}{S}$$

Since the right-hand side represents the dollar amount to be invested in the stock divided by the price of one share of the stock, it is equal to the number of shares to be held in the replicating portfolio. In other words,

*the derivative of the option price with respect to the underlying, called the **delta of the option,** has to be equal to the number of shares of stock held by the replicating portfolio.*

This result is the basis for extremely important problems in practice: the problem of **hedging** the risk of option positions, to be studied in chapter 9.

7.2.3   Black-Scholes Formula for the Call Option

Part of the reason why the approach of Black and Scholes (1973) was quickly accepted by practitioners and academics is that it provides us with an explicit formula for plain vanilla European call and put options. It is always useful to have a formula, even though these days it is somewhat less important because of the power of computational methods that have been developed to price options.

Denote by

$$N(x) := P[Z \le x] = \frac{1}{\sqrt{2\pi}} \int_{-\infty}^{x} e^{-\frac{y^2}{2}} \, dy$$

the **cumulative distribution function** of the standard normal random variable Z. We denote by $c(t, s)$ a deterministic function of the current time t and the current stock price s. Here is the famous **Black-Scholes formula for the European call option:**

THEOREM 7.2 (BLACK-SCHOLES FORMULA)   The price of the European call option with strike price $K > 0$, that is, a contingent claim with payoff $g(S(T)) = [S(T) - K]^+$, in the Merton-Black-Scholes model, at time t, when the stock price is s, is given by the function

$$c(t, s) = sN(d_1) - Ke^{-r(T-t)}N(d_2) \tag{7.13}$$

where

$$d_1 := \frac{1}{\sigma\sqrt{T-t}}[\log(s/K) + (r + \sigma^2/2)(T-t)] \tag{7.14}$$

$$d_2 := \frac{1}{\sigma\sqrt{T-t}}[\log(s/K) + (r - \sigma^2/2)(T-t)] = d_1 - \sigma\sqrt{T-t} \tag{7.15}$$

There are several ways of obtaining this formula, all of which are somewhat involved. One is to take a limit in the binomial tree approximation to the MBS model; another one is simply to check that the function $c(t, s)$ satisfies the Black-Scholes equation (7.9) (see Problem 9); still another way is to directly compute the expectation $E^*_{t,s}[e^{-r(T-t)}\{S(T) - K\}^+]$. We present this last method in section 7.9.

As for the put option, recall the put-call parity:

$$c(t, s) + Ke^{-r(T-t)} = p(t, s) + s$$

Using this formula it is easy to get (see Problem 9) the **Black-Scholes formula for the put option:**

$$p(t, s) = Ke^{-r(T-t)}N(-d_2) - sN(-d_1) \tag{7.16}$$

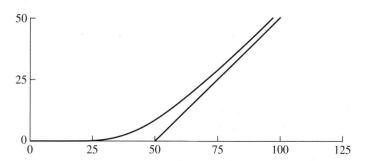

Figure 7.3
Black-Scholes values for a call option.

A graph of the Black-Scholes values for the price of European call and put options is given in figures 7.3 and 7.4.

In many situations we will have a model that is similar to but not quite the same as the Merton-Black-Scholes model. For this reason it is useful to have the following general rule, which we will use in following sections, for options on dividend-paying stocks, currency options, and so on. Its proof is the same as the proof of the preceding Black-Scholes formula.

GENERAL BLACK-SCHOLES PRICING RULE   Consider a market model in which we can trade in one risky security S and in the bank account with a constant interest rate r. Suppose that in this model the discounted wealth process of an investor satisfies the risk-neutral dynamics

$$d\bar{X}(t) = \bar{\pi}(t)\sigma\, dW^*(t)$$

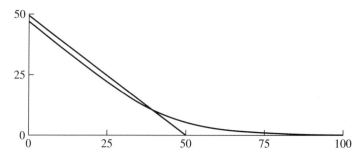

Figure 7.4
Black-Scholes values for a put option.

where $\pi(t)$ is the amount held in the underlying risky security S at time t. Moreover, suppose that the relationship between the "real-world" Brownian motion and the risk-neutral Brownian motion in this model is

$$W^*(t) = W(t) + \frac{\mu - \alpha}{\sigma}t$$

for some number α. Then in this market the Black-Scholes equation for a price of an option with the payoff $g(S(T))$ is given by

$$C_t + \frac{1}{2}\sigma^2 s^2 C_{ss} + \alpha s C_s - rC = 0, \qquad C(T, s) = g(s) \tag{7.17}$$

Moreover, for the European call option $g(s) = (s - K)^+$, we have the Black-Scholes formula

$$c(t, s) = s e^{(\alpha-r)(T-t)} N(d_1) - K e^{-r(T-t)} N(d_2) \tag{7.18}$$

where

$$d_1 := \frac{1}{\sigma\sqrt{T - t}}[\log(s/K) + (\alpha + \sigma^2/2)(T - t)] \tag{7.19}$$

$$d_2 := \frac{1}{\sigma\sqrt{T - t}}[\log(s/K) + (\alpha - \sigma^2/2)(T - t)] = d_1 - \sigma\sqrt{T - t} \tag{7.20}$$

7.2.4 Implied Volatility

If we analyze the Black-Scholes formula, we see that one very important parameter is the volatility σ of the stock. This parameter is not directly observable, so it has to be estimated. It can be estimated from historical data on prices of this stock. However, oftentimes practitioners prefer to get a feeling about what the market thinks the volatility will be equal to in the future. One way of doing so is to look at the price of a frequently traded option on this stock, say, a call option. Then we find the value of σ that, when inserted in the Black-Scholes formula, produces, as a result, the observed option price. More precisely, given known parameter values r, T, K, and s, denote by $BS(\sigma)$ the value of the Black-Scholes formula evaluated at σ. Suppose that the option price as observed in the market is $C(0)$. Then the **implied volatility** σ_{imp} is that value of σ that satisfies

$$BS(\sigma_{imp}) = C(0)$$

This value has to be found numerically, by trial and error. If the Merton-Black-Scholes model were indeed completely correct, it would make no difference whether we estimate

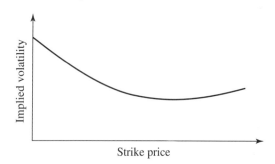

Figure 7.5
Volatility smile: The level of implied volatility differs for different strike levels.

the volatility from historical data or from present option prices. However, in reality, the volatility is not constant over time, and we are likely to get different values across different time periods. Even worse, suppose we computed the implied volatility by looking at a call option with strike price K_1. If the MBS model were correct, this should be equal to the volatility implied from the price of the call option on the same stock, but with a different strike price K_2. In general, this result does not occur, and we get different implied volatilities for different strike prices. The same is true for different maturities. The curve that is obtained when graphing strike prices against implied volatilities is called a **volatility smile** (even though it does not always have the shape of a smile); see figure 7.5. If the MBS model were correct, this curve would be a straight line parallel to the horizontal axis, at the height equal to the constant volatility σ of the stock. Since it is usually not a straight line, we conclude that there may be a need for more sophisticated models of volatility. For example, we could model the volatility as a stochastic process, randomly changing with time. Alternatively, we can try to model the stock price with models very different from the MBS model.

7.3 Pricing American Options

Many liquidly traded options are of the American type. Recall that we say that an option with payoff $g(t)$ is an **American option** if the holder of the option can exercise it at any time t before maturity T, and at that exercise time the holder gets paid $g(t)$. Mathematically, pricing these options is a problem considerably more difficult than pricing European options because it involves an optimization procedure—the holder has to decide when it is optimal to exercise the option. Our treatment of American options here is not always mathematically rigorous. Instead, we try to provide a combination of financial and mathematical intuition for the stated results.

7.3.1   Stopping Times and American Options

In order to present a probabilistic expression for the price of an American option, let us introduce the concept of a **stopping time:** A stopping time τ is a random variable taking values in the interval $[0, T]$ such that it does not look into the future. More precisely, we know whether τ happened by time t, that is, whether $\tau \leq t$, if t is the present time. A typical example is the first time the stock hits a certain level—we always know whether that has already happened or not (but we do not know if and when it will happen in the future). In contrast, consider the last time the stock hits a certain level during a given time horizon. This is a random variable that depends on what happens in the future. At any given point in the time interval before the end of the horizon we do not know whether that last time has already occurred or not. Therefore, that is not a stopping time. The holder of the American option can choose any stopping time to exercise the option. For example, the holder can wait until the stock price becomes sufficiently high.

Assume now that we are in a complete-market model, with a unique risk-neutral probability P^*. We now present the probabilistic expression for the price of an American option at time t, described in terms of stopping times:

THEOREM 7.3 (AMERICAN OPTION PRICE)   The price $A(0)$ of an American option with payoff $g(t)$ is given by

$$A(0) = \max_{0 \leq \tau \leq T} E^*[\bar{g}(\tau)] \tag{7.21}$$

where $\bar{g}(t)$ represents the discounted payoff. Here, the maximum is taken over all stopping times with values in the interval $[0, T]$.

We do not provide a rigorous proof of the theorem, but we give an intuitive justification of the previous formula: if we knew with certainty that the holder would exercise the option at a stopping time τ, then the value of the option would be equal to the value $E^*[\bar{g}(\tau)]$ of the corresponding European option with maturity τ. However, that stopping time is not known. The writer of the option only knows that the holder will try to exercise it at the time at which it has the highest value, so the writer prices the option by choosing among all possible stopping times the one corresponding to the highest expected value.

Remark   The rest of this section is somewhat technical, and may be skipped by a less curious reader.

We now present a more mathematical argument, but only from the perspective of the writer of the option, named Taf. Taf would like to ask for the option an amount of money that, appropriately invested in the market, guarantees that Taf can pay the option payoff when it is exercised. We say that the writer of the option is **hedged** (we discuss the concept of hedging in detail in chapter 9). In other words, Taf would like to have a wealth process with initial value x and portfolio strategy π^g that satisfies

$$X^{x,\pi^g}(t) \geq g(t), \quad \text{for all } t \leq T \tag{7.22}$$

We want to show that this hedging requirement implies that the option price at time zero has to be at least $A(0)$ as given by equation (7.21). That is, we want to show that if Taf follows a portfolio strategy such that the wealth process is enough to hedge the option in the sense of expression (7.22), then the initial capital x (the cost of the hedging wealth process) has to be larger than $A(0)$:

$$x \geq A(0) = \max_{0 \leq \tau \leq T} E^*[\bar{g}(\tau)] \tag{7.23}$$

Indeed, if, as is the case in standard models, the discounted wealth process $\bar{X}$ of the writer is a martingale with respect to the risk-neutral probability P^*, using the hedging requirement (7.22) we see that

$$x = E^*[\bar{X}(\tau)] \geq E^*[\bar{g}(\tau)], \quad \text{for all } \tau$$

(The first equality is the familiar budget constraint at time τ, a consequence of the martingale property.) Taking the supremum over τ yields inequality (7.23).

We have thus shown that Taf needs at least the amount $A(0)$ in order to be able to hedge the option, but it is not clear that this amount is sufficient to accomplish the hedge. The latter can also be shown, but that task is much harder.

In fact, we cheated a little bit in the previous argument, because the discounted payoff process of the American option (the hedging wealth process of the writer) might not be a martingale under the risk-neutral measure. If the holder of the option does not exercise the option at the optimal time, the writer may have extra money not needed for hedging, which he can consume (spend) outside the market. As long as the writer does not consume the extra money, his discounted hedging wealth process is a martingale (under P^*). However, once the writer consumes the extra money, it can be shown that his discounted wealth process becomes what is called a **supermartingale.** In particular, we have the inequality

$$E^*[\bar{X}(\tau)] \leq x$$

rather than the equality we have in the European (martingale) case. (Intuitively, the expected value of his future discounted wealth is less than it would be if he did not consume money.) Fortunately, our preceding argument still goes through even if only the inequality holds.

In fact, it can be shown that the writer's discounted hedging process is, in general, a supermartingale, but that it is a martingale prior to the (earliest) optimal exercise time. In other words, the writer does not have extra money to consume prior to the earliest optimal exercise time, but he may have some money for consumption after that time, if the holder has not exercised the option.

It is not easy to compute American option prices, especially in more complex models in which we might have several random variables (stocks, interest rates, volatilities, ...). In models with one random variable, such as the Merton-Black-Scholes model and the Cox-Ross-Rubinstein binomial model with one stock, these computations can be done using binomial trees or a PDE approach, as discussed in what follows.

7.3.2 Binomial Trees and American Options

It is particularly simple to compute prices of American options in the binomial Cox-Ross-Rubinstein model. Denote by $A(t)$ the time-t value of an American contingent claim with payoff $g(t)$. Then, as in chapter 4, we can prove the following **principle of dynamic programming** for the optimal stopping problem (7.21):

$$A(t) = \max\{g(t), E^*[e^{-r\Delta t} A(t + \Delta t)]\} \tag{7.24}$$

In words, *the value of the American option today is equal to the larger of the following two values: the payoff that can be collected today by exercising the option; or the value of continuing—the expected value under the risk-neutral measure of the discounted value of the option at the next exercise opportunity.*

This principle provides the **backward induction algorithm** for computing the price, because we know that at the end of the tree the value is equal to the payoff,

$$A(T) = g(T)$$

The algorithm is very similar to the algorithm we use to price a European option in a tree. The only difference is that, at every time step, we have to check whether the risk-neutral expectation is larger or smaller than the value of immediate exercise, that is, the payoff $g(t)$. In the binomial model, expression (7.24) becomes

$$A(t) = \max\{g(t), e^{-r\Delta t}[p^* A^u(t + \Delta t) + (1 - p^*)A^d(t + \Delta t)]\} \tag{7.25}$$

where $A^u(t + \Delta t)$ is the value of the option at time $t + \Delta t$ if the stock went up between t and $t + \Delta t$, and $A^d(t + \Delta t)$ is the option value at time $t + \Delta t$ if the stock went down.

Consider now the case in which the payoff is a function of the current stock price, $g(t) = g(S(t))$. As in the European case, expression (7.25) implies a very simple algorithm to compute the option price at time 0, illustrated in figure 7.6:

• Start at the end of the tree (the right-hand side), at time T, and compute the value of the option's payoff $g(S(T))$ at all time-T nodes, that is, for all possible values of $S(T)$.

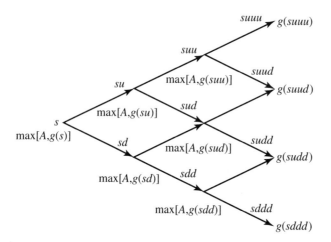

Figure 7.6
Backward induction for American options: At each node we compute the maximum of the values of continuing and of the current payoff.

- At a given $T - \Delta t$ node, compute the option value using equation (7.25) from the two option values at time T corresponding to the two branches from the $T - \Delta t$ node.

- Continue the previous step at $T - 2\Delta t$ nodes, and so on, until we reach time 0, that is, the leftmost end node of the tree. This value is the option price today, in the binomial model.

Example 7.2 (Binomial Tree and American Options)   Consider the same framework as in Example 7.1, that is, a two-period Cox-Ross-Rubinstein model with continuously compounded interest rate $r = 0.05$ and parameter values $S(0) = 100, u = 1.1$, and $d = 0.9$. The security we want to price is an American at-the-money put option, so that the strike price is $K = S(0) = 100$. We take $\Delta t = 1$. As before, we compute first the possible values of the stock prices at times 1 and 2, and payoff values $g(S(2)) = \max[100 - S(2), 0]$ at time 2; see figure 7.7. For example, the lower two nodes at time 2 result in the stock prices 99 and 81, hence the payoff values of 1 and 19, respectively. At the previous node the stock price is 90, so the payoff in case of immediate exercise would be 10. Recall that the risk-neutral probability is $p^* = 0.7564$. We can now compute the option value at the previous node as

$$\max\{10, e^{-r\Delta t}[p^* \cdot 1 + (1 - p^*) \cdot 19]\} = \max\{10, 5.1229\} = 10$$

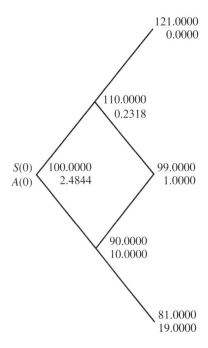

Figure 7.7
Computing an American option price in two periods.

Similarly, the top two nodes at time 2 have option payoff equal to 0 and 1, respectively, so that the top node at time 1 corresponds to the option value equal to

$$\max\{0, e^{-r\Delta t}[p^* \cdot 0 + (1 - p^*) \cdot 1]\} = 0.2318$$

Finally, from the option values at time 1, we compute the time-0 option price as

$$\max\{0, e^{-r\Delta t}[p^* \cdot 0.2318 + (1 - p^*) \cdot 10]\} = 2.4844$$

From the point of view of the holder, the option should not be immediately exercised at time 0, because the payoff would be zero; it is optimal to exercise at time 1 if the stock goes down, because the payoff is 10, which is larger than the value of waiting, equal to the price 5.1229 of the "unexercised" option. If the stock goes up at time 1, the option is out of the money, and it is not optimal to exercise.

7.3.3 PDEs and American Options*

In the case of European-type derivatives we showed that—among other possible approaches—we can find the price of an option as a solution to a partial differential equation (PDE). In this section we extend that approach to the case of American-type derivative securities with payoffs of the form $g(t) = g(S(t))$; that is, the payoff is a function of the value of the underlying. In particular, consider the Merton-Black-Scholes model with one stock that follows a geometric Brownian motion process and a bank account with constant interest rate r. As discussed in a previous section, the discounted option-price process $e^{-rt}A(t, S_t)$ is equal to the discounted wealth process that the writer of the option needs to have to be able to cover the option's payoff when the option is exercised. We conjecture that the price of the option is a deterministic function $A(t, s)$ of the present time and the present stock price, as it was in the European case. We recall that in the "risk-neutral world" the stock price satisfies the dynamics

$$dS(t) = rS(t)\,dt + \sigma S(t)\,dW^*(t)$$

Then, by Itô's rule, the discounted option price has to satisfy

$$d(e^{-rt}A) = e^{-rt}\left[A_t + \tfrac{1}{2}\sigma^2 S^2 A_{ss} + r(SA_s - A)\right]dt + [\ldots]\,dW^*$$

where the subscripts denote partial derivatives.

In the case of a European option, the drift would have to be zero, because the discounted price process is a P^*-martingale [by result (6.45)]. Here, however, as discussed in the previous section, the writer may be able to consume some money from the wealth process, in case the holder does not exercise at the optimal time. Therefore, the drift can also be negative (representing the consumption), and we get the following **free boundary problem:**

$$A_t + \tfrac{1}{2}\sigma^2 s^2 A_{ss} + r(sA_s - A) \le 0 \tag{7.26}$$

with the boundary conditions

$$A(t, s) \ge g(s), \qquad A(T, s) = g(s), \quad 0 < s < \infty$$

The first boundary condition says that the price of the option is at least as large as the payoff that the holder would get if the option were exercised immediately.

Let us use the name **continuation region** for the set of values (t, s) for which it is not optimal to exercise the option when the pair $(t, S(t))$ is in that region. Similarly, the **exercise region** is the set of (t, s) values for which it is optimal to exercise. When is it optimal to exercise the option? Intuitively, *it has to be optimal to exercise at those values of $(t, S(t))$ for which the value of the option becomes equal to the value of the payoff received in case of immediate exercise*, that is, when

$$A(t, S(t)) = g(S(t))$$

However, if this is not the case, so that

$$A(t, S(t)) > g(S(t))$$

then the value of continuing is larger than the value of exercising the option, and it is not optimal to exercise.

Continuing the heuristic discussion, recall that the writer cannot consume any money prior to the optimal exercise time, and so the drift of the wealth process has to be zero. This result implies that inequality (7.26) then has to hold as an equality, that is, the *Black-Scholes equation holds in the continuation region:*

$$A_t + \tfrac{1}{2}\sigma^2 s^2 A_{ss} + r(s A_s - A) = 0, \quad \text{if } A(t, s) > g(t, s)$$

However, if the writer is able to consume some of the money, then the pair $(t, S(t))$ has entered the exercise region, and the holder has not yet exercised the option. In other words, *if the Black-Scholes "equation" holds as strict inequality, then (t, s) must be in the exercise region:*

$$\text{If } A_t + \tfrac{1}{2}\sigma^2 s^2 A_{ss} + r(s A_s - A) < 0, \quad \text{then } A(t, s) = g(t, s)$$

We see that either we have the Black-Scholes equation holding as an equality, or equality $A(t, s) = g(s)$ holds. The **free boundary** is the boundary between the exercise region and the continuation region, that is, the curve that separates the two regions. It is called free because it is unknown and has to be computed as a part of the solution. Numerical methods have been developed for solving free boundary problems. They work well in the Merton-Black-Scholes model, when we have only one random variable, the stock price. In case we have more random variables, the Black-Scholes equation involves partial derivatives with respect to other variables, and it becomes less feasible to use those methods.

7.4   Options on Dividend-Paying Securities

Thus far, we have assumed that the underlying stock does not pay dividends. We now consider the case when the underlying pays dividends and the time and the amount of the payment are known. We assume that when the dividend is paid, the stock price falls down by the amount of the dividend (per share). (If it were certain that the stock would not fall by an amount at least as large as the dividend, there would be arbitrage. Can you tell why?) In reality, the stock price often falls by less than the dividend amount, mostly for tax reasons.

7.4.1 Binomial Model

Let us first consider the binomial model and assume that the dividends are proportional to the stock price, say, equal to $q_i S(t_i)$, for a dividend payment date t_i. The price of the stock right after the dividend payment, called **ex-dividend price,** is $S(t_i)(1 - q_i)$. If t_i is the first time a dividend is paid and is the ith step in the binomial tree, this ex-dividend price is simply $S(0)u^k d^{i-k}(1 - q_i)$, where k is the number of up moves. We can still use the binomial tree to compute the option price as before, simply by accounting for the reduction in the stock price each time the dividend is paid.

   The situation is a bit more complicated in case the amount of dividends is a known quantity, say D_i, at time t_i, independent of the price of the stock at that time. We could still try to use the binomial tree with the stock price reduced by D_i, but the tree would not be recombining: an "upward" change followed by the dividend payment and a "downward" change does not yield the same price of the stock as a "downward" change followed by the dividend payment and an "upward" change: $(us - D)d \neq (ds - D)u$. This fact creates computational problems. An alternative method that allows us to use the usual binomial tree procedure is to assume that the tree represents the price of the stock **net of dividends;** that is, the changes in the price are due only to the capital gains. Let us denote by S_G the price of the stock without the value of the future dividends. For notational simplicity, suppose that there is only one dividend payment D, paid at time τ. In this case the tree has to start with the initial value

$$S_G(0) := S(0) - e^{-r\tau} D$$

the initial price of the stock minus the present value of the dividend. Denote by $S_G(t_i)$ the price at time t_i obtained going forward in the tree as usual. After the first time step, the actual stock price would be

$$S(t_1) = S_G(t_1) + De^{-r(\tau - t_1)}$$

and so on, until the time the dividend is paid, after which S_G and S agree. The point is that we model S_G with the tree, not S. See the Problems section for an example.

   In practice it seems more realistic to assume, for individual stocks, that the dividend is independent of the price of the stock. Models in which the dividend is proportional to the value of the underlying may be appropriate for a stock index.

   In the case of an American call, it might be optimal to exercise early right before the stock pays a dividend. That possibility has to be included in the valuation of the option. We illustrate this case with an example, in which we use the pedestrian way of modeling the stock S, and not the process S_G.

Example 7.3 (Pricing an American Call on a Stock That Pays a Dividend)   Consider a two-period binomial setting with $S(0) = \$50$, $r = 2\%$, and $\Delta t = 1$. After one period the

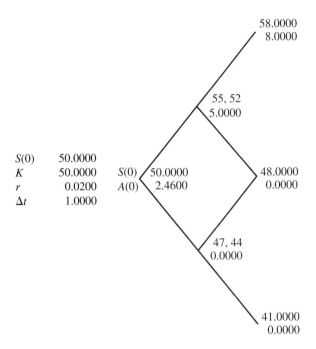

Figure 7.8
Pricing an American call on a dividend-paying stock.

price of the stock can go up to $55 or drop to $47, and it will pay (in both cases) a dividend of $3. If it goes up the first period, the second period it can go up to $58 or down to $48. If it goes down the first period, the second period it can go up to $48 or down to $41. We want to compute the price of an American call option with strike price $K = 50$ that matures at the end of the second period.

In figure 7.8 each node in the tree shows the price of the stock and the price of the option, which we compute in this example. After one period the stock has two prices: before and after the dividend. After the dividend the price falls by the amount of the dividend. Because of dividends we cannot work here with the probabilities under which the discounted stock price is a martingale. Instead, we find the replicating portfolio, formed by δ_1 shares of the stock and δ_0 dollars in the risk-free security. At maturity in the upper node we need to have

$$\delta_1 58 + \delta_0 e^{0.02} = 8$$
$$\delta_1 48 + \delta_0 e^{0.02} = 0$$

with solutions $\delta_1 = 0.8$ and $\delta_0 = -37.64$. These results give the price of the option at time 1 in the upper node as

$$0.8 \times 52 - 37.64 = 3.96$$

This price is lower than the value the holder would receive when exercising the option before the dividend, equal to $55 - 50 = 5$. Thus the value of the option is \$5, the maximum of the two, and the holder would actually exercise the option at this node. In the lower node the option price is zero, since the option will be out of the money regardless of what happens in the second period. Now we only need to compute the price of the option at the initial moment. We can do so either by computing the expected value under the risk-neutral probability, or by computing the price of the replicating portfolio. The latter procedure yields

$$\delta_1 55 + \delta_0 e^{0.02} = 5$$
$$\delta_1 47 + \delta_0 e^{0.02} = 0$$

with solutions $\delta_1 = 0.625$ and $\delta_0 = -28.79$. The price of the option is then

$$0.625 \times 50 - 28.79 = 2.46$$

Note that in both replication periods we avoided dealing with dividends: in the second period we started the replication after the dividend was paid, and in the first period we computed the replicating portfolio by considering its value before the dividend was paid. We could have done this example differently, but then we would have had to take account of receiving/paying the dividend into/from the replicating portfolio.

7.4.2   Merton-Black-Scholes Model

First, let us assume that the dividends are paid continuously, at a rate proportional to the price of the stock, with constant dividend yield q. In other words, we assume that the cumulative dividends up to time t are given by $\int_0^t q S(u)\, du$. This assumption may be a fair approximation to reality if S is an index, rather than a single stock. The total value of holding one share of the stock from time 0 to t is given by

$$G(t) := S(t) + \int_0^t q S(u)\, du$$

The corresponding wealth process will now have the dynamics

$$dX = (X - \pi)\, dB/B + \pi\, dG/S$$

where π is, as usual, the dollar amount invested in the stock (the rest is invested in the bank account B). The last term accounts for the dividend yield, as well as for the capital gains obtained from investing in the stock. If S is a geometric Brownian motion process with constant parameters μ and σ, and the risk-free rate r is constant, we get

$$dX(t) = [rX(t) + \pi(t)(\mu + q - r)]\, dt + \pi(t)\sigma\, dW(t) \tag{7.27}$$

Contingent claims in the market have to be priced under the probability measure (the risk-neutral probability), which makes the discounted wealth process a martingale. We see that this is the case if we get rid of the dt term containing $\mu + q - r$. In other words, we would have

$$dX(t) = rX(t) + \pi(t)\sigma\, dW^*(t)$$

where the risk-neutral Brownian motion is now given by

$$W^*(t) = W(t) + t(\mu + q - r)/\sigma$$

Substituting back in the Merton-Black-Scholes model, we get

$$dS(t) = S(t)[(r - q)\, dt + \sigma\, dW^*(t)] \tag{7.28}$$

So, the return rate of the stock has been replaced by the interest rate minus the dividend yield. Using the general rule (7.17), or repeating the arguments leading to the Black-Scholes equation, or using the Feynman-Kac theorem to find the price $C(t, s) = E^*_{t,s}[e^{-rT}C]$ of a claim $C = g(S(T))$, we get the following PDE for the option price:

$$C_t + \tfrac{1}{2}\sigma^2 s^2 C_{ss} + (r - q)s C_s - rC = 0, \qquad C(T, s) = g(s) \tag{7.29}$$

Also, using equation (7.18) (or repeating the arguments in the appendix to this chapter), we can compute directly the price of the European call option as

$$c(t, s) = s e^{-q(T-t)} N(d_1) - K e^{-r(T-t)} N(d_2) \tag{7.30}$$

where

$$d_1 = \frac{1}{\sigma\sqrt{T - t}}[\log(s/K) + (r - q + \sigma^2/2)(T \quad t)] \tag{7.31}$$

$$d_2 = \frac{1}{\sigma\sqrt{T - t}}[\log(s/K) + (r - q - \sigma^2/2)(T - t)] = d_1 - \sigma\sqrt{T - t} \tag{7.32}$$

There is another, more intuitive way to get this result. We note that the preceding formula is the same as the Black-Scholes formula for the call option on a non-dividend-paying stock, but with the stock price $s = S(t)$ replaced by $s e^{-q(T-t)}$ in the formula. In order to explain why this is the case, we can use Itô's rule to check that, if we denote by S^0 the process that satisfies the old dynamics, that is, with $q = 0$, then the process $S^0(t)e^{q(T-t)}$ satisfies the new dynamics (7.28), hence $S^0(t) = S(t)e^{-q(T-t)}$. At time T, after all the dividends have been paid out, we see that we have $S(T) = S^0(T)$. So, we can write the option price as $E_{t,s}^*[e^{-r(T-t)}\{S^0(T) - K\}^+]$. In other words, pricing the option on the stock $S(t)$ that pays dividends is the same as pricing the option on the stock S^0 paying no dividends, and with initial value $S^0(t) = S(t)e^{-q(T-t)}$. Consequently, we simply have to replace the initial value s in the Black-Scholes formula by the value $se^{-q(T-t)}$.

In the case in which dividends are paid out at discrete time points and the amounts are known, we apply an approach similar to that used in the discrete case. We assume that the Merton-Black-Scholes model is used for the capital gains process S_G equal to the stock price minus the present value of the dividends paid up to maturity T (rather than used for S itself). Note that at maturity $S_G(T) = S(T)$. Therefore, the option price is equal to

$$E^*[e^{-rT}g(S_G(T))]$$

Since S_G is modeled by the Merton-Black-Scholes model, we can use the Black-Scholes formula in which we substitute the initial stock price s by the initial value of S_G,

$$S_G(0) = S(0) - D(0)$$

where $D(0)$ is the present value of the dividends at time 0.

7.5   Other Types of Options

7.5.1   Currency Options

Consider an option that gives its owner the right to buy one unit of a foreign currency for K units of the domestic currency (which we call the "dollar"), at maturity T. This is a European call option on foreign currency. Mathematically, the payoff, evaluated in the domestic currency, is equal to

$$[Q(T) - K]^+$$

where $Q(T)$ is the exchange rate at time T, that is, the value in dollars of one unit of foreign currency at time T. Assume that the exchange-rate process is given by the Merton-Black-Scholes model

$$dQ(t) = Q(t)[\mu_Q\, dt + \sigma_Q\, dW(t)] \tag{7.33}$$

where μ_Q and σ_Q are constant coefficients.

We point out that the risk-free rate in the foreign country is similar to a dividend yield on a stock, because someone who holds the foreign currency will receive the corresponding interest. Consequently, it is not too surprising that *the price of the European call currency option is equal to the price of the European call option on a stock that pays a dividend at the continuous rate r_f equal to the foreign interest rate.*

In other words, the price is given by equation (7.30), with $q = r_f$ and $\sigma = \sigma_Q$. We recall that the forward price $F(t)$ for the foreign currency, also called the **forward exchange rate,** is given by

$$F(t) = Q(t)e^{(r-r_f)(T-t)}$$

where Q is given by equation (7.33), r is the domestic interest rate, and r_f is the foreign interest rate. We introduce the notation $f := F(t)$. Then the price of the call option is

$$c(t, f) = e^{-r(T-t)}[fN(d_1) - KN(d_2)] \tag{7.34}$$

where

$$d_1 = \frac{1}{\sigma_Q\sqrt{T-t}}\left[\log(f/K) + \left(\sigma_Q^2/2\right)(T-t)\right] \tag{7.35}$$

$$d_2 = \frac{1}{\sigma_Q\sqrt{T-t}}\left[\log(f/K) - \left(\sigma_Q^2/2\right)(T-t)\right] = d_1 - \sigma_Q\sqrt{T-t} \tag{7.36}$$

This is a convenient representation because it is often more useful to consider the forward (or futures) contract as the underlying security. The reason is that it can be less costly to hedge the risk of option positions by trading in forward (or futures) contracts on the underlying security with the same maturity date than by trading in the security itself, because of lower transaction costs.

In order to argue the preceding formula more rigorously, consider the possibility of replicating options payoffs by trading in the domestic bank account and the foreign bank account. Denote by $B(t) := e^{rt}$ the time-t value of one unit of domestic currency. The dollar value of one unit of the foreign account is

$$Q^*(t) := Q(t)e^{r_f t}$$

Itô's rule for products gives

$$dQ^* = Q^*[(\mu_Q + r_f)\,dt + \sigma_Q]\,dW$$

The wealth dynamics (in domestic currency) of a portfolio that consists of investing π dollars in the foreign account and the rest in the domestic account is given by

$$dX = \frac{X-\pi}{B}\,dB + \frac{\pi}{Q^*}\,dQ^* = [rX + \pi(\mu_Q + r_f - r)]\,dt + \pi\sigma_Q\,dW \tag{7.37}$$

This is exactly the same type of dynamics as in equation (7.27), with q replaced by r_f, so we conclude that the call option price is obtained in the same way as for the dividend-paying stock. Or we can use the general rule (7.18).

This approach produces a nice, compact formula. However, in practice, the Merton-Black-Scholes model is typically much less successful in fitting exchange-rate data than stock data. Therefore, other models have been developed for currency data.

7.5.2 Futures Options

The first successful model for pricing options on futures was proposed in Black (1976), and the corresponding formula for the European call option is called Black's futures formula. He suggested using the Merton-Black-Scholes model for the futures price itself, denoted here by F:

$$dF(t) = F(t)[\mu_F \, dt + \sigma_F \, dW(t)]$$

where μ_F and σ_F are constant parameters. **Black's futures formula** for the call option with the same maturity T as the futures contract is

$$c(t, f) = e^{-r(T-t)}[fN(d_1) - KN(d_2)] \tag{7.38}$$

where

$$d_1 = \frac{1}{\sigma_F \sqrt{T-t}} \left[\log(f/K) + \left(\sigma_F^2/2\right)(T - t) \right] \tag{7.39}$$

$$d_2 = \frac{1}{\sigma_F \sqrt{T-t}} \left[\log(f/K) - \left(\sigma_F^2/2\right)(T - t) \right] = d_1 - \sigma_F \sqrt{T-t} \tag{7.40}$$

Since in this model $F(t) = e^{r(T-t)}S(t)$, then, if S is modeled as a Merton-Black-Scholes process, the two processes have the same volatility, that is, $\sigma_F = \sigma$ (this result can be shown using Itô's rule for products; see Problem 30). It follows from formula (7.38) that the values of European call options on the futures contract and on the stock are the same when the maturities are the same. Intuitively, the reason is that $S(T) = F(T)$. This is not necessarily the case with American versions of these options, where it will depend on whether the futures price is typically below or above the spot price.

In order to justify Black's futures formula, consider a strategy that involves trading in futures and the bank account, with the amount held in futures denoted by π and the amount in the bank denoted by Y. Since it costs nothing to enter a long or a short position in the futures contract, the value (wealth process) of a strategy is equal to the amount in the bank account:

$$X(t) = Y(t)$$

However, the wealth process associated with such a strategy satisfies the dynamics (suppressing dependence on t)

$$dX = \frac{\pi}{F} dF + \frac{Y}{B} dB = \frac{\pi}{F} dF + rX \, dt$$

Then the discounted wealth process is given by

$$d\bar{X} = \frac{\bar{\pi}}{F} dF(t) = \bar{\pi}\mu_F \, dt + \bar{\pi}\sigma_F \, dW$$

We see that the risk-neutral Brownian motion is given by

$$W^*(t) = W(t) + \frac{\mu_F}{\sigma_F} t$$

Using the general rule (7.18) (or repeating the steps we performed for the original Black-Scholes formula), we get Black's futures formula (7.38). Also, from the general rule (7.17), we see that the corresponding PDE for the price function $C(t, f)$ of a futures option with payoff $g(f)$ is (denoting $\sigma = \sigma_F$)

$$C_t + \frac{1}{2}\sigma^2 s^2 C_{ff} - rC = 0, \qquad C(T, f) = g(f) \tag{7.41}$$

The solution for the call option is given in equations (7.38)–(7.40).

7.5.3   Exotic Options

The standard call and put options we have considered so far are sometimes called **plain vanilla** options. Options different from these are called **exotic options.** They often have a more complex structure. In particular, many exotic options depend on more variables than just the stock-price value at maturity T. For example, they might depend on the maximum, minimum, or average stock price on the interval $[0, T]$. We say that these are **path-dependent options,** because their payoff depends on what the path of the stock price has been up to maturity (rather than only on the price at maturity). Exotic options are usually more difficult to price, in terms of both explicit and numerical solutions. They are typically traded **over the counter,** which means traded directly between financial institutions and corporations, and not on exchanges. This way they can be tailored according to the needs of the trading parties. In particular, corporations often find that standard options are too rigid to provide protection from some specific risks, and they demand options with more complicated payoffs. There is virtually no limit on the number of possible different exotic options that can be invented. Here we only mention the most popular exotic options, for some of which there is an active over-the-counter market. To simplify the analysis, we restrict ourselves to the Merton-Black-Scholes model, and we assume that the stock does not pay dividends.

Packages   Packages are not really new options, but a combination of basic assets and call and put options. They are easily priced by pricing separately the components of the package.

Bermudan Options   Bermudan options are similar to American options, except that they can be exercised only at specific dates or during specific time intervals. Mathematically, the price is determined as a maximum of expectations taken over all stopping times taking values in the set of the possible exercise times.

Forward Start Options   Forward start options are paid for today, but start at some future time. For example, consider a European call option with maturity T and strike price equal to the stock-price value at time $t_1 < T$. We can think of this option as an at-the-money call option that starts at time t_1. In order to compute its price we first find its value at time t_1, and then at time $t = 0$. Denote by $\mathrm{BS}(T - t_1, S(0))$ the Black-Scholes price of the call option with time to maturity $T - t_1$, and the strike price equal to the today's stock price $S(0)$. Also note that in the "risk-neutral world" version of the Merton-Black-Scholes model [where the expected return of the stock is r and the Brownian motion process is $W^*(t) = W(t) + \frac{\mu - r}{\sigma} t$], we have

$$S(0) \frac{S(T)}{S(t_1)} = S(0) \exp\{\sigma[W^*(T) - W^*(t_1)] + (r - \sigma^2/2)(T - t_1)\}$$

By the definition of Brownian motion, the probability distribution of $W^*(T) - W^*(t_1)$ is the same as that of $W^*(T - t_1)$. Therefore, the distribution of the random variable $S(0)S(T)/S(t_1)$ is the same as that of the random variable $S(T - t_1)$. Using this, we compute the value at time t_1 of the option as

$$E_{t_1}^* \left[e^{-r(T - t_1)} \{S(T) - S(t_1)\}^+ \right] = E_{t_1}^* \left[e^{-r(T - t_1)} \frac{S(t_1)}{S(0)} \left(\frac{S(0)S(T)}{S(t_1)} - S(0) \right)^+ \right]$$

$$= \frac{S(t_1)}{S(0)} \mathrm{BS}(T - t_1, S(0))$$

The option value at time zero can now be computed as the expectation of its time-t_1 discounted value:

$$E_0^* \left[e^{-rt_1} \frac{S(t_1)}{S(0)} \mathrm{BS}(T - t_1, S(0)) \right] = \mathrm{BS}(T - t_1, S(0)) E_0^* \left[e^{-rt_1} \frac{S(t_1)}{S(0)} \right] = \mathrm{BS}(T - t_1, S(0))$$

where the last equality is due to the fact that the discounted stock price is a martingale, so $E_0^*[e^{-rt_1}S(t_1)] = S(0)$. We see that the price of the forward start at-the-money call option starting at the future date t_1 is the same as the price of the regular at-the-money call option with maturity $T - t_1$.

Compound Options   Compound options are options on options. For example, a call on a call option is an option to buy a call option with maturity T and strike price K at some exercise time $T_1 < T$, for some strike price K_1. The call on a call option should be exercised at time T_1 only if the strike price K_1 is lower than the price of the underlying call option at T_1. Therefore, in the Merton-Black-Scholes model, denoting by $\mathrm{BS}(T_1)$ the price of the underlying call option at time T_1, the price of the call on a call option at time 0 can be represented as

$$E_0^* e^{-rT_1} [\mathrm{BS}(T_1) - K_1]^+$$
$$= E_0^* e^{-rT_1} \left[E_{T_1}^* \left\{ e^{-r(T-T_1)} [S(T) - K]^+ \right\} - K_1 \right]^+$$
$$= E_0^* \left[\left\{ e^{-rT} [S(T) - K]^+ - e^{-rT_1} K_1 \right\} \mathbf{1}_{\{\mathrm{BS}(T_1) > K_1\}} \right]$$

where $\mathbf{1}_{\{A\}}$ is the indicator function that takes value 1 if the event A occurs and value zero otherwise. This term is a random variable that depends on $S(T_1)$, and the price of the stock $S(T)$ is another random variable. Therefore, we can numerically compute the price of the call on a call option in terms of the bivariate normal distribution function.

"As You Like It," or Chooser, Option   The "as you like it," or chooser, option is a contract that allows its holder to decide at a later time t_1 whether the option will be a call or a put. The time-t_1 value of this option is the maximum of the call and put values at time t_1

$$\max[c(t_1), p(t_1)]$$

If the call and the put have the same maturity $T > t_1$ and the same strike price K, the put-call parity can be used to deduce

$$\max[c(t_1), p(t_1)] = \max \left[c(t_1), c(t_1) + Ke^{-r(T-t_1)} - S(t_1) \right]$$
$$= c(t_1) + \max \left[0, Ke^{-r(T-t_1)} - S(t_1) \right]$$

The second term in the previous expression is the payoff at t_1 of a put option with strike price $Ke^{-r(T-t_1)}$. Therefore, the chooser option is a package consisting of a call option with maturity T and strike price K, and a put option with maturity t_1 and strike price $Ke^{-r(T-t_1)}$. Its price is the sum of the prices of the two options in the package.

Barrier Options   Barrier options are very popular because they cost less than their plain vanilla counterparts. However, these exotic options are also fairly difficult to price. They are less expensive because their payoff becomes zero if the price of the underlying asset crosses, or does not cross (depending on the type of option), a certain barrier. For example, an **up-and-in** call option has the payoff of the vanilla call option, but only if the asset price goes above a certain level L (the "barrier") at some point during the life of the option. Otherwise the payoff is zero. In contrast, an **up-and-out** call option has the same payoff as the regular call, unless the asset price goes above the barrier at least once, in which case the payoff is zero. These options are also called **knock-in** and **knock-out options** (respectively), for obvious reasons. There are also **down-and-in** and **down-and-out** versions of barrier options. If we denote

$$max(t) := \max_{0 \le u \le t} S(u) \tag{7.42}$$

the maximum of the price of the underlying asset on the interval $[0, t]$, the payoff of the up-and-in call option is $[S(T) - K]^+$ if $max(T) > L$, and zero otherwise. Therefore, the price of the option can be written as

$$E^* \left[e^{-rT} \{ S(T) - K \}^+ \mathbf{1}_{\{max(T) > L\}} \right]$$

This can be computed in the Merton-Black-Scholes model, because in that model there is an explicit expression for the joint density of Brownian motion process and its maximum. However, that computation assumes that the parties observe continuously whether the barrier is crossed or not. In reality, observations are taken only at discrete-time points (say, once a day). Methods have been developed that modify the price of the option to account for discrete versus continuous observations. There are also practical problems with replicating these options for hedging purposes, because the portfolio that replicates such an option depends heavily on the proximity to the barrier and on whether the asset price is below or above the barrier. This situation produces a discontinuity that makes the replicating portfolio take extreme values, which may be impractical in the real world.

Binary or Digital Option   A binary, or digital, option pays one dollar if the asset price ends up above a given strike price K, and zero dollars otherwise. The payoff is discontinuous, but it is not hard to compute the option price, at least in the Merton-Black-Scholes model (see Problem 24):

$$E^* \left[e^{-rT} \mathbf{1}_{\{S(T) > K\}} \right] = e^{-rT} P^*[S(T) > K] = e^{-rT} N(d_2) \tag{7.43}$$

where P^* is the risk-neutral probability and $N(d_2)$ is as in the Black-Scholes formula.

Lookback Option   Lookback options are like call or put options, except that the strike price is not a fixed number, but the maximum or the minimum of the asset price on the interval $[0, T]$. The payoff of the lookback call is $[max(T) - S(T)]$, where $max(T)$ is as defined in expression (7.42); the payoff of the lookback put is $[S(T) - min(T)]$, where

$min(T)$ is the minimum of S on $[0, T]$. There is an explicit formula for the price of these options in the Merton-Black-Scholes model.

Asian Option   The payoff of Asian options depends on the average of the price of the underlying on the interval $[0, T]$. As a result, the payoff of the option is less sensitive to the final value $S(T)$ of the underlying. In continuous time, the **arithmetic average** of S is

$$A(T) = \frac{1}{T} \int_0^T S(u)\, du$$

For example, the payoff of the average price call is $[A(T) - K]^+$. There is no explicit formula for the price of this option in the Merton-Black-Scholes model. However, in practice it is easier to replicate this option approximately than a regular call, because, as we get closer to maturity, we have increasingly precise knowledge about the amount of the payoff. There are numerical methods and approximate analytic methods for pricing these options. Moreover, if, instead of the arithmetic average we consider the **geometric average** of the price S, we can get an explicit formula for the Asian option price, because a geometric average of geometric Brownian motions is also a geometric Brownian motion; see Problems.

There are special modifications of the standard numerical methods, such as binomial trees and Black-Scholes partial differential equations, that are specifically designed to price a given exotic option efficiently. We refer the interested reader to the literature mentioned in the references.

Options on several assets may also be included in the exotic options category, but we discuss them separately in the next section.

7.6   Pricing in the Presence of Several Random Variables

Thus far we have focused on a setting with only one underlying risky asset and constant interest rate. There was only one source of randomness, stock movements in the discrete-time analysis, and one Brownian motion in continuous time. Pricing options becomes more complex in the following cases:

· Options on several risky assets

· One risky asset, but several random variables; for instance, random interest rate, random volatility, several Brownian motions in the model

We discuss in this section the pricing of options in such situations. As long as there are at least as many different assets as states in discrete time, and as many different risky assets as Brownian motions in continuous time, we usually remain in a complete-market model. In that case, there is a unique price, equal to the risk-neutral expectation. However, if we have more states than assets (in discrete time) or more Brownian motions than available risky assets (in continuous time), we may be forced to price an option that cannot be replicated, and the no-arbitrage price is no longer unique. In that case we have to suggest new ways of determining what the option price should be.

There are several ways of adapting the binomial tree approach to price options on several assets in discrete time. The interested reader may consult the references. Here we concentrate on continuous-time models, which allow a more compact presentation.

7.6.1 Options on Two Risky Assets

Let us extend the usual Black-Scholes model to the case of two stocks, S_1 and S_2. We first consider the following model:

$$dS_1 = S_1[\mu_1\, dt + \sigma_1\, dW_1]$$
$$dS_2 = S_2[\mu_2\, dt + \sigma_2\, dW_2] \tag{7.44}$$

where μ_1, μ_2, σ_1, and σ_2 are constant parameters, and W_1 and W_2 are Brownian motions, with **instantaneous correlation** ρ, $0 \leq \rho \leq 1$. Recall that this setup means that $E[W_1(t)W_2(t)] = \rho t$, for every t. It is worth mentioning that a model like this can be transformed into a model with two independent Brownian motions, B_1 and B_2. This transformation is possible because, given two independent Brownian motions B_1 and B_2, if we define

$$W_1 := B_1, \qquad W_2 := \rho B_1 + \sqrt{1 - \rho^2}\, B_2 \tag{7.45}$$

then W_1 and W_2 are two Brownian motions with instantaneous correlation ρ, as can be checked by computing the variances and covariances of W_1 and W_2. The model (7.44) can be rewritten as

$$dS_1 = S_1[\mu_1\, dt + \sigma_1\, dB_1]$$
$$dS_2 = S_2[\mu_2\, dt + \sigma_2\rho\, dB_1 + \sigma_2\sqrt{1 - \rho^2}\, dB_2] \tag{7.46}$$

The portfolio process is now two-dimensional, $\pi(t) = (\pi_1(t), \pi_2(t))$. The wealth process, suppressing the dependence on t, is

$$dX = \frac{\pi_1}{S_1}\, dS_1 + \frac{\pi_2}{S_2}\, dS_2 + \frac{X - (\pi_1 + \pi_2)}{B}\, dB$$

This expression gives

$$dX = [rX + \pi_1(\mu_1 - r) + \pi_2(\mu_2 - r)]\, dt + \pi_1\sigma_1\, dW_1 + \pi_2\sigma_2\, dW_2$$

In order for the discounted wealth process to be a martingale under the risk-neutral probability P^*, we need to have

$$dX = rX\,dt + \pi_1\sigma_1\,dW_1^* + \pi_2\sigma_2\,dW_2^* \tag{7.47}$$

for some P^*-Brownian motions W_i^* with correlation ρ. For that to be the case, we must have

$$W_i^*(t) = W_i(t) + t(\mu_i - r)/\sigma_i$$

Under this probability measure, the drift μ_i of stock S_i is replaced by the interest rate r. This is a complete-market model (because we have two stocks and two Brownian motions), and the unique price of a claim with payoff C maturing at time T is given by $E^*[\bar{C}]$, as usual.

Suppose now that the payoff is $C = g(S_1(T), S_2(T))$, a function of the prices of the stocks at maturity. Denote by $C(t, s_1, s_2)$ the price of this option at time t, when stock price values are s_1 and s_2. Using the two-dimensional Itô's rule, we see that (see Problem 33)

$$dC = \left[C_t + rS_1 C_{s_1} + rS_2 C_{s_2} + \frac{1}{2}\sigma_1^2 S_1^2 C_{s_1 s_1} + \frac{1}{2}\sigma_2^2 S_2^2 C_{s_2 s_2} + \rho\sigma_1\sigma_2 S_1 S_2 C_{s_1 s_2}\right]dt$$
$$+ \sigma_1 S_1 C_{s_1}\,dW_1^* + \sigma_2 S_2 C_{s_2}\,dW_2^* \tag{7.48}$$

Comparing the dt term with the wealth equation (7.47), or making the drift of the discounted C equal to zero, as in the one-asset case, we see that we need to have

$$C_t + \frac{1}{2}\sigma_1^2 s_1^2 C_{s_1 s_1} + \frac{1}{2}\sigma_2^2 s_2^2 C_{s_2 s_2} + \rho\sigma_1\sigma_2 s_1 s_2 C_{s_1 s_2} + r(s_1 C_{s_1} + s_2 C_{s_2} - C) = 0 \tag{7.49}$$

This is the **Black-Scholes equation for two assets.** The boundary condition is

$$C(T, s_1, s_2) = g(s_1, s_2)$$

The option can be priced by solving the PDE numerically. Comparing the dW terms in the wealth equation and the equation for dC, we also note that the portfolio that replicates this option is given by investing the following dollar amounts in each of the two stocks:

$$\pi_1^g = S_1 C_{s_1}, \qquad \pi_2^g = S_2 C_{s_2}$$

Example 7.4 (Exchange Option)   In the context of the model discussed in this section, consider the option to exchange one asset for another. This is an option that, at maturity, gives its holder the right to deliver asset S_1 and receive in exchange asset S_2. The payoff of this option is

$$g(S_1(T), S_2(T)) = [S_2(T) - S_1(T)]^+ = \max[S_2(T) - S_1(T), 0]$$

Since we have

$$(s_2 - s_1)^+ = s_1 \left(\frac{s_2}{s_1} - 1 \right)^+ \tag{7.50}$$

it is reasonable to expect that the option price will be of the form

$$C(t, s_1, s_2) = s_1 Q(t, z)$$

for some function Q and a new variable $z = s_2/s_1$. After some computations (see Problems) we can show that, if C satisfies equation (7.49), then Q has to satisfy

$$Q_t + \frac{1}{2}(\sigma_1^2 + \sigma_2^2 - 2\rho\sigma_1\sigma_2)z^2 Q_{zz} = 0 \tag{7.51}$$

with the boundary condition $Q(T, z) = (z - 1)^+$. We now recognize this PDE and the boundary condition as the Black-Scholes PDE corresponding to the price of a European call option with strike price $K = 1$, interest rate $r = 0$, and volatility

$$\sigma = \sqrt{\sigma_1^2 + \sigma_2^2 - 2\rho\sigma_1\sigma_2} \tag{7.52}$$

Using the regular Black-Scholes formula for Q, and the fact that $C = s_1 Q$, we get

$$C(t, s_1, s_2) = s_2 N(d_1) - s_1 N(d_2) \tag{7.53}$$

where

$$d_1 = \frac{1}{\sigma\sqrt{T - t}}[\log(s_2/s_1) + (\sigma^2/2)(T - t)] \tag{7.54}$$

$$d_2 = \frac{1}{\sigma\sqrt{T - t}}[\log(s_2/s_1) - (\sigma^2/2)(T - t)] = d_1 - \sigma\sqrt{T - t} \tag{7.55}$$

and σ is as in equation (7.52). Note that once we know how to price the exchange option, we can also price the options on a maximum or a minimum of two assets, because we have

$$\min[S_1(T), S_2(T)] = S_2(T) - \max[S_2(T) - S_1(T), 0]$$
$$\max[S_1(T), S_2(T)] = S_2(T) + \max[S_1(T) - S_2(T), 0]$$

and the second terms on the right-hand sides correspond to the payoff of an exchange option.

We present another, quite informal way of getting the price of the exchange option. (The reader can safely skip this paragraph.) We are motivated by expression (7.50). As usual, the price of the exchange option has to be the expected value, under the risk-neutral probability, of the discounted payoff; that is (recalling our notation $\bar{X}$ for the discounted value of X),

$$E^*[\bar{S}_1(T)\{Z(T) - 1\}^+] = S_1(0)E^* \left[\frac{\bar{S}_1(T)}{S_1(0)} \{Z(T) - 1\}^+ \right]$$

where $Z(t) = S_2(t)/S_1(t)$. We recall from equation (6.37) that expectations under a risk-neutral probability P^* are computed as $E^*[X] = E[M(T)X]$, for a given martingale M with expected value $E[M(T)] = 1$. It is then not surprising that, since

$$E^* \left[\frac{\bar{S}_1(T)}{S_1(0)} \right] = 1$$

multiplying by $\bar{S}_1(T)/S_1(0)$ inside the expectation is like changing the probability measure. In other words, we can think of the option price as

$$S_1(0)\tilde{E}[\{Z(T) - 1\}^+]$$

under a new probability measure $\tilde{P}$ (different from P and P^*). What is this measure? It turns out that it is the measure under which Z has to be a martingale. (An indication for this result is that

$$\tilde{E}[Z(T)] = E^* \left[\frac{\bar{S}_1(T)}{S_1(0)} Z(T) \right] = E^* \left[\frac{\bar{S}_2(T)}{S_1(0)} \right] = \frac{S_2(0)}{S_1(0)} = Z(0)$$

where we have used the fact that $\bar{S}_2$ is a martingale under the probability measure P^*.) Applying Itô's rule on $Z(t) = S_2(t)/S_1(t)$, and setting the dt term to zero (in order to have a martingale), we deduce that

$$dZ = Z(\sigma_1 d\tilde{W}_1 - \sigma_2 d\tilde{W}_2) \tag{7.56}$$

for some $\tilde{P}$-Brownian motions $\tilde{W}_i$. We now introduce the process

$$\tilde{W}(t) := \frac{\sigma_1 \tilde{W}_1(t) - \sigma_2 \tilde{W}_2(t)}{\sqrt{\sigma_1^2 + \sigma_2^2 - 2\rho\sigma_1\sigma_2}} \tag{7.57}$$

where σ_1, σ_2, and ρ are the parameters of equations (7.44). We can check, by computing the variance, that $\tilde{W}$ is a one-dimensional $\tilde{P}$-Brownian motion, too. (Intuitively, it is a weighted average of two Brownian motion processes.) Substituting equation (7.57) in equation (7.56), the stochastic differential equation for Z becomes

$$dZ = Z\sqrt{\sigma_1^2 + \sigma_2^2 - 2\rho\sigma_1\sigma_2}\, d\tilde{W}$$

This is the same dynamics as the risk-neutral dynamics of a single stock in the Merton-Black-Scholes model, with interest rate $r = 0$ and volatility σ. Therefore, we derive the same result as before. This method can be made rigorous, and goes under the name **change of numeraire,** studied later in the book. The reason for this name is that, by dividing by S_1, we effectively measure everything in the units of asset S_1, which then becomes our "numeraire."

7.6.2 Quantos

Quantos are financial contracts that involve more than one currency. For example, let $S(t)$ be a domestic equity index. A regular forward contract on this index has a payoff equal to $S(T) - F$ dollars (domestic currency). However, if the payoff is $S(T) - F$ units of foreign currency, that is a quanto product. We consider a setting with two risk-free accounts with interest rates r (domestic) and r_f (foreign), and in which the exchange rate Q—that is, the dollar value of one unit of foreign currency—satisfies

$$dQ(t) = Q(t)[\mu_Q \, dt + \sigma_Q \, dW(t)]$$

In order to see how to price quanto products, first recall the wealth equation (7.37): When we follow a portfolio strategy that invests π dollars in the foreign account and place the rest in the domestic account, the value of the portfolio in dollars becomes

$$dX(t) = [rX(t) + \pi(t)(\mu_Q + r_f - r)] \, dt + \pi(t)\sigma_Q \, dW(t) \qquad (7.58)$$

In order to make the discounted process $\bar{X}$ a martingale (in the domestic market) we need to have

$$dX(t) = rX(t) \, dt + \pi(t)\sigma_Q \, dW^*(t)$$

with W^* being a Brownian motion under the risk-neutral probability. Therefore,

$$W^*(t) = W(t) + t[\mu_Q - (r - r_f)]/\sigma_Q$$

Inserting this expression into the equation for dQ, we get

$$dQ(t) = Q(t)[(r - r_f) \, dt + \sigma_Q \, dW^*(t)]$$

Assume also that the domestic index S satisfies the risk-neutral dynamics (again in the domestic world)

$$dS(t) = S(t)[r \, dt + \sigma_S \, dZ^*(t)]$$

where Z^* is another Brownian motion under the risk-neutral probability, which has instantaneous correlation ρ with the Brownian motion W^*. We need two Brownian motion processes in our model because of the existence of two sources of uncertainty, one coming from the domestic index and another coming from the exchange rate. Consider also the product process SQ, with dynamics (from Itô's rule)

$$d[S(t)Q(t)] = S(t)Q(t)[(2r - r_f + \rho\sigma_Q\sigma_S)\,dt + \sigma_Q\,dW^*(t) + \sigma_S\,dZ^*(t)]$$

We have now the risk-neutral dynamics for processes S, Q, and SQ. Therefore, we can price (in dollars) the claims with payoff $g(Q(T), S(T))$ dollars, simply by taking the risk-neutral expectation

$$E^*[e^{-rT}g(Q(T), S(T))]$$

We can similarly price the payoffs of the form $g(Q(T), S(T)Q(T))$.

For example, suppose that we want to price a quanto forward with payoff $S(T) - F(t)$ units of foreign currency, which is the same as $[S(T) - F(t)]Q(T)$ units of domestic currency. The domestic value of the quanto at time t is

$$e^{-r(T-t)}\{E_t^*[S(T)Q(T)] - F(t)E_t^*[Q(T)]\}$$

where we use the fact that the forward price $F(t)$ is known at time t. If we want this value to be zero at time t (so that the cost of entering this contract is zero, as is the case with standard forward contracts), the forward price $F(t)$ has to be chosen so that

$$F(t) = \frac{E_t^*[S(T)Q(T)]}{E_t^*[Q(T)]} \tag{7.59}$$

Since the risk-neutral drift of the process SQ is $(2r - r_f + \rho\sigma_S\sigma_Q)$, we have (see Problem 36)

$$E_t^*[S(T)Q(T)] = S(t)Q(t)e^{(2r-r_f+\rho\sigma_S\sigma_Q)(T-t)}$$

Similarly,

$$E_t^*[Q(T)] = Q(t)e^{(r-r_f)(T-t)}$$

Substituting these in equation (7.59), we get

$$F(t) = S(t)e^{(r+\rho\sigma_S\sigma_Q)(T-t)}$$

This formula is not as intuitive as the one for the forward price of a regular forward contract. We see how the risk-neutral pricing framework is useful to get formulas like this in a relatively easy manner.

Word of Caution   The domestic risk-neutral two-dimensional Brownian motion (W^*, Z^*) is not the same as the foreign risk-neutral Brownian motion (W_f^*, Z_f^*). Indeed, consider the dynamics (from Itô's rule) of the exchange rate $1/Q$, which we would use to convert the units of domestic currency into the units of foreign currency:

$$d[1/Q(t)] = [1/Q(t)][(r_f - r + \sigma_Q^2)\, dt - \sigma_Q\, dW^*(t)]$$

However, by symmetry with the equation for dQ, we need to have

$$d[1/Q(t)] = [1/Q(t)][(r_f - r)\, dt - \sigma_Q\, dW_f^*(t)]$$

The result is that

$$W_f^*(t) = W^*(t) - \sigma_Q t$$

Similarly, S dollars in foreign currency, which is equal to S/Q, have the foreign risk-neutral dynamics (by Itô's rule)

$$d[S(t)/Q(t)] = [S(t)/Q(t)][(r_f - \rho\sigma_q\sigma_S)\, dt + \sigma_S\, dZ^*(t) - \sigma_Q\, dW_f^*(t)]$$

But the discounted stock price in foreign currency should be a martingale in the foreign risk-neutral world, meaning S/Q should have the dynamics

$$d[S(t)/Q(t)] = [S(t)/Q(t)][r_f\, dt + \sigma_S\, dZ_f^*(t) - \sigma_Q\, dW_f^*(t)]$$

Comparing the two equations, we get

$$Z_f^*(t) = Z^*(t) - \rho\sigma_Q t$$

Next, we want to study models in which there is only one risky asset, called stock as usual, but there are also other stochastic variables in the market. For example, the volatility of the stock may itself be a stochastic process changing randomly over time, and the interest rate might be stochastic, too. This flexibility produces more realistic models, but also presents more difficulties for pricing options. There are two main subclasses of models like these: complete- and incomplete-markets models. For a model to be a complete market, since there is only one risky asset, we need also to have only one Brownian motion process. If there are more Brownian motion processes, the model becomes one of incomplete markets, and the no-arbitrage price of options is no longer unique. For notational simplicity, we focus on models with stochastic volatility, while we usually keep the interest rate r constant. Here is a fairly general **stochastic volatility model:**

$$dS(t) = S(t)[\mu(t, S(t), V(t))\, dt + \sigma_{11}(t, S(t), V(t))\, dW_1(t) + \sigma_{12}(t, S(t), V(t))\, dW_2(t)]$$
$$dV(t) = \alpha(t, S(t), V(t))\, dt + \sigma_{21}(t, S(t), V(t))\, dW_1(t) + \sigma_{22}(t, S(t), V(t))\, dW_2(t)$$

Here, μ, α, and $\sigma_{ij}, i, j = 1, 2$, are some given deterministic functions of three variables t, S, and V, and W_1 and W_2 are two Brownian motions, independent or correlated. While this is a very flexible model, it is not usually easy to decide what the functions μ, α, and σ_{ij}

should be. Also, if W_1 and W_2 are not perfectly correlated, we have an incomplete-market model.

7.6.3 Stochastic Volatility with Complete Markets

Let us first consider a model with only one Brownian motion W:

$$dS(t) = S(t)[\mu \, dt + \sigma(t, S(t)) \, dW(t)] \tag{7.60}$$

In words, we generalize the Merton-Black-Scholes model by allowing the volatility to be a function of time and the current stock price. If the volatility is a deterministic function of time only, $\sigma = \sigma(t)$, it can be shown (see Problem 11) that the Black-Scholes formula for the call option remains the same, except that we have to replace the squared volatility σ^2 by its average

$$\frac{1}{T} \int_0^T \sigma^2(u) \, du$$

Similarly, if the interest rate is a deterministic function of time, we have to replace r by its average

$$\frac{1}{T} \int_0^T r(u) \, du$$

If the volatility and the interest rate are functions of time and the current stock price, we still have a complete-markets model, in which the unique risk-neutral measure is obtained by replacing the drift μ with the interest rate $r(t, S(t))$. The price of a European option with random payoff $g(T, S(T))$ at maturity T is given by

$$C(t, s) = E_{t,s}^* \left[e^{-\int_t^T r(u, S(u)) \, du} g(T, S(T)) \right]$$

Typically, this expression has to be computed numerically. The PDE for this price is the generalized Black-Scholes PDE:

$$C_t + \frac{1}{2} \sigma^2(t, s) C_{ss} + r(t, s)[sC_S - C] = 0$$

One early and popular model is the **constant elasticity of variance model** of Cox and Ross (1976), in which

$$\sigma(t, S) = \frac{\sigma}{S^\alpha}$$

for some constants $\sigma > 0$ and $0 \le \alpha < 1$.

Recall that oftentimes market participants try to estimate the volatility by looking at option prices and retrieving the implied volatility from the Black-Scholes formula. A similar exercise can be performed in this context, too: we observe option prices, and we try to find which function $\sigma(t, s)$ is consistent with those prices. That is, we try to find the function $\sigma(t, s)$ for which the theoretical option prices $C(t, s)$ agree with the observed option prices. In the context of binomial trees, the outcome would be an **implied tree.** This is a well studied area of research, and there is a rich literature on the subject.

7.6.4   Stochastic Volatility with Incomplete Markets; Market Price of Risk*

Consider now a stochastic volatility model with two Brownian motions W_1 and W_2:

$$dS(t) = S(t)[\mu(t, S(t), V(t)) \, dt + \sigma_1(t, S(t), V(t)) \, dW_1(t) + \sigma_2(t, S(t), V(t)) \, dW_2(t)]$$
$$dV(t) = \alpha(t, S(t), V(t)) \, dt + \gamma(t, S(t), V(t)) \, dW_2(t) \tag{7.61}$$

For concreteness, we assume that W_1 and W_2 are independent. This is now an incomplete-market model, and there is more than one risk-neutral probability. In the following expressions we suppress the dependence of the parameters of equations (7.61) on the variables S and V. In order to see that the model is incomplete, recall that under a risk-neutral probability P^*, the stock has to satisfy dynamics given by

$$dS(t) = S(t)[r(t) \, dt + \sigma_1(t) \, dW_1^*(t) + \sigma_2(t) \, dW_2^*(t)] \tag{7.62}$$

Denote by $\kappa(t)$ *any* stochastic process adapted to the information provided by W_1 and W_2 [that is, at time t the value of $\kappa(t)$ is fully determined by the values of $W_1(s)$ and $W_2(s), s \le t$]. It is easy to verify that equation (7.61) is equivalent to equation (7.62) if we set

$$W_1^*(t) = W_1(t) + \int_0^t \frac{1}{\sigma_1(u)} [\mu(u) - r(u) - \sigma_2(u)\kappa(u)] \, du$$

and

$$W_2^*(t) = W_2(t) + \int_0^t \kappa(u) \, du$$

(This result is checked by using $dW_2^* = dW_2 + \kappa \, dt$, and similarly for dW_1^*; see Problem 37.) Substituting in the expression for dV of equations (7.61), we get

$$dV(t) = [\alpha(t) - \kappa(t)\gamma(t)] \, dt + \gamma(t) \, dW_2^*(t) \tag{7.63}$$

Since equation (7.62) holds for *any* process $\kappa(t)$, we can state that *there are infinitely many risk-neutral probability measures in this model,* each one corresponding to a different **market price of risk** [this is the name usually given to the process $\kappa(t)$ for reasons related to the so-called utility pricing of options]. In practice, very often it is assumed that the market price of risk κ is a constant, and not a stochastic process. Then, if we denote by $C(t, s, v)$ the price of the option as a function of time, stock price S, and volatility process V, the two-dimensional Itô's rule, suppressing dependence on t, yields

$$dC = \left[C_t + \frac{1}{2} C_{ss} S^2 (\sigma_1^2 + \sigma_2^2) + \frac{1}{2} C_{vv} \gamma^2 + C_{sv} \gamma \sigma_2 + r S C_s + C_v (\alpha - \kappa \gamma) \right] dt$$
$$+ [\ldots] dW_1^* + [\ldots] dW_2^* \tag{7.64}$$

The dynamics of the discounted option price $\bar{C}$ are the same as the dynamics (7.64) of C, but with an additional term, $-r\bar{C}$, in the drift. Since the discounted price process has to be a martingale under a risk-neutral measure, its drift has to be zero, giving us the pricing PDE

$$C_t + \frac{1}{2} C_{ss} s^2 (\sigma_1^2 + \sigma_2^2) + \frac{1}{2} C_{vv} \gamma^2 + C_{sv} \gamma \sigma_2 + r(s C_s - C) + C_v (\alpha - \kappa \gamma) = 0$$

So, we have a different pricing PDE for each different market price of risk κ. We can treat κ simply as an additional unknown parameter that has to be estimated. In particular, we can try to get an **implied market price of risk** by matching the theoretical price $C(t, s, v)$ of a frequently traded option with its observed price.

Another approach to pricing in incomplete markets is to assume that the writer of the option has some utility (or risk) function and he chooses a price that is consistent with his attitude toward risk. We explore this approach next.

7.6.5   Utility Pricing in Incomplete Markets*

We present here an approach for pricing options in incomplete markets that is theoretically consistent with the utility function of the person trading the option. The main difference relative to the approach described previously is that the approach in this section depends on the risk preferences of the particular individual pricing the option, and not on the market price of risk κ, a quantity that is determined by what the market as a whole thinks of the risk associated with the underlying assets.

Consider a contingent claim with random payoff C at time T. We have the following definition:

*The **utility-based price** is the price at which the investor has zero demand for the option, relative to her utility function.*

This definition agrees with the unique no-arbitrage price of C in a complete-market model, and it specifies only one of the possible no-arbitrage prices in an incomplete-market model. In order to see, in an informal way, how this price is determined, denote by $\hat{X}(T)$ the optimal terminal wealth for the investor relative to her utility, and consider the expected utility $V(\delta; C(0))$ when holding δ units of claim C:

$$V(\delta; C(0)) := E[U(\hat{X}(T) + \delta C - \delta C(0))]$$

For example, if δ is negative, this function represents the utility of selling δ shares of C while receiving the price $C(0)$ per one unit of C. The utility-based price $C(0)$ of C is such a value for which the derivative $V'(0, C(0))$ of the maximum utility, with $\delta = 0$ units of C traded, is equal to zero. This statement means that the investor is indifferent between trading and not trading infinitesimally small amounts of the claim C. Computing the derivative $V'(0, C(0))$ and setting it equal to zero, and denoting $\hat{\lambda} = E[U'(\hat{X}(T))]$, we obtain

$$C(0) = \frac{1}{\hat{\lambda}} E[U'(\hat{X}(T))C] \tag{7.65}$$

Thus, if we know the optimal terminal wealth $\hat{X}(T)$ for the investor's problem of maximizing $E[U(X(T))]$, we can compute the utility-based price of a given claim C. The difficulty is that it is in general quite hard to find the optimal wealth in incomplete-market models.

Let us briefly discuss a connection of the utility-based pricing with risk-neutral pricing and with the duality/martingale method of chapter 4. (These results are quite deep, and we will not attempt to provide proofs; see Karatzas and Shreve, 1998, for an example.) Given the wealth process $X(t)$ of the investor, with initial value x, we recall that a risk-neutral density is a random variable $Z(T)$ such that

$$E[Z(T)\bar{X}(T)] = x$$

where $\bar{X}(T)$ is the discounted value of $X(T)$. In a complete market there is only one risk-neutral density $Z(T)$, and the price of an option with payoff C at time T can be found from the risk-neutral pricing expectation formula

$$C(0) = E[Z(T)\bar{C}]$$

In an incomplete market (such as the one of the previous section) there are many risk-neutral densities $Z_\kappa(T)$, each one corresponding to a different market price of risk process $\kappa(t)$. The question is, Can we find among all these market prices for risk the one, denoted $\hat{\kappa}$, for which the utility-based price would be given by the following expectation formula?

$$C(0) = E[Z_{\hat{\kappa}}(T)\bar{C}]$$

In order to do so, recall from chapter 4 (or argue now) that for a given utility function U and its dual function $\tilde{U}(z) = \max[U(x) - xz]$, the **duality relationship** (4.70) holds:

$$E[U(X^{x,\pi}(T))] \le E[\tilde{U}(\lambda \bar{Z}_\kappa(T))] + \lambda x \tag{7.66}$$

This is valid now for every risk-neutral density $Z_\kappa(T)$ and every positive number λ. Therefore, we can take infimum over the pairs $(\lambda, Z_\kappa(T))$ on the right-hand side to get

$$E[U(X^{x,\pi}(T))] \leq \inf_{\lambda,\kappa}\{E[\tilde{U}(\lambda\bar{Z}_\kappa(T))] + \lambda x\} \tag{7.67}$$

The optimization problem on the right-hand side is called the **dual problem** to the problem of maximizing the expected utility on the left-hand side. It can be shown, under some conditions on the model, that the optimal terminal wealth $\hat{X}(T)$ and the optimal pair $(\hat{\lambda}, \hat{\kappa})$ for the dual problem have to satisfy (here, $I = (U')^{-1}$)

$$\hat{X}(T) = I(\hat{\lambda}\bar{Z}_{\hat{\kappa}}(T)) \tag{7.68}$$

or, equivalently,

$$\hat{\lambda}\bar{Z}_{\hat{\kappa}}(T) = U'(\hat{X}(T)) \tag{7.69}$$

The utility-based price in equation (7.65), of a claim with payoff C at time T, is, therefore, indeed given by the risk-neutral pricing formula

$$C(0) = E[Z_{\hat{\kappa}}(T)\bar{C}]$$

In the risk-neutral terminology, this corresponds to pricing under the risk-neutral probability measure that is optimal for the dual problem. Here again the problem is that it is usually hard to find the optimal market price of risk $\hat{\kappa}$.

There is still another way of using the utility of the investor in order to solve the problem of pricing in incomplete markets. It is based on **certainty equivalence,** by which we mean that the price $C(0)$ of a payoff C should be such that the maximum utility without a long position in C should be the same as the maximum utility with a long position in C while paying the price $C(0)$ at time $t = 0$. In other words, assuming that without taking a position in C the investor starts with initial wealth x, the price $C(0)$ of the claim is chosen so that

$$\max E[U(X^x(T))] = \max E\left[U\left(X^{x-C(0)}(T) + C\right)\right]$$

where the maximum is taken over all admissible portfolio strategies. We have the same problem here as with the utility-based price—the maximum utilities in the last equality are hard to compute in incomplete markets.

The approaches from this section are not very popular in practice for options that can be efficiently hedged (meaning: approximately replicated) with underlying assets, but an approach of this kind may be necessary when trading financial contracts whose risk cannot be hedged by trading in available assets. The latter is typically the case in less developed markets, such as, for example, the market for energy derivatives (options on gas, electricity, and so on) or markets of developing countries.

7.7 Merton's Jump-Diffusion Model*

It can be argued that in the real world many economic processes exhibit occasional jumps; thus it may be useful to have models that incorporate jump processes. In particular, we may want to allow for the possibility that a stock price can experience sudden jumps, and we want to have models for pricing options on such a stock.

Merton (1976) extended the Merton-Black-Scholes diffusion model to a model that also has a jump component. He suggested that the number of jumps $N(t)$ between time 0 and time t should be a so-called **Poisson process,** governed by the **Poisson distribution:**

$$P[N(t) = k] = e^{-\lambda t} \frac{(\lambda t)^k}{k!} \tag{7.70}$$

where $\lambda > 0$ is the **jump intensity.** Moreover, if a jump happens at time t_i, the stock price goes from $S(t_i)$ to $X_i S(t_i)$, where X_i's are independent random variables with common distribution. More precisely, under the risk-neutral probability measure P^*, the stock price is given by

$$S(t) = S(0) \cdot X_1 \cdot X_2 \cdot \ldots \cdot X_{N(t)} \cdot e^{(r-\sigma^2/2-\lambda m)t+\sigma W^*(t)} \tag{7.71}$$

where we assume that N, W, and X_i are all independent of each other and we set

$$m := E^*[X] - 1$$

where X has the same distribution as the X_i's. The value m is chosen so that the discounted stock price $S(t)$ is still a martingale (under P^* probability). Indeed, we know that in the standard model $\bar{S}(t) = S(0) \exp\{-t\sigma^2/2 + \sigma W^*(t)\}$ is a P^*-martingale. In order to show that the discounted price in this jump-diffusion model is also a martingale, it is sufficient to show

$$E^*[X_1 \cdot X_2 \cdot \ldots \cdot X_{N(t)} \cdot e^{-\lambda m t}] = 1 \tag{7.72}$$

This point is demonstrated in Problem 38.

Under the "real-world" probability measure, we would simply replace the interest rate r with the actual expected rate of return μ.

Using Itô's rule for jump processes (not presented in this book), it can be shown that, under P^*, the stock price satisfies

$$dS(t) = S(t)(r - \lambda m)\, dt + S(t)\sigma\, dW^*(t) + dJ(t) \tag{7.73}$$

where $dJ(t) = 0$ if there is no jump at time t, and $dJ(t) = S(t)X_i - S(t)$ if the ith jump occurs at time t.

We now want to find an option pricing formula in this model. This procedure is somewhat delicate, since this is an incomplete-market model, hence there are many risk-neutral probability measures in the model and there is no unique no-arbitrage price for contingent claims. The market is incomplete because there are two sources of uncertainty, the Brownian motion process and the Poisson process, and only one risky security. As a consequence, the jump risk cannot be hedged away. Merton (1976) suggests using the risk-neutral probability specified earlier, which is the direct extension of the unique risk-neutral probability of the Merton-Black-Scholes model, with the corresponding change of the drift of the stock from $\mu - \lambda m$ to $r - \lambda m$. The economic reasoning is that the jumps in a given stock's price happen because of the arrival of new information specific to that particular stock (or the corresponding industry sector), which is, therefore, uncorrelated with the market. As such, this risk is a "nonsystematic" risk that cannot be diversified away. Thus we postulate that the jump component has the same distribution under the risk-neutral probability P^* used for pricing as under the "real-world" probability. This assumption holds because if a risk cannot be hedged (that is, "controlled" by investing in another security), prices are obtained as expected values under the real probability P (as is the case in insurance mathematics, for example).

We then use the following formula for the price $C(0)$ of a given European contingent claim with maturity T and random payoff $g(S(T))$:

$$C(0) = E^*[e^{-rT} g(S(T))] \tag{7.74}$$

Here, the expectation is taken under the probability P^*, described earlier. We now want to derive an expression as explicit as possible from this expectation. By conditioning on the number of jumps up to time T, that is, on the events $\{N(T) = k\}$, and using the independence among the variables in the model, we obtain **Merton's jump-diffusion option pricing formula**, as follows:

$$C(0) = \sum_{k=0}^{\infty} E^*[e^{-rT} g(S(T)) \mid N(T) = k] P^*[N(T) = k]$$

$$= \sum_{k=0}^{\infty} E^*\left[e^{-rT} g\left(S(0) \cdot X_1 \cdot X_2 \cdot \ldots \cdot X_k \cdot e^{(r-\sigma^2/2 - \lambda m)T + \sigma W^*(T)}\right)\right] e^{-\lambda T} \frac{(\lambda T)^k}{k!}$$

$$\tag{7.75}$$

If we knew the values of $X_1, \ldots, X_k$, then the expectation term in the sum would simply be the price of the option on the stock in the Black-Scholes model with initial value

$$S_k(0) := S(0) \cdot X_1 \cdot X_2 \cdot \ldots \cdot X_k \cdot e^{-\lambda m T}$$

Let us denote that price by $\mathrm{BS}(S_k(0))$. Using independence we have

$$
\begin{aligned}
E^*&\left[e^{-rT}g\left(S(0)\cdot X_1\cdot X_2\cdot\ldots\cdot X_k\cdot e^{(r-\sigma^2/2-\lambda m)T+\sigma W^*(T)}\right)\right]\\
&= E^*\left[E^*\left[e^{-rT}g\left(S_k(0)e^{(r-\sigma^2/2)T+\sigma W^*(T)}\right)\big|X_1,\ldots,X_k\right]\right]\\
&= E^*[\mathrm{BS}(S_k(0))]
\end{aligned}
$$

Then equation (7.75) can be written as

$$
C(0) = \sum_{k=0}^{\infty} e^{-\lambda T}\frac{(\lambda T)^k}{k!}E^*[\mathrm{BS}(S_k(0))] \tag{7.76}
$$

Expression (7.75) can be further simplified in the particular case in which the jump-size distribution is itself lognormal, that is, of the form

$$
X = e^{\alpha+\beta Z}
$$

where Z is a standard normal random variable under P^*. Then the product $X_1\cdot\ldots\cdot X_k$ is also lognormal, and so is the stock price $S(T)$ in Merton's jump-diffusion model. Now, when $S(T)$ is lognormal, then the expectations of the type $E^*[g(S(T))]$ can be computed similarly to the Black-Scholes formula. This derivation is left as an exercise in Problem 39, and we state the result here:

Let X have a lognormal distribution under P^*, $X = e^{\alpha+\beta Z}$, so that $\mathrm{Var}^*[\log(X)] = \beta^2$ and $m = e^{\alpha+\beta^2/2} - 1$. Denote

$$
\xi := \alpha + \beta^2/2, \qquad \sigma_k := \sigma^2 + k\beta^2/T, \qquad r_k := r - \lambda m + k\xi/T, \qquad \tilde{\lambda} =: \lambda(1+m)
$$

Then we have

$$
\mathrm{Var}^*[\log(X_1\cdot\ldots\cdot X_k)] = k\beta^2, \qquad E^*[X_1\cdot\ldots\cdot X_k] = e^{k\xi}
$$

Denoting by BS_k the Black-Scholes price of $g(S(T))$ when r is replaced by r_k and σ is replaced by σ_k, the option pricing formula (7.75) becomes, in this model,

$$
C(0) = \sum_{k=0}^{\infty} e^{-\tilde{\lambda}T}\frac{(\tilde{\lambda}T)^k}{k!}\mathrm{BS}_k \tag{7.77}
$$

7.8   Estimation of Variance and ARCH/GARCH Models

Another class of popular models, which we do not consider in detail, is a class of models based on time-series/econometrics analysis called ARCH/GARCH models (to satisfy the curiosity of the reader, GARCH stands for *generalized autoregressive conditional heteroskedasticity*). These are models in discrete time but continuous state space, as is usual for time-series models. Asset-price returns and associated volatilities are modeled in terms of the functional dependence of the current values on the past values, plus a random noise. In the limit when the time period goes to zero, models of this type usually converge to one of the continuous-time stochastic volatility models.

In order to motivate the ARCH/GARCH models, denote by

$$X_i = \log \frac{S(t_i)}{S(t_{i-1})}$$

the log-return on the interval $[t_{i-1}, t_i]$ of asset S. Then, given n observations, the usual estimate of the variance (squared volatility) of the log-returns is given by

$$\hat{\sigma}^2 = \frac{1}{n-1} \sum_{i=1}^{n} (X_i - \bar{X})^2$$

where

$$\bar{X} = \frac{1}{n} \sum_{i=1}^{n} X_i$$

is the sample average. Sometimes X_i represents relative returns, $X_i = [S(t_i) - S(t_{i-1})]/S(t_{i-1})$, rather than log-returns.

Suppose now that we estimate the volatility σ every day, using the observations from the last n days. Denote by σ_k the value of the volatility for day k. The model is usually set up so that σ_k^2 is actually not the variance, but the second moment, the expectation of X_k^2 conditional on the information up to time t_{k-1}:

$$\sigma_k^2 = E_{t_{k-1}} \left[X_k^2 \right] \tag{7.78}$$

When estimating this quantity, it may be desirable to give more weight to the more recent observations. This approach leads to models of the type

$$\sigma_k^2 = \sum_{i=1}^{n} w_i X_{k-i}^2 \tag{7.79}$$

where the weights w_i are positive and satisfy

$$\sum_{i=1}^{n} w_i = 1$$

A further extension is to include a term of the form αV^2, where α is a weight given to the long-run volatility V. Then the model becomes

$$\sigma_k^2 = \alpha V^2 + \sum_{i=1}^{n} w_i X_{k-i}^2, \qquad \alpha + \sum_{i=1}^{n} w_i = 1$$

This corresponds to the **ARCH model** suggested by Engle (1982). In that model, X_i is defined via

$$X_i = \sigma_i Z_i, \quad i = 1, \dots, n$$

where the Z_i's are standard normal random variables with Z_i independent of Z_j, for all $i \neq j$. Since σ_i depends only on the information up to time t_{i-1}, the distribution of X_i, conditional on the past, is normal. This result is consistent with equation (7.78). (Why?)

Consider now the case in which the weights are of the form

$$w_i = (1 - \lambda)\lambda^{i-1}$$

for some number $0 < \lambda < 1$. It can be verified that the weights add up to one. Moreover, we see that

$$w_i = \lambda w_{i-1}$$

In other words, the weight given to the observation of day $i - 1$ is equal to the weight of the observation of day i reduced by the factor λ. Expression (7.79) becomes

$$\sigma_k^2 = (1 - \lambda) \sum_{i=1}^{n} \lambda^{i-1} X_{k-i}^2$$

$$= (1 - \lambda) X_{k-1}^2 + (1 - \lambda) \sum_{i=2}^{n} \lambda^{i-1} X_{k-i}^2$$

$$= (1 - \lambda) X_{k-1}^2 + (1 - \lambda)\lambda \sum_{i=1}^{n} \lambda^{i-1} X_{k-1-i}^2 - (1 - \lambda)\lambda^n X_{k-1-n}^2$$

$$= (1 - \lambda) X_{k-1}^2 + \lambda \hat{\sigma}_{k-1}^2 - (1 - \lambda)\lambda^n X_{k-1-n}^2$$

If we assume that the number of observations n is large enough, so that the last term is negligible, we get

$$\sigma_k^2 = \lambda \hat{\sigma}_{k-1}^2 + (1 - \lambda) X_{k-1}^2$$

In other words, the current squared volatility is obtained as a weighted combination of the previous-day squared volatility and the previous-day squared return. A small value for λ puts more weight on the squared return, and a large value for λ puts more weight on the value of volatility obtained from past observations.

The following extension of this model, which includes the long-run volatility V, corresponds to the **GARCH(1,1) model** (introduced by Bollerslev, 1986):

$$\sigma_k^2 = \alpha_1 V^2 + \alpha_2 \sigma_{k-1}^2 + \alpha_3 X_{k-1}^2, \qquad \alpha_1 + \alpha_2 + \alpha_3 = 1 \tag{7.80}$$

In GARCH(p,q) models, we would use p past values of X_i and q past values of σ_i.

In multiple-variable models it is important to estimate covariances between different variables. Recall that the covariance σ_{XY} of two random variables X and Y is defined as

$$\sigma_{XY} := E[(X - E[X])(Y - E[Y])]$$

A standard estimate of the covariance is

$$\hat{\sigma}_{XY} = \frac{1}{n} \sum_{i=1}^{n} (X_i - \bar{X})(Y_i - \bar{Y})$$

We can also model the covariance $\sigma_{XY}(k)$ on day k in a way similar to that described for the ARCH/GARCH models. More precisely, we model $\sigma_{XY} = E[XY]$ here, rather than the covariance. For example, we can have the model

$$\sigma_{XY}(k) = \lambda \sigma_{XY}(k-1) + (1-\lambda) X_{k-1} Y_{k-1}$$

A GARCH(1,1) model would be

$$\sigma_{XY}(k) = \alpha_1 V^2 + \alpha_2 \sigma_{XY}(k-1) + \alpha_3 X_{k-1} Y_{k-1}$$

No matter which of these models we use, in practice we need to estimate the weights w_i, or α_i from past data using statistical techniques.

7.9 Appendix: Derivation of the Black-Scholes Formula

We prove the formula for the case $t = 0$ [the case for general t is similar, by considering $W^*(T) - W^*(t)$ instead of $W^*(T)$]. The price at $t = 0$ is given by the expectation

$$E^*[e^{-rT}\{S(T) - K\}^+] = I_1 - I_2 \tag{7.81}$$

where

$$I_1 = E^*\left[e^{-rT} S(T) \mathbf{1}_{\{S(T)>K\}}\right]; \qquad I_2 = K e^{-rT} E^*\left[\mathbf{1}_{\{S(T)>K\}}\right] \tag{7.82}$$

[Recall that $\mathbf{1}_{\{S(T)>K\}}$ is equal to 1 if $S(T) > K$ and is equal to 0 otherwise.] Since the stock price satisfies $dS(t) = S(t)[r\,dt + \sigma\,dW^*(t)]$ under the risk-neutral probability, we have, by analogy with equation (3.28),

$$S(T) = s \exp\left\{\sigma W^*(T) + \left(r - \tfrac{1}{2}\sigma^2\right)T\right\} \tag{7.83}$$

Suppose we want to have $S(T) > K$. What does this assumption mean in terms of $W^*(T)$? Taking logs on both sides of equation (7.83) and rearranging, we obtain

$$S(T) > K \quad \text{is equivalent to} \quad \sigma W^*(T) > \log K - \log s + \tfrac{1}{2}\sigma^2 T - rT \tag{7.84}$$

Under the risk-neutral probability the random variable $W^*(T)$ has the same distribution as $\sqrt{T}z$, where z is the standard normal random variable. If we write the right-hand side of expression (7.84) in terms of z, we get

$$z > \frac{1}{\sigma\sqrt{T}}\left(\log K - \log s + \frac{1}{2}\sigma^2 T - rT\right) = -d_2 \tag{7.85}$$

with d_2 as in equation (7.15), for $t = 0$.

We now compute I_2. We have

$$E^*\left[\mathbf{1}_{\{S(T)>K\}}\right] = P^*[S(T) > K] = P^*[z > -d_2] = P^*[z < d_2] = N(d_2)$$

Therefore,

$$I_2 = Ke^{-rT}N(d_2) \tag{7.86}$$

As for I_1, we have to do a bit of integration. We have

$$I_1 = e^{-rT}E^*\left[s \exp\left\{\sigma W^*(T) + \left(r - \tfrac{1}{2}\sigma^2\right)T\right\}\mathbf{1}_{\{S(T)>K\}}\right]$$

From equation (7.85), this can be written as

$$I_1 = s\int_{-d_2}^{\infty}\exp\left\{\sigma\sqrt{T}z - \tfrac{1}{2}\sigma^2 T\right\}n(z)\,dz$$

where

$$n(z) = \frac{1}{\sqrt{2\pi}}e^{-\frac{z^2}{2}}$$

is the standard normal density function. This can be rewritten as

$$I_1 = \frac{s}{\sqrt{2\pi}}\int_{-d_2}^{\infty}\exp\left\{-\frac{1}{2}\left(z - \sigma\sqrt{T}\right)^2\right\}dz$$

Using the change of variables

$$u = z - \sigma\sqrt{T}$$

and recalling that $d_1 = d_2 + \sigma\sqrt{T}$, we get

$$I_1 = \frac{s}{\sqrt{2\pi}} \int_{-d_1}^{\infty} \exp\left\{-\frac{1}{2}u^2\right\} du$$

But this means that

$$I_1 = sP^*[z > -d_1] = sP^*[z < d_1] = sN(d_1) \tag{7.87}$$

Equalities (7.86) and (7.87) together with equation (7.81) imply the Black-Scholes formula.

Summary

In the Cox-Ross-Rubinstein model, the price of European options can be easily computed by solving the binomial tree backward and computing one-step expectations of the discounted future values at each node of the tree. For American options, we only have to take one additional step: to compare the value of waiting with the value of exercising at each node of the tree.

In the Merton-Black-Scholes model the price function is a solution to a PDE, called the Black-Scholes equation. In the case of the European call option, the price has an analytic form, in terms of the cumulative normal distribution function. This is known as the Black-Scholes formula. The number of shares of the stock held in the replicating portfolio can be found as the derivative of the price function with respect to the stock value, and is called delta.

Typically, there are no analytic formulas for the prices of American options. They have to be found numerically. Theoretically, the price of an American option is the maximum of the prices of European options over all possible maturities, including random, stopping-time maturities, with the values between the initial time and the maturity time of the option. In the Merton-Black-Scholes model, the problem of computing an American option price becomes a so-called free boundary problem.

Formulas of the Black-Scholes type can also be found for European options with dividends, as well as for currency options, futures options, and some exotic options. The method can also be extended to models in which there is more than one risky asset, or more than one random variable.

In all these situations the price is uniquely determined, because markets are complete. In models with stochastic volatility and incomplete markets, we have to introduce another parameter, called market price of risk, to uniquely pin down the price of an option. Alternatively, we can embed the option pricing problem in a framework of utility maximization, in order to find the option price consistent with an investor's risk preferences. In the context of a jump-diffusion model, we can get a formula for option prices under special assumptions on the distribution of jumps in the stock price. The most popular stochastic volatility models in discrete time are the ARCH and GARCH models.

Problems

1. Consider a two-period CRR model with continuously compounded interest rate $r = 0.05$, $S(0) = 100$, $u = 1.1$, and $d = 0.9$. The payoff is the European at-the-money put option with strike price $K = S(0) = 100$. We take $\Delta t = 1$. Compute the price of the option at time $t = 0$.

†2. In a two-period CRR model with $r = 1\%$ per period, $S(0) = 100$, $u = 1.02$, and $d = 0.98$, consider an option that expires after two periods and pays the value of the squared stock price, $S^2(t)$, if the stock price $S(t)$ is higher than 100.00 when the option is exercised. Otherwise [when $S(t)$ is less than or equal to 100], the option pays zero. Find the price of the European version of this option.

3. Consider a model in which the price of the stock can go up 12% or down 8% per period. The interest rate is 5% per period. Compute the price of a security that pays $1,000 if the stock goes down for five consecutive periods and pays $40 if the stock goes up for five consecutive periods.

†4. Consider a single-period binomial model with two periods where the stock has an initial price of $100 and can go up 15% or down 5% in each period. The price of the European call option on this stock with strike price $115 and maturity in two periods is $5.424. What should be the price of the risk-free security that pays $1 after one period regardless of what happens? We assume, as usual, that the interest rate r per period is constant.

*5. Write a computer code for a program that would compute the price for a European call option in a CRR model in which

$$1 + r = e^{r\Delta t}, \qquad u = e^{\sigma\sqrt{\Delta t}}, \qquad d = \frac{1}{u}, \qquad \Delta t = T/n$$

The input of the program should consist of r, σ, K, $S(0)$, T, and n. The output should give the option price at time $t = 0$. Run the program for different values of n. You can check the correctness of your program by setting $K = 0$. What value should you get in this case? Finally, check your results by using the Black-Scholes formula and a table (or software) for the cumulative normal distribution function.

†6. Suppose that the stock price today is $S(t) = 2.00$, the interest rate is $r = 0\%$, and the time to maturity is three months. Consider an option whose Black-Scholes price is given

by the function

$$V(t, s) = s^2 e^{2(T-t)}$$

where the time is in annual terms. What is the option price today? What is the volatility of the stock equal to?

*7. Argue that formula (7.7) converges to the Black-Scholes formula (7.13) for the European call price, as $n \to \infty$, if we set $u = e^{\sigma \sqrt{\Delta t}}$ and $d = \frac{1}{u}$. {Hint: Use the central limit theorem, which says that the probability $P[a \leq X_p \leq b]$ for a binomial random variable X_p with parameters p and n is, in the limit, equal to the probability $P[(a - np)/\sqrt{np(1-p)} \leq Z \leq (b - np)/\sqrt{np(1-p)}]$, where Z is a standard normal random variable. Set $a = a_n$ and $b = \infty$, and compute the limits.}

*8. Let $C(t, s)$ be a price function (the value of the replicating portfolio) for the option $g(S(T))$ in the Merton-Black-Scholes model with interest rate r.

a. Express, in terms of the function $C(s, t)$ and its derivatives, the set of the pairs (s, t) for which the replicating portfolio borrows money from the bank. [Hint: the number of shares of S in the portfolio is given by $C_s(t, s)$; borrowing will take place if the amount held in the stock is larger than the value of the replicating portfolio.]

b. Suppose now that there are two interest rates in the market: r for lending and R for borrowing, $R > r$. Can you guess (without proof) what the Black-Scholes partial differential equation would look like in this case?

9. Find the Black-Scholes formula for the European put option by direct calculation of the expectation of its discounted value under the equivalent martingale measure, as is done for the call option in the appendix.

†10. Verify that the Black-Scholes formula for the European put option can be obtained from the formula for the call option using put-call parity. [Hint: You can use the fact that $1 - N(x) = N(-x)$ for the normal distribution function.]

11. Find the formula for the call option price in the Black-Scholes model in which the interest rate and the volatility are deterministic functions of time. For this purpose it is useful to know that the random variable

$$X = \int_0^t \sigma(u) \, dW(u)$$

with σ deterministic, has normal distribution, with mean zero and variance $\int_0^t \sigma^2(u) \, du$. (See Problem 14 in chapter 8 for this result.)

†12. In order to avoid the problem of implied volatilities being different for different strike prices and maturities, a student of the Black-Scholes theory suggests making the stock's

volatility σ a function of K and T, $\sigma(K, T)$. What is wrong with this suggestion, at least from the theoretical/modeling point of view? (In practice, though, traders might use different volatilities for pricing options with different maturities and strike prices.)

13. In this problem we want to compute the "Greeks," or sensitivities, of the call option price with respect to various parameters in the model. Specifically, in the notation of equations (7.13)–(7.15), show that the following expressions are valid for the partial derivatives of the call option price function $c(t, s)$:

$$c_s = N(d_1)$$

$$c_t = -\frac{sN'(d_1)\sigma}{2\sqrt{T-t}} - rKe^{-r(T-t)}N(d_2) \tag{7.88}$$

$$c_{ss} = \frac{N'(d_1)}{s\sigma\sqrt{T-t}}$$

Here, N' is the standard normal density function,

$$N'(x) = \frac{1}{\sqrt{2\pi}}e^{-x^2/2}$$

Using these expressions, prove that the Black-Scholes equation, that is, the first equation in equations (7.9), holds for the call option price $c(t, s)$.

†14. In a two-period CRR model with $r = 1\%$ per period, $S(0) = 100$, $u = 1.02$, and $d = 0.98$, consider an option that expires after two periods and pays the value of the squared stock price, $S^2(t)$, if the stock price $S(t)$ is higher than \$100.00 when the option is exercised. Otherwise [when $S(t)$ is less than or equal to 100], the option pays zero. Find the price of the American version of this option.

15. In the context of Example 7.2, compute the price of the American put option with the strike price $K = 101$.

†16. Find the price of a 3-month European call option with $K = 100$, $r = 0.05$, $S(0) = 100$, $u = 1.1$, and $d = 0.9$ in the binomial model, if a dividend amount of $D = \$5$ is to be paid at time $\tau = 1.5$ months. Use the binomial tree with time step $\Delta t = 1/12$ years to model the process $S_G(t) = S(t) - e^{-r(\tau - t)}D$ for $t < \tau$.

17. Find the price of the corresponding put option in the previous problem, without using put-call parity.

†18. Consider the following two-period setting: the price of a stock is \$50. Interest rate per period is 2%. After one period the price of the stock can go up to \$55 or drop to \$47, and it will pay (in both cases) a dividend of \$3. If it goes up the first period, the second period it can go up to \$57 or down to \$48. If it goes down the first period, the second period it can go

up to $48 or down to $41. Compute the price of an American put option with strike price $K = 45$ that matures at the end of the second period.

19. Compute the price of the corresponding American call option in the previous problem.

†20. Consider a Merton-Black-Scholes model with $r = 0.07$, $\sigma = 0.3$, $T = 0.5$ years, $S(0) = 100$, and a call option with the strike price $K = 100$. Using the normal distribution table (or an appropriate software program), find the price of the call option, when there are no dividends. Repeat this exercise when (a) the dividend rate is 3%; (b) the dividend of $3.00 is paid after three months.

21. Compute the price of the corresponding put option in the previous problem.

†22. In the context of the previous two problems, with no dividends, compute the price of the chooser option, for which the holder can choose at time $t_1 = 0.25$ years whether to hold the call or the put option.

23. In the context of the previous three problems, with no dividends, find the ("real-world") probabilities that the call and the put options will be exercised, if $\mu = 10\%$. (You will need a normal distribution table or software for this computation.)

†24. Provide a proof for expression (7.43) for the price of a digital option. Compute the price if the option pays $1.00 if the stock price at maturity is larger than $100.00, and it pays $0.00 otherwise. Use the same parameters as in the previous three problems.

25. Find the Black-Scholes formula for the option paying D dollars if $\min[S_1(T), S_2(T)] > K$, and zero otherwise, in the Black-Scholes continuous-time model:

$$dS_i(t) = S_i(t)[\mu_i \, dt + \sigma_i \, dW_i(t)]$$

$i = 1, 2$, where W_1 and W_2 are two independent Brownian motions.

†26. Let $S(0) = \$100.00$, $K_1 = \$92.00$, $K_2 = \$125.00$, and $r = 5\%$. Find the Black-Scholes formula for the option paying $10.00 in 3 months if $S(T) \leq K_1$ or if $S(T) \geq K_2$, and zero otherwise, in the Black-Scholes continuous-time model.

27. Consider the option with the payoff $g(S(T)) = [S(T)]^n$, in the Merton-Black-Scholes model. It can be shown that its price at time t has the form $C(t, s) = f(t, T)s^n$. Find the function $f(t, T)$ by the following two methods:

a. Computing the risk-neutral expected value

b. Substituting $C(t, s)$ in the Black-Scholes partial differential equation and its boundary condition; then, using this, getting an ordinary differential equation for $f(t, T)$ and solving it [Hint: for part a use the explicit form of $S(T)$; for part b the solution to the ordinary differential equation will be of the form $f(t, T) = e^{k(T-t)}$ for a constant k you have to determine.]

Chapter 7

*28. The price of a European call option is $8.23. The option is written on a non-dividend-paying stock with a current price of $100.00. The strike price is $95.00, the maturity is six months, and the risk-free interest rate is 6% per year. Find the implied volatility (you will have to find it numerically, possibly by trial and error, or using software that has a "root solver").

*29. Show that the Black-Scholes call option formula gives the value $(s - K)^+$ as we get closer to maturity, that is, as $t \to T$. Also show that the Black-Scholes call price tends to zero as the stock price tends to zero.

†30. Show that, if S is modeled by the Merton-Black-Scholes model, then S and its futures price have the same volatility.

31. Suppose that one euro can be purchased for U.S. $0.93. Suppose also that the risk-free interest rate in the European Union is 5% and in United States it is 6%, and that the volatility of the exchange rate is 11% per year. Find the dollar value of a six-month European call option on the euro with strike price $0.93.

†32. Compute the price of a European call on the yen. The current exchange rate is 108 and, the strike price is 110 yen per dollar, maturity is three months, and the price of a three-month T-bill is $98.45. We estimate the annual volatility of the yen-dollar exchange rate to be 15%. A three-month pure-discount yen-denominated risk-free bond trades at 993 yen (nominal 1,000).

33. Justify equation (7.48).

*34. Verify that equation (7.51) holds for the function $Q(t, z)$.

35. Consider a process X that satisfies

$$dX = X[\mu \, dt + \sigma \, dW]$$

for some constants μ and σ. Use Itô's rule to check that the solution is given by

$$X(T) = X(t) \exp\{\sigma[W(T) - W(t)] + (\mu - \sigma^2/2)(T - t)\}$$

Recall that if W is a normal distribution with mean zero and variance t, then

$$E[e^{\sigma W}] = e^{t\sigma^2/2}$$

Using this expression argue that

$$E_t[X(T)] = X(t)e^{\mu(T-t)}$$

36. Verify all the expressions obtained by applications of Itô's rule in the section on quantos (section 7.6.2).

*37. Check that equation (7.61) is equivalent to equation (7.62) for a given process κ and W_1^*, W_2^* as described in section 7.6.4.

*38. Show that equation (7.72) holds and argue that S is a P^*-martingale in Merton's jump-diffusion model. Hint: Compute the expectation in equation (7.72) by conditioning on the events $\{N(t) = k\}$ and using the fact that

$$e^x = \sum_{k=0}^{\infty} \frac{x^k}{k!}$$

*39. Show that equation (7.75) becomes equation (7.77) when the jump size X has log-normal distribution. Hint: Think of the usual Black-Scholes formula as a function of $\text{Var}^*[\log\{S(T)\}]$ and $E^*[S(T)]$.

Further Readings

The paper that started the literature on option pricing is Black and Scholes (1973). Merton (1973b) provides key interpretations, very influential in subsequent studies. The binomial model is first presented in Cox, Ross, and Rubinstein (1979). A standard textbook is Hull (2002). More advanced books include Bjork (1999), Musiela and Rutkowski (1997), and Wilmott (1998). The theoretical treatment of American options can be found in Karatzas and Shreve (1998). Foreign currency options are analyzed in Garman and Kohlhagen (1983). For options on futures, we recommend Ramaswamy and Sundaresan (1985). A good description of many exotic options and applications can be found in Nelken (2000). Some models of stochastic volatility are Cox and Ross (1976), Hull and White (1987), and Heston (1993). Advanced book treatments include Fouque, Papanicolau, and Sircar (2000) and Lewis (2000). Rubinstein (1994) is one of the papers on implied binomial trees. He (1990) considers the problem of convergence from discrete-time models (like trees) to continuous-time models. Pricing of options with jumps is studied in Merton (1976). ARCH and GARCH models are introduced by Engle (1982) and Bollerslev (1986). A good review can be found in Gourieroux (1997).

8 Fixed-Income Market Models and Derivatives

Although interest rates are an important factor in the prices of most securities, they are more important in fixed-income markets than in equity markets, because bond prices, forward rates, and their derivatives are more sensitive to the changes in interest rates than stock prices. Therefore, it becomes desirable to have models of interest rates, instead of just assuming that the interest rate is constant, as in the Merton-Black-Scholes model. In this chapter we present models of interest rates and their application to the pricing of general fixed-income derivatives, as well as pricing of simpler derivatives that do not require an explicit model of interest rates. In general, realistic models for interest rates tend to be more complex than models for stock prices, because we have to model the entire yield curve, that is, the rates for bonds with different maturities. The majority of popular interest-rate models have been developed in continuous-time settings, and it is for this reason that the bulk of this chapter is devoted to those settings.

As is customary when pricing fixed-income derivatives, we assume in this chapter that the following basic **principle for pricing interest-rate derivatives** holds:

The price at time t is equal to the expected value of the discounted payoff under some risk-neutral probability, conditional on the information available up to time t.

By risk-neutral probability we mean that the discounted prices of all assets are P-martingales. In this chapter we denote this pricing probability by P and the associated expectation functional by E, instead of P^* and E^*, since we do not consider the "real-world" probability anyway. Assuming a continuously compounded interest rate process r, the preceding principle means that the time-t price $C(t)$ of a given random payoff C with maturity T can be computed using the **expectation formula**

$$C(t) = E_t\left[e^{-\int_t^T r(u)du}C\right] \tag{8.1}$$

In particular, the zero-coupon T-bond that pays 1 dollar at time T has the price $P(t, T)$ at time t given by

$$P(t, T) = E_t\left[e^{-\int_t^T r(u)du}\right] \tag{8.2}$$

We always assume in this chapter that a bond pays 1 dollar at maturity.

8.1 Discrete-Time Interest-Rate Modeling

We now consider a discrete-time framework, with times $t = t_0 < t_1 < \cdots < t_n$. We denote by r_i the risk-free interest rate in the period $[t_i, t_{i+1}]$. The pricing formula (8.1) in discrete

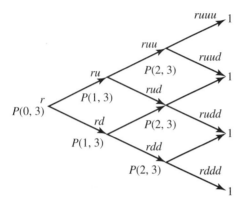

Figure 8.1
Interest-rate and bond-price values in a tree.

time becomes

$$C(t) = E_t \left[\frac{C}{\prod_{i=0}^{n-1}(1 + r_i)} \right] \tag{8.3}$$

where $\prod_{i=0}^{n-1}$ is notation that means the product of n terms with indicator i. It is clear from this formula that in order to price fixed-income securities it is convenient to model the interest rate as the basic random object, and to model it under the pricing probability P. Most models of interest rates are continuous-time models because of some analytical advantages. Here we present the main ideas and some specific models in discrete time.

8.1.1 Binomial Tree for the Interest Rate

In order to illustrate some of the main points, we first model the interest rate process as a binomial tree; see figure 8.1. As in the Cox-Ross-Rubinstein model for the stock price, we assume that the interest rate can go up or down. For simplicity, we also assume that the tree is recombining. The value at each node is the value of the interest rate to be used in the next time period. The probabilities of going up and down are the risk-neutral probabilities. Let us denote them by p and $1 - p$. That is, we assume that we are in the "risk-neutral world." We can now price interest-rate derivatives in this tree using equation (8.3). In particular, we can price pure discount bonds. As usual, we denote by $P(t, T)$ the price at time t of a pure discount bond that matures at $T \geq t$.

For example, consider a pure discount bond that matures after three periods. By definition, the value at time $t = 3$ is known: $P(3, 3) = 1$, at all the nodes at time $t = 3$. We can then go backward in the tree and compute the value at the previous nodes. For instance, at the uppermost node at time $t = 2$ the bond price would be

$$P^u(2, 3) = \frac{1}{1 + r^u(2)}[p \cdot 1 + (1 - p) \cdot 1]$$

where $r^u(2)$ is the interest rate at that node. The terms in square brackets are both 1 because we are considering the price of the bond one period before maturity, but as we go back in the tree, the terms in the square brackets will be the corresponding prices of the bond, which will change across different nodes.

Once we have computed the bond prices throughout the tree, we can also compute the prices of options on bonds by the same backward method. We show the whole procedure in a simple example, illustrated in Figure 8.2.

Example 8.1 (Bond Pricing in a Tree)   Consider a two-period setting, with dates $t = 0, 1, 2$. We assume that the interest rate at the initial date $t = 0$ is 5%. Suppose that the interest rate changes in the binomial tree according to an up factor $u = 1.1$ and a down factor $d = 0.9$. Therefore, at $t = 1$ the interest rate can be 5.5% or 4.5%, which are the rates that will prevail in the second period, depending on the node. At the initial time, $t = 0$, we would like to price a call option $C = [P(1, 2) - K]^+$ with maturity at $t = 1$, on a pure discount bond maturing at time $t = 2$, with strike price $K = 0.95$. We first have to compute the price of the bond throughout the tree. We assume that the risk-neutral probability is $p = 0.5$. This assumption gives us the following bond prices at time-1 nodes:

$$P^u(1, 2) = \frac{1}{1.055}(0.5 \cdot 1 + 0.5 \cdot 1) = 0.9479$$

$$P^d(1, 2) = \frac{1}{1.045}(0.5 \cdot 1 + 0.5 \cdot 1) = 0.9569$$

This result means that at $t = 0$ the price of the bond is

$$P(0, 2) = \frac{1}{1.05}(0.5 \cdot 0.9479 + 0.5 \cdot 0.9569) = 0.9071$$

The value of the option at maturity is either $(0.948 - 0.95)^+ = 0$ at the upper node or $(0.957 - 0.95)^+ = 0.0069$ at the lower node. Thus the price of the option at $t = 0$ is

$$C(0) = \frac{1}{1.05}(0.5 \cdot 0 + 0.5 \cdot 0.0069) = 0.0033$$

Therefore, we should pay (approximately) 0.0033 for the call on a bond that pays 1 dollar at time 2; see figure 8.2.

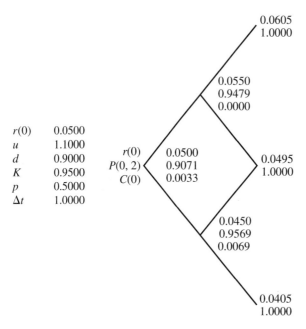

Figure 8.2
Pricing a call option on a bond.

A trader pricing interest-rate derivatives can take advantage of a large number of different outstanding bond issues at a given point in time. Using the information on existing bond prices, the trader can price derivatives whose payoff depends on the same underlying variable, the interest rate. Consider the case of modeling interest rates according to a binomial tree, as described in the previous example. We can retrieve the (implied) risk-neutral probabilities that make our interest-rate model consistent with existing prices and use those probabilities to price other interest-rate derivatives. We illustrate this point with another example.

Example 8.2 (Pricing Using Existing Bond Prices) Suppose that the one-year interest rate today is 4%. In our model one year from now, the one-year interest rate can only have two values: it can either go up to 5% or go down to 3%. Our market consists of a two-year pure discount bond with nominal value $100 that is trading at $92.278. We want to price a European call option on this bond, with maturity in one year and strike price 96. According to the model, one year from now, the price of a one-year pure discount bond will take one of the following two values (depending on the prevailing interest rate):

$$\frac{100}{1.05} = 95.238, \qquad \frac{100}{1.03} = 97.087$$

The absence of arbitrage implies that the price of the current two-year bond has to be equal to the price of the contract that pays the price of this bond one year from now (at which moment it will be a one-year bond). If we denote by p the risk-neutral probability that the interest rate will be 5% one year from now, and if our model is correct, it has to be the case that

$$92.278 = \frac{1}{1.04} \left[p \cdot 95.238 + (1 - p) \cdot 97.087 \right]$$

From this equation we compute $p = 0.605$. Now we can price the call option we are interested in as

$$\frac{1}{1.04} \left[p(95.238 - 96)^+ + (1 - p) \cdot (97.087 - 96)^+ \right]$$

$$= \frac{1}{1.04}(1 - 0.605) \cdot 1.087 = 0.413$$

8.1.2   Black-Derman-Toy Model

We present a similar example of a discrete-time binomial model that suggests a procedure for building a tree that matches properties of the observed term structure of interest rates and, in particular, a tree that is consistent with observed interest rates and their volatilities (Black, Derman, and Toy, 1990). We present this **matching of term structure** approach in the following example. We also say that we perform a **calibration** of the model to the data.

Example 8.3 (Black-Derman-Toy Model)   Suppose that we want to build a binomial tree with three periods, each corresponding to one year. The current one-year spot rate is $r_1 = 5\%$, the two-year spot rate is $r_2 = 6\%$, and the three-year spot rate is $r_3 = 6.5\%$. In addition, we estimate that the volatility of the current one-year spot rate is 8% and that the volatility of the one-year spot rate will be 7% one year from now. Here we use the term "volatility" for the standard deviation of the logarithm of the interest rate. We also assume that the real volatilities are equal to the risk-neutral volatilities (the standard deviations computed under risk-neutral probabilities). Finally, we assume that the risk-neutral probabilities of an upward movement and a downward movement of interest rates are equal to $p = 1 - p = 0.5$.

First, we find the one-year interest rates r^u and r^d one year from today that are consistent with the term structure we observe and with our volatility estimate. The mean of the log of the one-year interest rate, for probability of 0.5 at each node, is

$$E[\log(r_1)] = \mu_r = 0.5 \log r^u + 0.5 \log r^d$$

The variance of the log of the one-year interest rate is

$$\sigma_r^2 = 0.5(\mu_r - \log r^u)^2 + 0.5(\mu_r - \log r^d)^2$$

Substituting μ_r in the previous expression, it is straightforward to check that

$$\sigma_r = 0.5 \log \frac{r^u}{r^d} \tag{8.4}$$

We want this result to be equal to the observed value 0.08.

In addition, one year from now, according to our model, the price of the one-year pure discount bond with nominal value \$1 will have to be either $1/(1 + r^u)$ or $1/(1 + r^d)$. Then, since the current two-year rate is 6%, for our model to be consistent with the term structure and rule out the possibility of arbitrage opportunities, we need the today's price of the two-year pure discount bond (which will be the one-year bond one year from now) to be equal to the discounted expected value one year from now; that is,

$$\frac{1}{1.06^2} = \frac{1}{1.05} \left[0.5 \frac{1}{1 + r^u} + 0.5 \frac{1}{1 + r^d} \right] \tag{8.5}$$

Equation (8.4), with $\sigma_r = 0.08$, and equation (8.5) form a system of two equations with two unknowns. It is easy to verify that the solution to the system is $r^u = 7.57\%$ and $r^d = 6.45\%$.

Next, we want to derive the possible values of the one-year interest rate after two periods. After two periods there will be three possible values that we denote r^{uu}, r^{ud}, and r^{dd} with the usual interpretation: if the interest rate after one period is r^u, it can either go up to r^{uu} or down to r^{ud}. Similar notation applies if the rate after one period is r^d. We also assume that the tree is recombining; that is, if a one-year rate goes up in the first period and down in the second period, the resulting rate is the same as if the original rate first goes down and then up.

We now state the volatility and no-arbitrage conditions. After two periods, the three-year bond will be the one-year bond, whose price will depend on the one-year rate. At that time, the one-year rate will be r^{uu} with probability 0.25 (two independent up movements with probability 0.5 each), r^{dd} with probability 0.25, and r^{ud} with probability 0.5. In order to rule out arbitrage, we need the price of the three-year pure discount bond to be the discounted expected price of the one-year pure discount bond two periods from now; that is,

$$\frac{1}{1.065^3} = \frac{1}{1.06^2} \left(0.25 \frac{1}{1 + r^{uu}} + 0.5 \frac{1}{1 + r^{ud}} + 0.25 \frac{1}{1 + r^{dd}} \right) \tag{8.6}$$

We also want to match our volatility estimates. As we stated previously, our estimate is that the standard deviation of the log of the interest rate will be 7%. We assume that the standard deviation will be the same regardless of whether interest rates go up or down in the first period. Then, just as before, we have

$$0.07 = 0.5 \log \frac{r^{uu}}{r^{ud}} \tag{8.7}$$

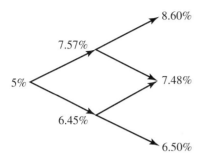

Figure 8.3
Interest rates matching the term structure and volatilities.

if the interest rate goes up in the first period, and

$$0.07 = 0.5 \log \frac{r^{ud}}{r^{dd}} \tag{8.8}$$

if the interest rate goes down in the first period. Equations (8.6)–(8.8) provide a system of three equations with three unknowns. It is straightforward to verify that the solution to the system is $r^{uu} = 8.60\%$, $r^{ud} = 7.48\%$, and $r^{dd} = 6.50\%$; see figure 8.3.

After we have computed the bond prices in the tree, we can use the tree for pricing options on a given bond, either by replication or by risk-neutral probabilities; see the Problems section.

8.1.3 Ho-Lee Model

Once we choose a tree for the interest-rate process, the bond prices are automatically determined. In practice, it would be ideal to use a tree that produces bond prices in agreement with observed market prices, or with market-price characteristics. We again illustrate the matching-of-term-structure idea, this time in the **Ho-Lee model.**

Denote by $r_i^l(j)$ the interest rate for the next j periods at time t_i at the node l. As in the Cox-Ross-Rubinstein tree model, l can be u (up) or d (down) one period after initial time. After two periods, l can be uu (up and up), ud, du, or dd, with the obvious interpretations. Analogous notation is applied after n periods. For example, $1/[1 + r_2^{ud}(3)]^3$ represents the price of the pure discount bond with nominal value \$1 and three periods left to maturity, evaluated two periods into the tree and when the term structure has gone up in one period and down in the other. The model also requires the tree to be recombining, that is, $ud = du$. The objective is to model changes of the whole term structure up or down at every time t_i.

We now introduce some additional notation for forward rates. At moment t_0, $f_0(j, k)$ represents the forward rate in the current term structure corresponding to periods j to k, $k > j$. That is,

$$[1 + r_0(j)]^j [1 + f_0(j, k)]^{k-j} = [1 + r_0(k)]^k \qquad (8.9)$$

Similarly, we denote by $f_i^l(j, k)$ the forward rate at moment t_i and node l, that is,

$$\left[1 + r_i^l(j)\right]^j \left[1 + f_i^l(j, k)\right]^{k-j} = \left[1 + r_i^l(k)\right]^k \qquad (8.10)$$

Suppose, as a starting point, that we know the whole term structure at moment t_0, that is, the value of interest rates of all maturities, $r_0(n)$, for any n. Suppose, also, that we know with certainty that at period t_1 the term structure will be the same as now. Then the price of the pure discount bond maturing j periods after time t_1 can be obtained in two ways, from $r_1(j)$ and from the corresponding forward rate, and to avoid arbitrage those values have to be the same:

$$\frac{1}{[1 + r_1(j)]^j} = \frac{1}{[1 + f_0(1, j + 1)]^j}$$

Here we suppressed the superscript l, since it is irrelevant. We now introduce the Ho-Lee model, which is a binomial randomization of the previous equation. More precisely, according to this model, one period from now we have

$$\frac{1}{\left[1 + r_1^u(j)\right]^j} = \frac{1}{[1 + f_0(1, j + 1)]^j} h^u(j) \qquad (8.11)$$

in the up state and

$$\frac{1}{\left[1 + r_1^d(j)\right]^j} = \frac{1}{[1 + f_0(1, j + 1)]^j} h^d(j) \qquad (8.12)$$

in the down state, with coefficients $h^u(j)$ and $h^d(j)$, which will be determined in the way we explain next.

First of all, we need $h^u(j)$ and $h^d(j)$ to be such that there is no arbitrage. We denote by p the risk-neutral probability of the up state and by $1 - p$ the risk-neutral probability of the down state. Consider the pure discount bond with maturity $j + 1$, which a period from now will have maturity j. In order to rule out arbitrage, the price of this bond has to be the present value of its expected price one period from now, where the expectation is taken according to the risk-neutral probability. Accordingly we have

$$\frac{1}{[1 + r_0(j + 1)]^{j+1}} = \frac{1}{1 + r_0(1)} \left[p \frac{1}{\left[1 + r_1^u(j)\right]^j} + (1 - p) \frac{1}{\left[1 + r_1^d(j)\right]^j} \right]$$

Replacing the future possible interest rates with their values according to equations (8.11) and (8.12), we get

$$\frac{1}{[1+r_0(j+1)]^{j+1}}$$

$$=\frac{1}{1+r_0(1)}\left[p\frac{1}{[1+f_0(1,j+1)]^j}h^u(j)+(1-p)\frac{1}{[1+f_0(1,j+1)]^j}h^d(j)\right]$$

$$=\frac{1}{1+r_0(1)}\frac{1}{[1+f_0(1,j+1)]^j}[ph^u(j)+(1-p)h^d(j)]$$

From this expression and equation (8.9) we see that we need to have

$$ph^u(j)+(1-p)h^d(j)=1 \tag{8.13}$$

for any value of j. Moreover, we want $h^u(j)$ and $h^d(j)$ to be such that the tree is recombining, that is, an up move followed by a down move results in the same bond prices as a down move followed by an up move. The price of a bond with maturity in j periods, after an up-down sequence in the term structure in this model, just as after one period, is

$$\frac{1}{\left[1+r_2^{ud}(j)\right]^j}=\frac{1}{\left[1+f_1^u(1,j+1)\right]^j}h^d(j)$$

Replacing the forward rate by its definition (8.10), we get

$$\frac{1}{\left[1+r_2^{ud}(j)\right]^j}=\frac{1+r_1^u(1)}{\left[1+r_1^u(j+1)\right]^{j+1}}h^d(j)$$

From equations (8.11) and (8.12) we can rewrite the previous expression as

$$\frac{1}{\left[1+r_2^{ud}(j)\right]^j}=\frac{1+f_0(1,2)}{h^u(1)}\frac{h^u(j+1)}{[1+f_0(1,j+2)]^{j+1}}h^d(j)$$

Replacing again the forward rates on the right-hand side by their definitions, we get

$$\frac{1}{\left[1+r_2^{ud}(j)\right]^j}=\frac{[1+r_0(2)]^2}{1+r_0(1)}\frac{1+r_0(1)}{[1+r_0(j+2)]^{j+2}}\frac{h^u(j+1)h^d(j)}{h^u(1)}$$

$$=\frac{[1+r_0(2)]^2}{[1+r_0(j+2)]^{j+2}}\frac{h^u(j+1)h^d(j)}{h^u(1)} \tag{8.14}$$

We now find the price of a bond with maturity in j periods, after a down-up sequence in the term structure. By repeating computations similar to those we just performed, we get the analogous result:

$$\frac{1}{\left[1 + r_2^{du}(j)\right]^j} = \frac{[1 + r_0(2)]^2}{[1 + r_0(j+2)]^{j+2}} \frac{h^d(j+1)h(j)}{h^d(1)} \tag{8.15}$$

Since we want expressions (8.14) and (8.15) to be equal, we need to have

$$\frac{h^u(j+1)h^d(j)}{h^u(1)} = \frac{h^d(j+1)h(j)}{h^d(1)} \tag{8.16}$$

Therefore, our objective is to choose $h^u(j)$ and $h^d(j)$ that solve equations (8.13) and (8.16). It is straightforward to verify that the pair

$$h^u(j) = \frac{1}{p + (1-p)\delta^j} \tag{8.17}$$

$$h^d(j) = \frac{\delta^j}{p + (1-p)\delta^j} \tag{8.18}$$

satisfies both equations for any $\delta > 0$. The parameter δ can be chosen so as to match the observed volatility. We illustrate this model with an example.

Example 8.4 (Ho-Lee Model)   Consider a three-period setting with spot rates $r_0(1) = 4\%$, $r_0(2) = 5\%$, and $r_0(3) = 5.5\%$. We assume that $p = 0.5$ and our estimate of δ is $\delta = 0.99$, so that $h^u(2) = 1.01005$, $h^u(1) = 1.005025$, $h^d(2) = 0.98995$, and $h^d(1) = 0.994975$. We want to construct the tree that corresponds to three pure discount bonds with nominal value $1 and maturity in one, two, and three periods; see figure 8.4. Their respective prices today are $P_0(1) = 1/1.04 = 0.9615$, $P_0(2) = 1/(1.05^2) = 0.9070$, and $P_0(3) = 1/(1.055^3) = 0.8516$. We can also compute the forward rates between the end of the first period and the end of the second period, $f_0(1, 2)$, and the forward rates between the end of the first period and the end of the third period, $f_0(1, 3)$, from $[1 + r_0(1)][1 + f_0(1, 2)] = [1 + r_0(2)]^2$, $[1 + r_0(1)][1 + f_0(1, 3)]^2 = [1 + r_0(3)]^3$. Substituting the corresponding values we get $f_0(1, 2) = 6.01\%$ and $f_0(1, 3) = 6.26\%$. After one period the one-period bond has a value of $1, by definition. The two-period bond will have a value, after one period, in the upper node equal to

$$P_1^u(1) = \frac{1}{1 + f_0(1, 2)} h^u(1) = 0.9481$$

and in the lower node

$$P_1^d(1) = \frac{1}{1 + f_0(1, 2)} h^d(1) = 0.9386$$

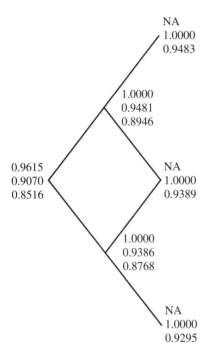

NA
1.0000
0.9483

1.0000
0.9481
0.8946

0.9615
0.9070
0.8516

NA
1.0000
0.9389

1.0000
0.9386
0.8768

NA
1.0000
0.9295

Figure 8.4
Prices of a one-, two- and three-period bond.

After two periods, the value of this bond is \$1. After one period the three-period bond has possible prices

$$P_1^u(2) = \frac{1}{[1 + f_0(1, 3)]^2} h^u(2) = 0.8946$$

in the upper node and

$$P_1^d(2) = \frac{1}{[1 + f_0(1, 3)]^2} h^d(2) = 0.8768$$

in the lower node. We now compute the prices of this bond after the second period, in which there will be three states. For that step, we have to take into account the new term structure, which depends on which node we are at.

First, suppose that the bond prices went up after one period. We have two bonds, the one-period bond with price $P_1^u(1) = 0.9481$ and the two-period bond with price $P_1^u(2) = 0.8946$, as computed previously, with corresponding rates $r_1^u(1) = 1/0.9481 - 1 = 5.48\%$ and $r_1^u(2) = (1/0.8946)^{1/2} - 1 = 5.73\%$. The forward rate $f_1(1, 2)^u$ between the end of period one and the end of period two at this node is given by the solution to $[1 + r_1^u(1)][1 + f_1^u(1,2)] = [1 + r_1^u(2)]^2$, which is $f_1^u(1,2) = 5.98\%$. Then, after two periods, if the bond prices go up in the first period, the price of the current one-period bond will be

$$P_2^{uu}(1) = \frac{1}{1 + f_1^u(1,2)} h^u(1) = 0.9483$$

in the upper node and

$$P_2^{ud}(1) = \frac{1}{1 + f_1^u(1,2)} h^d(1) = 0.9389$$

in the lower node.

Suppose now that, after one period, the bond prices drop. We have two bonds, the one-period bond with price $P_1^d(1) = 0.9386$ and the two-period bond with price $P_1^d(2) = 0.8768$, as computed previously, with corresponding rates $r_1^d(1) = 1/0.9386 - 1 = 6.54\%$ and $r_1^d(2) = (1/0.8768)^{1/2} - 1 = 6.80\%$. The forward rate $f_1^d(1,2)$ between the end of period one and the end of period two at this node is given by the solution to $[1 + r_1^d(1)][1 + f_1^d(1,2)] = [1 + r_2^d(2)]^2$, which is $f_1^d(1,2) = 7.05\%$. Then, after two periods, if the bond prices go down in the first period, the price of the current one-period bond will be

$$P_2^{du}(1) = \frac{1}{1 + f_1^d(1,2)} h^u(1) = 0.9389$$

in the upper node and

$$P_2^{dd}(1) = \frac{1}{1 + f_1^d(1,2)} h^d(1) = 0.9295$$

in the lower node. We observe that $P_2^{ud} = P_2^{du}$ as expected, given the restrictions we imposed on $h^u(j)$ and $h^d(j)$. After three periods the price of this bond is \$1 regardless of the node.

As usual, once we have computed the bond prices in the tree, we can use the tree for pricing options on a given bond, either by replication or by risk-neutral probabilities; see the Problems section.

8.2   Interest-Rate Models in Continuous Time

Historically, the first continuous-time models of fixed-income markets focused on the dynamics of the so-called **short rate** (or instantaneous interest rate) r. More precisely,

r is modeled as a diffusion process:

$$dr(t) = \mu(t, r(t)) \, dt + \sigma(t, r(t)) \, dW(t) \tag{8.19}$$

As in discrete time, the short rate here is typically modeled directly under the risk-neutral measure. We use the notation W in this chapter for the risk-neutral Brownian motion, not, as before, for the "real-world" Brownian motion. If the dimension of W is one, we call it a **one-factor model.** One-factor models were the first ones to be considered, and they still are very popular. However, most empirical studies suggest that two or three factors are necessary to have realistic models of the term structure of interest rates.

8.2.1   One-Factor Short-Rate Models

We list some popular one-factor interest-rate models.

Vasicek Model

$$dr = a(b - r) \, dt + \sigma \, dW$$

where $a, b, \sigma > 0$ are given constants. The Vasicek model is a classical one-factor model for interest rates. It is an example of a model that exhibits **mean reversion,** with the interest rate reverting to the value b. Indeed, if $r < b$, the drift $a(b - r)$ is positive and it pushes the process up toward the value b, while if $r > b$, it pushes the process down toward b. A disadvantage of the model is that the rate can become negative with positive probability. The main advantage of this model is that it results in simple formulas for bond and option prices.

Cox-Ingersoll-Ross (CIR) Model

$$dr = a(b - r) \, dt + \sigma \sqrt{r} \, dW \tag{8.20}$$

The Cox-Ingersoll-Ross model is another classical model. The interest rate cannot become negative because, if $r = 0$, the drift is ab, which is positive, and the diffusion term is zero; therefore, it can only increase. Explicit formulas for bond prices are available for this model. We will consider this model again in the equilibrium section.

Ho-Lee Model

$$dr = b(t) \, dt + \sigma \, dW$$

This is a continuous-time version of the discrete-time Ho-Lee model considered earlier. Here, $b(t)$ is a deterministic function, which is usually chosen so that the model matches observed market data.

Hull-White Model

$$dr = [b(t) - ar] \, dt + \sigma \, dW$$

The Hull-White model is similar to the Vasicek model, but the drift parameter $b(t)$ is a deterministic function of time rather than a constant. As in the Ho-Lee model, this approach provides more flexibility in matching the model to real data.

Black-Derman-Toy Model

$$dr = r[a(t) \, dt + \sigma \, dW]$$

The Black-Derman-Toy model resembles the Black-Scholes model for a stock price, except that the drift is a deterministic function of time. The discrete-time version of this model and its extensions are quite popular. The continuous-time model presents some theoretical difficulties.

What is the price of a zero-coupon bond in these models? First of all, it should be remarked that the market prices of liquid bonds are decided by supply and demand and other market factors, and not by using mathematical models. However, it is useful to have theoretical formulas for bond prices based on a model because we can then compare the values obtained by the formula to the market values, and we can find the model parameters that are consistent with the market prices. We can then use the model with so specified parameters to price securities that are not liquidly traded. Going back to the question of the time-t price $P(t, T)$ of a bond that pays one unit of currency at maturity time T, we recall our general risk-neutral pricing formula:

$$P(t, T) = E_t \left[1 \cdot e^{-\int_t^T r(u) du} \right] \tag{8.21}$$

More generally, we would compute the price $C(t, T)$ of a contingent claim with random payoff C at T, and paying dividends at rate $q(u)$ (possibly random), by the formula

$$C(t, T) = E_t \left[C \cdot e^{-\int_t^T r(u) du} + \int_t^T e^{-\int_t^u r(z) dz} q(u) \, du \right] \tag{8.22}$$

There is a potential subtle difficulty in arguing that this should be the price. In order for the no-arbitrage price to be given by equation (8.22), we would typically require that the claim C can be replicated by trading in the basic securities in the market, in this case by trading bonds. In standard models this is typically the case. In general, a bond-market model may be incomplete, and there might be more than one risk-neutral martingale probability measure, and it is not clear which one should be used for pricing. What is typically done in practice, and can be justified in theory, is to assume that the market, even if it is incomplete, uses one probability P for pricing all contingent claims, and it is this probability P under which we are modeling the interest rate.

If both the claim $C = C(r)$ and the dividend rate $q = q(r)$ are deterministic functions of the interest rate r, which is modeled by equation (8.19), according to Theorem 6.7 (Feynman-Kac), the price (8.22) is also given as a solution $C(t) = V(t, r)$ to the PDE

$$V_t + \frac{1}{2}\sigma^2 V_{rr} + \mu V_r - rV + q = 0, \qquad V(T, r) = C(r) \tag{8.23}$$

For example, for the zero-coupon bond maturing at T we would have $q \equiv 0$ and $C(r) \equiv 1$.

8.2.2 Bond Pricing in Affine Models

As we mentioned earlier, for most of the models that we have discussed we can find explicit formulas for the prices of bonds. We can do so because the Vasicek, Ho-Lee, CIR, and Hull-White models all belong to a class of so-called **models with affine term structure.** Affine models are defined as models in which the bond price has the form

$$P(t, T) = e^{A(t,T)-B(t,T)r(t)} \tag{8.24}$$

for some deterministic functions of time A and B. We want to find these functions for the models presented. Since $P(T, T) = 1$, we need to have

$$A(T, T) = 0, \qquad B(T, T) = 0 \tag{8.25}$$

We only consider the models in which the drift and the square of the diffusion coefficients of the process r in equation (8.19) are linear (or **affine**) functions of r, with time-dependent coefficients:

$$\mu(t, r) = \alpha(t)r + \beta(t) \tag{8.26}$$
$$\sigma^2(t, r) = \gamma(t)r + \delta(t) \tag{8.27}$$

We consider the PDE (8.23) (with V replaced by P), and we try a solution of the form (8.24). In particular, we substitute equations (8.26) and (8.27) in it, with $q = 0$, and after an easy calculation we get

$$A_t - \beta B + \frac{1}{2}\delta B^2 - r\left[1 + B_t + \alpha B - \frac{1}{2}\gamma B^2\right] = 0 \tag{8.28}$$

The term in the brackets in equation (8.28) has to be zero for all t, because the terms outside the brackets do not depend on r. Therefore, we get a nice result that the PDE separates into two ordinary differential equations (ODEs) for A and B:

$$B_t + \alpha B - \tfrac{1}{2}\gamma B^2 = -1 \tag{8.29}$$

$$A_t = \beta B - \tfrac{1}{2}\delta B^2 \tag{8.30}$$

Equation (8.29) for B is called a Ricatti ODE, and it can be solved for a unique solution satisfying $B(T, T) = 0$. Once we have found the solution, we can compute A from equation (8.30) as

$$A(t, T) = -\int_t^T \beta(u)B(u, T)\, du + \frac{1}{2}\int_t^T \delta(u)B^2(u, T)\, du \tag{8.31}$$

Note that $A(T, T) = 0$.

Example 8.5 (Bond Prices in the Vasicek Model)   Consider the Vasicek model in the form

$$dr(t) = [b - ar(t)]\, dt + \sigma\, dW(t)$$

with constant parameters b, a, and σ. The Ricatti ODE of equation (8.29) is now

$$B_t - aB = -1$$

The solution $B(t, T)$ that satisfies $B(T, T) = 1$ is given by

$$B(t, T) = \frac{1}{a}\left(1 - e^{-a(T-t)}\right)$$

The solution for A is

$$A(t, T) = -b\int_t^T B(u, T)\, du + \frac{\sigma^2}{2}\int_t^T B^2(u, T)\, du$$

A computation of the previous expression yields

$$A = \frac{1}{a^2}[(B - T + t)(ab - \sigma^2/2)] - \frac{1}{4a}\sigma^2 B^2$$

Parameters a, b, and σ can then be chosen to match some of the observed market variables, such as, for example, prices of bonds with three different maturities (which would result in a system of three equations with three unknowns).

8.2.3 HJM Forward-Rate Models

Recall the notion of the term structure of interest rates as the collection of spot rates of different maturities. When we have explicit expressions for bond prices as in the cases discussed earlier, we can compute the corresponding implicit spot rates and, therefore, the term structure of interest rates implied by the model. In particular, at moment $t = 0$, the spot rate with maturity at $t = T$, which we denote $R(T)$, is given by

$$R(T) = \frac{1}{T} \left(\frac{1}{P(0, T)} - 1 \right)$$

Therefore, each of the models we have discussed will imply a specific model of the term structure of interest rates. The difficulty is that we would have to check whether the term structure implied by the dynamics of the short (instantaneous) interest rate is consistent with spot rates and bond prices observed in the market. An alternative approach would be to model directly the spot rates or forward rates of different maturities as basic variables. Another advantage of this approach is that we can naturally introduce more than one factor in the model. The disadvantage of this approach is that the resulting models often are not Markovian, with the result that, in general, we cannot use the Feynman-Kac theorem and PDEs for pricing, and we cannot derive analytic formulas for prices.

Heath, Jarrow, and Morton (1990, 1992) introduced a new approach that consists in modeling the forward rates as the basic variables. The approach is called the **HJM model of the term structure.**

First, we have to define what we mean by forward rates in continuous time. In order to motivate the definition, consider the following way of constructing a **forward-rate investment:** At time t, $t < S < T$, we sell short one bond with maturity S, and, with the money we received ($P(t, S)$), we buy $P(t, S)/P(t, T)$ units of bonds with maturity T. At time S we have to pay 1 dollar (to cover the short position in the bond that matures at S), and we get $P(t, S)/P(t, T)$ dollars at time T from the other bond. In other words, this is a way of investing 1 dollar at future time S for a risk-free return between S and T. The continuous interest rate obtained by this investment during the period $[S, T]$ is called the **continuously compounded forward rate.** More precisely, it is the rate $R(t; S, T)$ such that

$$1 \cdot e^{R(t;S,T)(T-S)} = \frac{P(t, S)}{P(t, T)} \tag{8.32}$$

Taking logs, we get

$$R(t; S, T) = -\frac{\log P(t, T) - \log P(t, S)}{T - S} \tag{8.33}$$

If we take a limit as $S \to T$, we get the **instantaneous forward rate**, or just **forward rate**, $f(t, T)$, as

$$f(t, T) = -\frac{\partial \log P(t, T)}{\partial T} \tag{8.34}$$

Integrating this expression, we get

$$\log P(t, T) = -\int_t^T f(t, u) \, du$$

or

$$P(t, T) = e^{-\int_t^T f(t, u) du} \tag{8.35}$$

From equation (8.34), we see that

$$f(t, t) = -\left.\frac{\partial \log P(t, T)}{\partial T}\right|_{T=t} \tag{8.36}$$

However, from $P(t, T) = E_t[\exp\{-\int_t^T r(u) \, du\}]$, we get

$$\frac{\partial \log P(t, T)}{\partial T} = \frac{1}{P(t, T)} E_t \left[-r(T) e^{-\int_t^T r(u) du} \right]$$

As a consequence, we have

$$\left.\frac{\partial \log P(t, T)}{\partial T}\right|_{T=t} = E_t[-r(t)] = -r(t)$$

Comparing this result with equation (8.36), we see that

$$f(t, t) = r(t) \tag{8.37}$$

The HJM approach consists in modeling the dynamics of the continuous-time forward rate, rather than those of the short (instantaneous) interest rate, as

$$df(t, T) = \alpha(t, T) \, dt + \sigma^{Tr}(t, T) \, dW(t) \tag{8.38}$$

Here, W may be a multidimensional Brownian motion, in which case σ is a vector process. Note that this is not a single model, but a family of models for forward rates.

As we have seen, in the Merton-Black-Scholes model for stock prices, under the pricing measure (that is, in the risk-neutral world) the drift of the stock has to be equal to the interest rate. Something similar happens in the HJM framework, too. It turns out that *under the risk-neutral probability, and given the volatility structure $\sigma(t, T)$ for the forward rates, the drift structure $\alpha(t, T)$ is uniquely determined.* In fact, we have the following important result.

THEOREM 8.1   The drift process α and the volatility process σ in a given HJM forward-rate model have to satisfy the following **HJM drift condition:**

$$\alpha(t, T) = \sigma^{Tr}(t, T) \int_t^T \sigma(t, u)\, du \tag{8.39}$$

where σ^{Tr} is the vector σ transposed.

Proof   In order to simplify the notation, we assume that W is one-dimensional. Recall from calculus that $\frac{d}{dt}[\int_a^t f(t, x)\, dx] = f(t, t) + \int_a^t \frac{d}{dt} f(t, x)\, dx$. Using this expression, using equations (8.38) and (8.37), and changing the order of integration, we first get

$$d\left(-\int_t^T f(t, u)\, du\right) = f(t, t)\, dt - \int_t^T df(t, u)\, du$$

$$= r(t)\, dt - \left[\int_t^T \alpha(t, u)\, du\right] dt - \left[\int_t^T \sigma(t, u)\, du\right] dW(t) \tag{8.40}$$

Using this expression, the fact that $P(t, T) = \exp\{-\int_t^T f(t, u)\, du\}$, and Itô's rule, we find

$$\frac{dP(t, T)}{P(t, T)} = \left\{ r(t) - \left[\int_t^T \alpha(t, u)\right] du + \frac{1}{2}\left[\int_t^T \sigma(t, u)\, du\right]^2 \right\} dt$$

$$- \left[\int_t^T \sigma(t, u)\, du\right] dW(t)$$

However, under the risk-neutral probability, the drift of the bond prices has to equal $r(t)$ (in order to make the discounted bond prices P-martingales), and thus we must have

$$\int_t^T \alpha(t, u)\, du = \frac{1}{2}\left[\int_t^T \sigma(t, u)\, du\right]^2$$

Differentiating with respect to T we obtain the HJM drift condition (8.39).   ∎

The way the HJM framework may be used in practice is the following:

1. Independently of which model we will use, we first estimate, from observed bond prices, the initial forward-rate term structure $f(0, T)$ for all T, using the relation

$$f(0, T) = -\frac{\partial P(0, T)}{\partial T} \tag{8.41}$$

2. We choose the model by choosing volatility structure $\sigma(t, T)$ of the forward rates. By the HJM drift condition this also determines the drift of the forward rates.

3. We use the fact that $r(t) = f(t, t)$ and the forward rate dynamics (8.38) in order to price a given claim with random payoff C at time T, using the formula

$$C(t, T) = E_t \left[C \cdot e^{-\int_t^T r(u)du} \right]$$

Example 8.6 (Flat Term Structure)   Consider the case of a flat volatility structure

$$\sigma(t, T) \equiv \sigma$$

for some positive constant σ. This implies

$$\alpha(t, T) = \sigma \int_t^T \sigma \, du = \sigma^2 (T - t)$$

Therefore,

$$df(t, T) = \sigma^2 (T - t) \, dt + \sigma \, dW(t)$$

Integrating, we obtain

$$f(t, T) = f(0, T) + \sigma^2 t (T - t/2) + \sigma W(t)$$

Hence,

$$r(t) = f(t, t) = f(0, t) + \sigma^2 t^2/2 + \sigma W(t)$$

or

$$dr(t) = \left[\frac{\partial}{\partial T} f(0, t) + \sigma^2 t \right] dt + \sigma \, dW(t) \tag{8.42}$$

where $\frac{\partial}{\partial T} f(0, t)$ denotes the derivative of f with respect to the second argument, evaluated at the point $(0, t)$. This result is, in fact, a Ho-Lee model for the short (instantaneous) interest rate, that is, a model of the type

$$dr(t) = b(t) \, dt + \sigma \, dW(t)$$

for some deterministic function $b(t)$. If we choose $f(0, t)$ to be the observed initial term structure of forward rates, *we automatically get the Ho-Lee model with the drift function $b(t)$ chosen so as to fit the observed market data.* This would have been more difficult to do directly starting from the short-rate Ho-Lee model. What we mean is that, in that case, we would have had to find which function $b(t)$ fit the market data by first computing the theoretical bond prices and/or forward rates as functions of $b(t)$, and then choosing $b(t)$ to match the observed prices/rates. If our market data consisted of observed forward rates $f(0, T)$, we would get the same model as in equation (8.42), but we would have had to use more extensive computations.

It should be noted that this **calibration** or **matching** of the HJM model to the current term structure is not always easy. Looking at equations (8.41) and (8.42), we see that we actually need to construct the second derivative of the curve $f(0, T)$, which is observed only at discrete values of maturities T. This can be a potentially unstable procedure, and various methods have been suggested for doing it efficiently.

8.2.4   Change of Numeraire*

There is a useful trick for pricing options when the interest rate is random, which sometimes results in simple formulas. The trick consists in changing the "units of measurement," or **change of numeraire.** For example, if the value of an asset is measured in dollars, then the dollar currency is our numeraire. When we discount the value of an asset with the value of the bank account, then the bank account process is our numeraire (that is, the value of the asset is now expressed in units of the value of the bank account). In bond markets, it is often convenient to discount with the bond price.

More precisely, let $S(t)$ be the price process of a given asset. Let us fix a maturity time T and use the bond with maturity at T as the numeraire:

$$F(t) := \frac{S(t)}{P(t, T)} \tag{8.43}$$

We have denoted this process by F because it is an analogue of the theoretical forward price of equation (6.8) when we use bonds as risk-free assets.

More generally, in the Merton-Black-Scholes pricing theory we have used the risk-neutral probability under which the prices of all assets are martingales when using the bank account as the numeraire. Now, given an asset S, we denote by P^S *the probability under which the prices of all assets are martingales, when using S as the numeraire.* We call P^S the **risk-neutral probability for numeraire S.** When we use the bond with maturity T as the numeraire, we call the corresponding risk-neutral probability the T-**forward measure,** and we denote it by P^T. We denote by P the usual risk-neutral probability. We use similar notation for corresponding expectations.

We now deduce the very useful **relation between E expectation and E^S expectation:** Let $C(t)$ be a price process of an asset, given by (under the risk-neutral probability)

$$C(t) = E_t\left[e^{-\int_t^T r(u)du} C(T)\right]$$

However, since $C(t)/S(t)$ is a martingale under the P^S probability, we get

$$E_t^S\left[\frac{C(T)}{S(T)}\right] = \frac{C(t)}{S(t)} \tag{8.44}$$

Combining the last two equations, we obtain

$$E_t\left[e^{-\int_t^T r(u)du} C(T)\right] = S(t) E_t^S\left[\frac{C(T)}{S(T)}\right]$$ (8.45)

Sometimes it is easier to compute the right-hand side for a cleverly chosen numeraire S than to compute the left-hand side. We want to illustrate this point next.

8.2.5   Option Pricing with Random Interest Rate*

Consider a given asset S and the process F of equation (8.43) associated with it. We know that this process has to be a martingale under the P^T probability (defined earlier). We will restrict our analysis to a model in which

$$dF(t) = \sigma_F(t) F(t) dW^T(t)$$ (8.46)

for some P^T-Brownian motion W^T and some positive deterministic function of time $\sigma_F(t)$, such that $\int_0^T \sigma_F^2(u)\, du$ is finite. Then F is indeed a P^T-martingale (since it has zero drift). Let us now price a European call option

$$C = [S(T) - K]^+$$

in the preceding model. We use the representation (7.81) from the appendix of the previous chapter: we can write the price at $t = 0$ as

$$E\left[e^{-\int_0^T r(u)du}\{S(T) - K\}^+\right] = I_1 - I_2$$ (8.47)

where

$$I_1 = E\left[e^{-\int_0^T r(u)du} S(T)\mathbf{1}_{\{S(T)>K\}}\right]; \qquad I_2 = KE\left[e^{-\int_0^T r(u)du}\mathbf{1}_{\{S(T)>K\}}\right]$$ (8.48)

[Recall that $\mathbf{1}_{\{S(T)>K\}}$ is equal to 1 if $S(T) > K$ and is equal to 0 otherwise.] Let us first compute I_1. Using equation (8.45), we write

$$\begin{aligned}
I_1 &= S(0) E^S\left[\mathbf{1}_{\{S(T)>K\}}\right] \\
&= S(0) P^S[F(T) > K] \\
&= S(0) P^S\left[\frac{1}{F(T)} < \frac{1}{K}\right]
\end{aligned}$$ (8.49)

However, $1/F = P/S$ has to be a martingale under the P^S probability, hence of the form

$$d\left(\frac{1}{F(t)}\right) = \gamma(t)\frac{1}{F(t)} dW^S(t)$$

for some process γ. On the other hand, because of equation (8.46), using Itô's rule and the fact that the derivative of the function $f(x) = 1/x$ is $f'(x) = -1/x^2$, we also deduce that

$$d\left(\frac{1}{F(t)}\right) = \mu(t)\,dt + \sigma_F(t)\frac{1}{F(t)}[-dW^T(t)]$$

for some drift process μ. It is a consequence of the **Girsanov theorem** of stochastic calculus that, when we switch from one probability measure to another, equivalent probability measure, then the diffusion coefficient does not change, except, possibly, in its sign. Therefore, comparing the last two equations, and noting that $(-W^T)$ is also a Brownian motion, we conclude that we can take $\gamma \equiv \sigma_F$, hence

$$d\left(\frac{1}{F}\right) = \sigma_F\frac{1}{F}\,dW^S$$

Recalling that $F(0) = S(0)/P(0,T)$, it is easily verified that the solution to the previous SDE is given by

$$\frac{1}{F(T)} = \frac{P(0,T)}{S(0)}\exp\left\{\int_0^T \sigma_F(u)W^S(u) - \frac{1}{2}\int_0^T \sigma_F^2(u)\,du\right\} \tag{8.50}$$

Suppose we want to have $1/F(T) < 1/K$. Taking logs on both sides of equation (8.50) and rearranging, we obtain

$$1/F(T) < 1/K \quad \text{is equivalent to} \quad \int_0^T \sigma_F(u)W^S(u) < \log\frac{S(0)}{KP(0,T)} + \frac{1}{2}\int_0^T \sigma_F^2(u)\,du \tag{8.51}$$

We now use the following fact about stochastic integrals:

If $\sigma(t)$ is a deterministic function, then $\int_t^T \sigma(u)\,dW(u)$ is a normal random variable with mean zero and variance $\int_t^T \sigma^2(u)\,du$, if this last integral is finite.

This is not surprising if you think of the stochastic integral as a limit of finite sums. We leave the proof of this fact for Problem 16.

Denote

$$\Sigma_F(T) := \sqrt{\int_0^T \sigma_F^2(u)\,du} \tag{8.52}$$

By the preceding result, under P^S probability the random variable $\int_0^T \sigma_F(u)\,dW^S(u)$ has the same distribution as $\Sigma_F(T)z$, where z is the standard normal random variable. If we write the right-hand side of expression (8.51) in terms of z, we get

$$z < \frac{1}{\Sigma_F(T)} \left(\log \frac{S(0)}{K P(0, T)} + \frac{1}{2} \Sigma_F^2(T) \right) =: d_1 \tag{8.53}$$

Therefore, going back to equation (8.49), we get

$$I_1 = S(0) N(d_1) \tag{8.54}$$

where N is the cumulative standard normal distribution function and d_1 is defined in expression (8.53).

We now compute I_2. Using equation (8.45) again, taking into account definition (8.43), we write

$$I_2 = K P(0, T) E^T \left[\frac{1}{P(T, T)} \mathbf{1}_{\{S(T) > K\}} \right]$$

$$= K P(0, T) P^T [F(T) > K] \tag{8.55}$$

where we now use as numeraire the price of the bond with maturity at T. From equation (8.46) we conclude

$$F(T) = \frac{S(0)}{P(0, T)} \exp \left\{ \int_0^T \sigma_F(u) W^T(u) - \frac{1}{2} \int_0^T \sigma_F^2(u) \, du \right\} \tag{8.56}$$

A similar calculation then implies that

$$I_2 = K P(0, T) N(d_2) \tag{8.57}$$

where

$$d_2 = \frac{1}{\Sigma_F(T)} \left(\log \frac{S(0)}{K P(0, T)} - \frac{1}{2} \Sigma_F^2(T) \right) \tag{8.58}$$

We combine the previous computations in the following statement, known as **Merton's generalized option pricing formula:**

THEOREM 8.2   Consider a bond market with bond prices $P(t, T)$ and an asset price process S such that $F(t) = S(t)/P(t, T)$ satisfies equation (8.46), with σ_F deterministic. Then the price $C(0)$ of the European call option $C = [S(T) - K]^+$ in this market is given by

$$C(0) = S(0) N(d_1) - K P(0, T) N(d_2) \tag{8.59}$$

where d_2 is defined in equation (8.58) and d_1 is defined in expression (8.53).

Example 8.7 (Call Option Price in Affine Models)   Consider a call option with maturity at time T_1, written on a bond with maturity at time T_2, with $T_1 \leq T_2$. The payoff of the option is

$$C = [P(T_1, T_2) - K]^+$$

Here, the basic asset is the bond with maturity at T_2, so that in the preceding notation we set $S(t) = P(t, T_2)$, $T = T_1$. In affine models the corresponding process $F(t) = P(t, T_2)/P(t, T_1)$ is of the form

$$F(t) = e^{A(t,T_2)-A(t,T_1)-[B(t,T_2)-B(t,T_1)]r(t)}$$

for some deterministic functions A and B. As an example, consider the Vasicek model with

$$dr = a(b - r)\, dt + \sigma\, dW$$

Using Itô's rule we get

$$dF(t) = F(t)[\ldots]\, dt + F(t)\sigma_F(t)\, dW(t)$$

with

$$\sigma_F(t) = -\sigma[B(t, T_2) - B(t, T_1)]$$

We see that σ_F is a deterministic function, so we can use the preceding generalized option-pricing formula to price the call option.

8.2.6   BGM Market Model*

For frequently traded derivatives in developed markets the usual market practice is to use formulas of the Merton-Black-Scholes type as the benchmark. This means that the underlying process is assumed to follow a lognormal process. In this spirit, ideally, one would like to consider a model of forward rates of the type

$$df = \alpha f\, dt + \sigma f\, dW$$

for some deterministic function σ. Unfortunately, it can be shown that this process can "explode" to infinity. Mathematically, this outcome occurs because the drift process is proportional to the "quadratic" term $f \int_0^t f\, du$, because of the HJM drift condition. We describe here briefly a class of models that successfully circumvent this difficulty in the case of derivatives based on LIBOR rates, studied in more detail in the next section (LIBOR stands for London Interbank Offer Rate).

The forward LIBOR rate is defined using the discrete compounding version of equation (8.32):

$$1 \cdot [1 + \Delta T L(t, T_i)] = \frac{P(t, T_{i-1})}{P(t, T_i)} \tag{8.60}$$

In other words, we define the forward LIBOR rate for a future time period $[T_{i-1}, T_i]$ of a given fixed length ΔT as

$$L(t, T_i) := -\frac{P(t, T_i) - P(t, T_{i-1})}{\Delta T P(t, T_i)} \tag{8.61}$$

When this equation is written differently, we see that

$$L(t, T_i) = \frac{P(t, T_{i-1})}{\Delta T P(t, T_i)} - \frac{1}{\Delta T}$$

Since the second term is constant and the first term is the price of the bond with maturity T_{i-1} divided by the price of the bond with maturity T_i, the LIBOR rate should be a martingale under the T_i-forward measure. If we want it to be lognormal, it has to satisfy

$$dL(t, T_i) = L(t, T_i) \gamma(t, T_i) \, dW^{T_i}(t) \tag{8.62}$$

for some deterministic function γ. Therefore, under the risk-neutral probability we have

$$dL(t, T_i) = L(t, T_i)[\mu(t) \, dt + \gamma(t, T_i)] \, dW(t) \tag{8.63}$$

for some drift process $\mu(t)$. It can be shown that this is a special case of the HJM framework. Moreover, as we shall illustrate, it produces formulas for pricing derivatives based on the LIBOR rate that are consistent with the market practice. For this reason, and because it was developed by Brace, Gatarek, and Musiela (1997), it is called the **BGM market model** for LIBOR rates. Other researchers responsible for developing this and similar models are Miltersen, Sandmann, and Sondermann (1997), as well as Jamshidian (1997).

As an example, consider an option on the LIBOR rate called a **caplet,** with value at time T_i equal to

$$[L(T_{i-1}, T_i) - K]^+$$

where K is a constant. This is simply a call option on the LIBOR rate. By the change of numeraire formula (8.45), taking S to be the bond price, and using $P(T_i, T_i) = 1$, we get that the value of the caplet at time t is

$$P(t, T_i) E_t^{T_i} \{ [L(T_{i-1}, T_i) - K]^+ \}$$

where the expectation is taken under the T_i-forward measure. If we work in the BGM model (8.62), the LIBOR value $L(T_{i-1}, T_i)$ is lognormally distributed, and the value of this option is given by the Black-Scholes formula for a call option with strike price K, interest rate zero, and volatility determined from $\sigma^2(T_{i-1} - t) = \int_t^{T_{i-1}} \gamma^2(u, T_i)\, du$. When γ is constant, we get $\sigma = \gamma$ and a Black-Scholes type formula for the caplets called the **Black caplet formula.** Interestingly, this formula had been used in the market before the introduction of the BGM model. Thus the BGM model provides a theoretical justification for the market practice.

8.3   Swaps, Caps, and Floors

8.3.1   Interest-Rate Swaps and Swaptions

Let us recall the notion of an interest-rate swap: this contract stipulates that party A pays a floating rate to party B, while party B pays a fixed rate to party A, on a common notional principal amount. Within this general description, there are several specific types of swaps. In particular, here we consider the so-called **forward swap settled in arrears.** We denote by R the fixed interest rate and by $L(T_{i-1}, T_i)$ the floating interest rate corresponding to the time interval $[T_{i-1}, T_i]$, $i = 0, \ldots, n$. Here, L stands for LIBOR (London Interbank Offer Rate), since LIBOR is a floating rate often used in swap contracts. Both rates are expressed in annual terms. We assume that the payment dates, at which the difference between the fixed and the floating rate is paid, are $T_1, \ldots, T_n$, and that they are equally spaced, with interval width ΔT. The payoff of the swap that party A pays (the party paying the floating rate and receiving the fixed rate) at time T_i is a multiple of

$$C_i := \Delta T [L(T_{i-1}, T_i) - R]$$

This can be negative, in which case A receives the payment. Since the swap is a sequence of claims C_i, in order to price the swap (that is, compute at a given point in time the value of the swap) it is sufficient to price the claims C_i. Recall that we denote by $P(S, T)$ the time-S price of the zero-coupon bond with maturity $T \geq S$ and assume that the bonds pay one dollar at maturity, so that

$$P(T, T) = 1$$

By definition, we set the LIBOR rate to be the spot rate for the period $[T_{i-1}, T_i]$:

$$L(T_{i-1}, T_i) := \frac{1 - P(T_{i-1}, T_i)}{\Delta T\, P(T_{i-1}, T_i)} \tag{8.64}$$

where we divide by ΔT in order to derive the annual rate. Thus the payoff C_i is

$$C_i = \frac{1}{P(T_{i-1}, T_i)} - (1 + R\Delta T) \tag{8.65}$$

The second term is easy to price: the value at time $t < T_0$ of the constant amount $(1 + R\Delta T)$ paid at time $T_i > t$ is $(1 + R\Delta T)P(t, T_i)$. (Why?) As for the first term, we claim that the value at time $t < T_0$ of the payoff $1/P(T_{i-1}, T_i)$ paid at time T is equal to $P(t, T_{i-1})$. Indeed, if we invest $P(t, T_{i-1})$ at time t in buying a bond with maturity T_{i-1}, we get 1 dollar at time T_{i-1}, with which we can buy exactly $1/P(T_{i-1}, T_i)$ of bonds with maturity T_i, and hence collect $1/P(T_{i-1}, T_i)$ at time T_i.

Combining the preceding results, we see that the time-t price $C_i(t)$ of the payoff C_i is

$$C_i(t) = P(t, T_{i-1}) - (1 + R\Delta T)P(t, T_i) \tag{8.66}$$

Therefore, the price $S(t)$ of the swap at time t is

$$S(t) = \sum_{i=1}^{n} C_i(t) = \sum_{i=1}^{n} [P(t, T_{i-1}) - (1 + R\Delta T)P(t, T_i)]$$

Simplifying the previous expression (a bunch of terms cancel) we get the **price of the swap** in terms of the bond prices as

$$S(t) = P(t, T_0) - R\Delta T \sum_{i=1}^{n} P(t, T_i) - P(t, T_n) \tag{8.67}$$

The **swap rate** R is the fixed rate to be traded for the floating rate such that the cost of entering the swap at the initial time 0 is equal to zero. (In other words, there is no exchange of money at the initial time.) Then equation (8.67) implies that the swap rate is

$$R = \frac{P(0, T_0) - P(0, T_n)}{\Delta T \sum_{i=1}^{n} P(0, T_i)}$$

If, in addition, $T_0 = 0$, we get

$$R = \frac{1 - P(0, T_n)}{\Delta T \sum_{i=1}^{n} P(0, T_i)} \tag{8.68}$$

At least in theory, this is the rate that the parties in the swap contract should agree on if they want the initial cost of the contract to be zero.

There is another way to derive the swap price, without using the replication argument for pricing $1/P(T_{i-1}, T_i)$. For concreteness, assume a continuously compounded interest-rate process r, so that the price of the payoff C with maturity T can be computed as

$C(t) = E_t[\exp\{-\int_t^T r(u)\,du\}C]$, and the price of the zero-coupon bond paying 1 dollar at time T as $P(t, T) = E_t[\exp\{-\int_t^T r(u)\,du\}]$. Using this and equation (8.2) to compute the price of $1/P(T_{i-1}, T_i)$, we get (recalling the properties of conditional expectations):

$$
E_t\left[e^{-\int_t^{T_i} r(u)du}\frac{1}{P(T_{i-1}, T_i)}\right] = E_t\left[e^{-\int_t^{T_{i-1}} r(u)du}E_{T_{i-1}}\left[e^{-\int_{T_{i-1}}^{T_i} r(u)du}\right]\frac{1}{E_{T_{i-1}}\left[e^{-\int_{T_{i-1}}^{T_i} r(u)du}\right]}\right]
$$

$$
= E_t\left[e^{-\int_t^{T_{i-1}} r(u)du}\right]
$$

$$
= P(t, T_{i-1})
$$

This is the same result we obtained earlier for the first term of equation (8.66), which enabled us to price the swap.

Example 8.8 (Swap Pricing)   We want to price the position in a swap of an investor who receives a 10% fixed rate in semiannually paid coupons and pays the six-month LIBOR. The swap still has nine months left to maturity. At the last resetting date, the six-month LIBOR was 6%. The continuous three-month and nine-month rates are 5% and 7%, respectively. Nominal principal is 10,000. In the preceding notation, T_0 is three months in the past, T_1 is three months from now, and T_2 is nine months from now, $\Delta T = 0.5$. We cannot use the preceding formula directly, since $t > T_0$. Instead, we go back to equation (8.65) and see that the payoff three months from now, on one unit of the notional principal, is

$$
C_1 = \frac{1}{P(T_0, T_1)} - (1 + R\Delta T)
$$

and nine months from now it is

$$
C_2 = \frac{1}{P(T_1, T_2)} - (1 + R\Delta T)
$$

The first payoff is already known, and its price is simply obtained by multiplying by the price of the three-month bond. It is equal to

$$
C_1(t) = \left[\frac{1}{P(T_0, T_1)} - (1 + R\Delta T)\right]e^{-0.05 \cdot 0.25}
$$

The bond price $P = P(T_0, T_1)$ can be found from $P(1 + \Delta T L) = 1$, where $L = 0.06$ is the LIBOR rate. We get $P = 1/1.03$, and $C_1(t) = -0.0198$. The price of C_2 is found as in equation (8.66) to be

$$C_2(t) = P(t, T_1) - (1 + R\Delta T)P(t, T_2) = e^{-0.07 \cdot 0.25} - (1 + 0.1 \cdot 0.5)e^{-0.05 \cdot 0.75}$$

$$= -0.0087$$

Altogether, the value of the swap for the short position is

$$C(t) = C_1(t) + C_2(t) = -0.0285$$

Since our investor is long in the swap, his value is

$$10,000 \cdot 0.0285 = 285$$

for the notional principal of 10,000. We expected the swap to have a positive value for this investor, since the current term structure (in the 5–7% range) is lower than the fixed rate of 10% the investor is receiving.

A popular product derived from a swap is a **swaption:** It is an option to enter a swap contract with maturity T_n and payments at dates T_i, at a future date $T < T_1 < \cdots < T_n$, at a predetermined **swaption rate** $\tilde{R}$. Let us consider the swaption by which the holder has an option to start paying the fixed rate $\tilde{R}$ and receiving the floating rate, beginning at time T. The holder of the swaption would exercise it only if the swaption rate $\tilde{R}$ is no greater than the swap rate $R = R(T)$ at time T [which makes the value of the swap zero, as in equation (8.68)], for the swap starting at $t = T$ and maturing at $t = T_n$. Because, if $\tilde{R} > R(T)$, the holder could simply enter the swap at the rate $R(T)$ and be better off.

From equation (8.67) (with $t = T = T_0$), the swap price at time T is

$$S(T) = 1 - R\Delta T \sum_{i=1}^{n} P(T, T_i) - P(T, T_n) \tag{8.69}$$

The time-t value of the swaption is equal to the positive part of the time-t value of the swap, that is, equal to the time-t value of the payoff $S^+(T) = \max\{S(T), 0\}$. This statement is true because the swaption will be exercised at time T only if its value is positive at that time. Since $R\Delta T \sum_{i=1}^{n} P(T, T_i) + P(T, T_n)$ is the value of a coupon bond that pays coupons $R\Delta T$ at times T_i and matures at T_n, we see from equation (8.69) that $S^+(T)$ has the form of a put option on a coupon bond with strike price equal to 1. Hence, if we can price put options on coupon bonds, we can price a swaption. In the Problems section the reader is asked to show that the value of the swaption is also equal to the value of the cash flow of call options $[R(T) - \tilde{R}]^+ \Delta T$ paid at times $t = T_1, \ldots, T_n$, where $R(T)$ is again the swap rate at time T, for the swap starting at $t = T$ and maturing at $t = T_n$.

8.3.2 Caplets, Caps, and Floors

A **cap** is another popular interest-rate derivative. By holding a cap, the person who has to pay a floating interest rate is assured that the amount to be paid will never be more than a predetermined **cap rate.** Similarly, a **floor** guarantees that someone paying a floating interest rate will never pay less than a predetermined **floor rate.** Often, contracts include both caps and floors (and are called **collars**). Typically, the cap and the floor are set in such a way that their values offset each other: by accepting a floor, the debtor receives also a cap. Here we only consider caps (the analysis for floors is similar), and assume that the cap contract is for the interval $[0, T]$. A cap is a cash flow of several **caplets,** each with time T_i payoff given by

$$C = \Delta T [L(T_{i-1}, T_i) - R_C]^+$$

where $L = L(T_{i-1}, T_i)$ is the LIBOR spot rate and R_C is the cap rate, both expressed in annual terms; hence, we multiply by ΔT. We see that the holder of a caplet receives the difference between the LIBOR rate and the cap rate corresponding to the period ΔT if the LIBOR rate is higher than the cap rate.

Denote by P the bond price $P(T_{i-1}, T_i)$, and recall that $L\Delta T = 1/P - 1$. This relation implies that the caplet payoff is given by

$$C = \left(\frac{1}{P} - (1 + R_C \Delta T) \right)^+ = \frac{1 + R_C \Delta T}{P} \left(\frac{1}{1 + R_C \Delta T} - P \right)^+$$

Denoting

$$K = \frac{1}{1 + R_C \Delta T}$$

the payoff of the caplet at time T_i is

$$C = \frac{1}{KP} (K - P)^+$$

Note that this payoff is paid at time T, but it is known at time T_{i-1}. The price at moment T_{i-1} of the payoff C at T_i is $P \cdot C$: with $P \cdot C$ dollars we can buy C bonds with maturity T_i at time T_{i-1}, and that purchase guarantees the payoff C at time T_i. Therefore, the payoff C at time T_i is equivalent to the payoff

$$P \cdot C = \frac{1}{K} (K - P)^+$$

at time T_{i-1}. Consequently, we see that a caplet is equivalent to $1/K$ put options on the bond maturing at T_i, with option maturity equal to T_{i-1} and strike price equal to K. Hence, a cap is the same as a portfolio of put options on bonds, and it can be priced as such.

8.4   Credit/Default Risk

Most of the time in this book we assume that the party that has entered a financial contract will fulfill its obligations. In particular, we assume that the party that issues a bond will pay the face value at maturity. In practice, however, there is a risk that the debtor will default on its promise and that the creditor will receive only a portion of the face value. This type of risk is known as **default risk** or **credit risk.** One reason why corporate bonds provide higher returns than government bonds is that they involve higher default risk. (Let us mention, however, that empirical studies suggest that the default risk alone cannot explain the spread between interest rates of default-free and defaultable bonds.) In order to be able to hedge and trade credit risk, so-called **credit derivatives** have been introduced. For example, there are forward contracts on the spread between a corporate bond yield and the Treasury yield, or swaps on cash flows from a corporate bond and cash flows from a Treasury instrument. In this section we discuss some basic ideas on how to price fixed-income derivatives when there is a possibility of default.

There are two basic approaches. The early approach, initiated by Merton, using **value-based models** or **structural models,** assumes that the value of the firm issuing a bond is given by a certain stochastic process V. (In particular, it is usually convenient to model the value of the firm as a geometric Brownian motion.) The specific notion of "value of the firm" used in this setting is the value of the assets minus short-term liabities. It is assumed that at maturity T, if the default occurs, then the bondholders have the priority over the stockholders in collecting the remaining assets of the firm. In other words, if we denote by V the value of the firm, by E its equity (stocks), and by D the value of its total debt, then

$$E(T) = \max[V(T) - D, 0]$$

Thus equity is a call option on the value of the firm and can be priced as such. Similarly, bondholders receive

$$\min[V(T), D] = D - \max[D - V(T), 0]$$

which can be interpreted as the value of a default-free bond with face value D, minus a put option on the value of the firm.

More generally, default can be modeled as the event that arises when the process V, the value of the firm, hits a certain (low) level, which can be related to the nominal value of the debt D. Therefore, the payoff that will be paid is the full face value if the process V never hits the default level before maturity, and it is a **partially recovered value** if the process hits the default level before maturity. The problem with this approach is that it is difficult to measure the actual value process of a firm and estimate the parameters that will drive that value, as well as the fact that Brownian motion process may not be a good model for default risk.

A more recent approach, and one that is harder to interpret from an economic standpoint but that may be more practical for implementation purposes, is to model the default as a jump event of a jump process. This is called the **intensity-based approach** because it is usually assumed that the jump probability is determined by a jump-intensity process. Let us be more precise: for simplicity, we suppose that there is a random payment of C dollars at maturity if the default has not occurred and no payment at all if the default has occurred. Also for simplicity, the event of default is assumed to be independent of the payoff C and the interest rate. As a simple example, consider the case when the continuously compounded interest rate r is constant and when the risk-neutral probability of default is given by

$$P[\text{Default before time } t] = 1 - e^{-\lambda t}$$

for some constant intensity $\lambda > 0$. This corresponds to the probability of the first jump of a Poisson process. Denote by A the event that default has not occurred by time T. Recall the indicator function $\mathbf{1}_A$ that takes the value 1 if the event A happens (that is, no default) and 0 otherwise. Then, $P[A] = e^{-\lambda T}$. The price $C(0)$ of the claim C is

$$C(0) = E[e^{-rT}C\mathbf{1}_A] = E[e^{-rT}C]E[\mathbf{1}_A]$$

$$= E[e^{-rT}C]P[A] = E[e^{-rT}C]e^{-\lambda T}$$

That is, the price is given by

$$C(0) = E\left[e^{-(r+\lambda)T}C\right]$$

This is a very simple and intuitive result:

In this model, *the price of a defaultable claim is obtained by discounting at a higher rate* $r + \lambda$, rather than by r. The higher rate depends on the likelihood of default, as measured by λ.

Similar arguments show that this conclusion is also true when the interest rate is a stochastic process and the intensity $\lambda = \lambda(t)$ is a deterministic function of time. The price is then represented as

$$C(0) = E\left[e^{-\int_0^T [r(u)+\lambda(u)]du}C\right]$$

There are extensions of these results to more general specifications of the probability of default and of the form of partial payment in case the default occurs. One unpleasant feature of intensity-based models is that, in principle, in these models markets are incomplete, because, in general, the credit risk cannot be hedged. Thus contingent claims do not have unique no-arbitrage prices.

Finally, there are more elaborate approaches that model random changes of the credit rating of the firm. Credit ratings rely on a scale that indicates the risk of default of the firm. There are many different levels in these ratings, which include a threshold under which the company is considered high-risk (bonds below this rating are called junk bonds). The ratings are assigned by companies such as Standard & Poor's and Moody's. Rather than considering only "default" and "no-default" states of the world for the firm, the objective of these approaches is to model the gradual movements of the firm between different levels of creditworthiness, as a stochastic process. In practice, however, it is often difficult to find good data that would allow us to estimate the probabilities of those movements.

Summary

In fixed-income markets, investors trade derivative securities that depend on the movements of interest rates. In order to price bond derivatives in a tree model for the interest-rate process, we first have to compute bond prices by going backward in the tree. We can use the obtained prices to match the model parameters to the observed term structure of interest rates. Then we can price options on bonds, again by going backward in the tree.

As in the continuous-time stock-price models, the prices of bonds and bond options can be represented either as expected values under the risk-neutral measure or as solutions to PDEs. In the case of so-called affine models for the interest-rate process, the price of a bond can be found explicitly in terms of the current value of the interest rate.

A more recent approach is to model the instantaneous forward rates as diffusion processes. This is called the HJM (Heath-Jarrow-Morton) framework. In order to use it, we have to specify the volatility structure of the forward rates. Then the drift of the forward rates is automatically determined (under the risk-neutral measure) by the so-called HJM condition. An advantage of this approach is that it is easy to calibrate a model to the observed term structure of forward rates. A disadvantage is that, typically, we do not have closed-form solutions for prices of bonds and fixed-income derivatives.

In order to obtain closed-form solutions in some of the fixed-income models, it is sometimes useful to discount asset prices by a process other than the bank account. This technique is called change of numeraire. In particular, this method can be used to get a generalized Black-Scholes formula, in the situation when the interest-rate process may be random.

The values of some of the most popular interest-rate derivatives can be related to the values of bonds and bond options. In particular, a swap can be represented in terms of a coupon bond, while swaptions and caps can be priced in terms of put options on coupon bonds or pure discount bonds.

In fixed-income markets there is a significant danger of credit/default risk, meaning that the party that issues a bond may not be able to pay the full face value at maturity. Two main approaches to model the credit risk are the value-based approach and the intensity-based approach. In the simplest version of the latter approach, the price of a contingent claim is obtained by discounting at a rate higher than the interest rate.

Problems

1. Assume that the interest rate today is 6%. In the binomial tree model for interest rates with $p = 0.5$, $u = 1.1$, and $d = 0.9$, price the put option $[0.95 - P(1, 2)]^+$ with maturity $T = 1$, on the bond maturing at time $T = 2$.

†2. The price of three-month and nine-month T-bills are \$98.788 and \$96.270, respectively. In our model of the term structure, three months from today the six-month interest rate will be either 5.5% or 5% (in equivalent annual terms). Compute the price of a three-month European put written on the nine-month pure discount bond, with strike price \$97.5.

3. The one-month and two-month interest rates are 4% and 4.1%, respectively. Our model of the term structure says that one month from now the one-month interest rate will be either 3.5% or 4.5%. Compute the price of an interest rate derivative that pays \$1 in one month if the one-month interest rate is 4.5% and \$0.5 if the one-month interest rate is 3.5%. (**Note:** the interest rates quoted are the spot rates that have been annualized using compounding.)

†4. In Example 8.3 find the price of the at-the-money call option on the three-year bond, with option maturity equal to two years.

5. In the framework of Example 8.3 build a binomial tree if the current one-year spot rate is $r_1 = 4\%$, two-year spot rate is $r_2 = 5\%$, and three-year spot rate is $r_3 = 6\%$. In addition, it is estimated that the volatility of the current one-year spot rate is 3% and that one year from now the volatility of the one-year spot rate will be 3%. Assume that the risk-neutral probabilities are $p = 1 - p = 0.5$.

6. In the previous problem, find the price of the at-the-money call option on the three-year bond with option maturity equal to two years.

7. In the framework of Example 8.4 build a binomial tree if the current spot rates are $r_0(1) = 5\%$, $r_0(2) = 6\%$, and $r_0(3) = 6.5\%$. We assume that $p = 0.5$, and our estimate of δ is $\delta = 0.98$.

8. In the previous problem, find the price of the at-the-money put option on the three-year bond with option maturity equal to two years.

*9. Find the **bond price in the CIR model** (8.20). More precisely, show that in this model the bond price is given by

$$P(t, T) = L(T - t)e^{-r(t)B(T-t)}$$

where

$$L(s) = \left(\frac{2\beta e^{a+\beta s/2}}{(a + \beta)(e^{\beta s} - 1) + 2\beta} \right)^{\frac{2ab}{\sigma^2}}$$

$$B(s) = \frac{2\beta e^{\beta s} - 1}{(a + \beta)(e^{\beta s} - 1) + 2\beta}, \quad \beta = \sqrt{a^2 + 2\sigma^2}$$

†10. Show that the interest rate $r(t)$ in the Vasicek model has a normal distribution. [**Hint:** The Vasicek SDE can be solved for an explicit solution. It may help to find the SDE for the process $r(t)e^{at}$.] Show also that this distribution converges for $t \to \infty$.

11. Find the functions A and B in the continuous-time Ho-Lee model.

†12. In the previous problem, show that $P(t, T) = \frac{P(0,T)}{P(0,t)} \exp\{(T - t)[f(0, t) - r(t) - \frac{\sigma^2}{2}t(T - t)]\}$.

13. Find the interest-rate dynamics in the HJM model with

$$\sigma(t, T) = \sigma e^{-a(T-t)}$$

for given positive constants σ and a. In this model the forward-rates volatility goes down with shorter time to maturity. Does this model correspond to one of the short-rate models?

†14. Let $\sigma(t)$ be a deterministic function such that $\int_0^T \sigma^2(u)\, du$ is finite. Consider the process

$$Z(t) = e^{\int_0^t \sigma(u) dW(u) - \frac{1}{2} \int_0^t \sigma^2(u) du}$$

Use Itô's rule to show that this process satisfies

$$dZ = \sigma Z\, dW$$

Deduce that this process is a martingale process. Use this fact to find the moment-generating function

$$f(y) = E[e^{yX}]$$

of the random variable $X = \int_0^T \sigma(u)\, dW(u)$. Finally, argue that X is normally distributed, with mean zero and variance $\int_0^T \sigma^2(u)\, du$.

15. Consider two bond markets, forward and domestic, with the forward-rate dynamics, under the domestic risk-neutral measure, given by

$$df_D = \alpha_D\, dt + \sigma_D\, dW, \qquad df_F = \alpha_F\, dt + \sigma_F\, dW$$

where W is one-dimensional, for simplicity. Also suppose that the exchange rate Q, for exchanging domestic currency into one unit of foreign currency, is given by

$$dQ = Q[\mu \, dt + \sigma_Q \, dW]$$

also under the domestic risk-neutral measure. Show that the HJM drift condition for the foreign drift under the domestic risk-neutral measure is given by

$$\alpha_F(t, T) = \sigma_F(t, T) \left[\int_t^T \sigma_F(t, u) \, du - \sigma_Q(t) \right]$$

†16. Do you think that the put-call parity holds in the presence of default risk? Why?

**17. Show the following:

a. If the bond price satisfies $dP/P = m \, dt + v \, dW$, then the forward rate satisfies $df = \alpha \, dt + \sigma \, dW$, where

$$\alpha = \frac{\partial v}{\partial T} v - \frac{\partial m}{\partial T}, \qquad \sigma = -\frac{\partial v}{\partial T}$$

b. If f is given as in part a, then the short rate satisfies $dr = a \, dt + b \, dW$, where

$$a(t) = \frac{\partial f}{\partial T}(t, t) + \alpha(t, t), \qquad b(t) = \sigma(t, t)$$

c. If f is given as in part a, then $dP/P = [r + A + \|S\|^2/2] \, dt + S \, dW$, where

$$A = A(t, T) = -\int_t^T \alpha(t, s) \, ds, \qquad S = S(t, T) = -\int_t^T \sigma(t, s) \, ds$$

*18. Derive the Black-Scholes formula for the European put option directly using the "change of numeraire" technique. Note that you should use different numeraires for pricing $K\mathbf{1}_{\{S(T)<K\}}$ and $S(T)\mathbf{1}_{\{S(T)<K\}}$.

*19. Find the functions A and B in the continuous-time Hull-White model, and use Merton's generalized option pricing formula to find the expression for the price of the call option $[P(T_1, T_2) - K]^+$ on the bond in this model.

†20. You are a party to a swap deal with a notional principal of $100 that has four months left to maturity. The payments take place every three months. As a part of the swap deal you have to pay the three-month LIBOR rate, and in exchange you receive the fixed 8% rate (total annually) on the notional principal. The prices of the one-month and four-month risk-free pure discount bonds (nominal $100) are $99.6 and $98.2, respectively. At the last payment date the three-month LIBOR was 7%. Compute the value of the swap.

21. Compute the value of the following swap: the notional principal is \$100, the remaining life of the swap is nine months. You pay an 8% fixed rate on the notional principal annually, in semiannually paid coupons, and you receive the six-month LIBOR rate plus 1%. When the last payment took place the six-month LIBOR was 6%, the price of the three-month risk-free pure discount bond was \$98.50 (nominal \$100), and the price of a nine-month risk-free pure discount bond was \$95.

†22. Show that the value of the swaption $S^+(T)$ is equal to the value of the cash flow of call options $[R(T) - \tilde{R}]^+ \Delta T$ paid at times $t = T_1, \ldots, T_n$, where $R(T)$ is the swap rate at time T, for the swap starting at $t = T$ and maturing at $t = T_n$. [**Hint:** Use the principle for pricing interest-rate derivatives, properties of conditional expectations, and expression (8.68) in order to show that the value of this cash flow is equal to the value of $S^+(T)$.]

23. Denote $P = P(T_{i-1}, T_i)$, and let f be a given function. Show, using the expectation formula (8.1), that the time-t value of the payoff of $C = f(P)$ dollars paid at time T_i is the same as the time-t value of the payoff of $P \cdot C$ dollars paid at time T_{i-1}. Is this statement still true if we replace $P = P(T_{i-1}, T_i)$ with $P = P(T_i, T_{i+1})$?

†24. Consider a **floating-rate coupon bond** which pays a coupon c_i at time $T_i, i = 1, \ldots, n$, where the coupons are given by

$$c_i = (T_i - T_{i-1})L(T_{i-1}, T_i)$$

and $T_i - T_{i-1} = \Delta T$ is constant. Show that the value of this bond at time $t < T_0$ is equal to $P(t, T_0)$.

Further Readings

General descriptions of fixed-income securities markets and interest-rate derivatives are provided in Sundaresan (1997), Fabozzi (1999), Pelsser (2000), Brigo and Mercurio (2001), Martellini and Priaulet (2001), and Martellini, Priaulet, and Priaulet (2003). Some of the best-known models of the term structure of interest rates are Vasicek (1977), Cox, Ingersoll, and Ross (1985b), Ho and Lee (1986), Hull and White (1990), and Heath, Jarrow, and Morton (1992). The analysis of the change-of-numeraire technique is provided in Geman, El Karoui, and Rochet (1995). Examples of solutions to affine models are Jamshidian (1989) and Goldstein and Zapatero (1996). General treatments are Dai and Singleton (2000) and Duffie, Pan, and Singleton (2000). Market models were introduced in Brace, Gatarek, and Musiela (1997), Jamshidian (1997), and Miltersen, Sandmann, and Sondermann (1997). The first model of default risk was Merton (1977). Other approaches are Jarrow, Lando, and Turnbull (1997) and Duffie and Singleton (1999). An advanced textbook treatment is Bielecki and Rutkowski (2001).

9 Hedging

The term "hedging" implies the notion of protection. In financial markets the need for protection or hedging arises for two reasons. First, and this is the reason that justifies the existence of derivatives markets, derivatives enable market participants to eliminate some or all of the risks they face in conducting their line of business. The second, related, reason is that in the financial services industry a large part of the business of many intermediary companies consists in taking positions in derivatives, to satisfy the demand for derivatives by their client companies. As a result, companies that sell derivatives face possible losses. For them, hedging refers to the strategies they implement to eliminate or reduce the risks arising from having positions in derivatives sold to clients.

In this chapter we consider both types of hedging. First, we discuss the use of futures contracts for hedging purposes. We then study the ways in which options can be used for hedging and, more particularly, for creating desired payoff profiles. Finally, we discuss the problem of hedging of positions in derivatives and the sensitivity of options positions with respect to various market parameters.

9.1   Hedging with Futures

Futures are financial instruments ideally suited for hedging against various types of risks, by locking in today a specified price for an asset to be delivered in the future. For example, an airline company can lock in the cost of future purchases of oil by taking long positions in oil futures. Or, an oil company can lock in future sell prices by taking short positions in oil futures. In this section we ignore the marking-to-market feature of futures contracts, and we discuss them as if they were forward contracts.

9.1.1   Perfect Hedge

We first consider the ideal case in which the "hedger" (that is, the party that wants to use the futures contract to hedge some risk) is able to offset exactly the risk faced in the market by taking an equivalent but opposite position in the futures market. This approach is not always possible, because there might not be futures contracts available in the market that would exactly match the terms of the delivery and the assets to be delivered.

As an example, imagine a U.S. company that buys and sells products in the global market. Suppose first that the company has received an order to deliver its product six months from now to a European client, for 1 million euros. The company might be worried that the U.S. dollar/euro exchange rate might be very different six months from now. In particular, the company is concerned that the euro might be worth less relative to the dollar than it is worth now. It is easy to hedge this risk perfectly: the company can go short in six-month futures on euros, for 1 million euros. In other words, it takes an exactly opposite position to the one resulting from its business—it will receive 1 million euros six months from now as a payment for its product, and it enters a contract in which it will sell that amount of euros in six months, at a price that is known now, the current futures price. Six months from now the company's transactions in euros will cancel each other. This is the case of a **perfect hedge.**

Similarly, consider a company that will buy a product delivered by a European counter-party six months from now, for 1 million euros. The company might be worried about the euro becoming worth more relative to the dollar. This risk can be perfectly hedged by taking a long position in six-month futures on the euro, for 1 million euros.

9.1.2   Cross-Hedging; Basis Risk

When a company cannot take a futures position in the exact asset the company is interested in, it can try to use a futures position in a similar asset whose price is likely to be highly correlated with the asset of interest (for example, a similar type of oil or a similar agricultural commodity). The same problem arises with respect to the maturity: there might not be a futures contract with exactly the same maturity the company requires. The company will choose the contract with the closest possible maturity. In such a situation, we say that there is an **asset mismatch** or a **maturity mismatch.** The practice of choosing a futures contract different but related (in the underlying asset type or maturity) to the desired futures contract is called **cross-hedging.** We now study the basic aspects of cross-hedging.

Let us denote by $S_1(t)$ the spot price of the asset the hedger has to deliver at time T (if the hedger has to buy, the opposite reasoning holds). Suppose further that there is no futures contract with underlying S_1 or maturity T. Instead, there is a futures contract with underlying S_2 that is positively correlated to S_1 and with maturity $U \geq T$. We denote by $F_2(t, U)$ the futures price at time t of the contract maturing at time U on the asset S_2, which will be used for hedging. The hedger takes a long position in δ units of the futures $F_2(t, U)$. The number δ, which we want to compute, is called the **hedge ratio.** Let us also assume that the hedger holds (or receives) the amount $S_1(t)$ for the asset to be delivered at time T, with $S_1(t)$ specified at time t. We consider the risk exposure X per one unit of asset S_1:

$$X = S_1(t) - S_1(T) + \delta[F_2(T, U) - F_2(t, U)] \tag{9.1}$$

There are two components in this expression: the change in the value of the asset to be delivered at time T, and the payoff of holding the long position in the futures contract between t and T. Ideally, these two terms would offset each other. In particular, if the price of the underlying increases, the long position in the futures is likely to have a positive payoff and to offset the increase in the price of the underlying. At moment t, both $S_1(t)$ and $F_2(t, U)$ are known. The risk in the risk exposure X comes from the fact that the quantity

$$S_1(T) - \delta F_2(T, U)$$

is not known. This quantity is called the **basis.** The **basis risk** is measured by its variance conditional at time t:

$$\text{Var}_t[X] = \text{Var}_t[S_1(T)] + \delta^2 \text{Var}_t[F_2(T, U)] - 2\delta \text{Cov}_t[S_1(T), F_2(T, U)] \qquad (9.2)$$

[Since $S_1(t)$ and $F_2(t, U)$ are known at time t, their variances and covariance are zero.] We assume that the hedger wants to attain the lowest possible variance. Taking the derivative with respect to δ and setting it equal to zero gives us the optimal δ:

$$\delta = \frac{\text{Cov}_t[S_1(T), F_2(T, U)]}{\text{Var}_t[F_2(T, U)]} = \rho \frac{\sigma_S}{\sigma_F} \qquad (9.3)$$

where ρ is the correlation between $S_1(T)$ and $F_2(T, U)$, and σ_S^2 and σ_F^2 are their variances. The minimal variance is

$$\text{Var}_t[X] = \text{Var}_t[S_1(T)] - \frac{\text{Cov}_t^2[S_1(T), F_2(T, U)]}{\text{Var}_t[F_2(T, U)]} \qquad (9.4)$$

If there is a futures contract with underlying S_1 and maturity U, so that $S_1 = S_2$, and $U = T$, we have $S_1(T) = F_1(T) = F_2(T, U)$. This is the case of a perfect hedge we discussed earlier. In this case we have $\delta = 1$, and, using the fact that $\text{Cov}[S, S] = \text{Var}[S]$, we see that $\text{Var}_t[X] = 0$ and there is no basis risk involved.

Example 9.1 (Cross-Hedging Currency Risk)   Consider a U.S. firm that has a contract with a company in Surfland, a country whose official currency is called the *val*. The Surfland company will pay 1 million val to the U.S. firm six months from now. The U.S. firm wants to hedge its exposure to the exchange-rate risk. Unfortunately, there is no futures market for vals. However, there is a futures market for another currency, called the *playa*, of the country called Skiland. This currency is highly correlated with the Surfland val. Six-month futures contracts on playa are traded. The U.S. firm will short δ futures contracts on playa, maturing in six months, as a hedge against currency risk. Suppose that the exchange rates are $Q_1 = 0.1$ dollar/val (so that you have to pay 0.1 dollars in order to receive one val) and $Q_2 = 0.2$ dollar/playa (with similar interpretation). As a result, the playa/val exchange rate has to be $Q = Q_1/Q_2 = 0.5$ playa/val. Thus, at today's rates, 1 million vals is equivalent to 0.5 million playas. However, this figure does not mean that the company should short 0.5 million playas in the futures markets. If the company wants to minimize the variance of the exposure, it has to estimate the covariance $\text{Cov}[Q_1, Q_2]$ of the two exchange rates and the variance $\text{Var}[Q_2]$ of the dollar/playa exchange rate. Suppose that it is found from historical data that the standard deviations are $\sigma_{Q_1} = 0.03$ for the exchange rate on the val and $\sigma_{Q_2} = 0.02$ for the exchange rate on the playa, and that the correlation between the two is 0.9. Thus the covariance is equal to $0.9 \cdot 0.02 \cdot 0.03 = 0.00054$. We want to use formula (9.3) for the minimum variance hedge ratio. Since $U = T$, the value $F_2(T, T)$ is simply the value of the playa exchange rate at time T (rather than the value of a futures contract on playa). We get

$$\delta = 0.00054/0.0004 = 1.35$$

Therefore, for each val the U.S. company is trying to hedge, it should short an amount of playas equivalent to 1.35 vals. Since the company has risk exposure to 1 million vals, it should short $1,000,000 \cdot 1.35/2 = 675,000$ playas. If we compute the minimal variance (per unit of currency), we get 0.000171, which is quite a bit smaller than the variance of the dollar/val exchange rate, equal to $\sigma_{Q_1}^2 = 0.0009$.

We now discuss another interpretation of the parameter δ. Consider two different assets S_1 and S_2. It is often assumed that we have the following relationship of the **linear regression** type:

$$S_1(T) = a + bF_2(T, U) + \varepsilon(T) \tag{9.5}$$

where a and b are constants and ε is the error term, for example, a zero-mean normally distributed random variable. Classical regression theory tells us that the optimal δ of equation (9.3) is simply $\delta = b$. In this model, the minimal unit risk exposure becomes (up to a plus-minus sign)

$$X = a + bF_2(T, U) + \varepsilon(T) - S(t) + b[F_2(t, U) - F_2(T, U)]$$

$$= a + bF_2(t, U) - S(t) + \varepsilon(T)$$

The quantity $a + bF_2(t, U)$ can be thought of as the best guess for $S_1(U)$, and it is called the **target price,** while the quantity $\varepsilon(T) = a + bF_2(T, U) - S_1(T)$ determines the basis risk.

Oftentimes, the regression relationship is assumed between other quantities, such as the changes ΔS_1 of S_1 and ΔF_2 of F_2, rather than S_1 and F_2 themselves.

9.1.3 Rolling the Hedge Forward

Sometimes the objective is to hedge long-term obligations, while the available futures contracts are short-term. One possible strategy in this case is **rolling the hedge forward.** Under this strategy, the hedger enters the futures position at the available maturity, closes it out at maturity date, enters a new futures contract, closes it out at maturity date, and so on, until the expiration date of the obligation to be hedged. However, this strategy may be dangerous for two reasons. First, prices can move against the hedger in the meantime, and it may be hard to satisfy the appropriate margins. Second, this rolling of futures contracts signals to other market participants the objectives of the hedger, and they might be able to take advantage of that knowledge and implement strategies that will be costly to the hedger. A well-known example is the case of a company called Metallgesellschaft (MG), which in the early 1990s sold a large volume of long-term oil supply contracts, meaning that it promised to deliver oil at a future date at a predetermined fixed price. MG was hedging its obligations by rolling over futures contracts positions in oil. The price of oil actually fell, a trend which might have indicated that the supply contracts were even more favorable to MG. However, the hedging position in the futures contracts lost value, and the margin calls forced the management to abandon the contracts at a great loss.

9.1.4   Quantity Uncertainty

Another case not discussed in the previous analysis is the case in which the basis might be a nonlinear function of market variables. A typical example is the case in which the spot prices might be influenced by the size of the transaction and the size of the transaction is not known in advance. This is a case of **quantity uncertainty.** For instance, consider a farmer who wants to hedge the uncertainty about the price of corn. Depending on the nature of the relationship between the price and the size of the harvest, the optimal approach may actually be to take a hedge position of the opposite sign than in the usual case. On the one hand, for example, if there is no dependence between the harvest size and price of corn, the farmer will hedge by taking a short position in corn futures. On the other hand, suppose that if the harvest size is large in a particular year, the price of corn goes down. The profits may still be larger, because the amount sold is larger. And the other way round: smaller crops will make the price higher, but the farmer may experience losses because the amount sold is smaller. The farmer may want to hedge this latter risk and go long in corn futures. To recap, because of the negative correlation between the price and the size, the farmer's hedge position would be smaller, or even of the opposite sign, than otherwise, because this negative correlation already provides a **natural hedge** for the farmer's revenues.

9.2   Portfolios of Options as Trading Strategies

By taking simultaneous long and short positions, possibly in both call and put options, with various strike prices and maturities, an investor can design a portfolio with very different characteristics. Strategies of this type, which combine possibly several options and the underlying security, may be used for hedging purposes or for placing bets on the future movements of the underlying. We consider several examples, all of which are examples of **static positions,** meaning that we keep the initial position unchanged until maturity. The examples we give deal with very simple payoff shapes, but, in theory, *virtually any payoff function can be approximated as a combination of calls and puts with different strike prices.* In practice, however, there is only a limited number of strike prices that are traded.

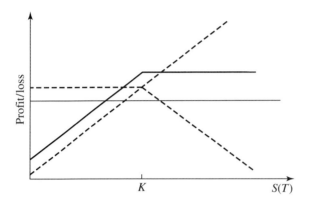

Figure 9.1
Covered call = long stock + short call.

9.2.1 Covered Calls and Protective Puts

A **covered call** is the strategy that consists in writing a call option and holding the underlying stock. Although a covered call implies a short position in a call, margin requirements are not imposed, since the holder of this position will always be able to deliver the stock if the option is exercised. The profit or loss of this strategy at maturity is shown in figure 9.1. The total profit or loss is the value of the payoff evaluated at the price level $S(T)$ of the underlying at maturity, minus the premium paid for the securities purchased, plus the premium received for the securities sold. A detailed explanation of how to compute the payoff is given in section 9.2.3 for the butterfly spread, while other payoffs of this section are further discussed in the Problems section. The dotted lines in the figures represent the profit or loss of the individual securities traded in the portfolio.

A **protective put** is a portfolio that consists in holding simultaneously a long position in the stock and a put on the stock. The payoff is presented in figure 9.2. The put protects the investor by providing insurance against the drop in the stock price: if the stock value goes down, the put value goes up.

9.2.2 Bull Spreads and Bear Spreads

A **bull spread** is the payoff in figure 9.3. It can be achieved by buying a call with strike price K_1 and selling a call with a higher strike price K_2, $K_2 > K_1$. The selling of the option with the higher strike price makes the upside potential (potential for profit) limited, but it means that this strategy requires less initial investment than buying a regular call. The investor holding this position gains if the stock price goes up.

A **bear spread** is the payoff in figure 9.4. The holder of this position gains if the stock price goes down. It can be achieved by buying a call with strike price K_2 and selling a call

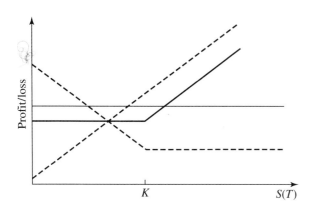

Figure 9.2
Protective put = long stock + long put.

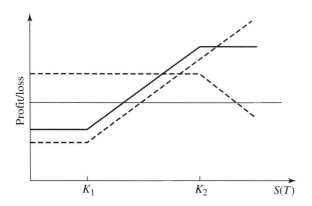

Figure 9.3
Bull spread profit/loss. Less expensive than a call, with less potential for profit.

with a lower strike price K_1. The purchase of the option with the higher strike price makes the downside potential (potential for loss) limited, but it means that this strategy brings less initial revenue than selling a regular call.

These payoffs can both be created using put options, too.

9.2.3   Butterfly Spreads

A **butterfly spread** is the combination of options whose payoff at maturity is represented in figure 9.5. We see that the payoff will be high if the underlying security S does not move far away from the value K_2, and it is otherwise low or zero.

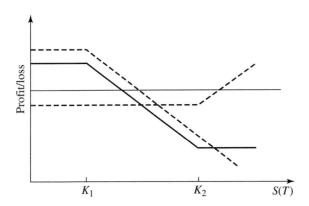

Figure 9.4
Bear spread profit/loss. Brings less money than selling a call, but loss potential is also lower.

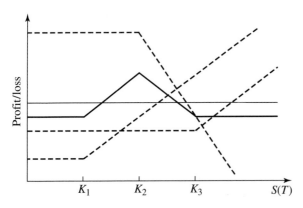

Figure 9.5
Butterfly spread profit/loss. Profit is made if the underlying does not move by much.

There are several ways in which this type of strategy can be implemented. One way is to buy two calls, one with "low" strike price K_1 and another with "high" strike price K_3, and sell two calls with strike price $K_2 = (K_1 + K_3)/2$ halfway between K_1 and K_3. The way to show this relation is to compute the payoff C as

$$V = [S(T) - K_1]^+ + [S(T) - K_3]^+ - 2[S(T) - K_2]^+ \tag{9.6}$$

For example, if $K_2 < S(T) < K_3$, we get

$$C = S(T) - K_1 - 2S(T) + 2K_2 = -S(T) + K_3$$

which is the equation for the line with the negative slope for S between K_2 and K_3 in figure 9.5, except it is moved down by the total initial cost of the portfolio. We leave it as an exercise in the Problems section to compute C for other values of S, as well as to compute the payoffs in other examples in this section.

Who would want to take a butterfly spread position (other than avid practitioners of yoga)? Looking at figure 9.5, you can see that this spread is appropriate for the investor who intends to make some profit if the stock stays close to the intermediate strike value (that is, if the volatility is low) and who wants to have a limited loss otherwise.

9.2.4   Straddles and Strangles

We mention two more option combinations with wild names. The payoff of a **straddle** is shown in figure 9.6. It is formed by buying a call and a put with the same strike price and the same maturity. The position results in profit if the stock price moves away from the strike price, and if it stays close to the strike price there is a limited loss, the cost of buying the options.

The payoff of a **strangle** (also called a **bottom vertical combination**!) is shown in figure 9.7. It is formed by buying a call and a put with the same maturity but different strike prices. Similarly to a straddle, the position results in profit if the stock price moves away from the strike price, and if it stays close to the strike price there is a limited loss, due to the cost of buying the call and put options.

All these strategies can be reversed, by going short (long) where the original strategy goes long (short). The profit/loss figures would be the same, except turned upside down. For example, a reverse straddle would lead to a (limited) profit if the stock price does not

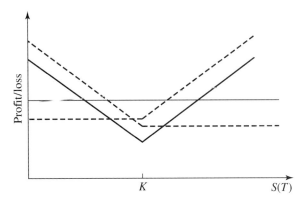

Figure 9.6
Straddle profit/loss. Profit is made when the underlying moves away from the strike price.

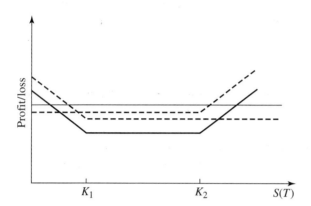

Figure 9.7
Strangle profit/loss. Profit is made if the underlying moves away from the two strike prices.

move away from the strike price, and otherwise may lead to (unlimited) losses, making it quite a risky position.

9.3   Hedging Options Positions; Delta Hedging

In this section we discuss the problem of an investment bank that has a position in options (for example, a short position in calls because a client wanted a long position in calls). The value of the position of the investment bank fluctuates as the time goes by. On the one hand, the bank may want to eliminate the risk that arises as a result of those fluctuations. On the other hand, the bank might want to hold that position for purely speculative reasons, without trying to hedge the risk completely. Here, we consider the former case, in which the investment bank is only interested in receiving a fee for the service (selling the option to the client) and tries to hedge the risk resulting from the position in options.

In a complete-markets setting, the no-arbitrage price of an option is equal to the cost of the strategy that replicates the option. This perfect replication, in theory, hedges against any risk of holding a position in the option. In practice, however, it is impossible to hedge against all the risks. In this section we discuss different ways in which the risk of holding positions in options is quantified in the market, as well as how market participants go about hedging against this risk. Mostly, we work in continuous-time complete-markets models. The problem of hedging in incomplete markets is usually quite difficult and outside the scope of this text.

We illustrate hedging methods by considering individual options. In practice, however, hedging takes place on a more comprehensive level, for a **book of options** a trader holds positions in. Even more globally, a risk-management department of an investment bank considers the overall risk of all the positions the bank is involved with. Nevertheless, it is important to understand the risk of holding a position in a single asset (options represent the most interesting example), because the comprehensive risk management is based on the same ideas as hedging the risk of a single position.

9.3.1 Delta Hedging in Discrete-Time Models

Instead of doing the general case, we illustrate how to hedge options using discrete-time models by examples. Suppose that our option trader Taf has sold a European call option for the price of $C(0) = 2.2715$. The option is written on a stock whose initial value is $S_0(0) = 55.5625$. (The stock-price values in this example are taken from a real data sample on Microsoft stock as discussed in section 9.3.4 and presented in figure 9.8.) The strike price is $K = 55$, and maturity is $T = 0.08$ years. Suppose that at maturity the stock price is $S(T) = 68.8125$. This means that Taf has to deliver $68.8125 - 55 = 13.8125$ at maturity. His total loss is $13.8125 - 2.2715 = 11.5410$. (We disregard the possibility of earning interest on the received option premium 2.2715.)

Taf does not know in advance whether he will make or lose money. Let us suppose he wants to hedge the risk of this position. Assume first that he adopts our simplest model, the single-period binomial model, and that he estimates the standard deviation of the (log) returns of the stock to be $\sigma = 0.32$. Using the CRR parametrization suggested in chapter 11, he assumes that the stock will take one of the two values

$$S^u = S(0)e^{\sigma\sqrt{T-t}} = 55.5625e^{0.32\sqrt{0.08}} = 60.826$$

$$S^d = S(0)e^{-\sigma\sqrt{T-t}} = 55.5625e^{-0.32\sqrt{0.08}} = 50.7544$$

Thus in his model the option payoff is either $60.826 - 55 = 5.826$ or zero. Suppose that he ignores the interest rate and sets $r = 0$. If he tries to replicate this payoff, he needs to solve the system

$$\delta_0 + 60.826\delta_1 = 5.826$$

$$\delta_0 + 50.7544\delta_1 = 0$$

for the amount of money δ_0 to be held in cash and the number δ_1 of shares of stock. As indicated by equation (3.48), δ_1 is the **delta** of the option, the change in the option value over the change in the price of the underlying, $\delta_1 = 5.826/10.0716 = 0.5784$. Thus Taf needs to buy 0.5784 shares of the stock. This purchase costs him $0.5784 \cdot 55.5625 = 32.1373$, or, after accounting for the received option price, $32.1373 - 2.2715 = 29.8658$. At maturity he has $0.5784 \cdot 68.8125 = 39.8011$ in stock. When the option is exercised, he has to deliver one share, or 68.8125 in stock, and he gets 55 from the option holder. His total profit or loss (assuming $r = 0$) is

$$-29.8658 + 39.8011 - 68.8125 + 55 = 9.9353 - 13.8125 = -3.8772$$

This is much less than 11.5410, the loss without hedging, but still substantial. In the Problems section we ask you to hedge a put option in this example. In fact, the put option will expire out of the money, so hedging was not necessary, but you do not know that in advance.

Let us now do this same exercise, but assuming a two-period model. Let us see if Taf has a smaller loss under this assumption. In the two-period model the up and down factors are given by

$$u = e^{\sigma\sqrt{(T-t)/2}} = e^{0.32\sqrt{0.04}} = 1.066, \qquad d = 1/u = 0.938$$

Instead of computing the replicating strategy, let us first find the risk-neutral probability.

$$p^* = (1 - d)/(u - d) = 0.4844$$

The option values at node one are

$$C^u(1) = p^*[S(0)u^2 - K]^+ + (1 - p^*)[S(0)ud - K]^+$$

$$= p^*8.1388 + (1 - p^*)0.5577 = 4.23$$

$$C^d(1) = p^*[S(0)ud - K]^+ + (1 - p^*)[S(0)d^2 - K]^+$$

$$= p^*0.5577 + (1 - p^*) \cdot 0 = 0.27$$

This gives us the delta at time zero as

$$\delta(0) = \frac{4.23 - 0.27}{S(0)u - S(0)d} = 0.5568$$

Therefore, Taf needs $0.5568 \cdot S(0) = 30.9372$ to buy 0.5568 shares of the stock. Since he obtained 2.2715 for the option, he needs to spend $30.9372 - 2.2715 = 28.6657$. Suppose that at time one ($t = 0.04$ years) the stock price is $S(1) = 61.25$. This does not quite correspond to the two-period model in which $S^u(1) = S(0)u = 59.2296$. Taf can now update the remaining part of his model by assuming that the stock will take either the value $61.25u = 65.2925$ or $61.25d = 57.4525$ at maturity. His new delta is

$$\delta(1) = \frac{(65.2925 - 55) - (57.4525 - 55)}{65.2925 - 57.4525} = 1$$

This result means that at time one he has to trade so as to have one share of the stock in his portfolio. He already has $0.5568 \cdot S(1) = 34.104$ in the stock, so he has to spend an additional $61.25 - 34.104 = 27.146$. Together with the initial cost of 28.6657, he has spent 55.8177. At maturity he has to deliver the share he has, and he gets $K = 55$ for it. Thus his total profit or loss is $-55.8177 + 55 = -0.8177$.

In this example, the loss in the two-period model is, indeed, much smaller than the loss using the single-period model. This result was partly due to chance. In order to obtain an even better hedge, at least on average, it is necessary to use models with more periods or continuous-time models. We will extend the preceding example to a Black-Scholes setting in section 9.3.4, and the loss for Taf in this example using that setting is smaller still. The mathematics is more sophisticated, but the main idea remains the same: hedge your position by holding the stock with the number of shares equal to the option's delta. This is called **delta hedging.**

9.3.2   Delta-Neutral Strategies

An option written on an underlying asset S is most sensitive to the changes in the value of S. Hence, the largest part of the risk comes from the price movements of asset S. The continuous-time quantity that measures the rate of change of the option value C with respect to the change in value of S is the first derivative of C with respect to S, and it is called the **delta of the option:**

$$\Delta_C := \frac{\partial C}{\partial S}$$

In order to explain further why this quantity is important, suppose for a moment that all other variables affecting the option value C are kept fixed, and think of C as a function of S only. We denote by ΔC the change in the value of the option. We have

$$\Delta C := C(S) - C(S(0)) = \frac{\Delta C}{\Delta S} \Delta S$$

where $\Delta S = S - S(0)$. If S is close to $S(0)$, $\Delta C / \Delta S$ becomes close to the first derivative Δ_C, and we have the first-order approximation of function C as

$$C(S) \approx C(S(0)) + \Delta_C[S - S(0)]$$

Suppose we are short C and we want to hedge the associated risk with respect to the movements of S by holding a position in S. We want the delta of the combined position (the option and the underlying asset) to be equal to zero, in order to eliminate the risk related to the uncertainty of the future value of S. The delta of a portfolio is defined in the same way as the delta of an option: it is the change in the value of the portfolio divided by the change in the value of the underlying asset. A zero delta for the combined position means that the portfolio does not change (at least not by much) in value if the price of the underlying asset changes. More precisely, we note that the first-order approximation for the value of the portfolio is

$$\pi(S) \approx \pi(S(0)) + \Delta_\pi[S - S(0)]$$

Thus, making Δ_π equal to zero we (approximately) eliminate the variability of the portfolio with respect to the changes of S.

Let us find the number of shares δ of S we should hold in the portfolio π in order to make Δ_π equal to zero. The delta of S is equal to one. (Why?) So, the delta Δ_π of the portfolio π that is short C (one option) and long δ shares of stock is

$$\Delta_\pi = -\Delta_C + \delta \cdot 1$$

(The minus sign comes from the short position in C.) Solving this expression for $\Delta_\pi = 0$, we conclude that *the delta of the portfolio is zero if it holds exactly Δ_C shares of the stock.* Such a portfolio is called **delta-neutral.** A portfolio is called **long delta** if its delta is positive, in which case its value will increase if the value of S increases, and it is called **short delta** if its delta is negative, in which case its value will decrease if the value of S increases, all other variables being constant.

An important point is that the value of delta changes frequently, partly because S changes its value frequently. Thus, in order to keep a portfolio delta-neutral, one has to trade frequently, adjusting the number of shares of S held in the portfolio. This approach is called a **dynamic hedging** strategy, as opposed to a static strategy of taking positions at time zero and holding them unchanged.

The reader may recall that in the Black-Scholes-Merton model, the perfect replication of a payoff $C = C(S_T)$ is achieved by holding exactly Δ_C shares of the underlying at all times. This means that *in that model all the risk is eliminated by continuously keeping the portfolio delta-neutral.* This result is not necessarily true in other models, or in practice, when one has to take into account the risks related to other factors such as the movements in volatility of S, the movements of the interest rate r, and others. In the next section we give the formula for the delta of the call and the put option in the Merton-Black-Scholes model, and then we illustrate it with an example of hedging an option, using real-world data.

9.3.3 Deltas of Calls and Puts

Recall the Black-Scholes formula (7.13) for the European call option:

$$c(t, s) = sN(d_1) - Ke^{-r(T-t)}N(d_2) \qquad (9.7)$$

where

$$d_1 = \frac{1}{\sigma\sqrt{T-t}}[\log(s/K) + (r + \sigma^2/2)(T-t)] \qquad (9.8)$$

$$d_2 = \frac{1}{\sigma\sqrt{T-t}}[\log(s/K) + (r - \sigma^2/2)(T-t)] = d_1 - \sigma\sqrt{T-t} \qquad (9.9)$$

The delta of the call option is the derivative $\frac{\partial}{\partial s}C(t, s)$ of the option price $C(t, s)$ with respect to the current stock price s. You are asked in Problem 13 to show that it is given by

$$\Delta_C = N(d_1) \qquad (9.10)$$

[This demonstration is not as easy as it appears from equation (9.7) because d_1 and d_2 also depend on s and have to be differentiated with respect to s.]

The theoretical perfect replication of the call option payoff would require holding exactly $N(d_1)$ shares of stock at all times. Note that this quantity is never larger than one [because $N(\cdot)$ is a probability], and thus holding one share or more of the stock is more than enough to hedge the call option payoff. The call's delta is also always positive, meaning that the replicating portfolio never goes short in the stock. The call option value increases when the stock price increases, and it decreases when the stock price decreases, whereas shorting the stock would result in a strategy with the reverse outcome.

From the put-call parity it is easily seen that the delta of the put option is given by

$$\Delta_P = N(d_1) - 1 \qquad (9.11)$$

This quantity is always negative and larger than -1, meaning that replicating the put requires going short in the stock, but never more than one share.

9.3.4 Example: Hedging a Call Option

We now illustrate hedging in the Merton-Black-Scholes model with an example using real data. We suppose that the trader Taf has sold a European call option, and, in order to hedge the risk of the short position in the option Taf uses the Black-Scholes replicating portfolio strategy. Taf will have to pay $[S(T) - K]^+$ at maturity T to the buyer of the option. With a perfect hedging strategy, Taf would initially invest the money collected from writing the call and, at maturity, would have the amount $[S(T) - K]^+$ in the replicating portfolio, exactly enough to cover the payment. In practice, however, the replication is unlikely to give the exact amount of the option payoff, for four main reasons:

1. Noncontinuous rebalancing of the replicating portfolio

2. Transaction costs involved in rebalancing frequently

3. Uncertainty about the exact value of volatility σ, which determines the number of shares in the replicating portfolio (and which, we recall, is assumed to be constant in the Black-Scholes-Merton model)

4. The fact that the model may not be realistic (for example, the stock price may not have a lognormal distribution)

We mention again that in practice it is unusual for a financial intermediary to try to replicate a single option, especially a simple vanilla option like a call or a put. More likely, the intermediary would try to hedge a whole book of options, or maybe a single deal involving a large trade in an exotic option contract.

In our example, we consider the price of Microsoft stock for 20 days in the year 2000. The results are presented in the table of figure 9.8. For simplicity, we take the interest rate r of the risk-free asset, the bank, to be zero. In order to estimate the volatility σ of the stock, we compute the standard error of the log-returns

$$Y_i = \log \frac{S(i+1)}{S(i)}$$

for those 20 days. (In reality, at day $t = 0$ we would not see the log-returns of the following 20 days, so we would have to use the standard error of historical log-returns.) This standard error s_Y is equal to 0.019978, and it estimates the standard deviation corresponding to one day. Remember that σ^2 denotes the variance of log-returns per unit time. More specifically, we denote by σ the annualized volatility. Therefore, assuming there are 252 trading days in a year, so that a day is equal to 1/252 years, the standard deviation of one day s_Y is an estimate of

$$\sigma \sqrt{\frac{1}{252}}$$

Hence, σ is estimated as

$$\sigma = 0.0199978\sqrt{252} = 0.317139$$

Taf sells a call option on this stock at day zero, with a strike price equal to $K = 55$ and maturity 20 days from now, which is about $T = 0.08$ years. Using these values of T and σ, the current value of the stock price $S(0) = 55.5625$, and the Black-Scholes formula, Taf computes the option price as $C(0, S(0)) = 2.2715$. Taf sells the option for this price (in practice, it would be this price plus a markup, the financial intermediation fee), and starts hedging it. In order to do so, Taf has to compute the delta of the option, which is equal to $N(d_1)$ in the Black-Scholes model, by formula (9.10). This gives the value 0.5629. On the first day Taf buys $\Delta(0) = 0.5629$ shares of the stock and borrows from the bank the difference

$$\Delta(0)S(0) - C(0, S(0))$$

between the price of the stock amount that has to be bought and the amount raised by selling the option. If the option was such that this difference was negative, Taf would deposit the extra money in the bank.

   Taf's replicating wealth process X (that is, the portfolio that replicates the call option) has an initial value equal to $X(0) = C(0, S(0))$. The next day the stock falls to $S(1) = 55.3750$. Taf's portfolio now has the value

$$X(1) = X(0) + \Delta(0)[S(1) - S(0)] = 2.1660$$

The new delta is computed using the new values $S(1) = 55.3750$ and $T - 1 = 19/252$, and is found to be $\Delta(1) = 0.5483$. The new delta is less than the old delta, which means Taf has to sell $\Delta(0) - \Delta(1)$ shares of the stock and deposit the proceeds in the bank. The next day $S(2) = 55.4375$, and the wealth value is

$$X(2) = X(1) + \Delta(1)[S(2) - S(1)] = 2.2003$$

Taf continues to trade this way every day until maturity. Taf also computes the theoretical value of the option for each day (this may not agree with the actual price for which the option is traded in the market). We see in figure 9.8 that the wealth process value follows closely the computed option value. In particular, at maturity, the option ends up in the money, and it is worth $S(19) - 55 = 13.8125$ dollars, which is the amount Taf has to deliver. At that time, the hedging or replicating portfolio includes one full share of the stock. The portfolio has the value $X(T) = \$13.6556$. So, in this particular transaction Taf loses $13.8125 - 13.6556 = 0.1569$ dollars. If, instead, Taf had not hedged the option position, there would have been a revenue of \$2.2715 for selling the option and a payment of \$13.8125 at maturity, leading to a substantially larger loss of \$11.5410.

   As we mentioned, in practice Taf would charge a price higher than the theoretical price of the option. In addition to charging a fee for the financial intermediary service, Taf would also like to have a protective cash "buffer" in case there is a difference between the value of the replicating portfolio and the payoff of the option, as in the example we just considered. In Problem 16 you are asked to repeat this example for a put option and with different values for σ and K.

Time	Stock Price	Call Price	Delta	Wealth
0	55.5625	2.2715	0.5629	2.2715
1	55.3750	2.1176	0.5483	2.1660
2	55.4375	2.1009	0.5539	2.2003
3	56.5625	2.7256	0.6481	2.8235
4	59.1250	4.5831	0.8268	4.4841
5	60.3125	5.5702	0.8899	5.4659
6	61.3125	6.4562	0.9313	6.3558
7	60.6250	5.7970	0.9166	5.7155
8	62.6875	7.7346	0.9724	7.6060
9	61.2500	6.3360	0.9507	6.2082
10	63.2500	8.2681	0.9873	8.1095
11	64.1875	9.1933	0.9953	9.0351
12	64.2500	9.2531	0.9972	9.0973
13	65.0000	10.0007	0.9992	9.8452
14	63.0000	8.0025	0.9974	7.8467
15	64.1875	9.1877	0.9997	9.0310
16	65.8125	10.8125	1.0000	10.6556
17	68.2500	13.2500	1.0000	13.0931
18	68.1250	13.1250	1.0000	12.9681
19	68.8125	13.8125	1.0000	13.6556

Figure 9.8
Replication experiment using Black-Scholes hedging on real data. The replicating wealth process closely follows the option value process.

9.3.5 Other Greeks

Option prices, or more generally, portfolio values, are sensitive to changes in many variables, not just the price of the underlying. This leads practitioners to consider the first and second derivatives of the option value with respect to those parameters, and use them similarly as the delta of an option or a portfolio. These derivatives are usually denoted by greek letters, and are known as **Greeks.** The standard Greeks for a portfolio with value X are

- **Delta:** $\Delta = \frac{\partial}{\partial s} X$
- **Theta:** $\Theta = \frac{\partial}{\partial t} X$
- **Gamma:** $\Gamma = \frac{\partial^2}{\partial s^2} X$
- **Vega:** $\mathcal{V} = \frac{\partial}{\partial \sigma} X$
- **rho:** $\rho = \frac{\partial}{\partial r} X$

where we have used the standard notation for the parameters of the Black-Scholes formula. In the Merton-Black-Scholes model an option or a portfolio value X depends only on the variables t and s (since σ and r are assumed constant); hence its Taylor series expansion is given by

$$X(t + \Delta t, s + \Delta s) = X(t, s) + \frac{\partial X(t, s)}{\partial s} \Delta S + \frac{\partial X(t, s)}{\partial t} \Delta t + \frac{1}{2} \frac{\partial^2 X(t, s)}{\partial s^2} \Delta S^2$$

$$+ \frac{1}{2} \frac{\partial^2 X(t, s)}{\partial t^2} \Delta t^2 + \frac{\partial^2 X(t, s)}{\partial s \partial t} \Delta S \Delta t + \cdots \qquad (9.12)$$

where

$$\Delta S = S(t + \Delta t) - S(t)$$

If we ignore the terms of order higher than Δt because they are small (although we have to keep the term involving ΔS^2, as in Ito's rule), we get the approximation

$$X(t + \Delta t, s + \Delta s) \approx X(t, s) + \Delta \cdot \Delta s + \Theta \cdot \Delta t + \tfrac{1}{2} \Gamma \cdot \Delta S^2 \qquad (9.13)$$

We see that we can reduce the variability of the portfolio by making Δ and Γ small. We cannot make Θ small directly, because this is the rate of change with respect to time and time changes no matter what. In fact, from the Black-Scholes partial differential equation (7.9), for an option with price $C(t, s)$ we have

$$\Theta + \frac{1}{2} \sigma^2 s^2 \Gamma + r(s\Delta - C) = 0 \qquad (9.14)$$

Thus the value of Θ is fixed once we fix the values of Δ and Γ, and it cannot be controlled independently of them. We also see that the only second derivative that is relevant to the approximate hedging is the one with respect to S, namely, the gamma of the option. The intuition for why gamma is important is the following: gamma is the rate of change of delta with respect to S, and delta is the number of shares in the replicating portfolio; hence, gamma is the rate of change of the replicating portfolio holdings with respect to changes in S; in other words, if gamma is high we have to rebalance more frequently in order to hedge against the movements of S. Gamma is a measure of the risk the hedger faces as a result of not rebalancing frequently.

If the portfolio X is delta-neutral, then equation (9.13) gives

$$\Delta X \approx \Theta \Delta t + \tfrac{1}{2} \Gamma \Delta S^2$$

Suppose that Θ is small. In that case, from this equation we see that a delta-neutral portfolio that is **gamma positive** is likely to increase in value no matter whether the stock price goes up or down, because gamma is multiplied by the square of the stock-price change. And the other way round, if a delta-neutral portfolio is **gamma negative,** it is likely to decrease in value no matter what the price of the underlying asset does. In this sense, it is good to be gamma positive.

9.3.6 Stochastic Volatility and Interest Rate

If the volatility σ and the interest rate r are also variable factors (arguably, they are stochastic in reality), then a portfolio value would depend on these variables, too. It would be a function $X(t, s, \sigma, r)$. The Taylor expansion of this function is

$$
\begin{aligned}
X(t + \Delta t, s + \Delta s, \sigma + \Delta\sigma, r + \Delta r) = X(t, s, \sigma, r) &+ \frac{\partial X}{\partial s}\Delta s + \frac{\partial X}{\partial \sigma}\Delta\sigma + \frac{\partial X}{\partial r}\Delta r \\
&+ \frac{\partial X}{\partial t}\Delta t + \frac{1}{2}\frac{\partial^2 X}{\partial s^2}\Delta S^2 + \frac{1}{2}\frac{\partial^2 X}{\partial \sigma^2}\Delta\sigma^2 \\
&+ \frac{1}{2}\frac{\partial^2 X}{\partial r^2}\Delta r^2 + \cdots
\end{aligned}
$$

We now have to worry about making vega and rho small, too. Although the Merton-Black-Scholes model assumes that r and σ are constant, in reality they change, and even if traders rely on the Merton-Black-Scholes model, they still use ρ and $\mathcal{V}$ as indicators of the sensitivity of the portfolio value with respect to changes in r and σ.

The following example exhibits a hedging strategy that deals with the types of risks we have discussed.

Example 9.2 (Hedging Using Greeks)   Denote by Γ the gamma of portfolio X, and by Γ_C the gamma of a contingent claim C. Taf wants to buy or sell n contracts of C in order to make the portfolio gamma-neutral. That is, Taf wants

$$\Gamma + n\Gamma_C = 0$$

hence

$$n = -\frac{\Gamma}{\Gamma_C}$$

However, taking this additional position in C will change the delta of the portfolio. Taf can then buy or sell some shares of the underlying asset in order to make the portfolio delta-neutral. This action does not change the gamma, because the underlying asset S has zero gamma. (Why?).

As an example, consider a delta-neutral portfolio X that has a gamma $\Gamma = -5,000$. A traded option has $\Delta_C = 0.4$ and $\Gamma_C = 2$. Taf does not like negative gamma and buys $n = 5,000/2 = 2,500$ option contracts, making the portfolio gamma-neutral. This step makes the delta of the portfolio equal to

$$\Delta_X = 2,500 \cdot 0.4 = 1,000$$

Thus Taf has to sell 1,000 shares of the underlying asset to keep the portfolio delta-neutral.

If Taf wants to make a portfolio vega-neutral, in addition to delta-neutral and gamma-neutral, then it is necessary to hold two different contingent claims written on the underlying asset. In this case Taf wants to have

$$\Gamma + n_1 \Gamma_1 + n_2 \Gamma_2 = 0$$

$$\mathcal{V} + n_1 \mathcal{V}_1 + n_2 \mathcal{V}_2 = 0$$

where n_i, Γ_i, and $\mathcal{V}_i$ are the number of contracts, the gamma, and the vega of claim i. This is a system of two equations with two unknowns that can typically be solved. At the end, Taf still has to adjust the number of shares in the new portfolio in order to make it delta-neutral, as before.

9.3.7   Formulas for Greeks

To conclude, we list here the formulas for Greeks of the European call option, in the Merton-Black-Scholes model:

$$\Delta = N(d_1)$$

$$\Theta = -\frac{sN'(d_1)\sigma}{2\sqrt{T-t}} - rKe^{-r(T-t)}N(d_2)$$

$$\Gamma = \frac{N'(d_1)}{s\sigma\sqrt{T-t}}$$

$$\mathcal{V} = s\sqrt{T-t}N'(d_1)$$

$$\rho = K(T-t)e^{-r(T-t)}N(d_2)$$

9.3.8   Portfolio Insurance

The protective put strategy that we discussed before provides a hedge against the drop in the value of the underlying asset. When an investor holds simultaneously the asset and a put on that asset, if the price of the asset drops below the strike price, the investor exercises the put and keeps the strike price. The strike price provides a floor (lower bound) to the value of the portfolio.

This strategy can be useful to institutions that have a large portfolio of assets and want to hedge downside risk (for example, mutual funds). They can achieve this purpose in two ways. First, they could buy puts on the assets. But these puts could be very expensive, or the desired type of puts might not be available (the maturity of the existing puts may not match the horizon of the investor). Alternatively, they can try to replicate a put whose underlying is the value of the portfolio, using dynamic hedging. The difference with our previous example of dynamic hedging is that the objective was to offset a short position in an option by replicating a long position in the same option. In the case of portfolio insurance, the objective is to replicate a position equivalent to a long position in the put, in addition to holding the portfolio of assets.

Replicating a put would involve shorting a certain amount of assets in the portfolio and having a long position in the risk-free asset. And it would also require constant rebalancing of the positions, since replicating strategies are dynamic strategies. In order to avoid transaction costs associated with frequent rebalancing, it may be cheaper to take short positions in futures contracts on the assets in the portfolio (or on an index correlated with the whole portfolio), since trading in futures generally involves smaller transaction costs than trading in the shares of the underlying asset. This strategy of "creating" a **synthetic put** on the portfolio value is called **portfolio insurance,** and it was used by many institutions in the United States in the 1980s. However, during a sudden drop in value of the U.S. market (the crash of October 1987), it turned out to be impossible to continue rebalancing the strategy in the required way, leading to big losses for the companies following the strategy. A major reason for these is the **loss of liquidity** that arises during a sudden market downturn— it is difficult to sell large quantities of assets (or take short positions in futures contracts on the assets) when the market is crashing. In fact, the attempt by all those companies to sell huge amounts of assets (or take short positions in futures) only made things worse and contributed to the market downturn: when the price of the underlying drops, the delta of the put also drops (increases in absolute value), with the result that in order to update the portfolio that replicates the put it is necessary to sell more of the underlying. Theoretically, replication is possible only in markets that are complete. A market that is not liquid and that experiences a sudden jump in prices is incomplete, and perfect replication is impossible.

9.4   Perfect Hedging in a Multivariable Continuous-Time Model

We now look at an extension of the Merton-Black-Scholes model to the case of a random volatility process $\sigma(t)$ and a random interest-rate process $r(t)$. However, we will still assume that markets are complete. Consider the following continuous-time model, driven by a one-dimensional, risk-neutral Brownian motion W^*:

$$dS(t) = S(t)[r(t)\,dt + \sigma(t)\,dW^*(t)]$$

$$dr(t) = a(t)\,dt + b(t)\,dW^*(t)$$

$$d\sigma(t) = c(t)\,dt + d(t)\,dW^*(t)$$

Here, $a(t)$, $b(t)$, $c(t)$, and $d(t)$ are, in general, functions of the current values of $S(t)$, $r(t)$, and $\sigma(t)$.

This is a continuous-time diffusion model, in which the price of an option C is a function $C(t, S(t), \sigma(t), r(t))$ of the random variables in the model. Even though the volatility and the interest rate are random, in this model the market is complete, since there is one risky asset S and one Brownian motion. If the option price C is a smooth function, using the multidimensional Itô's rule (3.62) on C and then discounting, the discounted option price $\bar{C}$ satisfies

$$d\bar{C} = [\ldots]\, dt + \left[\frac{\partial C}{\partial s} S\bar{\sigma} + \frac{\partial C}{\partial \sigma}\bar{d} + \frac{\partial C}{\partial r}\bar{b} \right] dW^*$$

In fact, since $\bar{C}$ has to be a martingale under the risk-neutral measure, the dt term has to be zero. However, the replicating wealth process X and the replicating portfolio π satisfy

$$d\bar{X} = \bar{\pi}\sigma\, dW^*$$

Comparing the two expressions, we see that **the portfolio that perfectly replicates C in this diffusion model with complete markets** is given by

$$\pi(t) = \sigma^{-1}(t) \left[\frac{\partial C}{\partial s} S(t)\sigma(t) + \frac{\partial C}{\partial \sigma} d(t) + \frac{\partial C}{\partial r} b(t) \right] \tag{9.15}$$

We see that the replicating (or hedging) portfolio is determined by Greeks other than just the delta of the option. In the special case of deterministic σ and r, in particular, with $b \equiv d \equiv 0$, we recover the Black-Scholes expression

$$\pi(t) = \frac{\partial C}{\partial s} S(t) = \Delta_C(t) S(t)$$

9.5 Hedging in Incomplete Markets

In general, perfect replication of a contingent claim C when markets are incomplete is not possible. Nevertheless, a trader can still try to set up a portfolio that is neutral with respect to relevant Greeks. An alternative strategy is to try to make the payoff $X(T)$ of the hedging portfolio as close as possible to the payoff C at maturity T of the claim. For example, a mathematically convenient formulation is to try to minimize the **quadratic error**

$$E[\{C - X^{x,\pi}(T)\}^2]$$

over all possible trading strategies π, starting with initial capital x. It is usually impossible to find nice explicit solutions to this problem. However, it can be done numerically in

many models. It is a problem of **stochastic optimization,** or **stochastic optimal control.**
In simple discrete-time models it can be formulated as an optimization problem of a **convex**
programming type.

A disadvantage of this formulation is that the profits are penalized in the same way as the
losses. A formulation that penalizes the losses only requires minimizing the expected loss

$$E[(C - X^{x,\pi}(T))^+]$$

The writer of the option loses money only if the payoff C is larger than the amount $X(T)$
in the hedging portfolio, so that the loss is the positive part of the difference $C - X(T)$.

More generally, we can formulate the hedging problem as the minimization of

$$E[L(C, X^{x,\pi}(T))]$$

where $L(c, x)$ is some loss function, appropriately defined. Or, in the tradition of the utility
theory, we can try to maximize expected utility

$$E[U(X^{x,\pi}(T) - C)]$$

of the profit we make, where U is a utility function.

Summary

Hedging is a trading activity that aims at reducing the risk of positions held by a market
participant. The simplest tool for hedging is futures contracts. In some cases trading in
futures can provide a perfect hedge, while in others, because of the mismatches in maturity
or the type of assets to be hedged, we are forced to cross-hedge using futures contracts
correlated with the prices of assets in which we have positions we want to hedge, or by
rolling the hedge forward. In such cases we say that there is a basis risk. In the case of
quantity uncertainty, hedging with futures can have unexpected features because of the
effect of the size of the contract on its price.

Call and put options can be used to create different payoff patterns at maturity. Using
combinations of calls and puts with names like butterfly spread, straddle, or strangle, profit
is made if the price of the underlying asset stays in a certain area or moves into an area, and
otherwise there is a loss.

A portfolio of assets is sensitive to various type of risks, such as changes in interest rate,
volatility, price of the assets underlying option contracts, and so on. The rates of change of
the portfolio value with respect to changes in various market variables are usually denoted by
Greek letters and thus called Greeks. For an option contract, the most important sensitivity is
the sensitivity with respect to the underlying asset, called delta. In order to make a portfolio

immune to the risk of the change in the underlying asset, we have to make it delta-neutral; that is, we want to keep delta small. In a perfect Black-Scholes market, we can completely get rid of the risk of an option position by delta hedging, that is, by keeping exactly delta shares of the underlying in the hedging portfolio. In practice, however, the portfolio may be exposed to other types of risks, such as interest-rate risk and volatility risk. In such cases, we have to consider other Greeks when constructing a hedge.

Perfect hedging is impossible in incomplete markets. Instead, we can try to accomplish approximate hedging. For example, we may want to make our portfolio value as close as possible to a given target value at a given date in the future. Such an approach typically requires use of numerical methods for optimization.

Problems

1. Suppose company A today enters a contract with company B for delivering 10,000 units of commodity c three months from today. Company A wants to hedge the risk of this position. Unfortunately, there is no futures market for commodity c. There is, however, a futures market for commodity d that includes a futures contract with maturity of three months. Suppose that it is found from historical data that the standard deviation of the commodity-c price is $\sigma_c = 0.02$, the standard deviation of the commodity-d three-month futures price is $\sigma_d = 0.01$, and the correlation between the two is 0.8. Find the hedging strategy with the minimal variance, and compute this minimal variance.

†2. Show that the payoff given by equation (9.6) is, indeed, equal to the payoff of the butterfly spread. Also show that the butterfly spread can be created by buying a put option with a low strike price, buying another put option with a high strike price, and selling two put options with the strike price in the middle.

3. Show that the payoffs of the bull spread and the bear spread can be created by selling and buying (a) call options and (b) put options. In other words, find an expression analogous to equation (9.6) for these options, and repeat the previous problem.

†4. The stock of the pharmaceutical company "Pills Galore" is trading at $103. The European calls and puts with strike price $100 and maturity in one month trade at $5.60 and $2.20, respectively. In the next three weeks the FDA will announce its decision about an important new drug the company would like to commercialize. You estimate that if the decision is positive the stock will jump to above $110, and if the decision is negative it will drop below $95. Is it possible to construct a strategy that will yield a profit if your estimates are correct? Explain.

5. The stock of "Scheme.com" is trading at $57. The price of a three-month T-bill is $98.5. A straddle with three-month European options with strike price $55 will have a positive

profit (the straddle payoff minus the straddle price) if the price of the stock is higher than $66.175 or lower than $43.825. Compute the price of the three-month European calls and puts with strike price $55.

†6. Consider a two-period binomial model with a stock that trades at $100. Each period the stock can go up 25% or down 20%. The interest rate is 10%. Your portfolio consists of one share of the stock. You want to trade so that the value of your modified portfolio will not drop below $90 at the end of the second period. Describe the steps to be taken in order to achieve this goal. Only the stock and the bank account are available for trading.

7. Repeat the previous problem, except that the stock can go up 20% or drop 5%. You want to guarantee that the value of your modified portfolio will not drop below $110 at the end of the second period.

8. In the context of section 9.3.1, perform the hedging of the corresponding put option, first in the single-period model, then in the two-period model.

9. Consider a binomial model with one period. The stock price is 100, and after one period it can go up to 115 or down to 90. The price of a European put with strike price 100 that matures at the end of the period is 5.5. Compute the portfolio that hedges a short position in the put (i.e., replicates the put).

†10. Consider a binomial model with a stock with starting price of $100. Each period the stock can go up 5% or drop 3%. An investment bank sells for $0.80 a European call option on the stock that matures after five periods and has a strike price of $120. Interest rate per period is 2%. Describe the steps to be taken by the investment bank in order to start hedging this short position at the moment the option is sold.

11. Suppose that the stock price today is $S(t) = 10$, the interest rate is $r = 0\%$, and the time to maturity is 0.5 years. Consider an option whose Black-Scholes price is given by the function

$$C(t, s) = s^2 e^{2(T-t)}$$

where time is in annual terms. If your portfolio is long 10 of these options and long or short N shares of the stock, what should the value of N be so that the portfolio is delta-neutral?

†12. In the previous problem suppose that another option with the same maturity is available with the Black-Scholes price given by the function

$$c(t, s) = s^3 e^{6(T-t)}$$

If you still hold 10 units of the first option, how many options of the second type and how many shares of the stock would you buy or sell to make a portfolio both delta-neutral and gamma-neutral (gamma equal to zero)?

13. Verify expression (9.10) for the delta of a call by differentiating the call price function (9.7). It will be helpful to recall that $N(\cdot)$ is a function corresponding to the standard normal distribution density; hence

$$\frac{d}{dx} N(x) = \frac{1}{\sqrt{2\pi}} e^{-\frac{x^2}{2}}$$

14. The delta of the call option is given by $N(d_1)$. Verify that the the delta of the put option is given by $N(d_1) - 1$, using the put-call parity.

15. You buy a put option with $N(d_1) = 0.7$, $K = 60$, $S(0) = 58$, and interest rate r $= 5\%$. How many shares of the stock should you buy or sell to have a delta-neutral position, that is, to have the delta of the portfolio equal to zero? You can use the solution to the previous problem.

*16. Produce tables analogous to the table in figure 9.8 for put options with strike prices $K = 50, 55, 60$. For $K = 55$, produce the tables for $\sigma = 0.31, 0.33$. What is the total profit or loss for Taf in each case? You can produce these tables in Excel, for example (see the book's web page).

17. What is the gamma of a portfolio consisting of 10 shares of stock S?

18. Verify that the expressions given in the text for all the Greeks of the European call option in the Black-Scholes model are indeed correct.

19. A pension fund manages a large portfolio whose current value is $2.7 billion. The value of the portfolio is assumed to satisfy the Black-Scholes model, with $\sigma = 0.25$. The interest rate is $r = 0.06$. For simplicity, we assume zero dividend rate. Taf, the skilled fund manager, wants to protect the portfolio by replicating a put option on its value, with strike price $K = 2.5$ billion and maturity $T = 1$ year. What amount does Taf have to sell from the portfolio today, or add to the portfolio, in order to start replicating the put option?

†20. The Black-Scholes price of a three-month European call with strike price 100 on a stock that trades at 95 is 1.33, and its delta is 0.3. The price of a three-month pure discount risk-free bond (nominal 100) is 99. You sell the option for 1.50 and hedge your position. One month later (the hedge has not been adjusted), the price of the stock is 97, the market price of the call is 1.41, and its delta is 0.36. You liquidate the portfolio (buy the call and undo the hedge). Assume a constant, continuous risk-free interest rate and compute the net profit or loss resulting from the trade.

21. You take a short position in 100 European call option contracts, with strike price $50 and maturity three months, on a stock that is trading at $52. The annual volatility of the stock is constant and equal to 22%. The annual, continuous risk-free interest rate is constant and equal to 5%. Suppose that you sold the options at a premium of 10% over the Black-Scholes

price. You hedge your portfolio with the underlying stock and the risk-free asset. The hedge is rebalanced weekly. After two weeks the portfolio is liquidated. Compute the final profit or loss if the price of the stock is $53.50 at the end of the first week and $51.125 at the end of the second week. Assume that one week is exactly $1/52$ year.

Further Readings

Good descriptions of trading strategies with options can be found in Hull (2002). For the basics on portfolio insurance see Leland (1980) and Leland and Rubinstein (1981). A more advanced (equilibrium) model is in Basak (1995). For the Metallgesellschaft case discussed in this chapter see Miller and Culp (1994).

10 Bond Hedging

In this chapter we consider the problem of measuring and hedging the risk of a portfolio of bonds. Prices of bonds are the result of three factors: the likelihood of default, the term structure of interest rates, and the time left until maturity or coupon payments. Time changes gradually and in a totally predictable way, so there is basically no risk associated with the last factor. We will ignore the risk of default and will focus on "risk-free bonds." Treasury securities constitute the only type of bonds that are considered completely free of default risk. The price risk of this type of bonds depends exclusively on interest rates. The approach we will use in this chapter is to consider bonds as derivatives whose underlying variable is the interest rate. A peculiarity of this underlying variable is that it is not directly traded in the markets (unlike the underlying of plain vanilla stock options, for example). Otherwise, the measures of risk used in bond portfolios are similar to those used for options (although they have different names). In the first section of this chapter we consider the main risk measure for bonds, called **duration.** Then we describe risk-hedging strategies. In bond management, this approach is called **immunization.** We finally study the measure of the second-order risk or **convexity.**

10.1 Duration

We first explore the notion of **Macaulay duration** for measuring interest-rate risk, introduced in Macaulay (1938). Although it is based on several restrictive assumptions, its simplicity and the fact that it captures the main factor that affects the bond price volatility make it the fundamental tool for bond portfolio management.

10.1.1 Definition and Interpretation

We first focus on the simplest case. Consider a default-free pure discount bond that will pay a nominal amount (say, $100) in exactly one period (for example, one year) from today. The one-year spot rate is r. Therefore, the price P of this bond is

$$P = \frac{100}{1+r} \tag{10.1}$$

An investor who holds the bond only has to worry about one type of risk, a possible change (more explicitly, an increase) in the interest rate. A small change ΔP in the price of the bond with respect to a small change in the interest rate Δr can be approximated as

$$\Delta P = \frac{\Delta P}{\Delta r} \cdot \Delta r \approx \frac{\partial P}{\partial r} \Delta r$$

Therefore, the natural measure of the risk of holding the bond is the derivative of the bond price with respect to the interest rate

$$\frac{\partial P}{\partial r} = -\frac{100}{(1+r)^2} = -\frac{P}{1+r} \tag{10.2}$$

We see that the effect on the price of the bond of an increase in the level of interest rate will be larger (in absolute value), the larger the price of the bond.

We can easily extend the same type of analysis to a pure discount bond that has several periods, say, T, to maturity. Suppose that the T-period spot rate is r. The price of the bond is

$$P = \frac{100}{(1+r)^T} \tag{10.3}$$

and its sensitivity to a change in the interest rate is

$$\frac{\partial P}{\partial r} = -T\frac{100}{(1+r)^{T+1}} = -T\frac{P}{1+r} \tag{10.4}$$

which is, of course, similar to equation (10.2), but with the additional factor of time left to maturity. That is, the price of a bond is more sensitive to a change in interest rates, the longer its maturity.

In practice, as we discussed in the introductory chapters, most of the bonds pay coupons. Consider a bond that pays coupons of size C_i at the end of each period, for T periods (we assume that the final coupon C_T includes the principal). Suppose further that the corresponding rates are denoted by $r_i, i = 1, 2, \ldots, T$, so that the price of the bond is

$$P = \sum_{i=1}^{T} \frac{C_i}{(1+r_i)^i} \tag{10.5}$$

We see that we cannot extend in a straightforward manner the analysis we performed for pure discount bonds, since the price of the bond is determined by a collection of interest rates that change with time. However, in practice, interest rates for different maturities are highly correlated, and they frequently (although not always) move in parallel; that is, if the one-year spot rate goes up, so does the five-year spot rate, for example. The problem is, then, to find a single number that will be a good representation of the whole term structure and whose changes will be a good summary of changes in the term structure. The obvious candidate is the **yield** or **internal rate of return** of the bond, as defined in the introductory chapters. We recall that the yield of our bond is the number y that satisfies

$$P = \sum_{i=1}^{T} \frac{C_i}{(1+y)^i} \qquad (10.6)$$

Comparing equations (10.5) and (10.6), it is clear that the yield depends only on the rates r_i that affect the price of the bond. For example, if all the rates r_i go up, the yield y also goes up. Then, similarly to our analysis of risk for pure discount bonds, we consider the derivative of the coupon bond with respect to its yield:

$$\frac{\partial P}{\partial y} = -\sum_{i=1}^{T} i \frac{C_i}{(1+y)^{i+1}} = -\frac{P}{1+y} \sum_{i=1}^{T} i \frac{\frac{C_i}{(1+y)^i}}{P} \qquad (10.7)$$

where the second equality is simply the result of multiplying and dividing by P. The second factor of equation (10.7) is called **duration** or **Macaulay duration.**

DEFINITION 10.1   The duration of a bond is a measure of the sensitivity of the bond to interest rate movements. More explicitly, the duration D of a bond that pays coupons C_i and has yield y and maturity T is given by

$$D := \sum_{i=1}^{T} i \frac{\frac{C_i}{(1+y)^i}}{P} \qquad (10.8)$$

It is clear from equation (10.7) that the sensitivity of a bond to interest-rate changes (measured through the changes in y) is larger, the larger the duration of the bond. The holder of a bond with high duration has more interest-rate-risk exposure than the holder of a bond with low duration.

From the duration formula (10.8) we can derive some intuition about this measure. The duration is a weighted average of all the time points i at which the bond makes a payment. For example, if the bond has a maturity of five years, $T = 5$, and it makes annual coupon payments, the duration will be a weighted average of the numbers $1, 2, 3, 4,$ and 5, which are the time points at which the coupon payments take place. Each of these numbers is assigned a weight $\frac{1}{P} \frac{C_i}{(1+y)^i}$. These are indeed true weights, as they add up to one, because

$$\sum_{i=1}^{T} \frac{C_i}{(1+y)^i} = P$$

The weight corresponding to time point i is the proportion of the value of the bond that corresponds to the payment received at i. This average places more weight on the time points that are more important for the value of the bond. For example, a bond that pays low coupons initially and large coupons later on will have higher duration than a bond that pays high coupons early and low coupons later. The extreme case is a bond that makes a single payment at maturity, a pure discount bond. In this case, all the weight is placed on the moment at which the single payment takes place, and *the duration of the pure discount bond is equal to its maturity*. The duration of a bond can be no higher than its maturity. The duration of a coupon bond is always lower than the duration of a pure discount bond with the same maturity.

In general, we can say that *the duration is to a coupon bond what maturity is to a zero-coupon bond.*

Example 10.1 (Computing Durations)   Consider a bond with a nominal value of $100 that pays a coupon of $8 at the end of each year and has five years left until maturity. Suppose that the yield of this bond is 5%. The price of the bond is

$$P = \sum_{i=1}^{5} \frac{8}{1.05^i} + \frac{100}{1.05^5} = 112.99$$

The duration of the bond is

$$D = \sum_{i=1}^{5} i \frac{\frac{8}{1.05^i}}{112.99} + 5\frac{\frac{100}{1.05^5}}{112.99} = 4.36$$

In this example, the duration of the bond is close to its maturity. However, this is only the case for relatively short-term bonds with relatively low coupons and relatively low interest rates. We illustrate this point with another example.

Example 10.2 (Different Yields)   Consider a bond with a nominal value of $100 that pays a coupon of $8 at the end of each year and has 30 years left until maturity. We first compute the duration for the case in which the yield of the bond is 5%. The price of the bond is

$$P = \sum_{i=1}^{30} i \frac{8}{1.05^i} + \frac{100}{1.05^{30}} = 146.12$$

The duration of the bond is

$$D = \sum_{i=1}^{30} i \frac{\frac{8}{1.05^i}}{146.12} + 5\frac{\frac{100}{1.05^{30}}}{146.12} = 14.82$$

We now compute the duration for a yield of 10%. The price of this bond is

$$P = \sum_{i=1}^{30} \frac{8}{1.1^i} + \frac{100}{1.1^{30}} = 81.15$$

The duration of this bond is

$$D = \sum_{i=1}^{30} i \frac{\frac{8}{1.1^i}}{81.15} + 5 \frac{\frac{100}{1.1^{30}}}{81.15} = 10.65$$

The duration decreases with the level of interest rates because the discounted value of the coupons is lower.

10.1.2 Duration and Change in Yield

Let us now make a connection between the duration and the derivative of the bond price with respect to the yield. As before, we have the approximation

$$\frac{\partial P}{\partial y} \approx \frac{\Delta P}{\Delta y} = \frac{\Delta P}{\Delta(1+y)} \tag{10.9}$$

where the denominator of the last fraction represents the change in $1 + y$, which is equal to the change in y. From equations (10.7), (10.8), and (10.9), we can see that, for a small change in y,

$$\frac{\Delta P}{\Delta(1+y)} \approx -D \frac{P}{1+y} \tag{10.10}$$

or

$$D \approx - \frac{\frac{\Delta P}{P}}{\frac{\Delta(1+y)}{1+y}} \tag{10.11}$$

The right-hand side of equation (10.11) is a standard notion in economics, called the **yield elasticity** of the price of the bond. In general, elasticity measures the proportional change in some economic variable as a result of a proportional change in a variable on which the former depends. In our particular case, expression (10.11) says that duration measures (approximately) the percentage change in price of a bond corresponding to a percentage change in $1 + y$.

Example 10.3 (Duration and Change in Bond Price)   Suppose that the duration of a bond is 5 and its yield is 6%. The investor holding this bond is worried about what will happen to its price if the yield increases to 7%, so that $1 + y$ increases from 1.06 to 1.07, which is close to 1%. From equation (10.11) the price of the bond will drop approximately 5%.

Since interest rates in general have relatively low values, an increase of y by 0.01 usually means an increase in $1 + y$ of approximately 1%. Therefore, the duration tells us the percentage drop in price we should expect as a result of an increase in interest rates of 1%.

As we have emphasized throughout this section, this analysis is only an approximation. In fact, it will be exact under two conditions:

· The term structure is **flat,** that is, all the spot rates are equal, $r_i = r$, for all i. In this case, the yield of any bond will be $y = r$, and it is an exact representation of the term structure.
· The term structure only experiences **parallel shifts;** that is, all the spot rates move by the same amount.

In practice, neither of these two conditions holds in general. As a result, alternative measures of duration have been suggested (see Gultekin and Rogalski, 1984, for a review of some of them). However, they are more complicated to compute and use, and they do not seem to work much better than the simple measure of duration of equation (10.8).

10.1.3   Duration of a Portfolio of Bonds

A very important observation for risk management is the fact that the concept of duration we have presented applies also to portfolios of bonds. That is, the price P we discussed earlier could be the price of a portfolio of risk-free bonds that will make payments C_i at times i, and we have the following useful property of duration that greatly simplifies the risk management of portfolios of bonds.

PROPOSITION 10.1   Suppose that the term structure is flat, so that the yield of all bonds is equal to the interest rate r. Then the duration of a portfolio of bonds is the weighted average of the bonds that are part of the portfolio. That is, consider a portfolio of bonds

$$P = \sum_{j=1}^{J} \alpha_j P_j$$

where α_j is the number (possibly negative, meaning short position) of the shares of bond P_j held in the portfolio. Then the duration of the portfolio is given by

$$D = \sum_{j=1}^{J} D_j \alpha_j \frac{P_j}{P} \qquad (10.12)$$

where D_j is the duration of bond P_j.

The reader is asked in Problem 2 to prove this result.

For hedging purposes, studied next, it is important to note that the duration changes as the yield and the time left to maturity change. Finally, we point out the similarity between the duration of a bond (or a portfolio of bonds) and the delta of an option (or a portfolio of options). Both parameters measure the sensitivity of a security or a portfolio to the changes in some underlying variable. In the same way that the delta of an option is the key measure used for hedging positions in options, duration is the key measure to hedge positions in bonds, as we see next.

10.2   Immunization

In this section we consider the problem of a portfolio manager whose portfolio consists exclusively of bonds and who is concerned about the interest-rate risk. The concept of a bond we consider here is a very broad one: by bonds we mean the right to receive given payments at future given dates. Of course, a pure discount bond falls in this category, but so does a bank loan, or any type of liability whose terms are completely specified and known in advance.

10.2.1   Matching Durations

A liability, that is, the obligation to pay a known amount at a future date, is equivalent to a short position in a pure discount bond maturing at that date. An example is an insurance company that collects insurance premiums and has to invest them so as to make future payments. The future payments of an insurance company are not predetermined but random. However, their total amount can often be accurately predicted.

A similar problem is faced by banks. Consider a bank that collects money from savings accounts that pay interest. The deposited amount is equivalent to a short position in a pure discount bond with maturity zero: at any moment, the depositor can withdraw the balance in the account, so the account is equivalent to a bond that matures immediately. (Typically, the depositor "renews" the investment by keeping the money in the account for some time.) Then, suppose that the bank invests the money by issuing a loan, say a 10-year mortgage at a fixed rate. If the interest on the savings account is 3% and the interest on the mortgage is 5%, the bank is poised to make a profit. Note that the bank has a portfolio of bonds: a short position in a bond with very short maturity (the savings account) and a long position in a coupon bond with long maturity (the mortgage). Suppose now that the interest rates in the economy go up and that, in order to be able to keep the deposits of its customers, the bank has to raise the interest to 6%. At that rate the bank will lose money. The interest-rate rise has affected the present value of the mortgage. The value of that mortgage is now lower because the future payments will be discounted at higher interest rates. The corresponding price P of equation (10.5) is lower.

The simplest solution for hedging this type of risk is the construction of a **dedicated portfolio.** The idea is to match the liabilities (the short positions in bonds) with the investments (the long position in bonds), so that the coupons in the long positions are identical in size and timing to the payments required by the liabilites. For example, the insurance company could invest its premiums in pure discount bonds with nominal values and maturities identical to the estimated liabilities.

However, a dedicated portfolio is not always feasible: the required pure discount bonds might not be available in the market; or, they might be available, but expensive, or too risky (and here we mean the risk of default). An alternative strategy for the bond portfolio manager is *to construct a long portfolio of bonds whose duration matches the duration of the portfolio of liabilities.*

The underlying idea of this strategy is the following. Suppose that the term structure is flat. Consider a manager who forms a portfolio consisting of a subportfolio of long bonds and a subportfolio of short bonds, so that they have the same initial value. The problem is that, as time goes by, the changes in interest rates can affect the values of these two subportfolios in different ways. The portfolio manager can address this risk by constructing a portfolio in which the interest-rate changes will have a similar effect on the subportfolio of long bonds and on the subportfolio of short bonds. This objective can be implemented by making sure that the durations of the two subportfolios are equal. From equation (10.7), if the prices P and the yields y of the subportfolios are equal, and if we make sure that the duration of the subportfolio of long bonds matches the duration of the subportfolio of short bonds, a small change in the term structure will have a similar impact on the value of both subportfolios, since their derivatives with respect to yield are the same. Furthermore, under the assumption of a flat term structure, it is straightforward to construct a portfolio with any target duration. We illustrate some of these points with an example.

Example 10.4 (Hedging by Immunization)   Suppose that the term structure is flat and the annual interest rate is 5%. We have a liability with a nominal value of $100, and the payment will take place in two years. In the market there are only two pure discount bonds: a one-year pure discount bond with nominal value $100 and a four-year pure discount bond with nominal value $100. We start with $90.70 in cash. We can check that this is the present value of the liability:

$$\frac{100}{1.05^2} = 90.70$$

In order to guarantee that we will be able to meet the payment in two years (approximately), we have to invest the money in a portfolio of bonds with the duration equal to the duration of the portfolio of short positions. In this case, there is only one liability with maturity in two years, equivalent to a short position in a pure discount bond with maturity in two years and, therefore, duration equal to two years. We want to invest in a portfolio with duration of two, as well. There are only two pure discount securities, with maturities (and, therefore, durations) equal to one and four. We take advantage of the property stated in proposition 10.1. We will invest a proportion α of the initial capital in the bond with duration 1 and the rest in the bond with duration 4. We solve

$$\alpha D_1 + (1 - \alpha)D_2 = \alpha + (1 - \alpha)4 = 2$$

The solution is $\alpha = 2/3$. Therefore, we invest $90.70 \times \frac{2}{3} = 60.47$ in the one-year bond and the rest, $90.70 - 60.47 = 30.23$, in the four-year bond. The price of the one-year bond is

$$\frac{100}{1.05} = 95.24$$

and therefore, we buy $60.47/95.24 = 0.63$ units of the one-year bond. Similarly, the price of the four-year bond is

$$\frac{100}{1.05^4} = 82.27$$

and we buy $30.23/82.27 = 0.37$ units of the four-year bond.

Suppose that immediately after investing in such a portfolio, interest rates go up to 6% (and the term structure remains flat). The present values of both the liability and the portfolio of bonds drop. The new values of the liability and the portfolio of bonds are

$$\frac{100}{1.06^2} = 89, \qquad 0.63\frac{100}{1.06} + 0.37\frac{100}{1.06^4} = 88.74$$

The drop in the value of the portfolio roughly matches the drop in the value of the liability.

Suppose now that, immediately after forming the portfolio of bonds, the interest rates drop to 4%. In this case, the value of the liability goes up. We hope that the value of the bonds will increase by roughly the same amount. The new values are

$$\frac{100}{1.04^2} = 92.46, \qquad 0.63\frac{100}{1.04} + 0.37\frac{100}{1.04^4} = 92.20$$

Again, the increase in the value of the portfolio approximately matches the increase in the value of the liability.

However, there are several problems with the previous analysis. First, this approach relies on the unrealistic assumptions that the term structure is flat and that all the interest-rate movements will be parallel shifts. This approach is valid as an approximation, but the quality of the approximation will depend on how close the term structure and its changes are to the assumptions.

Second, the duration changes as the interest rates move. Therefore, even if the durations match before an interest-rate jump, there is no guarantee they will match after the jump. We illustrate this problem in another example.

Example 10.5 (Change of Duration)   Consider the liability of the previous example and the portfolio of bonds formed for immunization purposes. Suppose that right after the portfolio of bonds is formed, the interest rates go down to 4%. As we computed in Example 10.4, the increase in the value of the portfolio will match the increase in the value of the liability. After the interest rate changes, the duration of the liability will still be equal to 2. However, the duration of the portfolio of bonds will not be equal to 2 anymore, since the relative weights of the securities will have changed. As we saw in Example 10.4, the new price of the portfolio of bonds is 92.20. The new weights of the one-year bond and the four-year bond are

$$\frac{0.63\frac{100}{1.04}}{92.20} = 0.66, \qquad \frac{0.37\frac{100}{1.04^4}}{92.20} = 0.34$$

The duration of the portfolio is

$$D = 0.66 \cdot 1 + 0.34 \cdot 4 = 2.02$$

The durations of the liability and the portfolio of bonds do not match anymore: the portfolio of bonds is more sensitive to an increase in interest rates and will lose more value than the liability if the rates go up.

In summary, similarly to the case of the delta of an option, duration is a dynamic variable. Hedging based on immunization requires a continuous adjustment of the portfolio. As with delta hedging, immunization guarantees that the values of the short and long positions move together "locally," that is, for a small change in the underlying and other independent variables. Beyond that situation, the portfolio is not immunized. This issue is related to the problem of convexity, which we discuss in section 10.3.

10.2.2   Duration and Immunization in Continuous Time

In some of the popular continuous-time models for bond interest rates (studied elsewhere in this book), there is a formula that relates the bond prices to the interest rate, and it is possible to compute explicitly the first derivative of the price of the bond with respect to the interest rate. Thus we can compute the continuous-time analogue of the duration. In general, for other models, it is possible to compute numerically the derivative of the price of a bond with respect to the interest rate or, in fact, to any other underlying factor. There are numerical techniques that can be used to compute this derivative, and they are described in the chapter on numerical methods (chapter 11), in the context of hedging options.

An advantage of using continuous-time models of the term structure as a starting point is that they typically do not result in a flat term structure or parallel shifts.

10.3   Convexity

The duration of a bond is a simple transformation of the derivative of the bond with respect to the yield. With the duration we try to measure the sensitivity of the price of the bond to a change in interest rates. In the previous sections we discussed the implicit assumptions in this approach: flat term structure and parallel shifts to the term structure. There is another problem, however, even if the previous two assumptions hold. By definition, the first derivative only measures "local" effects, that is, the price changes that result from an infinitesimal change in the yield value. However, in practice, interest rate changes are often relatively large, and the first derivative might not be a good approximation of their impact on the price of bonds. These are exactly the changes a portfolio manager is more concerned about.

Convexity is the measure of the error we are exposed to by using the first derivative to predict the impact of a change in interest rates on the price of a portfolio of bonds. If we consider the second derivative of the bond price with respect to yield, that is, if we take the derivative of the right-hand side of equation (10.7) with respect to the yield, we get

$$\frac{\partial^2 P}{\partial y^2} = \sum_{i=1}^{T} i(i+1) \frac{C_i}{(1+y)^{i+2}} \tag{10.13}$$

We see that it is positive, and therefore, the relationship between the price of a bond and its yield is convex. The stronger the convexity (the larger the second derivative), the larger the error we are exposed to by using the duration for immunization purposes.

The convexity is defined as

$$C = \frac{1}{P} \frac{\partial^2 P}{\partial y^2} \tag{10.14}$$

The improved approximation is obtained by including the second-order term in Taylor's expansion for the price:

$$\Delta P \approx -\frac{D}{1+y} P \Delta y + \frac{1}{2} C P (\Delta y)^2 \tag{10.15}$$

The comparison between the delta of a plain vanilla option and the duration of a bond can be extended to the gamma of an option and the convexity of a bond. In the same way that gamma is a measure of the stability of the delta of an option, convexity is a measure of the stability of duration. That is, as the interest rate changes, the duration of a bond changes. High convexity means that a shift of the term structure will have a relatively higher effect on duration of a bond. For example, a manager who has an immunized portfolio, but such that convexity of the short and long positions in bonds do not match, should expect that after a big shift in interest rates the portfolio will not be immunized anymore.

Summary

The most common everyday risk that bondholders face is the risk of the movement of interest rates in the market. These movements result in a change in a bond's yield, hence also in a change in the bond price. The change in the bond price for a given change in yield can be approximately predicted if we know the first derivative of the bond price with respect to the yield. The measure of this risk is expressed in terms of the first derivative, and it is called duration. It turns out that duration has another interpretation: it is equal to a weighted average of the times when the coupon payments are paid. Thus a coupon bond with duration equal to D is comparable to a zero-coupon bond with maturity equal to D.

Investors who face certain future payments as their liabilities can form a portfolio of bonds to be able to pay those amounts. Since duration approximately determines the change in the value of a portfolio of bonds, a bondholder can hedge, or immunize herself from the interest-rate risk by having a portfolio of bonds whose present value and duration are the same as the present value and duration of the liabilities. This method is called immunization, and it is similar to "delta-hedging" of options positions.

An even better estimate of the change in the bond price can be obtained by including the second derivative of the bond price with respect to the yield into the approximation formula. The related measure of risk is called convexity, because it measures how curved the price-yield curve is.

Problems

1. Compute the duration of a bond with a nominal value of $100 that pays a coupon of $3 every six months and has two years left until maturity. Suppose that the yield of the bond is 4%.

†2. Prove proposition 10.1.

3. Today is 01/01/02. On 06/30/03 we will have to make a payment of $100. We can only invest in a risk-free pure discount bond (nominal $100) that matures on 12/31/02 and in a risk-free coupon bond, nominal $100, that pays an annual coupon (on 12/31) of 8% on the nominal value, and matures on 12/31/04. Assume a flat term structure of 7%. How many units of each of the bonds should we buy in order to be immunized with respect to the duration?

4. In the context of the previous problem, suppose that right after the portfolio of bonds is formed, the interest rate goes up from 7% to 10%. Compute the new durations.

5. Suppose the term structure is flat, with $r = 6\%$. We have $5,000 in a checking account. One year from now we will have to make a payment of $5,300. The only risk-free bond in

the market is a two-year bond with nominal $100, paying semiannual coupons of 8% on the nominal value. The next coupon is to be paid in exactly six months. Describe the steps to be taken in order to be immunized with respect to the duration.

†6. Suppose that the annual interest rate is 4%. You have a liability with a nominal value of $300, and the payment will take place in two years. Construct the duration-immunizing portfolio that trades in two pure discount bonds: a one-year pure discount bond with nominal value $100 and a three-year pure discount bond with nominal value $100.

a. How many units of each bond should the portfolio hold?

b. If the rate drops to 3.5% after one year, is the value of all your positions at that time positive or negative? How much is it exactly?

7. Assume that the term structure is flat. Consider two pure discount bonds 1 and 2. Bond 1 matures in T years and bond 2 matures in $2T$ years. Is bond 2 "twice as sensitive to a 1% upward shift of the term structure" as bond 1?

†8. Consider a zero-coupon bond with nominal $100 and annual yield of 5%, with one year to maturity. You believe that after one week the yield will change from 5% to 5.5%. Find the expected change in the bond price in three ways:

a. Exactly, computing the new price

b. Approximately, using the initial duration

c. Approximately, using the initial duration and convexity

Further Readings

The notion of duration was introduced by Macaulay (1938). A discussion of its use for immunization purposes can be found in Bierwag (1977). Cox, Ingersoll, and Ross (1979) and Gultekin and Rogalski (1984) provide empirical studies on the use of different measures of duration for immunization purposes.

11 Numerical Methods

In practice it is very important to have efficient numerical methods for the computation of option prices and hedging strategies. For example, a company that needs a special option-type contract may ask several investment banks for a quote of the option price. The company may request an answer in a short period of time, and thereafter will buy the contract from the bank that has made the least expensive offer. Thus a bank has to be able to come up with a good estimate for the option price in a reasonably short period of time. It does not want to come up with too high a price because, in that case, the company will not buy the option from them. It does not want to come up with too low a price either, because then the likelihood of losing money becomes unacceptably high.

Another reason for the need for these methods is **risk management.** Banks are required by **regulatory agencies** to measure the risk of their positions on a regular basis. This risk is related to the values of options and other contracts the bank is involved with. Since there are hundreds of these contracts, a bank has to have efficient numerical methods to reevaluate them overnight.

In this chapter we describe the most popular numerical methods for finding prices of options. In particular, we discuss in more or less detail the following methods:

1. Binomial tree–based methods, which compute option prices by solving backward a binomial tree, or other types of trees.

2. Methods based on Monte Carlo simulation, which approximate the expected value of a random variable with the arithmetic average of its simulated values.

3. Finite-differences and other PDE methods, which compute values of a function satisfying the relevant partial differential equation when the PDE does not have an analytic solution.

11.1 Binomial Tree Methods

The binomial tree method computes an option price by solving backward a tree, computing the value of the option at each node of the tree.

11.1.1 Computations in the Cox-Ross-Rubinstein Model

We have already described how to compute option prices in the binomial Cox-Ross-Rubinstein model with one stock S and a bank account with constant continuous interest rate r. The numerical implementation is straightforward. Here we mention some additional details, relevant when conducting the numerical procedure. We denote by Δt the length of the time period between two time steps. We are given the model parameters $u > e^{r\Delta t}$ and $d < 1$, such that, during each time period, the stock $S(t)$ moves up to $uS(t)$ or down to $dS(t)$ with some probabilities p^* and $q^* := 1 - p^*$, respectively. For pricing options, we do not need to know the actual probabilities, but only the risk-neutral probabilities. Thus, p^* denotes the risk-neutral probability. We have computed p^* in equation (7.1) as

$$p^* = \frac{e^{r\Delta t} - d}{u - d}, \qquad q^* = \frac{u - e^{r\Delta t}}{u - d} \tag{11.1}$$

In addition, a common choice for u is

$$u = \frac{1}{d} \tag{11.2}$$

We need only one more condition to determine the numerical values of all the parameters. We derive this condition from the need to guarantee that the model is consistent with the volatility that we observe in the market: we estimate the value σ^2 of the variance of the stock's log-returns, $X_t := \log[S(t + \Delta t)/S(t)]$, per unit time, and we want to choose u so that in the model the variance of X_t equals the estimated variance. One reason why we use the variance of the log-returns is that it is a good approximation to the volatility of the continuous-time Merton-Black-Scholes model:

$$\text{Var}\left[\frac{dS(t)}{S(t)}\right] = \text{Var}[d \log S(t)] \approx \text{Var}[\log S(t + \Delta t) - \log S(t)] = \text{Var}\left[\log \frac{S(t + \Delta t)}{S(t)}\right]$$

We next analyze the implications of this restriction. On the interval of length Δt the estimated variance of the log-return X is $\sigma^2 \Delta t$. However, we can compute the theoretical variance as $\text{Var}[X] = E[X^2] - (E[X])^2$:

$$E[X] = E[\log\{S(t + \Delta t)/S(t)\}] = p \log u + (1 - p) \log d$$

$$E[X^2] = p(\log u)^2 + (1 - p)(\log d)^2$$

A short computation results in

$$\text{Var}[X] = p(\log u)^2 + (1 - p)(\log d)^2 - p^2(\log u)^2 - (1 - p)^2(\log d)^2$$
$$- 2p(1 - p) \log u \cdot \log d \tag{11.3}$$

The terms involving p^2, $(1 - p)^2$, and $p(1 - p)$ are small relative to p and $1 - p$ if p or $1 - p$ is small. Otherwise, if p is close to 0.5, these terms approximately cancel each other, since $\log d = -\log u$. In either case we can neglect them, and we see that the variance is approximately equal to

$$p(\log u)^2 + (1 - p)(\log d)^2$$

Since $d = 1/u$, we see that the variance is approximately $(\log u)^2$. We want this to be equal to the estimated variance:

$$(\log u)^2 = \sigma^2 \Delta t$$

This expression implies

$$u = e^{\sigma \sqrt{\Delta t}}, \qquad d = e^{-\sigma \sqrt{\Delta t}} \tag{11.4}$$

This is the choice of u and d suggested by Cox, Ross, and Rubinstein. This choice guarantees that the binomial model converges to the Merton-Black-Scholes model.

Example 11.1 (Pricing in a Tree)   As we did in Example 7.2, consider a Cox-Ross-Rubinstein model with continuously compounded interest rate $r = 0.05$, $S(0) = 100$, and $\sigma = 0.30$. The security we consider is an American at-the-money put option with strike price $K = S(0) = 100$. Suppose this is a six-month option, and we compute its price using two periods only, each of length three months, $\Delta t = 3/12 = 0.25$. In the Problems section the reader is asked to compute the price for smaller Δt, that is, for more time steps.

We have here

$$u = e^{\sigma \Delta t} = 1.0779, \qquad d = 1/u = 0.9277$$

The risk-neutral probability is

$$p^* = \frac{e^{r \Delta t} - d}{u - d} = 0.5650$$

We compute first the possible values of the stock prices at times 1 and 2, and payoff values $g(S(2)) = \max[100 - S(2), 0]$ at time 2. In figure 11.1, the values above the nodes are the stock price values, and the values below the nodes are the corresponding option values. For example, the lower two nodes at time 2 result in the stock prices 100 and 86.0708, hence the payoff values of 0 and 13.9292, respectively. At the previous node the stock price is 92.7743, so the payoff in the case of immediate exercise would be 7.2257.

We can now compute the option value at the previous node as

$$\max\{7.2257, e^{-r \Delta t}[p^* \cdot 0 + (1 - p^*) \cdot 13.9292]\} = \max\{7.2257, 5.9834\} = 7.2257$$

Similarly, the top two nodes at time 2 have an option payoff equal to 0, so that the top node at time 1 corresponds to the option value equal to

$$\max\{0, e^{-r \Delta t}[p^* \cdot 0 + (1 - p^*) \cdot 0]\} = 0$$

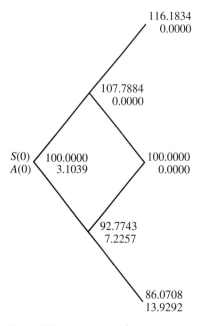

Figure 11.1
Computing an American option price in the two-period CRR model.

Finally, from the option values at time 1, we compute the time-0 option price as

$$\max\{0, e^{-r\Delta t}[p^* \cdot 0 + (1 - p^*) \cdot 7.2257]\} = 3.1039$$

From the holder's point of view, the option should not be exercised immediately at time 0 because it would pay zero; the holder should exercise at time 1 if the stock goes down, because the option pays 7.2257, which is larger than the value 5.9834 of waiting. The holder should not exercise at time 1 if the stock goes up, because the payoff is zero.

11.1.2 Computing Option Sensitivities

For hedging and risk management purposes it is important to be able to compute, at least approximately, the derivatives of the option price with respect to the parameters and variables in the model, such as σ, r, t, $S(0)$, and K. These derivatives measure how sensitive the option price is to the change in the value of the corresponding parameters.

For illustration purposes, we concentrate on the **delta** of the option, that is, the derivative with respect to the initial stock price $s = S(0)$. In other words, denoting by $C(s)$ the option price as a function of the initial underlying value s, we want to compute

$$\Delta_C := \frac{d}{ds} C(s) \tag{11.5}$$

One direct way of doing so is to compute $C(s)$ and compute $C(s + \Delta s)$ for some small Δs, and then approximate the delta by the **finite difference**

$$\Delta_C \approx \frac{C(s + \Delta s) - C(s)}{\Delta s} \tag{11.6}$$

The binomial model can be used for this purpose, as well as any other model in which we can compute the prices $C(s)$ and $C(s + \Delta s)$; see the Problems section.

The disadvantage of this method is that it requires building a new tree for the computation of $C(s + \Delta s)$. Another way to approximate the delta using only the original tree is

$$\Delta_C \approx \frac{C^u - C^d}{S(0)u - S(0)d} \tag{11.7}$$

where C^u and C^d are the option prices at the nodes after the first time period, C^u is the price corresponding to the stock price $S(0)u$, and C^d is the price corresponding to the stock price $S(0)d$. Actually, this is an estimate of delta at time Δt, not at the initial time 0, but it is nevertheless used in practice. In Example 11.1, the value of delta using this method would be estimated as

$$\Delta_C = (0 - 7.2257)/(107.7884 - 92.7743) = -0.4813$$

11.1.3   Extensions of the Tree Method

Variations on the basic tree approach are sometimes used. We discuss two of them. The first is the tree in which the risk-neutral probability is

$$p^* = 0.5$$

Hence this probability is independent of the number of time steps or volatility. Then we adjust the other parameters of the model so that the no-arbitrage conditions are satisfied and so that we match some properties of the real data. In particular, in this case we do not require $u = 1/d$, but instead we set

$$u = e^{(r-\sigma^2)\Delta t + \sigma\sqrt{\Delta t}}, \qquad d = e^{(r-\sigma^2)\Delta t - \sigma\sqrt{\Delta t}} \tag{11.8}$$

It is then easily verified that the variance condition (11.3) is satisfied. Second, the martingale condition

$$E^*[e^{-r\Delta t}S(\Delta t)] = S(0)$$

gives

$$p^*u + (1 - p^*)d = e^{r\Delta t}$$

Using expression (11.8), this condition would look like

$$e^{r\Delta t} = e^{r\Delta t}\left(\tfrac{1}{2}e^{-\sigma^2\Delta t+\sigma\sqrt{\Delta t}} + \tfrac{1}{2}e^{\sigma^2\Delta t+\sigma\sqrt{\Delta t}}\right) \tag{11.9}$$

In the Problems you are asked to show that the expression in the parentheses is approximately equal to one, for small Δt. You are also asked to compute option prices using this method.

Another popular variation is the **trinomial tree** approach. In this case the stock price can stay at the same level in the next time period, in addition to the possibility of going up or down. More precisely, the stock price S can go up to uS, down to dS, or stay at the same level S; see figure 11.2. The risk-neutral probabilities of these moves are denoted by p_1^*, p_2^*, and p_3^*.

This model is not necessarily a complete-markets model, since there are three possible outcomes at each node and only two securities to use for hedging, the stock and the bank account. Nevertheless, we can approximate complete-markets models, such as the Black-Scholes model, with trinomial trees. How do we choose the parameters? Here is one possibility: We can choose any value for u we like and we set $d = 1/u$. We now

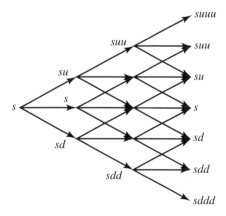

Figure 11.2
Trinomial tree with three time periods.

describe how to choose the probabilities p_i^*. If we discretize the Black-Scholes model in the risk-neutral world, we get

$$S(t + \Delta t) = S(t)[1 + r\Delta t + \sigma\sqrt{\Delta t}\,Z(t)]$$

where $Z(t)$ is a standard normal random variable. This shows that the conditional mean of the factor $F = S(t + \Delta t)/S(t)$ by which the stock price changes is

$$E_t[F] = 1 + r\Delta t$$

The variance is given by

$$\text{Var}_t[F] = \sigma^2 \Delta t$$

However, in our tree the mean is

$$E_t[F] = up_1^* + p_2^* + dp_3^*$$

and the second moment is

$$E_t[F^2] = u^2 p_1^* + p_2^* + d^2 p_3^*$$

Matching the mean and the variance, using the fact that $\text{Var}[F] = E[F^2] - (E[F])^2$, and requiring the probabilities to add up to one, we get the following system of equations:

$$p_1^* + p_2^* + p_3^* = 1$$

$$up_1^* + p_2^* + dp_3^* = 1 + r\Delta t$$

$$u^2 p_1^* + p_2^* + d^2 p_3^* = \sigma^2 \Delta t + (1 + r\Delta t)^2$$

For some values of u this system may give negative values. Then we need to change the value of u.

We compute the option value at a given node in a familiar way: as a discounted expected value of the three option values at the neighboring future nodes. That is, if the values at the three future nodes are C_1, C_2, and C_3, then the option value $C(t)$ at the current node is

$$C(t) = e^{-r\Delta t}[p_1^* C_1 + p_2^* C_2 + p_3^* C_3]$$

assuming that r is the continuously compounded interest rate.

11.2   Monte Carlo Simulation

Monte Carlo simulation is a simple and flexible way of computing European-style option prices and corresponding hedging portfolios. This method becomes relatively more efficient as the number of variables of the specific pricing problem increases. The reason is that while the cost of most methods (typically measured in computer time required) grows exponentially with the number of variables, in the case of Monte Carlo simulation it only grows linearly. Monte Carlo simulation can also be used for pricing American options, but this application is not straightforward, and we do not discuss it.

11.2.1 Monte Carlo Basics

Let us forget for a moment about option pricing and consider simply a random variable Y and its mean $E[Y]$. Suppose we cannot compute the mean explicitly, and instead we want to use a numerical method. Suppose also that we can simulate realizations of the random values Y (that is, consistent with its probability distribution) using some computer software. Denote

$$M = \text{The number of random realizations of } Y \tag{11.10}$$

obtained from independent simulations. We denote by Y_i the simulated values. We then form the average

$$\hat{\mu}_Y = \frac{1}{M} \sum_{i=1}^{M} Y_i$$

By the **law of large numbers** of probability theory, for large M the average $\hat{\mu}_Y$ is a good estimate for the mean $\mu_Y = E[Y]$ of Y:

$$E[Y] \approx \frac{1}{M} \sum_{i=1}^{M} Y_i \tag{11.11}$$

Now we are in business, since option prices are nothing else but risk-neutral expected values! Thus, if we can simulate the underlying asset price process and the interest rate process under the risk-neutral probability, we can estimate an option value by Monte Carlo.

Note that the variance of the sample average $\hat{\mu}_Y$ is

$$\mathrm{Var}\left[\frac{1}{M} \sum_{i=1}^{M} Y_i \right] = \frac{1}{M^2} \sum_{i=1}^{M} \mathrm{Var}[Y] = \frac{1}{M} \mathrm{Var}[Y]$$

Therefore, the standard error is

$$\frac{1}{\sqrt{M}} \sigma_Y \tag{11.12}$$

where σ_Y is the standard deviation of Y. We see that in order to improve the error by a factor of 10, for example, we need to increase the number M of simulations by a factor of 100.

In practice, we do not know the value of σ_Y. However, the standard error of our estimate can be approximated in the following way. Suppose we want to estimate the error of a Monte Carlo procedure when using $M = 100$ simulation runs. We perform a large number, denoted L, of experiments, each of which involves 100 simulation runs. Each of these experiments gives us an estimated value $\hat{\mu}_i$, $i = 1, \ldots, L$, for the mean of variable Y. The sample standard deviation s_μ of the sample consisting of $\hat{\mu}_i$'s is an estimate for the error of the Monte Carlo procedure using 100 simulation runs. In other words, denoting by $\bar{\mu}$ the sample mean of $\hat{\mu}_i$'s, we compute

$$s_\mu^2 = \frac{1}{L-1} \sum_{i=1}^{L} (\hat{\mu}_i - \bar{\mu})^2$$

as an estimate for the squared standard error of an individual estimate $\hat{\mu}_Y$.

11.2.2 Generating Random Numbers

Given that we know the distribution of a random variable Y, how do we simulate random values from its distribution? It turns out that most continuous distributions can be simulated if we can simulate values of the simplest distribution, a uniform distribution on the interval $[0, 1]$. There are standard algorithms that generate numbers in a way that mimics draws from a theoretical uniform distribution. These algorithms are incorporated into a large number of commercial software products, as functions typically called **random-number generators.** Most quantitative software programs have a feature that allows the user to simulate values from all typical distributions. Since random number generators use deterministic algorithms to produce numbers that only appear to be random, computer-generated random numbers are sometimes called **pseudorandom numbers.**

The most important distribution for us is the standard normal distribution. If you do not have access to a software program that would simulate values from this distribution, but you do have access to a random-number generator for the uniform distribution in the interval $[0, 1]$, one rough way of getting standard normal random values is as follows:

1. Simulate 12 values of uniform random numbers U_i, $i = 1, \ldots, 12$.

2. Compute $Z_1 = \sum_{i=1}^{12} U_i - 6$, to get an approximate standard normal random value.

3. Repeat this procedure M times to get a **random sample** of M standard normal random values $Z_1, \ldots, Z_M$.

An alternative is as follows:

1. Simulate M values of uniform random numbers U_i, $i = 1, \ldots, M$.

2. Compute $Z_i = N^{-1}(U_i)$, to get a sample of M standard normal random values.

Here, N^{-1} is the inverse function of the cumulative normal distribution function. The reason why this latter approach works is the following:

$$P[Z_i \leq x] = P[N^{-1}(U_i) \leq x] = P[U_i \leq N(x)] = N(x)$$

This shows that the distribution of Z_i is standard normal.

Excel Tip: Step (2) in the latter approach can be performed in Excel as

= NORMSINV(RAND())

When values Y_i from a normal random variable with mean μ and variance σ^2 are needed, we transform Z_i as follows:

$$Y_i = \sigma Z_i + \mu$$

Sometimes we need to simulate two random variables, Z_1 and Z_2, which have a bivariate standard normal distribution with correlation ρ. In order to do so, we simulate two independent standard normal variables Y_1 and Y_2, and then set

$$Z_1 = Y_1$$

$$Z_2 = \rho Y_1 + \sqrt{1 - \rho^2} Y_2$$

More generally, for the n-dimensional standard normal distribution with correlation ρ_{ij} between Z_i and Z_j, we simulate n independent normal variables $Y_1, \ldots, Y_n$ and then set

$$Z_i = \sum_{k=1}^{i} a_{ik} Y_k$$

where a_{ik} satisfy

$$\sum_k a_{ik}^2 = 1, \qquad \sum_k a_{ik} a_{jk} = \rho_{ij}$$

We cannot always solve this system for the values of a_{ij}'s, because not every choice of ρ_{ij}'s is consistent with a viable correlation structure.

11.2.3   Variance Reduction Techniques

As we showed in equation (11.12), the error of the estimate that results from Monte Carlo simulation decreases with the factor of $\sqrt{M}$, where M is the number of simulations. There are, however, a number of techniques that allow the reduction of the error without increasing the number of simulations. They are called, in general, **variance reduction** techniques. As the reader will notice, they usually go under somewhat peculiar names, but most are easy to understand. We describe some of them in this section.

Antithetic Variables   The technique of antithetic variables is the simplest, and it is very easy to use. We assume that our simulation is based on generating random values from a symmetric distribution, such as the standard normal distribution. We first compute an estimate $\hat{\mu}_1$ of the expectation $E[Y]$ by generating the values $Z_1, \ldots, Z_M$ of the standard normal distribution. Then we use those same simulated values, but with the opposite sign, $-Z_1, \ldots, -Z_M$, to compute a second estimate $\hat{\mu}_2$. Then we average them to get the final estimate:

$$\hat{\mu} = \frac{\hat{\mu}_1 + \hat{\mu}_2}{2}$$

The reason why this may be a good thing to do is that if $\hat{\mu}_1$ is above the true value of μ_Y, then $\hat{\mu}_2$ is likely to be below the true value; thus averaging them is likely to cancel some of the estimation error. In summary, if we are going to use M pseudorandom numbers from a symmetric distribution, we should generate $M/2$ numbers and use $M/2$ identical numbers but with the opposite sign. In addition to reducing the standard error of our estimate, we save time by generating only half of the random numbers.

Control Variates   Control variates is a technique that can be used if there are two random variables, X and Y, that have similar properties. Moreover, we have an analytic formula for $E[X]$, and we can compute it with high precision. We want to estimate $E[Y]$, for which we do not have an analytic formula. Then we pretend that we need to estimate $E[X]$ numerically, as well, so we compute its estimate $\hat{\mu}_X$, as well as the estimate $\hat{\mu}_Y$ of $E[Y]$. For both estimates we use the same random numbers from the Monte Carlo simulation and keep the Monte Carlo procedure as similar as possible. Then, because X and Y are supposed to be similar, we would expect that the error in estimating X is similar to the error in estimating $E[Y]$. That is,

$$E[X] - \hat{\mu}_X \approx E[Y] - \hat{\mu}_Y$$

or

$$E[Y] \approx \hat{\mu}_Y + E[X] - \hat{\mu}_X$$

This expression motivates the definition of a new estimate μ_Y^* of $E[Y]$ as

$$\mu_Y^* := \hat{\mu}_Y + E[X] - \hat{\mu}_X$$

For example, we could use this technique in the Merton-Black-Scholes model in order to compute a price of the Asian option with payoff

$$Y = \left(\frac{1}{T} \int_0^T S(u)\, du - K \right)^+$$

We could use the payoff of the call option $[S(T) - K]^+$ as the control variate, because we can compute analytically the price of the call. However, it is even better to use the Asian option based on the geometric average of the stock prices as the control variate, since that option does have an analytic solution (see Problem 11). The geometric mean of the stock prices at times t_i, $i = 1, \ldots, n$, is given by

$$[S(t_1) \cdot S(t_2) \cdot \cdots \cdot S(t_n)]^{\frac{1}{n}} \tag{11.13}$$

The continuous-time version of this expression is

$$\exp\left\{ \frac{1}{T} \int_0^T \log[S(u)]\, du \right\} \tag{11.14}$$

Many times it is better to use the estimate

$$\tilde{\mu}_Y^* = E[X] + \alpha(\hat{\mu}_Y - \hat{\mu}_X)$$

for a value of α different than 1. See Further Readings for details.

Quasi Monte Carlo   In order to motivate the quasi Monte Carlo approach, let us consider a two-dimensional case in which we want to generate random points in a plane. If we simulate uniformly distributed points (U_i, V_i) in a square, it may happen that the actual random numbers are not very uniformly distributed across the square, especially if we are using a relatively low number of points. The error of the Monte Carlo estimate would increase as a result. In order to circumvent this difficulty, mathematicians have invented so-called **quasi-random numbers** or **low-discrepancy sequences,** which are numbers that fill in the gaps in a given area (an interval, a square, a cube, . . .) in a uniform way, taking into account the distribution of the points already present in the sequence. In fact, these are not random numbers at all, but are often generated using sophisticated mathematical methods. The error associated with using these numbers is smaller than the Monte Carlo error, when the number of points is relatively low. This might be the method of choice for many applications, especially when it is desirable to use few random numbers. Since this method is more difficult to describe and less flexible to implement, we do not cover it in this text.

Importance Sampling   This is an approach in which we perform simulations from a conditional distribution rather than the original distribution. What is the motivation for this? Suppose, for example, that we want to price an option that is deep out of the money, so that there is a very high probability that the payoff will be zero. Then, if we sample from the original distribution, most of the simulated payoff values would be equal to zero, a procedure which is a waste of time, and, worse, we need a large number of simulations to get the right ratio of the values that are not zero relative to the zero values. So we may want to sample instead from a distribution conditional on the event that the payoff will not be zero. Then we will assign to the values we get from that conditional distribution a weight equal to the probability that the option is in the money. For example, for a put option with strike price K, the probability distribution function conditional on the option expiring in the money is, with $x \leq K$,

$$P[S(T) \leq x \mid S(T) \leq K] = \frac{P[S(T) \leq x, S(T) \leq K]}{P[S(T) \leq K]} = \frac{P[S(T) \leq x]}{P[S(T) \leq K]}$$

Then we generate M values Y_i, $i = 1, \ldots, M$, from the conditional distribution. In order to find the estimate of the price of the put, we compute

$$\left(\frac{1}{M} \sum_{i=1}^{M} (K - Y_i)^+ \right) P[S(T) \leq K]$$

11.2.4   Simulation in a Continuous-Time Multivariable Model

Thus far we have talked about Monte Carlo methods in a more or less abstract way, without actually describing how to simulate the values of the payoff we need to price. We will do so now. In order to illustrate the method, we consider the following extension of the Merton-Black-Scholes model, in which we also model the volatility as a diffusion process, directly in the risk-neutral world:

$$dS(t) = S(t)[r \, dt + \sigma(t)] \, dW^*(t)$$

$$d\sigma(t) = \alpha(t, \sigma(t), S(t)) \, dt + \beta(t, \sigma(t), S(t)) \, dW^*(t)$$

The Monte Carlo approach is ideally suited for such a model because we do not necessarily know analytic solutions with stochastic volatility, even for plain vanilla options, and because of the presence of the second random variable σ, which makes the binomial tree and the PDE approaches less efficient. Assuming that the functions α and β are such that there exists a unique solution (S, σ) to the preceding system of equations and such that S and σ are strictly positive processes, we will now describe how to simulate sample paths of those processes. Suppose that we consider an option that expires at T. We divide the interval $[0, T]$ into N periods of equal length

$$\Delta t = T/N$$

with the endpoints of the periods denoted t_k, $k = 0, \ldots, t_N$; $t_N = T$. We simulate, using any standard statistical package, independent values from the standard normal distribution, denoted

$$z_k, \quad k = 1, \ldots, N$$

Recall that the increments $\Delta W^*(t_k) = W^*(t_{k+1}) - W^*(t_k)$ of the Brownian motion W^* are independent normal random variables, with mean zero and variance Δt. Hence the sequence of values $\Delta W^*(t_k)$ has the same distribution as the sequence of values $\sqrt{\Delta t} z_k$. Therefore, we can simulate one sample path of S recursively using

$$S(t_{k+1}) = S(t_k) + S(t_k)[r\Delta t + \sigma(t_k)\sqrt{\Delta t} z_k]$$

We simultaneously perform a similar simulation for a sample path of σ, which we need in the simulation of $S(t_k)$:

$$\sigma(t_{k+1}) = \sigma(t_k) + \alpha(t_k, \sigma(t_k), S(t_k))\Delta t + \beta(t_k, \sigma(t_k), S(t_k))\sqrt{\Delta t} z_k$$

(This is called a **first-order scheme** or **Euler scheme** for simulating a solution to a stochastic differential equation. There are more efficient, higher-order schemes.)

We repeat the simulation for M sample paths, resulting in values $S^i(T)$, $i = 1, \ldots, M$. For each sample path i, we have to simulate a new sequence of standard normal values z_k^i, $k = 1, \ldots, N, i = 1, \ldots, M$. Consider now an option with payoff $g(S(T))$. By the law of large numbers we can approximate the option price

$$C(0) = E^*[e^{-rT} g(S(T))]$$

by the average over sample paths

$$\hat{C}(0) = \frac{1}{M} \sum_{i=1}^{M} e^{-rT} g(S^i(T))$$

If we were to use the PDE approach instead, in this framework we could compute the option price as a function $C(t, s, \sigma)$ that solves the PDE

$$C_t + \tfrac{1}{2}\sigma^2 s^2 C_{ss} + \tfrac{1}{2}\beta^2 C_{\sigma\sigma} + s\sigma\beta C_{s\sigma} + \alpha C_\sigma + r(sC_s - C) = 0, \quad C(T, s) = g(s) \quad (11.15)$$

We see that the dimension of the PDE increases with the number of random variables.

In order to get a good feeling about the performance of Monte Carlo, the reader should solve the relevant problems in the Problems section, using a software package such as Excel or Matlab. See also Example 11.2. An important implementation issue is what the relationship between the number of simulations M and the number of time steps N should be. A good rule of thumb (also shown to be theoretically justified) is this:

The number of simulated paths M should be of the order N^2, where N is the number of time steps, when using the first-order Euler scheme.

Given the amount of computational time to be devoted to the numerical exercise, this rule tells us how to allocate it between the discretization of the process and the number of simulations.

Example 11.2 (Option Pricing by Monte Carlo Simulation)   Consider the Merton-Black-Scholes model and the European call option with

$$S(0) = 65, \ T = 0.08, K = 55, r = 0, \sigma = 0.317$$

The SDE for the price S (in the risk-neutral world) is

$$dS = \sigma S \, dW^*$$

We can avoid the discretization, since we know that the solution is

$$S(T) = S(0)e^{\sigma W^*(T) - \frac{1}{2}\sigma^2 T}$$

We can simply simulate the values $W^*(T)$ as $z_i \sqrt{T}$, where z_i's are independent standard normal random values. We use Microsoft Excel's Visual Basic to write and execute a program to perform the simulation. Some simulation results are presented in figure 11.3. For example, using 100 simulation runs in one case we got that the price is 10.05885. The actual value, using the Black-Scholes formula, is 10.06513.

In another experiment, illustrated in figure 11.4, we pretend that we do not know the solution to the SDE for S, so we discretize it. In one particular case we ran 100 simulation runs for the paths of S, using 10 time periods. This produced a call price value equal to 10.04637, and it obviously required a longer time to do it than without discretization.

The standard error of these methods could be estimated by repeating many times the experiment of running 100 runs, and computing the sample standard deviation of the obtained option prices.

Excel Tip: In order to compute the Black-Scholes call option price by Monte Carlo we have created a user-defined function "BScallMC," using Visual Basic. In default mode,

		M	Call Price	Error
S	65	1	10.27463	0.209496
T	0.08	10	10.42471	0.359584
K	55	100	10.05885	−0.006277
r	0	1,000	10.06081	−0.004317
σ	0.317	10,000	10.06456	−0.00057

Figure 11.3
Monte Carlo with no SDE discretization: option price with 1–10,000 simulation runs.

N	M	Call Price	Error
1	1	10	−0.06513
3	10	10.4967	0.431572
10	100	10.04637	−0.01876
30	1,000	10.05136	−0.013765
100	10,000	10.06537	0.000242

Figure 11.4
Monte Carlo with SDE discretization: option price with 1–10,000 simulation runs and 1–100 discretization time steps. This method takes longer than without discretization.

Excel would compute the new values for this function each time we change parameter values on our spreadsheet. Since the computation of this function is slow, it may be a good idea to change the default mode to "Manual" in the menu of Excel calculation options. In this way you can control when to perform the calculations in the worksheet, rather than having them done automatically. Changing the mode of calculation can be done by going to

> Tools > Options > Calculation

Excel Tip: The Visual Basic and the program codes created in this language can be accessed by going to

> Tools > Macro > Visual Basic Editor

11.2.5   Computation of Hedging Portfolios by Finite Differences

Let us turn our attention now to the computation of the hedging portfolio π^C that replicates a European-style option with payoff $C = g(S(T))$. For the ease of exposition, we use the model of a stock price with stochastic volatility of the previous section. This illustration will make clear how this method is implemented in general.

Applying the two-dimensional Itô's rule (3.22) on the price process C of the option written on the stock with stochastic volatility, we get

$$dC(t, S(t), \sigma(t)) = [\ldots] dt + [S\sigma C_s + \beta C_\sigma] dW^*$$

where C_s and C_σ represent derivatives of the price of the option with respect to the stock price and the volatility, respectively (that is, the "delta" and the "vega" of the option). However, from the wealth equation (3.35), we know that the hedging wealth process (that is, the wealth process that replicates the value of the option) has $\pi^C \sigma \, dW^*$ as its dW^* term. Comparing the two, we deduce that the replicating portfolio can be found from the derivatives C_s and C_σ as

$$\pi^C = SC_s + \frac{\beta}{\sigma} C_\sigma$$

Can we compute C_s and C_σ (hence also the hedging portfolio π^C) by Monte Carlo simulation? The answer is yes, and we present the standard way of doing it. For example, let us describe how to compute the delta of the option, C_s, by simulation. Since C_s is the first derivative of the price C we can approximate it by the finite difference

$$\hat{C}_s(t, s, \sigma) = \frac{1}{\Delta s}[C(t, s + \Delta s, \sigma) - C(t, s, \sigma)]$$

for a small Δs. Furthermore, $C(t, s + \Delta s, \sigma)$ and $C(t, s, \sigma)$ can be simulated by Monte Carlo, since these are option prices. We denote by $\hat{C}$ the estimated values. For $\hat{C}(t, s + \Delta s, \sigma)$ we start the simulation of the process S with $S(t) = s + \Delta s$, while for $\hat{C}(t, s, \sigma)$ we start with $S(t) = s$. This method is called the **finite-difference approximation.** The convergence rate of the method is usually improved if we use the **central difference**

$$\frac{1}{2\Delta s}[\hat{C}(t, s + \Delta s, \sigma) - \hat{C}(t, s - \Delta s, \sigma)]$$

The random numbers generated in order to estimate $C(t, s, \sigma)$, should also be used to estimate $C(t, s + \Delta s, \sigma)$, instead of simulating new random numbers. This approach is called the method of **common random numbers.** The reason for this name is that the variance of the finite difference is given by

$$\frac{1}{(\Delta s)^2}(\text{Var}[\hat{C}(t, s, \sigma)] + \text{Var}[\hat{C}(t, s + \Delta s, \sigma)] - 2\text{Cov}[\hat{C}(t, s, \sigma), \hat{C}(t, s + \Delta s, \sigma)])$$

The covariance between $\hat{C}(t, s, \sigma)$ and $\hat{C}(t, s + \Delta s, \sigma)$ is positive if we use common random numbers; hence the total variance of the estimate is reduced.

We then proceed in a similar way to estimate C_σ:

$$\hat{C}_\sigma(t, s, \sigma) = \frac{1}{\Delta \sigma}[C(t, s, \sigma + \Delta \sigma) - C(t, s, \sigma)]$$

This expression would allow us to compute the necessary amount to be invested in the underlying stock as a part of the hedging portfolio.

11.2.6   Retrieval of Volatility Method for Hedging and Utility Maximization*

There is another simple way of computing the hedging portfolio π^C directly, without computing the derivatives of the option price. Recall that the discounted price process $\bar{C}$, equal to the discounted hedging wealth process, satisfies the equation (in the risk-neutral world)

$$d\bar{C} = \sigma \bar{\pi}^C dW^*$$

However, the Brownian motion itself satisfies the trivial equation

$$dW^* = 1 \cdot dW^*$$

From this, we can interpret, loosely speaking, the product $d\bar{C} \cdot dW^* = \sigma\bar{\pi}^C (dW^*)^2$ as the **instantaneous covariance** between the processes W^* and $\bar{C}$. We also know that $(dW^*)^2$ "behaves like" dt. From this interpretation, and recalling the definition of covariance, it is not surprising that, under technical conditions, we have

$$\sigma(t)\bar{\pi}^C(t) = \lim_{\Delta t \to 0} \frac{1}{\Delta t} E_t^*[\{\bar{C}(t+\Delta t) - \bar{C}(t)\}\{W^*(t+\Delta t) - W^*(t)\}]$$

Note that, by properties of conditional expectations, the following term is zero:

$$E_t^*[\bar{C}(t)\{W^*(t+\Delta t) - W^*(t)\}] = \bar{C}(t)E_t^*[W^*(t+\Delta t) - W^*(t)] = 0$$

Thus we can approximate $\bar{\pi}^C$ (using a small Δt) by

$$\bar{\pi}^C(t) \approx \sigma^{-1}(t)\frac{1}{\Delta t}E_t^*[\bar{C}(t+\Delta t)\{W^*(t+\Delta t) - W^*(t)\}] \qquad (11.16)$$

For a European option with payoff $g(S(T))$ we have

$$\bar{C}(t+\Delta t) = E_{t+\Delta t}^*[\bar{g}(S(T))]$$

and, again, by properties of conditional expectations, the conditional expectation of expression (11.16) is equal to

$$E_t^*[E_{t+\Delta t}^*\{\bar{g}(S(T))\}\{W^*(t+\Delta t) - W^*(t)\}]$$
$$= E_t^*[E_{t+\Delta t}^*\{\bar{g}(S(T))[W^*(t+\Delta t) - W^*(t)]\}]$$
$$= E_t^*[\bar{g}(S(T))\{W^*(t+\Delta t) - W^*(t)\}]$$

Therefore, from expression (11.16), $\bar{\pi}^C$ can be approximated by

$$\bar{\pi}^C(t) \approx \sigma^{-1}(t)\frac{1}{\Delta t}E_t^*[\bar{g}(S(T))\{W^*(t+\Delta t) - W^*(t)\}]$$

Consequently, since $W^*(t+\Delta t) - W^*(t)$ is distributed as a standard normal random variable multiplied by $\sqrt{\Delta t}$, we can get an **estimate $\hat{\pi}^C$ of the hedging portfolio** as

$$\hat{\pi}^C(t) = \frac{e^{r(T-t)}}{\sigma(t)M\sqrt{\Delta t}}\sum_{i=1}^{M}\bar{g}(S^i(T))z_1^i \qquad (11.17)$$

where z_1^i are independent standard normal random values used to simulate the sample paths S^i in the initial time period $[t, t + \Delta t]$.

The previous procedure is called the **retrieval of volatility method,** because it retrieves the volatility of the replicating wealth process. It is easily extended to the case when we have d stocks and d independent Brownian motions. Moreover, it can also be used for the utility maximization problem in complete markets. Namely, we know from equation (4.72) that the optimal portfolio for that problem is the one that replicates the contingent claim

$$\hat{X}(T) = I(\hat{\lambda}\bar{Z}(T))$$

The optimal portfolio $\hat{\pi}$ can be estimated as

$$\hat{\pi}(t) = \frac{e^{r(T-t)}}{\sigma(t)M\sqrt{\Delta t}} \sum_{i=1}^{M} \bar{I}(\hat{\lambda}\bar{Z}^i(T))z_1^i$$

where we have to simulate sample paths $Z^i(t)$ of the risk-neutral density process under the risk-neutral probability.

11.3   Numerical Solutions of PDEs; Finite-Difference Methods

In the Merton-Black-Scholes model and its many extensions, an option price can be determined as the solution to a partial differential equation (PDE). There are well-established numerical methods for solving PDEs that can be used to find option prices. We will consider the most widespread method, the **finite-difference method.** It is as easily applied to American options as to European options. However, it becomes less convenient, or even impossible, to use in models that have many random variables, as well as for some path-dependent options.

The Monte Carlo and tree methods are used to find the value of the option for the current stock price $C(0, S(0))$ only. Unlike these methods, the finite-difference method computes the option price $C(t, s)$ for "all" values of t and s. By "all" we mean on a **grid** covering a large range of t and s values. More precisely, the time horizon $[0, T]$ is divided into N periods, each of length $\Delta t = T/N$. Similarly, we choose a high value of the stock, which we denote $S_{\max}$, and we divide the interval $[0, S_{\max}]$ into M intervals of equal size $\Delta s = S_{\max}/M$. The stock price could, in principle, take larger values than $S_{\max}$, but they are unlikely. After a certain level, the option value would not change very much. For example, for a put option the option value would be practically zero for very large values of s. Similarly, the call option price would get close to the value s of the underlying stock for large values of s.

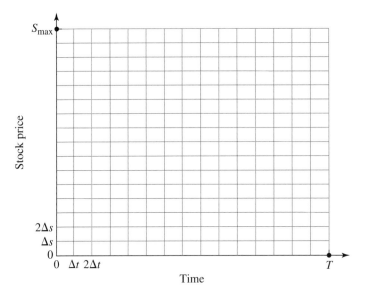

Figure 11.5
A grid for computing option price using finite differences.

The grid is shown in figure 11.5. We will denote the points in the grid $(i \Delta t, j \Delta s)$. The grid is chosen so that one of the points $(0, k\Delta s)$ on the y-axis corresponds to the current value $s = k\Delta s$ of the stock.

11.3.1 Implicit Finite-Difference Method

The idea of the finite-difference method is to replace the partial derivatives in the PDE by their difference approximations, which will produce a system of finite-difference equations, and then to solve the system thus obtained across the values of the grid. We denote by $C_{i,j}$ the value of the option at the point $(i \Delta t, j \Delta s)$.

We can approximate the first derivative of C at the point $(i \Delta t, j \Delta s)$ in the following three ways:

$$\frac{\partial C}{\partial s} \approx \frac{C_{i,j+1} - C_{i,j}}{\Delta s} \approx \frac{C_{i,j} - C_{i,j-1}}{\Delta s} \approx \frac{C_{i,j+1} - C_{i,j-1}}{2\Delta s} \tag{11.18}$$

Similarly for $\frac{\partial C}{\partial t}$, for example:

$$\frac{\partial C}{\partial t} \approx \frac{C_{i+1,j} - C_{i,j}}{\Delta t} \tag{11.19}$$

The second derivative $\frac{\partial^2 C}{\partial s^2}$ is the first derivative of the first derivative, and it can be approximated as

$$\frac{\partial^2 C}{\partial s^2} \approx \frac{1}{\Delta s}\left[\frac{C_{i,j+1}-C_{i,j}}{\Delta s} - \frac{C_{i,j}-C_{i,j-1}}{\Delta s}\right] = \frac{C_{i,j+1}+C_{i,j-1}-2C_{i,j}}{(\Delta s)^2} \qquad (11.20)$$

We now want to use these approximations to solve the Black-Scholes PDE

$$\frac{\partial C}{\partial t} + \frac{1}{2}\sigma^2 s^2 \frac{\partial^2 C}{\partial s^2} + r\left[s\frac{\partial C}{\partial s} - C\right] = 0$$

Substituting the finite-difference approximations for the derivatives, and $j\Delta s$ for s, we get

$$\frac{C_{i+1,j}-C_{i,j}}{\Delta t} + \frac{1}{2}\sigma^2 j^2 (\Delta s)^2 \frac{C_{i,j+1}+C_{i,j-1}-2C_{i,j}}{(\Delta s)^2}$$

$$+ r\left[j\Delta s \frac{C_{i,j+1}-C_{i,j-1}}{2\Delta s} - C_{i,j}\right] = 0 \qquad (11.21)$$

for $i=0,\ldots,N-1$, and $j=1,\ldots,M-1$. After a bit of algebra, this can be written as

$$C_{i+1,j} = a_j C_{i,j-1} + b_j C_{i,j} + c_j C_{i,j+1} \qquad (11.22)$$

for appropriately defined a_j, b_j, and c_j. In order to solve these equations inside the grid, we need to know the values along some of the grid's edges. We consider a put option as an example. We know that the value of the put option at maturity is $[K-S(T)]^+$, which gives

$$C_{N,j} = (K-j\Delta s)^+, \quad j=0,\ldots,M \qquad (11.23)$$

We also know that the value of the option is K when the stock price is zero, so

$$C_{i,0} = K, \quad i=0,\ldots,N \qquad (11.24)$$

Finally, we know that for the large values of s the option value is approximately zero, providing the condition

$$C_{i,M} = 0, \quad i=0,\ldots,N \qquad (11.25)$$

These **boundary conditions** are sufficient to find the option values inside the grid. We first look for the values at time $T-\Delta t$, corresponding to $i=N-1$. We get $M-1$ equations

$$C_{N,j} = a_j C_{N-1,j-1} + b_j C_{N-1,j} + c_j C_{N-1,j+1} \qquad (11.26)$$

Since $C_{N-1,0}=K$ and $C_{N-1,M}=0$, we have $M-1$ unknowns to solve for: $C_{N-1,1},\ldots,$ $C_{N-1,M-1}$. From the structure of equation (11.26), we can see that this system is relatively simple and can be solved by expressing $C_{N-1,2}$ in terms of $C_{N-1,1}$, using the first equation, then expressing $C_{N-1,3}$ in terms of $C_{N-1,2}$, and so on. After this step, we go on and find the values corresponding to $i = N - 2$, and so on, until we get the values at the initial time, when $i = 0$. One of these values corresponds to the current price of the stock and is the option price we are interested in.

In order to price an American put, we would follow a similar procedure, except that when computing the value $C_{i,j}$ of the option at $(i \Delta t, j \Delta s)$, we would compare it to the exercise value $(K - j \Delta s)^+$. If the exercise value is higher, we would replace the value of $C_{i,j}$ computed from the system of equations with the exercise value.

11.3.2 Explicit Finite-Difference Method

The explicit finite-difference method is a simplification of the implicit method. It is based on the assumption that the values of the partial derivatives $\frac{\partial C}{\partial s}$ and $\frac{\partial^2 C}{\partial s^2}$ are the same at the point (i, j) and at the point $(i + 1, j)$. Therefore, in the previous approximations we can replace i by $i + 1$, leading to

$$\frac{\partial C}{\partial s} \approx \frac{C_{i+1,j+1} - C_{i+1,j-1}}{\Delta s}$$

$$\frac{\partial^2 C}{\partial s^2} \approx \frac{C_{i+1,j+1} + C_{i+1,j-1} - 2C_{i+1,j}}{(\Delta s)^2}$$

This step results in the **explicit finite-difference method:**

$$\frac{C_{i+1,j} - C_{i,j}}{\Delta t} + \frac{1}{2}\sigma^2 j^2 (\Delta s)^2 \frac{C_{i+1,j+1} + C_{i+1,j-1} - 2C_{i+1,j}}{(\Delta s)^2}$$

$$+ r \left[j \Delta s \frac{C_{i+1,j+1} - C_{i+1,j-1}}{2\Delta s} - C_{i,j} \right] = 0 \tag{11.27}$$

The reason it leads to a simplification is that, after we find the values $C_{i+1,j-1}$, $C_{i+1,j}$, and $C_{i+1,j+1}$, we can find immediately the value of C_{ij}, since, from equation (11.27) we can write

$$C_{ij} = \tilde{a}_j C_{i+1,j-1} + \tilde{b}_j C_{i+1,j} + \tilde{c}_j C_{i+1,j+1} \tag{11.28}$$

for appropriately defined $\tilde{a}_j$, $\tilde{b}_j$, and $\tilde{c}_j$. We also see that this has the same form as finding the expectation of the future option price that has three possible values at each node, if we think of $\tilde{a}_j$, $\tilde{b}_j$, and $\tilde{c}_j$ as (discounted) risk-neutral probabilities. In other words, *the explicit finite-difference method is of the same type as the trinomial tree method.*

Numerically, the explicit scheme is less stable than the implicit scheme. There is a method in the middle of the two, called the **Crank-Nicholson method.** It is simply obtained by averaging the implicit and explicit methods. More precisely, we get equations of the type

$$C_{i+1,j} + C_{i,j} = a_j C_{i-1,j-1} + b_j C_{i,j} + c_j C_{i,j+1} + \tilde{a}_j C_{i+1,j-1} + \tilde{b}_j C_{i+1,j} + \tilde{c}_j C_{i+1,j+1}$$

This approach is not as simple as the explicit method, but it converges faster.

It should also be noted that it turns out that it is computationally more efficient to use the variable $u = \log(s)$ instead of s, and transform the Black-Scholes PDE in terms of this variable.

Summary

For the purposes of option pricing and risk management it is important to have efficient and flexible computational methods for calculating option prices, as well as the derivatives of those prices with respect to various model variables and parameters, called the Greeks. The three main computational methods are binomial trees, Monte Carlo simulation, and finite-difference methods.

The Cox-Ross-Rubinstein binomial tree model is easily implemented as a numerical algorithm. There are several ways to choose the parameters of the model. For example, we can match the means and the variances of the relative returns in the model with the observed historical means and variances. Or we can force the risk-neutral probabilities to be equal to one-half. Another variation is to have a trinomial tree, with three possible future values of the underlying price at each node of the tree. While simple and fast, the trees approach is difficult to implement for options on several assets and more complex asset-price models.

The Monte Carlo method is based on the fact that the mathematical expectation of a random variable can be approximated by the arithmetic average of a random sample of values from its distribution. The method is simple and flexible for European-type options, but not for American options. Moreover, in order to reduce the error n times, the number of simulations has to be increased n^2 times, which is relatively slowly. There are many variance reduction techniques designed to speed up the convergence of the Monte Carlo method to the true value. When simulating continuous-time diffusion models, we only have to simulate random samples from the standard normal distribution. These are used in discretized stochastic differential equations of the model variables in order to simulate their sample paths. Monte Carlo can also be used to compute Greeks and replicating portfolios.

The finite-difference method is a method for solving PDEs numerically. We replace the partial derivatives of a PDE by their finite-difference approximations and solve for the solution function across a grid of points that covers the area of interest. There are implicit and explicit finite-difference methods and their combinations. PDE methods are fast and flexible, but they cannot deal with models that have more than three or four random variables.

Problems

Note: For some of the problems the reader can find possibly helpful Excel spreadsheets at the web page **http://math.usc.edu/~cvitanic/book.html**

1. Simulate 1,000 paths of the Brownian motion W on the time interval $[0, 1]$, using 25 time periods. Estimate the mean and the variance of $W(1)$. Draw a graph of one of the paths.

†2. The one-year spot rate is 6%. According to your model of the term structure, you simulate the values of the one-year spot interest rate that could prevail in the market one year from now. You do only five simulations and get 6%, 6.52%, 6.32%, 5.93%, and 6.41%. Compute, using Monte Carlo, the rough approximation of the price of a one-year European call on the two-year pure discount bond with strike price 94.

3. Compute the price of the option in Example 11.1 with (a) 6 time steps, (b) 99 time steps, and (c) 100 time steps. Obviously, you may want to write a computer program to do the computation.

4. In the context of Example 11.1, compute the option price for $S(0) = 101$ and find an approximate value of the delta of the option. Do the same for the larger number of time steps: 6, 99, and 100.

5. In the context of the previous problem, estimate the value of the derivative of the option price with respect to the volatility, $\frac{d}{d\sigma}C(\sigma)$, by computing $C(\sigma + \Delta\sigma)$ for some $\Delta\sigma$ to be chosen by yourself.

6. In Example 11.1 compute the option price using $p^* = 0.5$.

7. Argue that equation (11.9) is approximately true for small Δt.

†8. Why do you think it is not easy to apply the Monte Carlo method to compute prices of American options?

9. a. Compute the price of a European call option using the trinomial tree method with two time periods. Use any parameter values you wish.

b. Do the same with ten time periods. For this calculation, it is better to use a computer.

*10. a. Using Monte Carlo and a software program, compute the price of the Asian option with payoff

$$Y = \left(\frac{1}{T} \int_0^T S(u)\, du - K \right)^+$$

in the Black-Scholes model. Choose any values for σ, T, K, $S(0)$, r, M, and N that you deem appropriate.

b. Use the corresponding call option as a control variate to get another estimate of the Asian option price. For this assignment, use the same number of simulations M as in part a.

c. Repeat part a using $M' = 10 \cdot M$ simulations. Is the new estimate closer to the estimate of part a or the estimate of part b? Which estimate do you think is better, part a or part b?

**11. Find the Black-Scholes formula for the call option on the discrete geometric mean (11.13), where the times t_i are equidistant, $t_{i+1} - t_i = \Delta t$, and the maturity is $T = t_n$. (Hint: find the distribution of the geometric means and compare it to the distribution of the stock price at time T.)

**†12. Explain why expression (11.14) is the continuous-time version of expression (11.13), and find the Black-Scholes formula for the call option on the continuous geometric mean (11.14).

**13. Use the call options formulas from the previous two problems as control variates (separately for each) to get another estimate of the price of the Asian option with arithmetic mean. Compare the results with Problem 10.

14. a. Using Monte Carlo and a software program, compute the price of the European call option in the Black-Scholes model. (Choose any values for σ, T, K, $S(0)$, r, M, and N that you deem appropriate.)

b. Repeat part a in the extension of the Black-Scholes model in which the volatility process σ satisfies

$$d\sigma(t) = 2[0.5 - \sigma(t)]\,dt + 0.1\sigma(t)\,dW^*(t)$$

15. Suppose that the interest rate is now 6% and satisfies the following Vasicek dynamics in the risk-neutral probability setting:

$$dr(t) = [0.02 - 0.2r(t)]\,dt + 0.15\,dW(t)$$

Compute, using Monte Carlo simulation, the price of a three-month zero-coupon bond.

16. Using Monte Carlo simulation and a software package, compute the value of the initial amount that the hedging portfolio should hold in the stock when replicating a European call option in the Black-Scholes model. [Choose any values for σ, T, K, $S(0)$, r, M, and Δs that you deem appropriate.] Then compute the exact value of this initial amount using the analytic formula, and compare the two values.

*17. Use the retrieval of volatility method to compute the initial value of the hedging portfolio of a European call option in the Black-Scholes model, with any parameters you wish to choose. Compare to the exact solution from the Black-Scholes formula.

**†18. Use the retrieval of volatility method to find the initial value of the optimal portfolio for maximizing the expected log-utility of terminal wealth $E[\log\{X^{x,\pi}(T)\}]$, in the Black-Scholes model, with any parameters you wish to choose. Compare to the exact analytic solution derived in chapter 4.

19. Find the Black-Scholes PDE after the change of variables $u = \log(s)$.

*20. Compute the Black-Scholes price of a call option using the implicit finite-difference scheme, the explicit finite-difference scheme, and the Crank-Nicholson scheme. Use any values of the parameters you wish, and compare with the analytic solution.

Further Readings

The tree method is introduced in Cox, Ross, and Rubinstein (1979). The introduction of the finite-difference method to price American options is due to Brennan and Schwartz (1977). A good review is also Brennan and Schwartz (1978). Textbook treatments are available in Kwok (1998) and Wilmott, Dewynne, and Howison (1993). Boyle (1977) introduced Monte Carlo methods to price European options. A comprehensive overview of this method and variance reduction techniques is in Boyle, Broadie, and Glasserman (1997); see also Fu, Laprise, Madan, Su, and Wu (2001). Monte Carlo methods have been recently extended with some success to the pricing of American options; see Bossaerts (1989), Carrière (1996), Longstaff and Schwartz (2001), and Ibáñez and Zapatero (in press). Duffie and Glynn (1995) provide important results concerning the efficient implementation of Monte Carlo simulation. The retrieval of volatility method is presented in Cvitanić, Goukasian, and Zapatero (2002). Analytic approximations to price options can be found in Geske and Johnson (1984) and Kim (1990). Simulation and numerical methods for PDEs have been applied lately with some success to the solution of the optimal consumption/portfolio problems studied in chapter 4. We mention here Monte Carlo approaches of Detemple, Garcia, and Rindisbacher (2003) and Cvitanić, Goukasian, and Zapatero (2003), and the use of numerical solutions to PDEs (or ODEs) in Kim and Omberg (1996), Brennan, Schwartz, and Lagnado (1997), Brennan and Xia (2001), and Xia (2001).

III EQUILIBRIUM MODELS

12 Equilibrium Fundamentals

In this chapter we introduce the concept of equilibrium, a key concept in economics. Its main application to finance is that it provides an alternative tool for asset pricing. We will review the basic types of equilibrium, as well as some of its main properties. We will also dwell on some technical aspects, not exempt from practical implications, such as the existence and uniqueness of equilibrium. In subsequent chapters, we will study in more detail each type of equilibrium and its applications. In this part of the book the risk-free asset is called a bond, for convenience.

Remark on the Reading Sequence   The reader interested only in the most popular equilibrium models in finance, the so-called CAPM model and its extensions, can go directly to chapters 13 and 14.

12.1   Concept of Equilibrium

12.1.1   Definition and Single-Period Case

In economics and finance models, we call the parameters whose values are given **exogenous.** We say that these are the **primitives** of the model. The values that are computed inside the model, using economic arguments, are called **endogenous.**

In the first part of the book we studied the so-called **partial equilibrium** problem for an agent: an investor that has to choose the optimal level of consumption and/or the optimal investment allocation, given a model. Our primitives were the preferences of the individual and the exact form of the dynamics of the market securities. The interest rate was also a part of our primitives. The investor has information about those dynamics and makes decisions based on that information. In the second part of the book we computed prices of securities based on the assumption that they were redundant: they could be replicated with existing securities. Our primitives were the prices of the basic securities, as well as the interest rate. The analysis in this setting was preference free. We were able to compute the price of a new security as a function of the prices of existing securities. In this part of the book we move one step further and solve endogenously for the prices of the basic securities. Our primitives will be the preferences of the individuals and the total amounts of goods and/or securities and the general form of their dynamics. The underlying idea is the cornerstone of economic analysis: supply equals demand. *Equilibrium is characterized by a set of prices such that the total demand of agents that behave optimally equals the total supply.* We illustrate some of the main ideas with a simple single-period example.

Suppose that our consumer Taf has a given level of wealth X. Taf has logarithmic utility for the consumption of a single good in the economy. We denote by c the number of units of the good that Taf consumes. Taf maximizes his utility and takes the price of the consumption good as given. Suppose also that Taf is the only person in the economy. The total supply of the consumption good in the economy is Q. An equilibrium is characterized by the price P of the good such that Taf's optimal consumption is Q. The solution to this problem is easy, since Taf's utility is increasing in consumption and there is no other use for wealth. As a result, Taf will use all the wealth to buy the consumption good, so that the optimal consumption $\hat{c}$ is such that

$$X = P\hat{c}$$

with the solution $\hat{c} = \frac{X}{P}$. The equilibrium price is $\hat{P} = \frac{X}{Q}$, the total wealth divided by the total supply of good. At this price, Taf optimally consumes the total amount of good in the economy, $\hat{c} = Q$, so that supply equals demand.

Consider now an extension of the previous example in which Taf cares about two consumption goods and his wealth equals X. The total supply of goods 1 and 2 is Q_1 and Q_2. As in the previous case, Taf will use all the wealth for consumption. However, the allocation of wealth between goods 1 and 2 will depend on their prices, P_1 and P_2. His maximization problem is given by

$$\max_{\{c_1,c_2\}} \{\alpha \log c_1 + (1-\alpha) \log c_2\}$$

such that

$$P_1 c_1 + P_2 c_2 = X$$

Solving for c_2 and substituting in the previous expression, we get

$$\max_{\{c_1\}} \left\{ \alpha \log c_1 + (1-\alpha) \log \left(\frac{X - P_1 c_1}{P_2} \right) \right\}$$

The optimal solution is

$$\hat{c}_1 = \frac{\alpha X}{P_1}$$

$$\hat{c}_2 = \frac{(1-\alpha)X}{P_2}$$

and the equilibrium prices, at which $\hat{c}_i = Q_i$, are

$$\hat{P}_1 = \frac{\alpha X}{Q_1}$$

$$\hat{P}_2 = \frac{(1-\alpha)X}{Q_2}$$

In the previous examples there is only one individual, whose wealth X is expressed in terms of money. A more compact and frequent formalization of equilibrium is the model in which the wealth of the agents consists of units of the consumption good. The amount of the consumption good each agent receives is called **endowment.** The term "endowment" is applied to any exogenously given amount of an economic variable, whether it is the consumption good or financial securities. We will distinguish between individual endowment and total, or **aggregate, endowment,** depending on whether it is the endowment of a given consumer or the endowment of all the agents in the economy.

In general, a more realistic equilibrium is the one that results from the interaction of several agents that own the totality of the goods in the economy. For example, consider an economy populated by two agents, A and B, that maximize utilities

$$\alpha \log c_1^A + (1 - \alpha) \log c_2^A, \qquad \beta \log c_1^B + (1 - \beta) \log c_2^B$$

respectively, where c_j^i represents consumption units of good j by individual i. We assume that these agents are endowed with the consumption goods in the number of units e_1^i and e_2^i. The total endowment of good i in this economy is $e_i = e_i^A + e_i^B$. The equilibrium condition is

$$c_i^A + c_i^B = e_i \tag{12.1}$$

When this is satisfied we say that the **markets clear.** Moreover, the **budget constraint** (the total amount consumed by agent i equals the total endowment of agent i) has to be satisfied:

$$P_1 c_1^i + P_2 c_2^i = P_1 e_1^i + P_2 e_2^i \tag{12.2}$$

We derive now the equilibrium prices. First, we solve for c_2^i as a function of c_1^i in the budget constraint,

$$c_2^i = \frac{P_1 e_1^i + P_2 e_2^i - P_1 c_1^i}{P_2}$$

We replace c_2^i by this expression in the utilities of the individuals. Then, by using the optimality conditions, also called **first-order conditions** or **FOC,** obtained by taking derivatives and setting them equal to zero, we get

$$\hat{c}_1^A = \frac{\alpha \left(P_1 e_1^A + P_2 e_2^A \right)}{P_1}$$

$$\hat{c}_1^B = \frac{\beta \left(P_1 e_1^B + P_2 e_2^B \right)}{P_1}$$

Using the equilibrium condition (12.1) in the market for good 1 we derive the following relationship between equilibrium prices:

$$\frac{P_1}{P_2} = \frac{\alpha e_2^A + \beta e_2^B}{(1 - \alpha)e_1^A + (1 - \beta)e_1^B}$$

The same relationship between the equilibrium prices holds if we use the optimality and the equilibrium conditions for good 2. Only the ratio of the prices is determined in equilibrium. Therefore, we can set the price of one of the goods to any arbitrary value and compute the price of the other good according to the equilibrium ratio. Typically, one of the prices, say the price of good 1, is set equal to one, so that the price of good 2 represents the number of units of good 1 you can buy with good 2. In this case, good 1 is called the **numeraire.**

We stress the fact that the price relationship derived from equilibrium in the market for good 1 guarantees equilibrium in the market for good 2. In general, when we have n markets we only need to solve for equilibrium in $n - 1$ markets. Equilibrium in the nth market follows automatically. This useful property is called **Walras' law.** We now prove it for the case of two agents and two goods in a one-period setting. Extensions to more agents, more goods, and multiple periods are straightforward.

THEOREM 12.1 (WALRAS' LAW)   Consider a single-period economy as described previously. Suppose that there are two agents with given utility functions and two consumption goods. The agents receive endowments e_i^j, $i = 1, 2$, $j = A, B$, where i represents the good and j the agent. Then equilibrium in one of the markets implies equilibrium in the other market.

Proof   Suppose that one of the markets, for example 1, is in equilibrium. Then,

$$c_1^A + c_1^B = e_1^A + e_1^B \tag{12.3}$$

We now add the two budget constraints to get

$$P_1(c_1^A + c_1^B) + P_2(c_2^A + c_2^B) = P_1(e_1^A + e_1^B) + P_2(e_2^A + e_2^B)$$

From the equilibrium in market 1 we can simplify the previous expression to get

$$P_2(c_2^A + c_2^B) = P_2(e_2^A + e_2^B)$$

Dividing both sides by P_2, equilibrium in market 2 follows.   ∎

We introduce the first example of equilibrium with financial markets in the next section.

12.1.2 A Two-Period Example

The notion of equilibrium in a multiperiod model is a straightforward extension of the equilibrium in a single-period model. The equilibrium condition that demand equals supply has to hold at every point in time. We consider here a simple two-period example. We point out that the terminology about "single-period" or "two-period" models is not completely uniform. Here we call the next model "two-period" because there is consumption at moments $t = 0$ and $t = 1$. However, in the rest of this book such a model would be called "single-period" because all the decisions have to be made at moment $t = 0$.

Suppose that there are two investors and a single consumption good. The investors can save or borrow money in the bond market at an interest rate r. For an equilibrium to exist, both the consumption-good market and the bond market have to clear. The bond market clears if the bond is in **zero net supply**: the amount one individual borrows is equal to the amount the other individual saves. Suppose that the optimization problems of the two individuals, A and B, in this economy are given as

$$\max_{\{c^A(0), c^A(1)\}} \{\log c^A(0) + \alpha \log c^A(1)\}$$
$$\max_{\{c^B(0), c^B(1)\}} \{\log c^B(0) + \beta \log c^B(1)\} \tag{12.4}$$

where $0 < \alpha$ and $\beta < 1$. The investors are endowed with amounts $e^i(j)$ of the good, where i is the individual and j the time at which he or she receives the endowment. In order to simplify, we use the consumption good as numeraire and normalize its price to 1 at each period (we can think of the consumption good as money). The budget constraints of the individuals are given by

$$c^i(1) = e^i(1) + [e^i(0) - c^i(0)](1 + r), \quad i = A, B$$

Substituting the budget constraint in the utility function (12.4) of the individuals, and using optimality conditions, we get

$$c^A(0) = \frac{e^A(1) + e^A(0)(1 + r)}{(1 + \alpha)(1 + r)}, \qquad c^B(0) = \frac{e^B(1) + e^B(0)(1 + r)}{(1 + \beta)(1 + r)}$$

From the equilibrium conditions $c^A(j) + c^B(j) = e^A(j) + e^B(j)$ (which, by the budget constraints, also imply that the bond market clears), we derive the equilibrium interest rate

$$1 + r = \frac{(1 + \beta)e^A(1) + (1 + \alpha)e^B(1)}{\alpha(1 + \beta)e^A(0) + \beta(1 + \alpha)e^B(0)}$$

In case both individuals have the same subjective discount factor, that is, $\alpha = \beta$, we get

$$1 + r = \frac{1}{\alpha} \cdot \frac{e^A(1) + e^B(1)}{e^A(0) + e^B(0)} \tag{12.5}$$

which is the equilibrium that would result in the case of a single agent, with endowment $e^A(i) + e^B(i)$ (see Problem 3).

In the previous example there is no uncertainty about the future states of the world. We now consider an example with uncertainty. In order to keep the notation as simple as possible, we consider an example with a single agent with logarithmic utility:

$$\max_{\{c\}} \{\log c(0) + \beta E[\log\{c(1)\}]\}$$

where the uncertainty is caused by the endowment process of the agent. We assume that $e(0)$ is known, while at moment $t = 1$ there are two possible states, 1 and 2, with probabilities p and $1 - p$. The random endowment $e(1)$ is $e_u(1)$ in state 1 and $e_d(1)$ in state 2. The agent has access to a bond with interest rate r. The interest rate has to be such that, in equilibrium, the agent consumes the endowment (in each state) and optimally invests zero in the bond. As in the previous example, we use the consumption good as numeraire and normalize its price to 1. The budget constraint of the agent is

$$c_i(1) = [e(0) - c(0)](1 + r) + e_i(1), \quad i = u, d \tag{12.6}$$

where i represents the state. The objective function of the individual becomes

$$\max_{\{c(0)\}} \{\log[c(0)] + \beta[p \log\{[e(0) - c(0)](1 + r) + e_u(1)\}$$
$$+ (1 - p) \log\{[e(0) - c(0)](1 + r) + e_d(1)\}]\}$$

The optimal $\hat{c}(0)$ is obtained from the optimality condition

$$\frac{1}{\hat{c}(0)} - \beta \left(p \frac{1+r}{[e(0) - \hat{c}(0)](1 + r) + e_u(1)} + (1 - p) \frac{1+r}{[e(0) - \hat{c}(0)](1 + r) + e_d(1)} \right) = 0 \tag{12.7}$$

At time $t = 0$ the optimal consumption of the agent has to be equal to the endowment, $\hat{c}(0) = e(0)$. This fact, together with equation (12.6), also guarantees that the investment in the bond market is zero. Substituting $\hat{c}(0) = e(0)$ in the optimality condition (12.7), we derive the equilibrium interest rate

$$1 + r = \frac{1}{e(0)\beta} \frac{e_u(1)e_d(1)}{pe_d(1) + (1 - p)e_u(1)} \tag{12.8}$$

12.1.3   Continuous-Time Equilibrium

The concept of equilibrium in continuous time is a direct extension of the discrete-time equilibrium discussed in the preceding paragraphs. We consider several examples in the next section.

12.2   Single-Agent and Multiagent Equilibrium

12.2.1   Representative Agent

We distinguish between **single-agent,** or **representative-agent, equilibrium** and **multiagent equilibrium.** In single-agent equilibrium we require the prices to be such that the agent optimally has to consume the totality of goods and hold the total supply of assets when they are in **positive supply,** and must have a zero demand for assets when they are in **zero net supply.** For example, stocks can be considered to be in positive supply in financial markets, while options are in zero net supply, since for an agent short an option there is an agent long the option. In a multiagent case we say that there is **aggregation** if we can find a single-agent equilibrium identical to the equilibrium of many agents. The single agent is then called the **representative agent.** Aggregation holds trivially in the case in which all the agents have identical utility functions and endowments. However, in general, aggregation does not have to hold. Aggregation has been shown to exist for those cases in which the agents have different utility functions but belong to a specific class. In particular, when the investors have utility functions that belong to the *constant relative risk aversion or CRRA* class, aggregation holds, in simple models. Two typical representatives of this class are the logarithmic and power utility.

12.2.2   Single-Period Aggregation

Consider an economy with two agents, A and B, who have the following preferences:

$$\max_{\{c\}}\{\log c^A(0) + \beta E[\log\{c^A(1)\}]\}$$

$$\max_{\{c\}}\left\{ \frac{(c^B(0))^\gamma}{\gamma} + \beta E\left[\frac{\{c^B(1)\}^\gamma}{\gamma} \right] \right\}$$

where $c^j(i)$ indicates consumption at moment i by agent j, $\beta < 1$ is a discount factor, and $\gamma < 1$ is a constant. These agents receive endowments of the consumption good at moments 0 and 1. At moment $t = 1$ there are two possible states, so that the random endowment of agent i can take values $e_u^i(1)$ with probability p and $e_d^i(1)$ with probability $1 - p$. The investors have access to a bond that pays interest at rate r. Since the amount invested in the bond at time 0 is $[e^j(0) - c^j(0)]$, the problems of the investors are equivalent to

$$\max_{\{c^A(0)\}} \left\{ \log[c^A(0)] + \beta \left[p \log \left\{ [e^A(0) - c^A(0)](1+r) + e_u^A(1) \right\} \right. \right.$$
$$\left. \left. + (1-p) \log \left\{ [e^A(0) - c^A(0)](1+r) + e_d^A(1) \right\} \right] \right\}$$

and

$$\max_{\{c^B(0)\}} \left\{ \frac{(c^B)^\gamma(0)}{\gamma} + \beta \left[p \left(\frac{\left\{ [e^B(0) - c^B(0)](1+r) + e_u^B(1) \right\}^\gamma}{\gamma} \right) \right. \right.$$
$$\left. \left. + (1-p) \left(\frac{\left\{ [e^B(0) - c^B(0)](1+r) + e_d^B(1) \right\}^\gamma}{\gamma} \right) \right] \right\}$$

We present now an example where the endowment is chosen so as to make the calculations easy.

Example 12.1 (Aggregation Property)   Suppose that the endowments of the individuals satisfy

$$\frac{1}{e^A(0)} = p\frac{1}{e_u^A(1)} + (1-p)\frac{1}{e_d^A(1)}$$
$$[e^B(0)]^{\gamma-1} = p[e_u^B(1)]^{\gamma-1} + (1-p)[e_d^B(1)]^{\gamma-1}$$

The first-order condition of agent A is

$$\frac{1}{c^A(0)} - \beta \left(p\frac{1+r}{[e^A(0) - c^A(0)](1+r) + e_u^A(1)} \right.$$
$$\left. + (1-p)\frac{1+r}{[e^A(0) - c^A(0)](1+r) + e_d^A(1)} \right) = 0$$

and the first-order condition of agent B is

$$[c^B(0)]^{\gamma-1} - \beta \left\{ p(1+r)\left[\{e^B(0) - c^B(0)\}(1+r) + e_u^B(1)\right]^{\gamma-1} \right.$$
$$\left. + (1-p)(1+r)\left[\{e^B(0) - c^B(0)\}(1+r) + e_d^B(1)\right]^{\gamma-1} \right\} = 0$$

Then it is straightforward to check (see Problem 4) that an equilibrium is obtained if

$$\hat{c}^i(j) = e^i(j), \qquad i = A, B, \ j = 0, 1$$

$$1 + r = \frac{1}{\beta}$$

Moreover, there is a representative agent with power utility with coefficient $\alpha < 1$ who optimally supports the same equilibrium; hence the "aggregation property" holds, as we argue next. First, we note that the first-order condition of this representative agent, whom we denote R, is

$$[c^R(0)]^{\alpha-1} - \beta\{p(1+r)[\{e^R(0) - c^R(0)\}(1+r) + e_u^R(1)]^{\alpha-1}$$
$$+ (1-p)(1+r)\{[e^R(0) - c^R(0)](1+r) + e_d^R(1)\}^{\alpha-1}\} = 0$$

Applying the equilibrium conditions

$$\hat{c}^R(j) = e^R(j), \quad j = 0, 1$$
$$1 + r = \frac{1}{\beta}$$

to the first-order condition equation, we get

$$[e^R(0)]^{\alpha-1} = p[e_u^R(1)]^{\alpha-1} + (1-p)[e_d^R(1)]^{\alpha-1} = 0 \tag{12.9}$$

As a representative agent, the investor R has endowments

$$e^R(j) = e^A(j) + e^B(j), \quad j = 0, 1$$

Substituting this expression and the expressions for the endowments of agents A and B into equation (12.9), our problem of finding such a representative agent is, then, equivalent to finding the value of α that satisfies

$$\left[p\frac{1}{e_u^A(1)} + (1-p)\frac{1}{e_d^A(1)}\right]^{-1} + \left\{p[e_u^B(1)]^{\gamma-1} + (1-p)[e_d^B(1)]^{\gamma-1}\right\}^{\frac{1}{\gamma-1}}$$
$$= \left\{p[e_u^A(1) + e_u^B(1)]^{\alpha-1} + (1-p)[e_d^A(1) + e_d^B(1)]^{\alpha-1}\right\}^{\frac{1}{\alpha-1}}$$

12.3   Pure Exchange Equilibrium

Equilibrium models are a very important branch of economics with many subfields. As we will show next, equilibrium models are also a very useful tool in financial economics, and they have given rise to some of the most influential research in the field. A full review of equilibrium models is beyond the scope of this book, and we will only consider some of the models that focus on the analysis of financial variables. The models we will consider in this chapter belong to the class of **pure exchange equilibria.** The solution of these models is simpler than that of more general models, and that simplicity allows the introduction of more complicated dynamics of the primitives and, therefore, more interesting results from a pricing point of view. We describe this notion in the different settings we consider throughout the book.

12.3.1 Basic Idea and Single-Period Case

In this book, we call a **pure exchange economy** an economy in which there is no modeling of the production of the goods. More precisely, the endowment is not the result of a production process over which the agents of the model have some control (for example, they could increase production by allocating more capital). The canonical pure exchange economy in finance is a model due to Robert E. Lucas, Jr., who received the Nobel Prize in Economics in 1995. He considers a discrete-time economy with an infinite number of periods. Here we introduce a simple single-period version to illustrate the concept. We assume that there are a finite number of states K in which the realizations of the endowment process are e_1, $e_2, \ldots, e_K$.

Consider a representative agent that maximizes utility from consumption, over one period, of a consumption good that can be interpreted as money,

$$\max_{\{\Pi\}} E[U(c)] \tag{12.10}$$

where $U(\cdot)$ is a utility function, c represents consumption, and Π is the proportion of the agent's wealth held in the stock. The stock represents ownership of a production process that will pay a stochastic amount e. Since this is a one-period economy, after the stock pays the amount e, it disappears. The endowment e can then be also interpreted as a liquidation value of the company whose ownership is represented by the stock. There is also a bond with interest rate r. This is a pure exchange economy because, despite the existence of the endowment e, there is no modeling of production and the probability distribution that characterizes e is exogenously given. The initial stock price is S, so that the return of the stock is $\frac{e}{S}$. Alternatively, we could have also considered the price of the bond as the endogenous variable. We choose here to fix the return on the bond and to find the equilibrium (expected) return of the stock. We now introduce the usual notion of equilibrium.

For financial markets to clear, the return of the stock has to be such that the investor optimally holds the totality of the stock, normalized to be one share for simplicity, and invests nothing in the bond. At maturity, the agent collects the payoff of the stock and consumes it, so that all the endowment of the consumption good is used.

In order to be consistent with our notion of equilibrium, we have to assume that the agent receives enough wealth to be able to hold the stock in equilibrium. To keep the notation as simple as possible, we assume that the agent initially receives the whole stock. We denote by Π the fraction of the share of the stock the investor will optimally hold. Upon realization of the uncertainty, the individual will consume the payoff of the portfolio,

$$c = S(1 - \Pi)(1 + r) + \Pi e \tag{12.11}$$

Therefore, the objective of the representative agent (12.10) is equivalent to

$$\max_{\{\Pi\}} E\left[U(S(1 - \Pi)(1 + r) + \Pi e)\right] \qquad (12.12)$$

The first-order condition is

$$E[(-S(1 + r) + e)U'(S(1 - \Pi)(1 + r) + \Pi e)] = 0 \qquad (12.13)$$

Since S and $(1 + r)$ are known, the previous equation can be restated as

$$S = \frac{1}{1 + r} \frac{E[eU'(S(1 - \Pi)(1 + r) + \Pi e)]}{E[U'(S(1 - \Pi)(1 + r) + \Pi e)]}$$

The equilibrium condition requires that $\Pi = 1$. Then the equilibrium price of the stock is

$$S = \frac{1}{1 + r} \frac{E[eU'(e)]}{E[U'(e)]} \qquad (12.14)$$

This result links equilibrium models to some of our basic no-arbitrage pricing results. More precisely, we have the following theorem:

THEOREM 12.2   In the preceding equilibrium, the price of the stock is the expected value of the future discounted payoff under an equivalent martingale measure.

Proof   Let $p_i = P[e = e_i]$. Equation (12.14) can be written as

$$S = \frac{1}{1 + r} \frac{\sum_{i=1}^{K} p_i e_i U'(e_i)}{E[U'(e)]} \qquad (12.15)$$

Consider new probabilities q_i given by

$$q_i := p_i \frac{U'(e_i)}{E[U'(e)]}$$

These indeed are probabilities: they add up to one since $\sum_{i=1}^{K} p_i U'(e_i) = E[U'(e)]$, and they are positive and less than one. From equation (12.15) we have

$$S = \frac{1}{1 + r} \sum_{i=1}^{K} q_i e_i = \frac{1}{1 + r} E^Q[e]$$

Thus the discounted stock under this new probability is a martingale.   ∎

We now present an example in which the returns are normally distributed.

Example 12.2 (Exponential Utility and Normal Returns)   Consider a representative agent who chooses an investment amount π in a single risky security. The objective of the agent is

$$\max_{\{\pi\}} \left\{ -E\left[e^{-\alpha X(1)}\right] \right\}$$

One dollar invested in the risk-free security at time 0 returns $1 + r$ dollars at time 1. For the risky security, one dollar returns R dollars, where R can be random. The budget constraint is

$$X(1) = [X(0) - \pi](1 + r) + \pi R$$

We assume that the risky return R is normally distributed with mean μ and standard deviation σ. The objective of the representative agent becomes

$$\max_{\{\pi\}} \left\{ -E\left[e^{-\alpha\{[X(0)-\pi](1+r)+\pi R\}}\right] \right\} = \max_{\{\pi\}} \left\{ -e^{-\alpha\{[X(0)-\pi](1+r)\}} e^{-\alpha\pi\mu+\frac{1}{2}(\alpha\pi\sigma)^2} \right\}$$

The last equality follows from the fact that, for a normal random variable with mean μ and variance σ^2, we have $E[e^{aX}] = e^{a\mu+\frac{1}{2}a^2\sigma^2}$. The preceding maximization is equivalent to $\max_{\{\pi\}}\{\pi[\mu - (1 + r)] - \frac{1}{2}\alpha\pi^2\sigma^2\}$ with the solution

$$\hat{\pi} = \frac{1}{\alpha}\frac{\mu - (1 + r)}{\sigma^2}$$

In this setting, a possible equilibrium problem is the following: Suppose that the standard deviation σ of the stochastic return is given. What would be the expected return μ at which the individual would optimally invest all of $X(0)$ in the risky security? That is, we want $\hat{\pi} = X(0)$. Then we would have to have

$$\mu = (1 + r) + X(0)\alpha\sigma^2 \tag{12.16}$$

Remark   Note that this example gives a relationship between the return of the stock, the interest rate, the risk aversion of the investor, and the variance of returns. Similar relations are obtained with other, more realistic equilibrium models, and these can be empirically tested. In the next section we mention the so-called equity premium puzzle, which arises from an empirically tested equilibrium relationship between these same variables and the mean and volatility of U.S. consumption data.

12.3.2   Multiperiod Discrete-Time Model

Discrete-time, multiperiod models are typically the setting of choice in macroeconomics analyses that study problems more complicated than pure exchange equilibria, but with simpler underlying dynamics. Numerical algorithms are then used to approximate the solution. In financial economics we are usually interested in closed-form solutions and complex dynamics (with fewer state variables), and continuous-time models seem more appropriate. We do not review multiperiod models here and refer the interested reader to the book by Stokey and Lucas (1989). However, we mention here an influential paper by Mehra and Prescott (1985). In the multiperiod discrete-time setting they consider a pure exchange equilibrium model with a representative agent with power utility $U(x) = x^\gamma / \gamma$. In equilibrium, there is a connection between the risk aversion of the agent, the mean returns of the risky and risk-free assets, and the mean and standard deviation of the growth rate of the agent's optimal consumption [somewhat similar to relation (12.16); see the remark following it]. Mehra and Prescott collect financial and consumption data for the 1889–1978 period, and find that the average real (adjusted for inflation) return of the stock market was 7%. For the same period, the average real risk-free rate was less than 1%, and the average growth of consumption was almost 2%. The difference between the two return rates is called the **equity premium.** The equilibrium relationship implies that a coefficient of risk aversion higher than $1 - \gamma = 50$ would be consistent with the observed data values. This is considered much higher than the typical risk aversion of average individuals. This fact, which many subsequent papers have tried to explain using various approaches, is called the **equity premium puzzle.**

12.3.3 Continuous-Time Pure Exchange Equilibrium

The representative agent receives an endowment of the consumption good at the rate $e(t)$ and consumes at the rate $c(t)$. We assume the following dynamics for e:

$$de(t) = e(t)[\alpha \, dt + \rho \, dW(t)] \tag{12.17}$$

where α and ρ are the constant drift and volatility and W is a one-dimensional Brownian motion. Thus the endowment is a geometric Brownian motion process.

The agent has access to a risk-free security whose dynamics is given by

$$dB(t) = B(t)r(t) \, dt$$

where r is the (possibly stochastic) interest rate, to be determined in equilibrium.

Suppose also that there is a stock in the economy whose price S is given by

$$dS(t) = S(t)[\mu(t) \, dt + \sigma(t) \, dW(t)]$$

The parameters of the stock process μ and σ will be determined in equilibrium and, therefore, are allowed to be stochastic.

Denoting by π the amount held in the stock, the wealth process of the agent satisfies

$$dX = \frac{\pi}{S} dS + \frac{X - \pi}{B} dB + (e - c) \, dt$$

After substituting for dS/S and dB/B, we get

$$dX = \pi\sigma\, dW + [(\mu - r)\pi + rX + e - c]\, dt$$

We recall, from chapter 4, the following notation for the market price of risk:

$$\theta(t) := \frac{\mu(t) - r(t)}{\sigma(t)}$$

and the state-price density process

$$dZ = -\theta Z\, dW$$

Using Itô's rule we obtain

$$d(\bar{Z}X) = \bar{Z}(\pi\sigma - \theta X)\, dW + \bar{Z}(e - c)\, dt \tag{12.18}$$

where $\bar{Z}$ denotes the discounted value of Z. Therefore, under technical conditions which we assume, the process

$$M(t) := \bar{Z}(t)X(t) + \int_0^t \bar{Z}(u)[c(u) - e(u)]\, du$$

is a martingale, implying $E_t[M(T)] = M(t)$. The consequence of this relation is the **self-financing condition**

$$\bar{Z}(t)X(t) = E_t\left[\bar{Z}(T)X(T) + \int_t^T \bar{Z}(u)[c(u) - e(u)]\, du\right] \tag{12.19}$$

In particular, with $t = 0$ we get the following **budget constraint:**

$$X(0) = E\left[\bar{Z}(T)X(T) + \int_0^T \bar{Z}(u)[c(u) - e(u)]\, du\right] \tag{12.20}$$

If the agent maximizes the utility from consumption only, with the no-bankruptcy requirement $X(T) \geq 0$, then the optimal strategy will consume all the wealth by time T, and we will have $X(T) = 0$. Moreover, if we assume that $X(0) = 0$ (so that the endowment is the only source of income), the budget constraint becomes

$$E\left[\int_0^T \bar{Z}(u)[c(u) - e(u)]\, du\right] = 0 \tag{12.21}$$

The objective of the representative agent is given by

$$\max_{\{c\}} E\left[\int_0^T e^{-\beta u} U(c(u))\, du\right]$$

and U is the utility function of the agent. Taking all this together with the budget constraint, we can transform this expression into the Lagrangian problem

$$\max_{\{c\}} E \left[\int_0^T \left(e^{-\beta u} U(c(u)) - \frac{1}{\lambda} \bar{Z}(u)[c(u) - e(u)] \right) du \right]$$

where it will be convenient to have $1/\lambda$ as the Lagrangian constant. We could solve the problem rigorously using the duality methods from chapter 4. However, we choose to be somewhat informal and simply take the derivative with respect to c in the previous expression, under the expectation and the integral signs, and set it equal to zero. This step results in the following expression for the optimal consumption:

$$\hat{c}(t) = I \left(\frac{1}{\lambda} e^{\beta t} \bar{Z}(t) \right) \tag{12.22}$$

where $I = (U')^{-1}$ is the inverse function of the marginal utility function, and λ is chosen so that the budget constraint (12.21) is satisfied. In equilibrium, all markets should clear. The aggregate consumption must be equal to the aggregate endowment at all times. The stock represents the wealth of the economy. The stock market clears if the aggregate wealth is equal to the total value of the stock held. In other words, the **market-clearing conditions** are

$$c(t) = e(t) \tag{12.23}$$

$$\pi(t) = X(t) \tag{12.24}$$

These conditions also imply that the investor optimally invests zero in the risk-free assets, thus guaranteeing that the risk-free market clears.

From equations (12.23) and (12.19), and if $X(T) = 0$, we see that $X(t) = 0$; hence also $\pi(t) = 0$. Thus the dW term in equation (12.18) has to be equal to zero, and we get the optimal amount held in the stock as

$$\hat{\pi}(t) = \frac{\theta(t)}{\sigma(t)} \hat{X}(t) \tag{12.25}$$

where $\hat{X}$ is the wealth of the individual. Under the preceding assumptions, this expression implies that $\pi(t) = X(t) \equiv 0$, consistent with condition (12.24).

Example 12.3 (Log Utility) The representative agent chooses optimal consumption according to

$$\max_{\{c\}} E \left[\int_0^T e^{-\beta t} \log c(t) \, dt \right]$$

From equation (12.22) the optimal consumption is

$$\hat{c}(t) = \lambda e^{\int_0^t [r(u) - \beta + \frac{1}{2}\theta^2(u)]du + \int_0^t \theta(u)dW(u)} \tag{12.26}$$

Since, in equilibrium, $\hat{c} = e$, by equations (12.17) and (12.26) and Itô's lemma we get

$$(r - \beta + \theta^2)\,dt + \theta\,dW_t = \alpha\,dt + \rho\,dW_t \tag{12.27}$$

For the equality to hold, both the dt and dW terms of equation (12.27) have to be equal. This step yields the following equilibrium conditions:

$$\theta = \rho$$
$$r = \alpha + \beta - \rho^2$$

Alternatively, we could assume that the agent maximizes

$$\max_\pi E[\log\{X(T)\}]$$

In this case the usual equilibrium condition replacing the $c = e$ condition is that his wealth is equal to the total stock value at all times,

$$X(t) = S(t)$$

However, we recall from chapter 4 that the optimal wealth is given by

$$\hat{X}(t) = \frac{x}{\bar{Z}(t)}$$

Using Itô's rule on $\hat{X} = x/\bar{Z}$ and equating the dt and dW terms, we get

$$\theta = \sigma$$

$$\mu = r + \sigma^2$$

The previous results do not change if the model parameters are stochastic, because of the use of log-utility.

12.4   Existence of Equilibrium

Equilibrium parameters cannot always be computed analytically. Many times they have to be computed numerically, if a numerical algorithm is feasible. Also, there are some interesting equilibrium results that do not require explicit computation of equilibrium parameters, as we will see. In this section we want to consider an even more basic issue: the existence of equilibrium. Whether we are planning to compute parameters numerically or trying to extract qualitative conclusions of an equilibrium model, we first need to guarantee that an equilibrium indeed exists. This is not a trivial issue, and, in fact, unless the model satisfies a minimum of technical conditions, the existence of an equilibrium cannot generally be guaranteed. There is an extensive literature on the existence of equilibrium. Here, in order to provide a feel for this problem, we focus on simple cases with one or two goods (in the continuous and discrete-time sections, respectively). The extension to cases of more than two goods is not trivial and typically relies on the so-called fixed point arguments. For an introduction to that technique, we refer the reader to the books by Mas-Collel, Whinston, and Green (1995) and Hildebrand and Kirman (1988).

12.4.1 Equilibrium Existence in Discrete Time

Consider a single-period economy, populated by J agents who care about consumption of two goods. The utility function of agent j is given by $U_j(c_1^j, c_2^j)$, $j = 1, 2, \ldots, J$. We assume that $U(\cdot, \cdot)$ is continuous, strictly increasing in both arguments, and strictly concave. The agents are endowed with units of the consumption goods. We denote the endowment of agent j by $e^j = (e_1^j, e_2^j)$, where at least one component for each agent is not zero. This assumption is important for technical reasons, and it also makes economic sense.

We denote by P_i the price of consumption good i. The problem of agent j is, then,

$$\max_{(c_1^j, c_2^j)} U_j\left(c_1^j, c_2^j\right) \tag{12.28}$$

such that

$$P_1 c_1^j + P_2 c_2^j = P_1 e_1^j + P_2 e_2^j$$

Substituting this budget constraint in the objective function of the agent, we find that the optimal consumption values $\hat{c}_1^j$ and $\hat{c}_2^j$ satisfy

$$\frac{\frac{\partial U^j(\hat{c}_1^j, \hat{c}_2^j)}{\partial c_2^j}}{\frac{\partial U^j(\hat{c}_1^j, \hat{c}_2^j)}{\partial c_1^j}} = \frac{P_2}{P_1} \tag{12.29}$$

Denote by $z_i^j(P)$, $P = (P_1, P_2)$, the good-i excess demand of agent j, defined as

$$z_i^j(P) := \hat{c}_i^j(P) - e_i^j \tag{12.30}$$

The economy is in equilibrium if there is a price vector $P^* = (P_1^*, P_2^*)$ such that

$$\sum_{j=1}^J z_i^j(P^*) =: Z_i(P^*) = 0, \quad i = 1, 2 \tag{12.31}$$

By Walras' law, if the market of one of the two goods clears, the other market also clears. It is then enough to show that there is a P^* such that $Z_2(P^*) = 0$, for example. Furthermore, from the condition of equation (12.29) it is clear that only the ratio of the prices matters. We can then fix one of the two prices (say, set $P_2 = 1$) and look for a value for the other price that yields an equilibrium. That is, the problem is to find a price P_1^* such that

$$Z_1(P_1^*, 1) = 0 \tag{12.32}$$

PROPOSITION 12.1 (EXISTENCE OF EQUILIBRIUM)   In the economy described previously there is a price P_1^* such that condition (12.32) is satisfied, and therefore, an equilibrium exists.

Proof   Given the properties of the utility functions of the individual and the assumptions about their endowments, it is clear from equation (12.29) that if the price P_1 goes to zero, $P_1 \to 0$, then the excess demand goes to infinity, $Z_1(P_1, 1) \to \infty$. Similarly, if $P_1 \to \infty$, then $Z_1(P_1, 1) \to -\sum_{j=1}^J e_1^j < 0$. By the properties of the utility functions and condition (12.29), it is also clear that $Z_1(\cdot, 1)$ is a continuous function, and there is a P_1^* such that $Z_1(P_1^*, 1) = 0$.   ∎

12.4.2   Equilibrium Existence in Continuous Time

We consider here a model of equilibrium in continuous-time complete markets with two agents. Similar results can be obtained for more than two agents. For simplicity, we assume that the only source of income for the agents is an endowment of the consumption good. The agents can consume this endowment or invest it in the financial markets, consisting of a stock and a bond, and they start with initial wealth equal to zero. Agents A and B maximize

$$\max_{\{c\}} E \left[\int_0^T e^{-\beta t} U_i(c^i(t)) \, dt \right], \quad i = A, B$$

Also for simplicity, we assume that the discount factor β is the same for both agents and constant. By definition, we say that the **market is in equilibrium** if

$$c^A(t) + c^B(t) = e(t) := e^A(t) + e^B(t) \tag{12.33}$$

for all $t \leq T$, where $e(t)$ is the rate of the total **aggregate endowment** at time t. Recall expression (12.19) [with $X(T) = 0$], which gives the value for the wealth processes X_A and X_B of the two agents:

$$\bar{Z}(t)X_i(t) = E_t \left[\int_t^T \bar{Z}(u)[c^i(u) - e^i(u)] \, du \right], \quad i = 1, 2 \tag{12.34}$$

If we add the two expressions and use equation (12.33), we see that the aggregate wealth in the economy is zero:

$$X_A(t) + X_B(t) = 0 \tag{12.35}$$

Since

$$d(X_A + X_B) = (\ldots)\, dt + \sigma\,(\pi^A + \pi^B)\, dW$$

we see that the stock market also clears:

$$\pi^A(t) + \pi^B(t) = 0 \tag{12.36}$$

and so does the bond market. The method we use is to construct a representative agent that behaves as the aggregate of the two agents.

Recall from equation (12.22) that the optimal consumption for the agents is of the form

$$\hat{c}^i(t) = I_i\left(\frac{1}{\lambda_i} e^{\beta t} \bar{Z}(t)\right)$$

where I_i is the inverse function of U_i'. Therefore, in equilibrium we have

$$e(t) = I_A\left(\frac{1}{\lambda_A} e^{\beta t} \bar{Z}(t)\right) + I_B\left(\frac{1}{\lambda_B} e^{\beta t} \bar{Z}(t)\right) \tag{12.37}$$

Equivalently, if we denote by $c = c^A + c^B$ the total **aggregate consumption** and introduce the function

$$I(y) = I_A\left(\frac{y}{\lambda_A}\right) + I_B\left(\frac{y}{\lambda_B}\right) \tag{12.38}$$

we can write

$$c(t) = I(e^{\beta t} \bar{Z}(t)) \tag{12.39}$$

If we can show that I is an inverse function of a derivative of some utility function U, such a function could be interpreted as a utility function of a representative agent. We will argue that this is indeed the case. We define the function

$$U(c) := \max_{c^A + c^B = c} [\lambda_A U_A(c^A) + \lambda_B U_B(c^B)] \tag{12.40}$$

We leave the proof that $U(c)$ in equation (12.40) satisfies the properties of a utility function as an exercise (see Problem 6). We first introduce a preliminary result.

PROPOSITION 12.2   The function I defined in equation (12.38) is the inverse of U', or, equivalently, the inverse function of I, denoted J, is equal to U'; that is,

If $I(J(c)) = c$, then $J(c) = U'(c)$

Proof   Assume that $I(J(c)) = c$ for some function J. We first show that the optimal values for the maximization problem of equation (12.40) are given by

$$\hat{c}^i = I_i \left(\frac{J(c)}{\lambda_i} \right), \quad i = 1, 2 \tag{12.41}$$

Let us check that $\hat{c}^A + \hat{c}^B = c$:

$$\hat{c}^A + \hat{c}^B = I_A \left(\frac{J(c)}{\lambda_A} \right) + I_B \left(\frac{J(c)}{\lambda_B} \right) = I(J(c)) = c$$

The optimality follows from the fact that by substituting the preceding values of $\hat{c}^i$ we get zero for the derivative with respect to c^A of the expression in the maximum in equation (12.40), that is, of the expression $\lambda_A U_A(c^A) + \lambda_B U_B(c - c^A)$ [recall also that $U_i'(I_i(y)) = y$]:

$$\lambda_A U_A' \left(I_A \left(\frac{J(c)}{\lambda_A} \right) \right) - \lambda_B U_B' \left(I_B \left(\frac{J(c)}{\lambda_B} \right) \right) = J(c) - J(c) = 0$$

Finally, let us show that $U'(c) = J(c)$:

$$U'(c) = \lambda_A U_A' \left(I_A \left(\frac{J(c)}{\lambda_A} \right) \right) \cdot \frac{d}{dc} I_A \left(\frac{J(c)}{\lambda_A} \right) + \lambda_B U_B' \left(I_B \left(\frac{J(c)}{\lambda_B} \right) \right) \frac{d}{dc} I_B \left(\frac{J(c)}{\lambda_B} \right)$$

$$= J(c) \cdot \frac{d}{dc} \left[I_A \left(\frac{J(c)}{\lambda_A} \right) + I_B \left(\frac{J(c)}{\lambda_B} \right) \right]$$

$$= J(c) \cdot \frac{d}{dc} c$$

$$= J(c) \qquad\qquad\qquad\qquad\qquad\qquad\qquad\qquad \blacksquare$$

We now denote $J(e) = J(e; \lambda_A, \lambda_B)$, to emphasize that the function J depends on the values of (λ_A, λ_B), and provide a **characterization of the existence of market equilibrium in terms of the representative agent in the economy:**

THEOREM 12.3   The market is in equilibrium if there exists a solution (λ_A, λ_B) to the system of equations

$$E\left[\int_0^T e^{-\beta t} J(e(t); \lambda_A, \lambda_B) \left[I_i\left(\frac{1}{\lambda_i} J(e(t); \lambda_A, \lambda_B)\right) - e^i(t)\right] dt\right] = 0, \quad i = A, B$$

$$(12.42)$$

and the market state-price density is defined by

$$\bar{Z}(t) := e^{-\beta t} J(e(t); \lambda_A, \lambda_B) \tag{12.43}$$

Proof   Expression (12.43) is obtained by inverting equation (12.39), setting $c = e$. We can now define consumption processes:

$$\hat{c}^i(t) = I_i\left(\frac{1}{\lambda_i} J(e(t); \lambda_A, \lambda_B)\right) \tag{12.44}$$

Then equations (12.42) imply that these consumption processes do satisfy the budget constraint, and hence can be supported by a self-financing strategy. Moreover, if we define the state-price density as in equation (12.43), we see from equation (12.22) that these consumption processes are optimal in this economy. As before, we check that $\hat{c}^A + \hat{c}^B = e$, so that the commodity market clears. This result, as shown previously, implies that the stock and the bond markets clear, too.   ∎

Technical Remark   It can be shown, under mild conditions on the model and the utility functions, that the values of λ_i satisfying equation (12.42) do exist. However, they are not unique, and, in particular, if a pair (λ_A, λ_B) solves equation (12.42), so does $(k\lambda_A, k\lambda_B)$, for any positive number $k > 0$.

12.4.3   Determining Market Parameters in Equilibrium

We now want to answer the following typical equilibrium question: Given that we know the dynamics of the aggregate endowment rate in the economy (which can be interpreted as the rate of the aggregate income), what are the values for the interest rate r and the market price of risk θ that would make the economy be in equilibrium?

In order to answer this question we specify the dynamics of e as follows:

$$de(t) = e(t)[\alpha\, dt + \rho\, dW(t)] \tag{12.45}$$

For simplicity, we assume α and ρ to be constant. From equation (12.39), $c = e$, and J being the inverse function to I, we know that

$$U'(e(t)) = J(e(t)) = e^{\beta t} \bar{Z}(t)$$

Thus, using Itô's rule and the dynamics of $\bar{Z}$, we have

$$U'(e(t)) = e^{\beta t}\bar{Z}(t)[(\beta - r(t))\,dt - \theta(t)\,dW(t)]$$

However, we also have

$$dU'(e(t)) = \left[U''(e(t))\alpha e(t) + \frac{1}{2}U'''(e(t))\rho^2 e^2(t)\right]dt + U''(e(t))\rho e(t)\,dW(t)$$

Comparing the dt and dW terms in the previous two equations, we obtain

$$r(t) = \beta - \frac{1}{U'(e(t))}\left[U''(e(t))\alpha e(t) + \frac{1}{2}U'''(e(t))\rho^2 e^2(t)\right] \qquad (12.46)$$

$$\theta(t) = -\frac{U''(e(t))}{U'(e(t))}\rho e(t) \qquad (12.47)$$

These two expressions give a complete characterization of the equilibrium interest rate and the equilibrium market price of risk in terms of the aggregate endowment in the economy (and its dynamics) and the utility of the representative agent. In other words, as usual, the equilibrium model allows us to make a connection between the interest rate of the risk-free asset, the risk premium of the risky asset, and the risk preferences and aggregate endowment of the agents in the economy.

Example 12.4 (Logarithmic Utility)   Assume that both agents have logarithmic utility, $U_i(c) = \log(c)$. Then the representative agent's utility function U is obtained by maximizing

$$\lambda_A \log(c^A) + \lambda_B \log(c - c^A)$$

which gives

$$\hat{c}^i = \frac{\lambda_i}{\lambda_A + \lambda_B}c$$

and

$$U(c) = (\lambda_A + \lambda_B)\log(c) + \lambda_A \log\left(\frac{\lambda_A}{\lambda_A + \lambda_B}\right) + \lambda_B \log\left(\frac{\lambda_B}{\lambda_A + \lambda_B}\right)$$

$$U'(c) = J(c) = \frac{1}{c}(\lambda_A + \lambda_B)$$

The values of λ_i are determined only up to a multiplicative constant, so we can freely set

$$\lambda_A + \lambda_B = e(0)$$

Then, solving for λ_i in equation (12.42), we get

$$\lambda_i = \frac{e(0)E\left[\int_0^T e^{-\beta t} e^i(t)/e(t)\, dt\right]}{\int_0^T e^{-\beta t}\, dt}$$

Since we set $\lambda_A + \lambda_B = e(0)$, the state-price density is given by

$$e^{\beta t}\bar{Z}(t) = J(e(t)) = \frac{e(0)}{e(t)}$$

and the optimal consumption processes are

$$\hat{c}^i(t) = I_i\left(\frac{e(0)}{\lambda_i e(t)}\right) = \frac{\lambda_i e(t)}{e(0)}$$

The market parameters in equilibrium are

$$r(t) = \beta + \alpha - \rho^2$$

$$\theta(t) = \rho$$

This is the same result as in the single-agent economy.

Example 12.5 (CCAPM—Consumption Capital Asset Pricing Model) Ideally, we would like to use equilibrium models for predicting the difference in return between the risk-free asset and the risky asset, if not in precise quantitative terms, then at least in a theoretically sound qualitative way. We see from $\theta = \sigma^{-1}(\mu - r)$ and equation (12.47) that we can write this difference as

$$\mu(t) - r(t) = -\frac{e(t)U''(e(t))}{U'(e(t))}\sigma\rho \tag{12.48}$$

This formula goes under the name **consumption-based capital asset pricing model,** or **CCAPM.** Note that the product of the dW terms of the risky asset S and the aggregate endowment e is $\sigma\rho Se$. Thus $\sigma\rho$ can be interpreted as the relative instantaneous covariance between S and $e = c$ (i.e., the instantaneous covariance divided by $S \cdot e$). Consequently, the CCAPM (12.48) tells us that *the difference $\mu - r$ of the returns of the risky and the risk-free asset is proportional to the (relatively instantaneous) covariance between the risky asset and the aggregate consumption.* In practice, a broad market index such as the S&P 500 can be used as a proxy for S, and there are also ways to estimate the aggregate consumption in the economy. Thus, in principle, we can test the CCAPM using available economic data, and use it for future predictions. However, there is one big difficulty: the estimation of $U''(e(t))/U'(e(t))$. In general, testing the CCAPM against empirical data usually shows that the CCAPM is, at best, only a very simplistic model of reality. It has to be extended and modified further in order to agree better with the empirical data. These efforts can be exerted in several directions, such as introducing more complex preferences (utility functions) for the agents, presence of transaction costs, liquidity problems, or other market frictions. For more on CAPM-type results see the next chapter.

Summary

An economy is in equilibrium if the prices are such that the total demand equals the total supply when the investors behave optimally. It is also required that in equilibrium the total aggregate consumption of all agents has to be equal to the aggregate endowment. The equilibrium prices depend on the investors' utility functions and their endowment. If the equilibrium with several agents is identical to the equilibrium with a single agent, we say that the aggregation property holds, and the single agent is called the representative agent.

In financial markets, one usually considers pure exchange equilibria, in which there is no modeling of the production of consumption goods. The equilibrium prices can be obtained as expected values under an equivalent martingale probability measure. The existence of equilibrium is not always guaranteed, and it can be a hard problem.

In continuous-time models, the optimal consumption processes can be computed from the aggregate endowment and the values of constants λ_i that can be found from the budget-constraint condition. It is convenient to present the solutions in terms of the representative agent's utility function, obtained by maximizing a weighted average of the individual agents' utility functions.

Equilibrium models help us to get relationships between the interest rate of the risk-free asset, the risk premium of the risky asset, and the risk preferences and aggregate endowment of the agents in the economy. In the consumption-based capital asset pricing model, CCAPM, derived from market equilibrium, the difference between the returns of the risky and the risk-free asset is proportional to the relative instantaneous covariance between the risky asset and aggregate consumption.

Problems

1. Recompute, as much as possible, all the examples in section 12.1 with the log-utility replaced by the power utility $U(x) = \sqrt{(x)}$.

†2. Recompute, as much as possible, all the examples in section 12.1 with the log-utility replaced by the exponential utility $U(x) = 1 - e^{-ax}$.

3. Show that the same equilibrium as in equation (12.5) would result in the case of a single agent, with endowment $e^A(i) + e^B(i)$.

4. Check that the equilibrium in Example 12.1 is obtained for the given values of r and $\hat{c}^i(j)$.

5. Consider the setting of Example 12.3, but with two agents with logarithmic utilities from consumption only, and identical constant discount parameter β. Show directly that the resulting equilibrium is identical to the equilibrium of the example, without using the end-of-the-chapter results.

6. Verify that U defined by equation (12.40) is a utility function. In other words, show that $U' > 0$ and $U'' < 0$, if the same is true for U_A and U_B.

7. Consider the framework of Example 12.4, but for the power utility $U_i(c) = \frac{c^\gamma}{\gamma}$. Find the following: the representative agent's utility function U; the values of λ_i [normalize by setting $\lambda_A^{1/(1-\gamma)} + \lambda_B^{1/(1-\gamma)} = e(0)$]; the state-price density $\bar{Z}$; the optimal consumption processes $\hat{c}^i$; and the equilibrium values for $r(t)$ and $\theta(t)$.

Further Readings

For a general treatment of equilibrium problems see Hildebrand and Kirman (1988) and Mas-Collel, Whinston, and Green (1995). A pathbreaking equilibrium model is Lucas (1978). A study of general macroeconomics equilibrium in dynamic settings can be found in Stokey and Lucas (1989). A very influential application of equilibrium models is in Mehra and Prescott (1985). The problem of complete-markets equilibrium in continuous time is analyzed in Karatzas, Lehoczky, and Shreve (1990). The problem of the existence of equilibrium in incomplete markets is beyond the scope of this book. On that topic, we mention the influential works of Duffie and Shafer (1985, 1986) and Cass (1991). Magill and Quinzii (1996) offer a comprehensive survey of this literature. In continuous time, see Cuoco and He (2001).

13 CAPM

In this chapter we present the most famous financial equilibrium model: the capital asset pricing model (CAPM), developed in the 1960s simultaneously by several scholars (William F. Sharpe, John Lintner, and Jan Mossin). The beauty of this model is its simplicity and the ease of its implementation. As a result, the CAPM became the benchmark of all asset pricing models and gave rise to the development of a whole strand of the literature that tested or extended the predictions of the CAPM. The CAPM was developed in a static, single-period setting. Its practical importance, however, triggered many intertemporal, multiperiod versions of the CAPM. As usual in this book, we will first present the simpler setting, then continue with more elaborate settings.

13.1 Basic CAPM

In this section we describe a version of the original CAPM model developed in a static, single-period setting. It is an **equilibrium model,** in the sense that it derives relationships between the prices of traded assets based on some strong assumptions about investors' behavior in the market.

13.1.1 CAPM Equilibrium Argument

The starting point of the CAPM is the mean-variance analysis presented in chapter 5. Securities are characterized by their return over the single period considered and by the standard deviation of this return. For a security i, we denote its stochastic return by R_i, with expected return μ_i, and standard deviation of the return σ_i.

As in the mean-variance chapter (chapter 5), we postulate a strong assumption that all the investors are interested only in the expected return and the variances and covariances of the securities. In order to justify this, we have to assume one of two possibilities:

• We can assume that the security returns are jointly normally distributed. If that is the case, the mean, the standard deviation, and the covariances provide a full characterization of the returns distribution, and the investors do not need other information.

• Alternatively, we can assume that the preferences of the investors can be described by a quadratic utility function. In this single-period setting, a quadratic utility function means that an investor with final wealth X chooses a portfolio π in order to achieve the objective

$$\max_{\{\pi\}} E[-AX^2 + BX]$$

where A and B are positive constants that characterize the risk aversion of the quadratic utility. Since we have

$$E[-AX^2 + BX] = -AE[X^2] + BE[X]$$

it is clear that, given a portfolio π, the investor's utility is a linear combination of the variances, the covariances, and the expected returns of the securities. These are the only parameters necessary to solve the optimization problem of the investor.

One of the criticisms of the CAPM is that neither of these two assumptions is very realistic. The assumption of the normality of returns has been frequently questioned, and many empirical studies seem to indicate that a symmetric distribution does not provide a good model for stock return behavior. The choice of the quadratic utility is problematic because this utility is increasing only in a limited range of the values of wealth, not for all positive values. Nevertheless, the CAPM serves as a benchmark asset pricing model.

Some other assumptions are needed in order for the CAPM to hold. We also assume that there are no market frictions. In particular, there are no transaction fees, and investors can short-sell without restrictions; they can also borrow and lend using the risk-free asset without limitations, at the same interest rate.

Recall now the mean-variance analysis of chapter 5. We supposed that there was a risk-free security in the market with return rate R. Under either of the two assumptions, the investor would only consider points on the efficient frontier as possible portfolios. In fact, we deduced the so-called **one-fund theorem,** which says that the investors will trade only in the risk-free asset and one portfolio (mutual fund) consisting of risky assets. Let us denote here that mutual fund by M.

The big **conclusion of the CAPM theory** is the following: if all investors are mean-variance investors and they all have the same beliefs about the means, the variances, and the covariances of the assets, they will all have their portfolio holdings only in the fund M and in the risk-free asset; hence, *the fund M has to be the* **market portfolio!** That is, *the investors have to hold exactly those assets that are traded in the market, and exactly in the proportion that a particular asset has as a part of the total market value.* Let us illustrate this point with an example.

Example 13.1 (Market Portfolio)   Consider a very simple market that consists of only two risky assets, A and B. Suppose that there are 1,000 shares of asset A with a market value of $4.00 per share, and 2,000 shares of asset B with a market value of $3.00 per share. Then the total **capitalization** of asset A is $4,000, and of asset B it is $6,000. The total market value is $10,000. The proportions $\Pi_A = 4,000/10,000 = \frac{2}{5}$, $\Pi_B = 6,000/10,000 = \frac{3}{5}$ are called **capitalization weights** of assets A and B. The CAPM equilibrium argument has a very simple conclusion: under its assumptions, it is optimal for investors to hold their money in the risk-free asset and the market; the market portion of the portfolio should have $\frac{2}{5} = 40\%$ of its worth in asset A and $\frac{3}{5} = 60\%$ in asset B. The way the investors should divide their money between the risk-free asset and the market depends on their mean-variance preferences.

Let us repeat again the CAPM equilibrium idea: if a security is traded, it has to be one of the securities that form portfolio M, because this is the only portfolio the investors will consider. Then, and this is the corollary of our analysis, the portfolio M has to be the market portfolio, which includes all the securities actually traded and also tells us in which proportions they should be held. The demand and supply of the investors will force the market portfolio to become efficient.

At first glance this looks like a much too simplistic way of modeling the market, and it is. The underlying assumptions of the CAPM equilibrium argument are much too strong to be realistic. However, they can be considered as an ideal market situation, and we can then come up with new models relative to this ideal situation.

13.1.2   Capital Market Line

Recall that with the risk-free asset the mean-variance efficient frontier is actually a straight line determined by the risk-free asset and one fund of risky assets. In the context of the CAPM theory where this fund is the market portfolio M, represented as a mean-variance point (σ_M, μ_M), this line is called the **capital market line.** Any efficient portfolio (σ, μ) on this line satisfies

$$\mu = R + \frac{\mu_M - R}{\sigma_M}\sigma$$

where R is the risk-free rate of return. The slope of this line $(\mu_M - R)/\sigma_M$ is called the **market price of risk,** and it tells us how much the expected return μ of a portfolio on the line will increase if its standard deviation increases by one unit.

Example 13.2 (Capital Market Line)   Our CAPM investor Taf considers a venture that is expected to return 16% after a year, with the uncertainty measured by a standard deviation of 50%. The risk-free rate is 5% and the market expected return is 9.5%, with the standard deviation 15%. If this venture was itself an efficient portfolio, it would be on the capital market line. Now, a portfolio on the capital market line with the standard deviation of 50% would have an expected return of

$$0.05 + \frac{0.095 - 0.05}{0.15}0.50 = 0.2$$

or 20%. We conclude that this venture is not on the capital market line. (Our conclusion does not necessarily mean it is a bad investment if combined with other investments.)

13.1.3 CAPM Formula

In the next, very important theorem, we state the main formalization of the CAPM, which is based on the previous analysis. It establishes the relationship of the return of an individual asset with the return of the market portfolio.

THEOREM 13.1 (CAPM)   In the equilibrium described previously, the expected return μ_i of any asset i has to satisfy the **CAPM formula**

$$\mu_i = R + \beta_i(\mu_M - R) \tag{13.1}$$

where the constant β_i is defined as

$$\beta_i = \frac{\sigma_{Mi}}{\sigma_M^2} \tag{13.2}$$

and σ_{Mi} is the covariance between the returns of the market portfolio M and the asset i.

Proof   Denote by Π_i^M the proportion of the asset i in the market portfolio. Then we know from chapter 5 that

$$\mu_M = \sum_{i=1}^{N} \Pi_i^M \mu_i$$

$$\sigma_M^2 = \sum_{i=1}^{N} \sum_{j=1}^{N} \Pi_i^M \Pi_j^M \sigma_{ij}$$

$$\sum_{i=1}^{N} \Pi_i^M = 1$$

Recall that the capital market line has the slope $\frac{\mu_M - R}{\sigma_M}$. Being on the efficient frontier, portfolio M has the highest possible slope of all the lines that contain the risk-free asset and any portfolio of risky assets. Thus the market portfolio proportions have to solve the maximization problem

$$\max_{\{\Pi_i\}} \frac{\mu_M - R}{\sigma_M} = \max_{\{\Pi_i\}} \frac{\sum_{i=1}^{N} \Pi_i(\mu_i - R)}{\left(\sum_{i=1}^{N} \sum_{j=1}^{N} \Pi_i \Pi_j \sigma_{ij}\right)^{1/2}} \tag{13.3}$$

where we have used the fact that $\sum_{i=1}^{N} \Pi_i R = R$. Taking the derivative of the expression we are trying to maximize with respect to Π_i at the point $\Pi_i = \Pi_i^M$, we get

$$\frac{(\mu_i - R)\sigma_M - (1/2)\left(\sum_{i=1}^{N}\sum_{j=1}^{N}\Pi_i^M\Pi_j^M\sigma_{ij}\right)^{-1/2} 2\left(\sum_{j=1}^{N}\Pi_j^M\sigma_{ij}\right)\sum_{i=1}^{N}\Pi_i^M(\mu_i - R)}{\sum_{i=1}^{N}\sum_{j=1}^{N}\Pi_i^M\Pi_j^M\sigma_{ij}}$$

$$= \frac{(\mu_i - R)\sigma_M - \sigma_M^{-1}\sigma_{Mi}(\mu_M - R)}{\sigma_M^2}$$

where we have used the expressions for μ_M and σ_M, and the fact that $\sigma_{Mi} = \sum_{j=1}^{N}\Pi_j^M\sigma_{ij}$. Setting this derivative equal to zero, we get

$$\mu_i - R = \frac{\sigma_{Mi}}{\sigma_M^2}(\mu_M - R) = \beta_i(\mu_M - R)$$

This is the CAPM expression we wanted to prove.   ∎

13.2   Economic Interpretations

The CAPM offers a nice interpretation about equilibrium returns through its key parameter, β, called (CAPM) **beta** of a given security. According to the CAPM, the equilibrium return of a risky security depends only on its beta, and securities or portfolios with a higher beta should offer in equilibrium a higher expected return. Beta is a normalized measure of the covariance of a given security with the market portfolio: securities whose prices (and, therefore, returns) are more affected by, and in the same direction as, market movements, should offer an expected return higher than those that are more independent of the market, assuming that the market beats the risk-free asset, that is, assuming $\mu_M > R$. In particular, an asset that may be very risky (high σ_i) but has a negative covariance with the market will have a low return. Such an asset can be used for diversification, to reduce the risk when combined with the market portfolio. Then investors will be willing to tolerate its lower rate of return.

13.2.1   Securities Market Line

From the definition we see that the beta of the market portfolio is one, while the beta of the risk-free security is zero. The graphical representation of the CAPM in the (β, μ) plane is called the **securities market line,** or **SML.** According to the CAPM, in equilibrium all securities and portfolios must fall on the SML. The SML is easily characterized by two points: the point $(0, R)$ that corresponds to a zero beta and the risk-free rate of return, and the point $(1, \mu_M)$ that corresponds to a beta of 1 and the market return.

13.2.2   Systematic and Nonsystematic Risk

The CAPM has another direct economic interpretation, which we now present. The difference $\mu_i - R$ is called the **expected excess rate of return.** Thus another way to state the CAPM is that the expected excess rate of return of an asset is equal to the product of its beta with the expected excess rate of return of the market portfolio.

Recall that we use the notation $R_i = [S_i(1) - S_i(0)]/S_i(0)$ for the (relative) return of the asset i. One possible way to study the relationship between $r_M := R_M - R$ of excess market returns and $r_i := R_i - R$ of security-i excess returns is to postulate that their means are linearly related (which is consistent with the CAPM), that is, to have a so-called **linear regression** model of r_i and r_M. In other words, we define random error terms ε_i such that the random variables r_i and r_M satisfy

$$r_i = a_i + b_i r_M + \epsilon_i \tag{13.4}$$

Denote by σ_{ϵ_i} their standard deviation. Under standard linear regression assumptions, that is, when ε_i's are independent and their means are equal to zero, it is the case that $b_i = \beta_i$. The prediction of the CAPM is that, in equilibrium, $a_i = 0$. Furthermore, if we take the covariance of r_i with r_m in expression (13.4), we get

$$\sigma_{iM} = \beta_i \sigma_M^2 + \text{Cov}[\epsilon_i, r_M]$$

which, by the definition of β, gives $\text{Cov}[\epsilon_i, r_M] = 0$. Taking now the variance of r_i, we get

$$\text{Var}[r_i] = \text{Var}[a_i + b_i r_M + \epsilon_i] = \beta_i^2 \text{Var}[r_M] + \text{Var}[\epsilon_i] + \text{Cov}[\epsilon_i, r_M] \tag{13.5}$$

or

$$\sigma_i^2 = \beta_i^2 \sigma_M^2 + \sigma_{\epsilon_i}^2 \tag{13.6}$$

In other words, the risk (variance) of security i can be decomposed into two parts: The first one, $\beta_i^2 \sigma_M^2$, is the part of the risk of the security that is related to the market, through its beta; this is called **market risk,** or **systematic risk** of the security. The second part, $\sigma_{\epsilon_i}^2$, is called **nonsystematic risk,** or **specific risk,** or **idiosyncratic risk,** or **firm/company-specific risk.** The CAPM postulates that, in equilibrium, the expected return of a company's stock should be related to its market risk: a security with a higher market risk (higher beta) should offer a higher expected return than a security with a lower market risk (lower beta). The specific risk is irrelevant. In particular, consider a security with high total risk (high σ_i^2), but low beta. In equilibrium, its expected return will be lower than the return of another security with a higher beta and lower total risk (that is, a security with lower specific risk). The reason is that the specific risk can be diversified away (by investing in other securities), while the market risk cannot be diversified, and thus it has to be rewarded with higher return. We illustrate this fact in the following example.

Example 13.3 (Diversifying Specific Risk)   Suppose, for simplicity, that all securities have the same specific risk $\sigma_{\epsilon_i}^2 = \sigma_\epsilon^2$ and that ϵ_i are independent of each other. Consider a portfolio that invests the same proportion $1/N$ in the N securities. We want to show that as the number of securities N grows, the specific risk of the portfolio goes to zero.

The variance σ_P^2 of our portfolio is given by

$$\sigma_P^2 = \mathrm{Var}\left[\frac{1}{N}\sum_{j=1}^N R_j\right] = \frac{1}{N^2}\sum_{j=1}^N\sum_{i=1}^N \sigma_{ji}$$

Using the fact that $\mathrm{Cov}[\epsilon_i, \epsilon_j] = 0$ for i different from j, and that $\mathrm{Cov}[\epsilon_i, r_M] = 0$, we get

$$\sigma_{ij} = \mathrm{Cov}[R_i, R_j] = \mathrm{Cov}[r_i, r_j] = \mathrm{Cov}[\beta_i r_M + \epsilon_i, \beta_j r_M + \epsilon_j] = \beta_i \beta_j \sigma_M^2$$

Recalling also equation (13.6), we get

$$\sigma_P^2 = \frac{1}{N^2}\sum_{i,j=1}^N \beta_j \beta_i \sigma_M^2 + \frac{1}{N^2}N\sigma_\epsilon^2$$

Since a covariance of a sum of random variables is equal to the sum of their covariances, then also the beta β_P of our portfolio is equal to $(1/N)\sum_{i=1}^N \beta_i$. Therefore, the first term on the right-hand side is $\beta_P^2 \sigma_M^2$. Thus the second term represents the specific risk of the portfolio and it goes to zero as N grows.

To recap, only the systematic risk is relevant for establishing the equilibrium expected returns of securities, since the specific risk is diversifiable.

Let us note that an asset that falls on the capital market line has to have specific risk equal to zero. Other assets with the same value of beta will have the same expected return according to the CAPM, but may have nonzero specific risk. Hence, they will fall to the right of the capital market line (see the Problems section).

Here is an example that illustrates how to find some of the parameters we are interested in, using the CAPM and the knowledge of other parameters:

Example 13.4 (Using the CAPM for Estimation)   Suppose that the expected return and standard deviation of the market portfolio are 11% and 20%, respectively. The expected return of security 1 is 6%. The expected return of security 2 is 10%, and its standard deviation is 18%. A portfolio that invests half of its value in security 1 and half in security 2 has a beta of 0.5. We want to find the specific risk of security 2 according to the CAPM. In order to compute this risk, we first need to find the beta of security 2. We know that we have

$$0.5\beta_1 + 0.5\beta_2 = 0.5$$

from which we get $\beta_1 = 1 - \beta_2$. We can now solve the system of two CAPM equations:

$$0.06 - r = (1 - \beta_2)(0.11 - r)$$

$$0.10 - r = \beta_2(0.11 - r)$$

to get $r = 5\%$ and $\beta_2 = 5/6$. From equation (13.6) we can now find that the specific risk $\sigma_{\epsilon_2}^2$ is equal to

$$\sigma_{\epsilon_2}^2 = 0.18^2 - (5/6)^2 0.20^2 = 0.0046$$

We emphasize again that according to the CAPM the best way to invest your money in risky assets is to invest it in the market portfolio (in practice approximated by mutual funds that mimic the market index). However, if you believe that CAPM assumptions are not quite satisfied, such as, in particular, that you have better information than other investors, you may also believe that you can do better than investing in the market portfolio (or that your mutual fund manager can do better).

13.2.3 Asset Pricing Implications: Performance Evaluation

The CAPM has had an enormous importance partly because it was the first purely financial equilibrium model, as opposed to equilibrium models that involve nonfinancial economic variables. Moreover, it has a number of important practical implications. If the model is close to being correct, it would give us a benchmark to evaluate securities and decide whether their price is right, or whether they are overvalued or undervalued.

The standard approach in order to evaluate a security is to start by collecting observations of excess returns r_i on the security and r_M on the market and run a regression as discussed earlier. For example, if we are collecting a sample of monthly returns, for a given month we measure the return on security i in excess of the risk-free return for that month (which can be taken to be the return on a pure discount government bond that has one month left to maturity at the beginning of the month). We then consider the following regression-type relationship:

$$\hat{r}_i = \hat{\alpha}_i + \hat{\beta}_i \hat{r}_M \tag{13.7}$$

where $\hat{\beta}$ is our estimate of the beta of security i (computed from the sample covariances and variances), $\hat{r}_i$ is the estimate (the sample average) of the mean return of the security i, and $\hat{r}_M$ is the market average estimated return. Then $\hat{\alpha}_i$ is defined by the preceding equation, and it represents our estimate of the "true" α, which is a measure of overpricing or underpricing of the security. If the CAPM is correct, then the "true" α is zero, $\alpha_i = 0$. Thus, if $\hat{\alpha}_i > 0$, the security seems to be paying on average a return that exceeds the return that it should pay in the CAPM equilibrium. Similarly, if $\hat{\alpha}_i < 0$, the security seems to be underperforming. The parameter α (or its estimate) is also called the **Jensen index.** A positive Jensen index means that a security is performing better than predicted by the CAPM and may be underpriced. Similarly, a negative Jensen index means that the security may be overpriced.

The problem with the Jensen index as a performance indicator is that it does not give an indication of the actual risk level of the security. For example, suppose that two securities have the same positive Jensen index but their betas are different. Arguably, the security with the lower beta is more attractive, because it provides on average the same level of performance above equilibrium but with a smaller risk.

Another measure of performance that considers this aspect of the security performance is the **Treynor index,** T_i, which is defined as

$$T_i = \frac{\mu_i - R}{\beta_i} \tag{13.8}$$

where $\mu_i - R$ is the expected excess return of the security. If the Treynor index of a given security is greater than the Treynor index $\mu_M - R$ of the market portfolio, then the security is performing better than it should according to the CAPM.

However, for beta to be the true indicator of risk, it is necessary to be able to achieve perfect diversification (i.e., to have specific risk equal to zero), as indicated in previous discussions. A problem when evaluating an individual security is that, by its nature, it is not diversified. Some investors try to pick a few securities that are performing better than the market. In that case, considering only the systematic risk might be a mistake, since a security could show a good performance when we use the CAPM as a benchmark, but it might have a high level of specific risk, which is not going to disappear if the portfolio is not well diversified. In such a case, the Treynor index is not satisfactory. A more appropriate measure of risk/return performance is then the **Sharpe index** or **Sharpe ratio,** S_i, defined as

$$S_i := \frac{\mu_i - R}{\sigma_i} \tag{13.9}$$

The higher the Sharpe index of a security, the better the security, in the mean-variance sense. In the CAPM the best we can do is to be on the capital market line, which corresponds to the Sharpe index of the market portfolio, $(\mu_M - R)/\sigma_M$.

These indexes are not independent, and their relationships are collected in the following proposition.

PROPOSITION 13.1   The following relations hold:

1. A good Jensen index ($\alpha_i > 0$) implies a good Treynor index ($T_i > \mu_M - R$) and the other way around: a good Treynor index implies a good Jensen index.

2. A bad Jensen index ($\alpha_i < 0$) implies a bad Treynor index ($T_i < \mu_M - R$) and the other way around: a bad Treynor index implies a bad Jensen index.

3. A good Sharpe index ($S_i > \frac{\mu_M - R}{\sigma_M}$) implies a good Treynor index. However, a good Treynor index can occur together with a bad Sharpe index ($S_i < \frac{\mu_M - R}{\sigma_M}$).

4. A bad Treynor index ($T_i < \mu_M - R$) implies a bad Sharpe index. However, a bad Sharpe index can occur together with a good Treynor index.

In the Problems section you are asked to argue this proposition.

13.2.4   Pricing Formulas

We now want to use the CAPM as a pricing tool; after all, the name suggests that it is a pricing model. We recall that the mean return of a given stock in the period $[0, 1]$ is defined as $\mu = \{E[S(1)] - S(0)\}/S(0)$, and, in the CAPM theory, is equal to $R + \beta(\mu_M - R)$. From these relations we can solve for $S(0)$ to find the following **CAPM pricing formula:**

$$S(0) = \frac{E[S(1)]}{1 + R + \beta(\mu_M - R)} \tag{13.10}$$

In other words, the today's price of an asset is its expected future price discounted by $1 + R + \beta(\mu_M - R)$.

Example 13.5 (CAPM Pricing)   Suppose that our investor Taf considers investing in a mutual fund whose beta is reported as 0.8. The fund has been returning an average excess return of 15% in the last five years. Thus, for lack of better information, Taf estimates the expected annual return to be 15% above the risk-free rate, which is equal to 5%. In other words, Taf expects one dollar invested today in the fund to return 1.2 dollars after a year. The market has also been returning an average excess return of 15%. Today's price of one share of the fund is $50.00. According to the CAPM, the price should be

$$S(0) = \frac{50 \cdot 1.2}{1 + 0.05 + 0.8 \cdot 0.15} = 51.28$$

It looks like the fund is not overvalued, and it might be a good investment opportunity.

We now derive another form of the pricing formula. Since the asset return is $S(1)/S(0) - 1$, we can write, denoting by R_M the market return and recalling the definition of beta (13.2),

$$\beta \sigma_M^2 = \text{Cov}[S(1)/S(0) - 1, R_M] = \text{Cov}[S(1), R_M]/S(0)$$

Substituting into the pricing formula (13.10), we get

$$S(0) = \frac{E[S(1)]}{1 + R + \text{Cov}[S(1), R_M](\mu_M - R)/\left[S(0)\sigma_M^2\right]}$$

Solving for $S(0)$ gives

$$S(0) = \frac{1}{1 + R}\left[E[S(1)] - \frac{1}{\sigma_M^2}\text{Cov}[S(1), R_M](\mu_M - R)\right] \tag{13.11}$$

We see that the asset price is the discounted value of its future expected value reduced by a term that is proportional to the covariance of the asset and the market returns. Thus, assuming $\mu_M > R$, if the asset is positively correlated with the market, its price is smaller than the discounted future expected value, and if it is negatively correlated with the market, its price is higher. Intuitively, this statement is true because in the latter case the asset has an additional diversification value. Formula (13.11) also shows that CAPM pricing is a linear procedure: the price of a linear combination $aS_1(1) + bS_2(1)$ of two assets is equal to the linear combination $aS_1(0) + bS_2(0)$ of the prices.

13.2.5   Empirical Tests

Given the relevance of the model, both from a financial economics and a practical standpoint, testing the CAPM has been the topic of a whole strand of the literature. One of the first papers that dealt with testing the CAPM was written by Eugene Fama and James Macbeth in 1973. The objective of the paper was to see whether there is a positive relationship between betas and returns. In order to test this CAPM prediction, a large number of monthly returns of individual securities are collected, and, as a proxy for the return on the market, monthly returns on a broad market index are used. The most popular index for this purpose is the S&P 500, but all broad market indexes are highly correlated, and the use of one over another does not yield major differences. Also, returns on the one-month pure discount government bonds are collected. The collected data are split into subperiods. The test involves a two-step procedure.

In the first step, all the securities in the sample are grouped in portfolios, in order to reduce the specific risk of individual securities. If this grouping were not done, a large data set would be needed in order to estimate beta. All the portfolios consist of the same number of securities. In order to decide the components of each portfolio, the beta of each individual security is computed by linear regression. Then the securities are ranked by their betas, and the portfolios are formed by grouping the securities according to their rankings: for example, the securities with the 10 highest betas form the first portfolio, the securities with the next 10 highest betas form the second portfolio, and so on. Each security is given equal weight in the portfolio. This is the end of the first step.

In the second step, the beta of each portfolio formed in the first step is computed for each subperiod. Then a new regression is performed, to examine whether the betas of the portfolios for a given subperiod are positively related to the returns of the portfolios in the next subperiod, as predicted by the CAPM. If the CAPM is correct, the regression coefficient should be statistically significant. Fama and Macbeth also tested other implications of the CAPM, like the fact that the CAPM relation is linear. They test this by including a quadratic term of beta in the linear regression: in this case, the regression coefficient should not be statistically significant.

This test failed to reject the CAPM and gave a big boost to the popularity of the model. Since then, many additional tests using other methodologies have been performed. Although the predictive power of the CAPM is not generally accepted, it is still a very important benchmark in practice, and it remains the most influential equilibrium pricing model.

13.3   Alternative Derivation of the CAPM*

Remark on Vector and Matrix Notation   In some of the sections in this part of the book it will be convenient to use matrix and vector notation. An N-dimensional vector x is a column of values $x = (x_1, \ldots, x_N)^{Tr}$, where ^{Tr} denotes the transpose operation, that is, transforming columns into rows and vice versa. We will need this notation for a product of two vectors:

$$x^{Tr} y = x_1 y_1 + \ldots + x_N y_N = \sum_{i=1}^{N} x_i y_i \qquad (13.12)$$

We present here an alternative derivation of the CAPM, with the investors having exponential utility rather than mean-variance preferences, and with the returns assumed to have a normal distribution. There are N risky assets in the market whose random return rates R_i are the entries in the N-dimensional vector $\vec{R} = (R_1, \ldots, R_N)^{Tr}$. As before, the risk-free rate of return is constant, denoted by R. We assume that $\vec{R}$ has an N-dimensional normal distribution, with a vector of expected return rates $\vec{\mu} = (\mu_1, \ldots, \mu_N)^{Tr}$, and the variance-covariance matrix $\Sigma = \{\sigma_{ij}\}$. Here, σ_{ij} is the covariance of R_i and R_j. There are J investors in the economy, and they have to decide how to allocate their initial wealth across the $N+1$ securities. We denote by π^j the N-dimensional portfolio of dollar amounts π_i^j invested in the risky security i by investor j. The objective of this investor is

$$\max_{\{\pi^j\}} E\left[-e^{-\gamma_j X_j(1)}\right] \tag{13.13}$$

where $X_j(1)$ is the final wealth of the investor,

$$X_j(1) = X_j(0) + (\pi^j)^{Tr}\vec{R} + \left(X_j(0) - \sum_{i=1}^{N}\pi_i^j\right)R \tag{13.14}$$

and γ_j is a constant that represents the degree of risk aversion of investor j. Probability theory tells us that for the normally distributed vector $\vec{R}$ with mean-vector $\vec{\mu}$ and variance-covariance matrix Σ we have

$$E\left[e^{-\gamma_j(\pi^j)^{Tr}\vec{R}}\right] = e^{-\gamma_j(\pi^j)^{Tr}\vec{\mu} - \frac{1}{2}\gamma_j^2(\pi^j)^{Tr}\Sigma\pi^j} \tag{13.15}$$

Therefore, the investor has to maximize

$$\max_{\{\pi^j\}} E\left[-e^{-\gamma_j\left((\pi^j)^{Tr}\vec{R} + \left(X_j(0) - \sum_{i=1}^{N}\pi_i^j\right)R\right)}\right]$$

$$= \max_{\{\pi^j\}}\left[-e^{-\gamma_j(\pi^j)^{Tr}\vec{\mu} - \frac{1}{2}\gamma_j^2(\pi^j)^{Tr}\Sigma\pi^j + \gamma_j(X_j(0) - (\pi^j)^{Tr}\mathbf{1})R}\right]$$

where $\mathbf{1}$ is an N-dimensional vector of ones and we have written $\sum_{i=1}^{N}\pi_i^j = (\pi^j)^{Tr}\mathbf{1}$. By taking derivatives of the previous expression with respect to π_i^j for all i, and setting them equal to zero, we find

$$\pi^j = \frac{1}{\gamma_j}\Sigma^{-1}\left(\vec{\mu} - R\mathbf{1}\right) \tag{13.16}$$

We now introduce the notion of equilibrium. For simplicity, we assume that each risky security is represented in the market by one share only.

DEFINITION 13.1   Denote by $\pi^M(t)$ the market portfolio at time t, that is, the N-dimensional vector of the values of N risky securities at time t. The market is in equilibrium if the aggregate demand of the investors is equal to the initial market portfolio, that is, if the following relationship holds:

$$\sum_{j=1}^{J}\pi^j = \pi^M(0) \tag{13.17}$$

We now show that the CAPM holds in equilibrium in the preceding setting.

THEOREM 13.2   In the equilibrium described by definition 13.1, we have the following CAPM relationship:

$$\mu_i - R = \beta_i(\mu_M - R) \tag{13.18}$$

where

$$\beta_i = \frac{\sigma_{iM}}{\sigma_M^2}$$

is the beta of asset i, $\mu_M = \sum_{i=1}^{N} \mu_i$ is the expected market return, and σ_{iM} is the covariance of the return R_i of asset i and the market return $R_M := \sum_{i=1}^{J} R_i$.

Proof   From the equilibrium condition (13.17) and the optimal portfolio expression (13.16), we get

$$\pi^M(0) = \left(\sum_{j=1}^{J} \frac{1}{\gamma_j}\right) \Sigma^{-1}(\vec{\mu} - R\mathbf{1}) \tag{13.19}$$

We now represent π^M as

$$\pi^M = \Pi^M X_M \tag{13.20}$$

where X_M is the initial aggregate stock value in the economy, and Π^M is an N-dimensional vector of the proportions of the market portfolio in the individual risky assets. The components of the vector Π^M add up to one. Since the return of a weighted average of assets is equal to the weighted average of their returns, we have

$$R_M = \vec{R}^{Tr}\Pi^M$$

Also, denoting by $\tilde{R}$ the vector whose components are equal to the components of vector $\vec{R}$ minus their expected values, by definition we have that the variance-covariance matrix is

$$\Sigma = E[\tilde{R}\tilde{R}^{Tr}]$$

where the expected value is taken for every element of the matrix. Using the last two expressions, for the vector σ_{NM} with components σ_{iM}, the covariances of securities i with the market portfolio, we get

$$\sigma_{NM} = E[\tilde{R}\tilde{R}_M] = E[\tilde{R}\tilde{R}^{Tr}\Pi^M] = \Sigma\Pi^M \tag{13.21}$$

Together with equation (13.20), this gives

$$\Sigma\pi^M(0) = \sigma_{NM}X_M \tag{13.22}$$

Using this fact and rearranging terms in equation (13.19), we see that

$$\left(\frac{X_M}{\sum_{j=1}^{J} \frac{1}{\gamma_j}}\right) \sigma_{NM} = \vec{\mu} - R\mathbf{1} \tag{13.23}$$

Multiplying both sides from the left by the transpose of the vector Π^M we get

$$\frac{X_M}{\sum_{j=1}^{J} \frac{1}{\gamma_j}} \sigma_M^2 = \mu_M - R \tag{13.24}$$

where we have used the fact that $(\Pi^M)^{Tr}\sigma_{NM}$ is the variance of the market (covariance of the market with itself) and $(\Pi^M)^{Tr}\vec{\mu} = \mu_M$. Therefore,

$$\frac{X_M}{\sum_{j=1}^{J} \frac{1}{\gamma_j}} = \frac{\mu_M - R}{\sigma_M^2}$$

and substituting in equation (13.23), we get the CAPM formula.   ∎

Remark 13.1   We point out that we obtain this result because we assume that the investors have exponential utility functions, although possibly with different degrees of risk aversion, and that the returns are normally distributed. The result does not hold for arbitrary utility functions or distributions.

13.4   Continuous-Time, Intertemporal CAPM*

In this section we present a continuous-time version of the CAPM, introduced by Robert C. Merton in 1973. It is also called the **intertemporal CAPM.** As in the basic CAPM, the market is assumed to be frictionless. That is, there are no transaction costs, investors can borrow and lend at the same risk-free rate, and there are no short-selling constraints.

The risk-free security, the bond or bank account, has the price B that satisfies the dynamics

$$dB(t) = B(t)r dt \tag{13.25}$$

where r is the constant interest rate. Investors can borrow at the continuous interest rate r by short-selling the bond (or borrowing from the bank). In addition, there are N risky securities whose prices S_i, $i = 1, 2, \ldots, N$, satisfy

$$dS_i(t) = S_i(t)\left[\mu_i dt + \sigma_i^{Tr} dW(t)\right] \tag{13.26}$$

where μ_i is the constant drift, σ_i is an M-dimensional vector of constants, and W is a M-dimensional vector of independent standard Brownian motions. For simplicity, let us assume that $N = M$ and that the $N \times N$ matrix σ, formed by stacking the N vectors σ_i as its columns, has full rank.

The economy is populated by J investors. We represent by π^j the N-dimensional portfolio vector of amounts invested in the N risky securities by investor j. The problem of each investor is to choose the portfolio π^j that maximizes the utility of the individual,

$$\max_{\{\pi^j\}} E[U^j(X_j(T))] \tag{13.27}$$

where $U^j(\cdot)$ is a utility function of agent j.

Remark 13.2   In the basic CAPM model discussed before we had to assume that either the utility of the investors is quadratic or the returns on the stocks are normally distributed. In this version of the intertemporal CAPM we allow for any utility function, but we require risky securities to follow geometric Brownian motion processes. This requirement is equivalent to the assumption of normality of returns in the static CAPM.

The wealth of individual investors is denoted by X_j and satisfies the following dynamics, by usual arguments:

$$dX_j(t) = [\{X_j(t) - [\pi^j(t)]^{Tr}\mathbf{1}\}r + \{\pi^j(t)\}^{Tr}\mu]\,dt + [\sigma\pi^j(t)]^{Tr}dW(t) \tag{13.28}$$

where $\mathbf{1}$ is a vector of ones and μ is the N-dimensional vector of drifts μ_i.

We recall the definition of the value function, or indirect utility,

$$V^j(t, x) = \max_{\{\pi^j\}} E_{t,x}[U^j(X_j(T))] \tag{13.29}$$

where $E_{t,x}$ denotes the expectation conditional on $X(t) = x$.

Recall expression (4.35) for the optimal portfolio in the case of one risky asset only. It can be shown that the analogue of that expression in the case of several risky assets is given by, for the investor j,

$$\pi^j(t) = -\frac{V_x^j(t, X_j(t))}{V_{xx}^j(t, X_j(t))}\left(\sigma^{Tr}\sigma\right)^{-1}(\mu - r\mathbf{1}) =: T^j(t, X_j(t))\left(\sigma^{Tr}\sigma\right)^{-1}(\mu - r\mathbf{1}) \tag{13.30}$$

where $T^j := -V_x^j/V_{xx}^j$ can be interpreted as the inverse of the "indirect absolute risk aversion." As before, V_x and V_{xx} denote the partial derivatives of V with respect to x.

For simplicity, we assume that each risky security is represented by only one share in the market. We denote the market portfolio by π^M and the aggregate stock market value by

X^M, which are then given by

$$\pi_i^M(t) = S_i(t), \qquad X^M(t) = \sum_{i=1}^{N} S_i(t) \tag{13.31}$$

We now define equilibrium in this market.

DEFINITION 13.2 (INTERTEMPORAL EQUILIBRIUM)   For a given volatility matrix σ, the equilibrium is characterized by a vector of the drifts μ such that, for any given stock i, the aggregate demand of all investors for that stock equals the total value of the stock. That is,

$$\sum_{j=1}^{J} \pi^j(t) = \pi^M(t) \tag{13.32}$$

Remark 13.3   We are assuming that the drifts of the stocks are constant. There is no reason why the drift in the equilibrium of the previous definition should be constant. Therefore, in general, we cannot guarantee the existence of such an equilibrium.

We now introduce some auxiliary notation. First, the "return rate" $\mu_M(t)$ of the market portfolio is

$$\mu_M(t) := \left(\frac{\pi^M(t)}{X^M(t)}\right)^{Tr} \mu \tag{13.33}$$

We also introduce a stochastic beta, which is the analogue of the static CAPM beta:

$$\beta_i(t) := \frac{\sigma_{iM}(t)}{\sigma_M^2(t)} \tag{13.34}$$

where σ_M^2 is the (stochastic) "variance" of the market portfolio, given by

$$\sigma_M^2(t) := \left(\frac{\pi^M(t)}{X^M(t)}\right)^{Tr} \sigma^{Tr} \sigma \frac{\pi^M(t)}{X^M(t)} \tag{13.35}$$

and σ_{iM} is the (stochastic) "covariance" between security i and the market portfolio,

$$\sigma_{iM}(t) := (\sigma_i)^{Tr} \sigma \frac{\pi^M(t)}{X^M(t)} \tag{13.36}$$

We present first an auxiliary result.

THEOREM 13.3 (ONE-FUND THEOREM)   Suppose that the equilibrium introduced in definition 13.2 holds. Investors will optimally invest only in the risk-free security and the market
portfolio.

Proof   From equations (13.30) and (13.32), we get

$$\pi^M(t) = \sum_{j=1}^{J} T^j(t, X_j(t))(\sigma^{Tr}\sigma)^{-1}(\mu - r\mathbf{1})$$

$$= T^M(t)(\sigma^{Tr}\sigma)^{-1}(\mu - r\mathbf{1}) \tag{13.37}$$

where $T^M(t) = \sum_{j=1}^{J} T^j(t, X_j(t))$, suppressing the dependence on X_j's. Therefore,

$$(\sigma^{Tr}\sigma)^{-1}(\mu - r\mathbf{1}) = \frac{1}{T_M(t)}\pi^M(t) \tag{13.38}$$

Substituting equation (13.38) in equation (13.30), we get

$$\pi^j(t) = \frac{T^j(t)}{T^M(t)}\pi^M(t) \tag{13.39}$$

This result proves our case: investor j invests the risky part of the portfolio in the market
portfolio in such a way that he holds $T^j(t)/T^M(t)$ shares of each stock. The rest is invested
in the risk-free security.   ∎

   We now introduce the main result.

THEOREM 13.4 (INTERTEMPORAL CAPM)   If the equilibrium described previously holds,
then for each individual security $i = 1, 2, \ldots, N$, its expected return rate has to satisfy

$$\mu_i - r = \beta_i(t)[\mu_M(t) - r] \tag{13.40}$$

where β_M and μ_M are as given by equations (13.33), (13.34), (13.35), and (13.36).

Proof   Suppose that the equilibrium holds, and, therefore, the one-fund result of equation (13.39) holds. From equation (13.38) we get

$$\mu - r\mathbf{1} = \frac{1}{T^M(t)}(\sigma^{Tr}\sigma)\pi^M(t) \tag{13.41}$$

If we multiply both sides of equation (13.41) from the left by $(\pi^M)^{Tr}(t)/X^M(t)$, we get

$$\mu_M(t) - r = \frac{1}{T^M(t)}\sigma_M^2 X^M(t) \tag{13.42}$$

It follows that

$$\frac{1}{T^M(t)} = \frac{\mu_M(t) - r}{\sigma_M^2} \frac{1}{X^M(t)} \tag{13.43}$$

and substituting in equation (13.41) we get

$$\mu - r\mathbf{1} = \frac{\mu_M(t) - r}{\sigma_M^2} (\sigma^{Tr}\sigma) \frac{\pi^M(t)}{X^M(t)} \tag{13.44}$$

Now, from equation (13.36), $(\sigma^{Tr}\sigma)\pi^M(t)/X^M(t)$ is the vector of "covariances" $\sigma_{iM}(t)$, $i = 1, 2, \ldots, N$, of the individual risky securities with the market portfolio. The last expression is, then, our intertemporal CAPM claim.   ∎

13.5 Consumption CAPM*

In this section we introduce an extension of the intertemporal CAPM presented in the previous section. This model was described by Breeden (1979) and has had great influence in the field because it can be empirically tested.

The setting of this model is similar to the setting of the intertemporal CAPM except that the investors maximize utility from consumption. The following is the analogue of equation (4.44) for the optimal consumption:

$$\frac{\partial U^j(t, c^j(t))}{\partial c} = \frac{\partial V^j(t, X_j(t))}{\partial x} \tag{13.45}$$

where $U^j(t, c)$ is the utility function of investor j and $V^j(t, c)$ is his indirect utility, similar to equation (13.29), and c^j and X_j are his consumption and wealth processes, respectively. For the consumption CAPM (CCAPM) to hold, we need to introduce the following assumption:

ASSUMPTION 13.1   The utility functions of all the investors are such that the optimal consumption is linear in wealth, that is,

$$c^j(t) = A_j X_j(t) + B_j \tag{13.46}$$

where A_j and B_j are constants and specific to the utility of investor j.

This assumption is satisfied for many utility functions in standard models. We now want to introduce the key parameter of this model, the so-called consumption beta. First, we define the **instantaneous covariance** $\sigma_{XY}(t)$ of the processes X and Y given by

$$dX(t) = (\ldots) dt + \sigma_X^{Tr}(t) dW_t, \qquad dY(t) = (\ldots) dt + \sigma_Y^{Tr}(t) dW_t$$

as the process

$$\sigma_{XY}(t) := \sigma_X^{Tr}(t)\sigma_Y(t) \tag{13.47}$$

Next, denote by $\pi^M(t)$ the market portfolio—that is, the N-dimensional vector of the values of the N securities in the market—and by $\Pi^M(t)$ the corresponding proportions—that is, the weights of the individual securities in the market portfolio. Denote also by σ_{NC} the vector of the instantaneous covariances of the logarithms of the N securities with the aggregate consumption, and define

$$\sigma_{MC} := (\Pi^M)^{Tr}\sigma_{NC}$$

which is interpreted as a "covariance" of the market portfolio with the aggregate consumption. Then, **consumption beta**, β_C, is defined by

$$\beta_C(t) := \frac{\sigma_{iC}(t)}{\sigma_{MC}(t)} \tag{13.48}$$

where $\sigma_{iC}(t)$ is the instantaneous covariance between the aggregate consumption and the logarithm of security i. We now introduce the main result.

THEOREM 13.5 (CONSUMPTION CAPM)   Suppose that the equilibrium described in definition 13.2 holds and that Assumption 13.1 is satisfied. Then the expected returns μ_i must satisfy

$$\mu_i - r\mathbf{1} = \beta_{iC}(t)[\mu_M(t) - r] \tag{13.49}$$

where $\mu_M(t) := (\Pi^M)^{Tr}(t)\mu$ is interpreted as the instantaneous expected return rate of the market portfolio.

Proof   As in the previous section, the optimal investment policy of investor j is given by

$$\pi^j(t) = T^j(t, X_j(t))(\sigma^{Tr}\sigma)^{-1}(\mu - r\mathbf{1}) \tag{13.50}$$

where $T^j = -V_x^j / V_{xx}^j$. Rearranging equation (13.50), we get

$$\sigma_{NX_j}(t) = T^j(t, X_j(t))(\mu - r\mathbf{1}) \tag{13.51}$$

where $\sigma_{NX_j}(t) = \sigma^{Tr}\sigma\pi^j(t)$ represents the N-dimensional vector of instantaneous covariances between the wealth of investor j and the logarithms of N stocks. Also, from the optimality condition (13.45) it follows that

$$T^j(t, X_j(t)) = \frac{\frac{\partial U^j(t,c^j(t))}{\partial c}}{\frac{\partial^2 U^j(t,c^j(t))}{\partial c^2} \cdot \frac{\partial c^j(t)}{\partial x}} = A^j(t, c^j(t))\left(\frac{1}{\frac{\partial c^j(t)}{\partial x}}\right) \tag{13.52}$$

where A^j is the inverse of the risk-aversion coefficient. Substituting this expression in equation (13.51) we get

$$\sigma_{NX_j}(t) = \frac{A^j(t, c^j(t))}{\frac{\partial c^j(t)}{\partial x}}(\mu - r\mathbf{1}) \tag{13.53}$$

However, given the linearity of optimal consumption in wealth from Assumption 13.1, we have

$$\sigma_{Nc^j}(t) = \sigma_{NX_j}(t) \left(\frac{\partial c^j(t)}{\partial x} \right) \tag{13.54}$$

with σ_{Nc^j} as the N-dimensional vector of instantaneous covariances of the logarithms of the N securities with the consumption of investor j. Therefore, substituting equation (13.54) in equation (13.53) we get

$$\sigma_{Nc^j}(t) = A^j(t, c^j(t))(\mu - r\mathbf{1}) \tag{13.55}$$

We now add expression (13.55) over all investors,

$$\sum_{j-1}^{J} \sigma_{Nc^j}(t) = \sigma_{NC}(t) = \left(\sum_{j=1}^{J} A^j(t, c^j(t)) \right) (\mu - r\mathbf{1}) = A_C(t)(\mu - r\mathbf{1}) \tag{13.56}$$

where we recall that $\sigma_{NC}(t)$ is the vector of instantaneous covariances of the logarithms of the N securities with the aggregate consumption, and $A_C := \sum_j A^j$. If we multiply both sides of equation (13.56) from the left by $(\Pi^M)^{Tr}(t)$, the N-dimensional vector of weights of the N securities in the market portfolio, we get

$$\sigma_{MC}(t) = A_C(t)[\mu_M(t) - r\mathbf{1}] \tag{13.57}$$

We can solve for $A_C(t)$ in equation (13.57) and substitute in equation (13.56) to get

$$\mu - r\mathbf{1} = \beta_{NC}(t)[\mu_M(t) - r\mathbf{1}] \tag{13.58}$$

where $\beta_{NC}(t)$ is the N-dimensional vector of consumption betas of the N-securities.　■

   As we mentioned earlier, this model has been very influential, especially in the empirical literature, because the aggregate consumption in an economy can be measured, thereby making this model amenable to empirical tests.

Remark　There is a discussion on the so-called consumption-based CAPM (CCAPM) in chapter 12.

Summary

The benchmark model for security returns is the capital asset pricing model, or CAPM. It assumes that all investors are identical and have mean-variance preferences. In equilibrium, it is then optimal to hold only the market portfolio of risky assets and the risk-free asset.

The consequence of the theory is that the return of a given security in excess of the risk-free return is proportional to the return of the market portfolio in excess of the risk-free return. The constant of proportionality is called beta, and it depends on the covariance of the security and the market.

In the CAPM theory the risk—that is, the variance of a security—is decomposed into a specific or idiosyncratic risk, which can be diversified, and the systematic or market risk, which cannot be diversified. The theory also provides ways of comparing relative performance of various securities through the quantities called the Jensen index, Treynor index, and Sharpe index. The CAPM formula can be transformed into a formula for the equilibrium price of a given security and used to decide whether a security is overpriced or underpriced. There is also a continuous-time version of the CAPM, called the intertemporal CAPM, and a consumption CAPM, the CCAPM.

Problems

1. Suppose the only securities you can buy are an asset A with a beta of 1.2 and a risk-free security. Your target is to hold a portfolio with a beta of 0.75. How should you divide your money between A and the risk-free security to achieve this purpose?

†2. In a CAPM market, the expected return of the market portfolio is 20%, and the risk-free rate is 7%. The market standard deviation is 40%. If you wish to have an expected return of 30%, what standard deviation should you be willing to tolerate? How would you attempt to achieve this value if you had $100.00 to invest? (Remark: Short-selling is allowed.)

3. Draw a graph of the capital market line in the (σ, μ) plane. What is the specific risk of a security that falls on the capital market line and why? Show on the graph where the securities with nonzero specific risk fall.

†4. Suppose that we estimate the standard deviation of a portfolio P to be 10%, the covariance between P and the market portfolio to be 0.00576, and the standard deviation of the market portfolio to be 8%. Find the idiosyncratic risk of P.

5. Suppose that the CAPM holds. The expected return and standard deviation of a risky security A are 10% and 15%, respectively. The risk-free rate is 6%, and the expected return

and standard deviation of the market portfolio are 12% and 15%. What proportion of the risk of A is systematic risk?

†6. The expected return and standard deviation of the market portfolio are 8% and 12%, respectively. The expected return of security A is 6%. The standard deviation of security B is 18%, and its specific risk is $(10\%)^2$. A portfolio that invests $\frac{1}{3}$ of its value in A and $\frac{2}{3}$ in B has a beta of 1. What are the risk-free rate and the expected return of B according to the CAPM?

7. Consider a market consisting of only two assets, A and B. There are 100 shares of asset A in the market, sold at a price per share equal to $1.00. There are 100 shares of asset B in the market, with a price of $2.00 per share. Asset A has an average return rate $\mu_A = 10\%$, and for asset B, $\mu_B = 6\%$. The risk-free interest rate is $R = 5\%$. Moreover, the standard deviation of the market return is $\sigma_M = 20\%$. Assume that the market satisfies the CAPM theory exactly.

a. What is the expected return rate of the market portfolio?

b. Find the beta of asset A and the beta of asset B.

c. What is the covariance σ_{MA} of the market with asset A?

d. An investment opportunity in this market offers an average return $\mu = 6\%$ with standard deviation $\sigma = 19\%$. Would your portfolio be efficient if you invested all the money in this opportunity? Why?

8. Provide arguments for the statements of Proposition 13.1. It may be useful to recall that correlation is always between -1 and 1, and, in particular, that $-\sigma_i\sigma_M \leq \sigma_{iM} \leq \sigma_i\sigma_M$.

9. The market portfolio is expected to return 15%, the risk-free asset returns 5%, and securities A and B are expected to return 12% and 16%, respectively. The correlations of the securities with the market are estimated to be 0.8 and 0.9, respectively, and the standard deviations of the returns are estimated as $\sigma_A = 0.3$, $\sigma_B = 0.6$, and $\sigma_M = 0.3$. Find Jensen, Treynor, and Sharpe indexes for the securities A and B.

†10. The risk-free rate, average return of portfolio P, and average return of the market portfolio are, respectively, 4%, 8%, and 8%. The estimated standard deviation of the market portfolio is 12%, and the estimated nonsystematic risk of portfolio P is 15%. The Jensen index for portfolio P is 1%. What can you say about the performance of portfolio P?

11. Suppose that you consider investing in a fund that invests 20% of its funds in the risk-free asset at the rate of 6%, and the remaining 80% in a portfolio with a beta of 0.9, with expected return of 25%. The market has been returning an average of 26%. Today's price of one share of the fund is $100. What is the today's theoretical CAPM price of one share?

Further Readings

The original papers that introduced the CAPM are Sharpe (1964), Lintner (1965), and Mossin (1966). For the use of the CAPM framework for portfolio performance evaluations, see Treynor (1965) and Jensen (1969). The intertemporal CAPM is due to Merton (1973a). The consumption CAPM can be found in Breeden (1979). It was extended in Duffie and Zame (1989). The empirical testing of the CAPM is presented in Fama and Macbeth (1973). Roll (1977) discusses some fundamental problems in testing the CAPM. Black (1972) studies the CAPM when investors do not have access to unlimited borrowing. Adler and Dumas (1983) consider the CAPM in an international setting. For a review of empirical tests and implications of the consumption CAPM, see Campbell, Lo, and MacKinlay (1996) and Cochrane (2001).

14 Multifactor Models

In this chapter we collect a series of results that are mostly an extension of the results of chapter 13. There is a model, however, that deserves independent consideration because of its formalization and application to many empirical tests: the arbitrage pricing theory (APT). We also discuss some examples of factor models that have been considered in the literature with some success at explaining securities returns. The continuous-time multifactor model is an extension of the intertemporal CAPM discussed in chapter 13.

14.1 Discrete-Time Multifactor Models

Recall the static CAPM formula,

$$\mu_i - R = \beta_i(\mu_M - R) \tag{14.1}$$

We can rewrite this expression as

$$\mu_i = A_i + \beta_i \mu_M \tag{14.2}$$

where $A_i = R(1 - \beta_i)$. Expression (14.2) is a **factor model** where the factor is the market portfolio. We first justify the introduction of multifactor models with an ad hoc argument. Suppose that we test the CAPM to see whether the model helps to explain securities returns. That is, we postulate that the returns of security i are given by

$$R_i = A_i + \beta_i R_M + \epsilon_i \tag{14.3}$$

where ϵ_i is the error term, or the part of the return that is not explained by the market. If we assume that ϵ_i is independent of R_M, a linear regression procedure will give us an unbiased estimate of β_i. We can extend this model to

$$R_i = A_i + \beta_i^{(M)} R_M + \beta_i^{(1)} F_1 + \beta_i^{(2)} F_2 + \cdots + \beta_i^{(N)} F_N + \epsilon_i \tag{14.4}$$

where $\beta_i^{(M)}$ is the beta with respect to the market, F_j, $j = 1, 2, \ldots, L$, are L **factors** that help explain returns, and the coefficients $\beta^{(j)}$, $j = 1, 2, \ldots, N$, are the betas with respect to the L factors, with an interpretation similar to the beta with respect to the market. The problem is to decide which are the relevant factors. Furthermore, if we include sufficiently many factors, it becomes easy to explain historical returns. The challenge is to choose factors that will be able to explain out-of-sample, future returns.

In an influential study, Chen, Roll, and Ross (1986) test a multifactor model with the following factors: interest rates, inflation, gross domestic product (GDP) growth, and the number of bankruptcies in the economy. Following the methodology of Fama and Macbeth (1973) described in chapter 13, they get very encouraging results. Another very influential multifactor model using the same methodology is presented in Fama and French (1992).

They show that the betas do not seem to be good predictors of the stock returns after the early 1960s. However, there are two financial variables that seem to do very well as predictors. First, the size of the company, measured by its market capitalization value (the price of each share multiplied by the number of shares). The smaller the size, the higher the expected return. Second, the **book-to-market ratio.** This is the number equal to the theoretical value of each share (the company's asset value per share minus the liability value per share, as recorded in the balance sheet) divided by the market price of each share. The higher the book-to-market ratio, the higher the expected return of the stock.

The APT model that we study in the next section provides a mathematical formalization of multifactor models. Here, we first present an example modified from Brennan (1995), of an equilibrium model that, starting with some particular preferences of the individuals in the economy, yields a multifactor equilibrium model.

Example 14.1 (Two-Factor Equilibrium)   Consider an economy with a set of risky securities and a risk-free security, populated by investors who try to maximize

$$\max_{\pi^j} E\left[-e^{-\alpha_j\{[X_j(1)-I(1)]/X_j(0)\}}\right] \tag{14.5}$$

where π^j is the vector of portfolio amounts to be invested in the risky securities by investor j, α_j is the coefficient of risk aversion of investor j, $X_j(0)$ is the initial wealth, $X_j(1)$ is the wealth of investor j at the end of one period, and $I(1)$ is the value at the end of the period of some benchmark portfolio, to be interpreted as a value of a market index. The rationale for this type of model is that many institutional investors measure their utility relative to a market index.

We will see that in equilibrium these preferences yield a multifactor model. We derive the equilibrium for the case of two assets, x and y, with returns R_i, $i = x, y$. We assume that these returns are normally distributed with expected return μ_i, standard deviation σ_i, and covariance σ_{xy}. For simplicity, we assume that all the investors start with initial capital $X_j(0) = 1$ and that $I(0) = 1$. The index gives weight ϕ to security x and $(1 - \phi)$ to security y. If we denote by π^j the investment in the security x (therefore, $1 - \pi^j$ goes into y), the problem of investor j is

$$\max_{\pi^j} E\left[-e^{-\alpha_j[(\pi^j-\phi)R_x+(\phi-\pi^j)R_y]}\right] \tag{14.6}$$

By the properties of the bivariate normal distribution, problem (14.6) is equivalent to

$$\max_{\pi^j}\left[-e^{-\alpha_j(\pi^j-\phi)(\mu_y-\mu_x)-\frac{1}{2}\alpha_j^2(\pi^j-\phi)^2\left(\sigma_x^2+\sigma_y^2-2\sigma_{xy}\right)}\right] \tag{14.7}$$

The solution to problem (14.7) is

$$\pi^j = \phi + \frac{\mu_x - \mu_y}{\alpha_j\Omega} \tag{14.8}$$

where $\Omega := \sigma_x^2 + \sigma_y^2 - 2\sigma_{xy}$. The aggregate wealth is equal to $\sum_{j=1}^{J} X_j(0) = J$, where J is the number of agents in the economy. We assume that the market portfolio consists of assets x and y. We denote by w the proportion of the market portfolio represented by security x, which then leaves a proportion $1 - w$ in security y. In equilibrium, the aggregate demand has to be equal to the aggregate supply; that is,

$$\sum_{j=1}^{J} \pi^j = \left(J\phi + \frac{\mu_x - \mu_y}{\Omega} \sum_{j=1}^{J} \frac{1}{\alpha_j} \right) = wJ \tag{14.9}$$

To simplify the notation, we set $\Gamma = \frac{1}{J} \sum_{j=1}^{J} (1/\alpha_j)$. In equilibrium, then, we have

$$\phi + \frac{\mu_x - \mu_y}{\Omega} \Gamma = w \tag{14.10}$$

and from here we get

$$\mu_x = \Omega(w - \phi)/\Gamma + \mu_y \tag{14.11}$$

By definition, the expected return of the market portfolio μ_M is

$$\mu_M = w\mu_x + (1 - w)\mu_y \tag{14.12}$$

Substituting equation (14.11) in equation (14.12), we get

$$\mu_M = w\Omega(w - \phi)/\Gamma + \mu_y \tag{14.13}$$

However, the expected return of the index portfolio μ_I is

$$\mu_I = \phi\mu_x + (1 - \phi)\mu_y \tag{14.14}$$

Substituting equation (14.11) in equation (14.14), we obtain

$$\mu_I = \phi\Omega(w - \phi)/\Gamma + \mu_y \tag{14.15}$$

From equation (14.13) and equation (14.15) we see that we can write equation (14.11) as

$$\mu_x = \frac{1 - \phi}{w - \phi}\mu_M + \frac{w - 1}{w - \phi}\mu_I \tag{14.16}$$

Equation (14.16) is a two-factor model. The expected return of a security is explained by two factors: the market portfolio (as in the CAPM) and a market index.

14.2   Arbitrage Pricing Theory (APT)

The arbitrage pricing theory (APT) model was introduced by Stephen Ross in 1976, and it offers a mathematical formalization of multifactor models. On the one hand, it does not impose a specific type of preference or normality of stock returns. On the other hand, it requires identification of the factors that explain the returns. We present next an informal statement of this result.

APT (STEPHEN A. ROSS, 1976)   Suppose there are N stocks in the economy, and for each stock i its return R_i is represented as

$$R_i = \mu_i + (\beta_i)^{Tr} F + \epsilon_i \tag{14.17}$$

where μ_i denotes the expected return, β_i is an L-dimensional vector of "betas" with respect to the factors, and F is an L-dimensional vector of factors with zero expected value. Random variables ϵ_i are assumed to be independent and identically distributed with zero mean and common variance σ_ϵ^2. Then, if there is no arbitrage and for large N, we have an approximate relationship

$$\mu_i \approx A + \beta_i^{Tr} f \tag{14.18}$$

where A is a constant scalar and f is a constant L-dimensional vector with elements denoted f_i.

Sketch of the Argument   For a rigorous proof see Huberman (1982). We only provide intuition, for the case $L = 1$. Denote by μ the vector of expected returns and by β the vector of betas. Also, denote by $\mathbf{1}$ the N-dimensional vector of ones. By linear algebra, we can decompose the vector μ as

$$\mu = A\mathbf{1} + f\beta + a \tag{14.19}$$

where A and f are constant scalars and a is a vector orthogonal to both $\mathbf{1}$ and β; that is,

$$a^{Tr}\mathbf{1} = \sum_{i=1}^{N} a_i = 0 \tag{14.20}$$

$$\beta^{Tr}a = \sum_{i=1}^{N} \beta_i a_i = 0 \tag{14.21}$$

We interpret a as a portfolio: the N elements of a represent the N weights in each of the risky securities. Condition (14.20) means that this portfolio has zero cost. Let us suppose now that all the elements of a are different from zero. (In general, that might not be the case. For the case in which some of the components are zero, we refer the reader to the complete proof in Huberman, 1982.) Now we can use a standard diversification argument. For a given number w consider the portfolio wa, that is, a portfolio whose weight i is equal to wa_i. From equations (14.19)–(14.21), the expected return of this portfolio is

$$\mu_w := E\left[w\sum_{i=1}^{N} a_i R_i\right] = w\sum_{i=1}^{N} a_i \mu_i = w\sum_{i=1}^{N} a_i^2 \tag{14.22}$$

where we have used the orthogonality of a with respect to β and $\mathbf{1}$. From equations (14.17) and (14.21), the variance of the portfolio wa comes from the ϵ terms:

$$\sigma_w^2 := \text{Var}\left[w\sum_{i=1}^{N} a_i R_i\right] = w^2 \sigma_\epsilon^2 \sum_{i=1}^{N} a_i^2 \tag{14.23}$$

We now want to argue that

$$\limsup_{N\to\infty} \frac{\sum_{i=1}^{N} a_i^2}{N} = 0 \tag{14.24}$$

In words, $\sum_{i=1}^{N} a_i^2$ grows more slowly than the number of securities N. If this is indeed the case, then most a_i's have to be small as N gets large, and from equation (14.19) the APT relation (14.18) approximately holds. Suppose that, instead of equation (14.24), we have

$$\limsup_{N\to\infty} \frac{\sum_{i=1}^{N} a_i^2}{N} = C$$

where C is a strictly positive but finite number. Then we can see, with $w = 1/N$, that the return of our portfolio μ_w converges to $C > 0$, while its variance σ_w^2 converges to zero. We consider this result to be arbitrage, hence impossible. A similar argument works if $C = \infty$, but with a different choice for w. Thus equation (14.24) has to hold in the absence of arbitrage.

The starting point of the APT is that the stock returns deviate from their means as a result of unexpected realizations of some factors (they can be economic or economic-related, such as political events). We can interpret the value F_i as a deviation of a factor, say Y_i, from its mean, that is, $F_i = Y_i - E[Y_i]$. For example, the GDP number is larger than expected, or inflation is lower than expected. Such a factor may have a systematic effect of making the stock returns deviate from their means. This approach is a plausible description of some of the dynamics of the economy. The interesting conclusion is that, if the returns realizations can be explained in such a way, in the absence of arbitrage the expected returns satisfy the approximate relationship (14.18). As in the case of the CAPM, equation (14.18) has very important pricing implications. A problem with implementing the APT is the selection of the factors that determine the equilibrium expected returns. The approaches of the numerous empirical papers on the APT vary from a simple selection of appealing factors to econometric techniques like factor analysis that try to identify the relevant variables.

14.3 Multifactor Models in Continuous Time*

Here we present the extension of the intertemporal CAPM to the intertemporal multifactor CAPM, also presented in Merton (1973a).

14.3.1 Model Parameters and Variables

The risk-free asset satisfies

$$dB(t) = B(t)r\,dt \tag{14.25}$$

where r is the constant interest rate at which investors can borrow or lend. The model in Merton (1973a) assumes an arbitrary number of risky securities and Brownian motion processes, with the number of risky securities possibly smaller than the number of Brownian motion processes. In order to keep the notation as simple and explicit as possible, here we present the case of two risky securities and two Brownian motion processes. Therefore, there are two risky securities ("stocks") that satisfy

$$dS_i(t) = S(t)\mu_i(t, Y(t))\,dt + \sigma_{i1}(t, Y(t))\,dW_1(t) + \sigma_{i2}(t, Y(t))\,dW_2(t), \quad i = 1, 2 \tag{14.26}$$

where μ_i is a function that depends (possibly) on time and a state variable Y; σ_{ij}, $j = 1, 2$, are also functions that depend on time and the state variable Y; and W_1 and W_2 are two independent standard Brownian motion processes. The state variable Y satisfies

$$dY(t) = \alpha(t, Y(t))\,dt + \rho_1(t, Y(t))\,dW_1(t) + \rho_2(t, Y(t))\,dW_2(t) \tag{14.27}$$

where α, ρ_1, and ρ_2 are also functions of time and the state variable. In order to keep the notation as simple as possible, here we only consider one state variable, but the results also hold for an arbitrary number of state variables. Since we are assuming the same number of Brownian motion processes and stocks, the market is complete, but a complete market also is not necessary for our results. We often suppress the state variable and the time variable in what follows.

There are J investors, and we represent by π^j the two-dimensional vector-portfolio of amounts π_1^j and π_2^j invested in the two risky securities by investor j.

The problem of each investor is to choose a portfolio process π^j that maximizes the utility of the individual,

$$\max_{\{\pi^j\}} E[U^j(X_j(T))] \tag{14.28}$$

where $U_j(\cdot)$ is a utility function and β is the subjective discount rate that we assume constant.

It can be checked as before that the wealth process of investor j satisfies

$$
\begin{aligned}
dX_j(t) = & \left\{ \left[X_j(t) - \pi_1^j(t) - \pi_2^j(t) \right] r + \pi_1^j(t)\mu_1(t) + \pi_2^j(t)\mu_2(t) \right\} dt \\
& + \left[\pi_1^j(t)\sigma_{11}(t) + \pi_2^j(t)\sigma_{21}(t) \right] dW_1(t) \\
& + \left[\pi_1^j(t)\sigma_{12}(t) + \pi_2^j(t)\sigma_{22}(t) \right] dW_2(t)
\end{aligned} \tag{14.29}
$$

14.3.2 Value Function and Optimal Portfolio

The value function or indirect utility depends on the state variable and wealth,

$$V^j(t, x_j, y) = \max_{\{\pi^j\}} E[U^j(X_j(T)) \mid X_j(t) = x_j, Y(t) = y] \tag{14.30}$$

where $E[\cdot \mid X_j(t) = x_j, Y(t) = y]$ denotes conditional expectation. We often suppress the variables x_j and y in our notation. We denote by Σ the 2×2 matrix formed by stacking the volatility components of the stocks; that is,

$$\Sigma = \begin{pmatrix} \sigma_{11} & \sigma_{12} \\ \sigma_{21} & \sigma_{22} \end{pmatrix}$$

We denote by μ the two-dimensional vector of expected returns and by $\mathbf{1}$ a two-dimensional vector of ones, so that

$$\mu - r\mathbf{1} = \begin{pmatrix} \mu_1 - r \\ \mu_2 - r \end{pmatrix}$$

Finally, we introduce σ_{YS}, the two-dimensional vector of "covariance" between the state variable and the stocks; that is,

$$\sigma_{YS} := \begin{pmatrix} \sigma_{Y1} \\ \sigma_{Y2} \end{pmatrix} := \Sigma \cdot \begin{pmatrix} \rho_1 \\ \rho_2 \end{pmatrix} = \begin{pmatrix} \sigma_{11}\rho_1 + \sigma_{12}\rho_2 \\ \sigma_{21}\rho_1 + \sigma_{22}\rho_2 \end{pmatrix} \tag{14.31}$$

We now want to find the two-dimensional vector π^j of optimal portfolio holdings for investor j. We use the HJB equation method of chapter 4 in its two-dimensional version. In particular, the reader is asked in Problem 2 to show that the HJB equation for the value function $V = V^j$ and portfolio $\pi^j = \pi = (\pi_1, \pi_2)$ is given by (denoting by subscripts the partial derivatives)

$$0 = V_t + \sup_{\pi_1, \pi_2} \left\{ \frac{V_{xx}}{2} [(\pi_1 \sigma_{11} + \pi_2 \sigma_{21})^2 + (\pi_1 \sigma_{12} + \pi_2 \sigma_{22})^2] \right. \tag{14.32}$$

$$+ V_x [(x - \pi_1 - \pi_2)r + \pi_1 \mu_1 + \pi_2 \mu_2] + \alpha V_y \tag{14.33}$$

$$\left. + \frac{V_{yy}}{2} (\rho_1^2 + \rho_2^2) + V_{xy} [\rho_1 (\pi_1 \sigma_{11} + \pi_2 \sigma_{21}) + \rho_2 (\pi_1 \sigma_{12} + \pi_2 \sigma_{22})] \right\} \tag{14.34}$$

Taking the derivatives with respect to π_k and setting them equal to zero, we get

$$0 = V_{xx} [(\pi_1 \sigma_{11} + \pi_2 \sigma_{21}) \sigma_{k1} + (\pi_1 \sigma_{12} + \pi_2 \sigma_{22}) \sigma_{k2}] + V_x [\mu_k - r] + V_{xy} [\rho_1 \sigma_{k1} + \rho_2 \sigma_{k2}]$$

These two equations can be written in a matrix form as

$$V_{xx} \Sigma \Sigma^{Tr} \pi = V_x (\mu - r\mathbf{1}) - V_{xy} \sigma_{YS}$$

From this, suppressing dependence on t, we get the optimal portfolio vector for agent j as

$$\pi^j = -\frac{\frac{\partial V^j}{\partial x_j}}{\frac{\partial^2 V^j}{\partial x_j^2}} (\Sigma \Sigma^{Tr})^{-1} (\mu - r\mathbf{1}) - \frac{\frac{\partial^2 V^j}{\partial y \partial x_j}}{\frac{\partial^2 V^j}{\partial x_j^2}} (\Sigma \Sigma^{Tr})^{-1} \sigma_{YS} \tag{14.35}$$

In the rest of the section, we will use the following notation:

$$T_j := -\frac{\frac{\partial V^j}{\partial x_j}}{\frac{\partial^2 V^j}{\partial x_j^2}}, \qquad H_j(t) := -\frac{\frac{\partial^2 V^j}{\partial y \partial x_j}}{\frac{\partial^2 V^j}{\partial x_j^2}} \tag{14.36}$$

so that equation (14.35) becomes

$$\pi^j = T_j (\Sigma \Sigma^{Tr})^{-1} [\mu(t) - r\mathbf{1}] + H_j (\Sigma \Sigma^{Tr})^{-1} \sigma_{YS} \tag{14.37}$$

We now introduce the equilibrium condition.

DEFINITION 14.1 (INTERTEMPORAL EQUILIBRIUM WITH STATE VARIABLES)   We denote by X_M the aggregate value of wealth in the economy; that is, $X_M := S_1 + S_2$. We also denote by π_i^M, $i = 1, 2$, the amount of the aggregate wealth that corresponds to each of the stocks. That is, $\pi_i^M = S_i$. For given volatility functions σ_{ij} and ρ_j, the equilibrium in the financial markets is characterized by drifts μ_i of the stock processes, $i = 1, 2$, such that the aggregate demand of all investors equals the total value of each stock, that is, such that

$$\sum_{j=1}^{J} \pi_i^j(t) = \pi_i^M(t) \tag{14.38}$$

As noted previously, an equilibrium might not exist. When there are state variables, the existence of an equilibrium is even more complicated. Thus, to guarantee the existence of an equilibrium, some assumptions are necessary about the preferences of the individuals and the structure of the prices and state-variable processes.

14.3.3 Separation Theorem

As in the case of the intertemporal CAPM, we introduce a preliminary result. We simplify the notation by introducing

$$T_M(t) := \sum_{j=1}^{J} T_j(t), \qquad H_M(t) := \sum_{j=1}^{J} H_j(t)$$

Furthermore, consider the two-dimensional vector

$$\begin{pmatrix} w_1 \\ w_2 \end{pmatrix} = (\Sigma\Sigma^{Tr})^{-1}\sigma_{YS} \tag{14.39}$$

and define

$$X_Y := w_1 + w_2 \tag{14.40}$$

so that the two components of $\frac{1}{X_Y}(\Sigma\Sigma^{Tr})^{-1}\sigma_{YS}$ add up to one.

PROPOSITION 14.1 (MUTUAL FUND SEPARATION)   Assume that an equilibrium exists. The optimal holdings of investor j in security i can be expressed as

$$\pi_i^j = \frac{T_j}{T_M}\pi_i^M + X_Y\left(H_j - T_j\frac{H_M}{T_M}\right)\frac{1}{X_Y}(\Sigma\Sigma^{Tr})^{-1}\sigma_{YS} \tag{14.41}$$

That is, the investors' holdings are a combination (in weights specific to each investor) of the following two portfolios:

1. The market portfolio, π^M.

2. The hedging portfolio with proportions given by the vector $\frac{1}{X_Y}(\Sigma\Sigma^{Tr})^{-1}\sigma_{YS}$, which is a portfolio that allocates weights according to the betas of the securities with respect to the state variable.

Proof   In equilibrium, we have from equation (14.37)

$$\pi^M = \sum_{j=1}^{J}\pi^j = T_M(\Sigma\Sigma^{Tr})^{-1}(\mu - r\mathbf{1}) + H_M(\Sigma\Sigma^{Tr})^{-1}\sigma_{YS} \tag{14.42}$$

Solving in equation (14.42) for $(\Sigma\Sigma^{Tr})^{-1}(\mu - r\mathbf{1})$ and substituting in equation (14.37), the result (14.41) follows. We multiply and divide by X_Y so that one of the terms can be interpreted as investing in a specific portfolio, the portfolio $\frac{1}{X_Y}(\Sigma\Sigma^{Tr})^{-1}\sigma_{YS}$, whose components are proportional to the covariance of each security with the state variable, times the inverse of the variance-covariance matrix of the securities, which is the definition of beta. ∎

As in the case of the standard intertemporal CAPM, the previous result states that in practice only a number of portfolios (two in our setting) are relevant: investors will optimally distribute their wealth among them in proportions that are investor-specific. One of the portfolios is the market portfolio. The other is a so-called **hedging portfolio:** it allocates weights in the securities in proportion to their covariance with the state variable. The investors use this portfolio to take care of possible shifts in the parameters that drive the stocks as a result of a change in the state variable.

14.3.4 Intertemporal Multifactor CAPM

We now introduce some auxiliary notation. First, we denote by $\Pi^j := \pi^j / X_j$ the vector of proportions invested in the stocks by investor j, and similarly Π^M denotes the vector of the market portfolio proportions. We also denote by μ_M and μ_Y the expected return of the mutual funds 1 and 2 of Proposition 14.1, that is, the market portfolio and the portfolio that invests in the stocks in proportion to the state-variable betas, respectively. We compute them next, getting

$$\mu_M = (\Pi^M)^{Tr}\mu \tag{14.43}$$

$$\mu_Y = \left(\frac{1}{X_Y}(\Sigma\Sigma^{Tr})^{-1}\sigma_{YS}\right)^{Tr}\mu \tag{14.44}$$

in the form of the weighted average of the expected returns of the securities. We denote by σ_{MS} the two-dimensional vector of "covariances" of the market portfolio with each of the two individual securities,

$$\sigma_{MS} := (\Sigma\Sigma^{Tr})\Pi^M := \begin{pmatrix}\sigma_{M1}\\\sigma_{M2}\end{pmatrix} = \begin{pmatrix}\sigma_{11}(\Pi_1^M\sigma_{11} + \Pi_2^M\sigma_{21}) + \sigma_{12}(\Pi_1^M\sigma_{12} + \Pi_2^M\sigma_{22})\\\sigma_{21}(\Pi_1^M\sigma_{11} + \Pi_2^M\sigma_{21}) + \sigma_{22}(\Pi_1^M\sigma_{12} + \Pi_2^M\sigma_{22})\end{pmatrix} \tag{14.45}$$

We denote by σ_M^2 the "variance" of the market portfolio; that is,

$$\sigma_M^2 = (\Pi^M)^{Tr}(\Sigma\Sigma^{Tr})\Pi^M$$
$$= (\Pi_1^M)^2(\sigma_{11}^2 + \sigma_{12}^2) + (\Pi_2^M)^2(\sigma_{21}^2 + \sigma_{22}^2) + 2\Pi_1^M\Pi_2^M(\sigma_{11}\sigma_{21} + \sigma_{12}\sigma_{22}) \tag{14.46}$$

Similarly, we denote by σ_Y^2 the "variance" of mutual fund 2 of Proposition 14.1, that is, the "variance" of the portfolio with weights proportional to the betas of the securities. More precisely, for the portfolio

$$\Pi^Y := \begin{pmatrix} \Pi_1^Y \\ \Pi_2^Y \end{pmatrix} := \frac{1}{X_Y}(\Sigma\Sigma^{Tr})^{-1}\sigma_{YS} \tag{14.47}$$

we compute

$$\sigma_Y^2 = \left(\frac{1}{X_Y}(\Sigma\Sigma^{Tr})^{-1}\sigma_{YS}\right)^{Tr}(\Sigma\Sigma^{Tr})\left(\frac{1}{X_Y}(\Sigma\Sigma^{Tr})^{-1}\sigma_{YS}\right) = (\Pi^Y)^{Tr}(\Sigma\Sigma^{Tr})\Pi^Y$$

$$= (\Pi_1^Y)^2(\sigma_{11}^2 + \sigma_{12}^2) + (\Pi_2^Y)^2(\sigma_{21}^2 + \sigma_{22}^2) + 2\Pi_1^Y\Pi_2^Y(\sigma_{11}\sigma_{21} + \sigma_{12}\sigma_{22}) \tag{14.48}$$

Also, we denote by σ_{MY} the "covariance" between the two mutual funds of Proposition 14.1, that is, the "covariance" between the market portfolio and the mutual fund that invests in the two securities in proportion to their state variable betas. In other words, we define

$$\sigma_{MY} = (\Pi^M)^{Tr}(\Sigma\Sigma^{Tr})\Pi^Y = \frac{1}{X_Y}(\Pi^M)^{Tr}\sigma_{YS} \tag{14.49}$$

where Π^Y is as in equation (14.47). Finally, in order to make the notation more compact, we define the following matrices,

$$\Gamma = \begin{pmatrix} \sigma_{M1} & \sigma_{M2}/X_Y \\ \sigma_{Y_1} & \sigma_{Y2}/X_Y \end{pmatrix} \tag{14.50}$$

and

$$\Omega = \begin{pmatrix} \sigma_M^2 & \sigma_{MY} \\ \sigma_{MY} & \sigma_Y^2 \end{pmatrix} \tag{14.51}$$

We point out that Γ is the matrix of "covariances" (elements of vectors $\sigma_{MS} = \Sigma\Sigma^{Tr}\Pi^M$, $\sigma_{YS}/X_Y = \Sigma\Sigma^{Tr}\Pi^Y$) between the two mutual funds of Proposition 14.1 and the two securities in the market, and Ω is the "variance-covariance" matrix of the two mutual funds of Proposition 14.1. We are now ready to introduce our main result.

THEOREM 14.1 (INTERTEMPORAL MULTIFACTOR CAPM, MERTON, 1973a)   If an equilibrium of definition 14.1 exists, the following pricing relationship must hold for the two stocks in the market:

$$\mu - r\mathbf{1} = \Gamma\Omega^{-1}\begin{pmatrix} \mu_M - r \\ \mu_Y - r \end{pmatrix} \tag{14.52}$$

That is, in equilibrium, the expected excess return of each security over the risk-free rate has to be equal to a weighted combination of the expected excess returns of the two mutual funds, the market portfolio, and another portfolio that invests in the two stocks in the market in proportion to their state variable betas. The weights of these expected excess returns are the extension of the CAPM beta, since Γ is a matrix of "covariances" and Ω^{-1} represents the inverse of a "variance-covariance" matrix.

Proof If we multiply both sides of equation (14.42) by $\Sigma\Sigma^{Tr}$ and solve for $(\mu - r\mathbf{1})$ we get, suppressing the time variable t,

$$\mu - r\mathbf{1} = (\Sigma\Sigma^{Tr})\Pi^M(X_M/T_M) - \sigma_{YS}(H_M/T_M)$$
$$= \sigma_{MS}(X_M/T_M) - \sigma_{YS}(H_M/T_M) \tag{14.53}$$

where we use equation (14.45). We now multiply both sides of equation (14.53) by the vector-row of the weights of the market portfolio, $(\Pi^M)^{Tr}$, to get

$$\mu_M - r = \sigma_M^2(X_M/T_M) - X_Y\sigma_{MY}(H_M/T_M) \tag{14.54}$$

where we use equations (14.46) and (14.49). Similarly, if we multiply both sides of equation (14.53) by the vector-row $(\Pi^Y)^{Tr}$ of the weights of mutual fund 2 of equation (14.42), we get

$$\mu_Y - r = \sigma_{MY}(X_M/T_M) - X_Y\sigma_Y^2(H_M/T_M) \tag{14.55}$$

where we use equations (14.49) and (14.48).

We observe that equation (14.53) can be written as

$$\mu - r\mathbf{1} = \Gamma^{Tr}\begin{pmatrix} X_M/T_M \\ -X_Y H_M/T_M \end{pmatrix} \tag{14.56}$$

where Γ is as in equation (14.50). Similarly, equations (14.54) and (14.55) can be jointly rewritten as

$$\begin{pmatrix} \mu_M(t) - r \\ \mu_Y(t) - r \end{pmatrix} = \Omega\begin{pmatrix} X_M(t)/T_M(t) \\ -X_Y H_M(t)/T_M(t) \end{pmatrix} \tag{14.57}$$

Solving for the matrix on the right-hand side in equation (14.57) and substituting in equation (14.56), the result of equation (14.52) follows. ∎

This theorem is an extension of the standard intertemporal CAPM and is the continuous-time extension of discrete-time multifactor models. We expect the number of factors to increase with the number of state variables. We leave the proof of this intuition for Problem 3.

Summary

The multifactor extension of the CAPM formula represents the mean return of an asset as a linear combination of the mean returns of several factors, not just a single factor (the market portfolio) as in the standard CAPM. The multifactor formula can be derived from equilibrium conditions similarly as in the standard CAPM, or, alternatively, it can be shown that it has to hold approximately in a model with many assets, in the absence of arbitrage. The latter is called the arbitrage pricing model, or APT. There is also a continuous-time version of multifactor models and the CAPM formula.

Problems

1. For an Internet retailing company (a company that sells goods on-line) you try to explain the expected return of its stock in a multifactor model. You use the following five factors: GDP growth, real interest rates, inflation, average cost of personal computers, and number of Internet provider companies in the market the company serves. What signs would you expect each of the betas to have?

2. Mimic the HJB equation approach from chapter 4 to argue that equation (14.32) holds for the value function $V(t, x, y)$.

*3. Extend the continuous-time multifactor CAPM to more than two factors.

Further Readings

Our discrete-time multifactor example is based on Brennan (1995) and Gómez and Zapatero (2003). The multifactor model in continuous time is presented in Merton (1973a). The arbitrage-pricing-theory model was introduced in Ross (1976a). The proof we sketch is due to Huberman (1982). A complementary paper is Dybvig and Ross (1985). Some well-known and successful multifactor models are Chen, Roll, and Ross (1986) and Fama and French (1992).

15 Other Pure Exchange Equilibria

The objective of this chapter is to provide an introduction to some of the most influential equilibrium models in financial economics, such as term-structure equilibria, informational equilibria, and equilibria with heterogeneous agents. We close the chapter with an introduction to international equilibrium. As in the rest of the book, we try to approach each topic first in a discrete-time setting and then using continuous-time tools.

15.1 Term-Structure Equilibria

In chapter 8 we studied different models of the term structure of interest rates. We assumed some dynamics for the interest-rate process, and from that we derived the prices of bonds of different maturities. The advantage of that approach is that we can incorporate in the interest-rate dynamics any properties that the interest rates display in the real markets. The drawback of the approach is the fact that the interest-rate process is completely ad hoc and no attempt is made to explain the properties of the interest rates by economic arguments. Alternatively, we can try to derive the interest-rate process as the result of economic forces. This attempt can be made using an equilibrium model. The advantage of this approach is that by studying the economic variables of the model, we can make predictions about possible changes in the term structure of interest rates. The drawback of this approach is that, as we have seen in this section of the book, it is in general hard to solve for equilibrium variables. As a result, tractable models are very often too simplistic, at the risk of deriving interest-rate processes that fall short of the properties the interest rates show in reality. In fact, in our presentation of the continuous-time version of the Lucas model we already derived the equilibrium dynamics of interest rates in a simple model. We can argue that, in general, any intertemporal pure exchange equilibrium model will produce an equilibrium process of interest rates. However, there are some specific models whose objective is to derive meaningful dynamics of interest rates. Some of these models have been very influential in practice, and we present them in this section. We present first the basic idea in discrete time, in order to provide some intuition.

15.1.1 Equilibrium Term Structure in Discrete Time

Models of the "term structure of interest rates" are typically cast in a continuous-time setting, and computations of the equilibrium interest rate are more elegant in some specific continuous-time models, as we will show. In this section we present a simple case of the term structure of interest rates in discrete time, and yet, in general, computing equilibrium interest rates in closed form is not a straightforward enterprise.

The notion of the term structure of interest rates in single-period models is not very interesting, since there is only one maturity date. We consider here a two-period equilibrium model with a representative agent. Suppose that the agent makes consumption and investment decisions in order to perform the maximization

$$\max E[\log c(1) + \beta \log X(2)] \tag{15.1}$$

where $c(1)$ represents the consumption at the end of the first period, $X(2)$ is the final wealth (or consumption at the end of the second period), and $\beta < 1$ is a constant discount factor. The market consists of a stock that has initial price $S(0)$ and pays a stochastic dividend $e(1)$ at moment $t = 1$ and a final stochastic dividend or liquidation value $e(2)$ at moment $t = 2$. The representative agent can invest in the stock and in a risk-free asset, called a bond, that pays an interest rate $r(1)$ in period 1 (known at the beginning of period 1) and $r(2)$ in period 2 (known at the beginning of period 2). The budget constraint of the representative agent is then

$$X(0) = \delta(0)S(0) + b(0)$$

$$X(1) = \delta(0)[S(1) + e(1)] + b(0)[1 + r(1)] = c(1) + \delta(1)S(1) + b(1)$$

$$\delta(1)e(2) + b(1)[1 + r(2)] = X(2) \tag{15.2}$$

where $X(0)$ is a given initial wealth level, δ represents the number of shares of the stock, and b is the amount invested in the bond. In equilibrium, the agent must hold the totality of the stock and invest nothing in the bond. Furthermore, the agent must consume the totality of the dividend paid by the stock.

The standard approach to solving this problem is of the dynamic programming type: we consider the problem at moment $t = 1$ for a given level of wealth and prices, find the optimal policies at that point, substitute them, and then solve the problem at the initial time. The problem of the investor at time 1 is

$$\max_{\{c(1),\delta(1),b(1)\}} \{\log c(1) + \beta E_1[\log X(2)]\}$$

subject to

$$c(1) + \delta(1)S(1) + b(1) = X(1)$$

$$\delta(1)e(2) + b(1)[1 + r(2)] = X(2)$$

Substituting these constraints in the objective of the investor, we get that the problem of the investor at time 1 is equivalent to

$$\max_{\{\delta(1),b(1)\}} \{\log[X(1) - \delta(1)S(1) - b(1)] + \beta E_1[\log\{\delta(1)e(2) + b(1)[1 + r(2)]\}]\}$$

The first-order conditions of this problem are

$$-\frac{S(1)}{X(1) - \delta(1)S(1) - b(1)} + \beta E_1\left[\frac{e(2)}{\delta(1)e(2) + b(1)[1 + r(2)]}\right] = 0$$

$$-\frac{1}{X(1) - \delta(1)S(1) - b(1)} + \beta E_1\left[\frac{1 + r(2)}{\delta(1)e(2) + b(1)[1 + r(2)]}\right] = 0$$

In equilibrium, the agent consumes the totality of the dividend, that is, $c(1) = X(1) - \delta(1)S(1) - b(1) = e(1)$, and invests the remaining wealth in the single existing stock, $\delta(1) = 1, b(1) = 0$. Substituting these two conditions in the second of the first-order equations, we get

$$1 + r(2) = \frac{1}{\beta e(1)E_1[1/e(2)]}$$

Thus the interest rate $r(2)$, determined at moment $t = 1$, depends on the realization of the dividend at moment 1 and on the distribution of the dividends in the second period.

In order to solve for the interest rate $r(1)$, we would have to solve our dynamic programming problem at time zero. We would need to solve for $\delta(1)$ and $b(1)$ from the preceding first-order conditions, then use them to compute the value function at time 1. With that and the budget constraint corresponding to $X(0)$, we could write the first-order condition for $\delta(0)$ and $b(0)$ and then find the equilibrium interest rate in a way similar to the one we used for finding $r(2)$. Unfortunately, a closed-form solution for $\delta(1)$ and $b(1)$ is feasible only if we make very specific assumptions about the probability distribution of the dividends $e(2)$. [For example, we could assume that $e(2)$ takes only two possible values.] In general, however, we may not be able to compute the equilibrium interest rate in a discrete-time model of this type.

15.1.2 Equilibrium Term Structure in Continuous Time; CIR model

The first model to exploit the advantages of continuous time as the appropriate framework for the analysis of the term structure of interest rates was the Cox, Ingersoll, and Ross (1985a, 1985b) CIR model, studied as a continuous-time equilibrium extension of the Lucas model. We present now a simplified version of their analysis.

Consider a representative agent that maximizes utility from final wealth (in the original work the agent maximizes utility from intertemporal consumption, but the results are similar),

$$\max_{\{\Pi\}} E[e^{-\beta T} \log\{X(T)\}] \tag{15.3}$$

where Π represents the vector of portfolio weights and β is the constant subjective discount rate. There are three securities in the financial market. There is a risky stock (the "production technology," in the terminology of Cox, Ingersoll, and Ross, 1985a, 1985b) that satisfies the dynamics

$$\frac{dS(t)}{S(t)} = \mu Y(t)\, dt + \sigma_1 \sqrt{Y(t)}\, dW_1(t) + \sigma_2 \sqrt{Y(t)}\, dW_2(t) \tag{15.4}$$

where μ is a constant, Y is a "state variable," σ_1 and σ_2 are two constant volatility parameters, and W_1 and W_2 are two independent Brownian motion processes. A key feature of the model is the particular form for the dynamics of the state variable Y, which is assumed to be

$$dY(t) = [aY(t) + b]\, dt + \sqrt{Y(t)}[\rho_1\, dW_1(t) + \rho_2\, dW_2(t)] \tag{15.5}$$

where a, b, ρ_1, and ρ_2 are constant. In addition to the stock, there is a "contingent claim" that satisfies the following dynamics:

$$\frac{dC(t)}{C(t)} = \alpha(t)\, dt + v_1\, dW_1(t) + v_2\, dW_2(t) \tag{15.6}$$

where α is the drift process, to be determined in equilibrium, and v_1 and v_2 are two known volatility parameters. From the point of view of the investor, the contingent claim is just another risky security. The difference between the stock and the contingent claim is that the stock will be in positive supply, while the claim will be in zero-net supply; that is, the aggregate demand for C will be zero. Finally, the investor has access to a bank account that pays a continuous (and possibly stochastic) interest rate r. Holdings in this bank account evolve according to

$$\frac{dB(t)}{B(t)} = r(t)\, dt \tag{15.7}$$

We now introduce the notion of equilibrium.

DEFINITION 15.1   Denote by $\Pi = (\Pi_1, \Pi_2)$ the two-dimensional vector of proportions of the wealth of the agent invested in the stock and in the contingent claim, respectively. An equilibrium is determined by processes r and α such that

$$\Pi_1(t) \equiv 1$$

$$\Pi_2(t) \equiv 0$$

for all $0 \le t \le T$.

We can now introduce the main result.

THEOREM 15.1 (CIR EQUILIBRIUM)   The equilibrium interest rate in the preceding model is given by

$$r(t) = \left[\mu - \left(\sigma_1^2 + \sigma_2^2 \right) \right] Y(t) \tag{15.8}$$

In particular, the equilibrium interest rate satisfies the dynamics of the following type:

$$dr(t) = \kappa [\bar{r} - r(t)] \, dt + \sqrt{r(t)} [\gamma_1 \, dW_1(t) + \gamma_2 \, dW_2(t)] \tag{15.9}$$

for some constants $\kappa, \bar{r}, \gamma_1$, and γ_2.

Proof   See Problem 1.   ∎

We see that the contingent claim, for this choice of the utility function, does not affect the equilibrium interest rate or its dynamics.

15.2   Informational Equilibria

An important modeling innovation took place in the late 1970s. On different fronts in the economics literature, scholars started questioning the influence of uncertainty about parameter models in economic decisions. Uncertainty about outcomes had been the main driving force of financial economic models since the late 1950s. However, models were always constructed on the basis that the agents knew the parameters of the model and the distribution of any uncertain outcomes. The new question is, What happens if the economic agent is not even sure about the parameters of the model or the distribution of the uncertain variables? For example, the investor may know that the stock returns are normally distributed but not be sure of the expected return. Possibly, the uncertainty about a parameter of the return distribution will affect the investment decision of the agent. This is the type of question we addressed in chapter 4. In this section we are interested in the equilibrium parameters in models with one or several agents with incomplete information. As we will see, in dynamic models (namely, continuous-time models) the presence of a representative agent with incomplete information is enough to cause significant effects on the dynamics of equilibrium parameters. However, in intertemporal models it is usually hard to compute equilibria when there are several different agents with incomplete information. The effects of the interaction of heterogenous agents with incomplete information are more easily studied in a static model. We present some of these models next.

15.2.1   Discrete-Time Models with Incomplete Information

We present the single-period model introduced by Grossman (1976). There are several agents that try to maximize their utility from the final wealth. The agents have incomplete information about the final value (liquidation value) of the risky security. More explicitly, each agent $j, j = 1, 2, \ldots, J$, maximizes

$$-E\left[e^{-\alpha_j X_j(1)}\right], \quad j = 1, 2, \ldots, J \tag{15.10}$$

where the constant α_j represents the coefficient of risk aversion and the final wealth $X_j(1)$ is random and given by

$$X_j(1) = \delta_j S(1) + [X_j(0) - \delta_j S(0)](1 + r) \tag{15.11}$$

in our usual notation. At moment $t = 0$ the agent observes the price $S(0)$ of the risky security and also gets partial information about the realization of its liquidation value $S(1)$. The signal of agent j is expressed as

$$Y_j := S(1) + \epsilon_j \tag{15.12}$$

where ϵ_j is the noise under which investor j sees the liquidation value of the stock. That is, the agents do not know the liquidation value of the stock, but each agent receives a private signal that is the realization of the final value of the stock plus some noise. We assume that, conditionally on observing Y_j's, the noise terms ϵ_j are independent and normally distributed with mean zero and common variance σ_ϵ^2. In this setting, for an agent j that observes a signal Y_j, the liquidation value of the stock at moment $t = 1$ is normally distributed conditional on Y_j, with mean Y_j and variance σ_ϵ^2. Consider now the random variable $\bar{Y}$, the average of the signals of all investors in this economy, that is,

$$\bar{Y} = \frac{1}{J} \sum_{j=1}^{J} Y_j \tag{15.13}$$

We first introduce an auxiliary result.

LEMMA 15.1   Suppose that an investor observes $\bar{Y}$. For this investor, the price $S(1)$ of the stock has a normal distribution with mean $\bar{Y}$ and variance $\frac{\sigma_\epsilon^2}{J}$, that is,

$$E[S(1)|\bar{Y}] = \bar{Y} \tag{15.14}$$

$$\mathrm{Var}[S(1)|\bar{Y}] = \frac{\sigma_\epsilon^2}{J} \tag{15.15}$$

Proof   By definition,

$$\bar{Y} = \frac{1}{J} \sum_{j=1}^{J} Y_j = \frac{1}{J} \sum_{j=1}^{J} [S(1) + \epsilon_j] = S(1) + \sum_{j=1}^{J} \frac{\epsilon_j}{J}$$

or,

$$S(1) = \bar{Y} - \sum_{j=1}^{J} \frac{\epsilon_j}{J}$$

Therefore,

$$E[S(1)|\bar{Y}] = \bar{Y} - E\left[\sum_{j=1}^{J} \frac{\epsilon_j}{J}\middle|\bar{Y}\right] = \bar{Y}$$

Also,

$$\text{Var}[S(1)|\bar{Y}] = \text{Var}\left[\sum_{j=1}^{J} \frac{\epsilon_j}{J}\middle|\bar{Y}\right] = \frac{1}{J^2}\sum_{j=1}^{J}\text{Var}[\epsilon_j|\bar{Y}] = \frac{1}{J^2}J\sigma_\epsilon^2 = \frac{\sigma_\epsilon^2}{J}$$

where we use the fact that ϵ_j's are independent conditionally on Y_j's.   ∎

Thus the standard deviation of $\bar{Y}$ is smaller than the standard deviation of the individual Y_j's, and any investor will be better off observing $\bar{Y}$ than Y_j. It turns out that in this setting there is an equilibrium price that is a linear function of $\bar{Y}$, and observing the price of the stock at moment $t = 0$ is equivalent to observing $\bar{Y}$. Before presenting the result, we introduce the notion of equilibrium in this setting.

DEFINITION 15.2   Denote the total number of existing shares of the stock by N. An equilibrium is given by an initial price $S(0)$ such that the total demand and supply meet; that is,

$$\sum_{j=1}^{J} \delta_j = N \tag{15.16}$$

Recall from chapter 4, expression (4.82), that the optimal investment strategy of agent j that observes $\bar{Y}$ is given by

$$\delta_j = \frac{E[S(1)|\bar{Y}] - (1+r)S(0)}{\alpha_j \text{Var}[S(1)|\bar{Y}]} \tag{15.17}$$

Now we state the main result as a theorem.

THEOREM 15.2   Suppose that all the agents know all the parameters of the economy, that is, they know the preference parameters of all other agents. The price $S(0)$ given by

$$S(0) = \frac{\bar{Y}}{1+r} - \frac{\sigma_\epsilon^2 N}{J(1+r) \sum_{j=1}^{J} \frac{1}{\alpha_j}} \tag{15.18}$$

is an equilibrium price.

Proof   If all investors know other agents' preferences and observe $S(0)$ as given by equation (15.18), they can back out the value of $\bar{Y}$ from it. Therefore, their information set includes $\bar{Y}$, and the expected value and the variance of the liquidation value of the stock are as expressed in Lemma 15.1. Then, we apply equation (15.17) and verify that the equilibrium condition (15.16) is satisfied.   ∎

The average of the price signals provides the investors with an aggregate of all the information in the economy and, therefore, dominates the individual signals perceived by the investors. In this setting, prices are called **fully revealing.** From equation (15.18) it is clear that if the signals revealed perfect information—that is, if the volatility of the noise terms were zero, $\sigma_\epsilon = 0$—then the equilibrium return on the stock would be equal to r (and not risky anymore). In general, however, the price of the stock will be lower than $\bar{Y}/(1+r)$, indicating that there is a risk premium embedded in the equilibrium price. That is, because there is uncertainty about the stock price $S(1)$, the average return on the stock in equilibrium is higher than without uncertainty. This risk premium [which we can measure by $S(0) - \bar{Y}/(1+r)$] is lower the higher the number of agents and, therefore, the amount of information existing in the economy. However, it is larger the more risk-averse the agents are on average, since the term $\sum_{j=1}^{J} 1/\alpha_j$ will be smaller.

15.2.2   Continuous-Time Models with Incomplete Information

In this section we consider a continuous-time pure exchange equilibrium model with a representative agent with incomplete information. The optimal strategy of this agent was studied in chapter 4. Obtaining explicit equilibrium prices with several agents with incomplete information (that varies across agents) is not feasible in general. However, some interesting results about equilibrium dynamics can be derived in single-agent models. We now describe the economy. There is a stock S that pays a continuous dividend rate e, satisfying the following geometric Brownian motion process:

$$\frac{de(t)}{e(t)} = \alpha \, dt + \rho \, dW(t) \tag{15.19}$$

The price of the stock satisfies

$$\frac{dS(t)}{S(t)} = [\mu(t) - e(t)]\,dt + \sigma\,dW(t) \tag{15.20}$$

where μ is the capital gains rate, to be determined in equilibrium. Therefore, an investor who holds the stock receives the following gains process, with a capital-gain and a dividend-yield component:

$$\frac{dG(t)}{S(t)} = \frac{dS(t)}{S(t)} + e(t)\,dt = \mu(t)\,dt + \sigma\,dW(t) \tag{15.21}$$

The risk-free asset satisfies

$$\frac{dB(t)}{B(t)} = r(t)\,dt \tag{15.22}$$

The (possibly) stochastic interest rate will be determined in equilibrium. We assume that there is a single agent in this economy, who does not see the true drift of the endowment process α. Instead, the agent has a prior distribution for the drift, assumed to be normally distributed, with initial mean $\tilde{\alpha}(0)$ and initial standard deviation $\delta(0)$. The agent sees the endowment and the stock-price process and modifies the prior according to the realizations of these processes. As discussed in chapter 4, the agent sees the price dynamics as driven by the **innovation process** $\tilde{W}$, a Brownian motion process, whose dynamics is

$$d\tilde{W}(t) = dW(t) + \frac{\alpha - \tilde{\alpha}(t)}{\rho}\,dt = \frac{1}{\rho}\left(\frac{de(t)}{e(t)} - \tilde{\alpha}(t)\,dt\right) \tag{15.23}$$

where the estimated dividend drift $\tilde{\alpha}$ and its estimated standard deviation δ change according to the following rule:

$$d\tilde{\alpha}(t) = \frac{\delta(t)}{\rho}\,d\tilde{W}(t) \tag{15.24}$$

$$d\delta(t) = -\delta^2(t)\,dt \tag{15.25}$$

Because the agent does not observe the original Brownian motion W, he "lives" in a different probability space, where uncertainty is explained by the Brownian motion $\tilde{W}$. For the agent, the stock-price dynamics can be written as

$$\frac{dS(t)}{S(t)} = [\tilde{\mu}(t) - e(t)]\, dt + \sigma\, d\tilde{W}(t) \tag{15.26}$$

for the process $\tilde{\mu} = E_t[\mu]$ to be determined in equilibrium. Note that, by comparing the preceding expressions for dS, μ and $\tilde{\mu}$ have to satisfy

$$\frac{\alpha - \tilde{\alpha}}{\rho} = \frac{\mu - \tilde{\mu}}{\sigma} \tag{15.27}$$

We assume that the agent maximizes logarithmic utility from consumption,

$$\max_{\{c,\pi\}} E\left[\int_0^T e^{-\beta t} \log c(t)\, dt \right] \tag{15.28}$$

where π represents the amount invested in the risky security. We recall the definition of the state-price density for the agent with incomplete information:

$$\tilde{Z}(t) = e^{-\frac{1}{2}\int_0^t \tilde{\theta}^2(s)ds - \int_0^t \tilde{\theta}(s)d\tilde{W}(s)} \tag{15.29}$$

with $\tilde{\theta} = \frac{\tilde{\mu}-r}{\sigma}$. The reader is asked in the Problems section to show that the optimal consumption and investment strategies of this agent are

$$\hat{c}(t) = \frac{1}{\hat{\lambda} e^{\int_0^t [\beta - r(s)]ds}\, \tilde{Z}(t)} \tag{15.30}$$

$$\hat{\pi}(t) = \frac{\tilde{\theta}(t)}{\sigma} \hat{X}(t) \tag{15.31}$$

where $\hat{\lambda}$ is a constant. We also recall the notion of equilibrium in this setting:

DEFINITION 15.3   Equilibrium is characterized by a set of parameters (μ, σ, r) such that the agent consumes the endowment/dividend process and invests all the wealth in the stock; that is,

$$\hat{c}(t) = e(t) \tag{15.32}$$

$$\hat{\pi}(t) = \hat{X}(t) \tag{15.33}$$

We are now in a position to introduce the equilibrium result.

THEOREM 15.3   In equilibrium, the interest rate, the drift of the stock price, and the volatility of the stock price are

$$r(t) = \tilde{\alpha}(t) + \beta - \rho^2 \qquad (15.34)$$

$$\mu = \alpha + \beta \qquad (15.35)$$

$$\sigma = \rho \qquad (15.36)$$

Proof   In equilibrium $c = e$, thus using Itô's rule in equations (15.19) and (15.30), and matching the drift and diffusion terms, we get $r = \tilde{\alpha}(t) + \beta - \tilde{\theta}^2$ and $\tilde{\theta} = \rho$. From this equation, we derive equation (15.34). Using this together with equations (15.31) and (15.33), we have that $\frac{\tilde{\theta}(t)}{\sigma} = \frac{\rho}{\sigma} = 1$, and then we derive equation (15.36). Since $\tilde{\theta} = \frac{\tilde{\mu}-r}{\sigma}$, we also get that $\tilde{\mu} = r + \sigma^2 = \tilde{\alpha} + \beta$, where the last equality is a result of equation (15.34). Using equation (15.27) we get equation (15.35). ∎

The equilibrium drift and volatility are those that would prevail in an equilibrium with full information. We have the following interesting corollary for the interest-rate dynamics:

COROLLARY 15.1   The equilibrium interest rate satisfies a mean-reverting process similar to the Vasicek model, but with time-varying speed of the mean reversion and volatility:

$$dr(t) = \frac{\delta(t)}{\rho}[\bar{r} - r(t)]\, dt + \frac{\delta(t)}{\rho}\, dW(t) \qquad (15.37)$$

with

$$\bar{r} = \alpha + \beta - \rho^2 \qquad (15.38)$$

Proof   See the Problems section. ∎

In expression (15.37), $\bar{r}$ represents the long-term mean of the interest rate. We can see that the speed of the mean reversion and the volatility are time-varying but deterministic (since δ is a deterministic function of time). Therefore, a relatively simple model of incomplete information with one representative agent yields appealing interest-rate dynamics.

15.3   Equilibrium with Heterogeneous Agents

In chapter 12 we considered the problem of the existence of equilibrium when there is more than one agent and possible differences between agents. However, the examples of equilibria we have presented so far are based on a single representative agent. Here we introduce the case of several heterogenous agents. When the agents are identical, the problem is in general equivalent to that of a single representative agent. Models with several heterogeneous agents are appealing because they are obviously more realistic and, furthermore, the equilibrium values are more complex and potentially more interesting from an economic standpoint, especially in continuous-time models. Unfortunately, in most of the cases it is not possible to solve for equilibrium in closed form. Here we present an example in discrete time, for intuition purposes. We also consider possible equilibria with heterogeneous agents in continuous time and present an interesting example.

15.3.1 Discrete-Time Equilibrium with Heterogeneous Agents

Agents can differ in several aspects. Here we will concentrate on two. Consider a simple pure exchange, single-period, two-state model with two agents, A and B. There is a stock S that pays a return R_1 in state 1 and R_2 in state 2. That is, an amount x invested in the stock pays $x(1 + R_i)$ in state i. We assume that there is a single share of the stock. Besides, there is a risk-free asset, called a bond, that pays an interest rate r regardless of the state. The two agents are endowed with initial wealth levels $X^A(0)$ and $X^B(0)$, respectively. In equilibrium, they must jointly hold the stock, and the sum of their holdings in the bond must be zero; that is, if we denote by δ^A and δ^B the number of shares of the stock each of them holds, then

$$\delta^A + \delta^B = 1$$

$$X^A(0) + X^B(0) = S(0) \tag{15.39}$$

We consider two possible cases of heterogeneity:

1. Suppose that the probability of state 1 is p and the probability of state 2 is $1 - p$. Suppose that both agents know this probability but they differ because they have different utility functions and maximize

$$\max_{\{\delta^A\}} E[\log\{X^A(1)\}] \tag{15.40}$$

and

$$\max_{\{\delta^B\}} E\left[\frac{\{X^B(1)\}^\gamma}{\gamma}\right] \tag{15.41}$$

respectively.

2. Suppose that both agents have the same type of utility function, say, the utility in expression (15.40), but they disagree about the likelihood of the states. The first investor believes that the probability of state 1 is p_1 (therefore, $1 - p_1$ is the probability of state 2), while the probability of state 1 for investor 2 is p_2.

We present the equilibrium interest rate in the following proposition:

PROPOSITION 15.1   Consider the economy described in item 1 in the preceding list. The equilibrium interest rate r solves the following nonlinear equation:

$$1 = \frac{X^B(0)}{X^A(0) + X^B(0)}(1+r)\frac{[(1-p)(r-R_2)]^{\frac{1}{\gamma-1}} - [p(R_1-r)]^{\frac{1}{\gamma-1}}}{p^{\frac{1}{\gamma-1}}(R_1-r)^{\frac{\gamma}{\gamma-1}} + (1-p)^{\frac{1}{\gamma-1}}(r-R_2)^{\frac{\gamma}{\gamma-1}}}$$

$$+ \frac{X^A(0)}{X^A(0) + X^B(0)}(1+r)\left[\frac{p}{r-R_2} + \frac{1-p}{R_1-r}\right] \qquad (15.42)$$

Proof   The proof is straightforward and may be accomplished by taking derivatives and using the equilibrium conditions (15.39); see Problem 4.   ∎

We point out that even in this simple single-period, two-state setting, in general it is not possible to derive the equilibrium interest rate analytically. We also make the observation that the equilibrium interest rate depends on the relative wealths of the agents of this economy, $X^i/(X^A + X^B)$. We now present the result for the second model.

PROPOSITION 15.2   Consider the model with heterogeneous agents described in item 2 in the list. The equilibrium interest rate r solves the following equation:

$$\frac{1}{1+r} = \frac{1}{r-R_2}\left(\frac{X^A(0)}{X^A(0)+X^B(0)}p_1 + \frac{X^B(0)}{X^A(0)+X^B(0)}p_2\right)$$

$$+ \frac{1}{R_1-r}\left(\frac{X^A(0)}{X^A(0)+X^B(0)}(1-p_1) + \frac{X_2(0)}{X^A(0)+X^B(0)}(1-p_2)\right) \qquad (15.43)$$

Proof   The proof is straightforward and may be accomplished by taking derivatives and using the equilibrium conditions (15.39); see the Problems section.   ∎

Observe that the equilibrium risk-free discount factor, that is, the left hand-side of equation (15.43), is a weighted average of the inverse $\frac{1}{R_i-r}$ of the spread between the return of the stock and the interest rate in each state. The weights are themselves weighted averages of the subjective probabilities of the two investors, with the weights being the relative wealth of each agent. That is, the agent with a higher share of the aggregate wealth of the economy has more impact on the equilibrium value than the agent with the lower share. This is a property that is shared by both types of models with heterogeneous agents.

15.3.2   Continuous-Time Equilibrium with Heterogeneous Agents

The continuous-time case of two agents with heterogeneous risk aversion usually does not have a known analytic solution from which the equilibrium parameters can be computed. The case of agents with different beliefs, however, can be solved in closed form, and we present the solution here. It is a simplified version of the model introduced by Detemple and Murthy (1994).

Consider two agents that we will call an "optimist" and a "pessimist," for reasons that will be clear later. Both agents maximize logarithmic utility from terminal wealth,

$$\max_{\{\Pi^i\}} E^i[\log X^i(T)] \tag{15.44}$$

where $i = O, P$ (O for "optimist" and P for "pessimist") and Π^i is the proportion invested in the risky security. We note that the expectation is indexed by the type of individual: as we explain next, the investors differ in their beliefs, and, therefore, they compute their expectations differently (using different probability measures).

The stock process satisfies

$$\frac{dS(t)}{S(t)} = \mu\, dt + \sigma\, dW(t) \tag{15.45}$$

where μ and σ are constant. The risk-free asset with possibly stochastic interest rate satisfies

$$\frac{dB(t)}{B(t)} = r(t)\, dt \tag{15.46}$$

Both agents observe the stock price and the interest rate. They also know σ. However, they do not observe the expected return of the stock process. Agent i believes that the expected return belongs to a distribution with mean μ^i. We assume that $\mu^O > \mu^P$ to justify our terminology of an "optimist" and a "pessimist." Both agents live in a setting of incomplete information, as introduced in chapter 4. We recall from that chapter that agent i sees the dynamics of the stock as

$$\frac{dS(t)}{S(t)} = \tilde{\mu}^i(t)\, dt + \sigma\, d\tilde{W}^i(t) \tag{15.47}$$

where $\tilde{\mu}^i(t)$ is the current estimate of the drift μ by the agent i, and $\tilde{W}^i$ is the "innovation" Brownian motion process,

$$\tilde{W}^i(t) := \frac{1}{\sigma}\left(\frac{dS(t)}{S(t)} - \tilde{\mu}^i(t)\, dt\right) \tag{15.48}$$

Thus each agent lives in a probability space where the respective $\tilde{W}^i$ is Brownian motion. We introduce the following notation:

$$\tilde{\theta}^i(t) = \frac{\tilde{\mu}^i(t) - r(t)}{\sigma} \tag{15.49}$$

We recall from chapter 4 that the optimal proportion invested in the risky security is given by

$$\hat{\Pi}^i(t) = \frac{\tilde{\theta}^i}{\sigma}, \quad i = O, P \tag{15.50}$$

The notion of equilibrium is as usual:

DEFINITION 15.4   In equilibrium, the agents hold the totality of the stock, that is,

$$\Pi^O(t)X^O(t) + \Pi^P(t)X^P(t) = S(t) \tag{15.51}$$

and they have the aggregate holding equal to zero in the risk-free asset, or, equivalently,

$$X^O(t) + X^P(t) = S(t) =: X(t) \tag{15.52}$$

where X represents the aggregate wealth.

We now introduce the main result of this section.

THEOREM 15.4   The equilibrium interest rate is given by

$$r(t) = \tilde{\mu}^O(t)\frac{X^O(t)}{X(t)} + \tilde{\mu}^P(t)\frac{X^P(t)}{X(t)} - \sigma^2 \tag{15.53}$$

Proof   The proof is a straightforward result of equations (15.50), (15.51), and (15.52). ∎

We point out that the equilibrium interest rate is explicit, unlike the discrete-time case, and, as in the discrete-time case, it is a weighted average of the equilibrium interest rates that would result if the agents agreed on their beliefs. The agent with a larger share of aggregate wealth has more impact on the equilibrium value.

If we assume that the prior distributions of μ for the two agents are normal distributions, we can get explicit expressions for $\tilde{\theta}$, as in chapter 4, and it is possible to write down the dynamics of the interest rate in this setting. This setting provides another interesting equilibrium model of the term structure.

15.4   International Equilibrium; Equilibrium with Two Prices

Another interesting application of pure exchange equilibrium models is the derivation of international finance variables, especially exchange rates. Foreign-exchange markets involve movements of large amounts of money (and the volume is increasing rapidly with the globalization of international markets). Moreover, exchange rates are the underlying variables of a large number of options and future contracts. As a result, the models that provide any insight about possible dynamics of exchange rates are potentially very useful, in the same way that models of interest rates are the basis for pricing many securities. From an economics point of view, an exchange rate is similar to a price: it is the ratio at which one unit of a domestic good can be traded for a foreign good. In practice, the difference between an exchange rate and a price is the fact that the exchange rate is common to a basket of goods (the goods sold in or by a given country) while prices are specific to individual goods. However, in pure exchange equilibrium models we usually assume one good per country, and then the distinction between the prices and the exchange rates is blurred. The models we will present here can be used as the models of relative prices between two goods or as exchange-rate models. We now present a discrete-time and a continuous-time international pure exchange equilibrium model.

15.4.1   Discrete-Time International Equilibrium

The basic model was introduced by Lucas (1982). In order to provide some intuition, we only present a stripped-down version of that model, a single-period model without uncertainty.

Consider an economy with two countries and two goods. Each country is populated by one agent: agent i is the agent of country i. Furthermore, each country specializes in the production of one good, different from the good produced by the other country. However, the two agents derive utility from consuming both goods. We denote by c_j^i, $i, j = 1, 2$ the consumption of good j by agent i. The utility of agent i is given by

$$\max_{\{c_1^i, c_2^i\}} \left\{ a_i \log c_1^i + b_i \log c_2^i \right\} \tag{15.54}$$

where a_i and b_i are constant and are an indication of the preferences of agent i. We allow the agents to have different preferences ($a_1 \neq a_2$ and/or $b_1 \neq b_2$) over the two consumption goods.

The agents are endowed with wealth X^i, and they have to decide how to allocate the wealth across both goods. However, one unit of good 1 is not necessarily worth the same as one unit of good 2. The relationship at which they are traded is determined in equilibrium, and we interpret it as the exchange rate. In practice, an exchange rate is the number of units of the currency of one country that have to be paid in order to purchase one unit of the currency of another country. In our model there is only one good in each country; therefore, we can assume that the price of good i in units of the currency of country i is 1. The exchange rate becomes the relationship at which the two goods are traded. We denote by q the number of units of good 1 that can be purchased with one unit of good 2. Therefore, the budget constraint of the agent of country 1 is

$$c_1^1 + q c_2^1 \leq X^1 \tag{15.55}$$

Similarly, the budget constraint of the agent of country 2 is

$$\frac{1}{q} c_1^2 + c_2^2 \leq X^2 \tag{15.56}$$

In order to keep the model as simple as possible, we assume that the endowment (the wealth) of individual i matches the total supply of good i. Therefore, the notion of equilibrium is the following.

DEFINITION 15.5   An equilibrium is characterized by an exchange rate q such that

$$c_1^1 + c_1^2 = X^1$$

$$c_2^1 + c_2^2 = X^2 \tag{15.57}$$

The main result follows:

PROPOSITION 15.3   The equilibrium exchange rate is given by

$$q = \frac{X^1}{X^2} \frac{b_1(a_2 + b_2)}{a_2(a_1 + b_1)} \tag{15.58}$$

Proof   You are asked in Problem 7 to prove this result.   ■

Even a model as simple as the one we have described permits interesting analysis. For example, the higher the aggregate endowment X^i of one good, the more units of that good will have to be paid for one unit of the other good.

15.4.2   Continuous-Time International Equilibrium

We present here a continuous-time version of the Lucas model of international equilibrium. We will use a specification of the utility function for which a closed-form solution of the equilibrium is possible. The model we present is discussed in detail in Zapatero (1995).

Consider an economy with two agents such as those described in the discrete-time example: they are the single agents of two different countries. Their utility functions are the equivalent of the utility functions described in the single-period model, and they maximize

$$\max_{\{c_1^i, c_2^i\}} E\left[\int_0^T e^{-\beta t} \{a_i \log[c_1^i(t)] + (1 - a_i) \log[c_2^i(t)]\} \, dt \right], \quad i = 1, 2 \tag{15.59}$$

where c_j^i represents the consumption rate of good j by agent i, with $i, j = 1, 2$. Both agents need to consume both goods. The goods are indexed as the agents because they are produced exclusively in the corresponding country.

Each country has a financial market with a stock and a bond. The bonds are securities that pay a continuous interest rate,

$$\frac{dB_i(t)}{B_i(t)} = r_i(t)\, dt, \quad i = 1, 2 \tag{15.60}$$

where r_i is the interest rate of country i, to be determined in equilibrium. The stock of country i pays a dividend rate e_i that satisfies

$$\frac{de_i(t)}{e_i(t)} = \alpha_i\, dt + \rho_i\, dW_i(t), \quad i = 1, 2 \tag{15.61}$$

where α_i and ρ_i are constant. We assume that W_1 and W_2 are independent. An investor who holds stock i receives a gain process G_i that has two components: a capital gains component (the price changes) and a dividend yield. The gains processes satisfy

$$\frac{dG_i(t)}{G_i(t)} = \mu_i(t)\, dt + \sigma_1^i(t)\, dW_1(t) + \sigma_2^i(t)\, dW_2(t) \tag{15.62}$$

where μ_i, σ_1^i, and σ_2^i are to be determined in equilibrium. We point out that, although the stock pays a dividend that depends only on one Brownian motion process, in equilibrium it is possible that the capital gains might depend on the Brownian motion process of the other country.

As usual, we assume that the securities of one country are expressed in units of the consumption good of that country. We denote the exchange rate by q, which we define as the number of units of good 1 that are required to buy one unit of good 2. Both agents have access to the securities and the good of the other country, through the exchange rate. The agent of country 1 will have to pay qc_2^1 in order to consume c_2^1 of the consumption good of country 2. Similarly, the agent of country 2 will have to pay c_1^2/q units of the good of country 2 (the "currency" of country 2) in order to consume c_1^2. We conjecture that the exchange rate satisfies the following type of dynamics in equilibrium:

$$\frac{dq(t)}{q(t)} = \gamma(t)\, dt + \nu_1(t)\, dW_1(t) + \nu_2(t)\, dW_2(t) \tag{15.63}$$

Here, γ, ν_1, and ν_2 will be determined in equilibrium.

We note that when the agent of country i invests in the risk-free asset of country j, $j \neq i$, the security is not risk-free anymore and has a stochastic component when measured in units of country i. We formalize this intuition in the following lemma:

LEMMA 15.2   The returns of the investments of the agent of country 1 in the bond and stock of country 2 satisfy the following equations,

$$\frac{d[q(t)B_2(t)]}{q(t)B_2(t)} = [\gamma(t) + r_2(t)]\,dt + v_1(t)\,dW_1(t) + v_2(t)\,dW_2(t) \tag{15.64}$$

$$\frac{d[q(t)G_2(t)]}{q(t)G_2(t)} = \left[\gamma(t) + \mu_2(t) + v_1(t)\sigma_1^2(t) + v_2(t)\sigma_2^2(t)\right]dt$$
$$+ \left[v_1(t) + \sigma_1^2(t)\right]dW_1(t) + \left[v_2(t) + \sigma_2^2\right]dW_2(t) \tag{15.65}$$

The returns of the investments of the agent of country 2 in the securities of country 1 satisfy

$$\frac{d[B_1(t)/q(t)]}{B_1(t)/q(t)} = \{r_1(t) - \gamma(t) + [v_1(t)]^2 + [v_2(t)]^2\}\,dt$$
$$- v_1(t)\,dW_1(t) - v_2(t)\,dW_2(t) \tag{15.66}$$

$$\frac{d[G_1(t)/q(t)]}{G_1(t)/q(t)} = \{\mu_1(t) - \gamma(t) + [v_1(t)]^2 + [v_2(t)]^2 - v_1(t)\sigma_1^1(t) - v_2(t)\sigma_2^1(t)\}\,dt$$
$$+ \left[\sigma_1^1(t) - v_1(t)\right]dW_1(t) + \left[\sigma_2^1 - v_2(t)\right]dW_2(t) \tag{15.67}$$

Proof   The reader is asked to prove this result in Problem 6.   ∎

We point out that now both agents face financial markets where there is a risk-free security (the "domestic" bond) and three risky securities (the two stocks and the "foreign" bond). However, there are only two Brownian motion processes. Therefore, equilibrium parameters must be such that one of the securities is redundant, or there will be an arbitrage opportunity. We now introduce the notion of equilibrium.

DEFINITION 15.6   An equilibrium is given by a set of parameters $\mu_i, \sigma_1^i, \sigma_2^i, r_i, \gamma$, and v_i, $i = 1, 2$, such that the agents optimally consume the aggregate endowment of each consumption good; that is,

$$c_1^1(t) + c_1^2(t) \equiv e_1(t)$$
$$c_2^1(t) + c_2^2(t) \equiv e_2(t) \tag{15.68}$$

for all $0 \leq t \leq T$. Also, the aggregate optimal holdings of the risky stocks are equal to the aggregate value of the stocks, and the aggregate optimal holdings in the bonds are zero.

For the particular case considered in this section, the equilibrium parameters can be computed explicitly. The proof is long and involves some technical considerations. We refer the reader to Zapatero (1995) for a detailed analysis. Here we present the main part of the result, the parameters that characterize the equilibrium exchange rate.

THEOREM 15.5   The parameters that characterize the dynamics (15.63) of the exchange rate in equilibrium are given by

$$\gamma = \alpha_1 - \alpha_2 + (\rho_2)^2 \tag{15.69}$$

$$\nu_1 = \rho_1 \tag{15.70}$$

$$\nu_2 = \rho_2 \tag{15.71}$$

Proof   See Zapatero (1995) for a proof.   ∎

In equilibrium, the exchange rate captures the difference in the expected growth and the volatility of the two consumption goods.

Summary

One application of equilibrium models is to derive the dynamics of the risk-free rate in the economy. For example, the continuous-time CIR model for the interest rate can be obtained as a result of a particular equilibrium. Interesting equilibria also result in models with partial information. The case of several agents with different beliefs about the parameters in the economy is called equilibrium with heterogeneous agents. In these models, the equilibrium interest rate typically depends on the weighted average of the relative wealth of the agents. Equilibrium models are also useful for determining the dynamics of the exchange rate in international economies with different currencies.

Problems

1. Show that equations (15.8) and (15.9) hold. Hint: Recall that in the one risky-asset case the optimal log portfolio proportion was $\Pi = \frac{\mu - r}{\sigma^2}$. Denote here by Σ the matrix with rows $\sqrt{Y}(\sigma_1, \sigma_2)$ and (ν_1, ν_2). Show that the analogue of the one-dimensional formula is

$$\Pi = \begin{pmatrix} \Pi_1 \\ \Pi_2 \end{pmatrix} = (\Sigma \Sigma^{Tr})^{-1} \begin{pmatrix} \mu Y - r \\ \alpha - r \end{pmatrix}$$

and use the equilibrium conditions.

2. Prove expressions (15.30) and (15.31) for the optimal strategy with incomplete information. Hint: You can show it similarly as in section 12.3.3, noting that the terminal wealth satisfies $X(T) = 0$ and that $d\bar{X} = \bar{\pi}\,dG/S - \bar{c}\,dt$.

3. Prove Corollary 15.1.

4. Prove Propositions 15.1 and 15.2.

5. Consider the equilibrium interest rate of (15.53). Derive the dynamics of the interest-rate process if the priors on μ_i are normally distributed and independent. Hint: There is a formula in this textbook for the dynamics of $\tilde{\mu}_i$ in this case.

6. Derive the dynamics of the returns of the investments in the foreign stocks and bonds in equations (15.64)–(15.67).

7. Prove Proposition 15.3.

Further Readings

A continuous-time equilibrium of the term structure is presented in Cox, Ingersoll, and Ross (1985a, 1985b). A discrete-time equilibrium with incomplete information is analyzed in Grossman (1976). A continuous-time equilibrium with agents with heterogeneous information can be found in Detemple and Murthy (1994). Extensions are discussed in Zapatero (1998) and Basak (2000). A continuous-time equilibrium with agents with different risk aversions is studied in Dumas (1989). Lucas (1982) considers a discrete-time international equilibrium. The continuous-time international equilibrium model presented here is as in Zapatero (1995). For a formal study of some of the properties of the type of equilibrium resulting in that model see Cass and Pavlova (2002).

16 Appendix: Probability Theory Essentials

For the convenience of the reader we list here the basics of probability theory, helpful for understanding the material of this book.

16.1 Discrete Random Variables

A **discrete random variable** X is a random quantity that can take values $x_1, \ldots, x_m, \ldots$ with probabilities

$$p_i = P[X = x_i]$$

The probabilities p_i are values between zero and one, and they add up to one. For example, let $X(t)$ be the number of market crashes between today and time t in the future. We define a market crash as a fall in the market index by at least 20% in one day. Suppose that we model the number of crashes as having the following **distribution:**

$$p_i := P[X(t) = i] = e^{-\lambda t} \frac{(\lambda t)^i}{i!}$$

for some positive number λ. It can be checked that $\sum_{i=1}^{\infty} p_i = 1$. This distribution is called the **Poisson distribution.**

It is often convenient to work with the **cumulative distribution function** $F_X(x)$, defined as

$$F_X(x) := P[X \leq x] \tag{16.1}$$

16.1.1 Expectation and Variance

Expected value, or **expectation,** or the **mean** $E[X]$ of a discrete random variable X, is its theoretical average, where the values are weighted by their probabilities:

$$E[X] = \sum_{i=1}^{\infty} p_i x_i \tag{16.2}$$

We implicitly assume that the summation in this expression can be done, in which case we say that the expectation exists. Often, we denote $E[X]$ by μ_X, or just μ.

The **sample average** of n observations $X_1, \ldots, X_n$ of the variable X is the random variable $\bar{X}$ defined by

$$\bar{X} = \frac{1}{n} \sum_{i=1}^{n} X_i \tag{16.3}$$

For two random variables X and Y, and two real numbers a and b, we have the following property of **linearity of expectation:**

$$E[aX + bY] = aE[X] + bE[Y] \tag{16.4}$$

Expectation $E[X]$ is the "average" value of X. In order to measure how far away from this value X is likely to fluctuate, we define the **variance** $\text{Var}[X]$ of X:

$$\text{Var}[X] := E[(X - E[X])^2] = E[X^2] - (E[X])^2 \tag{16.5}$$

In other words, the variance is the average value of the squared deviations $(X - E[X])^2$ from the mean. It is often denoted by σ_X^2 or just σ^2. For example, if X is constant, then $E[X] = X$ and $\text{Var}[X] = 0$. The square root of the variance σ_X is called the **standard deviation** because it measures the typical deviation from the mean of X. Given constant numbers a and b, we have

$$\text{Var}[aX + b] = a^2 \text{Var}[X], \qquad \sigma_{aX+b} = a\sigma_X \tag{16.6}$$

16.2 Continuous Random Variables

A random variable X is a **continuous random variable** if it can take a continuum of possible values and if its distribution can be defined through a function called a density. More precisely, X is a continuous random variable if there is a nonnegative function f_X, called the **density function,** such that

$$P[a \leq X \leq b] = \int_a^b f_X(x)\,dx \tag{16.7}$$

We define the cumulative distribution function as before, and it is easily seen that

$$f_X = \frac{d}{dx}F_X \tag{16.8}$$

For example, a stock price can be modeled as a continuous random variable, taking as its values real numbers in the interval $(0, \infty)$. (In reality, stock prices actually change by small discrete amounts.)

16.2.1 Expectation and Variance

For a continuous random variable X the definition of its expected value $E[X]$ is analogous to the discrete case, with summation replaced by integration and probabilities replaced by the density function:

$$E[X] = \int_{-\infty}^{\infty} x f_X(x) \, dx \tag{16.9}$$

This integral may not always exist, in which case we say that the expectation, or the **first moment** of X, does not exist. The variance is defined as before.

16.3   Several Random Variables

We often are interested in the relationship of two random quantities, such as the relationship between a particular stock and the market index or the relationship between two bonds of different maturities. The **joint distribution function** of two random variables X and Y is defined as

$$F_{X,Y}(x, y) := P[X \leq x, Y \leq y] \tag{16.10}$$

We say that they have a **joint density function** $f_{X,Y}$ if

$$F_{X,Y}(x, y) = \int_{-\infty}^{y} \int_{-\infty}^{x} f_{X,Y}(u, v) \, du \, dv \tag{16.11}$$

16.3.1   Independence

If there is no relationship between two random variables X and Y, we say that they are **independent.** Mathematically, X and Y are independent if

$$P[X \leq x, Y \leq y] = P[X \leq x]P[Y \leq y] \tag{16.12}$$

for all x, y. In other words, the probability of the intersection of an event involving X and an event involving Y is equal to the product of the probabilities of those events. In this case, *when the variables are independent, the mean of the product is equal to the product of the means:*

$$E[XY] = E[X] \cdot E[Y] \tag{16.13}$$

Moreover, *when the variables are independent, the variance of the sum is equal to the sum of the variances:*

$$\text{Var}[X + Y] = \text{Var}[X] + \text{Var}[Y] \tag{16.14}$$

It is also true that *two continuous variables are independent if and only if their joint density is equal to the product of* **marginal densities,** that is, if

$$f_{X,Y}(x, y) = f_X(x) f_Y(y)$$

16.3.2 Correlation and Covariance

In order to measure the level of dependence between two random variables, we introduce the notion of **covariance,** $\text{Cov}[X, Y]$:

$$\sigma_{XY} = \text{Cov}[X, Y] := E[(X - E[X])(Y - E[Y])] = E[XY] - E[X]E[Y] \qquad (16.15)$$

We see that the covariance is zero when X and Y are independent. For normal random variables (introduced in the next section), the opposite is also true: if X and Y are normally distributed and have covariance zero, then they are independent.

The covariance is often standardized to take values between 0 and 1. The quantity obtained in this way is called **correlation,** often denoted by the greek letter ρ, and we define it as follows:

$$\rho_{XY} = \text{Corr}[X, Y] := \frac{\sigma_{XY}}{\sigma_X \sigma_Y} \qquad (16.16)$$

The value of ρ is 1 or -1 when X and Y completely depend on each other in a linear fashion, that is, when $Y = a + bX$. Correlation and covariance are not necessarily good measures of nonlinear dependence between two variables. If the correlation is positive, the two variables tend to increase or decrease simultaneously. If the correlation is negative, then when X increases, Y tends to decrease, and vice versa.

Using covariance, we can now state **the formula for the variance of a linear combination of two random variables:**

$$\text{Var}[aX + bY] = a^2 \text{Var}[X] + b^2 \text{Var}[Y] + 2ab \text{Cov}[X, Y] \qquad (16.17)$$

16.4 Normal Random Variables

The most important continuous probability distribution is the **normal distribution,** or **Gaussian distribution.** A normal distribution is completely characterized by its mean μ and variance σ^2, and it has density of the form

$$f(x) = \frac{1}{\sigma\sqrt{2\pi}} e^{-\frac{(x-\mu)^2}{2\sigma^2}} \qquad (16.18)$$

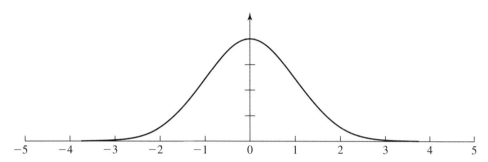

Figure 16.1
Graph of the standard normal density function.

We sometimes denote this distribution by $N(\mu, \sigma^2)$. The normal distribution with mean zero, $\mu = 0$, and variance one, $\sigma^2 = 1$, is called the **standard normal distribution** or Z-distribution, and a random variable with such a distribution is usually denoted by Z. Its density is

$$n(x) = \frac{1}{\sqrt{2\pi}} e^{-\frac{x^2}{2}} \qquad (16.19)$$

Figure 16.1 shows a graph of this function.

The standard normal distribution function is

$$N(x) = \frac{1}{\sqrt{2\pi}} \int_{-\infty}^{x} e^{-\frac{u^2}{2}} \, du \qquad (16.20)$$

This function cannot be computed explicitly, but it can be computed numerically, and most probability and statistics textbooks have a table for its values, including this book. Sometimes the functions n and N are denoted by φ and Φ, respectively.

A linear combination $aX + bY$ of normal random variables X and Y is also a normal random variable. We say that X and Y have a joint, **bivariate normal distribution** if their joint density is given by

$$f_{X,Y}(x, y) = \frac{1}{2\pi \sigma_X \sigma_Y \sqrt{1-\rho^2}} e^{-\frac{1}{2(1-\rho^2)} \left[\frac{(x-\mu_X)^2}{\sigma_X^2} + \frac{(y-\mu_Y)^2}{\sigma_Y^2} - \frac{2\rho(x-\mu_X)(y-\mu_Y)}{\sigma_X \sigma_Y} \right]} \qquad (16.21)$$

The main reason why the normal distribution is so prevalent is the so-called **central limit theorem,** which tells us that under not too restrictive conditions the distribution of a sum of n random variables can be approximated by the normal distribution, for n large. Here is the standard version of the central limit theorem, but there are other versions, with different conditions.

THEOREM 16.1 (CENTRAL LIMIT THEOREM)   Let $X_1, X_2, \ldots$ be a sequence of independent, identically distributed random variables, with mean μ and variance σ^2. Then

$$\lim_{n \to \infty} P\left[\frac{\sum_{i=1}^{n}(X_i - \mu)}{\sigma\sqrt{n}} \leq x\right] = N(x)$$

where $N(x)$ is the standard normal distribution function.

16.5   Properties of Conditional Expectations

First, we give some formal definitions, which are used for modeling information flows. A family of sets $\mathcal{F}$ is a σ-**algebra,** or σ-**field,** if the following conditions are satisfied:

1. The family $\mathcal{F}$ contains the empty set.
2. If A is contained in $\mathcal{F}$, then the complement of A is also in $\mathcal{F}$.
3. For any countable collection of sets in $\mathcal{F}$, their union is also in $\mathcal{F}$.

We say that a random variable X is **measurable** with respect to σ-algebra $\mathcal{F}$ if the events $\{\omega: X(\omega) \leq x\}$ are in $\mathcal{F}$, for all x. The smallest σ-algebra with respect to which X is measurable is called the σ-algebra **generated** by X.

Suppose we are given a finite set of random variables $\{X(0), \ldots, X(t)\}$. Denote by $\mathcal{F}(t)$ the set of events that describe the information generated by these random variables. More formally, to each random variable $X(i)$ we associate its σ-algebra $\mathcal{F}_i$ generated by $X(i)$, representing the information provided by $X(i)$. Then, $\mathcal{F}(t)$ is defined as the smallest σ-algebra containing the σ-algebras generated by $X(0), \ldots, X(t)$. This procedure can also be carried out for an infinite collection of random variables, representing values of a continuous-time stochastic process up to time t, that is, the set $\{X(s); 0 \leq s \leq t\}$. We again use the same notation $\mathcal{F}(t)$ to denote the information (σ-algebra) provided by the history of process X before and including time t.

Obviously, we have

$$\mathcal{F}(t) \subset \mathcal{F}(t + \Delta t)$$

because there is at least as much information at time $t + \Delta t$ as at time t. We call such a sequence of σ-algebras a **filtration.**

Consider now a given random variable Y. Under technical conditions, we can define the **conditional expectation** C of Y given a σ-algebra $\mathcal{F}$, denoted

$$C := E[Y|\mathcal{F}]$$

Formally, C is defined as the random variable measurable with respect to $\mathcal{F}$ for which

$$E[Y\mathbf{1}_A] = E[C\mathbf{1}_A] \text{ for all } A \in \mathcal{F}$$

Here, the indicator function $\mathbf{1}_A(\omega)$ is equal to one if $\omega \in A$, and it is zero otherwise. It is also characterized as the unique random variable C measurable with respect to $\mathcal{F}$ for which

$$E[Y - C] = 0, \qquad \text{Var}[X - C] \leq \text{Var}[X - Z]$$

for any other random variable Z measurable with respect to $\mathcal{F}$.

We can also define the conditional expectation of Y given the information provided by $X(i)$'s up to time t:

$$E_t[Y] := E[Y|\mathcal{F}(t)] = E[Y|X(s), 0 \leq s \leq t]$$

In the following list we present some useful properties of conditional expectations.

1. *If the information $\mathcal{F}(t)$ completely determines the value of Y, then $E_t[Y] = Y$.*

$$(16.22)$$

Intuitively, this conclusion follows because *if Y is known given information $\mathcal{F}(t)$, we can treat it as a constant.* More generally, we have the following:

2. *If the information $\mathcal{F}(t)$ completely determines the value of Y, then $E_t[YX] = Y E_t[X]$.*

$$(16.23)$$

The following property says that *if Y is independent of the information $\mathcal{F}(t)$, then, in order to find the expected value of Y, it does not matter whether we know that information or not:*

3. *If Y is independent of the random variables generating information $\mathcal{F}(t)$, then $E_t[Y] = E[Y]$.*

$$(16.24)$$

The final property, called the **law of iterated expectations,** says that *if we first average the values of Y knowing more information, and then we average knowing less information, we get the same average as if we had immediately averaged knowing less information:*

4. $E_t[E_{t+\Delta t}\{Y\}] = E_t[Y]$. $\hspace{4cm} (16.25)$

In particular, in the case of averaging with no information (i.e., taking the ordinary expected value), we get that *the expected value of a conditional expectation of Y is equal to the expected value of Y:*

5. $E[E_t\{Y\}] = E[Y]$. (16.26)

16.6   Martingale Definition

Given an information sequence (filtration) $\mathcal{F}(t)$ and a process $M(t)$ such that for each t, $M(t)$ is $\mathcal{F}(t)$-measurable, we say that $M(t)$ is a **martingale** if

$$E_t[M(t + \Delta t)] = M(t)$$ (16.27)

for all t and all $\Delta t > 0$. That is, the expected value of the future of the process, given the present and past information, is equal to the present value. In other words, the best predictor of the future value is the current value. By property (16.26), we see that a martingale process has constant expected value, which does not change with time,

$$E[M(t)] = E[M(0)]$$

Note that the martingale property depends on the probability under which we compute the expectations and on the chosen σ-algebra.

   We say that a process M is a **supermartingale** if

$$E_t[M(t + \Delta t)] \leq M(t)$$ (16.28)

and a **submartingale** if

$$E_t[M(t + \Delta t)] \geq M(t)$$ (16.29)

16.7   Random Walk and Brownian Motion

We present here a definition of the simple random walk process and its connection to Brownian motion. Let $X(i)$'s be independent random variables that take values 1 or -1 with probability one-half ("coin tosses"). Define

$$W(n) = X(1) + X(2) + \cdots + X(n)$$

In other words, this is a process that jumps up or down by one at each step. It is called a **simple random walk** process. By definition, it has independent increments; that is, for any set of times $0 \leq t_1 < t_2 < \cdots < t_n$, the random variables

$$W(t_2) - W(t_1), W(t_3) - W(t_2), \ldots, W(t_n) - W(t_{n-1})$$

are independent. It can also be checked that it is a martingale process, with respect to its own filtration. Define now the process

$$W_k(t) = \frac{1}{\sqrt{k}} W(kt)$$

if kt is an integer. Otherwise, we do linear interpolation between the integer values. It can be shown that when k tends to infinity, the process W_k converges to the Brownian motion process, as given in Definition 3.1.

References

Adler, M., and B. Dumas. (1983). "International Portfolio Choice and Corporation Finance: A Synthesis." *Journal of Finance* 38, 925–984.

Arrow, K. (1971). *Essays in the Theory of Risk Bearing.* Amsterdam: North Holland.

Basak, S. (1995). "A General Equilibrium Model of Portfolio Insurance." *Review of Financial Studies* 8, 1059–1090.

Basak, S. (2000). "A Model of Dynamic Equilibrium Asset Pricing with Heterogeneous Beliefs and Extraneous Risk." *Journal of Economic Dynamics and Control* 24, 63–95.

Basak, S., and A. Shapiro. (2001). "Value-at-Risk-Based Risk Management: Optimal Policies and Asset Prices." *Review of Financial Studies* 14, 371–405.

Bellman, R. (1957). *Dynamic Programming.* Princeton, NJ: Princeton University Press.

Bielecki, T., and M. Rutkowski. (2001). *Credit Risk: Modeling, Valuation and Hedging.* Berlin: Springer.

Bierwag, G. (1977). "Immunization, Duration and the Term Structure of Interest Rates." *Journal of Financial and Quantitative Analysis* 12, 725–743.

Bjork, T. (1999). *Arbitrage Theory in Continuous Time.* New York: Oxford University Press.

Black, F. (1972). "Capital Market Equilibrium with Restricted Borrowing." *Journal of Business* 45, 444–455.

Black, F. (1976). "The Pricing of Commodity Contracts." *Journal of Financial Economics* 3, 167–179.

Black, F., E. Derman, and W. Toy. (1990). "A One-Factor Model of Interest Rates and Its Application to Treasury Bond Options." *Financial Analysts Journal* 46, 33–39.

Black, F., and M. Scholes. (1973). "The Pricing of Options and Corporate Liabilities." *Journal of Political Economy* 81, 637–659.

Bodie, H., A. Kane, and A. Marcus. (2001). *Investments,* 5th ed. New York: McGraw-Hill/Irwin.

Bollerslev, T. (1986). "Generalized Autorregressive Conditional Heteroskedasticity." *Journal of Econometrics* 31, 307–327.

Bossaerts, P. (1989). "Simulation Estimators of Optimal Early Exercise." Working Paper, Carnegie-Mellon University.

Boyle, P. (1977). "Options: A Monte Carlo Approach." *Journal of Financial Economics* 4, 323–338.

Boyle, P., M. Broadie, and P. Glasserman. (1997). "Monte Carlo Methods for Security Pricing." *Journal of Economic Dynamics and Control* 21, 1267–1321.

Brace, A., D. Gatarek, and M. Musiela. (1997). The Market Model of Interest Rate Dynamics. *Mathematical Finance* 7, 127–154.

Breeden, D. (1979). "An Intertemporal Asset Pricing Model with Stochastic Consumption and Investment Opportunities." *Journal of Financial Economics* 7, 265–296.

Brennan, M. (1995). "The Individual Investor." *Journal of Financial Research* 1, 59–74.

Brennan, M., and E. Schwartz. (1977). "The Valuation of American Put Options." *Journal of Finance* 32, 449–462.

Brennan, M., and E. Schwartz. (1978). "Finite Difference Methods and Jump Processes Arising in the Pricing of Contingent Claims: A Synthesis." *Journal of Financial and Quantitative Analysis* 13, 462–474.

Brennan, M., E. Schwartz, and R. Lagnado. (1997). "Strategic Asset Allocation." *Journal of Economic Dynamics and Control* 21, 1377–1403.

Brennan, M., and Y. Xia. (2001). "Assessing Asset Pricing Anomalies." *Review of Financial Studies* 14, 905–945.

Brigo, D., and F. Mercurio. (2001). *Interest Rate Models: Theory and Practice.* Berlin: Springer.

Cadenillas, A., and S. Pliska. (1999). "Optimal Trading of a Security When There Are Taxes and Transaction Costs." *Finance and Stochastics* 3, 137–165.

Campbell, J., A. Lo, and G. MacKinlay. (1996). *The Econometrics of Financial Markets.* Princeton, NJ: Princeton University Press.

Carrière, J. (1996). "Valuation of the Early-Exercise Price for Options Using Simulations and Nonparametric Regression." *Insurance: Mathematics and Economics* 19, 19–30.

Cass, D. (1991). "Incomplete Financial Markets and Indeterminacy of Financial Equilibrium." In J.-J. Laffont (ed.), *Advances in Economic Theory,* 677–693. Cambridge: Cambridge University Press.

Cass, D., and A. Pavlova. (2002). "On Trees and Logs." *Journal of Economic Theory,* forthcoming.

Chen, N., R. Roll, and S. Ross. (1986). "Economic Forces and the Stock Market." *Journal of Business* 59, 383–403.

Cochrane, J. (2001). *Asset Pricing.* Princeton, NJ: Princeton University Press.

Constantinides, G. (1986). "Capital Market Equilibrium with Transaction Costs." *Journal of Political Economy* 94, 842–862.

Cox, J., and C.-F. Huang. (1989). "Optimal Consumption and Portfolio Policies When Asset Prices Follow a Diffusion Process." *Journal of Economic Theory* 49, 33–83.

Cox, J., J. Ingersoll, and S. Ross. (1979). "Duration and the Measurement of Basis Risk." *Journal of Business* 52, 51–61.

Cox, J., J. Ingersoll, and S. Ross. (1981). "The Relation between Forward Prices and Futures Prices." *Journal of Financial Economics* 9, 321–346.

Cox, J., J. Ingersoll, and S. Ross. (1985a). "An Intertemporal General Equilibrium Model of Asset Prices." *Econometrica* 53, 363–384.

Cox, J., J. Ingersoll, and S. Ross. (1985b). "A Theory of the Term Structure of Interest Rates." *Econometrica* 53, 385–407.

Cox, J., and S. Ross. (1976a). "The Valuation of Options for Alternative Stochastic Processes." *Journal of Financial Economics* 3, 145–166.

Cox, J., and S. Ross. (1976b). "A Survey of Some New Results in Financial Option Pricing Theory." *Journal of Finance* 31, 383–402.

Cox, J., S. Ross, and M. Rubinstein. (1979). "Option Pricing: A Simplified Approach." *Journal of Financial Economics* 7, 229–264.

Cuoco, D. (1997). "Optimal Consumption and Equilibrium Prices with Portfolio Constraints and Stochastic Income." *Journal of Economic Theory* 72, 33–73.

Cuoco, D., and H. He. (2001). "Dynamic Aggregation and Computation of Equilibria in Finite-Dimensional Economies with Incomplete Financial Markets." *Annals of Economics and Finance* 2, 265–296.

Cvitanić, J., L. Goukasian, and F. Zapatero. (2002). "Hedging with Monte Carlo Simulation." In E. Kontoghiorghes, B. Rustem, and S. Siokos (eds.), *Computational Methods in Decision-Making, Economics and Finance,* vol. 2, 339–353. Dordrecht, Netherlands: Kluwer Academic Publishers.

Cvitanić, J., L. Goukasian, and F. Zapatero. (2003). Monte Carlo Computation of Optimal Portfolios in Complete Markets. *Journal of Economic Dynamics and Control* 27, 971–986.

Cvitanić, J., and I. Karatzas. (1992). "Convex Duality in Constrained Portfolio Optimization." *Annals of Applied Probability* 2, 767–818.

Cvitanić, J., A. Lazrak, L. Martellini, and F. Zapatero. (2002). "Revisiting Treynor and Black (1973): An Intertemporal Model of Active Portfolio Management." Working Paper, University of Southern California.

Cvitanić, J., A. Lazrak, and T. Wang. (2003). "Sharpe Ratio as a Performance Measure in a Multi-Period Model." Working Paper, University of British Columbia.

Dai, Q., and K. Singleton. (2000). "Specification Analysis of Affine Term Structure Models." *Journal of Finance* 55, 1943–1978.

Dana, R.-A., and M. Jeanblanc. (2002). *Financial Markets in Continuous Time.* Berlin: Springer.

Davis, M., and A. Norman. (1990). "Portfolio Selection with Transaction Costs." *Mathematics of Operations Research* 15, 676–713.

Debreu, G. (1959). *Theory of Value.* New Haven, CT: Yale University Press.

Detemple, J. (1986). "Asset Pricing in a Production Economy with Incomplete Information." *Journal of Finance* 41, 383–391.

Detemple, J., R. Garcia, and M. Rindisbacher. (2003). "A Monte Carlo Approach for Optimal Portfolios." *Journal of Finance* 58, 401–446.

Detemple, J., and S. Murthy. (1994). "Intertemporal Asset Pricing with Heterogeneous Beliefs." *Journal of Economic Theory* 62, 294–320.

Dothan, U. (1990). *Prices in Financial Markets*. New York: Oxford University Press.

Dothan, U., and D. Feldman. (1986). "Equilibrium Interest Rates and Multiperiod Bonds in a Partially Observable Economy." *Journal of Finance* 41, 369–382.

Duffie, D. (1986). "Stochastic Equilibria: Existence, Spanning Number, and the 'No Expected Gain from Trade' Hypothesis." *Econometrica* 54, 1161–1184.

Duffie, D. (1989). *Futures Markets*. Upper Saddle River, NJ: Prentice Hall.

Duffie, D. (2001). *Dynamic Asset Pricing,* 3rd ed. Princeton, NJ: Princeton University Press.

Duffie, D., and P. Glynn. (1995). "Efficient Monte Carlo Estimation of Security Prices." *Annals of Applied Probability* 5, 897–905.

Duffie, D., and C.-F. Huang. (1985). "Implementing Arrow-Debreu Equilibria by Continuous Trading of a Few Long-Lived Securities." *Econometrica* 53, 1337–1356.

Duffie, D., and J. Pan. (1997). "An Overview of Value at Risk." *Journal of Derivatives* 4, 7–49.

Duffie, D., J. Pan, and K. Singleton. (2000). "Transform Analysis and Asset Pricing for Affine Jump-Diffusions." *Econometrica* 68, 1343–1376.

Duffie, D., and W. Shafer. (1985). "Equilibrium in Incomplete Markets I: A Basic Model of Generic Existence." *Journal of Mathematical Economics* 14, 285–300.

Duffie, D., and W. Shafer. (1986). "Equilibrium in Incomplete Markets II: Generic Existence in Stochastic Economies." *Journal of Mathematical Economics* 15, 199–216.

Duffie, D., and K. Singleton. (1999). "Modeling Term Structures of Defaultable Bonds." *Review of Financial Studies* 12, 687–720.

Duffie, D., and W. Zame. (1989). "The Consumption-Based Capital Asset Pricing Model." *Econometrica* 57, 1279–1297.

Dumas, B. (1989). "Two-Person Dynamic Equilibrium in the Capital Market." *Review of Financial Studies* 2, 157–188.

Dybvig, P., and S. Ross. (1985). "Yes, the APT Is Testable." *Journal of Finance* 40, 1173–1188.

Elliott, R., and P. Kopp. (1999). *Mathematics of Financial Markets*. Berlin: Springer.

Embrechts, P., C. Kluppelberg, and T. Mikosch. (1997). *Modeling Extremal Events for Insurance and Finance*. Berlin: Springer.

Engle, R. (1982). "Autoregressive Conditional Heteroskedasticity with Estimates of the Variance of United Kingdom Inflation." *Econometrica* 50, 987–1008.

Fabozzi, F. (1999). *Bond Markets, Analysis and Strategies,* 4th ed. Upper Saddle River, NJ: Prentice Hall.

Fabozzi, F., F. Modigliani, and F. Jones. (2002). *Capital Markets, Institutions and Instruments,* 3rd ed. Upper Saddle River, NJ: Prentice Hall.

Fama, E. (1976). *Foundations of Finance*. New York: Basic Books.

Fama, E., and K. French. (1992). "The Cross-Section of Expected Stock Returns." *Journal of Finance* 47, 427–465.

Fama, E., and J. Macbeth. (1973). "Risk, Return and Equilibrium: Empirical Tests." *Journal of Political Economy* 71, 607–636.

Fama, E., and M. Miller. (1972). *The Theory of Finance*. New York: Holt, Rinehart and Winston.

Fisher, I. (1965). *The Theory of Interest: As Determined by Impatience to Spend Income and Opportunity to Invest It,* New York: Augustus M. Kelley.

Fouque, J.-P., G. Papanicolau, and R. Sircar. (2000). *Derivatives in Financial Markets with Stochastic Volatility.* Cambridge: Cambridge University Press.

Fu, M., S. Laprise, D. Madan, Y. Su, and R. Wu. (2001). "Pricing American Options: A Comparison of Monte Carlo Simulation Approaches." *Journal of Computational Finance* 4, 39–88.

Garman, M., and S. Kohlhagen. (1983). "Foreign Currency Option Values." *Journal of International Money and Finance* 2, 231–238.

Geman, H., N. El Karoui, and J. Rochet. (1995). "Changes of Numeraire, Changes of Probability Measure and Option Pricing." *Journal of Applied Probability* 32, 443–458.

Gennotte, G. (1986). "Optimal Portfolio Choice under Incomplete Information." *Journal of Finance* 41, 733–746.

Geske, R., and H. Johnson. (1984). "The American Put Option Valued Analytically." *Journal of Finance* 39, 1511–1524.

Goldstein, R., and F. Zapatero. (1996). "General Equilibrium with Constant Relative Risk Aversion and Vasicek Interest Rates." *Mathematical Finance* 6, 331–340.

Gómez, J.-P., and F. Zapatero. (2003). "Asset Pricing Implications of Benchmarking: A Two-Factor CAPM." *European Journal of Finance,* forthcoming.

Gourieroux, C. (1997). *ARCH Models and Financial Applications.* Berlin: Springer.

Grossman, S. (1976). "On the Efficiency of Competitive Stock Markets Where Traders Have Diverse Information." *Journal of Finance* 31, 573–585.

Gultekin, N., and R. Rogalski. (1984). "Alternative Duration Specifications and the Measurement of Basis Risk: Empirical Tests." *Journal of Business* 57, 241–264.

Hansen, L., and R. Jagannathan. (1991). "Implications of Security Market Data for Models of Dynamic Economics." *Journal of Political Economy* 99, 225–262.

Harris, L. (2002). *Trading and Exchanges.* New York: Oxford University Press.

Harrison, M., and D. Kreps. (1979). "Martingales and Arbitrage in Multiperiod Securities Markets." *Journal of Economic Theory* 20, 381–408.

Harrison, M., and S. Pliska. (1981). "Martingales and Stochastic Integrals in the Theory of Continuous Trading." *Stochastic Processes and Their Applications* 11, 215–260.

He, H. (1990). "Convergence from Discrete- to Continuous-Time Contingent Claim Prices." *Review of Financial Studies* 3, 523–546.

He, H., and H. Pagés. (1991). "Consumption and Portfolio Policies with Incomplete Markets: The Infinite-Dimensional Case." *Journal of Economic Theory* 54, 259–305.

Heath, D., R. Jarrow, and A. Morton. (1990). "Bond Pricing and the Term Structure of Interest Rates: A Discrete Time Approximation." *Journal of Financial and Quantitative Analysis* 25, 419–440.

Heath, D., R. Jarrow, and A. Morton. (1992). "Bond Pricing and the Term Structure of the Interest Rates: A New Methodology for Contingent Claim Valuation." *Econometrica* 60, 77–106.

Heston, S. (1993). "A Closed-Form Solution for Options with Stochastic Volatility with Applications to Bond and Currency Options." *Review of Financial Studies* 6, 327–344.

Hildebrand, W., and A. Kirman. (1988). *Equilibrium Analysis.* London: North-Holland.

Hirshleifer, J. (1970). *Investment, Interest, and Capital.* Upper Saddle River, NJ: Prentice-Hall.

Ho, T., and S. Lee. (1986). "Term Structure Movements and Pricing Interest Rate Contingent Claims." *Journal of Finance* 41, 1011–1029.

Huberman, G. (1982). "A Simple Approach to Arbitrage Pricing Theory." *Journal of Economic Theory* 28, 183–191.

Hull, J. (2002). *Options, Futures, and Other Derivatives,* 5th ed. Upper Saddle River, NJ: Prentice Hall.

Hull, J., and A. White. (1987). "The Pricing of Options on Assets with Stochastic Volatilities." *Journal of Finance* 42, 281–300.

Hull, J., and A. White. (1990). "Pricing Interest-Rate Derivative Securities." *Review of Financial Studies* 3, 573–592.

Ibáñez, A., and F. Zapatero. (In press). "Monte Carlo Valuation of American Options through Computation of the Optimal Exercise Frontier." *Journal of Financial and Quantitative Analysis*.

Jamshidian, F. (1989). "An Exact Bond Pricing Formula." *Journal of Finance* 44, 205–209.

Jamshidian, F. (1997). "Libor and Swap Market Models and Measures." *Finance and Stochastics* 1, 293–330.

Jarrow, R., D. Lando, and S. Turnbull. (1997). "A Markov Model for the Term Structure of Credit Risk Spreads." *Review of Financial Studies* 10, 481–523.

Jensen, M. (1969). "Risk, the Pricing of Capital Assets, and the Evaluation of Investment Portfolios." *Journal of Business* 42, 167–247.

Jorion, P. (1997). *The Value at Risk: The New Benchmark for Controlling Market Risk.* Chicago: Irwin.

Karatzas, I., J. Lehoczky, and S. Shreve. (1987). "Optimal Portfolio and Consumption Decisions for a 'Small Investor' on a Finite Horizon." *SIAM Journal of Control and Optimization* 25, 1157–1186.

Karatzas, I., J. Lehoczky, and S. Shreve. (1990). "Existence and Uniqueness of Multiagent Equilibrium in a Stochastic, Dynamic, Consumption/Investment Model." *Mathematics of Operations Research* 15, 80–128.

Karatzas, I., J. Lehoczky, S. Shreve, and G.-L. Xu. (1991). "Martingale and Duality Methods for Utility Maximization in Incomplete Markets." *SIAM Journal of Control and Optimization* 29, 702–730.

Karatzas, I., and S. Shreve. (1997). *Brownian Motion and Stochastic Calculus,* 2nd ed. Berlin: Springer.

Karatzas, I., and S. Shreve. (1998). *Methods of Mathematical Finance.* Berlin: Springer.

Kim, I.-J. (1990). "The Analytic Valuation of American Options." *Review of Financial Studies* 3, 547–572.

Kim, T., and E. Omberg. (1996). "Dynamic Nonmyopic Portfolio Behavior." *Review of Financial Studies* 9, 141–161.

Kwok, Y. K. (1998). *Mathematical Models of Financial Derivatives.* Berlin: Springer.

Lamberton, D., and B. Lapeyre. (1997). *Introduction to Stochastic Calculus Applied to Finance.* London: Chapman & Hall.

Leland, H. (1980). "Who Should Buy Portfolio Insurance?" *Journal of Finance* 35, 581–594.

Leland, H., and M. Rubinstein. (1981). "Replicating Options with Positions in the Stock and Cash." *Financial Analysts Journal* 37, 63–72.

LeRoy, S. F., and J. Werner. (2001). *Principles of Financial Economics.* Cambridge: Cambridge University Press.

Lewis, A. (2000). *Option Valuation under Stochastic Volatility: With Mathematica Code.* Newport Beach, CA: Finance Press.

Lintner, J. (1965). "Security Prices, Risk and Maximal Gains from Diversification." *Journal of Finance* 20, 587–615.

Longstaff, F., and E. Schwartz. (2001). "Valuing American Options by Simulation: A Simple Least-Squares Approach." *Review of Financial Studies* 14, 113–148.

Lucas, R. (1978). "Asset Prices in an Exchange Economy." *Econometrica* 46, 1429–1445.

Lucas, R. (1982). "Interest Rates and Currency Prices in a Two-Country World." *Journal of Monetary Economics* 10, 335–360.

Macaulay, F. (1938). *Some Theoretical Problems Suggested by the Movements of Interest Rates, Bond Yields, and Stock Prices in the United States since 1856.* New York: National Bureau of Economic Research.

Magill, M., and M. Quinzii. (1996). *Theory of Incomplete Markets,* vol. 1. Cambridge, MA: MIT Press.

Markowitz, H. (1952). "Portfolio Selection." *Journal of Finance* 7, 77–91.

Martellini, L., and P. Priaulet. (2001). *Fixed-Income Securities: Dynamic Methods for Interest Rate Risk Pricing and Hedging.* New York: John Wiley.

Martellini, L., P. Priaulet, and S. Priaulet. (2003). *Fixed-Income Securities: Valuation, Risk Management and Portfolio Strategies.* New York: John Wiley.

Mas-Collel, A., M. Whinston, and J. Green. (1995). *Microeconomic Theory.* New York: Oxford University Press.

Mehra, R., and E. Prescott. (1985). "The Equity Premium: A Puzzle." *Journal of Monetary Economics* 15, 145–161.

Merton, R. (1969). "Lifetime Portfolio Selection under Uncertainty: The Continuous-Time Case." *Review of Economics and Statistics* 51, 247–257.

Merton, R. (1971). "Optimum Consumption and Portfolio Rules in a Continuous-Time Model." *Journal of Economic Theory* 3, 373–413.

Merton, R. (1973a). "An Intertemporal Capital Asset Pricing Model." *Econometrica* 41, 867–888.

Merton, R. (1973b). "Theory of Rational Option Pricing." *Bell Journal of Economics and Management* 4, 141–183.

Merton, R. (1976). "Option Pricing when Underlying Stock Returns Are Discontinuous." *Journal of Financial Economics* 3, 125–144.

Merton, R. (1977). "On the Pricing of Corporate Debt: The Risk Structure of Interest Rates." *Journal of Finance* 29, 449–479.

Miller, M., and C. Culp. (1994). "Risk Management Lessons from Metallgesellschaft." *Journal of Applied Corporate Finance* 7, 62–76.

Miltersen, K., K. Sandmann, and D. Sondermann. (1997). "Closed Form Solutions for Term Structure Derivatives with Log-Normal Interest Rates." *Journal of Finance* 52, 409–430.

Mossin, J. (1966). "Equilibrium in a Capital Asset Market." *Econometrica* 35, 768–783.

Musiela, M., and M. Rutkowski. (1997). *Martingale Methods in Financial Modeling.* Berlin: Springer.

Nelken, I. (2000). *Pricing, Hedging, and Trading Exotic Options.* New York: McGraw-Hill.

Oksendal, B. K. (1998). *Stochastic Differential Equations: An Introduction with Applications,* 5th ed. Berlin: Springer.

Pelsser, A. (2000). *Efficient Methods for Valuing Interest Rate Derivatives.* Berlin: Springer.

Pliska, S. (1997). *Introduction to Mathematical Finance: Discrete Time Models.* Malden, MA: Blackwell.

Pratt, J. (1964). "Risk Aversion in the Small and in the Large." *Econometrica* 32, 122–136.

Ramaswamy, K., and S. Sundaresan. (1985). "The Valuation of Options on Futures." *Journal of Finance* 60, 1319–1339.

Roll, R. (1977). "A Critique of the Asset Pricing Theory's Tests: Part I." *Journal of Financial Economics* 4, 129–176.

Ross, S. (1976a). "The Arbitrage Theory of Capital Asset Pricing." *Journal of Economic Theory* 13, 341–360.

Ross, S. (1976b). "Return, Risk and Arbitrage." In I. Friend and J. Bicksler, eds., *Risk and Return in Finance,* 189–217. Cambridge, MA: Ballinger.

Ross, S. (1978). "A Simpler Approach to the Valuation of Risky Streams." *Journal of Business* 51, 453–475.

Rubinstein, M. (1994). "Implied Binomial Trees." *Journal of Finance* 49, 771–818.

Samuelson, P. (1969). "Lifetime Portfolio Selection by Dynamic Stochastic Programming." *Review of Economics and Statistics* 51, 239–246.

Schroeder, M., and C. Skiadas. (2002). "Optimal Lifetime Consumption-Portfolio Strategies under Trading Constraints and Generalized Recursive Preferences." Working Paper, Northwestern University.

Sharpe, W. F. (1964). "Capital Asset Prices: A Theory of Market Equilibrium under Conditions of Risk." *Journal of Finance* 19, 425–442.

Sharpe, W. F., G. Alexander, F. Bailey, and W. C. Sharpe. (1998). *Investments,* 6th ed. Upper Saddle River, NJ: Prentice Hall.

Steele, M. (2000). *Stochastic Calculus and Financial Applications.* Berlin: Springer.

Stokey, N., and R. Lucas. (1989). *Recursive Methods in Economic Dynamics* (with Ed Prescott). Cambridge, MA: Harvard University Press.

Sundaresan, S. (1997). *Fixed Income Markets and Their Derivatives*. Cincinnati, OH: South-Western.

Treynor, J. (1965). "How to Rate Management Investment Funds." *Harvard Business Review* 43, 63–75.

Vasicek, O. (1977). "An Equilibrium Characterization of the Term Structure." *Journal of Financial Economics* 5, 177–188.

Wilmott, P. (1998). *Derivatives: The Theory and Practice of Financial Engineering.* New York: John Wiley.

Wilmott, P., J. Dewynne, and S. Howison. (1993). *Option Pricing: Mathematical Models and Computation.* Oxford: Oxford Financial Press.

Xia, Y. (2001). "Learning about Predictability: The Effect of Parameter Uncertainty on Dynamic Asset Allocation." *Journal of Finance* 56, 205–246.

Zapatero, F. (1995). "Equilibrium Asset Prices and Exchange Rates." *Journal of Economic Dynamics and Control* 19, 787–811.

Zapatero, F. (1998). "Effects of Financial Innovations on Market Volatility When Beliefs Are Heterogeneous." *Journal of Economic Dynamics and Control* 22, 597–626.

Index

Notation

$A(t, s)$ American option price

B bank account value

c consumption or consumption rate

$c(t, s)$ call option price

$C(t, s)$ price of a contingent claim

$p(t, s)$ put option price

P bond price

r interest rate

S stock price

t current time value

T maturity, terminal date

U utility function

V value function

W Brownian motion

X wealth process

Z state-price density

δ number of shares

ΔX change in value of X, $X(t_{i+1}) - X(t_i)$

μ drift of a diffusion process; mean return rate

π portfolio amount

Π portfolio proportion

ρ correlation coefficient

σ volatility, diffusion parameter

τ random time, stopping time

ω random outcome

$\bar{X}$ discounted value of X

$\hat{X}$ optimal value of X

$P[A]$ probability of event A

$E[X]$ expected value of X

$E_t[X]$ expected value of X conditional on information up to time t

$P^*[A]$, p^* risk-neutral probability

$E^*[X]$ expected value of X under the risk-neutral probability

$x := y$ x is defined to be y

σ^{Tr} matrix σ transposed

$\log(x)$ the natural logarithm $[\ln(x)]$

Normal Distribution Table

$$N(z) = P[Z \le z]$$

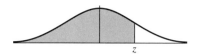

z	.00	.01	.02	.03	.04	.05	.06	.07	.08	.09
.0	.5000	.5040	.5080	.5120	.5160	.5199	.5239	.5279	.5319	.5359
.1	.5398	.5438	.5478	.5517	.5557	.5596	.5636	.5675	.5714	.5753
.2	.5793	.5832	.5871	.5910	.5948	.5987	.6026	.6064	.6103	.6141
.3	.6179	.6217	.6255	.6293	.6331	.6368	.6406	.6443	.6480	.6517
.4	.6554	.6591	.6628	.6664	.6700	.6736	.6772	.6808	.6844	.6879
.5	.6915	.6950	.6985	.7019	.7054	.7088	.7123	.7157	.7190	.7224
.6	.7257	.7291	.7324	.7357	.7389	.7422	.7454	.7486	.7517	.7549
.7	.7580	.7611	.7642	.7673	.7704	.7734	.7764	.7794	.7823	.7852
.8	.7881	.7910	.7939	.7967	.7995	.8023	.8051	.8078	.8106	.8133
.9	.8159	.8186	.8212	.8238	.8264	.8289	.8315	.8340	.8365	.8389
1.0	.8413	.8438	.8461	.8485	.8508	.8531	.8554	.8577	.8599	.8621
1.1	.8643	.8665	.8686	.8708	.8729	.8749	.8770	.8790	.8810	.8830
1.2	.8849	.8869	.8888	.8907	.8925	.8944	.8962	.8980	.8997	.9015
1.3	.9032	.9049	.9066	.9082	.9099	.9115	.9131	.9147	.9162	.9177
1.4	.9192	.9207	.9222	.9236	.9251	.9265	.9279	.9292	.9306	.9319
1.5	.9332	.9345	.9357	.9370	.9382	.9394	.9406	.9418	.9429	.9441
1.6	.9452	.9463	.9474	.9484	.9495	.9505	.9515	.9525	.9535	.9545
1.7	.9554	.9564	.9573	.9582	.9591	.9599	.9608	.9616	.9625	.9633
1.8	.9641	.9649	.9656	.9664	.9671	.9678	.9686	.9693	.9699	.9706
1.9	.9713	.9719	.9726	.9732	.9738	.9744	.9750	.9756	.9761	.9767
2.0	.9772	.9778	.9783	.9788	.9793	.9798	.9803	.9808	.9812	.9817
2.1	.9821	.9826	.9830	.9834	.9838	.9842	.9846	.9850	.9854	.9857
2.2	.9861	.9864	.9868	.9871	.9875	.9878	.9881	.9884	.9887	.9890
2.3	.9893	.9896	.9898	.9901	.9904	.9906	.9909	.9911	.9913	.9916
2.4	.9918	.9920	.9922	.9925	.9927	.9929	.9931	.9932	.9934	.9936
2.5	.9938	.9940	.9941	.9943	.9945	.9946	.9948	.9949	.9951	.9952
2.6	.9953	.9955	.9956	.9957	.9959	.9960	.9961	.9962	.9963	.9964
2.7	.9965	.9966	.9967	.9968	.9969	.9970	.9971	.9972	.9973	.9974
2.8	.9974	.9975	.9976	.9977	.9977	.9978	.9979	.9979	.9980	.9981
2.9	.9981	.9982	.9982	.9983	.9984	.9984	.9985	.9985	.9986	.9986
3.0	.9987	.9987	.9987	.9988	.9988	.9989	.9989	.9989	.9990	.9990
3.1	.9990	.9991	.9991	.9991	.9992	.9992	.9992	.9992	.9993	.9993
3.2	.9993	.9993	.9994	.9994	.9994	.9994	.9994	.9995	.9995	.9995
3.3	.9995	.9995	.9995	.9996	.9996	.9996	.9996	.9996	.9996	.9997
3.4	.9997	.9997	.9997	.9997	.9997	.9997	.9997	.9997	.9997	.9998